Eighth Edition

Corrections in America

An Introduction

Harry E. Allen, Ph.D.
SAN JOSE STATE UNIVERSITY

Clifford E. Simonsen, Ph.D.
CITY UNIVERSITY

PRENTICE HALL
Upper Saddle River, New Jersey 07458

Library of Congress Cataloging-in-Publication Data

Allen, Harry E.
    Corrections in America : an introduction / Harry E. Allen,
Clifford E. Simonsen. — 8th ed.
        p.   cm.
    Includes bibliographical references and index.
    ISBN 0-13-598038-0 (case cover)
    1. Corrections—United States.   I. Simonsen, Clifford E.
II. Title.
HV9304.A63   1998
364.6'0973—dc21   96-49655
                                                        CIP

Acquisitions Editor: *Neil Marquardt*
Editorial Assistant: *Rose Mary Florio*
Production Editor: *Adele M. Kupchik*
Managing Editor: *Mary Carnis*
Director of Manufacturing and Production: *Bruce Johnson*
Manufacturing Buyer: *Ed O'Dougherty*
Marketing Manager: *Frank Mortimer, Jr.*
Director, Image Resource Center: *Lori Morris-Nantz*
Photo Research Supervisor: *Melinda Lee Reo*
Image Permission Supervisor: *Kay Dellosa*
Permissions Assistant: *Debra Hewitson*
Photo Researcher: *Melinda Alexander*
Copy Editor: *Sally Ann Bailey*
Proofreader: *H. Muriel Adams*
Printer/Binder: *R. R. Donnelley & Sons, Harrisonburg, VA*
Formatting/page make-up: *Adele M. Kupchik/Robin Lucas/Julie Boddorf*
Design Director: *Marianne Frasco*
Interior Design: *Sheree Goodman Design*
Cover Illustration: *Greg Spalenka*

Inside Cover Photo Credits: *Front, Federal Bureau of Prisons; Back, UPI/Corbis-Bettmann*
Part Opening Photo Credits: *Part One, Corbis–Bettmann; Part Two, Frank Fournier/Contact Press Images; Part Three, AP/Wide World Photos; Part Four, Mark Terrill/AP/Wide World Photos; Part Five, Gary Wagner/Impact Visuals Photo & Graphics, Inc.; Part Six, UPI/Corbis–Bettman; Part Seven, David Woo/Stock Boston; Part Eight, Andrew Lichtenstein/Impact Visuals Photo & Graphics, Inc.*

© 1998, 1995 by Prentice-Hall, Inc.
Simon & Schuster / A ViacomCompany
Upper Saddle River, New Jersey 07458

Previous editions copyright ©1975, 1978, 1981, 1986, 1989, and 1992

Printed in the United States of America

10   9   8   7   6   5   4   3

ISBN 0-13-598038-0

Prentice-Hall International (UK) Limited, *London*
Prentice-Hall of Australia Pty. Limited, *Sydney*
Prentice-Hall Canada Inc., *Toronto*
Prentice-Hall Hispanoamericana, S.A., *Mexico*
Prentice-Hall of India Private Limited, *New Delhi*
Prentice-Hall of Japan, Inc., *Tokyo*
Simon & Schuster Asia Pte. Ltd., *Singapore*
Editora Prentice-Hall do Brasil, Ltda., *Rio de Janeiro*

Dedication

The authors would like to dedicate this edition to Fran. She has always supported them totally, from the time when she typed the first manuscript in the late hours of the night, to putting up with their long hours and craziness during this major overhaul. Now it's time for us to recognize her worth to us by our love, appreciation and support.

Brief Contents

Contents

CHAPTER 3: The Age of Prisons (1800 to the Present)   30

CHAPTER 4: The Pendulum of Correctional Ideologies   53

PART II: LAW AND THE LEGAL PROCESS   75

CHAPTER 16: Female Offenders   291

CHAPTER 17: Juvenile Offenders   316

CHAPTER 18: Special Category Offenders · 343

PART V: RIGHTS OF THE SENTENCED OFFENDER · 371

CHAPTER 19: Offender Rights in Confinement · 373

CHAPTER 20: The Death Penalty: The Ultimate Right   398

CHAPTER 21: The Rights of Ex-Offenders   426

Foreword

Harry Allen and Clifford Simonsen have done it again. The eighth edition of *Corrections in America* is a marked improvement over earlier editions. That the authors can continually improve on what is the standard for introductory textbooks on corrections is a testament to their expertise and continued involvement in the study of American corrections. The experience and knowledge of the authors inform every chapter in the text.

What is perhaps the most important change to the book in this edition is that Allen and Simonsen have purposefully gone beyond their well-established roles as experts on corrections. In this edition, the authors incorporate their pedagogical skill with their substantive knowledge. The eighth edition of *Corrections in America* is as thorough, comprehensive, and readable as its predecessors. This edition is also a much better teaching resource. In the eighth edition the authors have added a number of features which work to enhance the educational effectiveness of the presentation. Chapter introductions are better designed to alert the reader to important themes and topics which will appear in the chapters. The "CJ Bytes," "Correctional Briefs," and "Profiles" sections add depth and color to the writing and should bolster reader interest and attention.

The authors have also kept apace with developments in the field. Naturally, this edition includes updated data and references. Once again, Allen and Simonsen have integrated theory and research, classic and contemporary writings, and balanced the prescriptive with the descriptive. The expanded and improved chapter on female offenders is an example of the continual refinement of the coverage of substantive issues which has characterized the book over its long life. So too, the dedication of a complete chapter to the role of the private sector in corrections is timely recognition of our changing perceptions and practices.

Yet, with these important changes to the book, *Corrections in America* stays true to its tradition as an exemplary introductory textbook. All of the important topics and issues that have existed and now exist in corrections, as well as those concerns which are just now emerging, are noted and described. The book provides a wealth of information about the philosophy, people, practices, and problems of American corrections. Indeed, one reason why this book has survived to an eighth edition and is the leading text in the area is because the coverage of *Corrections in America* is comprehensive and exhaustive. This edition is no less complete than its predecessors.

I have often felt that the progression of *Corrections in America*, since its first appearance in 1975 through this latest edition, chronicles the recent history of American corrections. The table of contents of the book identifies the chronic, episodic, and recurrent issues that have captured attention over the past quarter century. It is interesting to watch topics emerge as a brief mention, rise to the status of a major chapter section (or even a whole chapter), and then recede to lesser prominence. In the final chapter, Allen and Simonsen continue to draw the reader's attention to what matters. It is not the controversy du jour that moves in and out of our attention, it is our approach to corrections and correctional policy. In concluding *Corrections in America*, Allen and Simonsen again teach us to focus on **Corrections of America**.

Lawrence F. Travis, III
Professor of Criminal Justice
Division of Criminal Justice
University of Cincinnati
Cincinnati, Ohio

Preface

Built on the foundation of its last seven editions, and with revisions based on user feedback and recommendations, we present *Corrections in America: An Introduction,* eighth edition. We, the authors, feel that our efforts will allow us to continue to provide the best introductory-level correctional text available.

Experts in crime and criminology, practitioners in the field of institutional and community corrections, and instructors who use this text every year make your authors proud and humble—and motivated us to attempt to do even more to continue to earn such praise.

In this new edition, we continue to attempt to provide a clear overview of each of the categories that make up corrections. We do not try to explore particular subjects in such great depth at the expense of other subjects that are important to the introductory student. We offer this new edition to the student and instructor not only as an educational experience but as an enjoyable awakening to the vast field of corrections and its impact on contemporary society. We hope the instructor will find the new pedagogical tools and other materials provided more helpful to their teaching experience, making it as effective and interesting as possible and remain academically and student friendly.

*B*ut the Tradition Continues

The eighth edition of *Corrections in America* has more revisions and changes than all of the previous seven editions. Most of the changes are based on reviews and comments of our colleagues and friends in academia and are aimed at making the text more accurate, complete, and useful as a teaching and learning tool. We continue to seek a balance between current and past research, grand and applied theory, and practical and predictive examples and issues. We have developed three new learning aids in this edition. The first new tool is called "Profiles," which describe especially useful examples of persons of note or notoriety at a particular time or point in the text. The second we call "CJ Bytes," aimed at providing interesting facts and definitions from corrections and criminal justice to the student aimed at the materials being covered in the text which reinforce but do not break the flow of the main textual materials. The third new feature is called "Correctional Briefs," which are short to long boxed examples of specific processes or programs that illustrate the points in the main body of the text in an interesting and illustrative manner. Another new feature is making the "Terms to Remember" at the end of each chapter appear in **boldface** in the text in order to enhance their learning potential. We have also redesigned and updated all tables, figures, and graphs to be more attractive and clear. We have also added many more photographs to emphasize issues discussed in the text and show the persons, facilities, and programs that are important to corrections.

The following features from the seventh edition continue to enhance the eighth:

- Its systems approach explores each element of corrections as an integrated and interrelated series of subsystems of persons, programs, and processes.

- Its unbiased presentation and the wide range of topics it covers make the text suitable for instructors who come from many points of view and orientation.

- Its end-of-chapter materials contain summaries, review questions, words to remember, extensive endnotes on points, plus recommended readings at the end of each part.

Special New Features

In addition to the new features just mentioned, we have added the following specific features and changes in the eighth edition:

- The authors have completely revised all the text and graphic materials to update them with materials and references that are the most current and relevant available.

- The first section of the book, Part I, dealing with history continues as four chapters, based on comments by users. Repetitive and redundant material has been removed and spread throughout the appropriate parts and chapters.

- The discussion of intermediate sanctions, which is designed to show the broad range of penalties that can be applied in terms of shocking the offenders or providing alternatives to incarceration for the nondangerous individuals, has been moved to Chapter 11, following probation, where it fits better as part of the correctional overall process.

- The coverage of female offenders has been greatly expanded and moved to Chapter 16, immediately following the chapter on male offenders so that both can be contrasted and compared. This effort responds to a call for a more balanced handling of the very latest research and data in regard to this fast-growing clientele group of corrections.

- The chapter on the death penalty, which now appears later in the text, has been streamlined and shortened, while still reflecting the latest data and problems in this critical sector of corrections and prisoners' rights.

- The chapter on juveniles has been restructured and repositioned to provide a more up-to-date view of this separate system. The impact of juvenile violence and crime is better covered by use of the most current data from NIJ, UCR, and OJJDP.

- The discussion of jails and detention facilities has been moved to Chapter 9, in Part III, as the start of the correctional process coverage. This is a more logical location, and the material has been completely updated and enhanced by input from the leadership of these facilities and AJA and NSA.

- In Part VI, a completely new arrangement has been used to relate these chapter to functions and tasks. Chapter 22 deals with custody functions and tasks, Chapter 23 deals with treatment functions and tasks, and Chapter 24 is a new chapter dealing with all the other specialized functions and tasks in corrections. This gives a much more comprehensive coverage to all these myriad tasks.

- We have included a complete new Chapter 28 under Part VII which deals with the private sector systems that have grown immensely since the last edition. The relationship between the public and private sectors is explored in depth and projections for future efforts examined.

- Current critical issues such as elderly inmates, juveniles treated as adults, gang violence, the increase in sex offenders, home detention, the impact of the ADA on corrections, and many others have been covered in the appropriate chapters, and several are covered in depth in the final chapter, which explores corrections as it enters the twenty-first century.

Organization of the Text

The text continues to be divided into eight "parts," with this edition containing twenty-nine, and we feel better balanced, chapters. The authors have been diligent in trying to cover as many as possible of the major changes and trends that have taken place since the seventh edition.

PART I: HISTORY AND EVOLUTION OF CORRECTIONS

This provides the basis of historical development and present philosophies in the handling of those who fall outside accepted norms of behavior. It continues to contain four chapters.

Chapter 1: Early History (2000 B.C. to A.D. 1700)
This chapter outlines the development of dealing with unacceptable behavior from tribalism to the beginnings of scientific enlightenment.

Chapter 2: A Century of Change (1700 to 1800)
This chapter examines the emergence of imprisonment as a form of punishment and atonement for crime.

Chapter 3: The Age of Prisons (1800 to the Present)
This chapter covers the development of prisons and penology from the development of the penitentiary to the modern era.

Chapter 4: Shifting Ideologies in Corrections
This chapter continues with innovations in corrections and the recent history of changes in philosophies and ideologies as concepts swing from one to the other.

PART II: LAW AND THE LEGAL PROCESS

This part deals with how the offender passes through and is dealt with by the judicial system after being charged with criminal acts.

Chapter 5: The Incidence of Crime

This chapter deals with misdemeanor and felony offenses (the two types that bring offenders into the system) and discusses how each are processed.

Chapter 6: The Correctional Filter

This chapter presents a different way to look at the filtering (formerly called "funneling") process as offenders move through the system, very few to incarceration.

Chapter 7: Sentencing

This chapter discusses indeterminate and determinate sentencing as widely different methods of attempting to deal with convicted offenders, as well as some promising alternatives to incarceration which are discussed in detail in Part III.

Chapter 8: Appellate Review

This chapter deals with the methods and routes of appeals and the current situation with the appellate logjam in the higher courts.

PART III: THE CORRECTIONAL PROCESS

This part has been placed where it should be to examine the major subsystems of the larger process called corrections and how they interact to provide options for correctional administrators and courts.

Chapter 9: Jails and Detention Facilities

This chapter has been revised and moved back to a more logical position at the start of the correctional process. This makes it clear that this sector has major impact on the rest of the processes.

Chapter 10: Probation

This chapter deals with the most frequently used sentencing option *before* incarceration and how it developed, where it is today, and where it seems to be going in the twenty-first century.

Chapter 11: Intermediate Sanctions

This chapter, a new one in the last edition, has been expanded in its dealing with offenders who do not fit into probation or parole, but who should also not be incarcerated, and the options that are available and developing.

Chapter 12: Imprisonment

This chapter deals with the processes, impacts, and potentials of imprisonment in the past and present systems in the United States.

Chapter 13: Parole

This chapter covers a system under attack, even though this major subsystem for community supervision over offenders after release from prison is growing in some aspects.

PART IV: THE CORRECTIONAL CLIENT

This part looks at the varied kinds of persons, or "clients," who end up somewhere in the corrections system, what they are like, and how they are handled.

Chapter 14: Jail Inmates
This chapter has been further developed and given more depth, drawing upon data and background material now available from more sources.

Chapter 15: Male Offenders
This chapter has been expanded to look at the major health, safety, and security issues for males in the institutions today, with a population explosion and rising percentages of violent prisoners.

Chapter 16: Female Offenders
This chapter has been vastly improved, building upon the growing body of knowledge in regard to this very special and fast growing population for the entire corrections system.

Chapter 17: Juvenile Offenders
This chapter has been cut down considerably and completely revised to reflect the changing attitudes toward juvenile offenders and the efforts to find ways to deal with the violent youths and gang members today.

Chapter 18: Special Category Offenders
This chapter expands on those categories of offenders who are not mainstream and have mental, physical, and health problems that require special programs. A new effort is made to examine the aging population that fills cells in correctional facilities.

PART V: THE RIGHTS OF CONVICTED OFFENDERS
This part examines the rights of offenders in a number of situations and legal environments in an effort to trace the development and applications of these rights.

Chapter 19: Prisoners' Rights in Confinement
This chapter, with extensive revision, looks at the conflicts between prisoner rights in confinement and the needs of administrators to manage a safe and secure institution.

Chapter 20: The Death Penalty: The Ultimate Right
This chapter has been completely revised but still explains the development of the death penalty and how it has been, and might be, applied to the few who are eventually executed in America.

Chapter 21: The Rights of Ex-Offenders
This chapter examines the barriers to reentry into society and the collateral consequences from these barriers for those former inmates who cannot find the most important right—a job.

PART VI: CORRECTIONS AS A PROFESSION
The continual battle between security and treatment are examined in light of the serious overcrowding, reduced budgets, and other issues of the mid-1990s.

Chapter 22: Custody Functions and Tasks

This chapter examines the management problems and issues involved with providing safety and security in a more violent and hard to manage population in America's prisons.

Chapter 23: Treatment Functions and Tasks

The death of the "medical model" and its impact on treatment in prisons and other correctional institutions is discussed, as well as the treatment services that are offered in a "get-tough" era for corrections.

Chapter 24: Specialized Functions and Tasks

This completely new chapter looks at the many other functions that must be performed in a safe and secure manner in correctional facilities in the nation.

PART VII: CORRECTIONAL SYSTEMS

This part looks at the correctional systems at the local, state, and federal levels (to include community corrections) and how they function and interact.

Chapter 25: State and Local Systems

This chapter contains a review of the major systems in the United States that deal with adult felons and how they are transforming in an overcrowded and legalistic period for incarceration. A special look is taken at major city and other correctional systems.

Chapter 26: The Federal System

This chapter has again been completely revised to reflect the changing nature of the kinds of criminals that are dealt with in federal institutions and programs, especially for drug offenses.

Chapter 27: Community-Based Systems

This chapter updates the efforts in the community at all jurisdictional levels to deal with the inmates that can be handled in some ways other than continued incarceration.

Chapter 28: Private Sector Systems

This chapter examines that part of the correctional picture that has grown from a passing reference just a few years ago to a huge new and fast-growing business sector. There is an overview of private correctional efforts along with the corporate entities who are working toward their acceptance as a valuable adjunct to public sector corrections in ways never before imagined.

PART VIII: THE FUTURE OF CORRECTIONS

This final part allows the authors to expound on just what the state of corrections is as we stand poised on the brink of the twenty-first century and where it might go next. Relevant issues and problems are reexamined in the context of the social nexus of our society today.

Chapter 29: Corrections Enters the Twenty-first Century

This chapter points out that the prison population topped a million in 1994, far ahead of predictions in the seventh edition. Inmates are seen as the products of drugs, homelessness, poverty, HIV infection, racism, and all the issues that impact the free society. A situation where harder sentencing could result in inmates that will cost society more for medical services than for its security is shown just over the horizon.

Acknowledgments

How does one begin to acknowledge the persons whose support, encouragement, assistance, and love have allowed us to develop, refine, and produce a book that has evolved through eight editions and well over twenty years? To try to acknowledge them individually would take several pages and we would still surely miss some of them. The list begins with our families and close personal friends; then our colleagues and reference groups in academia; professionals and practitioners in corrections and criminal justice at the federal, state, and local levels; and (perhaps most important) the hundreds of instructors and tens of thousands of students who have used the various editions of *Corrections in America: An Introduction* at colleges and universities throughout the world. To all of you we extend our deepest appreciation and gratitude for encouraging and assisting us in continuing to provide a text that seems to work.

We would, however, like to single out a few of the special persons who helped the authors turn their prose, ideas, and concepts for a book about corrections into a textbook that will continue to reach the users. First, our Criminal Justice editor, Neil Marquardt, gets kudos for leading us through this first complete edition produced by Prentice Hall with minimal problems and a lot of positive support. Neil fought for our ideas and concepts about improving a proven winner, rather than just staying with the status quo. Sally Ann Bailey, our copy editor, gets a special "thank you." She used her "magic red pencil" assiduously and helped us turn the words of two authors into a book that reads like the words of one. Mary Carnis, managing editor, was a calm and professional center in the midst of what often became a frantic effort to stay on schedule. This eighth edition received exceptional support from Adele Kupchik, our senior production editor, who listened to our sniveling about schedules and inspired us to meet them. Her expertise and good humor helped to get it done with fun. Marianne Frasco, art director, helped us understand the importance of the visual effect of this new edition. Frank Mortimer, Jr., marketing manager, got the word out to the sales staff and will be a great factor in keeping this text at the top of the lists in a tightly competitive field. Rose Mary Florio, Neil's editorial assistant, kept us calm and informed, coordinating our often frantic calls and concerns. Judy Cassillo, supplements editor, helped us get the right new tools included with this edition to make it fresh. Ed O'Dougherty, manufacturing buyer, made sure that everything was in place for final production. We can't forget to mention Robin Baliszewski, who got us through the hassles that occurred when the seventh edition moved over from Macmillan and steered us through the efforts to know Prentice Hall and made that edition a great success. We enjoyed working with her as an editor and know she will continue to help continue that success in her marketing position.

We also must offer continuing thanks to the National Criminal Justice Reference Service, the National Institute of Justice, and the Bureau of Justice

Statistics for their marvelous documents that provide critical and current data for our efforts. The Camps, George and Camille, deserve especially big "thanks" for allowing us to again use data from the many figures from their series of *Corrections Yearbooks* that always provide the latest data on adult corrections, probation and parole, jail systems, and juvenile corrections. Their efforts for the correctional system and correctional managers are legion and much appreciated.

Last, but by far not the least, we must again acknowledge our families, friends and significant others. While they have enjoyed with us whatever modest success we have had with this text, they have also had to put up with the periodic absences and the frenzy of revisions and changes. . . conducted in the heat of deadlines and often from long distances. Writing is a very lonely task, especially when it involves a very specific field, one that is not easy to discuss or share in the frantic throes of revision. We deeply appreciate the understanding and support we have gotten in these periods over the past twenty-plus years and love you all for understanding and caring.

About the Authors

Harry E. Allen
PH.D. IN SOCIOLOGY

Professor in the Administration of Justice Department at San Jose State University. Before joining San Jose State University in 1978, he served as Director of the Program for the Study of Crime and Delinquency at Ohio State University. Previously, he served as Executive Secretary of the Governor's Task Force on Corrections in the state of Ohio, after teaching at Florida State University's School of Criminology.

Professor Allen is the author or co-author of numerous texts and articles, including *Corrections in the Commmunity* with Edward Latessa. He has been very active in professional associations and is the only criminologist to serve as president of both the American Society of Criminology and the Academy of Criminal Justice Sciences. He received the Herbert Block Award for service to the American Society of Criminology, and is a Fellow in both the Western and the American Societies of Criminology. Currently, he is working on a textbook with Clifford Simonsen entitled *Terrorism and Criminal Justice*.

Clifford E. Simonsen
PH.D. IN PUBLIC ADMINISTRATION WITH MAJORS IN CRIMINAL JUSTICE ADMINISTRATION AND DEVIANCE

Director of the Institute for Public Safety and Security at City University in Seattle. He has held previous positions at the Program for the Study of Crime and Delinquency at the Ohio State University, Office of Research at the Washington Department of Social and Health Services, Chairman of the Law and Justice Program at City College, Manager, King County Department of Adult Detention, Associate Superintendent, Washington State Reformatory, and Chairman of the Corrections Department, Edmonds Community College.

Dr. Simonsen is the author of numerous articles and several books in the fields of crime, delinquency, and security. These include *Juvenile Justice In America*, *Private Security in America*, and *Security Administration*. He is an active member of the Academy of Criminal Justice Sciences, the American Correctional Association, and the American Society of Industrial Security.

History *and* Evolution *of* Corrections

CHAPTER ONE

Early History (2000 B.C. to A.D. 1700)

Overview

This text is not intended to be a history of corrections or a dissertation on its legal aspects. It is helpful, however, to know at least a little of the historical background—legal and social—to gain an improved understanding of the concepts we discuss later. In describing this background, we avoid technical jargon to keep misunderstanding to a minimum. Where appropriate, specific individuals and events that have influenced the history of corrections are detailed in the text for easy reference.

We begin by tracing the roots of corrections back to the early beginnings of civilization as we know it.

Behavior as a Continuum

Behavior in social groups, be they primitive tribes or complex modern nations, can be looked upon as points on a simple continuum, as shown in Figure 1-1. In all societies, certain acts or groups of acts have been universally discouraged, or *proscribed*. Such acts include murder, rape, kidnapping, and treason (or some form of rebellion against the group authority). By contrast, most societies have encouraged, or *prescribed,* such other behaviors as having children, marrying, hunting, growing food, and engaging in other activities that benefit the common welfare.

Behavior that is situated toward the center of the continuum from either end is usually controlled by a set of social rules called **folkways.** These rules are enforced by means of mild discouragement (the raising of an eyebrow, staring, or a look of shock) or by mild encouragement (applause or a smile). Actions farther out on either end of the continuum, which serve either to perpetuate or to threaten the group's existence, are controlled by a stronger set of rules called **mores.** In the beginning, mores were enforced by

The descent to hell is easy. The gates stand open day and night. But to reclimb the slope and escape to the upper air: this is labor.

—Virgil, *Aeneid,* Book 6

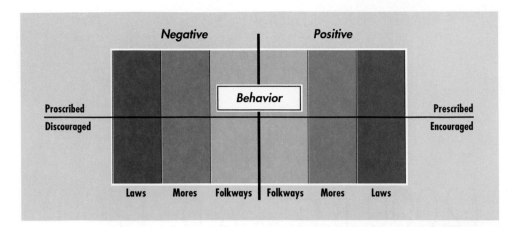

FIGURE

1.1

The Continuum
of Behavior

means of strong social discouragement (verbal abuse, beatings, temporary ostracism, or even banishment) or strong encouragement (dowries, secure social or financial status, or fertility rites), and those informal controls still protect certain mores today. But as societies became more complex, they devised more structured sanctions to prevent violation of the mores that were essential to the group's survival. These sanctions have been codified in the form of written rules, or **laws,** and the reward for obeying those laws is simply the ability to continue to function as a respected and productive member of society.

*R*edress of Wrongs

RETALIATION

The earliest remedy for wrongs done to one's person or property was simply to retaliate against the wrongdoer. In early primitive societies, *personal retaliation* was accepted and even encouraged by members of the tribal group. This ancient concept of personal revenge could hardly be considered "law." Yet it has influenced the development of most legal systems, especially English criminal law, from which most American criminal law derives.

The practice of personal retaliation was later augmented by the **blood feud,** in which the victim's family or tribe took revenge on the offender's family or tribe. Because this form of retaliation could easily escalate and result in an endless battle or *vendetta* between the injured factions, some method of control had to be devised to make blood feuds less costly and damaging.

The practice of retaliation usually begins to develop into a system of criminal law when it becomes customary for the victim of the wrongdoing to accept money or property in place of blood vengeance. This custom, when established, is usually dictated by tribal tradition and the relative positions of power between the injured party and the wrongdoer. Custom has always exerted great force among primitive societies. The acceptance of vengeance in the form of a payment (such as cattle, food, or personal services) was usually not compulsory, however, and victims were still free to take whatever vengeance they wished. Legal historians Albert Kocourek and John Wigmore described this pressure to retaliate:

> It must not be forgotten that the right of personal revenge was also in many cases a duty. A man was bound by all the force of religion to avenge the death of his kinsman. This duty was by universal practice imposed upon the

FOLKWAYS, MORES, AND LAW

Folkways are traditional social customs, including ways of thinking, feeling, or acting common to a social group of people. Mores are binding moral attitudes, habits, customs, and manners of a particular group of people. Laws are rules of conduct formally recognized as binding, defined and enforced by a controlling authority.

nearest male relative—the avenger of blood, as he is called in the Scripture accounts.[1]

The custom of atonement for wrongs by payment to appease the victim's family or tribe became known as *lex salica* (or **wergeld**, in Europe). It is still in effect in many Middle Eastern and Far Eastern countries, with the amount of payment based on the injured person's rank and position in the social group.

FINES AND PUNISHMENTS

How did these simple, voluntary programs become part of an official system of fines and punishments? As tribal leaders, elders, and (later) kings came into power,[2] they began to exert their authority on the negotiations. Wrongdoers could choose to stay away from the proceedings; this was their right. But if they refused to abide by the imposed sentence, they were declared to be outside the law of the tribe (nation, family), or an **outlaw.** There is little doubt that outlawry, or exile, was the first punishment imposed by society,[3] and it heralded the beginning of criminal law as we now know it.

Criminal law, even primitive criminal law, requires an element of public action against the wrongdoer—as in a pronouncement of outlawry. Before this element of public action, the backgrounds of criminal law and sanctions seem to have been parallel in most legal systems. The subsequent creation of legal codes and sanctions for different crimes either stressed or refined the vengeance factor, according to the particular society's values.

Early Codes

BABYLONIAN AND SUMERIAN CODES

Even primitive ethics demanded that a society express its vengeance within a system of regulations and rules. Moses was advised to follow the "eye for an eye and a tooth for a tooth" doctrine stated in Exodus 21:24, but this concept of *lex talionis* is far older than the Bible; it appears in the Sumerian codes (1860 B.C.) and in the 1750 B.C. code of King Hammurabi of Babylon, compiled over five hundred years before the Book of the Covenant (1250 B.C.).

As early societies developed language and writing skills, they began attempting to record the laws of their nations. While the Hammurabic Code is viewed by most historians as the first comprehensive attempt at codifying social interaction, the Sumerian codes preceded it by about a century, and the principle of *lex talionis* was evident in both. The punishments handed out under these codes were harsh and based on vengeance (or *talion*), in many cases being inflicted by the injured party. In the Babylonian code, over two dozen offenses called for the penalty of death. Both codes also prescribed mutilation, whipping, or forced labor as punishments for numerous crimes.

The kinds of punishments applied to slaves and bond servants have been cited by many scholars[4] as the origin of the punishments that in later law applied to all offenders. As stated by historian Gustav Radbruch,

> Applied earlier almost exclusively to slaves, [the mutilating penalties] became used more and more on freemen during the Carolingian period [A.D. 640–1012] and specially for offenses which betokened a base and servile

Two Ways to Pay for Homicide

Lex salica was the fine paid for homicide, and it varied according to the rank, sex, and age of the murdered person. In general, lex salica refers to a payment for death or injury. Wergeld, which means "man-money," originally referred to the death of an individual and the individual's supposed value to his or her family. It later referred to personal injury as well.

■

mentality. Up to the end of the Carolingian era, punishments "to hide and hair" were overwhelmingly reserved for slaves. Even death penalties occurred as slave punishments and account for the growing popularity of such penalties in Carolingian times. The aggravated death penalties, combining corporal and capital punishments, have their roots in the penal law governing slaves.[5]

The early punishments were considered synonymous with slavery; those punished even had their heads shaved, indicating the "mark of the slave."[6] In Roman days, the extensive use of penal servitude was spurred by the need for workers to perform hard labor in the great public works. The sentence to penal servitude was generally reserved for the lower classes; it usually meant life in chains, working in the mines or rowing in the galleys or ships, or building the public works planned by the government. The sentences carried with them the

Early congregate
confinement

—*COURTESY OF FEDERAL BUREAU OF PRISONS*

complete loss of citizenship and liberty and were classed, along with exile and death, as *capital punishment*. Penal servitude, or **civil death,** meant that the offender's property was confiscated in the name of the state and that his wife was declared a widow, eligible to remarry. To society, the criminal was, in effect, "dead."

CRIME AND SIN

Punishment of the individual in the name of the state also included the concept of superstitious revenge. Here crime was entangled with sin, and punishment in the form of *wergeld* (payment to the victim) or *friedensgeld* (payment to the state) was not sufficient. If society believed the crime might have offended a divinity, the accused had to undergo a long period of progressively harsher punishment in order to appease the gods. As time passed, the zone between church law and state law became more and more blurred, and the concept of personal responsibility for one's act was combined with the need to "**get right with God.**"[7] The early codes, even the Ten Commandments, were designed to make the offender's punishment acceptable to both society and God.

ROMAN AND GREEK CODES

In the sixth century A.D., Emperor Justinian of Rome wrote his code of laws, one of the most ambitious early efforts to match a desirable amount of punishment to all possible crimes. Roman art of the period depicts the "scales of justice," a metaphor that demanded the punishment balance the crime. Justinian's effort, as might be expected, bogged down in the morass of administrative details that were required to enforce it. The Code of Justinian did not survive the fall of the Roman Empire, but it left the foundation upon which most of the Western world's legal codes were eventually built.

In Greece, the harsh Code of Draco provided the same penalties for both citizens and slaves, incorporating many of the concepts used in primitive societies (for example, vengeance, outlawry, and blood feuds). The Greeks were the first society to allow any citizen to prosecute the offender in the name of the injured party, clearly illustrating that during that period, the public interest and protection of the social order were becoming more important than individual injury and individual vengeance.

THE MIDDLE AGES

The Middle Ages was a period of general disorder. Vast changes in the social structure and the growing influence of the Church on everyday life resulted in a divided system of justice. Reformation was viewed as a process of religious,

Early Code Makers

The Code of Hammurabi is estimated to have been written about 1750 B.C.

The Sumerian codes were those of kings Lipit-Ishtar and Eshnunna and are estimated to date from about 1860 B.C.

Draco, ruler of Greece in 621 B.C., drew up a very harsh and cruel code that used corporal punishment so extensively, it was said to be written not in ink but in blood.

Emperor Justinian I (A.D. 483–565) was a great preserver of Roman law who collected all imperial statutes, issued a digest of all writings of Roman jurists, and wrote a revised code and a textbook for students. His Corpus Juris Civilis became the foundation of law in most of continental Europe. ∎

The Inquisition had many ways to get the "truth"
—COURTESY OF CULVER PICTURES, INC.

not secular, redemption. As in early civilizations, the sinner had to pay two debts, one to society and another to God. The "ordeal" was the Church's substitute for a trial by the leadership of the secular group, until the practice was abolished in A.D. 1215. In trials by ordeal, guilt or innocence was determined by subjecting the accused to dangerous or painful tests, in the belief that those who were innocent would emerge unscathed, whereas the guilty would suffer agonies and die. The brutality of most trials by ordeal ensured a very high percentage of convictions.

The Church expanded the concept of crime to include some new areas, still reflected in modern codes. During the Middle Ages, sexual activity other than for procreation was seen as especially sinful. Sexual offenses usually involved either public or "unnatural" acts, and they provoked horrible punishments, as did heresy and witchcraft. The Church justified cruel reprisals as a means of saving the unfortunate sinner from the clutches of Satan. The zealous movement to stamp out heresy brought on **the Inquisition** and its use of the most vicious tortures imaginable to gain "confessions" and "repentance" from alleged heretics. Thousands of persons died at the hands of the inquisitioners in Spain and Holland, where these methods were the most extensively used. Punishment was not viewed as an end in itself, but as the offender's only hope of pacifying a wrathful God.

The Inquisition

The Inquisition was a tribunal established by the Catholic church in the Middle Ages with very wide powers for the suppression of heresy. The tribunal searched out heretics and other offenders rather than waiting for charges to be brought forward (somewhat in the manner of former Senator Joseph McCarthy, who rooted out so-called communists in the early 1950s). Emperor Frederick II made the Inquisition a formal institution in 1224, and it finally came to an end only in 1834. ∎

The main contribution of the medieval church to our study of corrections is the concept of *free will*. This idea assumes that individuals choose their actions, good or bad, and thus can be held fully responsible for them. The religious doctrines of eternal punishment, atonement, and spiritual conversion rest on the assumption that individuals who commit sins could have acted differently had they chosen to do so.

The early codes and their administration were usually based on the belief that punishment was necessary to avenge the victim. In early small tribal groups and less complex societies, direct compensation to the victim was used in place of revenge to prevent disintegration of the social structure through extended blood feuds. When those groups concentrated their power in a king or similar ruler, the concept of crime as an offense against the victim gave way to the idea that crime—however lowly the victim—was an offense against the state. In the process, *wergeld* was replaced by *friedensgeld*, and the administration of punishment became the responsibility of the king. Concentrating that power also led to a tendency to ignore victims and their losses, while concentrating on the crime and the criminal.

*P*unishment

CAPITAL AND CORPORAL PUNISHMENT

The most common forms of state punishment over the centuries have been death, torture, mutilation, branding, public humiliation, fines, forfeits of property, banishment, imprisonment, and transportation. These acts, and numerous variations on them, have always symbolized retribution for crimes. (Imprisonment and transportation are relatively modern penal practices and are discussed in later chapters.)

The death penalty (killing the offender) was the most universal form of punishment among early societies. There was little knowledge of behavior modification and other modern techniques to control violent persons, and often the feared offenders were condemned to death by hanging, crucifixion, burning at the stake, drowning, and any other cruel and unusual method the human mind could conceive. As technology advanced, methods for killing offenders became more sophisticated. In the belief that punishment, especially capital punishment, would act as a deterrent to others, societies carried out executions and lesser punishments in public.

Torture, mutilation, and branding fall in the general category of **corporal punishment** (any physical pain inflicted short of death). Many tortures were used to extract a "confession" from the accused, often resulting in the death penalty for an innocent person. Mutilation was often used in an attempt to match the crime with an "appropriate" punishment. (A liar's tongue was ripped out, a rapist's genitals were removed, a thief's hands were cut off.) Branding was still practiced as late as the nineteenth century in many countries, including the United States. Corporal punishment was considered to be a deterrent to other potential offenders.

The public humiliation of offenders was a popular practice in early America, utilizing such devices as the stocks, the pillory, ducking stools, the brank, and branding. The most significant aspect of those punishments was their *public nature*. Offenders were placed in the stocks (sitting down, hands and feet fastened into a locked frame) or in the pillory (standing, with head and hands fastened into a locked frame) and were flogged, spat upon, heaped with garbage, and reviled by all who passed by.

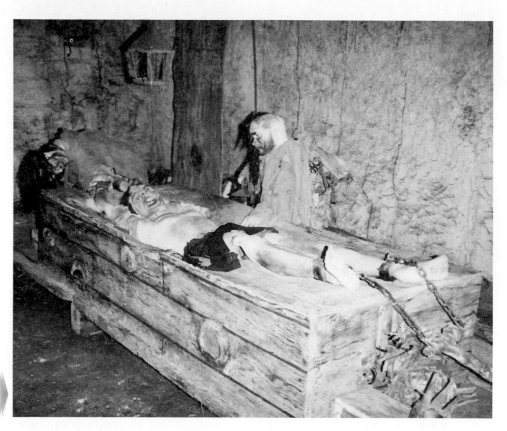

The "rack" was used for punishment
—*PHOTO BY HARRY ALLEN*

The ducking stool and the brank were used as common public punishments for gossips. The ducking stool was a chair or platform placed at the end of a long lever, allowing the operator on the bank of a stream to dunk the victim. The **brank** was a birdcagelike instrument placed over the offender's head, containing a plate of iron with sharp spikes in it that extended into the subject's mouth. Any movement of the mouth or tongue would result in painful injury.

Flogging (or whipping) has been a common punishment in almost all

The pillory was a way to provide public humiliation
—*COURTESY OF FEDERAL BUREAU OF PRISONS*

Western civilizations. The method was used particularly to preserve discipline in domestic, military, and academic settings. It was usually administered by a short lash at the end of a solid handle about three feet long, or by a whip made of nine knotted lines or cords fastened to a handle (the famed **cat-o'-nine-tails**), sometimes with sharp spikes worked into the knots. Flogging was a popular method of inducing confessions at heresy trials, as few victims could stand up long under the tongue of the lash. Caning remains a legal punishment in countries such as South Africa and Malaysia[8] and Singapore.[9]

DETERRENCE

The extensive use of capital and corporal punishment during the Middle Ages reflected, in part, a belief that public punishment would deter potential wrongdoers—a belief that the passing years have refuted: "It is plain that, however futile it may be, social revenge is the only honest, straightforward, and logical justification for punishing criminals. The claim for deterrence is belied by both history and logic."[10] No matter how society tried to "beat the devil" out of offenders, the only criminals who seemed to be deterred were the ones *tortured to death*. Later, enlightened thinkers began to seek more rational deterrents for crime by investigating its cause (see Chapter 2).

EMERGENCE OF SECULAR LAW

The problem of drawing up a set of laws that applied to the actions of men and women in earthly communities was compounded by Christian philosophers who insisted that law was made in heaven. In the fourth century A.D., St. Augustine recognized the need for justice, but only as decreed by God. The issue was somewhat clarified by Thomas Aquinas in the thirteenth century, when he distinguished among three laws: eternal law (*lex eterna*), natural law (*lex naturalis*), and human law (*lex humana*), all intended for the common good.[11] The last was considered valid only if it did not conflict with the other two.

Corporal punishment was a major correctional practice until the nineteenth century

—*COURTESY OF MARY EVANS PICTURE LIBRARY*

As time passed and the secular leaders (kings and other types of monarchs) became more powerful, they wanted to detach themselves from the divine legal order and its restrictions on their power. In the early fourteenth century, many scholars advocated the independence of the monarchy from the Pope. Dante, the Italian poet and philosopher, proposed the establishment of a world state completely under the rule of secular power.

England's lord chancellor Sir Thomas More opposed the forces advocating the unification of church and state and died on the executioner's block as a result. He refused to bend ecclesiastical law to suit the marital whims of his king, the fickle Henry VIII. Sir Thomas More was out of line with his day in another sense as well. As an advocate of the seemingly radical theory that punishment could not prevent crime, he was one of the first to see that prevention might require a close look at the social conditions that gave rise to crime. In the sixteenth century, unfortunately, this line of thought was too far ahead of its time, but Sir Thomas More's ideas persisted and eventually contributed much to the foundation of modern theories in criminology and penology.

The early background of law and punishment points up the significance of social revenge as a justification for individual or societal punishment against an offender. This rationale allowed the development of penal slavery and civil death as retaliation for wrongs against the crown. The idea of correcting an offender was entirely incidental to punishment. Imprisonment served purely for detention. Offenders condemned to the galleys or the sulfur mines suffered a form of social vengeance, often including the lash and other physical abuse, far more painful than was the loss of freedom alone. The offenders were placed in dungeons, galleys, or mines to receive punishment, not as punishment.

The idea of punishment to repay society and expiate one's transgressions against God explains in part why most punishments were cruel and barbarous. Presumably, the hardships of physical torture, social degradation, exile, or financial loss (the four fundamental types of punishment)[12] would be rewarded by eternal joy in heaven. Ironically, those punishments did little to halt the spread of crime: "Even in the era when extremely severe punishment was imposed for crimes of minor importance, no evidence can be found to support the view that punitive measures materially curtailed the volume of crime."[13]

EARLY PRISONS

What kinds of facilities for imprisonment existed during earlier ages? It is important to examine some aspects of the first institutions as they might possibly relate to later correctional practices. Some form of detention for offenders, whether temporary or permanent, has been a social institution from the earliest times. Offenders were, of course, always detained against their will, but the concept of imprisonment as a *punishment in itself* is a fairly recent one. Formerly, imprisonment was primarily a means of holding the accused until the authorities had decided on his or her real punishment, chosen from the variety just described. Even those condemned to penal servitude in the Roman public works must surely have been kept in some special place at night, regardless of how primitive. Unfortunately, little is known about this form of imprisonment. Most places of confinement were basically cages. Later, stone quarries and similar places designed for other purposes were used to house prisoners. The only early Roman place of confinement we know much about is the Mamertine Prison, a vast system of primitive dungeons built under the main sewer of Rome in 64 B.C.[14]

In the Middle Ages, after the fall of Rome, fortresses, castles, bridge abutments, and town gates were strongly and securely built to defend against roving bands of raiders. With the advent of gunpowder, however, those fortress cities lost much of their deterrent power. The massive structures were then used as places of confinement. Many became famous as places to house political prisoners.[15] It was not until the twelfth century that prison chambers were specifically included in castle plans.

The Christian church had followed the custom of **sanctuary** or asylum[16] since the time of Constantine, placing the wrongdoer in seclusion to create an atmosphere conducive to penitence. This form of imprisonment was modified into more formalized places of punishment within the walls of monasteries and abbeys. Long periods in solitary confinement for alleged transgressions against canon law were common. The prisons built during the Inquisition were similar in concept, if not in operation, to later cellular prisons in America. The idea of reformation through isolation and prayer had some influence on our first penitentiaries but, in general, the impact of such practices in this respect remains hard to evaluate.

WORKHOUSES

Bridewell, a workhouse, was created for the employment and housing of London's "riffraff" in 1557 and was based on the work ethic[17] that followed the breakup of feudalism and the increased migration of the rural populations to urban areas. The workhouse was so successful that by 1576 Parliament required the construction of a "Bridewell" in every county in England. The same unsettled social conditions prevailed in Holland, and the Dutch began building workhouses in 1596 that were soon copied all over Europe.

Unfortunately, workhouses did not typify the places of confinement used for minor offenders and other prisoners in the seventeenth and eighteenth centuries. Most cities had to make prisons out of buildings erected for some other purpose. No attempt was made to keep the young from the old, the well from the sick, or even the males from the females. No food was provided for those without money, and sanitary conditions were usually deplorable. Exploitation of inmates by other inmates and jailers resulted in the most vicious acts of violence. "Jail fever" (a common term for typhus), which was bred easily in such conditions, spread to surrounding cities and became the main method of keeping the country's population down. By the beginning of the eighteenth century, workhouses, prisons, and houses of correction in England and the rest of Europe had deteriorated into shocking conditions. Forcing criminals to exist in such miserable prisons became perhaps the most ruthless—if abstract—social revenge of all the punishments thus far described. "Out of sight, out of mind" was the watchword of that period, with the public seldom being aware of what happened behind the walls (ironically, a condition not unknown at the end of the twentieth century).

Summary

In this chapter, we observed the principle of punishment pass from an individual's response to a wrong, to a blood feud that involved the family, to an abstract action taken by some bureaucracy in the name of the state. That last approach to justice and punishment allowed the places of confinement to become human cesspools. It took the brilliant and dedicated reformers of the eighteenth century to establish the basis for modern penal philosophy, and their works are examined in the next chapter.

Review Questions

1. What are the differences among folkways, mores, and laws?
2. At what point in a society's development does retaliation begin to become criminal law?
3. What effect did the kings' increasing power have on punishment?
4. What was the first punishment imposed by society?
5. What is meant by *civil death*?
6. What is meant by *free will*?
7. What form of punishment has been most widely used?
8. What is meant by "deterrence as a result of punishment"?
9. What were some of the earliest forms of imprisonment?
10. From what does most American law derive?

Words to Remember

folkways	"blood feud"	cat-o'-nine-tails
mores	"get right with God"	*lex eterna*
laws	the Inquisition	sanctuary
outlaw	corporal punishment	Bridewell
civil death	brank	

Endnotes

1. Albert Kocourek and John Wigmore, *Evolution of Law*, Vol. 2, *Punitive and Ancient Legal Institutions* (Boston: Little, Brown, 1915), p. 124.
2. Ronald Akers, "Toward a Comparative Definition of Criminal Law," *Journal of Criminal Law, Criminology and Police Science* (1965): 301–306.
3. Kocourek and Wigmore, *Evolution of Law*, Vol. 2, p. 126.
4. Thorsten Sellin, "A Look at Prison History," *Federal Probation* (September 1967): 18.
5. Gustav Radbruch, *Elegantiae Juris Criminalis*, 2nd ed. (Basel, Switzerland: Verlag für Recht und Gesellschaft A.G., 1950), p. 5.
6. Slaves were also marked by branding on the forehead or by metal collars that could not easily be removed.
7. This religious requirement brought the two issues of sin and crime into the same arena and broadened the scope of the church courts. The offender was obligated to make restitution to both God and the state.
8. V. A. C. Catrell, *The Hanging Tree: Execution and the English People: 1770–1868* (New York: Oxford University Press, 1994).
9. Editors, "Guards Get Jail and Cane for Prisoner's Death," *The Straits Times*, March 21, 1996, p. 2.
10. Walter C. Reckless, *The Crime Problem*, 4th ed. (New York: Appleton-Century-Crofts, 1969), p. 497.
11. Stephen Schafer, *Theories in Criminology* (New York: Random House, 1969), p. 25.

12. Edwin H. Sutherland, *Criminology* (Philadelphia: J. B. Lippincott, 1924), p. 317.

13. Reckless, *The Crime Problem*, p. 504. There is no evidence that increased use of incarceration will lead to lower levels of crime. See David Biles, "Crime and the Use of Prisons," *Federal Probation* (June 1979): 39–43.

14. Norman Johnston, *The Human Cage: A Brief History of Prison Architecture* (Washington, D.C.: American Foundation, 1973), p. 5.

15. Ibid., p. 6.

16. The practice of granting a criminal sanctuary from punishment was generally reserved for holy places. It was abandoned in England in the seventeenth century.

17. Work ethic refers to the generally held belief in the Judeo-Christian world that hard work is good for both the soul and society.

CHAPTER TWO

A Century of Change (1700 to 1800)

Overview

As Chapter 1 suggests, the underlying principle of public revenge for private wrongs invariably tipped the scales of justice in favor of the state. Corporal and capital punishment were the rule. Executioners in sixteenth- and seventeenth-century Europe had at least thirty different methods of death from which to choose. These ranged from hanging and burning at the stake to more creative forms such as stretching the prisoner to death on the rack. Public punishment and degradation were commonly prescribed for even minor offenses. Imprisonment served only as a preface to the imposition of some gory punishment, carried out in the name of justice. With over two hundred crimes in England punishable by death, that nation witnessed some eight hundred public executions a year. As the seventeenth century drew to a close, the concept of retributive punishment by the state (with its implication that pity and justice are forever locked in opposition) was firmly entrenched in the laws of England and many other European countries.[1]

The vilest deeds like poison weeds
Bloom well in prison air;
It is only what is good in man
That wastes and withers there.
Pale anguish keeps the heavy gate
And the warder is Despair.

—Oscar Wilde, "The Ballad
of Reading Gaol"

The Age of Enlightenment and Reform

The events of the eighteenth century are especially important to the student of corrections. For it was during this period—later known as the Age of Enlightenment—that some of the most brilliant philosophers of our history recognized humanity's essential dignity and imperfection. The movement for reform was led by such giants as Charles Montesquieu, Voltaire, Cesare Beccaria, Jeremy Bentham, John Howard, and William Penn. The impact of their work, though not confined to any one area, was particularly constructive with regard to the treatment of criminals. Let us consider the contribution made by each.

MONTESQUIEU AND VOLTAIRE: THE FRENCH HUMANISTS

The French thinkers Montesquieu and Voltaire, along with Denis Diderot, epitomized the Age of Enlightenment's concern for the rights of humanity. In his essay *Persian Letters*,[2] Montesquieu used his mighty pen to bring the abuses of criminal law to public attention. Voltaire became involved in a number of trials that challenged the old ideas of legalized torture, criminal responsibility, and justice. The humanitarian efforts of those men paralleled the work of the most influential criminal law reformer of the era, Cesare Beccaria, founder of the **Classical School.**

The best-known work of Cesare Beccaria is *An Essay on Crimes and Punishment*—a primary influence in the transition from punishment to corrections. It established the following principles:

1. The basis of all social action must be the utilitarian conception of the greatest happiness for the greatest number.

2. Crime must be considered an injury to society, and the only rational measure of crime is the extent of that injury.

3. Prevention of crime is more important than punishment for crimes; indeed, punishment is justifiable only on the supposition that it helps to prevent criminal conduct. In preventing crime it is necessary to improve and publish the laws, so that the nation can understand and support them, to reward virtue, and to improve the public's education both in regard to legislation and to life.

4. In criminal procedures secret accusations and torture should be abolished. There should be speedy trials. The accused should be treated humanely before trial and must have every right and facility to bring forward evidence in his or her behalf. Turning state's evidence should be done away with, as it amounts to no more than the public authorization of treachery.

Charles Louis Secondat, Baron de la Brede et de Montesquieu (1689–1755), was a French historian and philosopher who analyzed law as an expression of justice. He believed that harsh punishment would undermine morality and that appealing to moral sentiment was a better means of preventing crime.

Voltaire (François Marie Arouet) (1694–1778) was the most versatile of the eighteenth-century philosophers, believing that the fear of shame was a deterrent to crime. He fought the legally sanctioned practice of torture, winning reversals—even after convicted felons had been executed—on convictions so obtained under the old code. He was imprisoned in the Bastille in 1726 and released on the condition that he leave France.

Denis Diderot (1713–1784) was a French encyclopedist and philosopher who was thrown into prison in 1749 for his work *Lettre sur les Aveugles* ("Letter on the Blind"), a strong attack on orthodox religion. He worked for twenty years on his twenty-eight-volume Encyclopedia, along with Voltaire, Montesquieu, and other great thinkers of the time. His Encyclopedia became a force in the fight for change in the eighteenth century.

Voltaire, one of the most enlightened eighteenth-century philosophers

—COURTESY OF CORBIS–BETTMANN

Cesare Bonesana, Marchese di Beccaria (1738–1794), wrote *An Essay on Crimes and Punishment*, which was published anonymously in 1764—the most exciting essay on law of the eighteenth century. It proposed a reorientation of criminal law toward humanistic goals. Beccaria suggested that judges should not interpret the law but, rather, that the law should be made more specific, as he believed the real measure of crime was its harm to society. He is regarded as the founder of the Classical School of Criminology.

Jeremy Bentham (1748–1832) was the greatest leader in the reform of English criminal law. He believed that if punishments were designed to negate whatever pleasure or gain the criminal derived from crime, the crime rate would go down. He wrote prodigiously on all aspects of criminal justice. Something of a crackpot in his later years, he devised his ultimate prison: the Panopticon. This monstrosity was never constructed, but debate over it slowed progress in English penology.

5. The purpose of punishment is to deter persons from the commission of crime and not to provide social revenge. Not severity, but certainty and swiftness in punishment, best secure this result. Punishment must be sure and swift and penalties determined strictly in accordance with the social damage wrought by the crime. Crimes against property should be punished solely by fines or by imprisonment when the person is unable to pay the fine. Banishment is an excellent punishment for crimes against the state. There should be no capital punishment. Life imprisonment is a better deterrent. Capital punishment is irreparable and hence makes no provision for possible mistakes and the desirability of later rectification.

6. Imprisonment should be more widely employed, but its mode of application should be greatly improved through providing better physical quarters and by separating and classifying the prisoners as to age, sex, and degree of criminality.[3]

When the essay was first published, Beccaria attempted to remain anonymous so as to "defend the truth without becoming her martyr."[4] After two hard years of writing, he felt he had made enough of a contribution, and he did his best to avoid persecution for his sharp criticism of the conditions of the time. It was soon evident, however, that he was not to be persecuted but hailed as a genius and, when his identity was disclosed, he was promptly invited to Paris by Domenico Morellet.[5] He did not want to leave Italy and his young wife, however, and when he finally made the trip, he had a miserable time. The great philosophers who came to Paris found the brilliant and fiery writer to be a shy, withdrawn, and slightly disturbed young man of twenty-six. He refused to debate with anyone and soon returned to Milan, never to journey away again. In later years he even refused an invitation from Catherine II of Russia to be her legislative adviser at court.

Although Beccaria himself did not seek or receive great personal fame, his small volume was praised as one of the most significant books produced by the Age of Enlightenment. Four of his newer ideas were incorporated into the French Code of Criminal Procedure in 1808 and into the French Penal Code of 1810:

1. An individual should be regarded as innocent until proven guilty.

2. An individual should not be forced to testify against himself or herself.

3. An individual should have the right to employ counsel and to cross-examine the state's witnesses.

4. An individual should have the right to a prompt and public trial and, in most cases, a trial by jury.

Among the philosophers inspired by Beccaria's ideas were the authors of the U.S. Constitution. It seems we owe a great deal to this shy Italian writer of the eighteenth century.[6]

BENTHAM AND THE HEDONISTIC CALCULUS

Jeremy Bentham was the leading reformer of the British criminal law system during the late eighteenth and early nineteenth centuries. He strongly advocated a system of graduated penalties to tie more closely the punishment to the crime. As political equality became a dominant philosophy, new penal policies were required to accommodate this change in emphasis. As Thorsten Sellin stated:

Older penal law had reflected the views dominant in societies where slavery or serfdom flourished, political inequality was the rule, and sovereignty was assumed to be resting in absolute monarchs. Now the most objectionable features of that law, which had favored the upper classes and had provided often arbitrary, brutal and revolting corporal and capital punishments for the lower classes, were to be removed and equality before the law established. Judicial torture for the purpose of extracting evidence was to be abolished, other than penal measures used to control some conduct previously punished as crime, and punishments made only severe enough to outweigh the gains expected by the criminal from his crime. This meant a more humane law, no doubt, applied without discrimination to all citizens alike in harmony with the new democratic ideas.[7]

Bentham believed that an individual's conduct could be influenced in a more scientific manner. Asserting that the main objective of an intelligent person is to achieve the most pleasure while receiving the least amount of pain, he developed his "**hedonistic calculus**,"[8] which he applied to all of his efforts to reform the criminal law. He, like Beccaria, believed punishment could act as a deterrent, but only if it were made appropriate to the crime. This line of thought, adopted by active reformers Samuel Romilly and Robert Peel in the early nineteenth century, has been instrumental in the development of the modern prison.

JOHN HOWARD

John Howard gave little thought to prisons or prison reform until he was appointed sheriff of Bedfordshire in 1773. The appointment opened his eyes to horrors he had never dreamed of. He was appalled by the conditions he found in the hulks and gaols and pressed for legislation to alleviate some of the abuses and improve sanitary conditions. He also traveled extensively on the European continent to examine prisons in other countries. He saw similarly deplorable conditions in

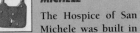

HOSPICE OF SAN MICHELE

The Hospice of San Michele was built in 1704 by Pope Clement XI. The pope himself placed an inscription over the door that remains to this day: "It is insufficient to restrain the wicked by punishment unless you render them virtuous by corrective discipline."

Sir Samuel Romilly (1757–1818), a follower of Bentham, was an able lawyer and the most effective leader in direct and persistent agitation for reform of the English criminal code. He pressed for construction of the first modern English prison, Millbank, in 1816. His prison idea was taken up by Romilly's followers, Sir James Mackintosh (1765–1832) and Sir Thomas Fowell Buxton (1786–1845).

Sir Robert Peel (1788–1850) was the leader in the English legislature for reform of the criminal code, pushing through programs devised by Bentham, Romilly, and others. He established the Irish constabulary, called the "Peelers" after the founder. In 1829, he started the London metropolitan police, known as "Bobbies," also after Sir Robert. He was active in all phases of criminal justice.

John Howard, early jail reformer

—*COURTESY OF FEDERAL BUREAU OF PRISONS*

most areas but was most impressed by some of the institutions in France and Italy. In 1777, he described those conditions and suggested reforms in his *State of Prisons.* In 1779, Parliament passed the Penitentiary Act, providing four principles for reform: secure and sanitary structures, systematic inspection, abolition of fees, and a reformatory regime.[9]

The Penitentiary Act resulted in the first penitentiary, located at Wyndomham in Norfolk, England, and operated by Sir Thomas Beever, the sheriff of Wyndomham. As we see later, the principles contained in the act, though lofty in concept, were hard to implement in the prevailing atmosphere of indifference. It is ironic that this great advocate for better prison conditions did himself die of **jail fever** (typhus) in the Russian Ukraine in 1790. John Howard's name has become synonymous with prison reform, and the John Howard Society has carried his ideas forward to this day.[10]

Houses of Correction, Workhouses, and Gaols

The proliferation of Bridewell-style houses of correction in England was originally intended as a humanitarian move and, in 1576, Parliament ordered that each county in England construct such an institution. They were not merely extensions of almshouses or poorhouses, but were actually penal institutions for all sorts of misdemeanants. Although the bloody penalties for major offenses were growing in number, not even the most callous would advocate harsh physical punishment for every offender. All sorts of rogues, from idlers to whores, were put into the Bridewells, where they were compelled to work under strict discipline at the direction of hard taskmasters. Today, the house of correction and the **workhouse** are regarded as synonymous. Actually, the workhouse was not intended as a penal institution, but as a place for the training and care of the poor. In practice, however, the two soon became indistinguishable, first in England and later in America. Conditions and practices in such institutions were no better than those in the gaols (jails) by the turn of the eighteenth century.

The use of **gaols** to detain prisoners has a grim and unsavory history. As the eighteenth century began, gaol administration was usually left up to the whim of the gaoler, who was usually under the control of the sheriff. Gaols were often used to extort huge fines from those who had the means, by holding those people indef-

Gaols and Gaolbirds

Gaols (jails) were used primarily as places of detention. Some prisoners waited to be tried, others could not pay their fines, and still others awaited execution. No attempt was made to segregate prisoners by age, sex, or crime. Food was often sold by the sheriff at inflated prices, and those who could not pay or have food brought in starved. Early efforts of reformers like John Howard helped clean up the gaols, but even today jails are usually the worst disgrace of the criminal justice system. *Gaolbird* (jailbird) was coined because of the large cagelike cells used to confine the prisoners in unsegregated bunches, like "birds in a cage." ∎

initely in pretrial confinement until they gave in and paid. The lot of the common "gaolbird" was surely not a happy one, and many of the prisoners perished long before their trial dates. The squalid and unhealthy conditions gave rise to epidemics of gaol fever (typhus) that spread to all levels of English life. John Howard claimed that more people died from this malady between 1773 and 1774 than those who were executed by the crown.[11] Ironically, prisoners, and not prison conditions, were blamed for the spread of the deadly disease, and even more sanguinary penalties for offenses were devised. Robert Caldwell describes the typical English gaol:

> Devoid of privacy and restrictions, its contaminated air heavy with the stench of unwashed bodies, human excrement, and the discharge of loathsome sores, the gaol bred the basest thoughts and the foulest deeds. The inmates made their own rules, and the weak and the innocent were exposed to the tyranny of the strong and the vicious. Prostitutes plied their trade with ease, often with the connivance and support of the gaolers, who thus sought to supplement their fees. Even virtuous women sold themselves to obtain food and clothing, and frequently the worst elements of the town used the gaol as they would a brothel. Thus, idleness, vice, perversion, profligacy, shameless exploitation, and ruthless cruelty were compounded in hotbeds of infection and cesspools of corruption. These were the common gaols of England.[12]

It is depressing to think that John Howard, shocked into humanitarian reform efforts when he found himself responsible for one of those human cesspools, was the only sheriff to undertake action against such institutions.

Transportation Systems

DEPORTATION TO THE AMERICAN COLONIES AND AUSTRALIA

One of the earliest forms of social vengeance was **banishment**. In primitive societies the offender was cast out into the wilderness, usually to be eaten by wild beasts or to succumb to the elements. As we have seen, imprisonment and capital punishment were later substituted for banishment. Banishment to penal servitude was, in effect, civil death. Banishment to the gaols, however, more often than not ended in physical death.

The wandering and jobless lower classes, in the period following the breakup of feudalism, were concentrated mostly in high-crime slums in the major cities. As economic conditions worsened, the number of imprisonable crimes was increased to the point that the available prisons were filled. In England, from 1596 to 1776, the pressure was partially relieved by the deportation or **transportation** of malefactors to the colonies in America. Estimates vary greatly of how many original American settlers arrived in chains. Margaret Wilson estimates between three and four hundred annually;[13] other authorities put the figure as high as two thousand a year. The use of convict labor was widespread before the adoption of slavery in the colonies. And even though the entering flow of dangerous felons was somewhat slowed by the introduction of slavery, the poor and the misdemeanant continued to come in great numbers.

Transportation to America was brought to an abrupt halt in 1776 by the American Revolution. But England still needed somewhere to send the criminals overloading its crowded institutions. Captain James Cook had discovered Australia in 1770, and soon the system of transportation was transferred to that continent. It was planned that the criminals would help tame that new and wild land. Over 135,000 felons were sent to Australia between 1787 and 1875, when the British finally abandoned the system.

The ships in which felons were transported have been described as "floating hells"—an understatement. The conditions below decks were worse than those of the gaols. Many died on the long voyages, but enough survived to make it a profitable venture for the shipowners, who fitted out ships specifically for that purpose.[14] Other nations turned to transportation in the nineteenth century, as we see later.

HULKS: A SORDID EPISODE

From 1776 until 1875, even with limited transportation to Australia, the increased prisoner loads wreaked havoc in England's few available facilities. The immediate solution to that problem created one of the most odious episodes in the history of penology and corrections: the use of old "hulks," abandoned or unusable transport ships anchored in rivers and harbors throughout the British Isles, to confine criminal offenders. The brutal and degrading conditions found in the gaols, houses of correction, and workhouses paled in comparison with the conditions found in those fetid and rotting human garbage dumps.

Those responsible for the hulks made no attempt to segregate young from old, hardened criminals from poor misdemeanants, or even men from women. Brutal flogging and degrading labor soon bred moral degeneration in both inmates and keepers. The hulks were originally intended only as a temporary solution to a problem, but they were not completely abandoned until 1858, eighty years later. (Hulks were used in California in the nineteenth century, and one state, Washington, considered the use of decommissioned U.S. Navy warships in 1976. New York City has also used a floating jail.) This episode in penal history becomes especially relevant when the problems of overcrowding in our maximum security prisons are examined.

Transportation

Transportation ships were hired transports employed to convey the convicts from England to New South Wales. Contractors received between twenty and thirty pounds per head. The more convicts carried, the greater the profit would be; thus as many as the ships would hold were usually crammed on board. As a result of such a state of confinement the most loathsome disease was common and the death rate was extremely high. One hundred and fifty-eight out of 502 who were placed on the *Neptune* in 1790 for conveyance to Australia died en route, and 95 out of the 300 in the holds of the *Hillsborough* in 1799, died on the voyage. Those who did arrive were so near dead that they could not stand, and it was necessary to sling them like goods and hoist them out of the ships: when first landed they died at the rate of 10 or 12 a day. The government attempted in 1802 to correct these evils by sending convicts twice a year in ships specially fitted out for the purpose and placed under the direction of a transport board and commanded by naval officers. Although the transports continued to be crowded, health conditions apparently had greatly improved, as it was reported in 1819 by Sir T. B. Martin, the head of the transport board, that, "within the past three years, only 53 out of 6,409, or at the rate of 1 in 112, had died. Out of the 10 transports which had recently sailed only one or two had died." Transportation of offenders involved private merchants to transport criminals, and they were essentially private business entrepreneurs "making a pound" off the backs of offenders. ∎

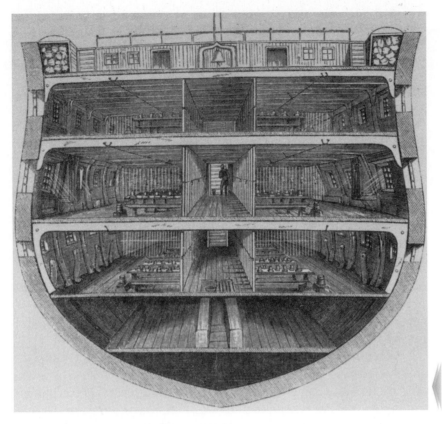

Convict hulk, nineteenth-century England

—COURTESY OF FEDERAL BUREAU OF PRISONS

Early Cellular Prisons

THE MAISON DE FORCE AT GHENT
AND THE HOSPICE OF SAN MICHELE

In his travels on the Continent, John Howard was most impressed by Jean-Jacques Vilain's **Maison de Force** (stronghouse) at Ghent, Belgium, and by the Hospice (hospital) of San Michele in Rome. Although those institutions had developed along individually different lines, both made lasting impressions on Howard. Both served as workhouses, but otherwise they had little in common: their differences were more important than their similarities.

Predecessors of the Belgian workhouses were those in neighboring Amsterdam, constructed around 1596. Most were intended to make a profit,[15] not

A floating prison used in New York City until 1996

—NEW YORK CITY DEPARTMENT OF CORRECTIONS

Convict Hulks

Convict hulks were among the earliest examples of imprisonment used as a method of dealing with criminals. The hulks, sometimes called "hell holes," were broken-down war vessels, stripped and anchored on bays and rivers around England. They were unsanitary, full of vermin, and unventilated. Disease ran rampant and often wiped out the whole prisoner population, and sometimes the crew and neighboring citizens as well. The last European hulk was maintained at Gibraltar as late as 1875. ∎

to exemplify humanitarian ideals, and were seen as a place to put rogues and able-bodied beggars to work. The workhouses were modeled after the Bridewell institution in England and followed a similar pattern of hard work and cruel punishment. By the eighteenth century, Belgium, too, was faced with increasing numbers of beggars and vagrants, and the government called on administrator and disciplinarian Jean-Jacques Vilain for help. His solution—the Maison de Force built in Ghent in 1773—followed the basic workhouse pattern established in Holland and England, but in many respects it was far more just and humane.

Vilain's efforts at improving the administration of the workhouse earned him an honored place in penal history. He was one of the first to develop a system of classification to separate women and children from hardened criminals, and felons from minor offenders. Although he was a stern disciplinarian, he was opposed to life imprisonment and cruel punishment. Rather, he defined discipline by the biblical rule, "If any man will not work, neither let him eat." Vilain's use of individual cells and a system of silence while working resembled the procedures observed at the Hospice of San Michele in Rome. His far-reaching concepts of fair and just treatment, when viewed against the harsh backdrop of that era, mark Vilain as a true visionary in the correctional field.

The **Hospice of San Michele** was designed for incorrigible boys and youths under the age of twenty. As such it is recognized as one of the first institutions to handle juvenile offenders exclusively. Prisoners were administered massive doses of Scripture and hard work in hopes that this regime would reform them. The rule of strict silence was enforced through the flogging of violators. The use of separate cells for sleeping and a large central hall for working became the model for penal institutions in the nineteenth century. This concept of expiation and penance, as applied to corrections, was new and exciting to John Howard, and his Puritan ethic enabled him to see the value of repentance and hard work as demonstrated by the program at San Michele. Under somewhat different policies, the Hospice of San Michele is still used today as a reformatory for delinquent boys.

The main concepts that carried over from the early cellular institutions were the monastic regime of silence and expiation, the central community work area, and individual cells for sleeping. The philosophy of penitence and monastic contemplation of past wrongs espoused by those institutions was reflected in the Quakers' early prison efforts in America.

WILLIAM PENN AND THE "GREAT LAW"

The American colonies were governed by the British under codes established by the Duke of York in 1676 and part of the older Hampshire code established in 1664. These codes were similar to those followed in England, and the use of capital and corporal punishment was the rule of the day. Branding, flogging, the stocks, the pillory, and the brank were also in use extensively.

The concept of more humanitarian treatment of offenders was brought to America by William Penn, the founder of Pennsylvania and leader of the Quakers. The Quaker movement was the touchstone of penal reform, not only in America, but also in Italy and England through its influence on such advocates as Beccaria and Howard. Compared with the other harsh colonial codes in force at the time, the **"Great Law"** of the Quakers was quite humane. This body of laws envisioned hard labor as a more effective punishment than death for serious crimes, and capital punishment was eliminated from the original codes. Later, in supplementary acts, murder and manslaughter were included as social crimes. Only premeditated murder was punishable by death, with other criminal acts treated according to the circumstances.

It is interesting to note that the Quakers' Great Law did away with most religious offenses and stuck to strictly secular criminal jurisprudence, a departure from the codes of other colonies and the earlier European codes. Under the Great Law, a "house of corrections" was established where most punishment was meted out in the form of hard labor. This was the first time that correctional confinement at hard labor was used as a punishment for serious crimes, and not merely as a preface to punishment scheduled for a later date.

The Quaker code of 1682 was in force until 1718, when it was repealed, ironically, just one day after the death of William Penn. The Great Law was replaced by the English Anglican code, and the mild Quaker philosophy gave way to harsh punishments. The new code was even worse than the previous codes of the Duke of York. Capital punishment was prescribed for thirteen offenses,[16] and mutilation, branding, and other corporal punishments were restored for many others.

The influence of Montesquieu, Voltaire, Beccaria, Bentham, Howard, and Penn was felt throughout colonial America. Much of the idealism embodied in the U.S. Constitution reflects the writings of those progressive eighteenth-century leaders. With their philosophies in mind, we can consider some of the major developments in correctional practice in that era of reform.

William Penn (1644–1718), an English Quaker, fought for religious freedom and individual rights. In 1681, he obtained a charter from King Charles II and founded the Quaker settlement of Pennsylvania.

THE WALNUT STREET JAIL

As we have seen, the world of the eighteenth century had prisons, but they were generally used as places of detention for minor offenders and for pretrial confinement. One of the earliest American attempts to operate a state prison for felons was located in an abandoned copper mine in Simsbury, Connecticut.[17] This underground prison began operation in 1773 and quickly became the site of America's first prison riots, in 1774. Although some have called it the first state prison, it was really not much more than a throwback to the sulfur pits of ancient Rome, and it did nothing to advance the state of American corrections. The prisoners were housed in long mine shafts, and the administration buildings were placed near the entrances. Underground mine shaft prisons constituted one of several American attempts to provide a special place in which to house and work convicted felons. The establishment of such a special facility was finally accomplished in Pennsylvania in 1790.

It is hard to imagine a time when there were no long-term penitentiaries for felons, but before 1790 that was the case. Ironically, in that year the first penitentiary in America, the prototype of the modern prison system, was born in the same city that spawned the fledgling United States as a nation. Philadelphia,

Benjamin Franklin (1706–1790) founded the American Philosophical Society in Philadelphia in 1743. He served as Pennsylvania's appointed agent to England and a member of the second Continental Congress (1777) to draft the Declaration of Independence, which he signed. He was plenipotentiary to France and negotiated to obtain that country's help in the Revolution. He was also a statesman, scientist, and philosopher.

Benjamin Rush (1745–1813), physician and political leader, was a member of both Continental Congresses (1776, 1777) and a signer of the Declaration of Independence. He established the first free dispensary in the United States (1786) and was an advocate of prison reform and humane treatment.

Pennsylvania, the home of the Declaration of Independence, is also—thanks to the Quakers—the home of the **Walnut Street Jail,**[18] the first true correctional institution in America.

Despite earlier efforts at prison reform, the Quakers had been thwarted in their humanistic goals by the repeal of Penn's Great Law in 1718. In 1776, the first American Penitentiary Act was passed, but its implementation was delayed because of the War of Independence. In 1790, with the Revolution behind them, the Quakers reasserted their concern with the treatment of convicted criminals.[19] After much prodding, they convinced the Pennsylvania legislature to declare a wing of the Walnut Street Jail a penitentiary house for all convicted felons except those sentenced to death.[20] Thus, although prisons, gaols, dungeons, and workhouses had been in existence for years, this wing was the first to be used exclusively for the correction of convicted felons.

Some of the concepts embodied in the Walnut Street Jail had their antecedents in the charter of William Penn in 1682. Those provisions, repressed by the harsh Anglican code, were that:

1. All prisoners were to be bailable.
2. Those wrongfully imprisoned could recover double damages.
3. Prisons were to be free as to fees, food, and lodging.
4. The lands and goods of felons were to be liable for confiscation and double restitution to injured parties.
5. All counties were to provide houses to replace the pillory, stocks, and the like.[21]

Although not all of the idealistic reforms were adopted, the direction of change had been established. The system of prison discipline developed at the Walnut Street Jail became known as the "Pennsylvania system." The Pennsylvania system was developed through the ideas and efforts of such reformers as Benjamin Franklin and Benjamin Rush, building on the humanitarian ideals of Howard, Bentham, Beccaria, and Montesquieu. Patriot and war hero William Bradford, who drafted the codes that implemented the system, praised the European reformers in the state legislature.

As originally conceived, the basic element of the **Pennsylvania system** called for solitary confinement without work. It was assumed that this method would result in quicker reformations. Offenders could reflect on their crimes all

The Walnut Street Jail

The Walnut Street Jail, typical of colonial jails before the innovation of solitary confinement for felons, is described in David J. Rothman, *Discovery of the Asylum* (Boston: Little, Brown, 1971), p. 55. "Jails in fact closely resembled the household in structure and routine. They lacked a distinct architecture and special procedures. When the Virginia burgess required that county prisons be 'good, strong, and substantial,' and explicitly recommended that they follow 'after the form of Virginia housing,' results were in keeping with these directions. The doors were perhaps somewhat sturdier, the locks slightly more impressive, but the general design of the jail was the same as for an ordinary residence. True to the household model, the keeper and his family resided in the jail, occupying one of its rooms; the prisoners lived several together in the others, with little to differentiate the keeper's quarters from their own. They wore no special clothing or uniforms and usually neither cuffs nor chains restrained their movements. They walked—not marched—about the jail. The workhouse model was so irrelevant that nowhere were they required to perform the slightest labor . . . ." ∎

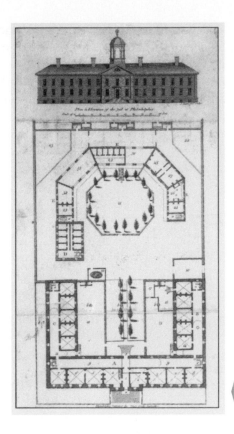

The Walnut Street Jail (Philadelphia, 1790), the first penitentiary in the New World

—*THE HISTORICAL SOCIETY OF PENNSYLVANIA*

day and would soon repent so they might rejoin humanity. The terrible effects of such isolation—physical and psychological—soon became apparent. Some kind of work had to be provided, as well as moral and religious instruction, to maintain the prisoners' mental and bodily health. The work schedule thus was from eight to ten hours a day, and the prisoner worked in isolation, usually on piecework or handicrafts.

More and more convicts were sent to the new state prison, and overcrowding shattered early hopes for its success. Even the original system of separate areas for women and children broke down with the flood of inmates. But despite the ultimate failure of the Walnut Street Jail program, it represented a major breakthrough for penology. New prisons were soon in demand throughout America, and the Walnut Street Jail was copied extensively, in at least ten states and many foreign countries.[22]

William Bradford (1721–1791), the "Patriot Printer of 1776," was one of the early advocates of a Continental Congress. He was a member of the Sons of Liberty, a political rival of Benjamin Franklin, and an active reformer of the harsh British codes. As a major in the army, he became a hero of the Revolution.

Summary

As the eighteenth century drew to a close, the move for prison reform was sparked by a new feeling of vigor and energy. The decade after the opening of the Walnut Street Jail was full of hope for the concepts embodied there, however imperfectly. It would be an oversimplification to say that the Walnut Street Jail was the world's first real attempt at a prison for convicted felons. The eighteenth century produced many such attempts, both in Europe and in America. Some of the principles behind the Walnut Street Jail, however, had a permanent influence on the development of correctional institutions throughout the world. Connecticut's abortive attempt to establish a state prison at Simsbury failed because the mine shafts could not be made habitable and because there was little public enthusiasm for the project. The Quakers' compassionate efforts, though much more humane, were doomed to failure by the lack of public and political support, incompetent personnel, and enforced idleness. With the industrial age came overcrowded prisons, which forced the new administrators to consider much larger and more productive kinds of institutions. As America entered the nineteenth century, it also entered an age of expansion. The prison movement adopted this growth-oriented philosophy, and as we see in the next chapter, the nineteenth and early twentieth centuries became the age of prisons.

Review Questions

1. What was Beccaria's main contribution to corrections?
2. What were John Howard's four principles for a penitentiary system?
3. Many reformers tried to improve prison conditions in the eighteenth century. Name at least three and describe their major contributions.

Words to Remember

Classical School	gaols	Hospice of San Michele
"hedonistic calculus"	banishment	the "Great Law"
jail fever	transportation	Walnut Street Jail
workhouse	Maison de Force	Pennsylvania system

Endnotes

1. For a historical view of the development of Western criminal justice systems up to the eighteenth century, see Herbert Johnson, *History of Criminal Justice* (Cincinnati: Anderson, 1988), pp. 23–112.

2. The *Persian Letters* was a satirical essay by Montesquieu on the abuses of current criminal law. The essay greatly influenced Beccaria. This, along with Voltaire's activities, led Beccaria to write his *Crimes and Punishment*.

3. Harry Elmer Barnes and Negley K. Teeters, *New Horizons in Criminology*, 3rd ed. (Englewood Cliffs, NJ: Prentice Hall, 1959), p. 322.

4. Cesare Beccaria, *An Essay on Crimes and Punishment* (Philadelphia: P. H. Nicklin, 1819).

5. Domenico Morellet (1727–1819) was a French philosopher who worked with Diderot on the *Encyclopedia*.

6. Beccaria's contributions to corrections as the father of modern criminology have been called into question in recent years. See Graeme Newman and Pietro Morongu, "Penological Reform and the Myth of Beccaria," *Criminology* 28 (1990): 325–346. Nonetheless, he remains the central figure in liberal penology.

7. Thorsten Sellin, "A Look at Prison History," *Federal Probation* (September 1967): 20.

8. Hedonistic calculus was a term devised by Jeremy Bentham to describe the idea that "to achieve the most pleasure and the least pain is the main objective of an intelligent man."

9. Barnes and Teeters, *New Horizons in Criminology*, p. 335. See also John Freeman, *Prisons Past and Present* (London: Heinemann, 1978), for an excellent set of papers celebrating Howard's contributions to prison reform.

10. The John Howard Society is a nonprofit organization supported by contributions. It

provides casework service to inmates and their families, and it also works to promote community understanding of prison problems and offers technical assistance to correctional agencies (608 South Dearborn St., Chicago, Illinois 60605).

11. John Howard, *The State of Prisons* (New York: E.P. Dutton, 1929).

12. Robert G. Caldwell, *Criminology* (New York: Ronald Press, 1965), p. 494.

13. Margaret Wilson, *The Crime of Punishment* (New York: Harcourt Brace and World, 1931), p. 224.

14. Alexis Durham, "Origins of Interest in the Privatization of Punishment: The Nineteenth and Twentieth Century American Experience," *Criminology* 27 (1989): 107–139. For an evaluation of modern private sector prisons, see Martin Sellers, "Private and Public Prisons: A Comparison of Costs, Programs and Facilities," *International Journal of Offender Therapy and Comparative Criminology* 33 (1989): 241–256; Nicole Casarez, "Furthering the Accountability Principle in Privatized Federal Corrections: The Need for Access to Private Prison Records," *University of Michigan Journal of Law Reform* 28 (1995): 24–303.

15. For a discussion of contemporary punishment for profit, see David Shichor, *Punishment for Profit: Private Prisons, Public Concerns* (Thousand Oaks, CA: Sage, 1995).

16. Only larceny was exempt from capital punishment. All other major crimes were punishable by death.

17. For a short history of this facility, see Charles W. Dean, "The Story of Newgate," *Federal Probation* (June 1977): 8–14. See also Alexis Durham, "Newgate of Connecticut: Origins and Early Days of an Early American Prison," *Justice Quarterly* 6 (1989): 89–116.

18. Barnes and Teeters, *New Horizons in Criminology,* p. 336.

19. Negley K. Teeters, *The Cradle of the Penitentiary* (Philadelphia: Pennsylvania Prison Society, 1955).

20. Donald R. Taft, *Criminology,* 3rd ed. (New York: Macmillan, 1956), p. 478.

21. Barnes, *The Story of Punishment,* p. 128.

22. Ibid.

CHAPTER THREE

The Age of Prisons (1800 to the Present)

Overview

The first two chapters have acquainted the student with how corrections has grown from individual to group punishment and then from group punishment to legal codes and punishment, accomplished by the country or state. We saw how the concept of penitence in the Walnut Street Jail grew to be a whole new concept—the penitentiary. In this chapter we shall examine how this simple concept grew into the vast network of prisons across America. First, we examine the two competing systems for prison design and construction for over a century.

To the builders of this nitemare
Though you may never get to
read these words I pity you;
For the cruelty of your minds have
designed this Hell;
If men's buildings are a reflection
of what they are,
This one portraits the ugliness of
all humanity.
IF ONLY YOU HAD SOME
COMPASSION

—on a prison wall

The Pennsylvania System

With the advent of the nineteenth century and the social upheaval produced by the Industrial Revolution, the citizens of Pennsylvania led the way in developing a penitentiary system. The Walnut Street Jail had been fairly effective for a decade, and that Pennsylvania system was copied extensively in both architectural design and administration (Table 3-1). But when the Philadelphia Society for the Alleviation of the Miseries of Public Prisons[1] observed the many emerging problems at the Walnut Street Jail, a radically new prison was proposed for the state. It was suggested that solitary confinement without labor continue to be used as the sole reformatory process.

The Western Penitentiary at Pittsburgh, built in 1826, was based on the cellular isolation wing of the Walnut Street Jail. Essentially, the Western Penitentiary amounted to a poor imitation of Bentham's proposed prison (Panopticon), an octagonal monstrosity that originally provided for solitary confinement and no labor. The legislature amended the program in 1829, maintaining

TABLE 3.1

American Prisons Built Before Auburn

Pennsylvania	Walnut Street Jail, Philadelphia	1790
New York	Newgate Prison, New York City	1797
New Jersey	State Penitentiary, Lamberton	1798
Kentucky	State Penitentiary, Frankfort	1800
Virginia	State Penitentiary, Richmond	1800
Massachusetts	State Prison, Charlestown	1805
Vermont	State Prison, Windsor	1809
Maryland	State Penitentiary, Baltimore	1812
New Hampshire	State Prison, Concord	1812
Ohio	State Penitentiary, Columbus	1816
Georgia	State Penitentiary, Milledgeville	1817

solitary confinement but adding the provision that inmates perform some labor in their cells. In 1833, the small dark cells were torn down, and larger **outside cells** were built. The efforts influenced the development of the Eastern Penitentiary, located in Philadelphia.

The Eastern Penitentiary became the model and primary exponent of the Pennsylvania, or "separate" system. This prison was built like a square wheel, with the cell blocks arranged like spokes around the hub, or central rotunda. The routine at Eastern—solitary confinement, silence, and labor in "outside"[2] cells—clearly stressed the separation of each inmate from the others (Figure 3-1a).

Although the Pennsylvania system aroused great international interest, it was adopted by only two other states. The New Jersey State Penitentiary in Trenton began operations in 1837 along the lines of the separate system—soon abandoned, however, in favor of that used at Auburn, New York. Rhode Island followed the same pattern as that in New Jersey. Its first prison, built in 1838 along the lines of the Eastern Penitentiary, abandoned the separate system by 1852. By contrast, many European countries wholeheartedly adopted the Pennsylvania model.[3]

The Auburn System

The major evils of the jails and other confinement facilities before 1800 were indiscriminate congregate confinement and enforced idleness. The rapid debasement of the prisoners when kept in filthy conditions, with men, women, and children thrown together under a regime of neglect and brutality, appalled the early reformers. The long-term prisons established in the last decade of the eighteenth century were not just a substitute for capital and corporal punishment; they were total administrative and custodial systems intended to remedy the evils of the old methods. In the first quarter of the nineteenth century, administrators experimented with many new systems. The leading contenders for the world's attention were the Eastern Penitentiary and the New York State Prison at Auburn, opened in 1819.

The Auburn prison administrators developed a system that was almost the opposite of that used at the Eastern Penitentiary. The building itself was based on a new "inside" cell design (Figure 3-1b),[4] and the cells were small when compared with those at Eastern. The small cells were designed just for sleeping, not for work.

Harry Elmer Barnes (1889–1968) was a great American educator and sociologist who coauthored many books on penology, punishment, and criminology.

Louis Dwight (1793–1854) organized the Prison Discipline Society of Boston. He was originally trained for the ministry but injured his lungs and could not preach. In 1824, he rode through the countryside distributing Bibles to prisoners. He was the most vocal advocate of the Auburn system and, as director of the Prison Discipline Society of Boston from 1825 to 1854, was the best source of information about that era of American prisons.

3.1

Cell Designs: (a)
"Outside Cell Design, (b)
"Inside" Cell Design

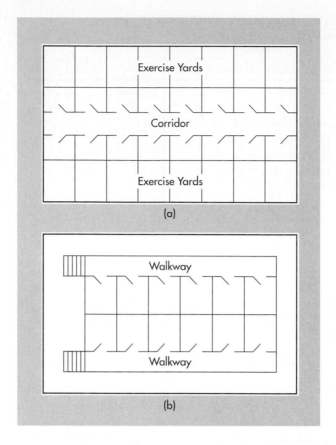

In addition, a new style of discipline was inaugurated at Auburn that became known as the Auburn, or "congregate," system.

In the early years of the Auburn prison, administrators tried an experiment to test the efficacy of the Pennsylvania system. They selected eighty of the most hardened convicts, placing them in solitary confinement and

A typical example of an
"inside" cell block

—*COURTESY OF THE GEORGIA
DEPARTMENT OF CORRECTIONS*

enforced idleness from Christmas 1821 through Christmas 1823. So many of those men succumbed to sickness and insanity that the experiment was discontinued. The Auburn administration thus claimed failure for solitary confinement when the method included idleness. Given the small **inside cells** in Auburn, their claim was no doubt a valid one. However, the Auburn experiment cannot be considered a fair test of the Pennsylvania system, because the latter system used large outside cells and provided for handicraft and other labor in the cells.[5]

DISCIPLINE AT AUBURN

An unfortunate by-product of the badly planned Auburn experiment was the use of solitary confinement as a means of punishment within the prison. The discipline regimen at Auburn also included congregate work in the shops during the day, separation of prisoners into small individual cells at night, silence at all times, lockstep marching formations, and a congregate mess at which the prisoners sat face-to-back.[6] There was great emphasis on silence. In the belief that verbal exchange between prisoners was contaminating, conversation was prevented by liberal use of the whip. An excellent description of the **Auburn system** in its early stages is quoted by Harry Elmer Barnes, drawn from a letter written by Louis Dwight:

> At Auburn we have a more beautiful example still of what may be done by proper discipline, in a prison well constructed. It is not possible to describe the pleasure which we feel in contemplating this noble institution, after wading through the fraud, and the material and moral filth of many prisons. We regard it as a model worthy of the world's imitation. We do not mean that there is nothing in this institution which admits of improvement; for there have been a few cases of unjustifiable severity in punishments; but, upon the whole, the institution is immensely elevated above the old penitentiaries.
>
> The whole establishment, from the gate to the sewer, is a specimen of neatness. The unremitted industry, the entire subordination and subdued feelings of the convicts, has probably no parallel among an equal number of criminals. In their solitary cells they spend the night, with no other book but the Bible, and at sunrise they proceed, in military order, under the eye of the turnkeys, in solid columns, with the lock march, to their workshops; thence, in the same order at the hour of breakfast, to the common hall, where they partake of their wholesome and frugal meal in silence. Not even a whisper is heard; though the silence is such that a whisper might be heard through the whole apartment. The convicts are seated, in single file, at narrow tables, with their backs towards the center, so that there can be no interchange of signs. If one has more food than he wants, he raises his left hand; and if another has less, he raises his right hand, and the waiter changes it. When they have done eating, at the ringing of a little bell, of the softest sound, they rise from the table, form the solid columns, and return, under the eye of the turnkeys, to the workshops. From one end of the shops to the other, it is the testimony of many witnesses, that they have passed more than three hundred convicts, without seeing one leave his work, or turn his head to gaze at them. There is the most perfect attention to business from morning till night, interrupted only by the time necessary to dine, and never by the fact that the whole body of prisoners has done its tasks, and the time is now their own,

An early Auburn-style prison
—*COURTESY OF FEDERAL BUREAU OF PRISONS*

and they can do as they please. At the close of the day, a little before sunset, the work is all laid aside at once, and the convicts return, in military order, to the solitary cells, where they partake of the frugal meal, which they were permitted to take from the kitchen, where it was furnished for them as they returned from the shops. After supper, they can, if they choose, read Scripture undisturbed and then reflect in silence on the errors of their lives. They must not disturb their fellow prisoners by even a whisper.[7]

TABLE *3.2*

American Prisons Built After Auburn (Through 1869)

New York (Sing Sing)	1825	Kentucky	1842
Pennsylvania (Pittsburgh)	1826	Indiana (Jeffersonville)	1842
Connecticut (Wethersford)	1827	Mississippi (Jackson)	1842
Massachusetts (a wing)	1829	Maine (Thomaston)	1845
Vermont	1831	New York (Clinton)	1845
Tennessee (Nashville)	1831	Texas (Huntsville)	1848
New Hampshire	1832	Minnesota (Stillwater)	1851
Illinois (Alton)	1833	California (San Quentin)	1852
Ohio (Columbus)	1834	Wisconsin (Waupun)	1852
Louisiana (Baton Rouge)	1835	Illinois (Joliet)	1858
Pennsylvania (Philadelphia)	1835	Indiana (Michigan City)	1860
Missouri (Jefferson City)	1836	Idaho (Boise)	1863
New Jersey (Trenton)	1837	Kansas (Lansing)	1864
Rhode Island (Providence)	1838	Nevada (Carson City)	1864
Michigan (Jackson)	1838	South Carolina (Columbia)	1865
Iowa (Ft. Madison)	1840	West Virginia (Moundsville)	1866
Alabama (Wetumpka)	1841	Nebraska (Lincoln)	1869
Georgia	1841		

The Auburn system became the pattern for over thirty state prisons in the next half century (see Table 3-2). Sing Sing Prison in New York followed the Auburn pattern in 1825. Wethersford Prison in Connecticut copied the Auburn system but used a more moderate form of those brutal punishments. Later prisons modeled their disciplinary systems after Wethersford.

Auburn's structural design—inside cells and wings composed of two to four tiers of cells (cell blocks)—became the model for most prisons built in the following 150 years. Variations on the Auburn concept are shown in Figure 3-2. The most popular of those types, first constructed in 1898 at Fresnes, France, became known as the "telephone pole" design. Regardless of the cell block arrangement, the inside cell design became the most common model in America.

One of the more important, but less noted, aspects of early prison architecture was the grand scale and sheer size of the institutions. "Bigger is better" (and cheaper) was the watchword of early prison builders. Huge gothic-style structures achieved an effect similar to that of the medieval cathedrals of Europe. They made

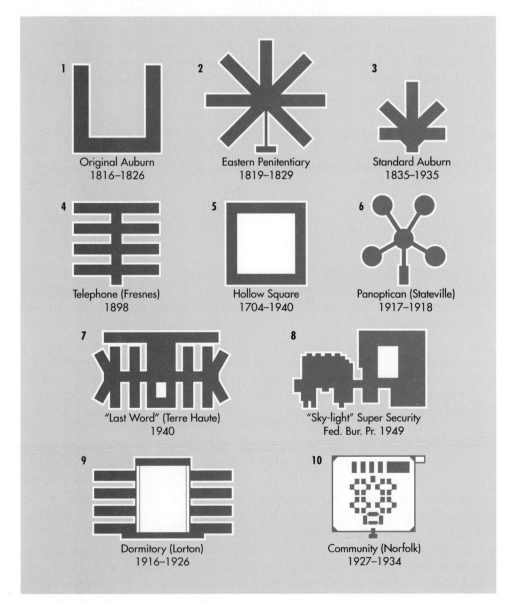

FIGURE

3.2

Types of Prisons

SOURCE: © Howard B. Gill, 1960. Reproduction permitted by Institute of Correctional Administration, Boston, Massachusetts.

1 Original Auburn 1816–1826

2 Eastern Penitentiary 1819–1829

3 Standard Auburn 1835–1935

4 Telephone (Fresnes) 1898

5 Hollow Square 1704–1940

6 Panoptican (Stateville) 1917–1918

7 "Last Word" (Terre Haute) 1940

8 "Sky-light" Super Security Fed. Bur. Pr. 1949

9 Dormitory (Lorton) 1916–1926

10 Community (Norfolk) 1927–1934

the people inside seem small and insignificant. This feeling was further enhanced by the stern discipline employed in these huge castles of despair. Size is discussed again in later chapters, but we should note here that the size of the early prisons gave rise to a subtle pressure to keep them filled with society's castoffs.

Prison Competition

The main theme in both the Pennsylvania and Auburn systems was the belief that a regimen of silence and penitence would prevent cross-infection and encourage improved behavior in the prisoner. Supporters of the Pennsylvania system claimed it was easier to control the prisoners, gave more consideration to their individual needs, prevented contamination by the complete separation of prisoners from one another, and provided more opportunity for meditation and penitence. Another advantage they cited was that prisoners could leave the Pennsylvania system with their background known only to a few administrators because they did not come in contact with other prisoners.

On the other hand, supporters of the Auburn, or congregate, system argued that it was cheaper to construct and get started, offered better vocational training, and produced more money for the state.[8] The persuasive power of economics finally decided the battle, and the **congregate system** was adopted in almost all other American prisons, even in Pennsylvania. The Western Penitentiary was converted in 1869, and finally, in 1913, the Eastern Penitentiary changed its system. The capitulation of the Pennsylvania system followed many long years of fierce controversy between the two systems. "The only gratifying feature of the controversy was that both systems were so greatly superior to the unspeakable . . . system which they displaced that their competition inevitably worked for the betterment of penal conditions."[9]

Rules

As was mentioned in Chapter 1, prisons can be viewed as yet another method to implement social vengeance for wrongs against society. Europeans examining the Auburn and Pennsylvania systems made a keen observation on the American society and its prisons:

> It must be acknowledged that the **penitentiary system** [emphasis added] in America is severe. While society in the United States gives the example of the most extended liberty, the prisons of the same country offer the spectacle of the most complete despotism.[10]

In this context, the individual citizen's sense of guilt when he or she inflicts brutal or cruel punishment on another is diffused by the need for revenge on criminal offenders as a class and for the protection of society. The "out-of-sight, out-of-mind" principle was especially evident in the early nineteenth-century prisons. Most of them were located far out in the countryside, free from either interference or inspection by the communities that supplied the prisoners. It is not too hard to understand why rules and procedures emphasized the smooth and undisturbed operation of the prison rather than the modification of the individual prisoner's behavior. Administrators were judged by the prison's production record and the number of escapes, not by the number of successful rehabilitations. Because of this, rules were designed to keep prisoners under total control. It is those early and well-established prison practices that have been the most difficult to overcome.

Elam Lynds, warden of Auburn and later of Sing Sing (which he built), was one of the most influential persons in the development of early prison discipline in America. He is described as having been a strict *disciplinarian* who believed that all convicts were cowards who could not be reformed until their spirit was broken. To this end, he devised a system of brutal punishments and degrading procedures, many of which remained as accepted practice until very recent times.

The imposition of silence was seen as the most important part of the discipline program. The rule of absolute silence and noncommunication was maintained and enforced by the immediate use of the lash for the slightest infraction. Flogging was advocated by Lynds as the most effective way to maintain order. He sometimes used a "cat" made of wire strands, but more often a rawhide whip. The stereotyped ex-con who always talks out of the side of his mouth actually developed earlier, in the "silent" prisons, to get around the silence rules.

Another bizarre form of discipline that was developed at Auburn was the **lockstep** formation. Prisoners were required to line up in close formation with their hands on the shoulders or under the arms of the prisoner in front. The line then moved rapidly toward its destination as the prisoners shuffled their feet in unison, without lifting them from the ground. Because this nonstop shuffle was "encouraged" by the use of the lash, any prisoner who fell out of lockstep risked a broken ankle or other serious injury from the steadily moving formation. Breaking the rule of silence during formation was considered especially objectionable and was punished viciously.

The use of degrading prison garb was also initiated at Auburn and Sing Sing. Early prisoners were allowed to wear the same clothing as the free society did. At Auburn and Sing Sing different colors were used for the first-time offenders and for repeaters. Bizarre outfits served to reveal the prisoners' classification at a glance, to institutionalize them further, and to facilitate identification of escapees. The famous **prison stripes** came into being in 1815 in New York. Only very recently were the stripes abandoned in most prisons but were returned by the Mississippi legislature in 1994.

The methods used to prevent conversation or communication during meals were also humiliating. As mentioned earlier, prisoners were required to sit face-to-back. They were given their meager, and usually bland and unsavory, meal to eat in silence. If they wanted more food, they would raise one hand; if they had too much, they raised the other. Any infraction of the rule of silence resulted in a flogging and the loss of a meal. This kind of entrenched procedure, very resistant to modern reforms, has been the source of many prison riots.

One of the earliest and most well-known forms of prison discipline was the "prison-within-a-prison," or solitary confinement, used as punishment for violation of institutional rules. Although the early experiment with total **solitary confinement** at Auburn showed it could not serve as the basis of a permanent prison system, the administrators saw its possibilities as a punishment for infractions of prison rules. Most of the prisons designed along the Auburn model, therefore, had a block of cells somewhere inside the walls, often referred to as the "hole." Usually, a sentence to solitary confinement was accompanied by reduced rations as well, consisting often of only bread and water. Solitary confinement is frequently used to discipline prisoners even today, although under more humane conditions.

PRISON STRIPES
A development of the various forms of attire used to degrade and identify prisoners. Wide alternating black-and-white horizontal bands were placed on the loose-fitting heavy cotton garments. Stripes were still in use in the South as late as the 1940s and 1950s. They have been generally replaced in most security prisons by blue denims or whites. Prison stripes are frequently found on prison chain gangs.

THE HOLE, OR SOLITARY CONFINEMENT
Usually located in the lower levels of the prison, most were small four-by-eight cells with no light and solid walls and doors, usually painted black. Time in the hole was ordinarily accompanied by reduced rations and the loss of all privileges. Today, solitary confinement is used for administrative or disciplinary segregation, commonly in cells similar to all others except for their single occupancy and loss of privileges such as television or radio.

The many new prisons that were constructed in the century after the Eastern Penitentiary and the Auburn Prison made few, if any, contributions to the development of penology or corrections. The two greatest innovations, which persist today, were prison industries and the massive structures using the interior cell block. Enforced silence was finally seen as a failure and abandoned. Cruel and barbaric punishments, though publicly decried, are still sometimes used—largely because most prisons are isolated from society and its controls. The development of corrections between 1800 and 1870, branching into procedures and philosophies that were unjust, still produced better methods than did the universally accepted capital and corporal punishment that preceded it. And in the following era, the swing toward a more realistic and humanistic correctional approach began.

Maconochie and Crofton: A New Approach

The reformatory system in America owes a great deal to the work of an Englishman, Captain Alexander Maconochie, and an Irishman, Sir Walter Crofton. Together they laid the foundation for reformative rather than purely punitive programs for the treatment of criminals.

MACONOCHIE AND THE INDETERMINATE SENTENCE

In 1840, Captain Maconochie was put in charge of the British penal colony on Norfolk Island, about a thousand miles off the coast of Australia. To this island were sent the criminals who were "twice condemned": they had been shipped to Australia from England and then from Australia to Norfolk. Conditions were so bad at Norfolk that men reprieved from the death penalty wept, and those who were to die thanked God.[11] That was the kind of hell Maconochie inherited.

A "sweat box" cell used for solitary confinement

—*PHOTO BY PETER C. UNSINGER*

The first thing Maconochie did was to eliminate the flat sentence,[12] a system that had allowed no hope of release until the full time had been served. Then he developed a "mark system" whereby a convict could earn freedom by hard work and good behavior. This put the burden of release on the convict. As Maconochie said, "When a man keeps the key of his own prison, he is soon persuaded to fit it into the lock." The system had five principles:

1. Release should not be based on the completing of a sentence for a set period of time, but on the completion of a determined and specified quantity of labor. In brief, time sentences should be abolished, and task sentences substituted.

2. The quantity of labor a prisoner must perform should be expressed in a number of "marks" that he must earn, by improvement of conduct, frugality of living, and habits of industry, before he can be released.

3. While in prison he should earn everything he receives. All sustenance and indulgences should be added to his debt of marks.

4. When qualified by discipline to do so, he should work in association with a small number of other prisoners, forming a group of six or seven, and the whole group should be answerable for the conduct and labor of each member.

5. In the final stage, a prisoner, while still obliged to earn his daily tally of marks, should be given a proprietary interest in his own labor and be subject to a less rigorous discipline, to prepare him for release into society.[13]

It is a sorry fact that Maconochie's visionary efforts toward rehabilitation were not appreciated or supported by the unenlightened bureaucrats above him. His results thus were disclaimed, and the colony fell back into its former brutalized routine almost as soon as he left it.

CROFTON AND THE IRISH SYSTEM

Fortunately, Maconochie's ideas did reach beyond the shores of Norfolk Island. His successful use of the indeterminate sentence[14] showed that imprisonment could be used to prepare a convict for eventual return to the community. If this were true, then the length of the sentence should not be an arbitrary period of time but should be related to the rehabilitation of the offender. Sir Walter Crofton of Ireland used that concept in developing what he called the "indeterminate system," which came to be known as the **Irish system**. He reasoned that if penitentiaries are places where offenders think about their crimes and can decide to stop their criminal misbehavior ("repent"), then there must be a mechanism to determine that this decision has in fact been made, as well as a mechanism for getting the inmate out when penitence has been done. The indeterminate sentence was believed to be the best mechanism.

The system Crofton devised—like Maconochie's—consisted of a series of stages, each bringing the convict closer to the free society. The first stage was composed of solitary confinement and monotonous work. The second stage was assignment to public works and a progression through various grades, each grade shortening the length of stay. The last stage was assignment to an intermediate prison where the prisoner worked without supervision and moved in and out of the free community. If the prisoner's conduct continued to be good and if he or she were able to find employment, then the offender returned to the community on a conditional pardon or **ticket-of-leave**. This ticket could be revoked at any time within the span of the original fixed sentence if the prisoner's conduct was not up to standards established by those who supervised the conditional pardon. Crofton's plan was the first effort to establish a system of **conditional liberty** in the community, the system we know today as *parole*.

The Reformatory Era (1870 to 1910)

Leaders in U.S. penology and prison administration met at the American Prison Congress of 1870[15] to discuss the direction that corrections practices should take. They were especially concerned about overcrowding, and they discussed what new kinds of prisons should be built to alleviate it. Many urged that Maconochie's and Crofton's plans be adopted in America. That idea was endorsed by the members, and the reformatory era in American corrections was born.

The first **reformatory** in America, built in Elmira, New York, in 1876, became the model for all those that followed. Zebulon Brockway, the first superintendent, had introduced some new educational methods at the Detroit House of Corrections, and he expanded on that concept at Elmira. Elmira was originally built for adult felons, but it was used instead for youths from sixteen to thirty years of age who were serving their first term in prison. One observer cited the following characteristics as the standards for Elmira, and many of those reappeared in its imitators:

1. The material structural establishment itself. The general plan and arrangements should be those of the Auburn system, modified and modernized; and 10 percent of the cells might well be constructed like those of the Pennsylvania system. The whole should be supplied with suitable modern sanitary appliances and with abundance of natural and artificial light.

2. Clothing—not degradingly distinctive, but uniform, . . . fitly representing the respective grades or standing of the prisoners . . .. Scrupulous cleanliness should be maintained and the prisoners appropriately groomed.

3. A liberal prison diet designed to promote vigor. Deprivation of food, by a general regulation, is deprecated . . . .

4. All the modern appliances for scientific physical culture; a gymnasium completely equipped with baths and apparatus; and facilities for field athletics.

5. Facilities for manual training sufficient for about one-third of the population . . . .. This special manual training covers, in addition to other exercises in other departments, mechanical and freehand drawing; sloyd [manual training] in wood and metals; cardboard constructive form work; clay modeling; cabinet making; clipping and filing; and iron molding.

6. Trade instruction based on the needs and capacities of individual prisoners. (Where a thousand prisoners are involved, thirty-six trades may be usefully taught.)

7. A regimental military organization with a band of music, swords for officers, and dummy guns for the rank and file of prisoners.

8. School of letters with a curriculum that reaches from an adaptation of the kindergarten . . . up to the usual high school course; and, in addition, special classes in college subjects . . . .

9. A well-selected library for circulation, consultation, and for occasional semi-social use.

10. The weekly institutional newspaper, in lieu of all outside newspapers, edited and printed by the prisoners under due censorship.

11. Recreating and diverting entertainments for the mass of the population, provided in the great auditorium; not any vaudeville or minstrel shows, but entertainments of such a class as the middle cultured people of a community would enjoy . . . .

12. Religious opportunities . . . adapted to the hereditary [and] habitual . . . denominational predilection of the individual prisoners.

13. Definitely planned, carefully directed, emotional occasions; not summoned, primarily, for either instruction, diversion, nor, specifically, for a common religious impression, but, figuratively, for a kind of irrigation.[16]

Zebulon Reed Brockway (1827–1920), along with Enoch C. Wines and Franklin Benjamin Sanborn, was the third member of the "big three" of penology in 1870. He served on many commissions to improve prisons and even founded the U.S. Army Disciplinary Barracks at Fort Leavenworth. Later, he was the first superintendent at the Elmira Reformatory, where he used military organization and discipline to govern the prisoners. His book, *Fifty Years of Prison Service* (1912), is a classic.

The only real differences between the programs at Elmira and those at the adult prisons were the emphasis on reforming youth, increased academic education, and more extensive trade training. Two significant features were adopted for the reformatories, though: the indeterminate sentence and a grading system based on marks that could lead to parole.

Elmira was copied, in one form or another, by seventeen states between 1876 and 1913 (Table 3-3). Brockway's leadership produced the first attempt to offer programs of education and reformation to all inmates, adult or youth. Trade training, academic education, and the military type of discipline utilized at Elmira undoubtedly also influenced the programs of many of the older prisoners. Some aspects of the indeterminate sentence and parole concepts were finally extended to the state prisons. It is not surprising that in an era when public education was considered to be the answer to so many problems in the outside world, it was viewed as the answer to crime as well. But because the same physical environment and the same underpaid and poorly qualified personnel found in prisons were also found in reformatories, those institutions were soon reduced to junior prisons with the usual routine. The same old "prison discipline" was still the most dominant feature in any penal program.

Elmira reformatory

—COURTESY FEDERAL BUREAU OF PRISONS

TABLE 3.3

Early Reformatories

New York (Elmira)	1876	Indiana (Jeffersonville)	1897
Michigan (Ionia)	1877	Wisconsin (GreenBay)	1898
Massachusetts (Concord)	1884	New Jersey (Rahway)	1901
Pennsylvania (Huntingdon)	1889	Washingon (Monroe)	1908–1909
Minnesota (St. Cloud)	1889	Oklahoma (Granite)	1910–1911
Colorado (Buena Vista)	1890	Maine (South Windham)	1912–1919
Illinois (Pontiac)	1891	Wyoming (Worland)	1912
Kansas (Hutchinson)	1895	Nebraska (Lincoln)	1912–1913
Ohio (Mansfield)	1896	Connecticut (Cheshire)	1913

Although the two main contributions of the reformatory era were the indeterminate sentence and parole, the seeds of education, vocational training, and individual rehabilitation had been sown. Even though such radical ideas could not flourish in the barren and hostile environment of that period, they took root and grew to fruition in later years.

Post–Civil War Prisons

The sixteen states that built prisons between 1870 and 1900 were almost all in the northern or western part of the country (Table 3-4). Their only claim to improvement was the introduction of plumbing and running water. All were of the Auburn type, and the only modifications in the older prison routine were the abandonment of the silent system and the use of the indeterminate sentence and parole.

In the South, devastated by the Civil War, the penitentiary system had been virtually wiped out. Some states attempted to solve their prison problems by leasing out their entire convict population to contractors.[17] Others took in contract work or devised combinations of both leasing out prisoners and taking in contracts. The freed blacks were thus replaced by yet another group of slaves: the convicted felons. The South was unique in that it ignored the Auburn and reformatory systems. The South's agrarian economy made exploitation of cheap labor both easy and desirable. A large portion of the prison population in the South was composed

TABLE 3.4

Post–Civil War Prisons

Oregon (Salem)	1871	New Mexico (Santa Fe)	1884
Iowa (Anamosa)	1873	Washington (Walla Walla)	1886
Arizona (Yuma)	1875	Michigan (Marquette)	1889
Colorado (Canon City)	1876	Montana (Deer Lodge)	1889
Illinois (Menard)	1878	North Carolina (Raleigh)	1889
California (Folsom)	1880	South Dakota (Sioux Falls)	1891
Kentucky (Eddyville)	1883	Tennessee (Brushy Mt.)	1895
North Dakota (Bismark)	1883	Utah (Salt Lake City)	1896

of plantation blacks who had no influence or resources, and they were treated with no mercy.[18] Leasing was eventually replaced by prison farms in most southern states, but the practice was not completely erased until the mid-1920s. This sordid period in penal history, brought to light again in the 1960s in Arkansas,[19] simply confirms the depths to which even so-called civilized people can sink in the treatment of their castoffs. The correctional experience in the South made only a negative contribution in regard to both procedure and discipline.

The Twentieth Century and the Industrial Prison

The introduction of handicrafts into the solitary Eastern Penitentiary cells represented the origin of prison industries in America. In continental Europe and England, the infamous efforts to provide labor in the workhouses and Bridewells had resulted in such fruitless activities as the treadmill. The modern pressure to provide vocational training or earnings for inmates did not concern early American prison administrators; rather, they wanted to make the prisons self-sustaining. Toward this goal, the prison workshops were merely extensions of the early factory workshops. When the factory production system was introduced into prisons and they began to show actual profits from their output, legislators were quickly convinced that prison industries were a sound operation. The Auburn system held out over the less efficient Pennsylvania system because it paid better returns on the taxpayer's investment. By the 1860s, the system of absolute silence had begun to fall apart because of the necessity for communication in the industrial shops. Early prison industries, in effect, exploited the available free labor for the sole purpose of perpetuating the institution itself. Some leaders in the field, however, saw that a change in emphasis could make the industries an important factor in prisoner rehabilitation.

A prison farm of the 1950s

—*COURTESY OF OHIO DEPARTMENT OF REHABILITATION AND CORRECTION*

John Herbert Dillinger (1902–1934) was an infamous American gangster and bank robber. He deserted the navy in 1923, and in 1924 was imprisoned for nine years following an assault to rob a grocery. He committed his first bank robbery in 1933. Another famous gangster, "Baby Face" Nelson, was part of his gang. Dillinger robbed and killed across the Midwest until he was killed by the FBI outside the Biograph Cinema in Chicago. Anna Sage, a madam and friend of Dillinger, betrayed him for the reward.

Bonnie Parker (1910–1934) and Clyde Barrow (1909–1934) were the leaders of the Barrow gang, which terrorized the Midwest in 1933 and 1934. They were gunned down in a Ford V-8 during a famous ambush in 1934. Clyde's dead hands clutched a shotgun with seven notches on the stock, Bonnie's a pistol with three. Bonnie had sent a song, "The Story of Bonnie and Clyde," to a music publisher to be released after her death. It caught the imagination of the country and was a hit, making pseudoheroes of these cheap killers (who were restored to fame again in the 1967 movie glorifying their exploits).

From the beginning of the twentieth century until 1940, the number of inmates in U.S. prisons increased by 174 percent.[20] Ten new Auburn-style prisons and one based on Bentham's Panopticon were built during this period—often referred to as the industrial era for prisons in America—which reached its zenith in 1935. The new prisons were considered "as cold and hard and abnormal as the prisoners whom they were intended to persuade toward better things."[21]

The **industrial prison** really had its origins in the profits turned by the first state prisons. Early in the nineteenth century, however, mechanics and cabinetmakers began to complain about the unfair competition they faced from the virtually free labor force available to prisons. The use of lease and contract systems aggravated the problem and led to a series of investigations that reached national prominence in 1886. The emergence of the labor union movement, coupled with abuses of the contract and lease systems of prison labor, eliminated those systems in the northern prisons by the end of the nineteenth century. They were replaced by piece-price[22] and state-account[23] systems. Opposition to prison industries resulted in enforced idleness among the increasing inmate population. This forced the adult prisons to adopt reformatory methods in some measure but made self-sustaining institutions a thing of the past.

The story of the prison industry's battle with organized labor is a history in itself and is not covered here. The beginning of the end for large-scale prison industries, which kept inmates employed in some kind of work, was the enactment of two federal laws controlling the character of prison products. The Hawes–Cooper Act, passed in 1929, required that prison products be subject to the laws of any state to which they were shipped. The Ahurst–Sumners Act, passed in 1935, essentially stopped the interstate transport of prison products by requiring that all prison products shipped out of the state be labeled with the prison name and by prohibiting interstate shipment where state laws forbade it. In 1940, the Ahurst–Sumners Act was amended to prohibit fully the interstate shipment of prison products.

A typical industrial prison— still around in the 1990s

—*COURTESY OF DEPARTMENT OF ADULT CORRECTIONS, STATE OF WASHINGTON*

Hawes–Cooper Act, Chap. 79

Be *it enacted by the Senate and House of Representatives of the United States of America in Congress assembled,* That all goods, wares, and merchandise manufactured, produced, or mined, wholly or in part, by convicts or prisoners, except convicts or prisoners on parole or probation, or in any penal and/or reformatory institutions, except commodities manufactured in Federal penal and correctional institutions for use by the Federal Government, transported into any State or Territory of the United States and remaining therein for use, consumption, sale, or storage, shall upon arrival and delivery in such State or Territory be subject to the operation and effect of the laws of such State or Territory to the same extent and in the same manner as though such goods, wares, and merchandise had been manufactured, produced, or mined in such State or Territory, and shall not be exempt therefrom by reason of being introduced in the original package or otherwise.

SEC. 2. This act shall take effect five years after the date of its approval. Approved, January 19, 1929. ■

The economic strains of the Great Depression, beginning with the Wall Street stock market crash in 1929 and spanning the period from 1929 to 1940, led thirty-three states to pass laws that prohibited the sale of prison products on the open market. Those statutes tolled the death knell for the industrial prison. With the exception of a few license plate and state furniture shops, most state prisons took a giant step backward to their original purposes: punishment and custody. Fortunately, another model was emerging at the same time: the "new penology" of the 1930s and the U.S. Bureau of Prisons under the leadership of Sanford Bates.

Ashurst–Sumners Act, Chap. 412

Be *it enacted by the Senate and House of Representatives of the United States of America in Congress assembled,* That it shall be unlawful for any person knowingly to transport or cause to be transported, in any manner or by any means whatsoever, or aid or assist in obtaining transportation for or in transporting any goods, wares, and merchandise manufactured, produced, or mined wholly or in part by convicts or prisoners (except convicts or prisoners on parole or probation), or in any penal or reformatory institution, from one State, Territory, Puerto Rico, Virgin Islands, or District of the United States, or place noncontiguous but subject to the jurisdiction thereof, or from any foreign country, into any State, Territory, Puerto Rico, Virgin Islands, or District of the United States, or place noncontiguous but subject to the jurisdiction thereof, where said goods, wares, and merchandise are intended by any person interested therein to be received, possessed, sold, or in any manner used, either in the original package or otherwise in violation of any law of such State, Territory, Puerto Rico, Virgin Islands, or District of the United States, or place noncontiguous but subject to the jurisdiction thereof. Nothing herein shall apply to commodities manufactured in Federal penal and correctional institutions for use by the Federal Government.

SEC. 2. All packages containing any goods, wares, and merchandise manufactured, produced, or mined wholly or in part by convicts or prisoners, except convicts or prisoners on parole or probation, or in any penal or reformatory institution, when shipped or transported in interstate or foreign commerce shall be plainly and clearly marked, so that the name and address of the shipper, the name and address of the consignee, the nature of the contents, and the name and location of the penal or reformatory institution where produced wholly or in part may be readily ascertained on an inspection of the outside of such package. ■

The Period of Transition (1935 to 1960)

The quarter century between 1935 and 1960 was one of great turmoil in the prisons. Administrators, stuck with the huge fortresses of the previous century, were now deprived of the ability to provide meaningful work for inmates. The Depression and the criminal excesses of the 1920s and 1930s hardened the public's attitude toward convict rehabilitation at a time when behavioral scientists were just beginning to propose hopeful reforms in prisoner treatment. J. Edgar Hoover, director of the Federal Bureau of Investigation (FBI), led the battle against "hoity-toity professors" and the "cream-puff school of criminology." His war on crime helped give the world the supermaximum prison, Alcatraz. Located on an island in San Francisco Bay, Alcatraz was constructed to house the hardest criminals in America. When it was built in 1934, it was seen as the answer to the outrages of such desperate criminals as John Dillinger, Bonnie and Clyde, and "Ma" Barker. Eventually, the U.S. Bureau of Prisons abandoned this idea as another failure.

ALCATRAZ

Starting in 1859, the twelve-acre island of Alcatraz in San Francisco Bay was the site of an army disciplinary barracks, which was replaced in 1909 by a military prison. In 1934 the military prison was converted to a federal prison that was considered virtually escapeproof. It was closed in 1963, due to high maintenance and service costs. It is now a National Park that receives thousands of visitors each year.

Early efforts toward diagnostic classification and casework were pioneered by such notables as Bernard Glueck at Sing Sing between 1915 and 1920, Edgar Doll and W. G. Ellis in New Jersey in 1925, and A. W. Stearns in Massachusetts in 1930. Sanford Bates introduced procedures into the U.S. Bureau of Prisons in 1934. Although sometimes "borrowing" principles from states across the nation, the U.S. Bureau of Prisons gradually emerged as the national leader in corrections, introducing many new concepts that have been copied by state systems. Two major contributions were diagnosis and classification and the use of professional personnel such as psychiatrists and psychologists to help rehabilitate inmates. The federal system also led the way to more humane treatment and better living conditions. But no matter how they were cleaned up, prisons remained monuments to idleness, monotony, frustration, and repression. Despite attempts to tear down the massive walls around some prisons, the forces of **lock psychosis** continued to hold out. Prison inmates were feared as the "convict bogey," who could be dealt with only by locking and relocking, counting and recounting.

It is not too surprising that the long hours of idleness, forbidding architecture, growing populations, and unnecessarily repressive controls created unbearable tensions among the inmates. The first riots in this country, as noted earlier, were at the mine-shaft prison in Simsbury, Connecticut. Riots at the Walnut Street Jail were reported in the early 1800s as well. The mid-nineteenth century, when prison industries provided extensive work for convicts, was a time of few riots. Presumably, either the inmates were too tired to riot or the control was too strict. As the prison industries died out, riots began to take place more regularly, adding evidence to the theory that enforced idleness causes restlessness and discontent among prisoners. There was a wave of riots in the prisons between 1929 and 1932. During World War II there were few problems, but in 1946 there was even a riot in Alcatraz, the superprison.

Whether the Alcatraz publicity offered an incentive or whether the rising prosperity of the 1950s simply presented too sharp a contrast with the bleak life on the inside, there was an explosion of prison discontent during that decade. Over three hundred prison riots have occurred since 1774, and 90 percent of those have occurred in the last four decades.[24] The American Correctional Association investigated the 1950s riots and reported what appeared to be the main causes:

- Inadequate financial support and official and public indifference
- Substandard personnel
- Enforced idleness
- Lack of professional leadership and professional programs
- Excessive size and overcrowding of institutions
- Political domination and motivation of management
- Unwise sentencing and parole practices[25]

The Modern Era

The "modern era" of corrections is generally considered to have begun about 1960, and it was characterized by a pattern of change that was to highlight the next decade. The 1960s in the United States were noted for turbulent and violent confrontations at almost every level of activity affecting human rights. The forces for change at work in the overall society were also reflected in great pressures for change in corrections. The dramatic reinterpretations of criminal law, the civil rights movement, violent and nonviolent demonstrations in the streets, the assassinations of a popular president and two other important national figures, the continuation of the longest and most unpopular war in American history—all of those outside pressures were also felt inside the walls of the nation's prisons. Reaction took the form of periodic violent prison riots and disorders. The U.S. Supreme Court emerged as the primary external agent for the enforced recognition of the basic rights of those swept up in the criminal justice system. This external pressure was generated by a long series of significant judicial interpretations. In addition, leadership and funding by the federal government were given to corrections administrators and planners at the state and local levels, enabling them to create, implement, and evaluate new standards, policies, and

Kate Clark ("Ma") Barker (1872–1935) was the co-leader of another infamous gang in the 1933 to 1934 era of crime waves in the Midwest. Her husband and four sons made up the nucleus of the gang. Alvin Karpis was also a member. They robbed banks and plundered around the St. Paul, Minnesota, area. In early 1935, "Ma" Barker and her husband, Fred, were surrounded and killed in a cabin on Lake Weir, Florida. She was found with a ubmachine gun in her hands.

practices. Unfortunately, aspiring politicians and the media have collectively generated and nurtured inaccurate stereotypes about offenders, blunting correctional gains and giving rise to more intractable problems.[26] The conservative movement in the political arena continues to cause a steady move to the right in corrections, wreaking havoc with the shrinking efforts at rehabilitation. The turmoil continues.

Internally Sought Reform

Early prisons were less secure than modern ones, and escape was far more common. It was easier to "disappear" into early American society with a new name and a new start. Inmate security and control, improved in recent years, have made escape from prisons difficult. And systems of identification and control, including computer banks of data on each of us, have made escape into society almost impossible.

When the prisons became so secure that relief and escape were cut off, the inmates' frustration and agitation turned inward. Prisoners in this "total institution"[27] used disturbances and riots to express their desire for reforms and changes in rules and conditions. Disturbances also served to resolve power struggles between prison gangs[28] and inmate groups. The early disturbances were characterized by disorganization and rapid dispersion; inmates used those methods to settle old grudges, refusing to fall in line behind any kind of leadership. In the 1960s and 1970s, disturbances were commonplace in most large state systems, reflecting the usual grievances: crowded living conditions, harsh rules, poor food, excessive punishment, and guard brutality.[29] Even the highly respected federal prison system was rocked in 1987 by large-scale hostage taking by Cuban inmates who feared deportation. The growing awareness of individual rights on the outside that began in the 1960s led inmates to seek the same rights inside prisons.

Beginning about 1966, the nature of the demands changed from those involving basic *conditions* to those concerning basic *rights*. In that year the Maryland Penitentiary in Baltimore was the scene of a riot involving over one thousand inmates. The warden claimed the disturbance was caused by heat waves and overcrowding, but "the riot had to have social overtones," said Joseph Bullock, a member of the state House of Delegates. "If they don't stop telling these people [blacks] about their rights," Bullock went on, "things will get worse."[30] Rioting and violence spilled over from the streets into the prisons of America. The "political prisoner" label, particularly for blacks and Chicanos, offered a more acceptable way for minority groups to state their feelings of deprivation. They struck out at a system that they perceived gave them an unequal start in life and then jailed them for failing to live up to the rules of that system.[31] Clearly, outside social behavior and conditions do carry over into prison. Little that is new in society starts in prison.

Change, though often temporary, does come about as a result of prison riots. More often today, new voices can help shape prison policies—through an inmate council, grievance procedures, conflict resolution,[32] or inmates serving on regular prison committees, following a collaborative model. Some systems also use an **ombudsman** as a link between the prisoner and the establishment. Correctional administrators have learned that the more diverse the correctional staff, the fewer the inmate assaults on other inmates and staff.[33] These methods are thought to be effective, and their continued use appears to be the trend for the future. Inmate self-government, tried in the 1800s at Elmira Reformatory in New York and more recently but unsuccessfully at the Washington State Penitentiary in Walla Walla, does not appear to offer the same promise as does selected individual representation.[34]

THE PRISON POPULATION BOOM

From 1980 to 1996, before the time of this writing, the number of prison inmates in the nation increased over 300 percent, from 330,000 to 1,054,000 prisoners. This population boom resulted from fear of crime, [35] fueled by politicians, the media, and such special interest groups as correctional and law enforcement officers and private prison builders. Proponents of prison building decry high crime rates and increased violence. Yet crime rates did not increase from 1980 to 1996, and there is substantial evidence that crime significantly declined over this time frame. The level of violence remained unchanged. Fear of violence, drive-by shootings, juvenile gangs struggling to control the drug trade, drug use, and racism have combined to create a "get-tough" environment.

The results, covered in more detail in later chapters, were rapid prison population expansion and prison construction, increased prison overcrowding, reduction of early release mechanisms from prison, and massive jail populations and jail construction. See Figure 3-3. Alternatives to prison—probation, parole, and "intermediate punishments"—also increased during this time, but did not significantly reduce the pressure to build correctional facilities. Alternatives are needed not only to the building of jails and prisons, but also for policies to buttress and expand corrections in the community. New ideas and programs are badly needed, as contemporary corrections appear to "be running on empty." Opportunities for change and growth exist for those students willing to advance correctional practice.

OMBUDSMAN
An appointed official who receives and investigates inmates' complaints against correctional practices, reports findings, and recommends corrective action without the inmates' having fear of reprisal.

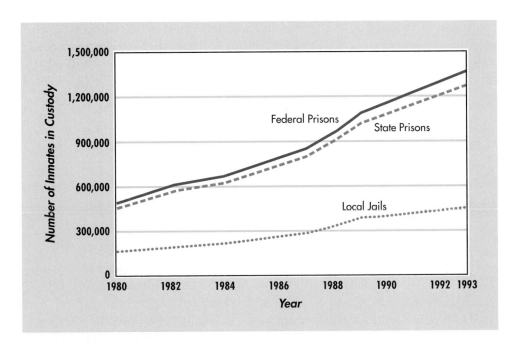

FIGURE

3.3

Number of Inmates In Custody, 1980–1993

SOURCE: A. Beck and D. Gilliard, Prisoners in 1994 (Washington, D.C.: U.S. Department of Justice, 1995), p. 2.

Summary

The period of transition saw a movement toward drastic measures, inside and outside the walls of America's prisons, to get across the point that mass-treatment prisons had failed. The giant fortresses to futility, built to house prisoners in silence and hard labor, were still being used for inmates no longer silent and forbidden to compete with outside labor. Those prisons were becoming the hulks of the twentieth century.

With a few exceptions, the principles established at the first prison congress in 1870—untried and untested to this day—were crushed by the administrators' need to maintain custody and control at any cost. As America entered the 1960s, the emphasis turned slowly toward the individual prisoner's needs, and some of the technology and ability that led us into the atomic age was finally focused on the problems of corrections.

The period following the emergence of the penitentiary as a social tool for the reintegration of the offender back into society was filled with hope. The Industrial Revolution provided a method for using the "captive" work force in productive, if not always totally effective, enterprises. The growth of industrial prisons, however, also resulted in the use of thousands of prisoners as slave labor. This brought opposition from labor organizations, do-gooders, and even penal administrators. Although the prison industries were shut down for understandable reasons, the resulting inactivity in the massive fortress prisons became a devastating factor in the development of corrections through the 1960s. Riots and unrest became a way of life in the huge monuments to the ideas of the nineteenth century.

The entry into corrections of psychologists, psychiatrists, and educators resulted in attempts to solve the problems of the idleness imposed on inmates in industrial prisons through methods predicated on the "medical model." Institutionalization soon took precedence over treatment, however, resulting in more obsession with "locks and clocks" and less support for a treatment model. The lack of consensus about the proper model for prisons to follow continued through the 1960s into the 1990s, and good intentions to reform the system continued to pave the road to chaos in America's prisons. It is said that a leopard cannot change its spots, and so removing the stripes from prisoners and calling them "residents" changed very little in American prisons. Without the commitment to total change in fortress prisons and penal policies, true reform can never take place.

Review Questions

1. What effect did the Industrial Revolution have on prisons and prison discipline?
2. Which of the two early nineteenth-century prison systems won out in America? Why?
3. What were the major differences between prisons and reformatories?
4. Why have so many riots occurred in prisons?
5. How were American prison industries reduced in correctional importance?

Words to Remember

outside cells

inside cells

Auburn system

congregate system

penitentiary system

lockstep

prison stripes

solitary confinement

Irish system

ticket-of-leave

conditional liberty

reformatory

industrial prison

lock psychosis

ombudsman

Endnotes

1. The Philadelphia Society for the Alleviation of the Miseries of Public Prisons was originally formed by a group of concerned citizens in 1787. Because of their continued efforts, the law of 1790 was passed, and the Walnut Street Jail was remodeled to accommodate felons in solitary confinement. The Society is now the Pennsylvania Prison Society (3 N. Second St., Philadelphia, Pennsylvania 19106-2208).

2. Outside cells were each about six feet wide, eight feet deep, and nine feet high, with a central corridor extending the length of the building in between. Some of them had individual yards added on the outside, with high walls between them.

3. That system, in modified form, is used to this day in Belgium, France, and West Germany. Additional international correctional material can be found in *The Prison Journal* 68 (Spring–Summer 1988); *Journal of Research in Crime and Delinquency* 25 (November 1988); *Corrections Today* 52 (July 1990); and Steven Adwell, "A Case for Single-Cell Occupancy in America's Prisons," *Federal Probation* 55:3 (1991): 64–67.

4. Inside cells are built back-to-back in tiers within a hollow building. Doors open onto galleries or runs that are eight to ten feet from the outside wall; cells are small and intended only for sleeping. The interior cell block has become characteristic of American prisons.

5. The argument continues. See the excellent discussion by Alexine Atherton, "Journal Perspective 1845–1986," *The Prison Journal* 68 (Spring–Summer 1987): 1–37, and Herbert Johnson, "Freedom and Prisons in the Land of the Free," chapter in *History of Criminal Justice* (Cincinnati: Anderson, 1988), pp. 149–168. For a detailed discussion of a Civil War prison, see Joseph Cangemi and Casimir Kowalski, *Andersonville Prison: Lessons in Organizational Failure* (Landham, MD: University Press of America, 1992).

6. Walter C. Reckless, *The Crime Problem,* 4th ed. (New York: Appleton-Century-Crofts, 1969), p. 548.

7. Harry Elmer Barnes, *The Story of Punishment,* 2nd ed. (Montclair, NJ: Patterson Smith, 1972), p. 136.

8. Robert G. Caldwell, *Criminology,* 2nd ed. (New York: Ronald Press, 1965), p. 506.

9. Barnes, *The Story of Punishment,* p. 140.

10. G. de Beaumont and A. de Tocqueville, *On the Penitentiary System in the United States and Its Application in France* (Philadelphia: Francis Lieber, 1833).

11. John V. Barry, "Captain Alexander Maconochie," *Victorian Historical Magazine* 27 (June 1957): 5.

12. Flat sentence refers to a specific period of time (for example, five years, ten years) in confinement for an offense, with no time off for any reason.

13. Harry Elmer Barnes and Negley K. Teeters, *New Horizons in Criminology,* 3rd ed. (Englewood Cliffs, NJ: Prentice Hall, 1959), p. 419.

14. An indeterminate sentence usually has broad beginning and end figures (three to five years, one to ten years, and so on), instead of a certain fixed period. Prisoners are allowed to earn their freedom by means of good conduct.

15. Progressive penologists of the era met in Cincinnati, Ohio, on October 12, 1870, to plan the ideal prison system. Two earlier attempts to gather had failed, but this meeting of the

American Prison Congress developed into the National Prison Association, later the American Correctional Association (8025 Laurel Lakes Court, Laurel, Maryland 20707).

16. Barnes and Teeters, *New Horizons in Criminology*, p. 426.

17. Georgia, Florida, Mississippi, Louisiana, and Arkansas, in particular, followed this procedure.

18. See Martha Myers, "Gender and Southern Punishment After the Civil War," *Criminology* 33:1 (1995): 17–46.

19. Tom Murton and Joe Hyams, *Accomplices to the Crime: The Arkansas Prison Scandal* (New York: Grove Press, 1967).

20. Margaret Calahan, *Historical Corrections Statistics in the United States: 1850–1984* (Washington, D.C.: U.S. Department of Justice, 1986), p. 36.

21. Wayne Morse, *The Attorney General's Survey of Release Procedures* (Washington, D.C.: U.S. Government Printing Office, 1940).

22. Under the piece-price system, a variation of the contract system, the contractor supplied the raw material and paid a price for each delivered finished product. Thailand currently uses this system.

23. In the state-account or public-account system, all employment and activity are under the direction of the state, and products are sold on the open market. The prisoner receives a very small wage, and the profit goes to the state. Usually binder twine, rope, and hemp sacks were produced this way; it provided a lot of work for prisoners, but little training. See American Correctional Association, *A Study of Prison Industry: History, Components, and Goals* (Washington, D.C.: U.S. Department of Justice, 1986).

24. Richard McCorkle, Terance Miethe, and Kriss Drass, "The Roots of Prison Violence," *Crime and Delinquency* 41:3 (1995): 317–331. See also Reginald Williams, "Lucasville: The Aftermath," *Corrections Today* 56:5 (1994): 64–76.

25. As cited in Barnes and Teeters, *New Horizons in Criminology*, p. 385.

26. John Irwin and James Austin, *It's About Time* (San Francisco: National Council on Crime and Delinquency, 1987), pp. 13–19. See also Steven Gorelick, "Join Our War: The Ideology in a Newspaper Crimefighting Campaign," *Crime and Delinquency* 35 (1989): 421–436, and *Corrections Today* 51 (February 1989).

27. Irving Goffman, "On the Characteristics of Total Institutions: Staff-Inmate Relations," in D. R. Cressey, ed., *The Prison* (New York: Holt, Rinehart and Winston, 1966), pp. 16–22. This concept refers to the sum of conditions created by a large number of people living around the clock within a close space, with tightly scheduled sequences of activity coordinated by a central authority.

28. George Knox et al., "Preliminary Results of the 1995 Adult Corrections Survey," *Journal of Gang Research* 3 (1996): 27–63. See also Rita Grant and Juanita Buford, "Working Together: Experts Unite to Combat Street and Prison Gangs, *Corrections Today* 56:5 (1994): 148–149.

29. Dan Dursky, "Who Are These People and Why Are They Suing You?" *Corrections Today* 51 (June 1989): 16–27, 114. See also the excellent review by John Conrad, "From Barbarism Toward Decency: Alabama's Long Road to Prison Reform," *Journal of Research in Crime and Delinquency* 26 (1989): 307–328.

30. *The New York Times,* July 9, 1966, p. 9.

31. James W. L. Park, "What Is a Political Prisoner? The Politics of Predators," *American Journal of Corrections* 34 (November–December 1972): 22–23. See also Robert Leger and Harvey Barnes, "Black Attitudes in Prison: A Sociological Analysis," *Journal of Criminal Justice* 14 (1986): 105–122.

32. Bill Love, "Program Curbs Prison Violence Through Conflict Resolution," *Corrections Today* 56:5 (1994): 144–147.

33. McCorkle et al., "The Roots of Prison Violence," p. 326.

34. Prison self-government systems in a total institution are subject to the pressures of the inmate subculture, making it very difficult to achieve the goals of true inmate representation.

35. Jill Furniss, "The Population Boom," *Corrections Today* 58:1 (1996): 38–43.

CHAPTER FOUR

The Pendulum of Correctional Ideologies

Overview

So far we have looked at the history and early developments of corrections, outlining the major construction of prisons and facilities that reflected the thoughts of those years. An underlying policy question explored in the first three chapters of your textbook concerned the role of criminal law and offenders: Who are offenders and what shall we do with them? The answers identified so far are that they are (1) evil and must be destroyed, (2) out of touch with God and need to repent, (3) poorly educated and ill-trained to function in modern society, and (4) sick and in need of being cured. These are commonly known as the punishment, reform, education, and medical models of corrections. In this chapter, we explore the philosophical bases on which these models are based and explain the rationales underlying current correctional developments. We need to understand why this nation has entered into an age of massive change and prison construction, what goals are being sought, and what the implications of the new programs and facilities might be.

In addressing the changes in programs, facilities, and philosophies, it is constructive to look at California, a state that built fourteen new prisons since the beginning of the "**War on Drugs**" (1982) and has another seventeen in the planning or construction phase. The $3 billion required to build just six prisons would be enough resources to hire an additional 53,000 new teachers for California classrooms, send 579,000 young persons to college, or enroll 538,000 children in Headstart programs. Building prisons reflects one set of ideologies regarding policies and priorities; educating and training children reflect another approach to handling crime. In this chapter, we identify correctional ideologies and their implications. We begin with an understanding of ideologies.

The popularity of incarceration as a response to crime has resulted in great swings in public and professional perceptions of the

The massive prison construction represented by a commitment by our nation to *plan for social failure* by spending billions of dollars to lock up hundreds of thousands of people while at the same time cutting billions of dollars for programs that would provide opportunity to young Americans.

—Steven Donziger,
The Real War on Crime

role of corrections. Underlying the field of corrections are three basic ideologies regarding the societal response to illegal behavior and the offender: punishment, treatment, and prevention. The different ideologies all attempt to answer the two simple questions: "Who are the offenders?" and "What should we do with (to) them?"

Conflicting Correctional Ideologies

To understand the current state of corrections, its problems and issues, and its possible future, we turn first to a discussion of ideologies. An **ideology**, according to *Webster's*, is "a systematic body of concepts, especially about human life or culture." A correctional ideology, then, refers to a body of ideas and practices that pertain to the treatment of offenders. Obviously, the actions of various correctional authorities and organizational units are shaped in large part by the particular ideologies to which they subscribe. In the history of treatment and punishment of offenders, the ideologies of different societies have supplied both the basis and the rationalization for the broad range of efforts—vengeful to semihumane—aimed at getting criminals off the streets. When a given effort is clearly a failure, the ideology eventually shifts to justify a different approach.

In modern times, a strong belief in the efficacy of one correctional ideology or another has sometimes led administrators to commit vast sums of public treasure to an unproved approach, thus shackling themselves to a possibly worthless plan for an indefinite period. By the same token, if the administrator's ideology happens to conflict with the approach favored by the society he or she serves, the administrator may try to resolve the conflict in one of two ways: by working out a compromise or by trying to sabotage the system. If the superintendent of a juvenile institution believes that society is trying to liberalize rules so rapidly that it threatens personal security, he or she may encourage or even trigger frequent escapes and walk-aways from the institution. In corrections, the backgrounds and ideologies of the keepers and the kept often diverge sharply, so it is difficult to convince both groups they can work toward a mutual goal.

Retribution

Philosophically, the term *retribution* generally means getting even with the perpetrator. The term *social revenge* suggests that an individual cannot exact punishment, but that the state will do so in their name.

Retribution assumes that the offenders willfully choose to commit the evil acts, are responsible for their own behavior, are likely to commit similar acts again, and should receive the punishment they richly deserve.

The "just deserts" movement in sentencing reflects the retribution philosophy. For many, it provides a justifiable rationale for support of the death penalty.

Many students of corrections, and penologists, have considerable difficulty with the concept of retribution, because it requires the state to make an offender suffer for the sake of suffering. To many, that idea runs counter to the Eighth Amendment's prohibition against cruel and unusual punishment. One respected criminologist has proposed that correctional punishments include electroshock in lieu of incarceration, as it can be calibrated, leaves less long-term emotional damage, is cheaper to administer, and would allow the victim the opportunity to witness the retribution. Is it possible that televising the electroshock sessions might act as a deterrent to other potential malefactors?   ∎

SOURCE: Graeme Newman, *Just and Painful: The Case for the Corporal Punishment of Criminals* (New York: Free Press, 1983).

Most of the ideologies applied to correctional actions over the years fall into one of three categories: **punishment, treatment,** or **prevention**. They often overlap, of course—punishment and treatment are usually justified as means to prevention, rather than as ends in themselves—but the division is useful for the purpose of this analysis.

The Punishment Ideology

The idea that punishment can result in the offense being "paid" for and that it can be expanded in effect from the specific criminal to the general public has been around from the earliest times. Most of the basic reasons for punishment can be placed in three general categories.

RETRIBUTION

Since the first system of laws was developed, punishment has been officially sanctioned as a means of regulating criminal behavior. The punishment ideology holds that the criminal is an enemy of society who deserves severe punishment, including banishment or death, for willfully breaking its rules. This philosophy has its roots in a societal need for retribution. As we noted in Chapter 1, punishment once was administered in the form of immediate and personal retribution, by either the victim or the victim's family. Society's authorization of punishment can be traced to that individual's need for retaliation and vengeance. Many theories try to explain the reason for the transfer of the vengeance motive from the individual to the state.

Philosophers have debated the reasons for this transfer to government of the victim's desire to strike back at the offender. Heinrich Oppenheimer lists several theories. Three of them are as follows:

1. In the *theological* view, retaliation fulfills a religious mission to punish the criminal.

2. In the *aesthetic* view, punishment resolves the social discord created by the offense and reestablishes a sense of harmony through requital.

3. In the *expiatory* view, guilt must be washed away through suffering. Ledger Wood advances a fourth explanation, a *utilitarian* theory. Punishment is considered to be a means of achieving beneficial and social consequences through application of a specific form and degree of punishment deemed most appropriate to the particular offender after careful individualized study of the offender.[1] [emphasis added]

DETERRENCE

Yet another reason for punishment of criminals is the belief that such actions have a **deterrent effect**, specifically on the offender or generally on others who might consider a similar act.[2] For punishment to serve as a deterrent, it must be swift, visible to others, closely linked to the forbidden action so that it discourages future recurrences of that crime, certain, and categorical (all persons committing a certain crime will receive the same punishment).[3] Furthermore, the state and its representatives must uphold superior values and conforming behavior to serve as irreproachable examples of good citizenship. Finally, after punishment, offenders must be allowed to resume their prior positions in society, without stigma or disability.

The failure of early penologists to recognize that uniform punishment was not as effective as selective and specialized punishment contributed to the failure of prisons based on the punishment ideology. Overpunishment has little deterrent effect as well, because when the compliance point has been passed and the punishment continues, the offender ceases to care about the crime. For example, even

A modern electronic control center

—*COURTESY OF GEORGIA DEPARTMENT OF CORRECTIONS*

Delaware's Infamous "Red Hannah"

The semiannual whipping and pillorying of criminals convicted at the present term of the court, of theft and other crimes, took place on Saturday. The attendance was small, probably not exceeding one hundred people, most of whom were boys. The following are the names of the "candidates," and the offenses for which they were sentenced:

- Joseph Derias, colored, horse stealing, 20 lashes, one hour in the pillory.
- Scott Wilson, larceny of clothing, 20 lashes.
- John Carpenter, colored, four cases of larceny (ice cream freezers, carriage reins, and a cow). He received 10 lashes in each case.
- John Conner, larceny of tomatoes, 5 lashes.
- John Smith, colored, house breaking, 20 lashes.
- John Brown, horse stealing, 20 lashes and one hour in the pillory.

—*Delawarean, May 27, 1876*

For centuries, the whipping post was a conspicuous part of Delaware's penal tradition. The first person to suffer the sanction was Robert Hutchinson, convicted of petty theft and sentenced to thirty nine lashes on June 3, 1679. Each town and county had its own whipping post, but the one that earned a prominent place in the history of American corrections was the notorious "Red Hannah." As the Wilmington *Journal Every Evening* once described it:

> In days gone by, the whipping post down in Kent County stood out brazenly in the open courtyard of the county jail not far from the old state house. It looked like an old-time octagonal pump without a handle. It had a slit near the top of it in which the equally old-time pillory boards might be inserted when needed for punitive use. There also were iron shackles for holding the prisoners while they were being whipped. That whipping post was painted red from top to bottom. Negro residents bestowed upon it the name of "Red Hannah." Of any prisoner who

Old Red Hannah, Delaware's whipping post (Courtesy of American Stock/Archive Photos)

had been whipped at the post it was said, "He has hugged Red Hannah!"

Red Hannah was a survivor. Despite public and local congressional pressure to ban whipping in the state, during the second half of the twentieth century, almost three hundred years after Robert Hutchinson received his thirty-nine lashes, old Red Hannah was still very much alive.

In 1963, the statutes that permitted whipping were challenged in the Delaware Supreme Court. The case was *State v. Cannon*, and the presiding judge held that the use of flogging to punish certain crimes did *not* violate either state or federal bans on cruel and unusual punishment. However, Red Hannah was ultimately laid to rest in 1973, when the statute authorizing the use of the lash was finally repealed by the Delaware legislature.

SOURCES: Robert G. Caldwell, *Red Hannah: Delaware's Whipping Post* (Philadelphia: University of Pennsylvania Press, 1947); *Delawarean*, May 27, 1876, p. 3; *Journal Every Evening*, August 2, 1938, p. 8; *State v. Cannon*, 55 Del. 587 (1963).

after an offender has successfully completed a punishment-oriented correctional process, the **stigma of conviction** and imprisonment is carried for the rest of the ex-offender's life.[4] Finding it almost impossible to get a job because of a criminal past, the ex-offender often decides, "If I'm going to have the name, I might as well play the game." At that point, neither the punishment nor the stigma is an effective deterrent, and the offender is likely to return to crime.

INCAPACITATION

A third reason to punish the offender derives from the concept of incapacitation. This theory finds no hope for the individual as far as rehabilitation is concerned and proposes that the only solution is temporarily to isolate, remove, or cripple such persons in some way. This approach is sometimes referred to as the *theory of disablement*, a euphemism for death, banishment, or mutilation. Ideally, the disablement should relate to the crime (for example, in some countries castration has been used to punish sex criminals). One variation of the isolation rationale of incapacitation is the selective incapacitation movement. Greenwood argued that prison overcrowding and the scarcity of beds in prisons require a policy of sending only repetitive or violent offenders to prison; he especially recommended prison for those who commit armed robbery.[5] Selective incapacitation[6] would thus result in better uses of correctional resources and more effective crime prevention, he believed. Miller and others[7] contended that if certain offenders committing repetitive criminal acts were categorically incarcerated and incapacitated for a mandatory period (three or even five years), significantly fewer crimes would have been committed in Columbus, Ohio, in 1975.

Current correctional technology does not permit our correctly identifying those who require incapacitation. Rather, the evidence is that we would probably incarcerate numerous noneligible (a "false positive" problem) persons and release to lesser confinement many of those eligible (a "false negative" problem) persons. Whatever benefits might accrue to this sentencing doctrine have thus far eluded corrections.

The Effect of Punishment

It is recognized that some punishment can be effective when applied in the right amounts and at the right time, and punishment may be a necessary predecessor to treatment, as few serious offenders readily seek or are amenable to treatment without some form of coercion or threat; but when the ideology of punishment is applied in a correctional institution, the result is usually negative for both the punished and the punisher. Correctional personnel tend to watch for minor rule infringements or nonconformism (horseplay, abusive language, skipping classes, etc.) so the punishment can be administered, and they overlook any positive actions by offenders.[8] Often the rules that are prepared for a punishment-oriented environment surround the offender with a wall of "do nots," leaving almost no leeway to "do" anything. As evidenced by a high crime rate, punishment by the law does not seem to create much respect for the law, even in jurisdictions where punishment may actually be swift, harsh, and certain. Overuse of punishment in a society that claims to be open and free creates a situation in which the punished can characterize their punishers as persecutors of the poor and helpless. The accusation turns attention away from crimes and gives rise to the concept of the "political prisoner." Thus minority group members are likely to blame their incarcerations on repression by the rich, on political persecution, or on attempted genocide. Punishments are then made more and more severe, in a hopeless effort to compensate for their ineffectiveness. Often such punishments motivate offenders to become more sophisticated criminals (rather than noncriminals) in the belief (no doubt valid) that the more skilled one is at a trade, the less likely one is to be caught. The offenders become hardened to the punishment, and the administrators learn to dole it out automatically as their only means of control.[9] Both parties are degraded in the process.

Selective Incapacitation

This doctrine of isolating the offender, or causing "social disablement," proposes adopting a policy of incarcerating those whose criminal behavior is so damaging or probable that nothing short of isolation will prevent recidivism. This "nothing-else-works" approach would require correctly identifying those offenders who would be eligible for longer-term imprisonment and diverting others into correctional alternatives. Thus we would be able to make maximum effective use of prison cells, a scarce resource, to protect society from the depredations of such dangerous and repetitive offenders.

Current correctional technology does not permit our correctly identifying those who require incapacitation. Rather, the evidence is that we would probably incarcerate numerous noneligibles (a "false positive" problem) and release to lesser confinement many of those eligible (a "false negative" problem). Whatever benefits might accrue to this sentencing doctrine have thus far eluded corrections. The difficulty is further spotlighted in the Report to the Nation on Crime and Justice:

> Career criminals, though few in number, account for most crime. Even though chronic repeat offenders (those with five or more arrests by age 18) make up

a relatively small proportion of all offenders, they commit a very high proportion of all crimes. The evidence includes data for juveniles and adults, males and females, and for urban and rural areas. In Wolfgang's Philadelphia study, chronic offenders accounted for 23% of all male offenders in the study, but they had committed 61% of all the crimes. Of all crimes by all members of the group studied, chronic offenders committed:

- 61% of all homicides
- 76% of all rapes
- 73% of all robberies
- 65% of all aggravated assaults

SOURCES: Marianne W. Zawitz, ed., *Report to the Nation on Crime and Justice* (Washington, D.C.: U.S. Department of Justice, Bureau of Justice Statistics, U.S. Government Printing Office, 1983), p. 35. Also Elmar Witekamp, Hans-Jurgen Kerner, and Volkard Schindler, "On the Dangerousness of Chronic/Habitual Offenders: A Reanalysis of the 1945 Philadelphia Birth Cohort Data," *Studies in Crime and Crime Prevention* 42:2 (1995): 157-175.

The argument that the use of punishment can halt crime is refuted by both history and science. Many factors contribute to make punishment the least effective means of reducing crime:

1. The use of punishment for deterrence must avoid the overseverity of application that arouses public sympathy for the offender.

2. Those persons most likely to be imprisoned are already accustomed to experiencing deprivations and frustration of personal goals routinely in daily life.

3. It is impossible to fashion a practical legal "slide rule" that will determine exact degrees of retribution appropriate for a list of crimes ranging from handkerchief theft to murder.

4. The simple application of naked coercion does not guarantee the subjects of its force will alter their behavior to conform to new legal norms or to improve their conformity with norms previously violated.

5. The possibility of deterrence varies with the chances of keeping the particular type of crime secret and consequently of avoiding social reprobation.[10]

It must be understood that the significance of punishment as an ideology in correctional practice lies in the viewpoint of the punished offenders. If they see the punishment as an unjust imposition of the will and power of the establishment, and if they are reinforced in that belief by their peers (other offenders), their punishment will only encourage them to maintain negative behavior patterns. By contrast, if offenders feel their punishment is both deserved and just, and their social group agrees, the punishment may have a startlingly different and more positive result. If a prosocial criminal (one who is not totally committed to a life of crime)

DETERMINATE SENTENCING

A fixed period of incarceration imposed on the offender by the sentencing court. The ideology underlying determinate sentencing is retribution, just deserts, or incapacitation.

A presumptive sentence is a term of imprisonment suggested by a policy-setting governmental agency, such as the state legislature or a sentencing council. The sentencing judge is expected to impose the indicated sentence, unless certain circumstances proven in court would require a different (longer or shorter) period of imprisonment.

A typical conversion for a community correction center

—COURTESY OF PENNSYLVANIA DEPARTMENT OF CORRECTIONS

PREDICTION

When practitioners and researchers attempt to identify who would commit future crimes over a period of time (or a career), they basically predict that a person will or will not get into difficulty ("criminal" or "noncriminal"). If one predicts "criminal" and the subject does not get into trouble, we create a "false positive" error. If the prediction is "noncriminal" and the subject commits a crime, the outcome is a "false negative." It is hoped that one would be accurate in identifying and correctly classifying subjects into the correct categories.

Even using the most sophisticated prediction devices and schedules based on extensive life-history information, inmate psychological test scores, official records and institutional information, and inmate responses to questionnaires, errors of prediction abound. On occasion, predictors made more incorrect than correct predictions!

is justly treated, that offender may abandon crime, but excessive punishment may push the offender over the edge and destroy every chance of reform. The punished and stigmatized offenders turn to those who are most like them for support and values. If they are embittered by the punishment they have received, they are likely to reject the very values the punishment was intended to reinforce.[11]

The punishment ideology is particularly attractive to those with a strong hostile urge just below the surface—although these people may appear to be upright and productive citizens. Thus justifications for the punishment ideology have been found in theories on theology, aesthetics, and utility, the idea being that the offender's suffering and expiation serve to cleanse and reestablish accord throughout the society as a whole. Although all kinds of logical arguments for punishment can be devised, it has been an obvious failure when set up as a uniform and inflexible response to negative behavior. The routine use of punishment in institutions designed to correct offenders can be viewed as more degrading to society than the offenses themselves in many cases.

The punishment ideology soon becomes a punishment procedure that is applied without regard to the individual nature of those being punished. Because of this, prisons become places where inmates look to one another for support and values, and the agents of the law become the enemy—one of the main reasons that many authorities on corrections refer to prisons as "schools of crime." The punishment ideology is a major factor in correctional programs. For a while it gave way to the therapeutic ideology, but around 1975 punitiveness became fashionable once again. Punitiveness has led legislatures to change sentencing from an indeterminate structure in which parole boards share the process of determining minimum and maximum sentence lengths. The new legislative initiatives abandon parole as an early release mechanism, install determinate/presumptive sentencing, and result in overcrowding of prisons. Punitiveness has led to a **brick-and-mortar** solution for the prison overcrowding situation: the building of more and more prisons is seen as the only answer.

James Austin and Aaron McVey[12] examined the effects of recent political policies designed to increase punishment by increasing the probability of an offender's being arrested, convicted, and imprisoned, and serving longer sentences. We extend their predictions by noting that, if current punishment trends continue, the nation

- will have 1.5 million prison inmates by the year 2000.
- will need to open a new 1,600-bed prison each week for the next five years just to keep even with prison growth.
- will need to hire 16,000 new correctional officers for each of the next five years.
- will have 63 percent of all African-American men behind bars by 2020.
- will have 600,000 elderly prisoners ("geriatric inmates") in prison by 2020.
- will remain number one in the rate of incarceration per 100,000 residents.
- will have almost 7 million persons under correctional control.

TREATMENT
Treatment begins with a diagnosis of an offender's needs, the designing of a program plan to address that person's needs, the application of the intended program with periodic monitoring, and updating and modification of the plan to maximize effectiveness.

Finally, the change in attitude has led to a painful search for alternatives to probation (regarded as *no punishment*) and imprisonment (regarded as *too expensive* a form of punishment). The emerging alternatives—known as intermediate punishments—promise relief from the pressures of prison overcrowding. In addition, the new wave of punitiveness has contributed to selective incapacitation, an important and effective tool for correctional administrators, but only if it is designed to suit an individual offender and an individual situation (see Chapter 10). General and uniform punishment is still the rule rather than the exception, however, and the movement toward a treatment or **preventive model** is slow.

THE TREATMENT IDEOLOGY

A major trend in corrections is to approach the offender much as one would the mentally ill, the neglected, or the underprivileged. This more humane ideology, reflected in the **treatment model**, sees the criminal behavior as just anoth-

Effective treatment programs can only start with open discussion and caring

—*PHOTO BY BOB DAEMMRICH, COURTESY OF STOCK BOSTON*

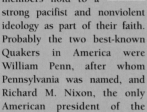
er manifestation of pathology that can be handled by some form of therapeutic activity. Although the criminal may be referred to as "sick," the treatment ideology is not analogous to a medical approach. The closest comparison with physical illness lies in the need for offenders to recognize the danger and undesirability of their criminal behavior and then to make significant efforts to rid themselves of that behavior. The treatment model does not "remove" criminal behavior, as one might remove an infected limb; rather, the "patient" (inmate) is made to see the rewards of positive behavior and is encouraged and equipped to adopt it as a model.

The treatment ideology does not encourage inmates to be coddled and allowed to do as they please within the institution. It is a fairly common belief among many elements of the criminal justice system that any program that is not punitive or restrictive is being "soft" or akin to "running a country club." In fact, some form of treatment ideology can be applied in even the most restrictive and security-oriented institution. The main difference between the treatment and punishment ideologies is that in the former, offenders are assigned to the institution for a correctional program intended to prepare them for readjustment to or reintegration into the community, not just for punishment and confinement. There is room for punishment and security in the treatment approach, but little room for treatment in the punitive approach. The more humane treatment methods are intended to be used in conjunction with the employment of authority in a constructive and positive manner, but inmates must be allowed to try, even if they fail. Authoritarian procedures, used alone, only give the offender more ammunition to support a self-image as an oppressed and impotent pawn of the power structure.

Recall that the field of corrections, especially in its early history in America, underwent significant change as innovators again sought the answers to those same two questions mentioned earlier, "Who are the offenders?" and "What should we do with them?" The treatment ideology contains four separate answers to those questions, commonly referred to as treatment doctrines.

The Quaker reform movement, arising in 1790, held that offenders were out of touch with God. The corresponding treatment approach was isolation. Prisoners were supplied with a Bible for reading and doing penitence. The doctrine for the Quakers was to help offenders find their way back to God; it was believed that once God was found, crime would cease.

The **reformatory movement** solutions, after 1890, provided somewhat different answers. Offenders were seen as disadvantaged, "unfortunate," persons whose education, training, and discipline had been inadequate. The educational doctrine answer was to provide education at a functional level, emphasis on vocational and occupational skills, and a regime of discipline that was aimed at the internalization of controls to prevent recurrence of criminal behavior when the prisoner was released.

The **medical model** that developed in the late 1920s and early 1930s, under the leadership of Sanford Bates and the U.S. Bureau of Prisons, saw the answers as lying within the individual. It then became necessary to diagnose the individual problem, develop a treatment program that might remedy it, and then apply treatment. When the "patient" was found to be well, he or she would be released to a program of aftercare in the community under the supervision of therapeutic parole officers who would continue casework therapy until the offender was "rehabilitated." The medical model offered hope of rehabilitation. It was the responsibility of corrections to "make the ill well." The "ill" would thus be passive recipients of beneficent therapy, like patients in a hospital.

Important foundations of the **treatment model** are the indeterminate sentence and the assumption that the offender can be treated and given early release when he or she has been "reformed." The minimum and maximum periods (such as a one- to five-year sentence) reflect the inability of the sentencing judge to know exactly when the prisoner would be reformed.

Before 1975, the federal system and all of the state systems had sentencing codes that were indeterminate, and boards of prison terms and parole, commonly called parole boards, were given broad discretion in determining when inmates were ready for release under parole supervision. Since 1976, more than half the states as well as the federal system have limited parole board discretion or abolished discretionary parole completely. In addition, the percentage of inmates released through parole board discretion declined from 72 percent to 39 percent. Twenty-three states now use guidelines to structure their release decisions.

The fourth doctrine emerged in the late 1960s. It is acceptable to use either 1965 or 1969 as the date of origin, but, whichever date is used, the form of treatment was a significant trend throughout the 1980s. Known as the **reintegration model,** the form of treatment made differing assumptions about the cause and solutions to crime and the criminal. The community was seen as the basic etiological factor, and the offender was considered to be the product of a local community that excluded, failed to provide for, or discriminated against the offender. Because the basic cause is regarded as community related, proponents thought it best to address the problem by using community resources that correctional personnel would be able to marshal or develop. These would include reducing poverty rates, investing in children, urban revitalization, Headstart programs, job training, among others. The offender's role requires active participation in the effort to resolve the difficulty; correctional personnel serve as brokers for services. Ideally, a community management approach is used, wherein several officers can specialize to maximize the delivery of opportunities to the offender, who is eager to reintegrate and become part of the community. All four doctrines require treatment and coexist in the correctional ideology called *treatment,* which we discuss in Chapter 22.

THE PREVENTION IDEOLOGY

As we mentioned earlier, the problem of crime cannot be separated from the individual offender. In a sense, the problem can be temporarily removed from the community whenever the offender is sent off to prison. Almost all offenders are

MEDICAL MODEL

This model in corrections implies that criminal behavior is comparable to a disease and that, if the disease (criminal behavior) can be diagnosed, it can be treated and the offender "cured." This model has been under attack from many points and has generally been replaced by individualized treatment to correct *behavior* instead of some underlying defect or disease.

INDETERMINATE SENTENCING

An indeterminate sentence is a sentence to incarceration pronounced by a judge that sets minimum and maximum periods of incarceration of the offender (such as "from one to five years"). The minimum term would establish the earliest release date (adjusted for certain time credits for, as an example, jail time during pretrial detention) or the date of first parole consideration to determine if the inmate should be released. At the maximum term, the inmate would have to be released.

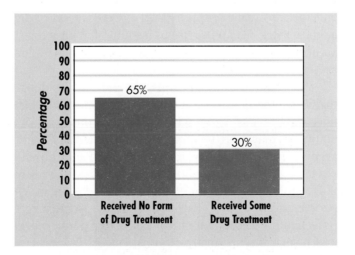

FIGURE

4.1

Recidivism Rates for Released Inmates in the District of Columbia, 1992

SOURCE: Steven Donziger, *The Real War on Crime* (New York: HarperCollins, 1996), p. 20.

eventually released, however, and the problem returns unless it has been effectively treated while the offender was in the prison. Because of the perceived minimal success of present correctional programs (recidivism rates range from 40 to 70 percent),[13] many communities and governmental agencies are turning to crime prevention as a possible solution. Prevention methods have a dual focus: on the individual and on the environment in which he or she lives. Much crime prevention activity is designed to steer potential delinquents away from a life of trouble. Such programs generally begin at the school level, where truancy and dropping out are often the precursors of criminal activity. Those early programs, for the most part, attempt to identify the first signs of criminal behavior.

Prediction is a complex process, even when it is carefully controlled.[14] The extensive studies by Sheldon and Eleanor Glueck illustrate the problems inherent in most prediction efforts.[15] Prevention programs in schools today aim to treat the problem child by providing specialized classes, vocational education, and counseling;[16] they do not aim to force the juvenile out of the picture by expulsion from school. The prevention ideology recognizes that problem children must have supportive help, or they are very likely to use crime as an outlet for unhappiness and insecurity.

Those who advocate the prevention ideology are well aware that total prevention of crime is probably impossible. The great sociologist, Emile Durkheim, believed crime in some form was an inevitable accompaniment to human society and that if serious crime were prevented, authorities would focus their attention on minor offenses.[17] Essentially, the prevention ideology holds that crime may at least be reduced through an attack on the social and emotional problems that encourage a child's criminal inclinations.

The individual's environment is recognized as a crucial focus in the prevention of crime; the prevention ideology emphasizes the need to structure the environment so criminal opportunity is minimized. As an example, it has been said that the greatest crime prevention device ever invented was the streetlight. The movement toward crime prevention through environmental design has great promise for the future. The object of such an approach is not only to provide barriers to crime (such as window bars, fences, locks, and airport security checks),[18] but also to enhance the existing features that tend to discourage crime (for example, more lighting around homes and apartment buildings, more windows in dark hallways, and community projects aimed at getting people to know their neighbors). The conditions that produce a high or low crime rate in a given area are not all physical, however; the environment includes the people, activities, pressures, and ideas to which an individual is exposed every day. The prevention ideology advocates the maximum use of resources in areas that have special problems such as poverty and overcrowding—funds should be allocated for crime prevention rather than for prison construction.[19]

In community corrections, the prevention ideology is combined with treatment. The emphasis is on the identification and treatment of the problems that have caused past criminal behavior, to prevent its recurrence. Eventually, the emphasis may lead to a closer, more interdependent relationship between the agencies now involved in crime prevention and those that provide community services. As they presently operate, criminal justice agencies actually tend to create more problems for minor offenders, instead of treating the problems that got those people into trouble.[20] If schools, churches, service agencies, and similar organizations could become more involved, before persons become entangled in the criminal justice system, many criminal careers could be prevented before they start.

Diversion and nonjudicial approaches to offenders are seen as potentially valuable alternatives to a more formal punishment-oriented reaction to the problem of crime.[21] A combination of prevention and treatment ideologies would be the most promising and humane organization of correctional beliefs and practices.

COMMUNITY CORRECTIONS
This describes sentences that provide alternatives to incarceration of offenders in prisons. These sentences often include participation in programs that are located in the same areas in which the offenders work and live. Community corrections sentences are designed to consider both the safety of the local residents as well as the treatment needs of offenders.

The Pendulum Swings

Since 1976, when crime took a temporary downturn, to 1990, high crime rates caused the forces of society to lean again toward the punishment ideology.[22] As the populations of the country's jails and prisons have grown to almost unmanageable proportions, administrators and legislatures have been more willing to accept the turn backward in order to have at least some way to cope with the growing and more violent criminal populations. The following chapters discuss the problems faced by harried and underfunded administrators trying to deal with institutions that are beyond bursting at the seams. Budgets are stripped of so-called frills such as *treatment* and must be used to add beds, food, and custody staff to house and feed inmates and protect society. The trend toward determinate sentences and "**get-tough**" **laws** at all levels exacerbates the situation. At best, treatment is difficult to carry out in a security institution. At worst, treatment is all but impossible to find. That pessimistic situation was the trend of the 1980s. The correctional "nonsystem" seems to be staggering toward the year 2000 in a continuing state of indecision as to what to embrace as its core ideology.[23] The signs seem clear, however, and the hope for treatment that dominated in the 1960s and 1970s seems lost now that the cry for "hard time" for offenders, poor economic conditions in inner-city blighted areas, and continued overcrowding exist at levels unprecedented in the short history of corrections in America.

Despite the increased reliance on punishment and the conservative backlash that has so negatively impacted corrections from the late 1980s to 1996, there remains strong support for both treatment and prevention among legislators[24] as well as the general public.[25] Perhaps the best analogy is of the pendulum and its

Teaching young students about corrections with an "officer-friendly" approach

—*COURTESY OF NEW YORK DEPARTMENT OF CORRECTIONS*

path as it moves from left to right. It will take major changes in the future for the pendulum of justice to move back toward the center. The task ahead for today's students will be both important and difficult as they track the path of the pendulum.

Contemporary Corrections

The need for correctional reforms and structured plans to achieve them have been documented by the **Wickersham Commission** (President Johnson's Task Force on Corrections) and the various state task forces. The early 1960s emerged as a period of seeking alternative methods, programs, treatment procedures, and designs for facilities. The most astonishing and significant findings included the following:

1. Long sentences are self-defeating in regard to rehabilitation.
2. Most offenders—perhaps as many as 85 percent—do not need to be incarcerated and could function better back in the community under supervision.
3. Most inmates derive maximum benefit from incarceration during their first two years; after that period, it becomes less and less likely that they could function as productive citizens if returned to society.
4. Community-based corrections are more realistic, less expensive, and at least as effective as incarceration.
5. Corrections, as a system, must encompass all aspects of rehabilitative service, including mental health, employment services, education, and social services.
6. Some offenders—because of their dangerousness—will require extensive incarceration and treatment programs especially designed and implemented in secure institutions. The staff in those institutions must be extensive and of high quality.
7. Most inmates are not mentally ill but suffer from a variety of educational, medical, psychological, maturational, economic, and interpersonal handicaps that are seldom reduced or resolved in contemporary correctional systems.
8. Inmates must be given the opportunity and capability to earn a living wage so as to compensate their victims and support their own families, keeping them off public assistance rolls.
9. The pay for inmates presently incarcerated is too low to be regarded as wages. Thus the rates of pay must be increased to at least the minimum wage on the outside for similar labor.
10. The private economic sector must be sought out and used to provide both training and work programs that will produce employable workers at the end of the corrections cycle.

Despite the evidence, three important developments in corrections have occurred over the last three decades. They are (1) the abandonment of the ideological basis for postadjudication handling of convicted offenders, commonly referred to as the *medical model;* (2) the shift to determinate sentencing, which places limits on the judge's power to determine how long the offender might serve in prison; and (3) a search for punishments that would be more effective than court-ordered probation and less severe than long-term incarceration, the so-called *intermediate punishments.*

By 1987, the majority of the states embraced determinate sentencing, abolishing parole release mechanisms in at least twenty-three states and imposing mandatory add-on time for use of a gun in crimes, sale of narcotics, and some especially brutal crimes. The reemergence of retribution in contemporary corrections has in part led to seriously overcrowded prisons, a deluge of lawsuits by prisoners seeking better conditions in incarceration, and an intense search for new alternatives to imprisonment[26] that would still provide public safety and constitutionally viable conditions for prisoners.[27] "Ironically, for a movement begun by fiscal conservatives, the new get-tough policy has turned out to be the most costly approach to corrections yet attempted."[28]

By 1993, correctional populations swelled to unparalleled numbers: 4.9 million adults, some 2.6 percent of the adult U.S. population. There were 909,000 men and women in the custody of state and federal prisons, 455,000 were in local jails on a given day, 2.8 million were on probation, and some 671,000 were on parole. See Figure 4-2 for a graphic presentation of the growth curves.

As law enforcement focused on the War on Drugs and gang violence primarily engendered over drug sales and turf issues, the number of committed drug offenders increased 900 percent from 1980 through 1992, equaling one-third of state and 60 percent of federal prison inmates. Violent offenders in prison accounted to 41 percent of the growth in number of prison inmates. Incarceration rates rose to 883 per 100,000 adult men, and the rate of incarceration of black men rose to eight times that of white men. During the same time frame, the number of adults on probation increased 205 percent, in jails rose 150 percent, and on parole increased 205 percent. Data on adults on all forms of correctional control are shown in Figure 4-3, and include the burgeoning prison alternatives of probation and intermediate punishments. The punishment ideology has contributed heavily to this growth.

The intermediate punishments that have emerged are new for American corrections; some even apply contemporary high-tech concepts to controlling

POSTADJUDICATION
This generally refers to the period after the offender has been found guilty by a judge or a jury and before the sentence has been pronounced. It is in this time frame that the court may consider alternatives to incarceration and use some intermediate sanction if the offender has a good record and appears able to be rehabilitated in the community without incarceration.

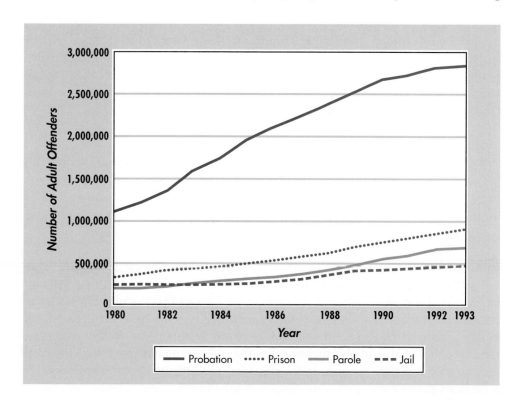

FIGURE

4.2

Adults in Jail, on Probation, in Prison, or on Parole in the United States, 1980–1993

SOURCE: Bureau of Justice Statistics, *Correctional Populations in the United States* (Washington, D.C.: U.S. Department of Justice, 1996), p. 1.

FIGURE

4.3

Adults in Jail, on
Probation, in Prison,
or on Parole, 1992

SOURCE: Bureau of Justice Statistics, *Correctional
Populations in the United States* (Washington,
D.C.: U.S. Department of Justice, 1995), p. 1.

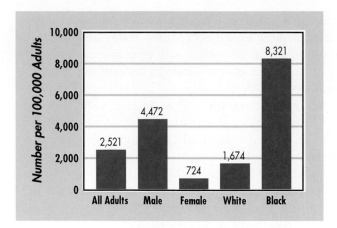

offenders. Those concepts are explored later in Chapter 9, but we introduce you here to the most common of the new alternatives. They include restitution programs, intensive supervised probation, house arrest, and electronic monitoring.

Intermediate Punishments

Restitution Programs

Usually a cash payment by the offender to the victim of an amount considered to offset the loss incurred by the victim or community–the amount of payment may be scaled down to the offender's earning capacity, and/or payment may be made in installments. Sometimes services directly or indirectly benefiting the victim may be substituted for cash payment.

Intensive Supervised Probation

A court-ordered program of community supervision by probation officers working with very small caseloads to provide intensive supervision–such programs are usually linked to impromptu drug testing, curfews, restitution, volunteer sponsors, probation fees, and other punitive intrusions. Sometimes (as in Georgia) two officers will share a caseload of up to forty probationers.

House Arrest

A more intensive program that requires the offender to remain secluded in his or her home except for work, grocery shopping, community restitution service, or other minor exceptions–frequently, house arrest may be intensified by requiring the offender to wear an electronic device that signals a computer monitor that the offender is present at home.

Electronic Monitoring

This program requires an offender to wear a bracelet or anklet that will emit an electronic signal, confirming via a telephone contact that the offender is located at a specific, required location. Some monitoring systems have the capability of emitting signals that can be picked up by cellular listening posts within a community, to signal to a computer monitor that the offender is moving within the community (not at home). Frequently, the electronic monitoring system is buttressed by scheduled probation officer visits, drug testing, and other surveillance options.

Some Effects of the War on Drugs

In the 1980s, a conservative crime prevention strategy commonly known as the "war on drugs" began in the United States. It adopts a narrow (and punitive) conception of the drug seller as a predatory offender willingly selling dangerous drugs to children and youths, amassing fortunes by corrupting innocent users, and ruining their lives. A policy of criminalization and enforcement was adopted; little effort or resources were devoted to treatment and habilitation.

Law enforcement went on an "arrest binge," increasing the volume of persons arrested and creating massive problems for other components of the criminal justice system. Prosecutors, defenders, judges, jailers, and prison administrators spend much of their days trying to move their caseloads before the next wave of incoming arrests. Effects include transferring judges to criminal cases, creating faster plea bargaining, forcing alternative control strategies (such as electronic monitoring and intensive supervision), shifting county inmates to state prisons by increasing the proportion of drug offenders committed to prisons, using temporary and makeshift holding facilities for inmates, forcing early release of sometimes dangerous inmates, and clogging both the courts and correctional systems.

Almost 60 percent of federal prison inmates are incarcerated for drug law violations; the national average for state systems is about 30 percent.

The war on drugs has diverted attention from the causes of drug use and social problems, contributed to the abandonment of the lower class in terms of new services, expanded the power of the state in light of the rights of the individual, legitimized intrusion of American politics into Latin and South American governments, and not reduced the volume of crime or drug use. Weir argues that cynical politicians have manipulated the public to attain their own agenda and goals and, in so doing, created a "dope fiend" stereotype to generate votes. The "war" has increased violence and enhanced gangster roles for minority inner-city youth. ∎

SOURCES: Christina Johns, *Power, Ideology and the War on Drugs* (Westport, CT: Praeger, 1992); John Klofas, "Drugs and Justice: The Impact of Drugs on Criminal Justice in a Metropolitan Community," *Crime and Delinquency* 39:2 (1993): 204-224; and William Weir, *In the Shadow of the Dope Fiend: America's War on Drugs.* (North Haven, CT: Archon Books, 1995.)

We must add a final note about contemporary developments in the modern era. American corrections has undertaken an enormous construction program, in what may be a futile effort to build enough cells to relieve overcrowding in prisons, penitentiaries, reformatories, corrections centers, and other facilities for incarceration. Imprisonment, generally acknowledged to cost the taxpayer about $25,000 per inmate annually, requires a larger and larger portion of the generally shrinking resources of government at all levels. Financing of prison construction, costing up to as much as $200,000 per bed, is borrowing against the future and flirting with bankruptcy for governmental jurisdictions.[29] Corrections has become so expensive that private entrepreneurs have provided correctional services at local jurisdictions and have proposed to provide correctional services for entire state systems at less cost and with greater effectiveness.

In addition to the direct costs of maintaining current jails and prisons, as well as underwriting the unprecedented construction program now underway, there are social costs seldom appreciated by the general public. In addition to the annual per inmate cost and debt retirement for prison construction, there are such collateral costs as loss of tax dollars for each incarcerated offender, increased child support and general welfare payments, loss of child support and alimony payments, increased delinquency from lack of parental support, foster home costs, and cross-generational dependence on welfare. Although no one knows the precise cost of incarceration—collateral, social, familial, psychological, and so on—it is no doubt staggering. Our current policy of overincarcerating offenders cannot be expected to continue without unacceptable drains on limited revenues from taxpayers and the public treasury.[30]

Summary

As we enter the twenty-first century, corrections in America is at a crossroads, a crisis unparalleled in the past two hundred years. The remainder of this text describes current developments and practices in corrections, innovations, proposed solutions, and ways to ease the crisis and improve the effectiveness of the system. To understand those recent developments, we need to explore the correctional ideologies detailed in this chapter. The explosion predicted from the conditions created by overcrowding, idleness, and lack of public concern erupted at Attica in the fall of 1971. The modern era became a period of seeking ways to prevent more such events: community-based corrections became the watchword for reform in corrections, and the "correctional filter" (discussed in Chapter 6) was supplied with more outlets for diverting inmates from seething, overcrowded prisons. Supreme Court decisions created further pressure for reform. The result, at least until the end of the 1970s, was a state of uneasy status quo. The status quo was broken in the beginning of the 1980s by riots at the New Mexico State Prison, which resulted in numerous brutal deaths and public outrage. Prison riots continued; in 1996, there were four prison riots over three days in federal prisons.

It appears now that some of the programs designed to relieve the problems in the overcrowded fortress prisons have in fact contributed to many of the conditions and made them even more ripe for violence. The fortress prisons are still here, they are even more overcrowded, and their maximum security clients are now the "bottom of the barrel" regarding behavioral problems.[31] This has caused an abandonment of the medical model and steady movement toward a model emphasizing custody and control over everything else in a futile effort to keep peace in the institutions and "protect society." The problem of selecting a philosophy or ideology that is effective and reflective of society's mood is a problem administrators will have to confront in the next decade.

Only when American society decides which ideology or combination of ideologies most deserves its support will the problems facing the correctional administrator be properly addressed. It may be that some combination will be the only possible answer, given the wide variety of problems and offenders. Some offenders may respond only to a punitive ideology, at least until we are able to develop treatment techniques that offer greater potential for success and are constitutionally acceptable. The offender who can respond to treatment, however, must be given a chance to receive it—without being totally free of control, as the protection of society remains the paramount concern. The prevention ideology offers great promise, but it seems too idealistic to suffice in and of itself. As prison populations become increasingly large and unmanageable, it may become necessary to introduce ex-offenders into the prison environment, as leavening and change agents working with the correctional administration. This is becoming more acceptable in the fields of probation and parole. Those ideas will undoubtedly lead to the development of other alternatives to incarceration, and some possibilities are outlined in later chapters. To comprehend the current issues in corrections, we must examine the decision process and options available to the prosecution, judiciary, and releasing authorities. That process and its options are described in the next chapter.

Review Questions

1. What basic ideologies have determined the handling of offenders over the years? Which is the oldest?
2. What criteria must be met if punishment is to act as a deterrent?
3. How does the treatment ideology differ from punishment? Are they necessarily exclusive of each other?
4. What are some of the changes presently taking place in the clientele of the correctional system?
5. How has the punishment ideology recently impacted on corrections?

Words to Remember

"War on Drugs"

punishment ideology

treatment ideology

prevention ideology

medical model

Wickersham Commission

theory of disablement

"brick-and-mortar" solution

preventive model

reformatory movement

stigma of conviction

reintegration model

diversion

"get-tough" laws

deterrent effect

treatment model

Endnotes

1. Elmer H. Johnson, *Crime, Correction, and Society* (Homewood, IL: Dorsey Press, 1974), p. 173. See also Dean Spader, "Megatrends in Criminal Justice Theory," *American Journal of Criminal Law* 13:2 (1986): 157–198, and Alexandar Fatic, *Punishment and Restorative Crime Handling*. Aldershot, UK: Avebury, 1995.

2. Norman Carlson, "A More Balanced Correctional Philosophy," *FBI Law Enforcement Bulletin* 46 (January 1977): 22–25. See also Jerry Parker and H. G. Grasmick, "Linking Actual and Perceived Certainty of Punishment," *Criminology* 17 (November 1979): 366–379, and Michael Leiber, Anne Woodrick, and Michele Roudebush, "Religion, Discriminatory Attitudes, and Orientation of Juvenile Justice Personnel," *Criminology* 33:3 (1995): 431–449.

3. See Raymond Paternoster for a review of the evidence on the deterrent effects of punishment, "The Deterrent Effect of the Perceived Certainty and Severity of Punishment: A Review of the Evidence and Issues," *Justice Quarterly* 4 (June 1987): 173–217.

4. John Irwin and James Austin, *It's About Time* (San Francisco: National Council on Crime and Delinquency, 1987), pp. 12–14. See also Joel Waldfogel, "The Effect of Criminal Conviction on Income and the Trust 'Reposed in the Workmen,'" *Journal of Human Resources* 29:1 (1994): 62–81, and Shelley Albright and Furjen Denq, "Employer Attitudes Toward Hiring Ex-Offenders," *The Prison Journal* 76:2 (1996): 118–137.

5. Peter B. Greenwood, *Selective Incapacitation* (Santa Monica, CA: Rand Corporation, 1983). See also M. Gottfredson and T. Hirschi, "The True Value of Lambda Would Appear to Be Zero: An Essay on Criminal Careers, Selective Incapacitation, Cohort Studies, and Related Topics," *Criminology* 24 (May 1986): 213–233, and Scott Decker and Barbara Salert, "Predicting the Career Criminal: An Empirical Test of the Greenwood Scale," *Journal of Criminal Law and Criminology* 77 (1986): 215–236.

6. Incapacitation remains a hotly debated topic in corrections. See David Rowe, Wayne Osgood, and Alan Nicewander, "A Latent Trait Approach to Identifying Criminal Careers," *Criminology* 28 (May 1990): 237–270; Rolf Loeber and Howard Snyder, "Rate of Offending in Juvenile Careers," *Criminology* 28 (February 1990): 97–109; Rudy Haapanen, *Relative Incapacitation and the Serious*

Offender (New York: Springer-Verlag, 1990); and Daniel Nagin, David Farrington, and Terrie Moffit, "Life Course Trajectories of Different Types of Offenders," *Criminology* 33:1 (1995): 111–139.

7. Stuart Miller, Simon Dinitz, and John Conrad, *Careers of the Violent* (Lexington, MA: Lexington Books, 1982).

8. More than half of the prison inmates will be charged with prison rule violations during their current sentences. See James Stephan, *Prison Rule Violations* (Washington, D.C.: U.S. Bureau of Justice Statistics, 1989). See also Mary Finn, "Disciplinary Incidents in Prison: Effects of Race, Economic Status, Urban Residence, and Prior Imprisonment," *Journal of Offender Rehabilitation* 22:1/2 (1995): 143–156.

9. See the comments on the Alabama "dog house" by John Conrad, "From Barbarism Toward Decency: Alabama's Long Road to Prison Reform," *Journal of Research in Crime and Delinquency* 26 (November 1989): 307–328, and David Lovell and Ron Jemelka, "When Inmates Misbehave: The Costs of Discipline," *The Prison Journal* 76:2 (1996): 165–179.

10. Johnson, *Crime, Correction, and Society,* pp. 361–365. A European view of punishment can be found in Andrew von Hirsch, "'Neoclassicism,' Proportionality and the Rationale for Punishment: Thoughts on the Scandinavian Debate," *Crime and Delinquency* 29 (January 1983): 52–70. See also Walter Dickey, *What Every Policymaker Should Know About Imprisonment and the Crime Rate* (Washington, D.C.: Campaign for an Effective Crime Policy, 1995).

11. There is a current rebirth of the punishment ideology, described in detail by Donald E. J. MacNamara, "The Medical Model in Corrections: Requiescat in Pace," *Criminology* 14 (February 1977): 439–448. For a counterargument, see Daniel Glaser, "The Counterproductivity of Conservative Thinking About Crime," in E. Sagarin, ed., *Criminology: New Concerns* (Beverly Hills, CA: Sage, 1979), pp. 89–104. For inmate views on punishment, see Mansfield Frazier, *From Behind the Wall: Commentary on Crime, Punishment, Race and the Underclass by a Prison Inmate* (New York: Paragon, 1995), and Victor Hassine, *A Life Without Parole: Living in Prison Today* (Los Angeles: Roxbury, 1996).

12. James Austin and Aaron McVey, *The 1989 NCCD Prison Population Forecast: The Impact of the War on Drugs* (San Francisco: National Council on Crime and Delinquency, 1989), p. 13.

13. Allen Beck and Bernard Shipley, *Recidivism of Prisoners Released in 1983* (Washington, D.C.: U.S. Bureau of Justice Statistics, 1989).

14. For a discussion of prediction, see Haapanen, *Relative Incapacitation and the Serious Offender.*

15. See John Lamb and R. Sampson, "Unraveling Families and Delinquency: A Re-analysis of the Gluecks' Data," *Criminology* 26 (1988): 355–380. See also Martin Larzelere and Gerald Patterson, "Parental Management: Mediator of the Effect of Socioeconomic Status of Early Delinquency," *Criminology* 28 (1990): 301–324, and Carolyn Smith and Terence Thornberry, "The Relationship Between Childhood Maltreatment and Adolescent Involvement in Delinquency," *Criminology* 33:4 (1995): 219–234.

16. June Andrew, "Violence and Poor Reading," *Criminology* 17 (November 1979): 361–365. See also Carol Veneziano, "Applying the Skill-Deficit Concept of Deviance to Juvenile Delinquents," *Juvenile and Family Court Journal* 40 (1989): 45–51. But see Stephen Cox, William Davidson, and Timothy Bynum, "A Meta-analytic Assessment of Delinquency-Related Outcomes of Alternative Education Programs," *Crime and Delinquency* 41:2 (1995): 219–234.

17. Emile Durkheim, *Division of Labor in Society,* trans. George Simpson (Glencoe, IL: Free Press, 1947).

18. William Minor, "Skyjacking Crime Control Models," *Journal of Criminal Law and Criminology* 66 (March 1975): 94–105. See also Barry Poyner and William Fawcett, *Design for Inherent Security: Guidelines for Nonresidential Buildings* (London: Construction Industry Research and Information Associates, 1995), and Mary Smith, *Crime Prevention Through Environmental Design in Parking Facilities* (Washington, D. C.: U.S. Department of Justice, 1996).

19. C. Ray Jeffery, *Crime Prevention Through Environmental Design,* 2nd ed. (Beverly Hills, CA: Sage, 1977). See also Garland White, "Neighborhood Permeability and Burglary Rates," *Justice Quarterly* 7 (March 1990): 11–56, and Tim Hope, "Community Crime Prevention," in

Michael Tonry and David Farrington, eds., *Building a Safer Society* (Chicago: University of Chicago Press, 1995), pp. 21–89.

20. Scott Decker, "A Systematic Analysis of Diversion: Net Widening and Beyond," *Journal of Criminal Justice* 13 (1985): 207–216. See also Minoru Yokoyama, "Net-widening of the Juvenile Justice System in Japan," *Criminal Justice Review* 14 (1989): 43–53.

21. James Austin, Karen Joe, Barry Krisberg, and Patricia Steele, *The Impact of Juvenile Court Sanctions: A Court That Works* (San Francisco: National Council on Crime and Delinquency, 1990).

22. That trend has stopped. The National Crime Survey of victims indicates that crime has dropped 17 percent since 1981, the peak year. See Joseph Bessette et al., *Criminal Victimization 1988* (Washington, D.C.: U.S. Bureau of Justice Statistics, 1989), and Federal Bureau of Identification, *Uniform Crime Report 1994* (Washington, D. C.: U.S. Department of Justice, 1995). Uniform crime rates started to decrease in 1990.

23. Harry E. Allen, Edward Latessa and Gennaro Vito, "Corrections in America: 2000 A.D.," *Corrections Today* 50 (1987): 92–96.

24. T. Flanagan, E. McGarrell, and A. Lizotte, "Ideology and Crime Control Policy Positions in a State Legislature," *Journal of Criminal Justice* 17 (1989): 87–101, and Marla Sandys and Edmund McGarrell, "Attitudes Toward Capital Punishment Among Indiana Legislators," *Justice Quarterly* 11:4 (1994): 651–677.

25. F. Cullen et al., "Public Support for Correctional Treatment: The Tenacity of Rehabilitative Ideology," *Criminal Justice and Behavior* 17 (1990): 5–18; Frances Cullen, "Social Support as an Organizing Concept for Criminology," *Justice Quarterly* 11:4 (1995): 527–559.

26. See the special topic issue of *Crime and Delinquency* 36 (January 1990) for discussions of the major innovations.

27. For a discussion of the forces that have contributed to the contemporary scene, see Marilyn McShane and Frank Williams, "Running on Empty: Creativity and the Correctional Agenda," *Crime and Delinquency* 35 (October 1989): 562–576. See also Edward Latessa and Harry Allen, *Corrections in the Community* (Cincinnati: Anderson, 1997).

28. Latessa and Allen, *Corrections in the Community*, p. 57. See also Philip Zimbardo, *Transforming California's Prisons into Expensive Old Age Homes for Felons: Economic Hidden Costs and Consequences for California's Taxpayers* (San Francisco: Center on Juvenile and Criminal Justice, 1994).

29. Irwin and Austin, *It's About Time*, pp. 9–11.

30. Donziger, *The Real War on Crime,* pp. 47–54.

31. Jom Doyle, "Former Illinois Warden Assails Pelican Bay Guards," *San Francisco Chronicle,* September 29, 1993, p. A-15.

Suggested Readings: Part I

Austin, James. *Parole Outcomes in California*. Madison, WI: National Council on Crime and Delinquency, 1989.

Austin, James, and Aaron McVey. *The Impact of the War on Drugs*. San Francisco: National Council on Crime and Delinquency, 1989.

Bagdikian, Ben H. *The Shame of Prisons*. New York: Pocket Books, 1972.

Baiamonte, John. *Spirit of Vengeance: Nativism and Louisiana Justice, 1921–1924*. Baton Rouge: Louisiana State University Press, 1986.

Barnes, Harry Elmer. *The Story of Punishment,* 2nd ed. Montclair, NJ: Patterson Smith, 1972.

Barnes, Harry Elmer, and Negley K. Teeters. *New Horizons in Criminology,* 2nd ed. Englewood Cliffs, NJ: Prentice Hall, 1959.

Baunach, Phyllis Jo. *Mothers in Prison*. New Brunswick, NJ: Transaction, 1985.

Brockway, Zebulon Reed. *Fifty Years of Prison Service*. Montclair, NJ: Patterson Smith, 1969.

Carter, Robert M., Daniel Glaser, and Leslie T. Wilkins. *Correctional Institutions*. New York: J. B. Lippincott, 1972.

Cohen, Albert, George Cole, and Robert Bailey. *Prison Violence*. Lexington, MA: D. C. Heath, 1976.

Cullen, Francis, and Karen Gilbert. *Reaffirming Rehabilitation*. Cincinnati: Anderson, 1982.

Donziger, Steven, *The Real War on Crime*. New York: HarperCollins, 1996.

Greenwood, Peter, and Susan Turner. *Selective Incapacitation Revisited: Why the High-Rate Offenders Are Hard to Predict*. Santa Monica, CA: Rand Corporation, 1987.

Hassine, Victor. *Life Without Parole: Living in Prison Today*. Los Angeles: Roxbury, 1996.

Irwin, John, and James Austin. *It's About Time*. San Francisco: National Council on Crime and Delinquency, 1987.

Jacoby, Joseph. *Classics of Criminology*. Prospect Heights, IL: Waveland, 1988.

Jeffery, C. R., ed. *Biology and Crime*. Beverly Hills, CA: Sage, 1979.

John, Herbert. *History of Criminal Justice*. Cincinnati: Anderson, 1988.

Johnston, Norman. *The Human Cage: A Brief History of Prison Architecture*. New York: Walker, 1973.

Latessa, Edward, and Harry Allen. *Corrections in the Community*. Cincinnati: Anderson, 1997.

Martin, Randy, Robert Mutchnick, and Timothy Austin. *Criminological Thought: Pioneers Past and Present*. New York: Macmillan, 1990.

Mauer, Mark. *Young Black Men and the Criminal Justice System*. Washington, D.C.: Sentencing Project, 1990.

McCarthy, Belinda, ed. *Intermediate Punishments*. Monsey, NY: Willow Tree Press, 1987.

Nagel, William. *The New Red Barn*. New York: Walker, 1973.

National Advisory Commission on Criminal Justice Standards and Goals. *Corrections*. Washington, D.C.: U.S. Department of Justice, 1973.

Petersilia, Joan. *Racial Disparities in the Criminal Justice System*. Santa Monica, CA: Rand Corporation, 1983.

———. *The Influence of Criminal Justice Research*. Santa Monica, CA: Rand Corporation, 1987.

President's Commission on Law Enforcement and Administration of Justice. *Task Force Report: Corrections*. Washington, D.C.: U.S. Government Printing Office, 1967.

Rothman, David J. *The Discovery of the Asylum*. Boston: Little, Brown, 1971.

Scacco, Anthony. *Rape in Prison*. Springfield, IL: Charles C. Thomas, 1975.

U.S. Bureau of Justice Assistance. *Electronic Monitoring in Intensive Probation and Parole Programs*. Washington, D.C.: Bureau of Justice Assistance, 1989.

U.S. General Accounting Office. *Prison Crowding: Issues Facing the Nation's Prison System*. Washington, D.C., 1989.

Urban Institute. *Comparison of Privately and Publicly Operated Facilities in Kentucky and Massachusetts*. Washington, D.C.: The Institute, 1989.

Wilbanks, William. *The Myth of a Racist Criminal Justice System*. Monterey, CA: Brooks/Cole, 1986.

Law *and the* Legal Process

CHAPTER FIVE

The Incidence *of* Crime

Overview

In Part I, we introduced you to the historical development of the fascinating field of corrections, noting those major philosophical changes that influenced the approach, facilities, and thrusts of various eras of corrections: classical, industrial, reform, educational, prison, and the medical model. We examined how those ideologies compete in handling law violating offenders, and how recent developments in prison construction, intermediate punishments, and punishment approaches have influenced the last quarter-decade of this century.

We now turn to issues that deal with crime: the volume and patterns of law offending in this nation; processes by which offenders are assigned to the major components of the justice system (probation, prisons, and parole, for example); and how sentencing practices influence correctional practices, programs, and facilities. We end this section with a brief discussion of appellate review of conviction and sentences, as well as possible capital punishment to be inflicted on a few of the more serious offenders. In later sections of this textbook we will examine correctional processes, clients, and rights, as well as professionals in the field of corrections working at state, federal, and community settings. We begin our examination of this section with an inquiry into crime rates and, surprisingly, what appears to be an outbreak of *lawfulness* in America as we move toward the end of the 1990s. We offer a somewhat dazzling array of statistical data, gleaned from the many (sometimes conflicting) sources of criminal justice data, to give the student a "feel" for the overall origin and incidence of crime. As throughout this text, we do not attempt to present news flashes, but examples of the kinds of trends and ways to express where corrections is moving on the continuum of the criminal justice scene in America.

> Crime is normal because a society exempt from it is utterly impossible.
>
> —Emile Durkheim

Common-Law Origins of Crime

Most crimes fall into one of two categories, felonies or misdemeanors. Felonies are a group of offenses considered in most societies serious enough to deserve severe punishment or even death. Although they vary somewhat in their specific names, the major *felony* crimes are remarkably similar for all jurisdictions. In the United States, we have come to define most common-law crimes as felonies, because we inherited many of their designations from the English common-law statutes. Under the common law, which developed by history and precedent, there were three categories of crime: **treason, felony,** and **misdemeanor.**[1] Originally, the distinction between felonies and misdemeanors was based on the fact that all felonies were capital offenses, also involving forfeiture of all lands and property of the perpetrator, whereas misdemeanors called for lesser penalties. Even though the United States adopted many aspects of English common law, the severity of felony punishment was later modified to reflect the American way of life.

The distinction between a felony and a misdemeanor in America is generally based either on the type of institution in which the offender would be incarcerated or the length of the sentence imposed. Most felony convictions require a sentence of at least one year in a state prison. This guideline is not infallible, but it serves as a good rule of thumb in determining which crimes are generally considered felonies. Most legal agencies tend to lump the various kinds of felonies into categories that pertain to the social harm involved: offenses against the person, offenses against the habitation, offenses against property, offenses against morality and decency, and so on (see Table 5-1). Figure 5-1 shows only seven **index crimes**; the FBI chose not to include arson in the crime clock because the figures on this eighth category are too new to be accu-

TABLE 5.1

Estimated Number of Prisoners in Custody of State Correctional Authorities by the Most Serious Offense, 1984–1993

Most Serious Offense	Number of Inmates in State Prison	
	1984	1993
All offenses	417,389	828,371
Violent offenses	227,300	394,500
Murder	46,800	90,200
Manslaughter	13,000	14,600
Rape	18,400	32,600
Other sexual assault	14,200	48,800
Robbery	89,800	119,100
Assault	34,000	73,200
Other violent	11,100	16,000
Property offenses	133,100	192,200
Burglary	71,400	95,000
Larceny	26,100	34,700
Motor vehicle theft	5,200	20,400
Fraud	16,600	21,100
Other property	13,900	21,000
Drug offenses	31,700	186,000
Public-order offenses	21,900	52,100
Other/unspecified	3,400	3,500

SOURCE: Tracy Snell, *Correctional Populations in the United States, 1993* (Washington, D.C.: U.S. Department of Justice, 1995),

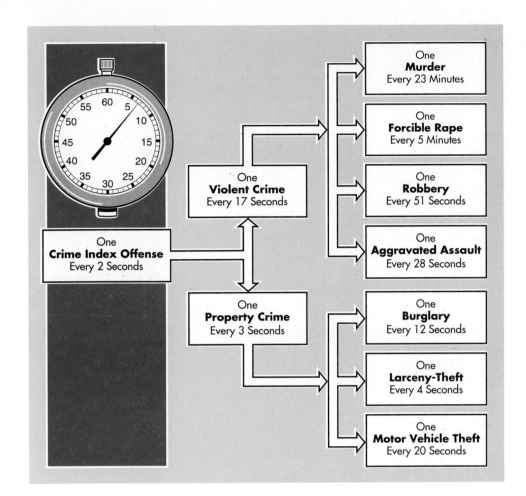

F I G U R E

5.1

Crime Clock, 1994

SOURCE: Adapted from Federal Bureau of Investigation, *Uniform Crime Reports for the United States, 1994,* (Washington, D.C., U.S. Government Printing Office, 1995).

rate. We will look at those categories and the correctional clients they produce, but first we examine trends in crime in the United States over the last half-decade (1990–1994).

First, we do not need to point out that crime in America is unacceptably high, particularly in the violent crime category. Second, crime has been *decreasing* in the nation for at least the last five years; the number of offenses known has decreased over 3 percent since 1990, and the rate per 100,000 inhabitants has decreased almost 8 percent. These data were supplied by the Federal Bureau of Investigation in the *Uniform Crime Report 1994,* which reports crimes known to police and aggregated at the federal level to be reported every year.[2] Third, the other major crime trend indicator, the National Crime Victimization Survey, indicates that crime has dropped significantly in almost every type of crime. Since 1976 to 1991, the rate of victimization has dropped

- 17 percent for robbery
- 21 percent for aggravated assault
- 37 percent for theft crimes
- 40 percent for household burglary.[3]

The **NCVS** was changed in 1992, rendering difficult any comparisons with more recent years. What is evident, however, is that high fear of and concern about crime has not abated. Gangs, drive-by shootings, drug-related violence, and arson of churches have garnered crime coverage, raising fear of crime and hardening attitudes

Crimes Against the Person

The four index crimes against the person are defined as follows:

Criminal homicide, which refers to murder and nonnegligent manslaughter, is the willful (nonnegligent) killing of one human being by another.

Forcible rape is the carnal knowledge of another person forcibly and against their will. Assaults or attempts to commit forcible rape by force or threat of force are also included; however, statutory rape (sex with a minor without force) and other sex offenses are not included in this category.

Robbery is the taking or attempting to take anything of value from the care, custody, or control of a person or persons by force or threat of force and violence and/or putting the victim in fear.

Aggravated assault is an unlawful attack by one person upon another for the purpose of inflicting severe or aggravated bodily injury. This type of assault is usually accompanied by the use of a weapon or by means likely to produce death or great bodily harm. Aggravated assault attempts are also included because it is not necessary that an injury result when a gun, knife, or other weapon is used that could and probably would result in a serious injury if the crime were successfully completed.

■

toward criminals. Cynical politicians have played on public fears during election campaigns,[4] inflaming citizen hostility and creating a perception of "dope fiends" and out-of-control crime. The nation is experiencing less crime, and the decrease, while not exactly an outbreak of lawfulness, is a welcomed trend.

Felonies

CRIMES AGAINST THE PERSON

Four of the eight major, or "index," crimes cited in the FBI's *Uniform Crime Reports* (*UCRs*) are usually labeled **crimes against the person**.[5] These four crime categories (murder and nonnegligent manslaughter, aggravated assault, **forcible rape,** and robbery) are the so-called headline crimes, which create public fear

A crime in progress

—PHOTO BY G. MARCHE, *COURTESY OF FPG INTERNATIONAL*

and promote support for get tough laws and stronger law enforcement. Despite their shock effect, the four offenses accounted for only 5.5 percent of the arrests for index crimes reported in 1994 (622,155 out of 11,341,585).[6] The emphasis placed on those crimes is demonstrated by the higher percentage that is cleared by arrest: it is only logical that the principal resources of our law enforcement agencies should be marshaled to solve the crimes the public fears most. An average of 49 percent of the crimes in these four categories are cleared by arrest, compared with only 15.7 percent in crimes against property. Murder and nonnegligent manslaughter led with a clearance rate of 64 percent, aggravated assault follows with 56 percent, forcible rape has a 52 percent rate of clearance, and robbery has only a 24 percent rate.[7]

As shown in Table 5-1, a nationwide survey of 828,371 prisoners in custody of state correctional authorities in 1993 detailed the offenses for which these inmates were currently incarcerated (instant offense): violent offenses (48 percent), property offenses (23 percent), and drug offense (22 percent) predominated. An estimated 61 percent of the offenders in custody had been incarcerated at least once before.

It is clear from the analysis of the processing of murder cases that they are considered important and get more thorough attention than do less publicized crimes. At one time or another, murder has been a capital offense on the statutes of nearly all of the countries in the Western world. An attempt to understand the correctional client who commits crimes against the person might well begin with the murderer, as described in the *UCR* for 1994. Because murder is usually considered the most completely reported, cleared, and resolved crime, it is a good vehicle for examining the offender who commits crimes against the person (see Tables 5-2 and 5-3).

First, we cannot fail to observe that a disproportionate number of blacks are victims of murder (49.5 percent) and the offenders arrested for murder (53 percent). In 1994, 92 percent of the black murder victims were slain by black offenders, and 83 percent of the white murder victims were slain by white offenders. Males were

TABLE 5.2

Murder Circumstances Distributed by Percentage, 1966–1994

Year	Total Number	Romantic Triangle and Lovers' Quarrels	Other Arguments	Known Felony Type	Suspected Felony Type
1966	10,950	8.5%	40.9%	14.8%	7.0%
1969	14,640	7.0	41.3	19.3	7.2
1972	18,520	7.1	41.2	22.1	5.3
1975	20,510	7.3	37.9	23.0	9.4
1978	18,714	2.7	42.8	16.7	5.6
1979	20,591	2.4	42.9	16.9	5.3
1980	21,860	2.3	44.6	17.7	6.7
1981	20,053	2.5	42.2	17.2	5.5
1986	20,613	2.8	45.6	25.0	4.8
1988	20,675	1.7	32.5	19.0	1.3
1989	21,500	2.0	33.2	21.4	0.8
1990	23,438	2.0	32.3	20.8	0.7
1991	24,703	1.4	30.6	21.4	1.0
1992	23,760	1.5	28.9	21.7	1.2
1994	22,076	—	—	—	—

SOURCE: Federal Bureau of Investigation, *Uniform Crime Reports in the United States*, 1981, 1986, 1988 (Washington, D.C.: U.S. Department of Justice, 1982, 1987, 1989, 1995), 1981 data, p. 37; 1986 data, p. 39; 1988 data, p. 18; 1989–1992 data

TABLE 5.3

Murder Circumstances Distributed by Percentage, 1993

Type	Percent
Felony/suspected felony type	19.1 %
Romantic triangle	2.0
Brawl due to alcohol/drugs	2.0
Arguments	28.1
Juvenile gang/gangland killing	5.2
Others	5.7
Unknown	28.1
	100.0%

SOURCE: FBI, *Crime in the United States 1994* (Washington, D.C.: U.S. Department of Justice, 1995), p. 20.

more often slain by males (87 percent), but nine out of ten females were slain by males. It is also notable that over 54 percent of the persons arrested for murder in 1994 were under twenty-five years old. Those between eighteen and twenty-four, in fact, accounted for thirty in one hundred of the arrests for murder. Murder is the best example for understanding the eight index crimes (see Table 5-1).[8]

The American murderer is often a young male who kills his victim during an argument or over a family problem. The profile of the circumstances under which murder occurs is shown in Table 5-2. Although there is serious public alarm and concern about murderers, as prisoners they are usually the least problematic of all offenders. They are frequently given "honor" status and some work in the least secured areas of correctional facilities.

The rates of prosecution and conviction for aggravated assault and forcible rape are very similar to those for murder. Although a number of studies on rape suggest that the actual crime rate may be as much as three to five times the reported crime rate, that probability does not change the fact that many of the persons convicted and sentenced to state prisons are young and aggressive and have committed prior violent offenses. The data in Table 5-4 suggest injuries from crime.

TABLE 5.4

The Cost of Crime, 1992

Average loss per crime, 1992	
Mean loss, all crimes	$524
Personal crimes	$218
Crimes of violence	206
Rape	234
Robbery	555
Assault	124
Household crimes	$914
Personal and household theft	221
Burglary	834
Motor vehicle theft	3,990

NOTE: Data include all forms of economic loss, medical expenses, and time lost from work because of the crime.
*Includes crimes involving no loss.

SOURCE: Patsy Klaus, *The Costs of Crime to Victims* (Washington, D.C.: U.S. Department of Justice, 1994), p. 1.

CRIMES AGAINST PROPERTY

Of the estimated 1,053,738 individuals who are under correctional supervision in America's prisons each day, a rate of 346 per 100,000 Americans, the largest single group are placed there for **drug offenses** (22 percent), followed by robbery (14 percent). Even with the low clearance by arrest percentages, the sheer volume of the property crimes tends to keep our prisons full (23 percent of all prisoners). Reported incidents of burglary, for example, totaled 2,712,156 in 1994,[9] and the clearance by arrest rate for burglary was 13 percent. Similar low clearance by arrest figures apply to both larceny (20 percent) and auto theft (14 percent), with convictions for all three offenses still providing thousands of new clients for the correctional system.

The offender against property is usually young. For those under the age of eighteen, the number of auto theft cases alone that must be referred to juvenile authorities is over 44 percent of the total arrests for those offenses. The same is true for 34 percent of the larceny arrests and 35 percent of the reported burglary arrests. Persons under the age of twenty-one accounted for 46 percent of the larceny arrests and 60 percent of the arrests for auto theft; persons under the age of twenty-five accounted for 63 percent of the burglary arrests.[10] Crimes against the person may account for the longer sentences, but crimes against property contribute most to the volume in the correctional pipelines.

Burglary is usually considered a crime against the habitation and is the most common crime reported in the crime index. There were almost 2.7 million burglaries reported in 1994, a decrease of 5 percent over 1993.[11] Because a large percentage of burglary is committed in dwellings, it is a crime that alarms citizens. That fear prevails even though trends since 1990 show an 8 percent decline in residential burglary under both daytime and nighttime circumstances. Two out of every three burglaries in 1994 were residential in nature. Sixty-seven percent of all burglaries involved forcible entry, 25 percent were unlawful entries (without force), and the remainder were forcible entry attempts. More (59 percent) residential burglaries occurred during the daytime, but almost two out of three non-residential burglaries occurred during nighttime hours.

There is a great amount of fear (sometimes resulting in the victim's overreaction) that forcible entry into one's home may result in violence against the victim's person. The homeowner's zeal for self-preservation results in a number of tragic shooting accidents each year, even though burglars are actually seldom violent. It has been estimated that property worth billions of dollars each year is taken to obtain money for drugs, but that claim has been seriously challenged.[12] Because the crime of burglary requires stealth and cunning, offenders are seldom caught at the scene, but rather when they attempt to sell ("fence") the stolen goods.

Although the clearance by arrest rate was only 13 percent in 1994, that figure is deceptive.[13] Some burglaries are perpetrated by more than one offender, but in other cases one person may be responsible for numerous offenses. Unless arrested offenders choose to confess to more than the offense for which they were caught, many thousands of burglaries go unsolved.

CRIMES AGAINST MORALITY AND DECENCY

Crimes that tend to get even more publicity than murder are those that have a sexual connotation, especially when against children. Child molesters, for example, excite widespread public alarm and high interest on the part of the media.[14] (They sell newspapers!) Those who abuse or molest children also assume the lowest

ACTS BETWEEN CONSENTING ADULTS

Acts between consenting adults are generally defined as sexual activity that does not involve coercion or force and that takes place in private. They are generally considered not the law's business and represent previously criminal acts that have been decriminalized.

position in the inmate social system in most prisons. Other bizarre sex crimes, with the possible exception of "straight" rape, are also considered repulsive by the inmate subculture. Rape is at least vaguely linked to manhood and perceived as "macho" by the inmate subculture. Although homosexuals are looked upon as "weirdos" in prisons, they can also be welcomed as willing sex objects by other inmates, although sexual behaviors create dissension and trouble for correctional administrators.[15] Many of the so-called acts between consenting adults are now removed from most criminal codes,[16] leaving only the forcible assaultive homosexuals to be sent to prison. This aggravates an already growing problem of control in single sex institutions.

Rape has been traditionally one of the most underreported crimes in America. It has been argued that the stigma and prosecution problems for the *victim* in this type of offense are often more damaging than the penalty for the *offender*. There were 106,096 forcible rapes reported in 1994, but some experts believe there were actually many times that number. Although the victim has good reason to remember his or her assailant, past experience has resulted in low arrest rates. In 1994, however, 52 percent of forcible rapes were cleared by arrest, a trend that seems to be improving after decades of very low clearances.[17]

In the case of rape, usually the only witness is the victim. In the absence of physical or other testimonial evidence, the rapist thus often goes free. Although there were 106,096 rapes reported in 1994, only 29,791 resulted in an arrest.[18] The rapist, then, is young, probably from an urban area, usually black, and has raped someone of his own race. This person represents another aggressive problem for the correctional administrator. Many states have made the crime of rape, as well as many other crimes against morality and decency, a nonprobational offense.[19] This means that most of such offenders will spend some time—and frequently a long time—in prison before they can hope to be back on the streets. Sex crimes that involve extremely peculiar acts or psychopathic personalities are discussed in Chapter 20.

DOMESTIC CRIMES

Two more major crimes deserve attention before we turn to misdemeanors: *domestic violence* and *sexual abuse of children*. Both fall within the **domestic crimes** category, but the *UCR* does not permit collecting detailed information for those types of offenses. Both are viewed with considerable disdain by the public, which holds strong opinions on what should be done, opinions based on misinformed underestimates about the volume of such crimes.

Police Response to Spouse Abuse

Police departments throughout the country are beginning to educate officers about the dynamics of domestic violence, and are adopting official policies encouraging or requiring officers to arrest suspects in domestic violence incidents. State laws are expanding officers' legal authority to arrest in these cases. In most states, officers are now permitted—or in some states (such as California) required—to arrest suspects in misdemeanor domestic violence incidents without obtaining a warrant even if they did not witness the crime, provided they have probable cause to believe a crime has been committed by the person being arrested.

SOURCE: Gail Goolkasian, *Confronting Domestic Violence: The Role of Criminal Court Judges* (Washington, D.C.: U.S. Department of Justice, 1986), p. 3. ∎

Spouse Abuse

A catchall description for battering and **spouse abuse** refers to serious, repetitive, and harmful crimes that can impact behavior across many generations. Children unfortunately learn that "this is the way parents and families ought to act." *Domestic violence* refers to assaultive behavior between adults who are married, are cohabitating, or have either an ongoing or a former existing interpersonal relationship. About nineteen females are battered for every one male.[20]

The lethal consequences of spouse battering are detailed by the FBI, which reported that 30 percent of all murdered females were slain by either their boyfriends or their husbands.[21] Rarely is spouse abuse a single incident; a battered woman faces a high probability of being attacked again and again, especially if she does not call the police. Battering tends to escalate in both severity and frequency over time.

Law enforcement officers called to the scene of a domestic disturbance have generally (until the last decade) been wary of intervening, not only because of the danger to the officers themselves,[22] but also because there was no general policy that required a formal action. Thus the earlier police responses were to physically separate and calm both persons and make referrals to social service agencies. Often the officers would have to return to the same address in a short time, to repeat the generally ineffective nonintervention. Now there is a growing consensus across the nation that the best policy is to arrest the batterer (or both parties if the aggressor can not be readily determined), and for prosecutors and judges to use criminal sanctions to force a cessation of the battering as well as to provide treatment for batterers.[23] Court-ordered counseling and education programs can stop domestic abuse, but only if court orders contain enforcement sanctions and compliance is monitored. Yet much remains to be done to initiate safe havens for the battered spouse, train counselors, find community funding, educate justice personnel, and intervene successfully in the battered spouse syndrome.[24]

CHANGING THE BATTERER

"The judge told him, in no uncertain terms, that the law doesn't allow him to assault me just because I'm his wife. He said that he'll send him to jail if he's brought back for another offense. Right there in the courtroom ... you should have seen the look on his face. I think he knew the judge wasn't kidding, and that's when he decided to do something about it."

—former battered wife

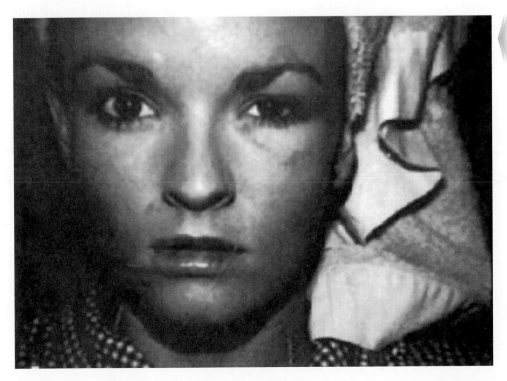

Battered and bruised Nicole Brown Simpson

—PHOTO BY WLM/TV REUTER, COURTESY OF ARCHIVE PHOTOS

Sexual Abuse of Children

Tens of thousands of children a year are mistreated by a parent or household member in **child sexual abuse** cases. Acts involve sexual behavior with an inappropriate person who is too young or too closely related by blood, kinship, or marriage.[25] It has been clearly shown that long-term psychological damage, twisted lives, children growing into adults unable to love or be loved, delinquent behavior, and other damages result from sexual abuse of children.[26] The actual number of victims is unknown but is undoubtedly many times the number that come to the attention of authorities.

Sexual abusers of children are most frequently related to their victims—such as fathers, stepfathers, uncles, aunts, or other relatives—although a small percentage of the offenders are strangers. Most offenders misuse their positions of intimate relationship by engaging in sexually oriented and intrusive behaviors with their children, wards, and loved ones.

Such sexual abusers seldom are committed to prison, where they would occupy despised positions in the inmate social system and would themselves be targeted for assault by other inmates. Instead, little is done to protect abused children in this country. For example, some 90 percent[27] of the relatively few cases brought to the attention of authorities do not go forward to prosecution, thus allowing abusers to escape any deterrent penalty and continue further abuse of their original victims or other children.

Young children are often believed to have little capability to report an incident accurately. Furthermore, adults whom the child trusts enough to tell about the abuse may believe the report to be a fabrication, fantasy, or lie. Even if the child is believed, parents and health professionals are reluctant to carry the case to law enforcement authorities, primarily for fear that legal proceedings will have a greater negative impact on the victim than the initial act. Prosecutors face an inability to prove that the crime occurred, much less to gather sufficient evidence to secure conviction. The rules of evidence preventing hearsay are predicated on the belief that children are unreliable, incompetent, or not creditable as witnesses. Even a sensitive prosecutor, trained in special techniques for prosecuting cases of child sexual abuse, has some reluctance about exposing a child to the grinding impact of an adversarial court trial.

If sexually abused children are to be protected effectively, states will have to reform their statutes to abolish the special competency requirements for children (which some twenty states have already done), and legislatures will need to create special hearsay exceptions that would meet constitutional muster. Each prosecutor's office should have at least one attorney specially trained in child abuse cases, and both community health and child development professionals should be tapped for assistance at trial, as well as for interviewing the abused child. Finally, judges should also be specially trained and, if necessary, should permit closed-circuit televised testimony and videotaped depositions.[28] Child sexual abuse is widespread, and the victims must often suffer in silence, largely unprotected by the justice or correctional systems.

White-Collar and Corporate Crime

A third area of growing public concern about crime involves **white-collar offenses**: crimes that are committed by persons acting in their legitimate roles in business or government. Such offenders include a wide range of offenders, for example, elected officials, businesspersons, dentists and other professionals, automobile

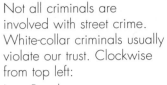

Not all criminals are involved with street crime. White-collar criminals usually violate our trust. Clockwise from top left:

Ivan Boesky
—PHOTO BY E. PETERSON, COURTESY OF UPI/CORBIS-BETTMAN NEWSPHOTOS

Charles Keating
—PHOTO BY SAM JONES, COURTESY OF AP/WIDE WORLD PHOTOS

Michael Milken
—PHOTO BY MARK PETERSON, COURTESY OF MARK PETERSON/REUTERS/CORBIS-BETTMANN NEWSPHOTOS

Pete Rose
—PHOTO BY MARK LYONS, COURTESY OF AP/WIDE WORLD PHOTOS

Leona Helmsley
—PHOTO BY DAVID CANTOR, COURTESY

mechanics, corporate polluters of the environment, embezzlers, persons who accept bribes and excessive gratuities, those who sell power or influence, tax evaders, those who make false insurance claims, persons of the cloth who take funds donated by their congregations for personal gain, stockbrokers who use inside information for profit, and many others who commit such crimes of greed and immoral behavior. Recent offenders in those categories include Reverend Jim Bakker, baseball great Pete Rose, former Speaker of the House James Wright, stockbroker and inside trader Ivan Boesky, Congressman David Durenburger, and hotel tycoon Leona Helmsley.

Most white-collar offenders have positive self-concepts and do not regard their actions as crime or themselves as criminals. Rather, they tend to rationalize their acts as "sharp business practices" or as claiming money they feel due to them for their substantial efforts. Such offenses are seldom detected, much less prosecuted. There is no reliable estimate of the financial damage from white-collar and corporate crime, although the total may well exceed $200 billion per year.[29]

Marshall Clinard argues that the auto, defense, and pharmaceutical corporate giants have abused the public's trust, defied democratic principles, endangered the public and the environment, subverted the democratic process, and engaged in widespread bribery of elected officials at home and abroad.[30] Clinard argues further that self-regulation and the regulatory machinery are ineffective in controlling corporate abuses of this nature. (The savings-and-loan scandal has been estimated to eventually cost the taxpayers $500 billion.) Clinard advocates stiffer penalties, heavy fines for abusers' corporate executives, and fines and imprisonment for top corporate managers. Finally, he calls for widespread publication of offenders' names and crimes, as well as cancellation of incorporation status (a "corporate death penalty") if further violations occur.

Imprisonment for white-collar criminals, when it does occur, is most likely to be for short periods in minimum security federal facilities. The infrequency of incarceration as a sanction for white-collar offenders does not, however, mean that they go unpunished.[31] Civil and regulatory agencies often impose huge fines and remove critical licenses needed to continue operating, resulting in humiliation, bankruptcy, and loss of the means to make a living in such a position of trust. James Inciadri argues that white-collar criminals are increasingly being punished, despite earlier research findings.[32] There is some evidence that the likelihood of incarceration can have a deterrent effect on at least some types of white-collar criminals.[33] Such offenders will likely become clients of probation, alternative sanctions, and parole agencies in the future.

Misdemeanors

THE STATISTICS

Although the number of arrests for index crimes reported in 1994 reached a total of 2,384,244, the total number of arrests was 11,877,188.[34] By the time that many reported arrests are bargained down and finally resolved, a huge number of misdemeanants are being handled by local detention facilities and jails. It is obvious that this problem touches all of the related subsystems of the criminal justice system, affecting plans, workloads, and personnel.

A misdemeanor conviction usually brings a sentence of less than one year, usually served at a local jail or county workhouse rather than a state prison. A misdemeanor can also be punished by the assessment of a fine. This broad definition varies from jurisdiction to jurisdiction, but the standard of less than one year's imprisonment is fairly common.

ALCOHOLICS AND THE REVOLVING DOOR

In some parts of the country, one can stagger down the sidewalk in drunken splendor and seldom run afoul of the law.[35] In most areas, however, the "**common drunk**" is the most typical client for the misdemeanor facilities. Over 30 percent of misdemeanor arrests are for drunkenness or offenses directly related to drinking. One study found that 43 percent of the states' imprisoned male felons were drinking at the time they committed their crimes, and one in three was under the influence of an illegal drug. It is estimated that over two million arrests are made each year for public drunkenness alone.[36] Of course, this creates several problems for the police, not the least of which is the need for great numbers of personnel to handle the drunks. The second area to feel the crunch of the huge volume is the lower-court system. Packed dockets result in "assembly-line justice" in order for the courts to function at all. It is estimated that approximately 50 percent of the convicted jail population could be treated in facilities other than jails, if such facilities were available (Alcoholics Anonymous, antabus, group therapy, social learning programs, continuity of services, etc.).

Alcoholism is a major problem in America. In terms of numbers, it is our leading drug abuse problem. It is estimated that there are at least 12 million alcoholics in the United States, most of whom do not recognize their problem. The **skid rows**[37] of America are populated with the derelicts and dregs of a society that treats the drinking problem as a criminal offense. Most of the offenders arrested for public drunkenness are chronic, having been arrested for the same offense many times before. The conditions in most jails allow for little more than a drying-out period, followed by the inevitable return of the offender to the streets and the bottle.

The alcoholic is neither deterred nor cured by frequent trips to jail. All that is accomplished is the provision of a brief period of sobriety and removal from public view. The system of misdemeanant corrections is unable to deal with the alcoholic, either medically or from a social standpoint, and jail is usually the only available local response.

SKID ROWS

Skid rows were used in logging work in the Pacific Northwest as a route through the underbrush and timber for dragging logs to the rivers. The most famous of the skid rows ended up in Puget Sound in Seattle, Washington, near what is now called Pioneer Square. The poorer sections of the city were situated along the course of the skid row, and thus it became associated with being down on one's luck or "being on the skids."

The public drunk: criminal or victim?

—PHOTO BY JOEL GORDON, COURTESY OF JOEL GORDON PHOTOGRAPHY

In several court cases, petitioners have attempted to draw an analogy between public drunkenness for an **alcoholic** and the logic of *Robinson* v. *California*. In that 1961 California case, the U.S. Supreme Court found that an individual could not be punished simply for being a drug addict. The argument for applying that logic to the alcoholic was finally reviewed in 1968 by the Supreme Court in the case of *Powell* v. *Texas*. The Court found that being drunk in public was not a compulsion symptomatic of the disease; therefore, arrest and confinement for it did not constitute cruel and unusual punishment. This decision was a setback for those attempting to decriminalize the drunkenness laws, but the Court has not completely barred the door to alternative constitutional approaches to the problem in the future.

The sheer volume of drunkenness cases makes it imperative to discover alternatives to the automatic jailing of the chronic drunk. One study of only six chronic offenders in Washington, D.C., found that the group had amassed a total of 1,409 arrests for drunkenness and had spent, altogether, over 125 years behind bars.[38] The increasing use of alternatives to incarceration for alcoholics and drunkenness offenders suggests that such methods are proving somewhat effective in rehabilitating chronic offenders, especially compared with more conventional techniques. The most popular form of diverting alcoholics from the criminal justice system is the detoxification center, now being used in numerous jurisdictions

The **detoxification** center is a civil treatment–oriented alternative to the police station as the processing point for offenders whose only crime is drunkenness. Offenders are retained there until they have been restored to a stable and sober condition. The option of treatment beyond the initial drying-out period[39] is usually left up to the individual, and in most detoxification centers, the majority elect to stay for more treatment. Detoxification centers are usually staffed with medical and other professional personnel to determine the exact needs of each individual. In the case of serious complications, the patient can be transferred to a public hospital for more extensive care.

FIGURE 5.2

Comprehensive Public Inebriate Diversionary Program

SOURCE: National Institute of Law Enforcement and Criminal Justice, *Diversion of the Public Inebriate from the Criminal Justice System* (Washington, D.C.: U.S. Department of Justice, 1973), p. 7.

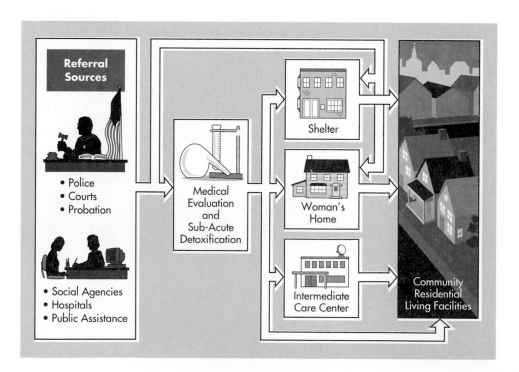

The removal of over two million such "customers" from the annual workload of the country's law enforcement agencies, permitting the agencies to concentrate on more serious threats, would be no small step toward the reduction of major crime in America.[40] One model for a comprehensive system for the diversion of the public drunk is shown in Figure 5-2.

TRENDS NOT FAVORING MISDEMEANANTS

An estimated 459,804 persons were confined in the nation's local jails on June 30, 1994. Although that trend follows the same alarmingly higher rate as that for U.S. prisons, jail inmates are especially difficult to manage in the local communities' restricted environs. In the twelve months ending on June 30, 1994, over 9.8 million persons had passed through the nation's jails. Although a substantial portion of them were repeaters, if each had been a first-timer, then almost 4 percent of the population of the United States would have gone to jail in that twelve-month period alone![41]

The public has begun to get tough on the drinking driver, however, and has replaced the drunk with the person arrested for driving while intoxicated (**DWI**) or driving under the influence (**DUI**).[42] From 1993 to 1994, the number of persons arrested for drunkenness decreased from 561,636 to 539,951 (down 4.3 percent), whereas the number arrested for DWI/DUI decreased over 4.3 percent, from 1,060,581 to 1,014,859.[43] In a system already overloaded, the efforts to crack down on the DWI/DUI with stiffer and longer sentences has begun to be felt strongly. As organizations such as Mothers Against Drunk Drivers (MADD)[44] try to slow the carnage on American highways, this problem may become in the next

Jailing Drunk Drivers

Drunk driving is one of the most serious public health and safety problems facing the American people and their policymakers. In a two-year period, 50,000 Americans die as a result of drunk driving—almost as many American lives as were lost in the entire ten years of the Vietnam War. Conservative estimates place the annual economic loss from drunk driving accidents at $21 to $24 billion for property damage alone.

In the past, state laws dealing with drunk driving ran the gamut of sanctions from release with warning, through moderate to heavy fines, to suspension and revocation of licenses, and—rarely—to incarceration. Enforcement, too, varies considerably from one jurisdiction to the next.

In the last few years, a growing awareness of the magnitude of the problem, coupled with the actions of citizen groups, has led many states to reform both their laws and their enforcement. Since 1981, more than thirty states have enacted legislation directed at drunk driving control, most often by prescribing more severe sanctions such as mandatory confinement. When researchers examined the effects of mandatory confinement for drunk drivers the findings revealed the following:

- When mandatory confinement is introduced and well publicized, drunk driver arrests usually decrease.

- The introduction of mandatory confinement imposes new and heavy demands on courts, incarceration facilities, and probation services.

- The adoption of mandatory confinement is frequently accompanied by increased public concern about drunk driving and is associated with a decline in traffic fatalities.

- Mandatory confinement can be imposed either through legislation or through judicial policy.

- The implementation of mandatory confinement often requires additional resources for the criminal justice system.

- Appropriate systemwide planning can minimize dysfunction and substantially reduce the impact of mandatory confinement on criminal justice operations.

- Publicity is crucial to enhance the deterrent effects.

- Special attention for repeat offenders and scofflaws will require a mechanism to identify scofflaws incorporated into the routine screening of license renewal and registration applications at the motor vehicle department. ∎

SOURCE: U.S. Department of Justice, *Jailing Drunk Drivers* (Washington, D.C.: U.S. Department of Justice, 1984), pp. 1–2.

decade the most significant administrative issue to face managers of local jails. The effects of MADD as a social movement have interacted with the passage of DUI laws, and both the jail and probation populations have been increased as a result, while decreasing the rates of death on the highway.[45]

Summary

Does the misdemeanor offender graduate to more serious crime? Or is he or she usually a felon to begin with, who has plea bargained down a charge? The answer seems to be yes to both questions. It is a common practice to plea bargain a felony charge down to a misdemeanor, especially in the case of a first offense. But some studies show that misdemeanants (excluding the drunkenness offenders) tend to repeat their acts and eventually are convicted of a felony. How, then, do we go about drawing a line between a misdemeanor and a felony?

The definition of a misdemeanor, as mentioned earlier, varies from state to state. The legal definition is usually rooted in the statutes, according to how severe the penalty is for the act, the level of government at which the offender is tried, or some specific list of offenses. In many cases, the term is a catchall, with any crime not specifically listed as a felony automatically considered a misdemeanor. The gray area between a misdemeanor and a felony is even further confounded in some jurisdictions that attempt to differentiate between "high" or "gross" misdemeanors and the regular garden variety. In general, however, the term misdemeanor applies to such offenses as drunkenness, vagrancy, disorderly conduct, breach of the peace, minor assaults, larcenies of small amounts, small-scale gambling and other forms of vice, shoplifting, and other minor offenses.

Most felonies also contain the elements of some misdemeanor. If they have a weak felony case, prosecutors will often try to persuade the defendant to plead guilty to a lesser, included offense. This usually saves the state time and money if the accused accepts the deal. It also gives the offender one more opportunity to remain free of a felony record. Almost nothing is known about the empirical disposition of misdemeanor offenders in America, and so any attempt to state the frequency with which prosecutors use this form of plea bargaining would be mere conjecture. Plea bargaining is discussed in more detail in Chapter 6.

Crime Statistics and Imprisonment

Crime statistics are complex, but data strongly suggest that locking people up has scarcely led to a reduction in crime. As James Austin and John Irwin point out in their 1993 National Council on Crime and Delinquency pamphlet *Does Imprisonment Reduce Crime?*, the states with the highest crime rates also have the highest imprisonment rates. "If the imprisonment/crime reduction hypothesis were valid," they write, "the safest jurisdiction in the country would be Washington D.C. which has by far the highest imprisonment rate in the world (1,168 per 100,000 residents) (National Council on Crime and Delinquency, 1993). And from 1960 to 1991, although there have been fluctuations in crime rates, "the fact remains that in the face of a 165 percent increase in imprisonment rates, the overall UCR crime rate has increased by over 200 percent, property crimes by nearly 200 percent, and violent crime by over 370 percent." ■

SOURCE: Jerome H. Skolnick. "What Not to Do About Crime—The American Society of Criminology 1994 Presidential Address," *Criminology* 33:1 (1995): 8.

Many felonies and misdemeanors are similar. The main difference, as noted earlier, lies in the kind of processing that offenders can expect, depending on whether they are handled as felons or as misdemeanants. The convicted felon can expect to receive, in the majority of cases, a better chance for probation services, institutional programs, and parole services when released. On the other hand, as the system now works, those advantages are more than offset by the loss of civil rights and later employment problems that make a felony conviction a serious and permanent handicap.[46] Although there are efforts under way to adopt licensing standards and restore civil rights for ex-offenders, movement in that area has been extremely slow. For this reason, many offenders avoid the stigma of a felony conviction by the expedient of a misdemeanor guilty plea. The correctional system must be adapted to offer similar services to all convicted offenders, whether or not they are felons. A false distinction between the offenses does not change the basic problems that led the offender to commit the act in the first place. When correctional treatment can be placed on a sensible continuum, so that procedures are related to the needs of the individual offender, the stigma of being called a felon will be reduced and real corrections can be made.

The problem of treating different levels of crimes in different ways is one of the basic tenets of the medical model for rehabilitation. This model assumes laws can be devised to make the punishment fit the crime, a noble premise but one that eluded both the Emperor Justinian and Gilbert and Sullivan's *Mikado*. The process of treating the criminal and causing real behavioral change has proved to be so costly and difficult that it seems doomed to total eclipse by the turn of the century. Also, although the legal differentiation between a misdemeanor and a felony is convenient in the criminal justice process, it holds little significance for the true classification, treatment, and behavioral control of individual offenders. Those who commit (or who are at least convicted for) misdemeanors can turn out to have worse or better custody and/or treatment problems than those who are labeled as felons. Perhaps the future will see a more effective utilization of the medical model, but it is doubtful that change will take place before the year 2000.[47]

Review Questions

1. What are the four main crimes against the person?
2. Explain why the clearance-by-arrest rate is higher for crimes against the person than for other crimes.
3. Explain why the drunken driver represents a serious problem in the correctional system.
4. Explain the difference between a felony and a misdemeanor.
5. What are spouse batterers, and what can be done to lessen the battering problem?
6. Define child sexual abuse. Why are so few cases brought into court?
7. What problems does the drunk driver pose for society? What possible solutions are there to this problem?
8. What dangers do corporate crimes pose to the public?

$\mathcal{W}$ords to Remember

treason	forcible rape	common drunk
felony	domestic crime	skid rows
misdemeanor	drug offenses	alcoholic
index crime	spouse abuse	detoxification
NCVS	child sexual abuse	DWI/DUI
crimes against person	white-collar offenses	

$\mathcal{E}$ndnotes

1. Rollin M. Perkins, *Criminal Law and Procedure,* 4th ed. (Mineola, NY: Foundation Press, 1972), p. 4. For a more recent discussion of the classification issues, see Daniel Glaser, "Reconceiving Some Confounding Domains of Criminology: Issues of Terminology, Theory and Practice," in Joan McCord, ed., *Advances in Criminological Theory,* Vol. 3 (New Brunswick, NJ: Transaction, 1992), pp. 23–46.

2. Federal Bureau of Investigation, *Uniform Crime Report 1994* (Washington, D.C.: U.S. Department of Justice, 1995), p. 7.

3. Trends calculated from Kathleen Maguire, Ann Pastore, and Timothy Flanagan, eds., *Sourcebook of Criminal Justice Statistics 1992* (Washington, D.C.: U.S. Department of Justice, 1995), p. 245.

4. Jerome Skolnick, "What Not to Do About Crime," *Criminology* 33:1 (1995): 1–16; Frances Cullen, "Social Support as an Organizing Concept for Criminology," *Justice Quarterly* 11:4 (1994): 527–559; and Harry Allen, "The American Dream and Crime in the Twenty-First Century," *Justice Quarterly* 12:3 (1995): 427–445.

5. Federal Bureau of Investigation, *Uniform Crime Report 1994* (Washington, D.C.: U.S. Department of Justice, 1995), p. 19.

6. Federal Bureau of Investigation, *Uniform Crime Report 1994,* p. 225.

7. Ibid., p. 207.

8. Ibid., p. 20.

9. Ibid., p. 39. See Louise Biron and Carol Ladoucer, "The Boy Next Door: Local Teen-Age Burglars in Montreal," *Security Journal* 2:4 (1991): 200–204; Paul Cromwell, James Olson, and D'Aunn Avary, "How Residential Burglars Choose Targets: An Ethnographic Analysis," *Security Journal* 2:4 (1991): 195–199; and Richard Wright, Robert Logie, and Scott Decker, "Criminal Expertise and Offender Decision Making: An Experimental Study of the Target Selection Process in Residential Burglary," *Journal of Research in Crime and Delinquency* 32:1 (1995): 39–53.

10. Ibid., pp. 227–228.

11. Ibid., p. 38.

12. The Drug Abuse Foundation, *Heroin Addiction: The Issues* (Washington, D.C.: Drug Abuse Foundation, 1973). See also Robert MacCoun and Peter Reuter, "Are the Wages of Sin $30 an Hour? Economic Aspects of Street-Level Dealing," *Crime and Delinquency* 38:4 (1992): 477–491, and Arthur Kellerman, Lori Westphal, and Laurie Fischer, "Weapon Involvement in Home Invasion Crimes," *Journal of the American Medical Association* 273:2 (1995): 1759–1762.

13. Federal Bureau of Investigation, *Uniform Crime Report 1994,* p. 207. See also Richard Wright, Scott Decker, Allison Redfern, et al., "A Snowball's Chance in Hell: Doing Fieldwork with Active Residential Burglars," *Journal of Research in Crime and Delinquency* 29:2 (1992): 148–161, and Steve Brandl and James Frank, "The Relationship Between Detective Effort and the Disposition of Burglary and Robbery Investigations," *American Journal of Police* 13:3 (1994): 149–160.

14. Keith Kaufman, Anne Wallace, and Charles Jackson, "Comparing Female and Male Perpetrators' Modus Operandi: Victims' Reports of Sexual Abuse," *Journal of Interpersonal Violence* 10:3 (1995): 322–333.

15. Richard Tewksbury found that homosexual activities were at lower than expected rates and frequency in his Ohio prison study. See Richard Tewksbury, "Measures of Sexual Behavior in an Ohio Prison," *Federal Prisons Journal* 1 (1989): 34–39. See also the special issues of *The Prison Journal* 69 (Spring–Summer and Fall–Winter 1989); Helen Eigenberg, "Homosexuality in Male Prisons: Demonstrating the Need for a Social Constructionist Approach," *Criminal Justice Review* 17:2 (1992): 219–234; and Paul Van den Ven, "Talking with Juvenile Delinquents About Gay Males and Lesbians: Implications for Combating Homophobia," *Adolescence* 30:117 (1995): 19–42.

16. Victor Hassie, *Life Without Parole: Living In Prisons Today* (Los Angeles: Roxbury, 1996), pp. 71–76, 85–90, and 111–116.

17. Federal Bureau of Investigation, *Uniform Crime Report 1992* (Washington, D.C.: U.S. Department of Justice, 1992), pp. 23–24. See also Patsy Klaus and Marshall DeBerry, *The Crime of Rape* (Washington, D.C.: U.S. Department of Justice, 1985); Robert Hazelwood and Janet Warren, "The Serial Rapist: His Characteristics and Victims (Part I)," *FBI Law Enforcement Bulletin* 58 (1989): 10–17; Patricia Frazier and Eugene Bordiga, "Rape Trauma Syndrome: A Review of Case Law and Psychological Research," *Law and Human Behavior* 16:3 (1992): 293–311; and Loretta Stalans and Arthur Lorigio, eds., "Responding to Violence Against Women," *Crime and Delinquency* 41:4 (1995): 387–556 (special issue).

18. Federal Bureau of Investigation, *Uniform Crime Report 1994,* p. 227.

19. In Ohio this can apply generally to any repeat of dangerous offenders. The court must consider the likelihood that the offender will commit another offense; the nature and circumstance of the offense; and the history, character, and condition of the offender. Those who fall into the nonprobationable category generally serve much longer prison terms. For a discussion of prediction in justice, see Norval Morris and Marc Miller, *Predictions of Dangerousness in the Criminal Law* (Washington, D.C.: U.S. Department of Justice, 1987); John Weisz et al., "Differential Prediction of Young Adult Arrests for Property and Personal Crimes: Findings of a Cohort Follow-Up Study of Violent Boys," *Journal of Child Psychology and Psychiatry* 32:5 (1991): 783–792; and Reginald Wilkins, Charles Austin, and Susan Baugh, eds., "Stemming the Violence," *Corrections Today* 56:5 (1994): 64–153 (special issue).

20. Gail Gooklasian, *Confronting Domestic Violence: The Role of Criminal Court Judges* (Washington, D.C.: U.S. Department of Justice, 1986). See also Kirk Williams and Richard Hawkins, "Wife Assault, Costs of Arrest, and the Deterrence Process," *Journal of Research in Crime and Delinquency* 29:3 (1992): 292–310; Jay Osofsky, "The Effects of Exposure to Violence on Young Children," *American Psychologist* 50:9 (1995): 782–788; and Freda Briggs, ed., *From Victim to Offender: How Child Sexual Abuse Victims Become Offenders* (St. Leonards, Australia: Allen and Unwin), 1995. On domestic violence, see Helen Tauchen and Ann Witte, *The Dynamics of Domestic Violence: Does Arrest Matter?* (Cambridge, MA: National Bureau of Economic Research, 1994).

21. Two particularly useful reports are by Patrick Langan and Christopher Innes, *Preventing Domestic Violence Against Women* (Washington, D.C.: U.S. Department of Justice, 1986), and Anita Timrots and Michael Rand, *Violent Crime by Strangers and Nonstrangers* (Washington, D.C.: U.S. Department of Justice, 1987). See also Karen Stout, "Intimate Femicide: A National Demographic Overview," *Journal of Interpersonal Violence* 6:4 (1991): 476–485, and Angela Carsilles, "No-Drop Policies in the Prevention of Domestic Violence Cases: Guarantees of Action of Dangerous Situations," *Fordham Law Review* 63:3 (1994): 853–882.

22. Robert Menzies, "Psychiatrists in Blue: Police Apprehension of Mental Disorder and Dangerousness," *Criminology* 25 (1987): 429–454.

23. Delbert Elliott and his colleagues have recently evaluated the three police dispositions (mediation, separation, arrest) and found no difference by disposition. Franklin Dunford, David Huizinga, and Delbert Elliott, "The Role of Arrest in Domestic Assault: The Omaha Police Experiment," *Criminology* 28 (1990): 183–206. See also David Hirschel, Ira Hutchison, and Charles Dean, "The Failure of Arrest to Deter Spouse Abuse," *Journal of Research in Crime and Delinquency* 29:1 (1992): 7–33, and Christopher Carlson and Frank Nidley, "Mandatory Penalties, Victim Compensation, and the Judicial Processing of Domestic Abuse Assault Cases," *Crime and Delinquency* 41:1 (1995): 132–149.

24. Mark Hamm, "Domestic Violence: Legislative Attitudes Toward a Coherent Public Policy," *Journal of Crime and Justice* 12 (1989): 37–39. A review of the historical treatment of wives and spouse abuse can be found in David Hirschel, Ira Hutchison, Charles Dean, et al., "Review Essay on the Law Enforcement Response to Spouse Abuse: Past, Present, and Future," *Justice Quarterly* 9:2 (1992): 247–283.

25. Debra Whitcomb, *Prosecution of Child Sexual Abuse: Innovations in Practice* (Washington, D.C.: U.S. Department of Justice, 1985), p. 1. Also see Gail Stevens, "Grandfathers as Incest Perpetrators: Dirty Old Men or Predatory Offenders?" *Journal of Crime and Justice* 18:2 (1995): 127–141.

26. Brent Morrow and Gwendolyn Sorell, "Factors Affecting Self-Esteem, Depression, and Negative Behaviors in Sexually Abused Female Adolescents," *Journal of Marriage and the Family* 51 (1989): 677–686. See also Christopher Bagley, "The Long-Term Psychological Effects of Child Abuse: A Review of Some British and Canadian Studies of Victims and Their Families," *Annals of Sex Research* 4:1 (1990): 23–48.

27. James Stewart, "From the Director," in Whitcomb, *Prosecution of Child Sexual Abuse: Innovations in Practice*, p. 1. See also Lorie Fridell, "Decision-Making of the District Attorney: Diverting or Prosecuting Intrafamilial Child Sexual Abuse Offenders," *Criminal Justice Policy Review* 4:3 (1990): 249–267.

28. David McCord, "Expert Psychological Testimony About Child Complaints in Sexual Abuse Prosecutions: A Foray into the Admissibility of Novel Psychological Evidence," *Journal of Criminal Law and Criminology* 77 (1986): 1–68. See also Catherine Whitaker, *Teenage Victims* (Washington, D.C.: U.S. Department of Justice, 1986); Ellen Gray, *Child Abuse: Prelude to Delinquency* (Washington, D.C.: U.S. Department of Justice, 1986); and Mary Mason, "A Judicial Dilemma: Expert Witness Testimony in Child Abuse Cases," *Journal of Psychiatry and the Law* 19:3–4 (1991): 185–219. For a note of caution, see Philip Jenkins, *Intimate Enemies: Moral Panics in Contemporary Great Britain* (New York: Aldine de Gruyter, 1992).

29. *U.S. News and World Report,* May 20, 1985, p. 83. See also Tony Poveda, "White-Collar Crime and the Justice Department: The Institutionalization of a Concept," *Crime, Law and Social Change* 17:3 (1992): 235–252.

30. Marshall Clinard, *Corporate Corruption: The Abuse of Power* (Westport, CT: Praeger, 1990). See also Stephen Rackmill, "Understanding and Sanctioning the White Collar Offender," *Federal Probation* 56:2 (1992): 26–33.

31. Mark Cohen, "Corporate Crime and Punishment: A Study of Social Harm and Sentencing Practices in Federal Courts, 1984–1987," *American Criminal Law Review* 25 (1989): 605–660. See also Pamela Busy, "Fraud by Fright: White Collar Crime by Health Care Providers," *North Carolina Law Review* 7 (1989): 426–550, and Hazel Croall, "Sentencing the Business Offender," *Howard Journal of Criminal Justice* 30:4 (1991): 280–292.

32. James Inciardi, *Criminal Justice* (New York: Harcourt Brace Jovanovich, 1990), p. 99.

33. Steve Klepper and Daniel Nagin, "The Deterrent Effect of Perceived Certainty and Severity of Punishment Revisited," *Criminology* 27 (November 1989): 721–743. See the special issue on sentencing the corporation, John Coffee, Mark Cohen, Jonathan Macey, et al., "A National Conference on Sentencing of the Corporation," *Boston University Law Review* 71:2 (1990): 153–189, and David Weisberg, Elin Waring, and Ellen Chayet, "Specific Deterrence in a Sample of Offenders Convicted of White-Collar Crimes," *Criminology* 33:4 (1995): 587–607.

34. Federal Bureau of Investigation, *Uniform Crime Report 1994,* p. 227.

35. President's Commission on Law Enforcement and Administration of Justice, *The Challenge of Crime in a Free Society* (Washington, D.C.: U.S. Government Printing Office, 1967), p. 234.

36. Ibid., p. 233.

37. See David Whitford, "The Skid Row Merry-Go-Round," *Corrections Magazine* 9 (1983): 29–36. See also Malcomb Ramsey, *Downtown Drinkers: The Perceptions and Fears of the Public in a City Centre* (London: Home Office, 1989).

38. President's Commission, *The Challenge of Crime in a Free Society,* p. 233.

39. Drying out refers to the period required for the alcoholic's body to readjust to a lowered level of alcohol. This often presents a very severe shock to the system, resulting in withdrawal symptoms like those experienced by the drug user who goes "cold turkey."

40. John Snortum, Ragnar Hauge, and Dale Berger, "Deterring Alcohol-Impaired Driving: A Comparative Analysis of Compliance in Norway and the United States," *Justice Quarterly* 3 (1986): 139–165. See also Andreas Muller, "Business Recession, Alcohol Consumption, Drinking and Driving Laws: Impact on Oklahoma Motor Vehicle Facilities and Fatal Crashes," *American Journal of Public Health* 79 (1989): 1366–1370, and Ralph Weisheit and John Klofas, "Social Status of DUI Offenders in Jail," *International Journal of the Addictions* 27:7 (1992): 793–816.

41. Craig Perkins, James Stephan, and Allen Beck, *Jails and Jail Inmates 1993–94* (Washington, D.C.: U.S. Department of Justice, 1995), p. 13.

42. DWI and DUI are terms used for persons arrested for driving while under the influence. Though generally related to alcohol, the categories include driving while under the influence of drugs and other substances, whether obtained legally or by prescription. See the special issue by Herbert Moskowitz, ed., "Problems with DWI Arrests, Convictions, and Sentencing," *Alcohol, Drugs and Driving* 7:3–4 (1992): 173–265.

43. Federal Bureau of Investigation, *Uniform Crime Report 1994*, p. 168.

44. MADD, which stands for "Mothers Against Drunk Driving," is a group formed by the mothers of the victims of accidents caused by drunk drivers.

45. Patrick Kinkade, Matthew Leone, and Thomas Wacker, "Probation and the Drunk Driver: A Cost of Being MADD," *Federal Probation* 56:2 (1992): 6–15.

46. U.S. Office of the Pardon Attorney, *Civil Disabilities of Convicted Felons: A State-by-State Survey* (Washington, D.C.: U.S. Department of Justice, 1992). See also Deborah Sunta, John Edwards, and Roger Boe, eds., "Employing Offenders," *Forum on Corrections Research* 8:1) (1996): 3–51 (special issue).

47. Malcolm Feeley and Jonathan Simon, "The New Penology: Notes on the Emerging Strategy of Corrections and Its Implications," *Criminology* 30:4 (1992): 449–474. See also Steven Donziger, *The Real War on Crime* (New York: HarperCollins, 1996), pp. 195–219.

CHAPTER SIX

The Correctional Filter

*O*verview

In our examination of the dimensions of and trends of crime in America, we now come to the concept of a correctional filter, representing the various sentencing options, the diversion of offenders from the prison-bound population that sometimes confuses us as to what is actually occurring in the criminal justice system. At every point in this "filter" certain types of offenders and cases are shunted into alternative dispositions, most of which involve some type of correctional supervision other than prison. Those who finally evade those filter points and are placed under custody and supervision in prisons are, for the most part, the worst of the worst. Here, in this chapter, we examine the processes, flows, and rationales of the correctional filter and turn to the sentencing and appeals processes in succeeding chapters . . . important parts to understand in the interactions of criminal law, public opinions and the criminal offenders' ultimate destination in the correctional continuum.

*T*he Correctional Process

The first requirement for any correctional process to occur is a *client* (otherwise known as an inmate, resident, or patient). Whether we examine the largest maximum security prison in the nation[1] or a rural jail,[2] the common denominator is always some individual who has been placed there for detention, punishment, or rehabilitation. Why was one person incarcerated while another was freed or placed under some other kind of supervision in his or her home community? American corrections is a diversified mix of facilities, theories, techniques, programs, and practices. This amalgam is also part of a poorly articulated combination of police, courts, juvenile authorities, probation, prisons, and parole that is somewhat simplistically referred to as our criminal justice system.

In the halls of justice, the only justice is in the halls.

—Lenny Bruce

The nonsystematic nature of criminal justice in America can be better understood by examining the prevailing sentiments and goals at the two extremes of the process: police and corrections. The police, in their law-and-order role, are working hard to get offenders off the streets and out of the community. If offenders are locked up, no matter how temporarily, they are no longer a police problem. In this role, police are often viewed by the public as agents of banishment. In the course of their work, the police see offenders at their worst, often while they are committing the offense and in contact with the victim of the crime. It is therefore understandable that police reaction to offenders sometimes leans toward the ideologies of retribution and punishment, rather than reintegration and rehabilitation.

Correctional personnel, on the other hand, are attempting to get the offender out of the system and reintegrated into society. Accomplishing that involves taking calculated risks and the inevitable release of some offenders who do return to crime. Usually, only the worst risks fail to abide by the law; unfortunately, those failures are the only examples of "corrected" felons who come into recontact with the police. Thus the police—already overworked and saddled with an often thankless job—view correctional attempts to reintegrate former offenders into their communities as a public threat and an extra work burden.

The offender, if caught, passes through most of the different stages of the criminal justice (non)system on the way to prison. Many do not pass through every procedural step but are filtered out of the system at different stations along the way. Therefore, it is essential to examine this screening process, called the *correctional filter,* to determine at what point and for what reasons certain offenders are filtered out of the system short of actual incarceration.

Walter C. Reckless (1899–1989), a member of the "Chicago School" of criminology, developed the containment theory as another way to explain criminal behavior. His theory stated that the tendency to commit unlawful acts is determined by the type, or quality, of the self-concept the individual has, and its ability to "contain" the act.

Elements of the Criminal Justice System

The popular myth that our criminal justice system provides fair and uniform treatment of offenders was exploded by our own Department of Justice:

Police make arrests all the time in protecting society

—*PHOTO BY DOROTHY LITTELL, COURTESY OF TEXASTOCK, INC.*

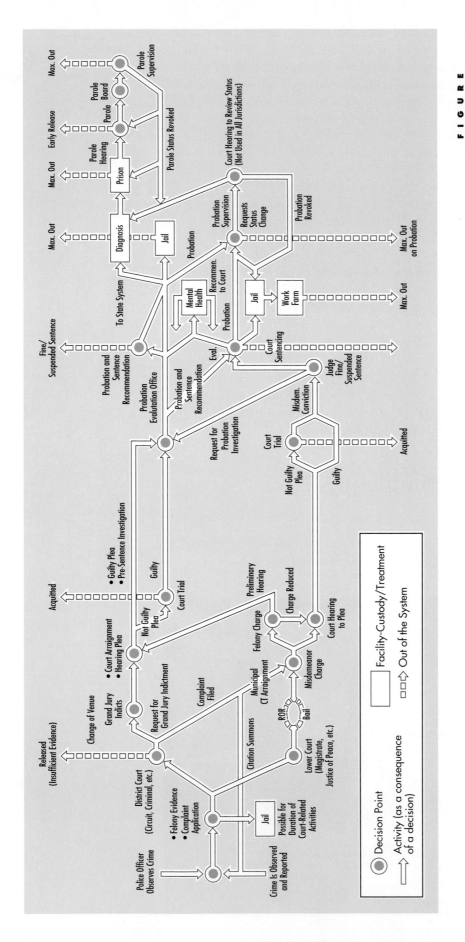

Police Officer Observes Crime

Crime Is Observed and Reported

District Court (Circuit, Criminal, etc.)
• Felony Evidence
• Complaint Application

Jail Possible for Duration of Court-Related Activities

Released (Insufficient Evidence)

Change of Venue

Grand Jury Indicts

Request for Grand Jury Indictment

Complaint Filed

Citation Summons

Municipal CT Arraignment

Lower Court (Magistrate, Justice of Peace, etc.)

ROR
Bail

Misdemeanor Charge

Felony Charge

Charge Reduced

Preliminary Hearing

Court Hearing to Plea

Acquitted

Court Arraignment
• Court Arraignment
• Hearing Plea

Not Guilty Plea

Court Trial

Guilty

Guilty Plea
• Pre-Sentence Investigation

Request for Probation Investigation

Not Guilty Plea

Court Trial

Guilty

Misdem. Conviction

Acquitted

Judge Fine / Suspended Sentence

Probation Evaluation Office

Probation and Sentence Recommendation

Fine / Suspended Sentence

To State System

Probation and Sentence Recommendation

Eval.

Mental Health

Recommen. to Court

Probation

Court Sentencing

Jail

Work Farm

Max. Out

Diagnosis

Jail

Probation

Probation Supervision

Requests Status Change

Probation Revoked

Max. Out on Probation

Court Hearing to Review Status (Not Used in All Jurisdictions)

Max. Out

Prison

Diagnosis

Parole Status Revoked

Parole Hearing

Max. Out

Early Release

Parole Hearing

Parole Board

Parole

Parole Supervision

Max. Out

○ Decision Point

● Activity (as a consequence of a decision)

⟶

☐ Facility-Custody/Treatment

▭▭▭⇨ Out of the System

FIGURE 6.1

The Criminal Justice System

SOURCE: National Clearinghouse for Correctional Programming and Architecture, Correctional Environments (Washington, D.C.: U.S. Department of Justice, 1973), p. 46.

A substantial obstacle to development of effective corrections lies in its relationship to police and courts, the other subsystems of the criminal justice system. Corrections inherits any inefficiency, inequity, and improper discrimination that may have occurred in any earlier step of the criminal justice process. Its clients come to it from the other subsystems; it is the consistent heir to their defects.

The contemporary view is to consider society's institutionalized response to crime as the criminal justice system and its activities as the criminal justice process. This model envisions interdependent and interrelated agencies and programs that will provide a coordinated and consistent response to crime. The model, however, remains a model—it does not exist in fact. Although cooperation between the various components has improved noticeably in some localities, it cannot be said that a criminal justice "system" really exists.[3]

The American criminal justice system is, in fact, many separate systems of institutions, processes, and procedures. The thousands of American villages, towns, cities, counties, states—and even the federal government—all have criminal justice "systems" of sorts. Though they may appear similar in that all function to apprehend, prosecute, convict, and sentence lawbreakers, no two are exactly alike.

A diagrammatic representation of the flow of offenders through police, prosecution courts, and corrections is shown in Figure 6-1. This diagram emphasizes the points at which the "typical" criminal justice system provides alternative courses of action, so that many suspects may be filtered out of the system before they even come close to a correctional institution.

The criminal justice system is composed of three separate subsystems—police, courts, and corrections—each with its own tasks. Those subsystems are by no means mutually exclusive of one another, however, and what is done in one has a direct effect on another. Courts receive their raw material from the police, the corrections sector receives clients from the courts, and the cycle goes on when the released offenders are again arrested by the police.

Any increased success by the police, or shift in enforcement policy in terms of more arrests or more drug arrests, seriously impacts the courts and corrections by overloading already heavy work schedules and facilities. Also, if corrections cannot succeed in its reintegration efforts, the police are overloaded with repeat offenders (recidivists). This circular process is the focal point for much controversy among the three parts. We examine each subsystem and its effect on the correctional filter.

DISCRETION AND THE POLICE

Among the criminal justice subsystems, particularly corrections, there has been an increasing focus on those situations and circumstances in which guidelines, operating policies, and procedures are missing, contradictory, or unwritten. The potential abuse of discretionary power has become an area for considerable concern and angry debate. With that concern in mind, evident in all subsystems, we now examine such **discretion** in the police sector.

Decision making in most administrative agencies is usually the responsibility of an organization's top executive. This individual is probably the highest paid, best educated, most experienced, and most mature individual in the organization.

The executive is given a staff to marshal the information needed to make decisions and usually is given sufficient time to deliberate on them.

The police system, it can be argued, appears to be just the opposite—sort of an upside-down pyramid. The decision to arrest or not to arrest, to shoot or not to shoot, is usually made in a split second and often by young, inexperienced officers at the bottom of the organizational ladder. In most cases they are also in the lowest pay bracket, with little education, experience, or maturity. They have no staff to give them data, but must make decisions based on whatever training they do have and the way they perceive the situation at the moment. It is small wonder that the use of this broad discretionary power at the lowest levels tends to arouse a general distrust of police statistics and to create hostility among the subsystems.

As mentioned before, the principal document used to determine the crime rates in America is the FBI's *UCR*,[4] although increasing emphasis is being placed on victimization studies. This report is an accumulation of crimes known to the police from over sixteen thousand police agencies in America. Significantly, the agencies that contribute data to the *UCR* do so on a *voluntary* basis. The report was started in 1930 by the Committee on Uniform Crime Records of the International Association of the Chiefs of Police. Since that time, its statistical coverage has extended to 98 percent of the population in America. The expression "crimes known to the police" was explained in the *UCR* for 1992:

> Law enforcement does not purport to know the total volume of crime because of the many criminal actions which are not reported to official sources.

Felony Sentencing in State Courts 1992

In 1992 state courts convicted nearly 900,000 adults of a felony. Forty-four percent of convicted felons were sentenced to a state prison, and 26 percent were sentenced to a local jail (usually for a year or less). The remaining 30 percent were sentenced to straight probation with no jail or prison time to serve.

- State courts convicted 893,600 adults of a felony in 1992.

- From 1988 to 1992 the volume of felony convictions rose 34 percent. Convictions rose the most for aggravated assault (up 57 percent) and drug trafficking (up 53 percent).

- The growth in convictions outpaced that in adult arrests. Despite the relatively large increase in convictions, processing was not slower in 1992 than in 1988. In both years average elapsed time from arrest to sentencing was around seven months.

- The proportions of felons sentenced to incarceration or probation in 1992 were generally unchanged from 1988. Prison sentences accounted for 44 percent of felony sentences in both years.

- State courts sentenced 44 percent of convicted felons to a state prison, 26 percent to a local jail, and 30 percent to straight probation with no jail or prison time to serve.

- Felons sentenced to a state prison in 1992 had an average sentence of six and one-half years but were likely to serve roughly a third of that sentence—or about two and one-half years—before release, assuming that current release policies continued.

- The average sentence to local jail was seven months. The average probation sentence was about four years. In addition, a fine was imposed on 18 percent of convicted felons, restitution on 16 percent, community service on 6 percent, and treatment was ordered for 7 percent.

- Of the total number of convicted felons in 1992, 92 percent had pleaded guilty to their crime. The remaining 8 percent had been found guilty at trial.

- Nationally, of the felons convicted in 1992, 52 percent were white, 47 percent were black, and 1 percent were of other races. ∎

SOURCE: Patrick Langan and Helen Graziadei, *Felony Sentencing in State Courts 1992* (Washington, D.C., U.S. Department of Justice, 1995), p. 1.

Estimates as to the level of unreported crime can be developed through costly victim surveys but this does not eliminate the reluctance of the victim to report all criminal actions to law enforcement agencies. In light of this situation, the best source for obtaining usable crime counts is the next logical universe, which is the offenses known to the police. The crimes used in the crime index are those considered to be the most constantly reported and provide the capability to compute meaningful crime trends and crime rates.[5]

NATIONAL CRIME STATISTICS

The *UCR* program is the product of a voluntary cooperative law enforcement effort to produce national crime statistics. Approximately sixteen thousand law enforcement agencies, covering some 97 percent of the U.S. population, submit monthly and annual reports to the FBI so that information can be assembled to depict the current crime problem.

In addition to this entirely voluntary source of crime data, National Crime Victimization Surveys (NCVSs) are conducted by the U.S. Bureau of the Census and the Bureau of Justice Statistics. The NCVS data indicate that the *UCR* vastly underestimates the volume of crime. With the exception of homicide and motor vehicle theft, there are from two to five times more Type I offenses (serious crimes) reported annually by the NCVS than are reported by the *UCR*.

In 1993, however, the *UCR* indicated that index crime had actually decreased by 2.9 percent in 1992 over 1991. This is in agreement with the NCVS data, which strongly state that crime has decreased approximately 14 percent since 1978; and victimization rates declined an additional 3 percent for men and 10 percent for blacks, 1993–1994. Urban and rural areas experienced an eight percent decline in victimization rates.[6] Since the NCVS data are more comprehensive (and the *UCR* seems to be following that trend) and are less sensitive to political factors, we can conclude that crime may actually be decreasing in the United States.

Over 13,991,675 crime index offenses were reported by law enforcement agencies in 1994. During that same period, 509,812 individuals were admitted to prisons in America.[7] Where did the remaining 13,481,863 offenders disappear to? This situation and these statistics show the correctional filter in action.

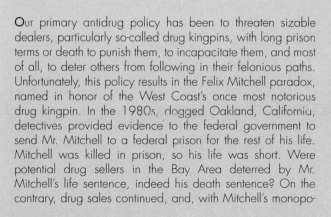

Drug Policy and Paradox

Our primary antidrug policy has been to threaten sizable dealers, particularly so-called drug kingpins, with long prison terms or death to punish them, to incapacitate them, and most of all, to deter others from following in their felonious paths. Unfortunately, this policy results in the Felix Mitchell paradox, named in honor of the West Coast's once most notorious drug kingpin. In the 1980s, dogged Oakland, California, detectives provided evidence to the federal government to send Mr. Mitchell to a federal prison for the rest of his life. Mitchell was killed in prison, so his life was short. Were potential drug sellers in the Bay Area deterred by Mr. Mitchell's life sentence, indeed his death sentence? On the contrary, drug sales continued, and, with Mitchell's monopo-

listic pricing eliminated, competition reduced the price of crack-cocaine. The main effect of Mitchell's imprisonment was to destabilize the market, lowering drug prices and increasing violence as rival gang members challenged each other for market share. The aftermath saw a rise in drive-by shootings, street homicides, and felonious assaults. By indirection, effective law enforcement, followed by incapacitation, had stimulated serious random violence.

SOURCE: Jerome H. Skolnick. "What Not to Do About Crime—The American Society of Criminology 1994 Presidential Address," *Criminology* 33:1 (1995): p. 10.

First, most crimes known to the police are never solved. The rate of clearance by arrest for various crimes varies greatly, from 64 percent for murder to 13 percent for burglary.[8] The aggregate number of serious (index) crimes **cleared by arrest**[9] in 1994 was only 20 percent, with a 49 percent clearance for violent crimes and 16 percent for property crimes. Of course, this means that 80 percent (eight out of ten index crimes) did not result in an offender's entering the criminal justice system. Even if we assume that any one criminal may be responsible for many offenses, there is a great amount of filtering at the entry point, leaving us with only about three million offenses cleared by arrest in 1994.

THE PROSECUTOR'S DECISION

The next step in the flow of criminals is the prosecutor's office. It is here that prosecutors implement their broad discretionary power to dismiss the charges or reduce them to charges for which the defendant will plead guilty. Recent studies indicate that as many as 50 to 90 percent of the felony cases initiated by the police are dismissed by prosecutors.[10] U.S. attorneys declined to prosecute in 39 percent of the offenses investigated by federal law enforcement agencies in 1993.[11] A high percentage of charges not dismissed are reduced through **plea bargaining** to a less serious charge to which the defendant agrees to plead guilty. The usual explanation for this further action of the correctional filter is that high caseloads and limited resources force prosecutors to dispense with much of their caseload as quickly as possible in order to avoid overwhelming their own offices and the courts. The time factor does not explain, however, why some cases are prosecuted and others dismissed. Here, the wide discretionary power given to prosecutors becomes a crucial issue, and prosecutors consider such factors as the case's strength, even-handedness, harm done to the victim, and the attorneys' personal attributes.[12]

In fact, prosecutors' effectiveness is usually measured by the number of convictions they get while in office. Because their political survival depends on their success in securing convictions, it is not too surprising that they will dismiss or bargain away the cases that show little promise of conviction. They may even bargain for probation without prosecution (deferred prosecution) in cases they cannot possibly win. The general public is seldom concerned with the prosecutors' methods of obtaining convictions, as long as they get them.[13]

When a case finally reaches the trial court, the prosecutor earnestly prepares for a real battle, not for justice, but for a *conviction*. His or her professional reputation is at stake. Therefore, the prosecutor must resort to all the oratory and psychological trickery that can be mobilized. He or she is ethically no better and no worse than the defense lawyer in this judicial bout. The average trial, unfortunately, becomes more a show or contest than a struggle for justice. The judge acts as referee—to see there is something like fair play. The jury sits in amazement, at times flattered at the compliments paid them by the lawyers, and at times incensed at the threats and insults exchanged by the lawyers in reckless fashion. During the court recess, the two lawyers may often be seen slapping each other on the back in perfect amity. Here is a basic American institution in action, with tragic implications that most Americans do not grasp.[14] The prosecutor's discretion to dismiss or bargain further helps explain the gap between the number of reported crimes and the number of actual imprisonments.

Because this part of the decision process is so critical to the offenders, it is helpful to review it in detail. The decision to charge an offender occurs after the police have made their arrest and presented their information to the prosecuting

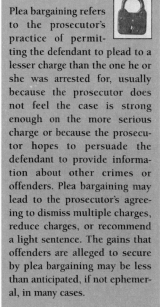

PLEA BARGAINING

Plea bargaining refers to the prosecutor's practice of permitting the defendant to plead to a lesser charge than the one he or she was arrested for, usually because the prosecutor does not feel the case is strong enough on the more serious charge or because the prosecutor hopes to persuade the defendant to provide information about other crimes or offenders. Plea bargaining may lead to the prosecutor's agreeing to dismiss multiple charges, reduce charges, or recommend a light sentence. The gains that offenders are alleged to secure by plea bargaining may be less than anticipated, if not ephemeral, in many cases.

attorney. Except in those few police departments with legal advisers on call twenty-four hours a day, the prosecutors are the first legally trained individuals to examine the facts. It is their job to decide whether to charge the suspect or to dismiss ("**no-paper**" or *nolle prosequi*[15]) the case.

The legal decision to proceed will be made only if the alleged crime contains certain elements.[16] There must be a narrowly defined unlawful act and the presence of criminal intent. The offender must have intended to commit the unlawful act, or the case is on shaky legal ground. Many crimes may include a number of lesser crimes within their definition. Alternatives to the charge of first-degree murder, which is very difficult to prove, might be unpremeditated murder (manslaughter), aggravated assault, assault with intent to kill, and so on. With a bit of imagination, good prosecutors can make the intent and the acts match up well enough to ensure a fairly strong case for conviction. If they think they can get a defendant to plead guilty to a lesser charge (and accept a lesser penalty), they may well bargain for it. Often, if the defendant will not accept the lesser charge, the case is dropped because of its low potential for conviction if pursued (thereby saving public funds and also maintaining the good track record the prosecutor needs for reelection or advancement). At least 90 percent of the defendants convicted will have pled guilty (**no contest**) to a charge.

Aside from the "legal sufficiency" issue, the prosecutor will also consider a complaint from an extralegal standpoint. Often the most important extralegal considerations are determined by the matter of equity or by department policy. Age, sex, race, prior convictions, and similar factors have no bearing on guilt, but they are obviously taken into account in the charging decision.[17] If established department policy diverts all first offenders or all those under the age of eighteen to nonjudicial programs, the prosecutor will act accordingly. By the same token, a tough departmental position on certain offenses means that almost everyone who commits such an offense will be charged and processed through the courts.

The initial screening by the prosecuting attorney is the most important step in the criminal justice system for most suspects. Although more statistics are being gathered on this critical process, it is still a cloudy area. As early as 1933, criminologist N. Baker wrote as follows:

> How much more significant it would be to have figures on the situations arising behind closed doors in the prosecutor's office. Court statistics are enlightening to such an extent that it is now almost commonplace to designate the prosecutor as the most powerful official in local government. If we had some means of checking the decisions of the prosecutor when the question "to prosecute or not to prosecute?" arises, such figures would go much farther to substantiate such a statement.[18]

Plea bargaining has been studied in detail since Alaska abolished it in 1975. Generally, those studies have found that the plea has little impact on the length of the prison sentence and that the alleged process of the police's overcharging on multiple crimes is not as widespread as was previously assumed. Defendants may not necessarily benefit from plea negotiations. Jack Call, David England, and Susette Talarico reviewed the evaluations and concluded that plea bargaining by judges and prosecutors can be effectively controlled, that abolishing plea bargaining will result in more trials but that the system can accommodate them, and that its reduction or elimination will not result in either significantly longer or more severe sentences. Plea bargaining has been eliminated not only in Alaska but also

PHRENOLOGISTS
Persons who believed you could tell whether a person had criminal tendencies by the shape of the skull and by bumps on the head.

PROBATION
Probation is a sentence imposed by the court that does not involve confinement and imposes conditions to restrain the offender's actions in the community. The court retains authority to modify the conditions of sentence or to resentence the offender if he or she violates the conditions.

Race and Criminal Justice

Whites and African-Americans live in completely different worlds when it comes to race and the criminal justice system. Three points about race are paramount. First, arrest rates indicate that African-Americans commit more crime than white relative to the population. Second, there are so many more African-Americans than whites in our prisons that the difference cannot be explained by higher crime among African-Americans—racial discrimination is also at work, and it penalizes African-Americans at almost every juncture in the criminal justice system. Third, whether the cause is higher crime or discrimination or both, this country is on the verge of

a social catastrophe because of the sheer number of African-Americans behind bars—numbers that continue to rise with breathtaking speed and frightening implications. The reason: our criminal justice policies are preventing many African-Americans from claiming their stake in the American dream, thereby contributing to the destruction of our national ideal of racial harmony. ∎

SOURCE: Steven R. Donziger, ed., *The Real War on Crime* (New York: HarperCollins, 1996), p. 99.

in Detroit and Denver, among other jurisdictions. In the military services, neither the U.S. Air Force nor the Coast Guard allows plea bargaining.[19]

THE COURT'S DILEMMA

The criminal court is at the core of the American criminal justice system. The courts are highly structured, deeply venerated, and circumscribed by law and tradition. The rest of the system is dependent on and responsible to the courts.[20] The police and their procedures are molded and restricted by the courts' decisions, prosecutors must weigh the legal and extralegal issues surrounding the cases before them in light of the court that will try them, and the correctional system is dependent on the court for its workload. The formal processes that take place in the courtroom are not merely symbolic but are often crucial for the protection of the individual suspect and society.[21]

Judges are either elected or appointed to office. In either case, they can be put in a position in which they owe a political debt to their backers. Because of

The courtroom is a place of drama and tedium

—*PHOTO BY JANET CENTURY, COURTESY OF CENTURY PHOTOGRAPHY*

Criminals come to justice when drug deals going down are thwarted by arrest

—PHOTO BY HUGH PATRICK BROWN, COURTESY OF SYGMA

the corrupt practices of a very few judges, it is often felt that judges in general are responsive only to pressure groups and will dismiss cases if told to do so by those in power. Actually, the discretion of a judge in a criminal court is quite limited.

Dean Wigmore is credited with the term *sporting theory* of justice as a description of a court trial.[22] The trial can boil down to a legal contest between two highly skilled lawyers, with the judge playing the role of a referee. Our adversary system of justice pits two lawyers against each other in an attempt to prove the suspect's technical guilt or innocence. The judge, who may be considerably less skilled at law than either the prosecutor or the defense attorney, simply determines the outcome of various procedural disputes. If the judge makes one wrong decision, the offender may question it on appeal, and that alone can suffice to overturn the conviction. It is a basic concept of the American system of justice to permit many guilty persons to go free rather than risk convicting one innocent person because the procedures that protect his or her rights were not observed to the letter.

The courts, like the prosecutor, work in several ways to narrow the correctional filter.[23] Cases may be dismissed at the early stages of the trial because the court finds there was a mistake in either the charges or the facts. The court itself may allow damaging or false evidence to be admitted, which would cause the case to be reversed later by an appellate court. Also, both the prosecutor and the court may divert the offender into treatment systems that are alternatives to the state's correctional institutions. Thus many potential correctional clients who enter the court process are filtered out and do not actually end up in prison.

Although prosecuting attorneys may have good cause to believe a certain suspect committed a particular offense, cause to charge that suspect, and cause to bring the suspect to trial, they sometimes make errors. Their errors are usually brought to the court's attention by the defense attorney during the suspect's preliminary appearance before the judge. A judge who is convinced at this point that the charges are in error can dismiss the case. He or she will usually accompany the dismissal with a few unkind words to the prosecutor for presenting such a poor case. It is that kind of problem that the ambitious prosecutor seeks to avoid at all costs.

Ernesto Miranda (1942–1976) was the principal in the Supreme Court case that established now famous "Miranda Warning," in 1966. This warning of constitutional rights requires the officer must advise the defendant prior to questioning. Miranda was killed in a bar in an argument over cards at the age of thirty-four. The killer was arrested and carefully "Mirandized."

Sometimes, though seldom as often as television might lead us to think, the case against a suspect falls apart during the trial. The defense lawyers make critical motions in attempts to suppress evidence or restrict certain testimony. The judges must rule on these crucial issues, knowing their ruling might be reversed on appeal. If they make a decision that later is appealed and overruled, their reputation may suffer. On the other hand, they may agree with the motions and dismiss the case at that point, saving the state the expense and bother of a long string of appeals. In either case, yet another client may be filtered out of the correctional system.

In earlier days, the choices for a judge were relatively simple. The suspect would be found guilty and sentenced to prison, or innocent and then released. A few were found not guilty by reason of insanity, but most of those convicted were sentenced to the prisons of early nineteenth- and twentieth-century America. Today, a guilty finding means the judge must choose among a broad range of alternative paths. A few of them are mentioned here, and most are covered in detail in later chapters.

Probation has become by far the most popular alternative to incarceration in state prisons. Judges have seen this approach as an opportunity to allow guilty individuals who present little or no danger to society to continue a productive life, on condition of good behavior. Probation is used in as many as 60 percent of the cases in some states. A variation on probation, called **shock probation,** has been initiated in at least fourteen states, including Ohio, Kentucky, and Indiana. In this system the offender is given the maximum sentence for a crime, then released after a short taste of prison life (up to ninety days) and returned to the community on regular probation. Judges find the system a desirable way to punish specific offenders whose crimes are slightly more serious than those for which regular probation is clearly an effective and appropriate remedy.[24] Shock incarceration, usually based on a military training model and allowing early release from prison, is increasingly popular.

Shock probation is a specific deterrence-based sentence to prison, designed to give the offender a taste of incarceration in the belief that it will deter future criminal activity. The sentencing court can later recall the offender and place him or her on probation with conditions similar to regular probation.

Another method of diverting clients from the corrections system is, instead, to place them in the mental health system. Many states have psychopathic-offender or habitual-offender statutes[25] that allow the court to have offenders examined

Community Residential Centers (Halfway Houses)

Halfway houses are nonconfining residential facilities for adjudicated adults or juveniles, or those subject to criminal or juvenile proceedings. They are intended as an alternative to confinement for persons not suited for probation or who need a period of readjustment to the community after imprisonment.

It is common to refer to halfway houses providing services for probationers as "quarter-way houses." For those servicing parolees, the term would be "halfway houses." For those providing assistance to persons who are assigned to halfway houses as an intensive alternative to prison commitment, the term would be "three-quarter houses."

Many more halfway houses provide services for juveniles than for adults, and some houses specialize by client or treatment modality: women only, prerelease federal furloughees, alcohol abusers, narcotics abusers, developmentally disabled, and so on.   ■

and committed after conviction but before sentencing. Still other states have systems offering that path before conviction. The pleas of **incompetency to stand trial** and **not guilty by reason of insanity**[26] are also available to the defendant in most jurisdictions. In addition, about 40 percent of the states have passed laws that would allow a person who might plead not guilty by reason of insanity to be convicted as "guilty but mentally ill," requiring the commitment to prison and, usually, later treatment for mental illness.

All of these procedures provide a temporary or permanent escape from the corrections system and further accelerate the filtering process. One result of the filtering process, it appears, is that the offenders who are eventually incarcerated are significantly different in composition from all those who are originally arrested.

Even those offenders who are found guilty and sentenced to the corrections system are often destined for units other than prisons. A broad range of community correctional programs[27] has sprung up across the nation. Some (such as community residential centers or **halfway houses**) are designed to provide housing and treatment while the offender attempts to maintain family and job ties in the community. The sharply increased emphasis on and use of those programs herald the beginning of the end of treatment methods predicated on the fortress prisons of the past. Judges are more inclined to choose a treatment option that provides a measure of humanity and hope. The community-based correctional programs are believed to offer great promise in that regard.

Although these are the most widespread options for judges in their sentencing decisions, others are available as well. In several jurisdictions, for minor crimes, a fine or restitution to the victim may be required in place of a prison sentence. Public service has also been used as a substitute for prison. Weekend or evening imprisonment, community work orders, and attendance centers have also been used instead of full-time incarceration. All recognize the importance of allowing offenders to remain in the community and hold their jobs while paying for their crimes in some reasonable way. (For a more detailed discussion of these programs, see Chapter 11.)

Another Look at Crime Statistics

You can now see that the extent of the crime picture in America depends on where a person is in the system with respect to the **correctional filter** (see Figure 6-2). Statistics are helpful, as they keep us informed about how many

Justice for the Famous

The trial of O. J. Simpson provided the nation with a compelling yet somewhat distorted view of the inner workings of the criminal justice system. It touched on several of the critical issues that hinder the creation of an effective crime policy: domestic violence, racism, police bias, and the role of the media. It also highlighted the difficulties courts have in dispensing justice to the accused and in providing crime victims with a degree of closure to their experiences. It did not, however, give a true picture of what the criminal justice system is like for the majority of people who enter it—people who, unlike O. J. Simpson, are of limited financial means and have no status as celebrities. ∎

SOURCE: Steven R. Donziger, ed., *The Real War on Crime*. (New York: HarperCollins, 1996), p. 180.

people have been arrested, prosecuted, convicted, acquitted, committed, and placed on probation or parole. But they can also be deceptive, because so many cases fall out of the process along the way. It is far too easy for the beginning student of corrections or criminal justice to assume that the number and characteristics of prisoners in our correctional institutions reflect an accurate picture of the crime problem. The preceding description of the filtering process, with its limiting effect on the number of offenders actually incarcerated, suggests the error of such an assumption. There is a great discrepancy between the number of actual crimes (reported and unreported) and the number of incarcerated felons.

To help the student understand the correctional filter better, a concrete example of the California filter is given in Table 6-1. During 1995, a total of 216,384 arrested persons were processed through the funnel and 39 percent of the arrestees were not incarcerated. Those not incarcerated received release at the station house or at the first case review by the prosecutor, were dismissed by the prosecutor (later) or court, were diverted to drug treatment, or were found not guilty at trial.

Stated somewhat differently, of every one hundred persons arrested for an index crime in California in 1995, slightly over sixty-nine were found guilty and sentenced. Most of the sentenced offenders received a combination of jail time followed by probation. About seven received straight probation, and more than fourteen were sent to prison. Lest the significance of this finding be lost, we repeat: for every one hundred persons arrested for felonies in California, only fourteen were imprisoned.

FIGURE

6.2

Outcomes for Arrest Felony Crimes, 1994

SOURCES: Federal Bureau of Investigation, *Crime in the United States 1995* (Washington, D.C.: U.S. Department of Justice, 1995). Figure adapted from C. Silberman, *Criminal Violence, Criminal Justice* (New York: Random House, 1978), pp. 257-261.

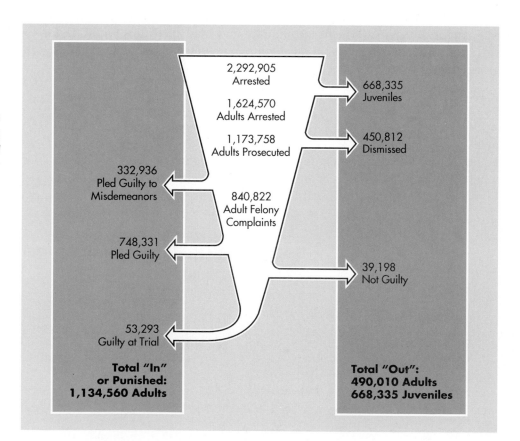

2,292,905 Arrested
1,624,570 Adults Arrested
1,173,758 Adults Prosecuted
840,822 Adult Felony Complaints

668,335 Juveniles
450,812 Dismissed
39,198 Not Guilty

332,936 Pled Guilty to Misdemeanors
748,331 Pled Guilty
53,293 Guilty at Trial

Total "In" or Punished: 1,134,560 Adults

Total "Out": 490,010 Adults 668,335 Juveniles

TABLE *6.1*

The Correctional Filter in California (for 216,384 Felony Arrests), 1995

Dispositions of arrested persons		
Stationhouse release	3.5%	
Prosecutorial denial of complaint	11.5	15.0% filtered out
Complaint filed		
Misdemeanor	31.9	
Felony	53.1	
	100.0%	
Dispositions of filed complaints		
Dismissed by court, prosecutor	13.2%	
Diversion	3.8	
Found not guilty at trial	0.3	17.3% filtered out
Guilty and sentenced	69.3	
	86.6%	
Sentence dispositions		
Probation*	6.6%	
Probation and jail	44.6	
Jail	3.0	
Imprisoned	14.2	
Fines/other	0.9	
	69.3%	

*Includes Fines and Other (2.6%). All other cases have not been cleared, are waiting trial, in trial, or convicted and not yet sentenced.

SOURCE: California Department of Corrections, 1996.

Summary

When you consider that most of the early studies of crime were conducted in regard to incarcerated offenders in adult prisons, it is small wonder that some of our theories are often found to be unsound. There is no doubt that statistics can help us in deciding new procedures or processes, but statistics regarding criminal justice have some strange characteristics that must be taken into consideration. Law professor Thorsten Sellin, discussing the problems of analyzing crime records, stated the following as his "second principle": "The value of criminal statistics as a basis for the measurement of criminality in geographic areas decreases as the procedure takes us farther away from the offense itself."[28] Because prisons usually represent the furthest possible point from the offense, clearly we must be skeptical about drawing conclusions from statistics that originate from prison populations.

The correctional filter offers us both a problem and an advantage. The problem is that the number of incarcerated felons is quite different from the number of crimes known to the police or from arrest figures shown in the *UCR*. This means that those programs aimed at the small sample of criminals who actually end up in prison are working with only the tip of the iceberg. The advantage such knowledge gives the criminal justice administrators is the recognition that their efforts must be redirected toward the real crime problems. Without a thorough knowledge of the filtering process, much effort could be wasted on a very small part of the problem.

In the following chapters and discussions about law and the correctional process, we examine sentencing practices and alternatives available. While following the discussions, keep in mind the drastic effect the correctional filter exerts on those who cannot manage to avoid imprisonment. Recall the famous line from George Orwell's political satire, *Animal Farm*: "All animals are equal, but some are more equal than others."[29]

Review Questions

1. What are the main elements of the criminal justice system?
2. What are the *Uniform Crime Reports (UCRs)*?
3. What effect does the correctional filter have on crime statistics?
4. What are the National Crime Surveys (NCVS), and what do they suggest about crime in the United States?
5. Define correctional filter and indicate how the accused escape from incarceration through the filter.
6. How are arrested persons (the suspected) different from those imprisoned at the end of the correctional filter?
7. What does the defendant gain by plea bargaining? The prosecutor?
8. Describe the correctional filter at work in California.

Words to Remember

discretion	no paper	not guilty by reason of insanity
cleared by arrest	no contest	incompetency to stand trial
UCR	shock probation	correctional filter
plea bargaining	halfway houses	

Endnotes

1. The largest prison in the United States is the California Men's Colony at San Luis Obispo. Built in 1954 and with a capacity of 3,859 inmates, it held 6,414 in 1995. American Correctional Association, *Directory 1996* (Laurel, MD: American Correctional Association, 1996), p. 32.

2. See Larry Mays and Joel Thompson, "Mayberry Revisited: The Characteristics and Operations of America's Small Jails," *Justice Quarterly* 5 (1988): 421–440. See also the special topics edition of *Corrections Today* 30 (December 1988) and *American Jails* 6:6 (February 1993).

3. National Advisory Commission on Criminal Justice Standards and Goals, *Corrections* (Washington, D.C.: U.S. Department of Justice, 1973), pp. 5–6. But see John Klofas, "Drugs and Justice, The Impact of Drugs on Criminal Justice in a Metropolitan Community," *Crime and Delinquency* 39:2 (1993): 204–224.

4. See Edwin Zedlewski, "Deterrence Findings and Data Sources: A Comparison of the Uniform Crime Reports and the National Crime Victimization Surveys," *Journal of Research in Crime and Delinquency* 20 (July 1983): 262–276. A more recent statement of the differences can be found in Scott Menard, Alfred Blumstein, David McDowell, et al., "Residual Gains, Reliability, and the UCR–NCVS Relationship: A Comment on Blumstein, Cohen, and Rosenfeld," *Criminology* 30:1 (1992): 105–132.

5. Federal Bureau of Investigation, *Crime in the United States: 1992 (Uniform Crime Report)* (Washington, D.C.: U.S. Government Printing Office, 1993).

6. Craig Perkins and Patsy Klaus, *Criminal Victimization 1994* (Washington, D.C.: U.S. Department of Justice, 1996), p. 4.

7. Federal Bureau of Investigation, *Uniform Crime Reports in the United States 1994* (Washington, D.C.: U.S. Government Printing Office, 1995), p. 5. Admission data were taken from George M. and Camille Graham Camp, *The Corrections Yearbook: 1995* (New Salem, NY: Criminal Justice Institute, 1995), p. 10.

8. Federal Bureau of Investigation, *Uniform Crime Report*, (1995), p. 207.

9. In the *Uniform Crime Reports* program, police clear a crime when they have identified the offender, have sufficient evidence to charge the offender, and actually take the offender into custody.

10. In 1975, Alaska abolished plea bargaining. In 1986, approximately 56 percent of all felony arrests were not prosecuted, and 7 percent of the felony arrests were reduced to misdemeanors. Alan Barnes, *Disparities Between Felony Charges at the Time of Arrest and Those at the Time of Prosecution* (Anchorage: Alaska Statistical Analysis Unit, 1988).

11. Bureau of Justice Statistics, *Federal Criminal Case Processing: 1982–1993* (Washington, D.C.: U.S. Department of Justice, 1996), p. 5.

12. John Wooldredge, "The Impact of Jurisdiction Size on Guilty Pleas in 569 State Courts," *Sociology and Social Research* 74 (1989): 26–33.

13. Joseph Sanborn, "A Historical Sketch of Plea Bargaining," *Justice Quarterly* 3 (1986): 111–138. See also Douglas Smith, "The Plea Bargaining Controversy," *Journal of Criminal Law and Criminology* 77 (1986): 949–967; Barbara Nienstedt, James Riggs, and Thomas Epperlein, *Targeting Serious and Repetitive Offenders: The Effect of Crime Control Legislation in Arizona* (Phoenix: Arizona Statistical Analysis Center, 1988); and Samuel Walker, *Taming the System: The Control of Discretion in Criminal Justice* (New York: Oxford University Press, 1993). For a statistical analysis of charge reduction, see Calesta Albonetti, "Charge Reduction: An Analysis of Prosecutorial Discretion in Burglary and Robbery Cases," *Journal of Quantitative Criminology* 8:3 (1992): 317–333. See also Pamela Bucy, "The Poor Fit of Traditional Evidentiary and Sophisticated Crime: An Empirical Analysis of Health Care Fraud Prosecutors," *Federal Law Review* 63:2 (1994): 383–538.

14. Harry Elmer Barnes and Negley T. Teeters, *New Horizons in Criminology,* 3rd ed. (Englewood Cliffs, NJ: PrenticeHall, 1959), p. 242. See also John Dawson, *Prosecutors in State Courts, 1990* (Washington, D.C.: U.S. Department of Justice, 1992).

15. A no-paper action generally means that the prosecutor has decided there is not enough likelihood of conviction to warrant securing an indictment. See also James Garofalo, "Police, Prosecutors, and Felony Case Attrition," *Journal of Criminal Justice* 19:5 (1980), 439–449.

16. The expression *elements of a crime* refers to specific and precise statutory conditions of fact that must exist in order for that crime to have taken place. (For example, it must be dark for "burglary in the night season" to take place.)

17. Josephina McDonough, "Gender Differences in Informal Processing: A Look at Charge Bargaining and Sentence Reduction in Washington, D.C.," *Journal of Research in Crime and Delinquency* 77 (1986): 949–967. See Cassia Spohn, John Gruhl, and Susan Welch, "The Impact of the Ethnicity and Gender of Defendants on the Decision to Reject or Dismiss Felony Charges," *Criminology* 25 (1987): 175–190. See also Peter Kraska, "The Processing of Drug Arrestees: Questioning the Assumption of an Ambivalent Reaction," *Journal of Criminal Justice* 20:6 (1992): 517–525, and Elizabeth Lear, "Contemplating the Successive Prosecution Phenomenon in the Federal System," *The Journal of Criminal Law and Criminology* 85:3 (1995): 625–675.

18. N. Baker, "The Prosecutor-Initiation of Prosecution," *Journal of Criminal Law, Criminology and Police Science* 23 (1933): 771. See also I. D. Macphail, "Safeguards in the Scottish Criminal Justice System," *Criminal Law Review* (March 1992): 144–152.

19. Jack Call et al., "Abolition of Plea Bargaining in the Coast Guard," *Journal of Criminal Justice* 11 (1983): 351–358. Considerable interest in plea bargaining has developed in the last ten years, and the process has become more open to the public. In Indiana, for example,

prosecutors are required to inform victims of plea bargains before they may be finalized. See Robert Davis, "Victim/Witness Noncooperation: A Second Look at a Persistent Phenomenon," *Journal of Criminal Justice* 11 (1983): 287–299. See also Edwin Villmoare and Virginia Neto, *Victim Appearances at Sentencing Under California's Victims' Bill of Rights* (Washington, D.C.: U.S. Department of Justice, 1987), and Dean Champion, "Private Counsels and Public Offenders: A Look at Weak Cases, Prior Records, and Leniency in Plea Bargaining," *Journal of Consulting and Clinical Psychology* 56 (1988): 710–714. See also the more recent Richard Cole, "Prosecutorial Discretion in the Military Justice System: Is It Time for a Change?" *American Journal of Criminal Law* 19:3 (1992): 395–410.

20. Mary Lee Luskin and Robert C. Luskin, "Why So Fast, Why So Slow: Explaining Case Processing Time," *Journal of Criminal Law and Criminology* 77 (1986): 190–214. For a concrete example of these principles, see Marianne Means, "Ginsberg's Senate Appearance a Defining Moment," *Seattle Times*, July 25, 1993, p. 7.

21. For an intense discussion of the legal system and plea bargaining, see Ralph Adam Fine, *Escape of the Guilty* (New York: Dodd, Mead, 1986). A more recent empirical study is by Roy Flemming, Peter Nardulli, and James Eisenstein, *The Craft of Justice: Politics and Work in Criminal Court Communities* (Philadelphia: University of Pennsylvania Press, 1992).

22. John Henry Wigmore (1863–1943) was probably the world's foremost authority on the law of evidence. His *Treatise on the Anglo-American System of Evidence Trials at Common Law*, written in 1904–1905, is generally regarded as one of the world's greatest law books. He had great influence on the reform of evidentiary law. Roscoe Pound, *Criminal Justice in America* (New York: Holt, Rinehart and Winston, 1929), p. 163.

23. Alissa Worden, "The Judge's Role in Plea Bargaining: An Analysis of Judges' Agreement with Prosecutors' Sentencing Recommendations," *Justice Quarterly* 122 (1995): 257–278.

24. On the other hand, shock probation may work to expose the offender to the least desirable elements of both probation and incarceration, an argument used by many opponents of the plan. See David Petersen and Paul Friday, "Shock of Imprisonment: Short-Term Incarceration as a Treatment Technique," *International Journal of Criminology and Penology* 1 (November 1973): 319–326. The most sophisticated analysis of shock probation to date is by Gennaro Vito and Harry E. Allen, "Shock Probation in Ohio: A Comparison of Outcomes," *International Journal of Offender Therapy and Comparative Criminology* 25 (1981): 70–75. These researchers found that incarceration may be the main factor that increases recidivism among shock probationers.

25. Psychopathic-offender and habitual-offender statutes received a great impetus in the late 1930s and early 1940s. Their main function is permitting an examination to determine if the offender is psychopathic or a habitual criminal, as a basis for possible commitment. See Tara Valinchus and George Roundtree, "Burnout Phenomenon in Antisocial Personality Disorder: Myth or Reality?" *International Journal of Comparative and Applied Criminal Justice* 16:1 (1992): 101–114.

26. Pleading not guilty by reason of insanity (NGRI) may not be quite as advantageous for defendants as was once commonly believed. See Jeraldine Branff, Thomas Arvanites, and Henry Steadman, "Detention Patterns of Successful and Unsuccessful Insanity Defendants," *Criminology* 21 (August 1983): 439–448. See also Henry Steadman et al., "Maintenance of an Insanity Defense Under Montana's `Abolition' of the Insanity Defense," *American Journal of Psychiatry* 146 (1989): 357–360; Lisa Callahan et al., "Measuring the Effects of the Guilty But Mentally Ill (GBMI) Verdict: Georgia's 1982 GBMI Reform," *Law and Human Behavior* 16:4 (1992): 447–462; and Bruce Arrigo, *The Contours of Psychiatric Justice: A Postmodern Critique of Mental Illness, Criminal Insanity, and the Law* (New York: Garland, 1996).

27. Community corrections generally refers to programs that take place in the community or draw heavily on community resources in their operation. See Rhonda Reeves, "Corrections in the Community," *Corrections Today* 54:8 (1992): 74–79. Also see Edward Latessa and Harry Allen, *Corrections in the Community* (Cincinnati: Anderson, 1997).

28. Thorsten Sellin, "The Significance of Records of Crime," *Law Quarterly Review* 67 (October 1951): 498.

29. George Orwell, *Animal Farm* (New York: Harcourt Brace and World, 1954).

CHAPTER SEVEN

Sentencing

Overview

Perhaps no part of the criminal justice system has more criticism or controversy than the court's effort to make, as William S. Gilbert noted, the punishment fit the crime. This chapter examines that critical decision and acquaints the reader with some of the effects that such decisions have on prison populations and their impact as shown in the correctional filter.

Those who criticize the court's efforts to apply "justice" while dealing with public opinion, jail and prison overcrowding, and legislative restrictions on the judge's discretion need to have a better understanding of the sentencing process: we must consider the incidences of crime, that is, the sheer volume of cases when looking at the sentencing decisions made in America's courts. This chapter reviews the material already covered and prepares the student for the appellate process covered in Chapter 8.

The Sentencing Decision

Defendants who reach the sentencing stage of the criminal proceeding are those who have not yet escaped the correctional filter. They have either pled guilty to or have been found guilty of a crime in a jury or **bench trial**.[1] The court must now decide how to dispose of them. Making a sentencing decision is often the most complicated and difficult task for the sentencing judge.

This decision is exacerbated by the nationwide problem of high incarceration rates, despite a two-decade building or renovation binge in every state. As shown by Figure 7-1, this rate ranges from as high of 636 per 100,000 population in Texas to a low of 78 per 100,000 population in North Dakota. The United States continues to incarcerate more persons per 100,000 population than any other democracy in the Western world (except for the

My object all sublime
I shall achieve in time—
To let the punishment fit the crime,
The punishment fit the crime.

—William S. Gilbert, *The Mikado*

Granting Felons Probation

A high percentage of felony offenders in California were committed to prison in 1986; about one in three persons convicted of felony offenses was imprisoned in California in that year, compared to one in ten in 1970. This has resulted in a critically overcrowded prison system, holding over 64,000 inmates, that was an estimated 100,000 by 1994.

To find an answer to the crisis, California has embarked on a "bricks-and-mortar" attempt to construct enough prison cells to accommodate the over capacity problem (the prisons are operating at 80 percent over their rated capacities). California opened four new prisons in 1986 (about 2,600 new beds) and plans to open twelve new facilities in the immediate future. Even that effort is not likely to produce sufficient beds to accommodate the projected population.

Judges in California, faced with the problem of having to sentence felons and acutely aware of the prison overcrowding crisis, have responded by sentencing adults convicted of felony crimes to probation. Over one-third of the probationers in California are felony probationers.

Joan Petersilia and others studied the probation outcomes of felons granted probation and found that, over a forty-month period, 65 percent of the study group were arrested, 51 percent were reconvicted (new crime), and one in three were incarcerated. Some three out of four (75 percent) of the new charges filed against the study group were for major crimes directly threatening public safety: robbery, theft, burglary, and other violent crimes.

Sentencing judges' decisions are made in a social context that includes prison-bed availability. Whenever prison beds are a scarce commodity, sentencing dispositions will need to include alternatives to incarceration. In California's example, the option cited above had deleterious implications for public safety. The legislature in the state is now considering providing more alternatives for sentencing judges in their important decisions. ∎

SOURCE: Outcome figures are from Joan Petersilia et al., *Granting Felons Probation* (Santa Monica, CA: Rand Corporation, 1985).

Russian Republic, which is still emerging from communism). Rising rates of violent street crime and increasing numbers of drug offenders, along with the trend of longer determinate sentences, make the sentencing decision more complex than it has ever been.

RAPID CHANGE IN SENTENCING

By 1930, and continuing up to 1974, most states and federal courts employed the **indeterminate sentencing** structure; that is, the judge would impose a prison sentence with both a minimum and a maximum term in years, such as two years minimum to five years maximum or five years minimum to twenty years maximum. The wide range of sentence lengths reflected the correctional system's dominant goal of rehabilitation and its belief that once the offender had been rehabilitated, the parole board would detect the change and order the prisoner's release. Parole boards actually determined the length of the sentence served using their authority of **discretionary release.**

Beginning in 1975, however, American sentencing laws and practices started to undergo a rapid change, a fundamental restructuring of the sentencing process. The causes of this change have been identified as follows:[2]

1. Prison uprisings (such as at Attica in New York, and others in New Mexico, Oklahoma, California, and Florida) indicated that inmates were discontented with the rhetoric of rehabilitation and the reality of the prison environment.

2. The abuse of discretion caused concerns about individual rights, as prosecutors, judges, and parole boards were immune from review and some practiced arbitrary uses of discretion.

3. Court orders and decisions led to a movement that demanded accountability in official decision making and outcomes.

Rank	State	Number	Rank	State	Number
1	Texas	636	26	Kentucky	288
2	Louisiana	530	27	Tennessee	277
3	Oklahoma	508	28	Idaho	258
4	South Carolina	494	29	Indiana	258
5	Nevada	460	30	Wyoming	254
6	Arizona	459	31	Kansas	249
7	Georgia	456	32	South Dakota	240
8	Alabama	450	33	Pennsylvania	235
9	Michigan	428	34	New Mexico	220
10	Mississippi	408	35	Hawaii*	202
11	Florida	406	36	Washington	201
12	Maryland	395	37	Montana	194
13	Virginia	395	38	Iowa	192
14	Delaware*	393	39	Wisconsin	187
15	California	384	40	Rhode Island*	186
16	Ohio	377	41	New Hampshire	177
17	New York	367	42	Oregon	175
18	Arkansas	353	43	Massachusetts	171
19	Missouri	338	44	Vermont*	168
20	North Carolina	322	45	Nebraska	159
21	Connecticut*	321	46	Utah	155
22	Alaska*	317	47	Maine	118
23	Illinois	310	48	West Virginia	106
24	New Jersey	310	49	Minnesota	100
25	Colorado	289	50	North Dakota	78

Inmates per 100,000 people in state prisons, June 1, 1994.
* Prisons and local jails in these states form an integrated system; data include both jail and prison populations.

FIGURE

7.1

Incarceration Rates by State, 1994

SOURCE: Patrick Langan and Helen Graziadei, *Felony Sentencing in State Courts 1992* (Washington, D.C.: U.S. Department of Justice, 1995), p. 1.

4. The rehabilitation ideal was challenged both empirically and ideologically, which undermined the rationale of the indeterminate sentence's "parole after rehabilitation" corollary.

5. Experimental and statistical studies of judicial sentencing found substantial disparity and both racial and class discrimination.[3] Such inconsistencies and disparities fostered the conclusion that sentencing practices were unfair.

6. Crime control and corrections became a political football,[4] useful for those seeking election to public office. Such political opportunists led the general public to believe that lenient judges and parole boards were releasing dangerous offenders back into the community, with little concern for public safety.

NEW GOALS

Although corrections in the 1970s generally reflected the utilitarian goal of rehabilitation, the dialogue and arguments from the reform movement brought other primary goals to the forefront in the 1980s, such as the incapacitation of persons likely to commit future crimes and its variant of **selective incapacitation,** in which the highest-risk offenders would receive much longer sentences in order to prevent

FIGURE 7.2

Mandatory Prison Term Statutes in the United States

SOURCE: James Austin, Charles Jones, John Kramer, and Phil Renniger, *National Assessment of Structured Sentencing* (Washington, D.C.: Department of Justice, 1996), pp. 24-25.

Key

R Repeat/Habitual	**N** Narcotics/Drugs	**S** Sex Offenses
D Drunk Driving	**P** Possession of Weapons	**O** Other

	R	D	N	P	S	O		R	D	N	P	S	O
Alabama	R	D	N	P	-	-	Montana	R	D	N	P	-	-
Alaska	R	-	N	P	-	O	Nebraska	R	D	-	-	S	-
Arizona	R	D	N	P	S	-	Nevada	R	-	N	P	-	-
Arkansas	R	-	N	P	-	-	New Hampshire	R	D	-	P	S	-
California	R	-	N	P	S	O	New Jersey	R	D	N	P	S	-
Colorado	R	D	N	P	S	O	New Mexico	R	D	-	P	-	-
Connecticut	-	D	N	P	S	-	New York	R	-	-	-	-	-
Delaware	R	-	N	P	-	-	North Carolina	R	D	N	-	S	-
District of Columbia	-	-	N	P	-	O	North Dakota	-	D	N	P	-	-
Florida	R	-	N	P	-	-	Ohio	R	D	-	P	-	-
Georgia	R	D	N	P	S	-	Oklahoma	R	-	-	P	-	-
Hawaii	R	-	-	P	-	O	Oregon	-	D	-	-	-	-
Idaho	R	D	N	P	S	-	Pennsylvania	R	D	N	P	S	O
Illinois	R	D	N	P	S	O	Rhode Island	R	D	N	P	S	O
Indiana	R	-	N	P	-	-	South Carolina	R	-	N	P	-	-
Iowa	R	-	N	P	-	-	South Dakota	-	-	N	P	-	-
Kansas	-	D	-	-	-	-	Tennessee	-	D	-	-	-	-
Kentucky	R	D	-	P	S	-	Texas	R	D	-	P	-	-
Louisiana	R	-	-	P	-	-	Utah	R	-	-	-	S	-
Maine	-	D	-	P	-	-	Vermont	R	-	-	P	-	-
Maryland	R	-	N	P	-	-	Virginia	-	D	-	P	-	O
Massachusetts	-	D	N	P	-	-	Washington	R	-	-	-	S	O
Michigan	R	D	N	P	-	-	West Virginia	R	-	N	P	-	-
Minnesota	R	-	N	P	-	-	Wisconsin	R	D	N	P	S	O
Mississippi	R	-	N	P	-	-	Wyoming	R	-	-	-	-	-
Missouri	R	-	N	P	-	-							

any more criminal activity.[5] Since the mid-1990s, the **"Three Strikes and You're Out"** laws have become popular with the public and legislators. The specific deterrence of sentenced offenders—and the general deterrence of those contemplating committing a crime—were legitimized as social policy goals. In addition, the retributionist goal became attractive, inasmuch as it would impose deserved punishment. (Such a **"just deserts"** goal looks backward to the offender's personal culpability, focuses on the nature of the act, and considers the harm done.)[6]

REFORM OPTIONS

As a result of the reform movement, sentencing practices were changed, in the belief that such practices would limit disparity and discretion and establish more detailed criteria for sentencing or new sentencing institutions. These contradictory options included:

(1) abolishing plea bargaining;
(2) establishing plea-bargaining rules and guidelines;
(3) setting mandatory minimum sentences;
(4) establishing statutory determinate sentencing;

(5) setting voluntary or descriptive sentencing guidelines or presumptive or prescriptive sentencing guidelines;

(6) creating sentencing councils;

(7) requiring judges to provide reasons for their sentences;

(8) setting parole guidelines to limit parole board discretion;

(9) abolishing parole;

(10) adopting or modifying good-time procedures; and

(11) routinizing appellate review of sentences.[7]

Clarence E. Gideon (1911-1976), was the subject of the Supreme Court decision that determined the right to counsel in a non-capital case, wrote his writ of certiorari by hand on a lined yellow pad. Made famous by the book and movie about the case, called *Gideon's Trumpet,* he died a pauper in a Fort Lauderdale medical center.

Those options represent only the principal steps designed to limit unbridled discretion, lessen discrimination, make sentencing more fair, and enhance justice.

REFORM EFFECTS

In just over a decade, the dramatic changes in sentencing structures and practices became evident. Release by a parole board was abolished in at least twelve states,[8] and parole **sentencing guidelines** had been established in eight others. In 1987, the U.S. federal sentencing guidelines were promulgated. More than ten states used determinate sentencing (with a known release date), and at least forty-eight states established mandatory minimum sentences for at least one crime. Several states adopted statewide sentencing councils, and at least fifty jurisdictions drew up local sentencing guidelines. It is against that background of concern and change that we shall look at the sentencing decision.

PREDICTING BEHAVIOR

If the sentence had no purpose except to punish the offender, as was the case until fairly recently, the judge's job would be easily prescribed by statute. In modern times, however, the sentence is also intended to be the cornerstone for reintegration. Those broadly divergent objectives create a paradox that may force judges to choose between equally unwise alternatives based on the *offense* rather

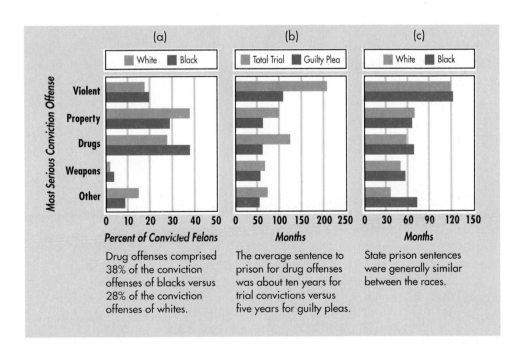

FIGURES

7.3, 7.4, & 7.5

(a) Offense Distribution of Persons Convicted of a Felony In State Courts, by Race, 1992

(b) Average Sentence to State Prison, by Offense and Nature of Conviction, 1992

(c) Average Sentence to State Prison for a Felony Imposed by State Courts, by Offense and Race, 1992

SOURCE: Patrick Langan and Robyn Cohen, *State Court Sentencing of Convicted Felons, 1992* (Washington, D.C.: U.S. Department of Justice, 1996), p. 13, p. 41, and p. 13, respectively.

than the *offender*. The choice is often further complicated by subtle pressures from police, prosecutors, and the public to incarcerate certain offenders for long periods of time.

One of the main problems with the sentencing decision is that it requires that judges predict human behavior. As judges ask themselves if specific offenders will respond to prison positively or perhaps benefit more from psychiatric help while on probation, they have little factual information to guide them. In the final analysis, most judges must rely on a presentence investigation and their own intuition, experience, and imagination to produce the best decision.

THE PRESENTENCE INVESTIGATION

Most of the states make a **presentence report** mandatory for offenses for which imprisonment can be more than one year. It is estimated that over 85 percent of the states do prepare some kind of presentence report on felony cases, although there may be extreme variation in the report's usefulness and quality. The presentence report, if properly researched and prepared, can be an extremely valuable document for trial judges in their sentence decisions.

The presentence investigation is usually prepared by the court's probation officer or by a staff of social workers. Privately commissioned presentence investigation reports prepared for the court,[9] as well as creation of local agencies to prepare individualized client-specific sentencing plans that stress nonincarceration sanctions[10] (as is the case in North Carolina), also serve to assist sentencing judges. The defense attorney usually reviews, and may challenge, points in the presentence report to help the judge make a sentencing decision based on information from all of the sources.[11]

Walter C. Reckless pointed out the essential elements of a workable presentence investigation report. He said that a presentence investigation report, when written up and presented to the judge, should include in summary form such information as:

1. present offense (including the person's attitudes toward it and his role in it);
2. previous criminal record and family situation (including tensions and discord and the factors affecting his happiness);
3. neighborhood environment and school and educational history;
4. employment history (especially the skills and the efficiency and stability as a worker);
5. associates and participation;
6. habits (including alcohol, gambling, promiscuity, and so forth);
7. physical and mental health (as reported by various sources and by special examinations); and
8. summary and recommendations.

Although most presentence investigations will emphasize such objective facts in a case as age, grade reached in school, number of children, and so on, it is important that the investigating officer capture as much subjective content as possible, especially how the defendant looks at his or her situation and the meaning of various plights and difficulties to him or her. The defendant's perspective on life and the way he approaches it, as well as his or her attitudes toward the objects and the relationships of his or her milieu, are the most crucial items in a presentence investigation, just as they are in more elaborate case studies. Subjective data,

Severity levels of conviction offense		Criminal History Score						
		0	1	2	3	4	5	6 or more
• Unauthorized use of motor vehicle • Possession of marijuana	I	12	12	12	15	18	21	24 23–25
• Theft-related crimes ($150–2,500) • Sale of marijuana	II	12	12	14	17	20	23	27 25–29
• Theft crimes ($150–2,500)	III	12	13	16	19	22 21–23	27 25–29	32 30–34
• Burglary-felony intent • Receiving stolen goods ($150–2,500)	IV	12	15	18	21	25 24–26	32 30–34	41 37–45
• Simple robbery	V	18	23	27	30 29–31	38 36–40	46 43–49	54 50–58
• Assault, 2nd degree	VI	21	26	30	34 33–35	44 42–46	54 50–58	65 60–70
• Aggravated robbery	VII	24 23–25	32 30–34	41 38–44	49 45–53	65 60–70	81 75–87	97 90–104
• Assault, 1st degree • Criminal sexual conduct, 1st degree	VIII	43 41–45	54 50–58	65 60–70	76 71–81	95 89–101	113 106–120	132 124–140
• Murder, 3rd degree	IX	97 94–100	119 116–122	127 124–130	149 143–155	176 168–184	205 195–215	230 218–242
• Murder, 2nd degree	X	116 111–121	140 133–147	162 153–171	203 192–214	243 231–255	284 270–298	324 309–339

Italicized numbers within the lighter boxes denote the range within which a judge may sentence without the sentence being deemed a departure. First-degree murder is excluded from the guidelines by law and is punished by life imprisonment.

FIGURE
7.6

Minnesota Sentencing Guidelines Grid (Presumptive Sentence Length in Months)

SOURCE: Minnesota Sentencing Guidelines Commission, *Report to the Legislature, 1983* (St. Paul, MN: Minnesota Sentencing Guidelines Commission, 1983), p. 14.

in short, give the more revealing clues as to what has shaped the destiny of the defendant so far and what the future possibilities are.[12]

The presentence investigation report gives the judge a comprehensive and factual overview of the offender, his or her crime, nature, history, habits, personality, problems, needs, and risks. It also usually contains a recommendation to the court of an appropriate disposition for the case. Judges tend to accept the presentence recommendation at a rate of about 83 percent for probation and 87 percent for imprisonment.[13]

The presentence report serves many functions. Not only is it of immediate use in determining an appropriate sentence, but it also is used by correctional agencies or institutions for classification and program activities assignments. It will aid the probation officer in handling the case, should probation be the sentence imposed. It will also follow the offender to parole, at which time it will be used by the parole officer in planning and supervising the case. Appellate review courts use

A judge hands out a sentence to a convicted criminal

—PHOTO BY MICHAEL NEWMAN, COURTESY OF PHOTOEDIT

the document when considering an appeal of sentence, and the presentence investigation reports also offer a data base from which to conduct research on convicted offenders, case flows, and court management.[14]

JUDICIAL VERSUS ADMINISTRATIVE SENTENCING

Traditionally, the sentencing process has involved a judicial determination of the appropriate punishment for a specific crime. There have been extensive changes in judicial power in the last century, however, particularly over the last decade.[15] In the early days, when a judge sentenced an offender to ten years in prison, it was almost certain that the offender would serve ten years to the day. As administrative forms of sentence shortening (involving such matters as good time, pardon, parole, and clemency) became more common, the correlation between the judge's sentence and the time the offender served largely disappeared. In practice, courts using indeterminate sentencing can establish minimum and maximum sentences within the sentencing statutes, but the actual length of the sentence is often left up to the administrators of the correctional system—to the executive rather than the judicial branch of government.

A comparison of the judicial and administrative styles of decision making in sentencing reveals some similar criteria:

Dollree Mapp was the principal in the Supreme Court case of Mapp v. Ohio that established clear guidelines under the Amendment against illegal search and seizure. Nine years later she was re-arrested, this time for illegal possession of drugs. A proper search warrant, using standards under Mapp v. Ohio resulted in a 20-year sentence.

1. [a] determination of how much time is right for the kind of crime at issue, with the decisionmaker's own sense of values and expectations usually (but not always) heavily influenced by the pressures of his environment and what he perceives to be the norms of his colleagues.[16]

2. classification within that crime category of the offender's particular act as mitigated, average, or aggravated.

3. offender's past criminal record (slight, average, or aggravated).

4. offender's extent of repentance, attitude toward available treatment, and official prognosis of his or her reformability.

5. anticipated public (usually meaning law enforcement) reaction to a proposed disposition.

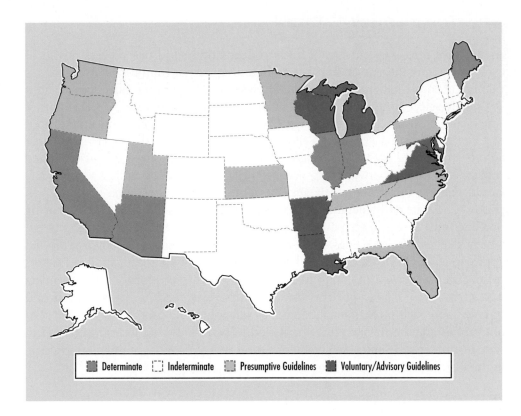

FIGURE 7.7

Types of Sentencing
Practices in the United
States, 1994

SOURCE: Bureau of Justice Statistics, *National Assessment of Structured Sentencing* (Washington, D.C.: U.S. Department of Justice, 1996), p. 12.

Legend: ■ Determinate ⬚ Indeterminate ▨ Presumptive Guidelines ■ Voluntary/Advisory Guidelines

Not all of these criteria are used or even relevant in every case, and many other variables may be raised because of the existence of particular facts (such as strong middle-class background and allegiance) or the peculiarities or hang-ups of an individual decision maker. Something approximating the given basic list, however, appears to comprise the critical factors in most sentence fixing. Presumably, very similar criteria are involved in prosecutorial sentence bargaining at the pre-arraignment stage.[17]

Presumptive Sentencing

One alternative to limit sentencing disparity is the presumptive sentencing system, in which the state legislature sets minimum, average, and maximum terms, allowing the judge to select a term based on the characteristics of the offender and aggravating circumstances. The sentence imposed will be the time served, less any credits against the sentence that the offender earns (such as credit for time served in jail, good behavior in prison, program participation, and so on). California has a presumptive sentencing structure that provides three options to the sentencing judge, as seen here for the crime of burglary:

1. aggravating circumstances—seven years
2. presumptive (average) sentence—five years
3. mitigating circumstances—three years

Ordinarily, the judge would decide if the offender were to be placed on probation or sentenced to prison (the "in-out" decision). Assuming imprisonment to be the answer, the judge would impose the average sentence of five years, unless mitigating circumstances were present at the time of the offense (for example, if the offender were under the influence of a controlled substance or had a weak personality and was easily led into committing a crime for peer approval, and so on). If mitigating circumstances were proven, the judge would impose the least sentence (three years). However, if aggravating circumstances were proven, the judge must impose the highest sentence (seven years). Some examples of aggravating circumstances are gross bodily harm to victim, prior incarceration in prison, vulnerability of victim (over sixty years of age, blind, paraplegic, etc.). ■

PRACTICAL PROBLEMS IN SENTENCING

As we have seen previously, a flowchart of the criminal justice process reveals at every step along the way an imbalance of input to output (number of arrests versus number of incarcerations). Many cases are winnowed out in the early stages, and it is a highly select group of prisoners who end up in the Atticas and San Quentins of America. In a statistical sense, the negative selection process that admits the offender to prison may be considered more discriminating than the positive one that admits students to Ivy League colleges. But for the practical need to spread limited resources over an overwhelming number of cases, scores of additional offenders would join each of the relatively small proportion of offenders who do end up in prison. The state and federal correctional systems are finite in size. The sentencing decision must take into account the decisions at the other end of the funnel process, which determine release rates. The system can become blocked if sentences do not approximately balance releases, and dangerous overcrowding can result. At worst, prison overcrowding can contribute to judicial overuse of probation for offenders whose risk level is too high. This can result in overworked probation officers and unacceptably high probation failure rates by offenders who continue to commit serious crimes and are revoked from probation to be resentenced to imprisonment in state institutions.[18] Sentencing, therefore, must reflect both the number of prisoners in the institutions and the limited resources for handling them.[19]

PROBLEMS IN SETTING PRISON TERMS

In the past, the determination of prison terms has been left largely to the courts. Decisions were made within the broad parameters of **plea bargaining**[20] and statutory limitations. The courts generally established maximum sentences and parole boards determined the actual lengths of confinement according to limits established by the court and by law. In the past decade, however, control over the sentencing process has become more of a concern to state legislatures. Concerns about disparate sentences and other abuses or perceived abuses of the system have resulted in six basic strategies to formalize legislative control over the sentencing process:

> *Determinate sentencing*—sentencing systems under which parole boards no longer may release prisoners before their sentences (minus good time)[21] have expired;

> *Mandatory prison terms*—statutes through which legislatures require a prison term always to be imposed for convictions for certain offenses or offenders;

Disparate Sentencing for Crack and Cocaine Use

In 1986, Congress created sentencing disparity for two of the most popular types of cocaine: powder and crack (crystal). The former is the preferred form for whites.

Sale of five grams of crack cocaine—barely a teaspoonful—results in a minimum of five years in federal prison for the violator. It requires one hundred times that amount of powdered cocaine, the type preferred by whites, to result in a comparable sentence. About 90 percent of those convicted of

crack cocaine are black, but only 30 percent of those convicted of selling powder cocaine are black. When the U.S. Sentencing Commission recommended changing the sentencing guidelines to equalize sentencing, both the US House and Senate voted to block any change in the 100 to 1 ratio. ∎

SOURCE: Michael Isokoff, "Crack, Coke, and Race," *Newsweek,* November 6, 1995, p. 77.

Sentencing Guidelines

In an attempt to limit if not remove sentencing disparity, many jurisdictions have implemented a set of guidelines to help judges decide what sentence ought to be imposed, given the seriousness of the offense and characteristics of the offender. Guidelines are based on past experience of a large number of sentencing judges and represent average sentences imposed by his or her peers in similar cases. Obviously, inasmuch as the determinations are guidelines, judges are not *required* to impose the recommended sentence (but, at least, must state in writing the reasons for ignoring the guidelines).

One such guideline to determine sentence length is from Minnesota. Across the top of the guideline grid is a score for the characteristics the offender brings to the sentencing hearing: number of prior juvenile adjudications, adult misdemeanor and felony convictions; number of times the offender has been previously incarcerated, employment status or educational attainment; whether the offender escaped or was on probation or parole at the time of the instant offense, and so

on. Obviously, the higher the score, the worse the criminal history (and the longer the recommended sentence).

The severity of the offense is found on the left side of the grid, ranked from least severe to highest (murder in the second degree) offense. After the judge calculates the criminal history score, she or he locates the offense category and reads across to see what other judges have given in terms of sentence length. The sentencing judge then imposes a sanction within the suggested range.

Although this procedure may appear to be a mechanical and impersonal manner of determining sentence length, it will remove much of the disparity in sentencing. Obviously, guidelines of this sort must be periodically updated so they reflect the most recent practices. Minnesota has reduced sentencing disparity through the effective use of guidelines. ∎

SOURCE: For more information, see Herbert Koppel, *Sentencing Practices in 13 States* (Washington, D.C.: U.S. Department of Justice, 1983).

Sentencing guidelines—procedures designed to structure sentencing decisions based on measures of offense severity and criminal history;

Parole guidelines—procedures designed to structure parole release decisions based on measurable offender criteria;

Good-time policies—statutes that allow for reducing a prison term based on an offender's behavior in prison; and

A "jury of peers" is sworn in for their civic duty

—*PHOTO BY JIM PICKERELL, COURTESY OF STOCK BOSTON*

Emergency crowding provisions—policies that relieve prison crowding by systematically making inmates eligible for release sooner.[22]

Prison populations are increasing in almost every state. Policies for setting prison terms influence the size of prison populations by both the number that are sentenced and the length of time that they stay in prison. As a result, many states have attempted to find ways to modify prison terms and reduce population pressures. Those methods include the following: sentencing guidelines[23] that use available prison capacity as a consideration in setting the length of terms (such as those in Minnesota and Florida);[24] mechanisms for accelerating good time; and direct release of certain prisoners—usually those already close to their release date—under administrative provisions (such as emergency crowding laws, the use of commutation, sentence revisions, and early-release programs).[25]

Figure 7-8 demonstrates the amount of discretion in sentencing between jurisdictions. The determinate sentencing states—California, Colorado, Connecticut, Illinois, Indiana, Maine, Minnesota, New Mexico, North Carolina, and Washington—tend to afford the least amount of discretion. Offenders usually receive fixed sentences and they are served in full, minus good-time credits. Generally in those states, parole boards continue to handle revocations and good-time decisions.

Such a sentencing structure limits "judicial imperialism" in sentencing, as the legislature heavily influences the sentence length. Whether there are unforeseen problems in **presumptive sentencing** remains to be proven, but California's prison population problems may well be due to a corollary of presumptive sentencing: abolition of parole board early release authority that has been used to control prison overcrowding in the past.

Mandatory prison term statutes exist in forty-eight states. Those statutes apply for certain crimes of violence and for habitual criminals, and the court's discretion in such cases (regarding, for example, probation, fines, and suspended sentences) has been eliminated by statute. In some states the imposition of a prison term is constrained by sentencing guidelines. Guidelines are usually set by a governor's commission, whose members usually represent a cross section of the state population. As noted by a recent study,

> A sentencing commission in each state monitors the use of the guidelines and departures from the recommended sentences by the judiciary. Written explanations are required from judges who depart from guideline ranges. The Minnesota Sentencing Guidelines Commission states that "while the sentencing guidelines are advisory to the sentencing judge, departures from the presumptive sentences established in the guidelines should be made only when substantial and compelling circumstances exist." Pennsylvania sentencing guidelines stipulate that court failure to explain sentences deviating from the recommendations "shall be grounds for vacating the sentence and resentencing the defendant." Furthermore, if the court does not consider the guidelines or inaccurately or inappropriately applies them, an imposed sentence may be vacated upon appeal to a higher court by either the defense or the prosecution.[26]

The range and particular format for sentencing guidelines can include such things as specifically worded statutes and grids with a range of judicial options. Parole guidelines are sometimes closely prescribed, and sometimes wide discretion is afforded to the parole board. The amount of flexibility in such decisions can directly enhance or detract from the efforts to relieve crowded prison conditions.

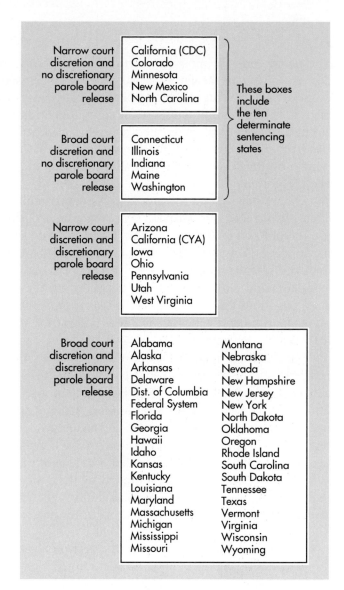

Narrow court discretion and no discretionary parole board release
- California (CDC)
- Colorado
- Minnesota
- New Mexico
- North Carolina

Broad court discretion and no discretionary parole board release
- Connecticut
- Illinois
- Indiana
- Maine
- Washington

These boxes include the ten determinate sentencing states

Narrow court discretion and discretionary parole board release
- Arizona
- California (CYA)
- Iowa
- Ohio
- Pennsylvania
- Utah
- West Virginia

Broad court discretion and discretionary parole board release
- Alabama
- Alaska
- Arkansas
- Delaware
- Dist. of Columbia
- Federal System
- Florida
- Georgia
- Hawaii
- Idaho
- Kansas
- Kentucky
- Louisiana
- Maryland
- Massachusetts
- Michigan
- Mississippi
- Missouri
- Montana
- Nebraska
- Nevada
- New Hampshire
- New Jersey
- New York
- North Dakota
- Oklahoma
- Oregon
- Rhode Island
- South Carolina
- South Dakota
- Tennessee
- Texas
- Vermont
- Virginia
- Wisconsin
- Wyoming

FIGURE

7.8

Sentencing Discretion Between Jurisdictions, 1995

SOURCE: Bureau of Justice Statistics, *Setting Prison Terms* (Washington, D.C.: U.S. Department of Justice, 1989, p.4.

Because most parole decisions are not based on time but on perceived "risk to the community," tighter and tighter criteria make it difficult to manage prison population size by such decisions.

Good-time policies are another way to control behavior in the institutions and to control population pressures as well. The threat of losing up to one-third of their sentences by poor conduct does act as a control over some inmates' behavior. Our review of the changes in sentencing practices and their consequences in the last decade clearly shows the shifts that have taken place. Although discretion in determining sentence length has been somewhat removed from the sentencing judge and parole board, it was reduced by legislatures through their enactment of new sentencing structures. In turn, in many jurisdictions, the prosecutor's discretion was increased. The prison populations will continue to climb as more and more offenders are committed and serve longer and longer sentences. American corrections appears to be on a collision course with a standard of human decency: the Eighth Amendment to the U.S. Constitution which forbids cruel and unusual punishment. To understand the situation, it is necessary to look at the problems with the penal codes.

Problems with Penal Codes

The penal codes of most jurisdictions are a potpourri of social thinking from past eras. Most of the earlier penal codes were devised in response to a specific event or set of events, often after a particularly heinous crime or repugnant act. Such acts bring public pressure on legislators and, if that pressure is persistent enough, a new law is created with an attached formula for punishment. Unfortunately, those laws, with punishments that are often irrationally severe, remain on the books for decades after the incident and the legislators have long been forgotten.

Many states are in the process of updating and revising their entire criminal codes. It is a long and arduous task, however, and there is a great temptation to use the old as a model for the new. Many feel that sentence fixing should not be part of penal legislation. The obvious failure of the early penal codes, designed to mete out specific punishments for specific offenses, has reinforced the belief that legislators and judges should be excluded from the sentence-fixing process. One alternative that was advocated is the use of professional psychologists, trained to understand human behavior, as a replacement for legislators and jurists in fixing the penalties for crimes.

In 1967 President Johnson's Crime Commission reported that "a common characteristic of American penal codes is the severity of sentence available for almost all felony offenses."[27] That background of severity has inhibited meaningful change in penal codes. In examining sentencing practices, one must review both the system of criminal justice and the erratic quality of justice dispensed by that system. Failure to observe the difference between justice *in* the law and justice *before* the law can result in unfair criticism of the judge.

The Model Penal Code,[28] drafted by the American Law Institute, addresses the problems of severity and inconsistency of present penal codes with regard to sentencing. Imprisonment is seen as a last resort, to be used only when

1. there is undue risk that during the period of suspended sentence or probation the defendant will commit another crime;
2. the defendant is in need of correctional treatment that can be provided most effectively by commitment to an institution; or
3. a lesser sentence will depreciate the seriousness of the defendant's crime.[29]

Another issue in penal code revision is the disparity of sentencing for the same or similar offenses. The emphasis today is on reintegration, but prisoners who feel that they have been unfairly treated in sentencing may well reject all efforts to reintegrate them. This kind of disparity also destroys public confidence in the criminal justice system. The elimination or revision of antiquated statutes and the adoption of principles that are widely accepted by both the judiciary and correctional administrators will go a long way toward encouraging consistent and appropriate sentencing.

Models for Sentencing

How should the jurist arrive at the proper length of sentence for an offender? The present system, sometimes referred to as the "hunch" system,[30] results in discriminatory sentences by the same judge, and between different judges, for the same

The Role of Sentencing Commissions with Restorative Justice

When the purposes of sentencing commissions are presented in the literature, typically issues of fairness, equity, and consistency arise; sometimes the more systemic and prescriptive goals of increased retribution, more directed incapacitation for violent offenders, or cost effectiveness are offered. Research, evaluations, and other measurements of success are thus oriented around numbers and percentages incarcerated, length of incarceration, and comparison groups of offenders in other geographic or temporal venues.

This is not surprising, since the rhetoric of the day is so disposed, but even a slightly distant review of this situation reveals a glaring omission in policy, practice, and research—the victim. It is as if a collective decision was made to measure justice as punishment, with some small dissent to include rehabilitation, but every bit of it offender-oriented.

A growing number of observers from inside and outside the criminal justice system are expressing their concern over this imbalance, and while it may not yet have reached the stage of a movement, there is enough activity that sentencing commissions would do well to anticipate the future and attempt to blend a victim focus into their agenda.

Generally referred to as "restorative justice," this philosophy puts the victim and the community at the center. The primary concern is to right the wrong, using the offender as a vehicle where possible; true involvement of the victim in the process—more than the allocution opportunity now sometimes extended to the victim.

Sentencing commissions can take five steps to improve focus on the victim:

1. Involve victims as commission members and in discussions. Involvement is the key to understanding the perspective and acknowledging the legitimacy of their role.

2. Include a goal of restoring the victim for the commission—if it is not, why should anyone expect victim restoration to be an aim of the criminal justice process?

3. Train and orient staff and the public to their responsibility. Training is paramount to many technical matters concerning calculation of guidelines, completing of forms and impacts of commission rules. Shouldn't the effect on the primary victim be a centerpiece of concern rather than an afterthought, or worse, ignored?

4. Insure policies and procedures are in place to allow victim involvement and restoration. The most obvious example is restitution. One of the most oft cited conditions of probation, few jurisdictions have in place any semblance of a professional system to identify, collect, track, and disburse restitution. The methods are available through the private sector if not other public agencies.

5. Measure success by identifying how victims and communities are restored, using measures such as restitution collected; community service hours; percentage of victims given the opportunity for a face-to-face dialogue with their offender or to sit on an impact panel; and results of surveys. If we spend all our time collecting data on how we affect offenders, it sends a message that we don't care about the effect on victims.

As confounding as it already is to try to sort out commission responsibilities, broadening the role to include restorative justice may very well be a welcome diversion from the "how tough can we get" debate, and can create new allies for some beleaguered commissions. Victim advocates are a growing force on the justice scene and having them side-by-side with sentencing commissions is much preferable to having them head-to-head. In any case, as we strive toward the elusive goal of a fair and balanced justice delivery system, this is the right thing to do. ∎

SOURCE: Thomas J. Quinn, *Sentencing Commission News*, April 1996, Issue 3.

---

offenses. Over a quarter of a century ago, reformers felt that it should be no great task to set up a diagnostic clinic for the administration of sentenced persons. In the clinic, impartial, disinterested scientists would function under conditions that never exist in the courts.[31] Diagnostic clinics have been very slow in coming, but at least the presentence clinic is in wider use than it was before.

At the 1971 National Conference on Corrections in Williamsburg, Virginia, eight points were made in regard to more appropriate sentencing:

1. It should be mandatory that trial judges have presentence reports in all felony cases. These reports should be prepared by qualified probation or corrections officers. The report should also be made a part of the record for any sentence appeal which may be permitted.

2. Diagnostic facilities should be made available to all judges.

3. Jury sentencing should be abolished.

4. Sentencing judges should be required to record the reasons for each sentence. These reasons are to be made known to the defendant, with copies to the corrections personnel involved and to the appellate courts in those instances in which the sentences are appealed.

5. Sentencing judges should educate their communities on the philosophy of sentencing

6. Defense counsel and the prosecutor should be consulted by the judge before imposing sentence.

7. Probation officers and judges should receive instructions in sentencing and perhaps attend sentencing institutes.

8. Trial judges should be elected or appointed in as nonpolitical a way as possible.[32]

Another approach to sentencing reform has been devised by David Fogel, the executive director of the Illinois Law Enforcement Commission. In his **justice model**, which groups crimes into five categories, each category would have a flat sentence of from two to twenty-five years, depending on the offense. Sentencing judges would be allowed a 20 percent leeway in either direction under this legislative plan, but each circumstance that might affect the severity of the sentence would be spelled out in detail.[33]

A discussion of sentencing would be incomplete without mentioning the policy implications of the increasing demand for deterrence. Some writers now argue that those states that imprison more of the offender population (rather than use community corrections) would have lower crime rates if the proportion of persons sentenced to prison were to increase. Though this may appeal to conservatives who believe that the criminal justice system can affect the rates of crime and serve as a deterrent, the data on the effects of higher imprisonment rates do not bear out the presumed effects. In both the United States and Canada, the rates of crime do not go down with increased imprisonment.[34] Instead, the rates of crime go up when the proportion of offenders per 100,000 who are sentenced to prison is raised. We thus may need to start thinking about the continued use of imprisonment to deter others from committing crime when studies show that it has just the opposite effect.[35]

Summary

In the past fifteen years, we have witnessed a revolution in sentencing in the United States. Among the changes imposed are the abolition of the parole board's authority to release offenders at their discretion and the adoption of sentencing guidelines for judges. Changes also include shifting to mandatory prison sentences for specified crimes, adoption of presumptive sentences, and other efforts to limit discretion and disparity in sentencing and length of time served in prison. So widespread have the changes been that only three states (North Dakota, Virginia, and Wyoming) have left their sentencing laws unchanged.[36]

In addition to the sentencing law changes, sharp increases have occurred in the number of persons incarcerated. Never in the history of the United States have we had so many and such a large proportion of the public incarcerated in prisons. While reasons for the sudden increase are not exactly understood, it is obvious that corrections is once again in crisis and on a collision course with the Eighth Amendment's prohibition of cruel and unusual punishment. The next chapter examines some of the legal issues, including appeals of sentences before and during incarceration.

Review Questions

1. What is the principal reason for the judge's diminished sentencing power?
2. What are some of the aids available to help the judge decide what sentence to impose?
3. What factors have led to the rapid changes in the sentencing structures in the United States?
4. Identify the basic policy goals of sentencing, and define each.
5. What roles can the presentence investigation report play in corrections?
6. Explain the concept of presumptive sentencing.
7. In what ways can a prosecutor influence sentence length?
8. Why are prison populations increasing?
9. Cite the advantages and disadvantages of the indeterminate sentence.
10. What problems can arise when adult felony offenders are placed on probation?
11. What are some implications of overcrowded prisons for the sentencing decision?

Words to Remember

bench trial
indeterminate sentencing
discretionary release
three strikes and you're out

just deserts
sentencing guidelines
presentence report
plea bargaining

good-time policies
justice model

Endnotes

1. Brian Reaves and Phiny Smith, *Felony Defendants in Large Urban Counties 1992* (Washington, D.C.: U.S. Department of Justice, 1995), p. 26. Of the 48,330 felony convictions in large urban counties in 1991, 91 percent were the result of guilty pleas; 9 percent were found guilty by a jury.

2. National Institute of Corrections, *Research on Sentencing: The Search for Reform* (Washington, D.C.: U.S. Department of Justice, December 1983). But see David Kopel, *Prison Blues: How America's Foolish Sentencing Policies Endanger Public Safety* (Washington, D.C.: Cato Institute, 1994).

3. For an examination of how the offender's race biases sentence length, see R. D. Peterson and J. Hagan, "Changing Conceptions of Race and Sentencing Outcomes," *American Sociological Review* 49 (1984): 56–70. See also Christopher Turk and Neal Shover, "Research Note: The Origin of Sentencing Reforms," *Justice Quarterly* 3 (1986): 329–342; Leo Carroll and Claire Cornell, "Racial Composition, Sentencing Reforms, and Rates of Incarceration," *Justice Quarterly* 2 (1985): 473–490; and Marjorie Zatz, "The Changing Forms of Racial/Ethnic Biases in Sentencing," *Journal of Research in Crime and Delinquency* 24 (1987): 69–92. In another study, race was not related to the imposed length of prison term. See Stephen Klein, Joan Petersilia, and Susan Turner, "Race and Imprisonment Decisions in California," *Science* 247 (1990):

812–816. Also see Nelson James, *Disparities in Processing Felony Arrests in New York State* (Albany: New York State Division of Criminal Justice, 1995).

4. John Irwin and James Austin, *It's About Time* (San Francisco: National Council on Crime and Delinquency, 1987), p. 15. See also Sheldon Messinger and John Berecochea, "Don't Stay Too Long but Come Back Soon: Reflections on the Size and Vicissitudes of California's Prisoner Population," paper presented at the Conference on California Growth and Its Influence on Correctional Policy (University of California, Berkeley, May 10, 1990). See especially Steven Donziger, *The Real War on Crime* (New York: HarperCollins, 1996).

5. John Blackman and J. Welsh, "Selective Incapacitation: Sentencing According to Risk," *Crime and Delinquency* 29 (1983): 504–528. See also Peter Greenwood and Susan Turner, *Selective Incapacitation Revisited: Why the High-Rate Offenders Are Hard to Predict* (Santa Monica, CA: Rand Corporation, 1987), and Anne Rettenberg, "Drug Policy Director Calls for Increasing Prison Capacity," *Criminal Justice Newsletter* 20 (May 15, 1989): 7. And Franklin Zimring and Gordon Hawkins, *Incapacitation: Penal Confinement and the Restraint of Crime* (New York: Oxford University Press, Studies in Crime and Public Policy, 1995).

6. For a discussion of the federal just deserts juvenile code, see Craig Fischer, "As Model Code Nears Completion, Practitioners Ask 'What Code?' " *Criminal Justice Newsletter* 17 (October 15, 1986): 5–7, and Michael Tony, *Sentencing Matters* (New York: Oxford University Press, 1996).

7. Sandra Shane-Dubow, Alice Brown, and Erik Olsen, *Sentencing Reform in the United States: History, Content, and Effect* (Washington, D.C.: U.S. Department of Justice, 1985). See also Turk and Shover, "Research Note," note 3.

8. Peggy Burke, *Abolishing Parole: Why the Emperor Has No Clothes* (Lexington, KY: APPA, 1995).

9. Thomas Gitchoff and George Rush, "The Criminological Case Evaluation and Sentencing Recommendation: An Idea Whose Time Has Come," *International Journal of Offender Therapy and Comparative Criminology* 33 (1989): 77–83.

10. Laura Donnelly and Stevens Clarke, *North Carolina's Community Penalties Program: An Evaluation of Its Impact on Felony Sentencing in 1987–88* (Chapel Hill: University of North Carolina, 1990).

11. Walter Dickey, "The Lawyer and Accuracy of the Presentence Report," *Federal Probation* 43 (June 1979): 28–39. See also David Roberts, "Effects of Court Officials on Sentence Severity: Do Judges Make a Difference?" *Criminology* 22 (February 1984): 135–138.

12. Walter C. Reckless, *The Crime Problem,* 4th ed. (New York: Appleton-Century-Crofts, 1967), pp. 673–674.

13. The degree of agreement may also depend on the report preparer's knowing the negotiated plea and the proposed sentence to which the prosecutor and the defense counsel have agreed.

14. See J. M. Schmolesky and T. K. Thorson, "The Importance of the Presentence Investigation Report After Sentencing," *Criminal Law Bulletin* 18 (1982): 406–441, and Loraine Geltsthorpe and Peter Raynor, "Organizational Effectiveness of Probation Officers' Reports to Sentencers," *British Journal of Criminology* 35:2 (1995): 188–200.

15. Paul Wice, "Leadership," *Justice System Journal* 17:2 (1995): 271–372.

16. Peter Brimelow, "Judicial Imperialism," *Forbes,* June 1, 1987, pp. 109–112.

17. Caleb Foote, "The Sentencing Function," in Roscoe Pound, ed., *A Program for Prison Reform* (Cambridge, MA.: American Trial Lawyers Foundation, 1973), p. 30. There are variations in the amount of plea bargaining by organizational demands as well as population of the jurisdiction. See John Wooldredge, "The Importance of Jurisdiction Size on Guilty Pleas in 569 State Courts," *Sociology and Social Research* 74 (1989): 26–33, and Mike McCorville and Chester Mirsky, "Guilty Plea Courts: A Social Disciplinary Model of Criminal Justice," *Social Problems* 42:2 (1995): 216–234.

18. Lawrence Greenfield, *Probation and Parole 1984* (Washington, D.C.: U.S. Department of Justice, 1986), pp. 2–3. See also Joan Petersilia and Susan Turner, "Comparing Intensive and Regular Supervision for High-Risk Probationers: Early Results from an Experiment in California," *Crime and Delinquency* 36 (1990): 146–161.

19. Tamasak Wicharaya, *Simple Theory, Hard Penalty: The Impact of Sentencing Reforms on State Courts, Prisons, and Crime* (Albany: State University of New York Press, 1995).

20. For an exploration of courtroom work groups and their effects on sentencing, see Douglas Thompson, "How Plea Bargaining Shapes Intensive Probation Supervision Policy Goals," *Crime and Delinquency* 36 (1990): 156–161.

21. Craig Fischer, "To Ease Crowding, Rhode Island Inmates Get 90 Days 'Good Time,'" *Criminal Justice Newsletter* 21 (June 15, 1990): 2–4. For a criticism of determinate sentencing coupled with reduction of power of the parole board to release offenders early, see James Austin, *Parole Outcome in California: The Consequences of Determinate Sentencing, Punishment, and Incapacitation on Parole Performance* (Madison, WI: National Council on Crime and Delinquency, 1989).

22. Bureau of Justice Statistics, *Setting Prison Terms* (Washington, D.C.: U.S. Department of Justice, 1983).

23. Harvey Silets and Susan Brenner, "Commentary on the Preliminary Draft of the Sentencing Guidelines Issued by the United States Sentencing Commission in September 1986," *Journal of Criminal Law and Criminology* 77 (1986): 1069–1111. See also Michael Block and William Rhodes, "The Impact of the Federal Sentencing Guidelines," *NIJ Reports* (1987): 2–13.

24. Herbert Koppel, *Sentencing Practices in 13 States* (Washington, D.C.: U.S. Department of Justice, 1984), p. 5.

25. Bureau of Justice Statistics, *Setting Prison Terms,* p. 2. See also Herbert Koppel, *Time Served in Prison* (Washington, D.C.: U.S. Department of Justice, 1984); Mark Cunniff, *Felony Sentencing in 18 Local Jurisdictions* (Washington, D.C.: U.S. Department of Justice, 1985); and Alexander Smith, Harriet Pollack, and F. Warren Benton, "Sentencing Problems: A Pragmatic View," *Federal Probation* 51 (1987): 67–74.

26. President's Commission on Law Enforcement and Administration of Justice, *The Challenge of Crime in a Free Society* (Washington, D.C.: U.S. Government Printing Office, 1967), p. 142. For a recent evaluation of Minnesota's sentencing guidelines, see Stephen Coleman and Katheryn Guthrie, *Sentencing Effectiveness in Preventing Crime* (St. Paul, MN: Criminal Justice Statistical Analysis Center, 1988). Also see Stewart D'Alessio and Lisa Stolzenberg, "The Impact of Sentencing Guidelines on Jail Incarceration in Minnesota," *Criminology* 33:2 (1995): 283–302.

27. President's Commission on Law Enforcement and Administration of Justice, *The Challenge of Crime in a Free Society*, p. 142.

28. American Law Institute, *Model Penal Code, Proposed Official Draft* (Philadelphia: ALI, 1962), p. 73.

29. Ibid.

30. Harry Elmer Barnes and Negley Teeters, *New Horizons in Criminology,* 3rd ed. (Englewood Cliffs, NJ: Prentice Hall, 1959), p. 264.

31. Ibid., p. 264.

32. Eds., *Report of National Conference on Corrections* (Washington, D.C.: U.S. Government Printing Office, 1971), pp. 2–3.

33. Michael Serrill, "Critics of Corrections Speak Out," *Corrections Magazine* (March 1976): 23.

34. James Austin and David McVey, *The 1989 NCCD Prison Population Forecast: The Impact of the War on Drugs* (San Francisco: National Council on Crime and Delinquency, 1989), p. 6. Conservatives are likely to argue that the decline in crime volume and rates that began in 1990 are a direct result of harsher punishment. Yet crime, as measured by the National Crime Victimization Survey, began to drop in 1981 and dropped about 20 percent since that time. A cause of a phenomenon has to precede the effect. The crime rates began to drop long before increases in sentence length and harsher laws began.

35. David Biles, "Crime and the Use of Prisons," *Federal Probation* 43 (June 1979): 39–43. For a discussion of using prisons to incapacitate offenders, see Todd Clear and D. Barry, "Some Conceptual Issues in Incapacitating Offenders," *Crime and Delinquency* 29 (October 1983): 529–545; and Edmund McGarrell and Timothy Flanagan, "Measuring and Explaining Legislator Crime Control Ideology," *Journal of Research in Crime and Delinquency* 24 (1987): 102–118.

36. Turk and Shover, "Research Note," p. 330.

CHAPTER EIGHT

Appellate Review

Overview

Our examination of legal issues surrounding corrections for offenders and law violators would not be complete without integrating the path of appeals from the convictions, penalties imposed, conditions of imprisonment, questions about civil rights violations, and such things as use of force. The prison walls are no more seen to be a "stone curtain" between the persons imprisoned and the free society. They are still granted many of the same rights guaranteed by the United States Constitution. Prisoner rights will be discussed in detail in Part IV. This chapter looks at such items as motions to vacate sentences, habeas corpus, and civil rights. We begin with basic tenets of the justice system in America. The many legal cases which are involved with corrections are presented here in the most basic form. Serious students of corrections, whether future academicians or practitioners, should become very familiar with those key cases.

The Issue of Due Process

A basic tenet of the criminal justice process in America is that every defendant is presumed innocent until proven guilty. Not only does our system demand proof of guilt, but it also requires that the proof be obtained fairly and legally. The process of appellate review helps ensure that it will be. In effect, the appellate review acts as a shield for the defendant caught up in the processes of criminal trial, incarceration, or supervision in the community. The state has considerable resources to prosecute those it considers offenders, and the Constitution protects us from the kind of government "railroading" that could deprive us of life, liberty, or property without the benefit of **due process** of law. Due process has been a constitutional right for all Americans under federal law

> Courts have held that prison officials have an affirmative duty to prevent inmates from acquiring and possessing dangerous instruments that could be used to assault other inmates.... Officials will continue to be liable when they possess knowledge of real risks to inmates and do not act reasonably to prevent assaults from occurring.
>
> —Michael Vaughn
> and Rolando del Carmen

since the passage of the Fourteenth Amendment in 1868. It was not until the "criminal law revolution" of the 1960s, however, that the due process clause of the Fourteenth Amendment was also made binding on all of the states through a series of Supreme Court decisions. In the field of corrections, like every other segment of criminal justice, those decisions have created a climate of great challenge and rapid change. This chapter includes a brief examination of the appeal process and procedure, a glance at several significant cases, and an analysis of trends that appear to be emerging in pending appeals.

One of the problems with due process of law is not that it is *due*—that is, something we are entitled to—but rather determining how *much* of it is due.[1] Only a few decades ago, very few criminal cases were appealed. Since the case of *Gideon v. Wainwright,* however, the picture has radically changed. The securing of the right to counsel for all defendants, stemming from that landmark decision, has opened the floodgates in the review courts across America. In some jurisdictions the rate of appeals is as high as 90 percent of all convictions (see Figure 8-1).[2] Collateral attack,[3] or the filing of an appeal in the federal system while the state case is still undecided—almost unknown before the 1960—is now routine in most state courts. The result of this overload in the review system has been a monumental increase in the workload for state and federal judges.[4] It has also created extended periods of litigation, often stretched out over several years, that have eroded any lingering belief a conviction for a criminal offense must be considered final. The review procedure has as many as eleven steps in some state systems, and it is not unusual for a defendant to explore at least four or five. The eleven steps are as follows:

1. New trial motion filed in court where conviction was imposed.
2. Appeal to state intermediate appellate court (in states where there is no intermediate appellate court, this step would not be available).
3. Appeal to state supreme court.
4. Petition to U.S. Supreme Court to review state court decision in appeal.
5. Postconviction proceeding in state trial court.

RAILROADED

The term *railroaded* has become part of American slang. Its origins lie in the practice by early state prisons of having a train pick up prisoners at various points, jails, and counties along the way and drop them at the prison. Sometimes local undesirables were put on the prison train to end up in prison under less than due process conditions.

FOURTEENTH AMENDMENT

All persons born and naturalized in the United States, and subject to the jurisdiction thereof, are citizens of the United States and of the State wherein they reside. No State shall make or enforce any law which shall abridge the privileges or immunities of citizens of the United States: nor shall any State deprive any person of life, liberty, or property, without due process of law, nor deny to any person within its jurisdiction the equal protection of the law.

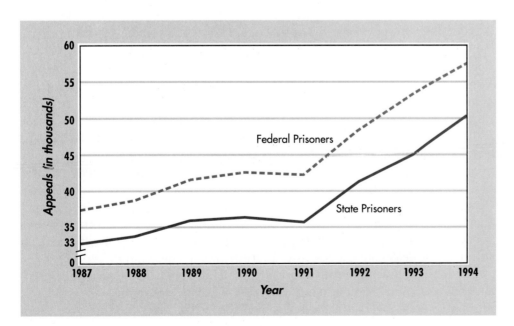

FIGURE

8.1

Petitions Filed in U.S. District Courts by State and Federal Prisoners

SOURCE: Kathleen Maguire and Ann Pastore, eds., *Sourcebook of Criminal Justice Statistics* (Washington, D.C.: U.S. Department of Justice, 1995), p. 499.

6. Appeal of postconviction proceeding to state intermediate appellate court.

7. Appeal to state supreme court.

8. Petition to U.S. Supreme Court to review state court decision on appeal from postconviction proceeding.

9. Habeas corpus petition in federal district court.

10. Appeal to U.S. Court of Appeals.

11. Petition to U.S. Supreme Court to review court of appeals decision on habeas corpus petition.[5]

It is easy to see why the review process can take so long, especially when some steps may be used several times in a single appeal, with reviews of the same case taking place simultaneously in different court systems. Thus due process may be a long and complicated procedure and, when appeal is part of the scheme, it can become a seemingly endless cycle.

The Path of a Criminal Case

There are so many points in the criminal proceeding to which appellate actions can be directed that it is worthwhile to reexamine the steps in which the courts become participants (see Figure 8-2). The first point at which most defendants come into contact with the criminal justice system is at the time of their *arrest,* usually by a police officer. Even at this early step, the potential for a later appeal is great. It is all too true that the "guilty often go free because the constable blundered." A suspect's Fourth and Fifth Amendment rights have been clearly established by decisions such as *Mapp* v. *Ohio* and *Miranda* v. *Arizona* (covered later in this chapter). The failure of law enforcement officers to comply with the procedural safeguards established as a result of those landmark cases can mean an overturned conviction in a later review court.[6]

The next stage of the criminal justice process is usually the *initial appearance* before a judge. Often the court in which this appearance takes place may not actually have the jurisdiction to try the defendant, but the defendant has the right to state his or her case before a court as soon as possible after arrest.[7] This initial appearance is usually accompanied by the presentation of a complaint by the prosecution. The judge at the initial appearance has several tasks to perform, and the failure to perform them correctly can result—as with the arresting officer—in a successful appeal at a later time. The defendant must be made aware of the charges against him or her and warned against making any self-incriminating statements. If the accused is to be assigned an attorney at state expense, this procedure is initiated. When the initial court does not have the jurisdiction to try a particular case, a decision must be made on the continued detention of the accused (in the case of dangerous persons), or some arrangement must be made for the accused's release prior to trial before the court of primary jurisdiction. The defendant can be released on his or her own **recognizance**[8] or may be required to post bail. In the first instance, the judge believes the defendant will appear in court as required because he or she has nothing to gain—and a reputation to lose—by running away. In the second, the defendant posts a certain sum of money that is forfeited if he or she fails to appear. In both cases, the object is to encourage the defendant's appearance at further proceedings on the case.

If the case does not fall under the initial court's jurisdiction, the defendant has the right to request a *preliminary hearing,* to examine the merits of binding the case over to a higher court. The preliminary hearing gives both

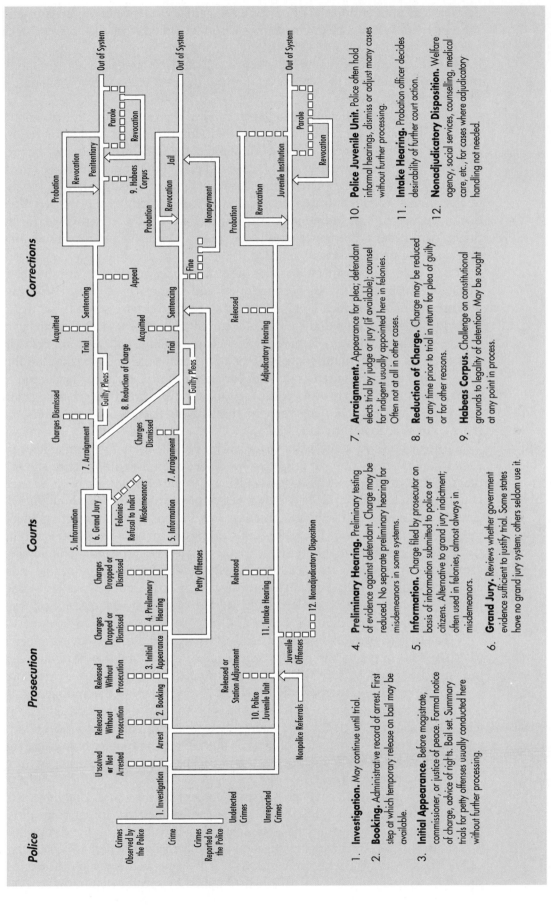

Police | Prosecution | Courts | Corrections

1. **Investigation.** May continue until trial.

2. **Booking.** Administrative record of arrest. First step at which temporary release on bail may be available.

3. **Initial Appearance.** Before magistrate, commissioner, or justice of peace. Formal notice of charge, advice of rights. Bail set. Summary trials for petty offenses usually conducted here without further processing.

4. **Preliminary Hearing.** Preliminary testing of evidence against defendant. Charge may be reduced. No separate preliminary hearing for misdemeanors in some systems.

5. **Information.** Charge filed by prosecutor on basis of information submitted to police or citizens. Alternative to grand jury indictment; often used in felonies, almost always in misdemeanors.

6. **Grand Jury.** Reviews whether government evidence sufficient to justify trial. Some states have no grand jury system; others seldom use it.

7. **Arraignment.** Appearance for plea; defendant elects trial by judge or jury (if available); counsel for indigent usually appointed here in felonies. Often not at all in other cases.

8. **Reduction of Charge.** Charge may be reduced at any time prior to trial in return for plea of guilty or for other reasons.

9. **Habeas Corpus.** Challenge on constitutional grounds to legality of detention. May be sought at any point in process.

10. **Police Juvenile Unit.** Police often hold informal hearings, dismiss or adjust many cases without further processing.

11. **Intake Hearing.** Probation officer decides desirability of further court action.

12. **Nonadjudicatory Disposition.** Welfare agency, social services, counselling, medical care, etc., for cases where adjudicatory handling not needed.

FIGURE
8.2

General Flow of the Criminal Justice System

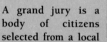
defense and prosecution the opportunity to gather evidence and witnesses and present them informally. It constitutes a sort of preview of the case for both sides and for the judge. To the defendant, the preliminary hearing offers an informal evaluation of his or her chances in the later trial. It is at this point that many defendants decide to plead guilty to their charge or to negotiate a plea to a lesser charge.[9]

The next step is the filing of a *formal criminal charge* in the court that will try the case. If a federal crime punishable by death, imprisonment, hard labor, or loss of civil or political privileges has been committed, the filing of charges may be preceded by another review of the facts by a grand jury. If the grand jury agrees there is probable cause that the offense has occurred and the defendant might have done it, a document is issued that constitutes the formal charging of the accused. This document is called an **indictment**. A defendant has a right to participate in the preliminary hearing but is not usually allowed to appear before the **grand jury** unless special permission is obtained.

The federal government permits the waiver of a grand jury in noncapital cases, and the grand jury has been used less and less in recent years. (Watergate was one instance in which a grand jury was considered necessary.) If the grand jury inquiry is not required, the prosecutor simply files a document called an *information,* which contains the formal criminal charge. Many challenges are made in regard to this portion of the process. Some of the challenges must be made at this time, or they cannot be used as grounds for later appeal. In fact, the resolution of issues raised at this point—in regard to search and seizure, police interrogation techniques, and other questions as to the admissibility of evidence—may consume more court time than the actual trial.

The next critical point is the *arraignment,* the offender's first formal appearance before the trial court. At this point the defendant is asked how he or she will plead. If the defendant chooses to stand mute, a plea of "not guilty" is entered automatically. It is when the defendant pleads guilty at this point (in about 90 percent of the cases) that the judge must be careful about procedural errors which might result in an appeal. The defendant who pleads guilty must understand the nature of the charges and the consequences of a guilty plea. The judge should have some basis for accepting the plea, usually evidence from the prosecutor that indicates or establishes guilt. Although there usually is little error on this last point, probably because those who plead guilty seldom appeal, it is another legal basis for appeals.

The *trial,* so memorably dramatized on television and in the movies, appears to be the main target for the appellate procedure. It is the trial that best illustrates the impact of our adversary system[10] on the process of criminal justice. Grounds for appeal abound in the trial, from the selection of the jury to the finding of guilt or innocence. The burden of proof of guilt is on the prosecution throughout the trial. Many defense motions[11] are made only to establish grounds for later efforts at appeal. After a determination of guilt or innocence, the trial is completed. The effect of most appeals is to require that a new trial be held—not to ensure an overturned conviction for the accused.

The last step in the court process is sentencing by the court. The judge usually prescribes the sentence, but the procedure can be done by a jury in some jurisdictions. In the case of a guilty plea, the sentencing usually follows the completion of a pretrial or presentencing investigation of the defendant, who has become the convicted offender. The sentencing process has not generated many appeal actions, probably because sentences are usually determined by specific statutes rather than

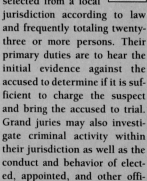

Members of the Texas Supreme Court listen to an attorney present his case before the court

—PHOTO BY MIKE BOROFF, *COURTESY OF TEXASTOCK, INC.*

by the judge's discretion. Excessive or cruel sentencing practices do come under appeal, however, and the indeterminate sentence has been attacked many times.

The Mechanics of an Appeal

Now that we have seen the points at which appealable errors are most likely to occur, the effects of some of the major cases, and the potential of future appeals, it is important to know how one makes an appeal following a criminal conviction. The process is highly fragmented and cumbersome, but a basic scheme applies to most jurisdictions. Although there are many alternatives to this basic model, it covers most of the avenues for appeals.

The entire process stems, of course, from a conviction of guilt by some court system at the municipal, county, state, or federal level. In each case, the procedure for appeal is determined by the court of record for that case. Those appeals, known as postconviction remedies, were not generally available until after the seventeenth century. They are usually made by the defendant. The state is unlikely to appeal a decision, regardless of the outcome: If the accused is convicted, that is the result the state was after, and if the accused is declared innocent, the state cannot appeal—the Constitution guarantees that someone who is found innocent cannot be placed in **double jeopardy** (subjected to a second trial, by the same jurisdiction, on the same facts). The effect of an appropriately introduced appeal is a stay in the execution of the original sentence until the appeal is decided. As soon as possible, if not immediately after the sentence is pronounced, the defendant's counsel must either move for a new trial or make an appeal on some reasonable grounds, as appellate courts usually make short work of "frivolous" appeals. But as long ago as 1933, the significance of the appeal process was firmly established:

> Appellate courts do not *reverse* [emphasis added] decisions simply because they disagree with them. Reversal must proceed from error of law and such error must be substantial. But if this account is to be veracious I must call attention to a fact familiar to every experienced lawyer, yet not apparent in the classical literature of the law, and probably not consciously admitted even to themselves by most appellate judges. Practically every decision of a lower court can be reversed. By that I mean practically every record contains some erroneous rulings [and] they can nearly always find some error if they want grounds for reversal.[12]

JAILHOUSE LAWYERS

Inmates claiming to have some legal knowledge, who counsel and assist other inmates in the preparation of legal documents such as habeas corpus, pleadings, and appeals to higher courts.

Each state has an appellate tribunal that serves as the **court of last resort**. The titles vary (as shown by Figure 8-3), but no matter what the title, a pathway for appeal is open to all in the American judicial system.

THE COURTS OF APPEAL

Table 8-1 illustrates the court of appeal of each state, by level of jurisdiction. The level immediately above the trial court is usually called the **court of appeals**. In some states, and in the federal system, there is more than one level of appeal. In those cases, the highest level of appellate court is generally called the **supreme court**. The Supreme Court of the United States is the court of last resort; cases decided there are considered final. The U.S. Supreme Court will usually hear cases from the state systems only after the defendant has exhausted all state remedies and the case has been finally adjudicated.[13]

In most state systems, the court of appeals reviews the trial court's decisions for judicial error. The facts in the case are not in question, and the trial court's decisions on that aspect of the case are binding on the appellate court. Because of that aspect of appellate review, evidence on the facts of the case is not presented to the

FIGURE 8.3

Parallels between State Court Systems and the Federal Court System

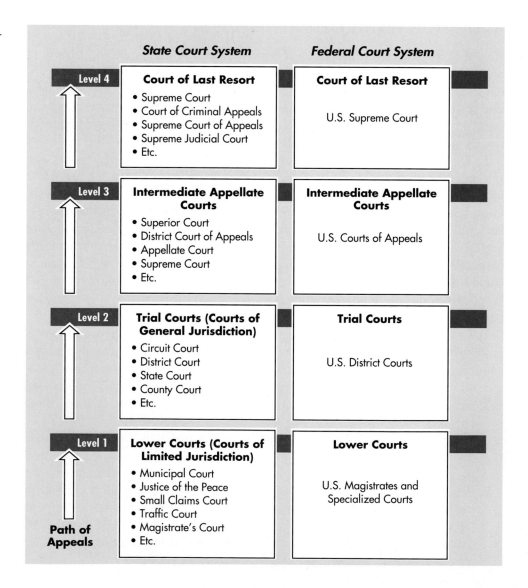

TABLE *8.1*

Courts of Appeal by Level of Jurisdiction and Organization, by State

State	Courts of Last Resort	Courts of Intermediate Appeals
Alabama	Supreme court	Court of civil appeals
		Court of criminal appeals
Alaska	Supreme court	Court of civil appeals
Arizona	Supreme court	Court of criminal appeals
Arkansas	Supreme court	None
California	Supreme court	Court of appeals (2 departments)
Colorado	Supreme court	Court of appeals
Connecticut	Supreme court	None
Delaware	Supreme court	None
District of Columbia	Court of appeals	None
Florida	Supreme court	Court of appeals (4 districts)
Georgia	Supreme court	Court of appeals
Hawaii	Supreme court	None
Idaho	Supreme court	Court of appeals
Illinois	Supreme court	Appellate court (5 districts)
Indiana	Supreme court	Court of appeals
Iowa	Supreme court	None
Kansas	Supreme court	None
Kentucky	Court of appeals	None
Louisiana	Supreme court	Court of appeals
Maine	Supreme judicial court	None
Maryland	Court of appeals	Court of special appeals
Massachusetts	Supreme judicial court	None
Michigan	Supreme court	Court of appeals
Minnesota	Supreme court	None
Mississippi	Supreme court	None
Missouri	Supreme court	Court of appeals (3 districts)
Montana	Supreme court	None
Nebraska	Supreme court	None
Nevada	Supreme court	None
New Hampshire	Supreme court	None
New Jersey	Supreme court	Appellate division of superior court
New Mexico	Supreme court	Court of appeals
New York	Court of appeals	Appellate division of supreme court (4 departments)
North Carolina	Supreme court	Court of appeals
North Dakota	Supreme court	None
Ohio	Supreme court	Court of appeals
Oklahoma	Supreme court	
	Court of criminal appeals (3 districts)	Court of appeals
Oregon	Supreme court	Court of appeals
Pennsylvania	Supreme court	Superior court
Rhode Island	Supreme court	None
South Carolina	Supreme court	None
South Dakota	Supreme court	None
Tennessee	Supreme court	Court of appeals
		Court of criminal appeals
Texas	Supreme court	Court of civil appeals (14 districts)
	Court of criminal appeals	
Utah	Supreme court	None
Vermont	Supreme court	None
Virginia	Supreme court of appeals	None
Washington	Supreme court	Court of appeals
West Virginia	Supreme court of appeals	None
Wisconsin	Supreme court	None
Wyoming	Supreme court	None

SOURCE: *National Survey of Court Organization* (Washington, D.C.: U.S. Department of Justice, 1971), p. 4.

court of appeals; rather, the review is based on the trial record. An appellate court cannot reverse the factual findings of the trial court unless they are totally erroneous. In states that have a second level of review, the trial record and the intermediary court's decision are examined. Usually, the refusal to hear an appeal over a lower appellate court's ruling is the same as upholding the decision, and the case stops there, unless an appeal is filed separately in a federal court of appeals on some constitutional issue.

The federal court system currently includes ninety-four trial courts (federal district courts) and thirteen intermediary review courts (courts of appeal) between the state trial courts and the U.S. Supreme Court. The federal courts of appeals are spread across the country in "circuits" to facilitate servicing the ninety-four trial courts. Federal courts are restricted in their powers to, "cases arising under the Constitution, federal laws, or treaties, all cases affecting ambassadors, public ministers, and consuls, admiralty and maritime cases, controversies where the United States is a party, controversies between states, between a state and a citizen of another state, between citizens of the same state claiming lands under grants from different states, and in cases between a state or citizens of a state and foreign states, citizens, or subjects."[14]

The federal courts of appeals are similar to the state courts of appeals in that they review for error the cases tried by the federal district courts:

> The Supreme Court is the ultimate interpreter of the Constitution and federal statutes. It reviews the decisions of the courts of appeals and some direct appeals from district courts. The Supreme Court also reviews the decisions of state courts involving matters of federal constitutional rights where the case has been finally adjudicated in the state court system. Besides its appellate function, the Court has original jurisdiction in suits where a state is a party and in controversies involving ambassadors, ministers, and consuls.[15]

Appeals from Behind the Walls

In the early twentieth century, most appeals were based on the issues in the trial. In the 1960s, appeals began to move toward issues related to individual rights under the U.S. Constitution.[16] Using the Fourteenth Amendment as a lever, the Supreme Court affirmed those rights to individuals in the separate states on a piecemeal basis. Under the "hands-off" doctrine established by Chief Justice Felix Frankfurter, the Court had restricted its early decisions to the actions of judges. Later, abandoning the Frankfurter policy, the Court began to impose procedural guidelines on law enforcement, corrections, and every other element of the criminal justice system. Constitutional rights of prisoners (discussed in Part IV) were more sharply defined by the appellate courts' decisions. Many of these appeals came from desperate people behind prison walls,[17] and those appeals continued to increase (civil rights appeals increased *389 percent* between 1977 and 1994, for example).[18]

Reform by Judicial Decree

Corrections, as a social system, is above all a political unit established by an authorizing mandate, supported by tax revenues, and subject to political influences. It reflects both the system of justice and the overall sociocultural environment. The

Selected Amendments to the U.S. Constitution

FOURTH AMENDMENT

The right of the people to be secure in their persons, houses, papers, and effects, against unreasonable searches and seizures, shall not be violated, and no warrants shall issue, but upon probable cause, supported by oath or affirmation, and particularly describing the place to be searched, and the person or things to be seized.

FIFTH AMENDMENT

No person shall be held to answer for a capital, or otherwise infamous crime, unless a presentment or indictment of a Grand Jury, except in cases arising in the land or naval forces, or the Militia, when in actual service in time of War or public danger; nor shall any person be subject for the same offense to twice be put in jeopardy of life or limb; nor shall be compelled in any criminal case to be a witness against himself, nor be deprived of life, liberty, or property, without due process of law; nor shall private property be taken for public use, without just compensation.

SIXTH AMENDMENT

In all criminal prosecutions, the accused shall enjoy the right to a speedy and public trial, by an impartial jury of the state or district wherein the crime shall have been committed, which district shall have been previously ascertained by law, and to be informed of the nature and cause of the accusation; to be confronted with the witnesses against him, to have compulsory process for obtaining witnesses in his favor, and to have the Assistance of Counsel for his defense.

EIGHTH AMENDMENT

Excessive bail shall not be required, nor excessive fines imposed, nor cruel and unusual punishment inflicted. ∎

---

latter is the source of externally induced reform. In externally induced reform, changes are effected by individuals or groups outside the correctional system.[19]

At the state and local levels, correctional reform is usually accomplished through legislative or executive action. Examples of reform by legislation range from the complete revision of a state's criminal code to passage of simple amendments to bills, allowing such benefits as educational and home furloughs. The executive branch of government can also exert a direct effect on correctional reform through executive orders. Those orders can accomplish small but important changes, such as the abolition of mail censorship,[20] the appointment of a task force of involved citizens to seek correctional reform,[21] and the withholding of support for clearly unsound correctional programs.[22]

Between 1960 and 1972, American criminal law passed from a state of *evolution* to a state of *revolution*.[23] The step-by-step extension to the states of the various federal constitutional guarantees of individual rights was clearly the goal of the courts' quiet but effective revolution. The decisions of the much maligned—or revered—Warren Court are more readily understood when viewed from that perspective. During the 1960s, nearly all of the guarantees of the Fourth, Fifth, Sixth, and Eighth Amendments to the Constitution were made binding on the states, although the Rehnquist Court attempted to undo some of these advances.

As previously mentioned, the Fourteenth Amendment (due process clause) provided the primary leverage in the landmark decisions that impacted corrections. The extension of constitutional guarantees to all persons accused in state proceedings has produced dramatic and significant changes in criminal law and

THE COURT-APPOINTED MASTER

A "court master" is a person knowledgeable in correctional administration and operations who has been appointed by the court to assist in the specific issues which arise in the case of a specific institution or system of institutions. The precise duties and powers depend on the terms of the court decree or settlement and include taking testimony, discovery of evidence, and monitoring implementation of the court-ordered changes. The "master" is required to submit a "Report of Proceedings" for the court, and such reports may include suggestions for additional charges for the court to consider and order to be addressed. Correctional administrators are generally leery of court masters, whose salaries and expenses they are frequently required to pay.

criminal procedures and important effects on corrections through appeals related to major landmark decisions.

It should be pointed out that in addition to these cases, from the 1960s and 1970s the Supreme Court also entertained cases concerning the civil rights of inmates, using the Civil Rights Act of 1871. As we approach the twenty-first century, many prisons in most states are under court orders or are facing constitutional challenges under Chapter 42, U.S. Code Section 1983.[24] Many states are being sued, and federal masters have been appointed to oversee the conditions in state prisons. The national situation as of June 30, 1994 can be found in Table 8-2.

Two major results of inmate litigation were the development of new mind-sets by correctional administrators, and nationwide standards were developed to demonstrate to the courts that the level of practice in the institutions being sued were the best the industry could provide.[25] Although litigation is always a trying situation, it may well be the best way to affect change in correctional settings. The threat of federal court suits has brought about significant changes in practices, policies, and procedures.

Court Orders and Court Decrees

Inmates in state and federal prisons have increasingly petitioned the Court for relief under a variety of statutes. All functions and services of the correctional institutions have been examined. These include use of force, indifference to medical needs, cruel and unusual punishment, food services, overcrowding, religious issues, lack of psychological services, right to treatment, and conditions of confinement, to mention only a few. It seems that there are few things done in prisons that inmates will not take action against. In mid-1994, the entire prison systems of fifteen states, and another seventeen individual prisons, were court ordered or had court-ordered consent decrees to make changes. A total of sixty institutions were involved, and seventeen court-appointed masters were assigned to oversee the court orders. In the Juvenile Justice systems, at the same time frame, the entire juvenile corrections systems of fifteen states were under court orders, generally to improve conditions of confinement, reduce overcrowding, and improve services (especially medical services). Institutions in the Juvenile Justice systems of nine states were under court order, typically to improve conditions and programs. Another sixteen states had at least one institution under court order.

In summary, you can see how external pressure from the courts, especially the U.S. Supreme Court, has modified and clarified the criminal law and offered basic constitutional guarantees to all persons, including those incarcerated in state and federal prisons. Such pressures can be expected to continue, marching under the banner of the Fourteenth Amendment, until all other federal constitutional protection provisions are also imposed on the states.[26]

This effort to return the control over prison conditions to the courts has resulted in well over four thousand court decisions in the past two decades. The return of the power of the courts over correctional administration is a hopeful sign for the modern era. The erosion of that power, which had its gradual beginning in 1970, and the subsequent assumption of power by the executive branch have been at the core of many of the problems we noted at the beginning of the chapter.[27]

External pressure is also brought to bear by private organizations and some groups composed of former prisoners. The John Howard Association,[28] the

TABLE *8.2*

Departments and Institutions Under Court Order/Consent Decree (as of June 30, 1994)

State	Adult					Juvenile				
	Entire Dept. Under Order	Master or Monitor Assigned	One or More Inst. Under Order to Imprv Cond	Master or Monitor Assigned	Number of Institutions	Entire Dept. Under Order	Master or Monitor Assigned	One or More Inst. Under Order to Imprv Cond	Master or Monitor Assigned	Number of Institutions
AL	No		No				Yes	No		
AK	Yes	Yes	Yes	No	13	No				
AZ	Yes	Yes	Yes	Yes	1		Yes	No		
CA	No		Yes	Yes	3	Yes	Yes	No		
CO	No		Yes	No	8	No		No		
CT	Yes		Yes	Yes	4	Yes	Yes	No		
DE	No		Yes	No	2	No		No		
FL	No		No			Yes	No	Yes	No	2
GA	Yes	No	Yes	No	6	No		No		
HI	No		Yes	Yes	2	No		No		
IL	No		Yes	Yes	1					
IN	No		Yes	No	8					
IA	No		Yes	Yes	1	No				
KS	Yes	No	Yes	No	2	No		No		
KY	Yes	No	Yes	No	2	No		No		
LA	No		Yes	Yes	6					
MD	No		Yes	No	4	No		No		
MI	No		Yes	Yes	7	No		No		
MS	Yes	No	No			No		No		
MO	Yes	No	Yes	No	9	No		No		
NV	Yes	Yes	Yes	Yes	1	No		No		
NH	Yes	No	Yes	No	1	Yes	No	No		
NM	No		Yes	Yes	5	No		No		
NY	No		Yes	Yes	2	No		Yes	Yes	1
NC	No		Yes	No	65	No		No		
OH	Yes	No	Yes	No	4	No		No		
OK	No		No			Yes	Yes	Yes	Yes	5
PA	Yes	No	Yes	Yes	1	Yes	Yes	Yes	Yes	1
RI	Yes	No	Yes	No	All	Yes	Yes	No		
SC	Yes	No	No			No		No		
TN	No		No			No		Yes	No	4
UT	No		Yes	Yes	All	No		No		
VA	Yes	No	No			No		No		
WA	No		No			No		Yes	No	2
WV	No		Yes	Yes	1					
WI	No		Yes	No		No		No		
FPB	No		Yes	No	1					

SOURCE: American Correctional Association, *Directory of Juvenile and Adult Correctional Agencies and Paroling Authorities* (Lanham, MD: American Correctional Association, 1996), p. xx.

American Correctional Association,[29] and the National Council on Crime and Delinquency[30] seek reform through prison certification visits and suggestions to correctional administrators. These efforts help keep the major problem areas in corrections before the public's view. Organizations of ex-offenders who work with prisoners, such as the Seventh Step Foundation,[31] Man-to-Man,[32] and the Fortune Society,[33] also seek correctional reform.

Appeals Flood the Courts

A flood of appeals made with the help of court-appointed lawyers and jailhouse lawyers filled the dockets of the appeals courts, beginning in the 1960s and accelerating through the mid-1990s. As rights were established in the obvious areas outside prison walls (arrest, search, and seizure; privacy and intrusion; cruel and unusual punishment), they were eventually tested with regard to events inside the walls as well. The autonomous and discretionary control over inmates was finally lifted, as the right to counsel moved into the prison as well as the courtroom. A milestone case was decided in the 1967–1968 Supreme Court term, when *Mempa* v. *Rhay*[34] extended the right to counsel to state probation revocation hearings, previously considered an essentially administrative action. The Court held that the application of a deferred sentence was a "critical point" in the proceeding.

The right to counsel for defendants both inside and outside the walls of America's prisons has strained the entire criminal justice system. As more and more aspects of the criminal justice system are challenged, often by court-appointed lawyers, the real problem becomes the need for a routine way to solve correctional problems, not reduce the flow of frivolous cases into the system.

The criminal courts have been forced to become almost administrative in nature because of the overload of cases. Because as many as 90 percent of convictions

Prison inmate in law library

through jury or bench trials are appealed, the review courts are equally inundated. The National Advisory Commission on Criminal Justice Standards and Goals expended much effort in trying to find ways to reduce the court caseload. The first recommendations that were made included a number of alternatives.

SCREENING

One of the methods suggested was to place more stress on **screening,** as the guidelines for screening offenders vary greatly from jurisdiction to jurisdiction. To help in drawing up criteria for screening suspected offenders out of the process, the following suggestions were made by the commission:

> An accused should be screened out of the criminal justice system if there is no reasonable likelihood that the evidence admissible against him would be sufficient to obtain a conviction and sustain it on appeal. In screening on this basis, the prosecutor should consider the value of a conviction in reducing future offenses, as well as the probability of conviction and affirmation of that conviction on appeal.
>
> An accused should be screened out of the criminal justice system when the benefits to be derived from prosecution or diversion would be outweighed by the costs of such action.[35]

Tightening the correctional filter at this point would result in a great workload reduction throughout the rest of the criminal justice system.

Many of the lawsuits filed by inmates that allege violations of constitutional and civil rights have merit, and much has been done to improve the quality of life in prison settings.[36] Yet there are undoubtedly many, perhaps a large proportion, of suits that are spurious and frivolous litigations. The American Correctional Association has suggested that such suits can be discouraged by the following actions:

1. Having the incarcerated complainant pay fees to the court when cases are filed and resolved.
2. Limiting the number of lawsuits an inmate may file annually.
3. Requiring the complainant to certify that the claims being raised have not been adjudicated before.
4. Having the judiciary require that court permission be secured before filing additional claims.[37]

DIVERSION

Another effort in the drive to reduce the number of cases brought to trial is the **diversion** of offenders before conviction. Diversion is quite different from screening because it assumes the individual will participate in some treatment program in return for removal from the criminal justice process before trial. In screening, the individual is dropped out of the process before it really begins, with no threat of continued prosecution or promise of special programs for his or her cooperation. Diversion programs may be run by agencies within the criminal justice system or by private and public agencies entirely outside it. The primary benefit from both screening and diversion programs is their ability to offer services to offenders without placing the stigma of further criminalization on them. Overcriminalization, usually a result of too many antiquated laws remaining on the books, is one of the reasons so many cases sit on dockets. The National Advisory Commission suggested guidelines for when diversion should take place:

> In appropriate cases, offenders should be diverted into noncriminal programs before formal trial or conviction.
>
> Such diversion is appropriate where there is a substantial likelihood that conviction could be obtained and the benefits to society from channeling an offender into an available noncriminal diversion program outweigh any harm done to society by abandoning criminal prosecution.[38]

Diversion programs are another recognition of the situational nature of many crimes. By expanding the base of available services and keeping the offender out of the damaging stages of the criminal justice process, society gives the offender a much better chance to adjust in the community. The "drug court" movement is a recent example of a promising diversion program.[39]

RESTRICTIONS VERSUS INNOVATIONS

Until about 1988, the federal courts were able to keep their dockets (workload) reasonably current, despite the increased volume of cases. However, the expanded war on drugs to reduce trafficking and sales of illegal substances has led to a wave of cases and resultant backlogs. Collateral and postconviction appeals have not abated to accommodate this vastly increased workload for the courts.

Proposed solutions to overcrowding in the courts range from the conservative effort to limit access to appellate and federal district courts,[40] to more constructive recommendations from the U.S. Federal Courts Study Committee.[41] The latter's suggestions include filing drug cases in state rather than federal courts to help cope with the surge in volume of drug-related cases. Other suggestions recommend the repeal of mandatory minimum sentence provisions of the federal statutes and reassessing federal sentencing guidelines, which some believe reduce the effective court processing of cases.

Some state appellate courts have responded to caseload growth in a variety of ways that Congress and the federal courts might well copy. Those coping strategies include adding judgeships, creating new or expanding existing appellate courts, deciding cases without published opinions or writing memo opinions, temporarily assigning judges from the retired ranks or from lower courts, and reducing panel sizes. Expediting hearings, limiting oral arguments, and setting time limits on arguments and briefs are other mechanisms that could be utilized.[42] The reduction of protections of cherished constitutional rights in the name of expediency to meet a crisis or facilitate vague political goals in the name of a war on drugs (regardless of the nobility of the espoused goals) poses some serious and unacceptable threats to every citizen, convicted criminal or not.

The Battle for Rights Continues

As we have shown, the appellate system has brought rights and reform to the criminal justice system as a whole and to the sector known as corrections in particular.[43] If the stone walls that surround our American fortress prisons cannot be torn down, then at least the basic rights available to those outside must be brought in. This process has only begun, the courts are whittling down the dictatorial powers formerly held by prison administrators. The entire department, of at least one or more institutions, is under a court order in thirty-four states in regard to adult offenders.[44]

The basic rights granted to citizens under most of the constitutional amendments have been extended to the inmates in our prisons. In the years to come, the peripheral issues will be examined. Two of the most controversial issues continue to be the right to treatment and its corollary—the right to refuse treatment. Those issues stem from the widespread use of the treatment model in most of our adult correctional systems. Lack of prison industries and enforced idleness have encouraged the development of treatment programs to fill time.[45] The long-term value of such programs is questionable at best, and they are coming under attack.

Following an interim decision in *Wyatt* v. *Stickney*,[46] in which the U.S. District Court held that the states had to provide adequate treatment for patients involuntarily confined in mental institutions, the U.S. Supreme Court also ruled on this issue in *O'Connor* v. *Donaldson*.[47] The decision in that case leaves little question that civilly committed mentally ill persons have a right to treatment. The Court stated that every person has a constitutional right to liberty. It also concluded that

> A state cannot constitutionally confine . . . a nondangerous individual who is capable of surviving safely in freedom by himself or with the help of willing and responsible family members or friends. Since the jury found, upon ample evidence, that O'Connor, as an agent of the State, knowingly did so confine Donaldson, it properly concluded that O'Connor violated Donaldson's constitutional right to freedom.[48]

Before the Supreme Court as this book goes to press is a case about whether a state can continue to confine a violent sexual predator who is considered likely to recommit his crime, but who has served his complete sentence and does not meet the criteria for commitment as mentally ill.

Because the justification for the indefinite commitment of mentally disturbed offenders (that is, the "incompetent to stand trial," the "not guilty by reason of insanity," and, by some court interpretations, those adjudicated psychopathic offenders) is a need for treatment,[49] the right might easily be extended to this class of residents of mental health institutions.

As in the right to treatment for the mentally ill, cases supporting the right to rehabilitation have been argued on both statutory and constitutional grounds. For instance, if state statutes clearly define the purpose of confinement as rehabilitation, the major responsibility of the administering organization could easily be conceived of as providing rehabilitation opportunities. A number of states include in their criminal codes some reference to the rehabilitative goals of incarceration. Ohio, for example, even changed the name of its state department responsible for incarcerating offenders to the Department of Rehabilitation and Correction. Although those statutes state rehabilitative purposes, the enforcement of rights based on the statutes has been delayed because societal values emphasize other goals and because corrections appears to lack knowledge of proven rehabilitative methods.

Arguments for a constitutional right to treatment derived from the Eighth Amendment prohibition of cruel and unusual punishment were made applicable to state actions in 1962.[50] Since that time, federal courts have increasingly intervened in prison administration, making decisions on the right-to-treatment issue. Some decisions uphold the view that governmental entities have no constitutional duty to rehabilitate prisoners.[51] Others withhold constitutional affirmation of

The "Landmark Cases" of the 1960s and 1970s

MAPP V. OHIO. The case of *Mapp* v. *Ohio* (exclusionary rule), 367 U.S. 643 (1960), opened a Pandora's box of Fourteenth Amendment rulings. A crack in the armor of state proceedings, it paved the way for the flood of cases heard by the Court during the next decade, in reference not only to illegally obtained evidence but also to all areas of individual rights.

ROBINSON V. CALIFORNIA. In the case of *Robinson* v. *California* (cruel and unusual punishment), 370 U.S. 660 (1962), the Eighth Amendment's clause forbidding cruel and unusual punishment was made binding on state proceedings.

GIDEON V. WAINWRIGHT. In the crucial decision of *Gideon* v. *Wainwright* (right to counsel), 372 U.S. 335 (1963), the Court held that defendants in noncapital cases are entitled to assistance of counsel at trial as a matter of right. This right was extended to state proceedings, again under the provisions of the Fourteenth Amendment. This story was written about in the book *"Gideon's Trumpet,"* which showed how even a poor, uneducated man could appeal to the Supreme Court of the United States with a yellow legal pad written in pencil.

MIRANDA V. ARIZONA. The application of the Fifth Amendment protections against self-incrimination was influenced by *Gideon* v. *Wainwright*, 392 U.S. 335 (1963). For the first time, in the 1966 decision of *Miranda* v. *Arizona*, 384 U.S. 436, a set of specific and detailed police warnings to the arrested person (and now the prison inmate) were required, through the due process clause, at specific and distinct points in the criminal process.

JOHNSON V. AVERY. A significant 1969 decision provided prisoners in state penal institutions with legal assistance in preparing habeas corpus proceedings. In *Johnson* v. *Avery*, 393 U.S. 483, the Court held that states not providing adequate legal assistance would have to put up with "jailhouse lawyers," prisoners determined to research and conduct their own and others' appeals.

FURMAN V. GEORGIA. In *Furman* v. *Georgia*, 408 U.S. 238 (1972), the issue of cruel and unusual punishment as applied to the death penalty was raised in a petition by several states for clarification of that long-standing dilemma. In June 1972, the U.S. Supreme Court held that any statute which permits a jury to demand the death penalty is unconstitutional. ∎

the right to rehabilitation but conclude that the absence of rehabilitation programs, in conjunction with other prison conditions, may result in the setting of a specific prison being defined as cruel and unusual punishment.

The courts have yet to define specifically a right to rehabilitation, but many feel the constitutional identification is inevitable, if not imminent. The right to treatment for the mentally ill has progressed slowly through the courts.[52] The impediment of defensive and punitive public opinion has delayed implementation of the humanitarian philosophy of a right to treatment for prisoners, but that right should not be ignored. The indications are numerous and strong that the time for such recognition is near and that collateral consequences will be substantial. Practitioners in the field of corrections thus would do well to anticipate and prepare for the likely effects of this new emphasis.

Obviously, the resolution of this problem could decide whether the future of corrections lies in real correction efforts or a return to old-fashioned imprisonment. Unless some highly effective treatments for criminal behavior are found, backed by solid evaluation, the treatment programs are in serious trouble.

Appeals will continue until inmates behind prison walls are granted the same constitutionally guaranteed protections accorded to their counterparts in the free world, except those obviously denied by incarceration such as the

The Justices' Caseload versus Constitutional Rights

The Court's caseload has increased steadily to a current total of over 7,700 cases on the docket per term. In 1945, there were only 1,460 cases. Plenary review, with oral arguments by attorneys, is granted to less than 120–150 cases per term. Formal written opinions were delivered in only 93 cases in 1993. Approximately 70 additional cases were disposed of without granting plenary review. The publication of a term's written opinions, including concurring opinions, dissenting opinions and orders, approaches 7,000 pages. Some opinions are revised a dozen or more times before they are announced.

In 1996, the U.S. Congress passed the Antiterrorism and Effective Death Penalty Act, a controversial part of which was tougher limits on death penalty appeals. In essence, the Congress tried to limit state prisoners to one appeal in a federal court, seeking speedier resolution to capital punishment cases. Some had labeled the ability of prisoners to file successive habeas corpus petitions as frivolous attempts to delay executions. The U.S. Supreme Court unanimously decided that Congress could not block death row prisoners' efforts to reach that Court, even if the inmates on death row had to file habeas corpus petitions directly with the U.S. Supreme Court. ∎

SOURCE: Dan Freedman, "Death Row Appeals Restricted," *The San Francisco Examiner,* June 28, 1996, p. A-8.

right to privacy, to choose one's associates, and freedom of movement.[53] Whenever appeals do fail, however, convicted and sentenced offenders must pay a debt to society in the correctional process—the subject we take up in Part III.

The Aging Court

The last decade saw major changes in the makeup of the Supreme Court, and even more change is under way as we move into the next century. The average age of the Supreme Court members, including the relatively junior members, was sixty-four

Current Supreme Court Justices

—PHOTO BY RICHARD STRAUSS/ SMITHSONIAN INSTITUTION, COURTESY OF THE SUPREME COURT HISTORICAL SOCIETY

and a half after retirements of Justices Brennan and Marshall. The appointment of President Clinton's first member of the Court was confirmed easily. Judge Ruth Bader Ginsberg became the second female member of the Supreme Court and also considerably lowered the average age of the justices. It seems clear that Justice Blackmun (eighty-five) and Stevens (seventy-three) may leave the Court during the next few years. If relatively young jurists are nominated and appointed by President Clinton, the year 2000 could see a Supreme Court with an average age of near sixty, a Court that could influence our laws well into the early years of the twenty-first century.

Summary

As the decade of the 1990s closes and the twenty-first century looms directly ahead, the aging of the U.S. Supreme Court can figure directly into the future of corrections in America. The conservative trend has abated somewhat and will continue to be more so in the Clinton presidency. Of course, the sweeping decisions of the 1950s and 1960s will not be reversed in a wholesale manner, but there seems to be a hardening of conservative attitudes in America, and the pendulum of political opinion may be slow in moving away from the right. Many changes that the Clinton-appointed Court decides upon will have a direct effect on the corrections field, and they are a matter for close scrutiny by both students and serious professionals with a fairly viable understanding of how the appeal system works and the changes on the horizon as we enter the twenty-first century. The next part will let us look into the correctional processes and institutions that provide the basic structure for the correctional system.

Review Questions

1. Explain the difference between a court of appeals and a supreme court.
2. Who was Clarence Gideon? Explain the actions he took to make his appeal.
3. Why is there such a logjam in the appellate system? What are some suggestions for easing the pressure?
4. What rights does an inmate have? What rights does an inmate not have?
5. Explain why the rights of inmates began to be extensively defined in the 1960s.
6. What are appeals, and what options are available to appeal courts when a decision is made?
7. What might be done to cut down on frivolous appeals?
8. How can appeal courts manage caseloads more efficiently?

Words to Remember

due process	indictment	affirmation
Gideon v. *Wainwright*	grand jury	screening
initial appearance	double jeopardy	diversion
recognizance	reverse	
preliminary hearing	court of last resort	

# Endnotes

1. For an excellent discussion of the amount of process due offenders, see John Conrad, "The Rights of Wrongdoers," *Criminal Justice Research Bulletin* 3 (1987): 18-24 and Editors, "Supreme Court Review," *Journal of Criminal Law and Criminology* 83:4 (1993): 693–717.

2. Because plea bargaining reduces the offender's ability to appeal, it is not surprising that most appeals arise from trials. Trials typically involve crimes against the person and sentences of five years or less. Defendants are not particularly successful; offenders win about 20 percent of the time and have their convictions overturned in only about 10 percent of their appeals. See National Center for State Courts, *Understanding Reversible Error in Criminal Appeals: Final Report* (Williamsburg, VA: National Center for State Courts, 1989); David Neubauer, "Research Note: A Polychotomous Measure of Appellate Court Outcomes: The Case of Criminal Appeals," *Justice System Journal* 16:1 (1992): 75–87. See also Jimmy Williams, "Role of Appellants, Sentencing Guidelines, Decision Making in Criminal Appeals," *Journal of Criminal Justice* 23:1 (1995): 83–91.

3. National Advisory Commission on Criminal Justice Standards and Goals, *Courts* (Washington, D.C.: U.S. Government Printing Office, 1973), p. 113. For an excellent review of legal trends and issues in corrections, see Rolando del Carmen, "Legal Issues and Liabilities in Community Corrections," paper presented at the annual meeting of the Academy of Criminal Justice Sciences, Chicago, 1984. See also William C. Collins, *Correctional Law 1986* (Olympia, WA: Collins, 1986); Henry Campbell Black, *Black's Law Dictionary* (St. Paul, MN: West, 1991), p. 179; and Lloyd Weinreb, *Leading Constitutional Cases in Criminal Justice* (Westbury, NY: Foundation Press, 1993).

4. Although the number of criminal trials in the United States increased relatively little from 1983 to 1994, the number of appeals increased 53 percent. See also Daniel Gillis, *The Federal Civil Justice System* (Washington, D.C.: U.S. Department of Justice, 1987); Michael Tolley, "The Impact of Reform on Substance: Court Reform and the Work of the Maryland Court of Appeals," *Justice System Journal* 15:3 (1992): 765–781; and Kathleen Maguire and Ann Pastore, eds., *Sourcebook of Criminal Justice Statistics* (Washington, D.C.: U.S. Department of Justice, 1995), p. 499.

5. National Advisory Commission, *Courts,* p. 113.

6. One study found that appeals based on *Miranda* issues were successful only 0.5 percent of the time. See Karen Guy and Robert Huckabee, "Going Free on a Technicality: Another Look at the Effect of the *Miranda* Decision on the Criminal Justice Process," *Criminal Justice Research Bulletin* 4 (1988): 1–3. In 1989 the U.S. Supreme Court watered down the *Miranda* warnings from a "clear and unequivocal" offer of appointed counsel to a revised warning that "reasonably conveys" the suspect's rights. See David Altman, "Coercion and Clarity: The Supreme Court Approves Altered *Miranda* Warnings," *Journal of Criminal Law and Criminology* 80 (1990): 1086–1111. The referenced case is *Duckworth* v. *Eagen,* 109 S. Ct. 2875 (1989). See also Rudolph Alexander, "The *Mapp, Escobedo,* and *Miranda* Decisions: Do They Serve a Liberal or Conservative Agenda?" *Criminal Justice Policy Review* 4:1 (1990): 39–52.

7. This is what is generally called the right to habeas corpus. See James Basta, "Habeas Corpus: Unresolved Standard of Review on Mixed Questions for State Prisoners," *Journal of Criminal Law and Criminology* 83:4 (1993): 978–997. On the issue of speedy trial, see Steven Wernikoff, "Sixth Amendment: Extending Sixth Amendment Speedy Trial Protection to Defendants Unaware of Their Indictments," *Journal of Criminal Law and Criminology* 83:4) (1993): 804–835. The case is *Doggett* v. *United States,* 112 S. Ct. 2866 (1992). See also Thomas Schneider and Robert Dars, "Speedy Trial in Homicide Court," *Criminal Justice* 9:4 (1995): pp. 24–29.

8. See Chris Eskridge, *Pretrial Release Programming* (New York: Clark Boardman, 1983), pp. 33–59; Keith Cooprider, "Pretrial Bond Supervision: An Empirical Analysis with Policy Implications," *Federal Probation* 56:3 (1992): 41–49; and Brian Reeves and Jacob Perez, *Pretrial Release of Felony Defendants, 1992* (Washington, D.C.: U.S. Department of Justice, 1994).

9. This is a classic example of plea bargaining (see Chapter 7). See also Terance Miethe, "Charging and Plea Bargaining Practices Under Determinate Sentencing: An Investigation of the Hydraulic Effect of Discretion," *Journal of Criminal Law and Criminology* 78 (1987): 155–176, and James Nelson, *The Impact of Restrictions on Pre- and Post-Indictment Plea Bargaining in Bronx County* (Albany: New York State Division of Criminal Justice, 1994).

10. The adversary system refers to the battle between the prosecution and defense attorneys during a trial when each cross-examines and attacks the witnesses and facts presented by the other. See Gary Goodpaster, "On the Theory of American Adversary Criminal Trial," *Journal of Criminal Law and Criminology* 78 (1987): 118–154. See also Stephen Schulhofer, "The Future of the Adversary System," *Justice Quarterly* 3 (1986): 83–93. Opinions critical of the adversarial model can be found in Gordon Van Kessel, "Adversary Excesses in the American Criminal Trial," *Notre Dame Law Review* 67:3 (1992): 403–552.

11. Such motions usually concern the admissibility of evidence and are aimed to suppress the presentation of evidence that might hurt the defense attorney's case. See David Doyle, "Fourteenth Amendment: Admitting Evidence of Battered Child Syndrome to Prove Intent," *Journal of Criminal Law and Criminology* 83:4 (1993): 894–919, and Beth Dwerman, "The Supreme Court's Prohibition of Gender-based Peremtory Challenges," *Journal of Criminal Law and Criminology* 85:4 (1995): 1028–1061.

12. Joseph N. Ulman, *The Judge Takes the Stand* (New York: Alfred A. Knopf, 1933), pp. 265–266.

13. The increasingly conservative U.S. Supreme Court continues to restrict access to habeas corpus relief for state prisoners, both on collateral and postconviction appeals. See Richard Powers, "State Prisoners' Access to Federal Habeas Corpus: Restrictions Increase," *Criminal Law Bulletin* 24 (1989): 444–453, and Donald Zeithaml, "Constitutional Right to State Capital Collateral Appeal: The Due Process of Executing a Convict Without Attorney Representation," *Journal of Criminal Law and Criminology* 80 (1990): 1190–1210. See the case of *Murray v. Giarrantano,* 109 S. Ct. 2765 (1989), and Christopher Smith, "Judicial Policy Making and Habeas Corpus Reform," *Criminal Justice Policy Review* 7:1 (1995): 91–114.

14. U.S. Constitution, Article III, Section 2. See also Jonathan Lonner, "Official Government Abductions in the Presence of Extradition Treaties," *Journal of Criminal Law and Criminology* 83:4 (1993): 998–1023.

15. John Palmer, *Constitutional Rights for Prisoners* (Cincinnati: Anderson, 1973), p. 10.

16. Thomas Marvel and Sue Lindgren, *The Growth of Appeals* (Washington, D.C.: U.S. Department of Justice, 1985), p. 2.

17. Prison jailhouse lawyers can resist controls and conditions placed on them by correctional institutions by assisting in filing lawsuits and have been described as "primitive rebels." See Dragan Milovanovic and Jim Thomas, "Overcoming the Absurd: Prisoner Litigation as Primitive Rebellion," *Social Problems* 36 (1989): 48–60, and Hawkeye Gross, *Tales from the Joint* (Boulder, CO: Palladin Press, 1995).

18. Ibid., p. 3. See also Samuel Jan Braken, "Prison Reform Litigation: Has the Revolution Gone Too Far?" *Corrections Today* 49 (1987): 160–168. Increases in litigation are symptoms of inherent problems in institutions; curtailing litigation will not solve those problems. See Jim Thomas, "The `Reality' of Prisoner Litigation: Repackaging the Data," *New England Journal of Criminal and Civil Confinement* 15 (1989): 27–54. See also Tolley, "The Impact of Reform on Substance," and Michael Vaughn and Rolando del Carmen, "Civil Liability Against Prison Officials for Inmate-Inmate Assault," *The Prison Journal* 75:1 (1995): 68–69.

19. See John Conrad, "The Rights of Wrongdoers," Richard Cole and Jack Call, "When Courts Find Jail and Prison Crowding Unconstitutional," *Federal Probation* 56:1 (1991): 29–39; and Steven Donziger, *The Real War on Crime* (New York: HarperCollins, 1996).

20. J. J. Gilligan, Governor, Ohio, Administrative Orders 814, 814A, 814B, August 5, 1971.

21. For example, Ohio Citizens' Task Force on Corrections, February 1971, and Wisconsin Citizens' Study Committee on Offender Rehabilitation, May 1971. See also Barry Feld, "Violent Youth and Public Policy," *Minnesota Law Review* 79:5 (1995): 965–1168.

22. An example of such withdrawal is the abolition of prison farm programs throughout the nation. Farming has ceased to be a relevant vocational training vehicle for primarily urban offenders, and in most states the programs are too expensive to operate.

23. Editors of Criminal Law Reporter, *The Criminal Law Revolution and Its Aftermath, 1960–71* (Washington, D.C.: BNA Books, 1972).

24. Joseph Pellicciotti, "42 U.S. Code Section 1983 and Correctional Officials' Liability: A Look at the New Century," *Journal of Contemporary Criminal Justice* 3 (August 1987): 1–9, and Rudolph Alexander, "The U.S. Supreme Court and an Inmate's Right to Refuse Mental Health Treatment," *Criminal Justice Policy Review* 5:3 (1991): 225–240. For a sharp contrast, see William Ziegelmueller, "Sixth Amendment: Due Process On Drugs: The Implications of Forcibly Medicating Pretrial Detainees with Antipsychotic Drugs," *Journal of Criminal Law and Criminology* 83:4 (1993): 836–867.

25. Rod Miller, "Standards and the Courts," *Corrections Today* 54(3) (1992): 58–60, and Virginia Joint Legislative Audit and Review Commission, *Oversight of Health and Safety in Local Jails* (Richmond: Commonwealth of Virginia, 1995).

26. The high-water mark for inmate suits against conditions may have been *Bell v. Wolfish,* 441 U.S. 520 (1979), and *Rhodes v. Chapman,* 452 U.S. 337 (1981). Both cases reflect the conservatism of U.S. Supreme Court appointees made by Presidents Nixon and Reagan. See Michael Fieweger, "Consent Decrees in Prison and Jail Reform—Relaxed Standard of Review for Government Motions to Modify Consent Decrees," *Journal of Criminal Law and Criminology* 83:4 (1993): 1024–1054.

27. Howard K. Gill, based on comments before the Philadelphia Bar Association and in *William and Mary Law Review* 5 (1964): 30–45. See also Agnes Baro, "The Loss of Local Control over Prison Administration," *Justice Quarterly* 5 (1988): 457–473; Mary Kay Harris, Russ Immarigeon, Cathryn Jo Rosen, et al., "Judicial Intervention in Local Jails, Part I," *Prison Journal* 70:2 (1990): 1–85; Mary Kay Harris, Marvin Zalman, Allen Breed, et al., "Judicial Intervention in Local Jails, Part II," *Prison Journal* 71:1 (1991): 1–92; and Bradley Chilton and David Nice, "Triggering Federal and Court Intervention in State Prison Reform," *Prison Journal* 73:1 (1993): 30–45.

28. The John Howard Association, named after the famous prison reformer, seeks reform by visits and inspections to prison systems (537 S. Dearborn St., Chicago, Illinois 60605).

29. The American Correctional Association, the major professional organization of practicing penologists, was founded in 1870. It publishes the professional journal of corrections, *Corrections Today* (8025 Laurel Lakes Court, Laurel, Maryland 20707).

30. The National Council on Crime and Delinquency is a voluntary citizens' organization that operates a clearinghouse for criminal justice information and attempts to develop innovations in corrections and influence legislation (NCCD Center, 685 Market St., San Francisco, California 94105).

31. Seventh Step Foundation is an ex-offender organization formed by Bill Sands, who wrote the book *My Shadow Ran Fast.* This organization works inside and outside prisons in a manner similar to that of Alcoholics Anonymous (136 E. Maple, Independence, Missouri 64058).

32. Man-to-Man Associates, Inc., is a volunteer organization that contacts programmed release prisoners six months before their actual release and starts their adjustment. Members meet prisoners on their release day and provide help wherever needed (935 E. Broad Street, Columbus, Ohio 43215).

33. Fortune Society is an ex-offender organization with the goal of helping former inmates back into society by providing limited shelter and help in finding a job (39 W. 19th St., New York, New York 10011).

34. *Mempa v. Rhay,* 389 U.S. 128, 2d Cir. 3023 (1968). A petitioner filed a habeas corpus claiming a denial of the right to counsel at the probation revocation and sentencing proceedings. The Supreme Court of the State of Washington denied the petition. The U.S. Supreme Court reversed the previous decision, asserting the necessity that counsel be present at such a hearing. The U.S. Supreme Court, in an act reflective of conservative retrenchment, has enabled the federal government to seize assets to disable a defendant's defense. The right to retain private counsel in certain circumstances is under attack. See Melinda Hardy, "Applicability of Right to Counsel of Choice to Forfeiture of Attorney's Fees," *Journal of Criminal Law and Criminology* 80 (1990):

1154–1189, and Mitchel Miller and Lance Silva, "Drug Enforcement's Double-Edged Sword: An Assessment of Asset Forfeiture Programs," *Justice Quarterly* 11:2 (1994): 313–335.

35. National Advisory Commission, *Courts*, p. 20.

36. Steven Nay, "Constitutional Compliance: Avoiding Inmate Litigation," *Corrections Today* 49 (1987): 186–191. See also Jim Thomas, Devin Keeler, and Kathy Harris, "Issues and Misconceptions in Prisoner Litigation: A Critical View," *Criminology* 24 (1986): 775–797, and the theme issue: "Correctional Health Care," *Corrections Today* 54:7 (1992): 1–152.

37. Debra Anderson, *Curbing the Abuses of Inmate Litigation* (College Park, MD.: American Correctional Association, 1987). See also W. J. Bryan, "Jails and Courts: A Cooperative Effort," *American Jails* 6:3 (1992): 51–52.

38. National Advisory Commission, *Courts*, p. 32. See James Inciardi and Duane McBride, *Treatment Alternatives to Street Crime: History, Experiences, and Issues* (Rockville, MD: U.S. National Institute on Drug Abuse, 1991).

39. Arthur Lurigio and Gad Benziger, eds., *Drugs and Community Corrections* (Chicago: Loyola University Press, 1996), and Edward Latessa and Harry Allen, *Corrections in the Community* (Cincinnati: Anderson, 1997), p. 402.

40. Powers, "State Prisoners' Access to Federal Habeas Corpus.: Restrictions Increase," pp. 445-446.

41. Peter Brimelow, "Judicial Imperialism," *Forbes,* June 1, 1987, pp. 109–112. See also U.S. Federal Courts Study Committee, *Report of the Federal Courts Study Committee: April 2, 1990* (Philadelphia: U.S. Federal Courts Study Committee, 1990).

42. Thomas Marvell, "State Appellate Court Responses to Caseload Growth," *Judicature* 72 (1989): 282–291.

43. Sue Davis and Donald Songer, "The Changing Role of the United States Court of Appeals: The Flow of Litigation Revisited," *Justice System Journal* 13 (1989): 323–340, and Ralph Henham, "Sentencing Policy and the Role of the Court of Appeal," *Howard Journal of Criminal Justice* 34:3 (1995): 218–227.

44. American Correctional Association, *ACA Directory 1993* (Laurel Heights, MD: American Correctional Association, 1993), p. xx.

45. Under a consent decree, South Carolina has agreed to establish full-time programming for general population inmates in its twenty-eight institutions, as well as for those in protective custody. See Nay, "Institutional Compliance," p. 190.

46. *Wyatt v. Stickney,* 325 F. Supp. 781 (M.D. Ala. 1971), 344 F. Supp. 373, and 374 F. Supp. 387 (1972). See also *Wyatt v. Aderholt,* 503 F. 2d 1305 (1974).

47. *O'Connor v. Donaldson,* 43 L.W. 4929 (1975).

48. *O'Connor v. Donaldson* at 4933.

49. Issues over inadequate mental health and medical service abound, and court orders in these areas are frequent. See, in particular, *Cody v. Hillard,* 599 F. Supp. 1015 (D.S.D. 1984) and the consent decree of 1985 for *Ruiz v. Estelle,* 670 F. 2d 1115 (1982). See also Ben Crouch and James Marquart, "Resolving the Paradox of Reform: Litigation, Prisoner Violence, and Perceptions of Risk," *Justice Quarterly* 7 (1990): 103–123. In 1992, the U.S. Supreme Court held in *Foucha v. Louisiana* (112 S. Ct. 1780, 1992) that an insanity acquitee may be involuntarily detained under civil confinement only as long as both mentally ill and dangerous, but no longer. See Paul Robinson, "Foreword: The Criminal-Civil Distinction and Dangerous Blameless Offenders," *Journal of Criminal Law and Criminology* 83:4 (1993): 693–717.

50. *Robinson v. California,* 370 U.S. 660 (1962).

51. See *McLaramore v. State,* 257 S.C. 413 (1972).

52. See the special theme issues of *The Prison Journal* 69 (1989), especially Scott Darnell, "No More Victims: Alternative Treatment Methods for the Incarcerated Sex Offender," 1: 83–87, and Michael Vaughn and Allen Sapp, "Less Than Utopian: Sex Offender Treatment in a Milieu of Power Struggles, Status Positioning, and Inmate Manipulation in State Correctional Institutions," 2: 73–89.

53. *Kaimowitz v. Michigan Department of Mental Health,* 42 U.S. L.W. 2063 (Michigan Cir. Ct., 1973).

$\mathcal{R}$ecommended Readings: Part II

Austin, James, and Marci Brown. *Ranking the Nation's Most Punitive and Costly States*. San Francisco: National Council on Crime and Delinquency, 1989.

Blumstein, Alfred, Jacqueline Cohen, Jeffery Roth, and Christy Visher. *Criminal Careers and Career Criminals*. Washington, D.C.: National Academy Press, 1986.

Branham, Lynn. *The Use of Incarceration in the United States: A Look at the Present and the Future*. Washington, D.C.: Criminal Justice Section, American Bar Association, 1992.

Burnham, David. *Above the Law: Secret Deals, Political Fixes, and Other Misadventures of the U.S. Department of Justice*. New York: Scribner, 1966.

Donziger, Steven. *The Real War on Crime*. New York: HarperCollins. 1996.

Early, Barbara, and Stephen Early. *Prisoners' Rights in America*. Chicago: Nelson Hall, 1986.

Fairchild, Erika, and V. J. Webb. *The Politics of Crime and Criminal Justice*. Beverly Hills, CA: Sage, 1985.

Federal Courts Study Committee. *Report of the Federal Courts Study Committee: April 1, 1990*. Philadelphia: Federal Courts Study Committee, 1990.

Gaskins, Carla. *Felony Case Processing in State Courts, 1986*. Washington, D.C.: U.S. Bureau of Justice Statistics, 1990.

Hester, Thomas, and Carol Kaplan. *Federal Criminal Cases, 1980–1987*. Washington, D.C.: U.S. Bureau of Justice Statistics, 1989.

Langan, Patrick. *Felony Sentences in State Courts, 1990*. Washington, D.C.: U.S. Bureau of Justice Statistics, 1993.

McDonald, Douglas, Judith Greene, and Charles Worzella. *Day Fines in American Courts: The Staten Island and Milwaukee Experiments*. Washington, D.C.: U. S. National Institute of Justice, 1992.

Meierhoefer, Barbara. *The General Effect of Mandatory Minimum Prison Terms: A Longitudinal Study of Federal Sentences Imposed*. Washington, D.C.: Federal Judicial Center, 1992.

National Advisory Commission on Criminal Justice Standards and Goals. *Courts*. Washington, D.C.: U.S. Department of Justice, 1973.

National Center for State Courts. *Understanding Reversible Error in Criminal Appeals: Final Report*. Williamsburg, VA: National Center for State Courts, 1989.

National Council on Crime and Delinquency. *Criminal Justice Sentencing Policy Statement*. San Francisco: National Council on Crime and Delinquency, 1992.

Packer, Herbert L. *The Limits of the Criminal Sanction*. Stanford, CA: Stanford University Press, 1968.

Petersilia, Joan. *The Influence of Criminal Justice Research*. Santa Monica, CA: Rand Corporation, 1987.

Reiss, Albert, and Jeffrey Roth, eds. *Understanding and Preventing Violence*. Washington, D.C.: National Academy Press, 1993.

The
Correctional
Process

CHAPTER NINE

Jails *and* Detention Facilities

Overview

Now that the student has explored the overall history, philosophies, and legal processes for dealing with the misdemeanants and felons in America, it is time to examine those processes and the facilities designed to deal with them. Many processes have been used across the centuries to develop specific outcomes of trials and sentencing authorities. Statements such as "the prisoner shall be hanged by the neck until dead" and "the prisoner shall be drawn and quartered and his parts scattered to the four points of the compass" have evoked the kind of feeling of certainty that justice has been served in the extreme cases. But most crime—despite media images—does not involve such extreme measures, sensational headlines, and sound bytes in contemporary society. While homicides have averaged about twenty-five thousand each year in the last decade, these figures represent only about 2 percent of the more than ten *million* crimes per year of all types reported in the *UCR*. What processes deal with the other 98 percent of the crime that is not involved with homicide? Where do these "other" offenders go, and how are they processed? The sensational, but infrequent, reportage from death row and the coverage of the booking desk of a local jail may seem vastly disparate media events, but the latter is where *all* the action in the criminal justice system starts.

The chapters of Part III will lead the student from the apprehension of an offender to the eventual disposition of the prisoner and his or her return to society. It is clear that our society has developed many different processes, and institutions are needed to meet the primary mission of corrections—to protect society. This chapter will take a look at jails and detention centers as the very first step in an often long and convoluted road in the name of justice that eventually will return the offender to society, having paid a debt for crimes committed whether great or small. The

Education like training rises in importance as jails elevate their job requirements, particularly with the advent of the direct supervision jail.

—Ken Kerle, Executive Editor,
American Jails, 1992

- Receive individuals pending arraignment and hold them awaiting trial, conviction, or sentencing
- Readmit probation, parole, and bail-bond violators and absconders
- Temporarily detain juveniles pending transfer to juvenile authorities
- Hold mentally ill persons pending their movement to appropriate health facilities
- Hold individuals for the military, for protective custody, for contempt, and for the courts as witnesses
- Release convicted inmates to the community upon completion of sentence
- Transfer inmates to federal, state, or other authorities
- House inmates for federal, state, or other authorities because of crowding of their facilities
- Relinquish custody of temporary detainees to juvenile and medical authorities
- Sometimes operate community-based programs with electronic monitoring or other types of supervision.

"scales of justice" attempt to balance the crime and the appropriate punishment, and this process starts with apprehension by the police and booking at a local facility.

Jails: A Grim History

The housing of offenders and suspected criminals in local detention facilities is a practice as old as the definition of crime. The process and practices at the local gaol, lockup, workhouse, stockade, hulk,[1] detention center, or jail have changed little over the centuries. Only recently has there been any serious attempt to provide programs or treatment for jail inmates, and even those efforts must be carefully monitored or officials are likely to abandon them.[2] Originally devised as a place to lock up and restrain all classes of misfits, the jail has a long and sordid history.[3] As we discussed in Chapter 2, John Howard was made keenly aware of the appalling jail conditions in eighteenth-century England when he found himself the proprietor of one of its worst. His effort to reform the practices and improve the conditions in the gaols and prisons of England and the rest of Europe parallels the periodic attempts by American reformers to clean up our jails.

The early jails in America were similar to those in Europe. Most were composed of small rooms in which as many as twenty to thirty prisoners were jammed together. The purpose of jails, as originally conceived by Henry II of England when he ordered the construction of the first official English jail at the Assize of Clarendon in 1166, was to detain suspected or accused offenders until they could be brought before a court. Seldom were the jails adequately heated or ventilated, and food was either sold by the jailer or brought in by family or friends. Conditions within the early jails defy description, and the problems of overcrowding and poor sanitation continue to plague many jails today. A few are exemplary, but at best most are warehouses for the misdemeanant, vagrant, petty offender, and common drunk.[4] At worst, they are overcrowded, understaffed, underfunded "festering sores," as described by a former director of the Law Enforcement Assistance Administration. The jail, perhaps more than any other

Police officer reads "Miranda" (suspect rights) to arrested suspect at station

—PHOTO BY JOHN COLETTI, COURTESY OF PICTURE CUBE , INC.

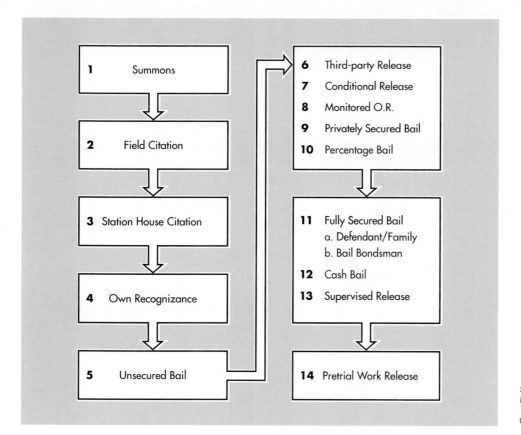

1	Summons
2	Field Citation
3	Station House Citation
4	Own Recognizance
5	Unsecured Bail

6	Third-party Release
7	Conditional Release
8	Monitored O.R.
9	Privately Secured Bail
10	Percentage Bail

11	Fully Secured Bail a. Defendant/Family b. Bail Bondsman
12	Cash Bail
13	Supervised Release

| 14 | Pretrial Work Release |

FIGURE

9.1

Pretrial Alternatives
to Detention

SOURCE: Bureau of Justice Statistics. *Jail, Pre- and Post-Jail Trial Alternatives to Jail Incarceration*, Vol. 1 (Washington, D.C.: U.S. Government Printing Office, 1977), p. 8.

segment of the correctional system, is resistant to change and tends to deteriorate more quickly than it can be improved. Jails are the "cloacal region of corrections."[5]

Felons, misdemeanants, and some juveniles in both of these categories make up the major population of jails. However, additional categories of **jail inmates** include mentally ill persons for whom there are no other facilities, parolees and probationers awaiting hearings, federal prisoners awaiting pickup by marshals, and offenders sentenced to departments of corrections for whom there is not yet space but who cannot be released.

The jail has been at the end of the line for receiving public and governmental support since the days when John Howard inherited the abomination at Bedfordshire in 1773. Though public attention may turn to jails from time to time—when politicians or the media expose a particularly appalling situation—the jails quickly revert to their original deplorable state. In the last few years, a number of new facilities based on new management concepts have been constructed to provide better conditions and programs for the misdemeanant prisoner and felony detainee, but these are all too few. Community programs and facilities are sometimes used to provide work and educational programs for short-term sentenced prisoners—again, not very often.[6]

Of all the problems that plague the criminal justice system, none is more confused and irrational than the question of what should be done with the offender in the period preceding trial. In the United States, the concept of "innocent until proven guilty" creates many problems for the local jail. Pretrial detention and procedures for pretrial liberty have been the subject of hot debate among personnel in the criminal justice system for many decades.[7] The **presumption of innocence** is difficult to maintain once the defendant has been arrested and detained in jail. The police find that presumption difficult to accept if they have acted on probable cause (high probability of guilt) in first making the arrest. Several projects studying

Charles Manson (1934–), The leader of the infamous Manson "family," was convicted and sentenced to death, along with Susan Atkins, Patricia Krenwinkle, Leslie Van Houten, and Charles Watson, for the Tate-Folger-LaBianca Hollywood murders. The 1976 moratorium on the death penalty reduced them all to life. Manson has come up for parole many times but is still incarcerated.

FIGURE

9.2

General Processing Path
in Jails

Booking

- Searching (by arresting/corrections officer)
- Receipting from police (no liability issues, injuries)
- Booking documents
- Holding cell (for assignment)

Classification and Cell Assignment

- Determine security level (max./med./min.)
- Offense classification (felony/misdemeanor)
- Personal characteristics (male/female/juvenile)
- Shower and cleansing
- Issue jail clothing (color coded)

Movements to/from:

- Courts ·
- Meals
- Other jurisdictions
- Other facilities in system
- Programs (work, exercise, etc.)

Visiting Schedules

- Attorneys
- Family/friends
- Criminal investigators

Release

- Institutional authorities if sentenced
- Society if acquitted

A "new era" jail without bars on the doors

—COURTESY OF THE STATE OF CALIFORNIA
DEPARTMENT OF CORRECTIONS

the effects of pretrial decisions on sentencing offer evidence that this period is critical to later correctional efforts.[8] It is even more difficult for the public to realize that "not guilty" does not necessarily mean that the offender is "innocent" and may actually have committed the crime. Not guilty simply means that the *guilt* for the offense for which the defendant was charged and tried was not established "beyond a reasonable doubt."

That is especially true when we consider that the Sixth Amendment to the Constitution guarantees a "speedy and public trial." According to twelve major jurisdictions that examined felony case-processing time, the average time for a felony case to be filed in court was 3.5 months, and the average time for being indicted and bound over for trial was 4.75 months. Those electing for a trial showed the longest time frames, a little over 7 months for filing in court to 7.5 months for indictment and being bound over for trial.[9] This presents a problem for the innocent person being held, for he or she looks more guilty with each passing day in confinement. A later study found that the median number of days from arrest to adjudication for felony defendants (in the largest 75 U.S. counties) was 86 days in general, somewhat longer (105 days) for violent offenders and somewhat shorter (77 days) for those charged with offenses against property. Some 73 percent of all convicted offenders in this study received sentences to incarceration.[10]

The most effective way to deal with the nondangerous or to protect the innocent is either to keep them out of jail or to release them as soon as possible. Pretrial diversion, electronic monitoring,[11] weekend confinement, community work orders,[12] increased use of bail and personal recognizance, more extensive use of fines (including day fines[13] and time payments), and various forms of work and study release all are viable alternatives to the destructive and expensive enforced idleness of most jails. Jails have proved highly resistant to change in the past and can be expected to remain so in the future. Until jails as we know them become mere relics, replaced by integrated community correctional centers,[14] the best policy is to search for ways to keep people out of them and still protect the citizenry.

The answer to the problem of the "second-generation" jails built in the early 1980s was to develop the concept of the "new- or third-generation jail"—a facility designed for maximum interaction between the staff and inmates of our newer large jurisdiction facilities. As described by Spears and Taylor,

> First, the correctional facility—the physical plant—can be considered a technological tool. It greatly influences what equipment can be used and which inmate management philosophy can be applied. There are three types, or generations, of jails, providing varying degrees of staff and inmate interaction depending on the physical barriers built into them.
>
> **First-generation jails** are designed to provide linear remote surveillance, where cells are lined in rows and the staff walk down a central corridor and/or catwalks. The "wheel spoke" or Y-shaped designs allow staff to observe inmate behavior only on an intermittent and infrequent basis. This interaction is generally through bars.
>
> **Second-generation jails** are designed to provide indirect surveillance of inmate behavior. Instead of staff having to walk around the outsides of cells, they stay in a secure control booth surrounded by the inmate housing. Bars are replaced with security glass. This increases the staff's visual surveillance, but verbal interaction with the inmate population is still infrequent.

Third- (new-) generation jails are designed to make the most of staff interaction with the inmate population by placing them inside the inmate housing unit. This direct surveillance allows staff to change from being an inmate behavior monitor to being an inmate behavior manager. By supervising the inmates' activities directly, staff can help to actively change their behavior patterns, rather than just reacting to them.[15]

Third-generation or **direct-supervision jails** are increasingly being built across the nation. This new management strategy places correctional officers in direct contact with inmates, requiring new ways of interacting and controlling residents in cell areas (now known as "pods"). The line officer becomes more self-dependent; the main locus of authority and daily decision-making shifts from staff supervisor to line officers. Supervisors must now conduct performance evaluations of officers based on such expected behaviors as the following:

1. Being in daily contact with inmates in pods;
2. Refraining from doing or saying anything that would belittle or degrade an inmate;
3. Reporting promptly critical information to superior officers (inmate escape plans, for example);
4. Engaging in continual visual observation of inmates; and
5. Investigating activity appearing out of the ordinary.[16]

The direct-supervision strategy is believed to reduce inmate violation of and formal processing for contraband possession, destruction of property, escapes, insolence, suicides, and violence problems.[17]

JAILS TODAY

Urban dwellers in America have responded to the need for local lockups and correctional facilities in a number of ways. The most common confinement facility is the lockup, but the size and quality of these facilities vary greatly. There is quite a difference between the one-cell lockup[18] of a small southern town and those of the gigantic facilities of New York City and Los Angeles. (The counterpart of the city lockup is the county jail, but jails, lockups, detention facilities, workhouses, and a number of other units are commonly referred to as jails. We refer to all of

Officers working in a police command center

—*PHOTO BY JAMES SHAFFER, COURTESY OF PHOTOEDIT*

these facilities as city or county jails, except when it is more relevant to refer to them by another designation.) Policies and programs vary greatly among cities and counties, but some general descriptions and suggestions can be made for small, medium, and large systems. Eighty percent of U.S. jails hold fewer than 50 up to 249 inmates, yet the 25 largest jail systems held almost one in three jail inmates (see Table 9-1).

Jail Populations and Characteristics

Although it is always difficult to obtain accurate data regarding jails and jail populations, the 1994 study of jail inmates, from the U.S. Department of Justice, provides current and reliable information.[19]

Table 9-2 indicates that more than 490,400 persons were held in locally operated jails in June 1994, an increase of 7.5 percent over the 1993 total and 46 percent greater than that of 1983. The latest profile of jail inmates reflected the traditional twofold function of a jail: a place for the temporary detention of the

TABLE 9.1

The 25 Largest Local Jail Jurisdictions: Number of Facilities and Inmates and Average Daily Population, Midyear 1994

Jurisdiction	Number of Facilities	Number of Inmates	Average Daily Population
Los Angeles County, CA	9	20,113	19,725
New York City, NY	15	18,171	18,091
Harris County, TX	4	10,716	10,282
Dallas County, TX	6	9,715	9,321
Cook County, IL	/	9,092	8,950
Dade County, FL	7	6,338	6,656
San Diego County, CA	11	5,487	5,651
Orleans Parish, LA	11	5,351	5,231
Tarrant County, TX	4	5,317	5,167
Shelby County, TN	2	5,124	4,891
Maricopa County, AZ	7	5,170	4,862
Orange County, CA	3	4,987	4,836
Philadelphia City, PA	5	4,696	4,799
Santa Clara County, CA	8	4,303	4,103
Bexar County, TX	/	4,301	3,882
San Bernardino County, CA	2	3,136	3,188
Broward County, FL	3	3,367	3,165
Orange County, FL	/	3,470	3,162
Baltimore City, MD	5	3,350	3,160
Alameda County, CA	3	3,330	3,098
Sacramento County, CA	2	2,954	2,852
Fulton County, GA	4	2,684	2,524
Travis County, TX	3	2,636	2,463
Wayne County, MI	3	2,499	2,400
Duval County, FL	3	2,775	2,383

NOTE: The jurisdictions are ranked by their average daily population in 1994.
Based on the average daily population for the year ending June 30.

SOURCE: Perkins, Craig A., et al. Jails and Jail Inmates 1993–94 (Washington, D.C.: U.S. Department of Justice, April 1995), p. 7.

TABLE 9.2

Number and Average Daily Population of Men, Women, and Juveniles in Local Jails, Midyear 1994

All inmates	490,442
Adults	483,717
Male	434,838
Female	48,879
Juveniles	6,725
Held as adults	5,139
Held as juveniles	1,586

NOTE: Detailed data for 1993 were estimated and rounded to the nearest 100.

SOURCE: Perkins, Craig A. et al., *Jails and Jail Inmates 1993–94* (Washington, D.C.: U.S. Department of Justice, April 1995), p. 4.

unconvicted and a confinement facility where many convicted persons, predominantly misdemeanants, serve out their sentences.[20] Slightly more than five out of every ten jail inmates had not been convicted of a crime. Compared with state and federal prisons, jails held a much smaller percentage of inmates for violent crimes but larger proportions for property and public order offenses.

In 1994, 51 percent of jail inmates stood accused but not convicted of a crime. Most of those who had counsel were being represented by court-appointed lawyers, public defenders, or legal aid attorneys. A large percentage of all unconvicted inmates remained in jail, even though bail had been set for them by the authorities.

Blacks outnumbered any other category in the nation's jails (44 percent compared with 39 percent for whites, and 15 percent for Hispanics), by far exceeding the blacks' 12 percent share of the U.S. population. There were proportionately more blacks incarcerated in the nation in 1991 than in South Africa, a country noted for overt racist policies. Black males in the United States are incarcerated at a rate four times that of black males in South Africa: 3,109 versus 729 per 100,000 black male population.[21] Inmates belonging to other minority groups in the United States accounted for only 1 percent of all jail inmates.[22]

The 1994 adult jail populations consisted predominantly of males (94 percent). Most inmates were young men in their twenties. There was an amazing number of admissions and releases in 1991 (over twenty million), a total of about

TABLE 9.3

Conviction Status of Adult Jail Inmates by Sex, Midyear 1993

	Number of Adult Jail Inmates
Total	455,500
Convicted	226,600
Male	203,900
Female	22,700
Unconvicted	228,900
Male	207,600
Female	21,300

NOTE: The number of convicted inmates may be undercounted because some jail records do not distinguish between inmates who are unconvicted and those who are convicted but waiting to be sentenced. In the *1989 Survey of Inmates in Local Jails*, U.S. Department of Justice, 1990, about 57% of inmates were convicted.

SOURCE: Perkins, Craig A., et al. *Jails and Jail Inmates 1993–94* (Washington, D.C.: U.S. Department of Justice, April 1995), p. 5.

7 percent of the national population, if each case represented one individual! (Of course, those numbers represent multiple arrests in most cases.) Four out of five of all jail inmates were housed in the 505 (**Big 505**) jurisdictions with an average daily jail population of over one hundred, representing 813 jails.

The Problems of Overcrowding

Pressure from state correctional systems to reduce institutional populations is rapidly changing the makeup of our jails (and probationers), with serious offenders being housed with local drunks and misdemeanants. Already overcrowded and difficult to control, many jails have become dumping grounds where little is done but locking up and feeding the population. The following description, while it appeared in a 1979 article in *Corrections Magazine,* is still valid and applicable today:

> "The best I have is worse than the worst conditions at the state pen," said one exasperated Mississippi county attorney. "And I have a feeling it may be like this all over the country."

> "Asking which jails are the worst is like asking, like kids do, whether you'd rather die by burning or freezing," says Ronald Goldfarb, an attorney and author of the book *Jails.* "They are all pretty awful. And whatever the problems on the state level, they are worse in the jails."

> No one denies that the prisoners suffer from crowded multiple cells, a lack of fresh air and exercise, rampant illness, vermin, and idleness. "It's a madhouse back there," said one young Alabama jailer. "They're sodomizing each other and beating each other up all the time."

> Some of the stories are grotesque. In August of last year, two Mississippi prisoners were found hanged in their cell after their request for transfer to the state prison was denied; a protest note was found nearby. In Tennessee, in 1975, a juvenile status offender, unable to get medication he needed, acted out his frustration by setting fire to a mattress. Toxic fumes from the polyurethane material spread through the jail, killing forty-two people, including staff, visitors, and inmates. In 1977, in Meridian, Mississippi, two state prisoners started a fire in their cell and pushed a third inmate, a local inebriate, into the blaze.[23]

Although there have been many improvements, the dismal picture just described remains, relatively, all too accurate. The improvements in many physical facilities have been set back by overcrowding and by the more violent populations. More than one in four of the largest jails were under court order to limit population in 1991, and there were 434 additional court orders to the "Big 505" to improve specific conditions of confinement (food service, medical services, fire hazards, inmate classification, segregation policies, etc.).

As noted in Table 9-1, the twenty-five largest jails in the United States held 31 percent of the nation's total jail inmates, most exceeding their capacity. Most jail administrators acknowledge that all flexibility in a jail, in regard to classification and housing, is lost when the jail is at 90 percent of capacity. It is obvious that those jails with unused capacity will be the smaller jails. A major cause of overcrowding in facilities is the pressure to close other facilities that do not meet acceptable standards.[24] Between 1972 and 1993, the number of jails available to house adult prisoners dropped from 3,921 to 3,304. That number of jail facilities will most likely continue to decline into the twenty-first century. It is clear that rated capacities (total beds) for jails have risen sharply to 475,224 (over 100 percent) in the same time period. The explanation for this trend is due largely to the fact that most new jails that replace the old, smaller facilities are built to hold many more beds. Although most of the old, decrepit jails probably deserved to be closed, the expanding populations and related problems have been left to a system with a continuing limited capacity to handle them, regardless of how poorly. Overcrowding and idleness have thus become the rule in jails that have not expanded beyond the traditional brick and mortar approach to jail crowding.

Immediate housing options to reduce overcrowding include conversion of an abandoned motel to a jail annex, purchase of manufactured housing units (modular units that can be interconnected), construction of a canvas tent-based housing community, leasing bed space from other jurisdictions, house arrest for work-release prisoners, electronic monitoring of defendants not otherwise eligible for pretrial release, double-bunking an existing facility, and contracting with community residential programs for alcohol- and drug-dependent inmates in need of such services.[25] Regrettably, 112 of the nation's 505 largest jails (the Big 505) are under court order to alleviate crowded living units.[26]

Jail Structure and Design

Most jails are fairly uniform in their basic structure. Usually they are designed to operate with a minimum staff and still provide secure confinement for the inmates ("second-generation jails"). In the older jails, a large central cagelike structure called the **bullpen** is used for most of the nonviolent prisoners and the drunks (for the latter group, the structure is called the "tank"). Larger jails may contain several bullpens and a **drunk tank**. The central area is usually surrounded by rows of cells, facing inward toward the bullpens. Like keepers of caged animals, officials often limit contact with inmates by passing food into the bullpens and cells through slots in the doors. Thus the already minimal contact between inmates and staff is reduced still further. Although the lack of contact is usually justified in the name of security, it compounds the already highly impersonal atmosphere in most second-generation jails.

Sanitary facilities are another major problem, especially in the older jails. Even where there is adequate plumbing, the inmates' frustration is too often vented on those objects. The lack of privacy and the personal degradation associated with the open use of sanitary facilities heighten the resentment and dehumanization, leading inmates to vandalize the already limited sanitary equipment. Many jails visited by the 1970 National Jail Census did not have any functioning flush toilets; buckets and similarly medieval expedients still prevailed in several American jails. Although toilets are a problem, the need for adequate showers and washroom facilities is even more critical.

The large percentage of drunks and others placed in the tank, some filthy with their own vomit and excrement, are often left in an unsanitary condition because of a lack of adequate cleanup facilities. As stated in the National Advisory Commission, "If cleanliness is next to godliness, most jails are securely in the province of hell."[27]

A small, six-cell jail has few luxuries
—*PHOTO BY CLIFF SIMONSEN*

In the rush to construct a new third-generation of jails, financed largely with the last vestiges of the funds from the Law Enforcement Assistance Administration, there is much more adherence to standards and the involvement of staff in every aspect of inmate activity. But the most expensive portion of every corrections budget is people, so the new jails are often built to isolate staff in control centers that operate electronic equipment to move people around the facilities. The amount of space and the requirement for access to natural light make the new jails much more humane and less oppressive.[28] Overcrowding pressures, however, may cause many of those facilities to disregard the mandated standards, just so they can keep up with population growth. The result is the same frustration that causes vandalism to equipment and deterioration of morale in inmates. Jail managers and jail advisory boards must continually innovate to maintain control of overcrowded facilities.

Problems with Personnel

The structures used to house our jails reflect the multitude of problems connected with those facilities.[29] Certainly, the lack of adequate personnel is a crucial factor.[30] Most jails are operated by the law enforcement agency that has jurisdiction in the particular area. Because most of the full-time jail personnel are county police officers, dedicated to putting offenders into jail, the primary emphasis is on custodial convenience rather than correctional services. The philosophy behind that includes an almost fanatical concern with security, leaving the responsibility for the jails' internal operation to the inmates themselves. It is that situation which has produced the most reprehensible conditions in many of the large municipal jails. When jail personnel are not sworn officers but low-paid custodial individuals, the conditions become still worse. The need for preservice and inservice training of jailers[31] and other jail personnel has been clearly perceived by jail inspectors.[32] The

TABLE 9.4			
Jail Staffing, 1983–1993			
	1983	*1988*	*1993*
Number of staff	64,600	99,631	65,500
Number of inmates per staff	3.5	3.4	2.8
Annual operating cost per inmate	$9,360	$10,639	$14,667

SOURCE: Craig A. Perkins et al., *Jails and Jail Inmates 1993–1994*. (Washington, D.C.:, U.S. Department of Justice, 1995), p. 5.

immediate requirement is not an influx of professional staff, but extensive training aimed at breaking the habitual work patterns of uninterested, politically appointed, and unqualified jail personnel.[33]

One problem with upgrading personnel and facilities has its roots in the long history of the jail's separate **fee system**, which stems from a practice in early England. The office of sheriff in those days was a position of pomp and prestige but little work. The distasteful duty of caring for the jail and its inmates was usually sold as a concession to a keeper, or gaoler. Fees for maintaining the inmates were extracted from their families, friends, or estates. Under that system, the greater the number of inmates and the longer they were kept, the more income would accrue to the jailer. To increase his profit, the jailer cut his expenses to a minimum and operated the jail as cheaply as possible. The system remained unquestioned until 1773, when John Howard became the sheriff of Bedfordshire.

The fee system was used in America for many years, until it was largely replaced by a variation on itself. The inmates themselves are no longer required to pay for the jailer from the county treasury. In some states, this per diem fee is paid by the state or by federal agencies with which the jail has a contract. Leasing bed space from other jurisdictions is a more current example. Some states (such as California) pay their counties to incarcerate state-sentenced offenders with short sentences. Not surprisingly, a system that pays the sheriff to arrest and jail as many persons as possible is often exploited by the sheriffs who inherit it. Not until a professional police officer position of sheriff and a civil service program are devised to replace fee systems in every jurisdiction will the corruption they encourage be eliminated.

The standards for jailers and related personnel have been a matter of concern for many years:

> The key to success on your job and in pursuing a course of independent study . . . is self-discipline. You have to work at it on a regular basis when at times you would prefer to relax.

> Make no mistake about it. The position of jail officer has assumed an importance that was not recognized even ten years ago. In the next decade you will see the training requirements and courses for study for those who would aspire to a career in corrections equal in length to the training and study required for other people in law enforcement.

> The way of the world is change. For the professional jailer this fact means a continued life-long career of study and continuous training. This course is but a necessary first step.[34]

It is clear that the upgrading of personnel and their reorientation to this new and challenging mission is as critical in the jail system as it is anywhere else in the criminal justice system.[35]

Alternatives to Jail

There are various alternatives to jail available to the pretrial defendant as well as to the convicted misdemeanant. We cover a few of those alternatives now.

Extended confinement of innocent persons, as with pretrial detention of the unadjudicated felon and later found not guilty, is a serious problem. The defendant who is innocent and is exposed through pretrial confinement to the conditions of most jails will probably build up considerable animosity toward the criminal justice system and corrections in particular. The convicted offender eventually sent to a correctional institution also will have negative feelings about the inequities of a system that appears to confine arbitrarily some defendants before trial while releasing others.

OTHER DISPOSITIONS FOR THE MISDEMEANANT

The confusion in defining and enforcing misdemeanor statutes is reflected in the absence of uniform techniques and systems for dealing with misdemeanants. Although different states vary greatly in their approaches, and jurisdictions within states may also be inconsistent, some patterns are fairly constant.[36] As we mentioned earlier, the bulk of the misdemeanor cases are disposed of through confinement or probation. There are other alternatives for disposition as well, the most prevalent being the use of fines.

Fines are often called **price-tag justice**. In the case of misdemeanor offenses, the fine is in many cases offered as an alternative to a period of confinement, meaning the offender who cannot pay is confined, in effect, for being poor rather than for being guilty. The sheer number of misdemeanor cases the lower courts must hear presents a major obstacle to all but the most cursory justice. Some lower courts may hear as many as one hundred or more misdemeanor cases in a single morning. It is difficult, under such circumstances, to conduct any kind of in-depth diagnosis of the offender, the offense, or the offender's ability to pay a fine. The amount of fine for a particular crime is virtually standardized, and paying it is like paying forfeited bail. For the individual unable to pay, a term in the lockup is the only alternative. In some cases, however, fines can be paid on the installment plan. That procedure gives offenders a chance to keep their jobs or seek work to pay the fine. Combined with weekend confinement and community work orders, the installment plan has greatly improved misdemeanor justice.

As part of the increased enthusiasm for intermediate punishments and search for a graduated progression of intermediate sanctions (see Chapter 11), courts have increasingly begun to use fines and day fines (a sliding dollar amount determined by the offender's daily wages). The Vera Institute of Justice implemented a project to demonstrate and then evaluate the efficacy of using day fines in Staten Island, New York. The project demonstrated the following:

1. The day-fine concept could be implemented in a typical American court of limited jurisdiction.

2. Day fines could substitute for fixed fines ("the same or similar amount to be imposed on all defendants convicted of similar offenses").

FINES

A fine is a penalty imposed on a convicted person by a court that requires him or her to pay a specified amount of money. The fine is a cash payment of a dollar amount assessed by the judge in an individual case or determined by a published schedule of penalties. Fines may be paid in installments in many jurisdictions or by use of the offender's credit card. Many jurisdictions now base the dollar amounts of a fine on an offender's daily earnings (day fines), a practice common in some European and South American countries.

3. Fine amounts were higher for more affluent offenders under the day-fine system.

4. Overall revenues increased.

5. High rates of collection could be sustained despite the higher average day-fine amounts.

6. The deep skepticism among criminal justice professionals about the court's ability to enforce and collect such fines was unfounded.[37]

Both fines and day fines are likely to be used more extensively by courts to achieve a graduated progression of penalties for less serious crimes as well as to reduce jail overcrowding.

WEEKEND CONFINEMENT

To lessen the negative impacts of short-term incarceration and allow offenders to retain current employment, some jurisdictions permit sentences to be served during non-working weekends. Such weekend confinement generally requires a guilty misdemeanant to check into the jail on Friday after work and leave Sunday morning, sometimes early enough to permit church attendance. A **weekender** serving his or her sentence over a number of months would generally be credited with three days of confinement per weekend. Minimum security facilities (not the maximum security jails) are appropriate for such offenders.

COMMUNITY WORK ORDERS

Sentencing judges sometimes order misdemeanants to perform a period of service to the community as a substitute for, or in partial satisfaction of, a fine. This disposition is generally a condition of a suspended (or partially suspended) sentence or of probation. It can be used in a variety of ways: a sentence in itself, work in lieu of cash fine, a condition of suspended sentence, or a condition of probation.

The offender "volunteers" his or her services to a community agency for a certain number of hours per week over a specified period of time. The total number of hours, often assessed as the legal minimum wage, is determined often by the amount of the fine that would have been imposed or by the portion of the fine that is suspended.

Other alternatives for the misdemeanant are probation without adjudication and the suspended sentence. Both are variations on the same theme: holding formal disposition over the head of the offender for a period of time, often under specified conditions, and then nullifying the conviction. In probation without adjudication (also known as deferred prosecution), offenders can forgo prosecution as long as they meet certain established conditions, usually for a specific period of time.[38] The suspended sentence is used whenever offenders obviously do not require supervision to ensure their good behavior. This alternative is usually used for first offenders considered to be so impressed with their arrest and conviction that further sanctions against them would be of little positive value.

The extent to which these alternatives are employed is not really known, as there has been little research in the area. It is apparent that the misdemeanants, like adult felons, often fall out of the correctional funnel before it narrows. If they did not, the jails of the country simply could not hold them.

Over the last two decades, the health care of jail inmates has been the subject of endless litigation,[39] included in civil rights mandates,[40] addressed

Sentencing to Service

In 1986, the Minnesota Department of Corrections established a Sentencing to Service jail reduction program in conjunction with the Minnesota Department of Natural Resources. Certain nondangerous offenders age 18–25 were sentenced to work on county and state operated work teams to beautify forests and recreational trails, and assist in natural resource management work projects. It was found that participating offenders strongly preferred to be working than sitting idle in jail cells, and that they tended to work hard and developed a sense of ownership and pride in their assigned work projects. Supervising officers found the workers easier to manage at night, since they are tired and tend to go to bed early. Staff also reported prisoner attitudes as improved and conflicts rare. Initial analyses in 1991 indicate the project is cost-effective and has a potential to return $5 in services for every $1 of expenditure, that some 86% successfully completed their programs, and that over $1 million was saved by using

Women's chain gang at Estrella jail as part of Sheriff Joe Arpaio's war on crime. (Photo by Tim Zielenbach, courtesy of Contact Press Images).

this work program, including the approximately 21,000 jail days saved. ∎

SOURCE: John McLagan, "Sentencing to Service," *American Jails* 5:6 (1992): 28–32.

---

through court orders,[41] and mandated through state regulation. It is clear that provision of adequate inmate health and mental health care[42] is no longer an option but is compulsory. Across the nation and particularly in the Big 505 jails, their managers[43] are taking steps to meet these mandates, including the following:

1. Determining the real costs of and identifying existing community medical service providers[44] and adopting health maintenance organization (HMO) models;[45]
2. Resolving security issues for transporting inmates to hospitals and medical care appointments;
3. Innovating scheduling for medical staff;
4. Providing special housing (for geriatrics, tuberculosis patients,[46] early-stage HIV inmates,[47] pregnant inmates, etc.);
5. Seeking accreditation (sometimes as a defense against litigation and claims of deliberate indifference); and
6. Planning for future problems.

Demands of this nature will require jail managers to find ways to creatively adopt proven techniques and implement innovations[48] that would permit continued quality health care while curtailing costs of services.[49]

ALTERNATIVES TO JAIL AT THE PRETRIAL STAGE

Incarceration is one of the most severe punishments meted out by the American criminal justice system. Yet over one-half of all persons in local jails are awaiting trial. In effect, we are using our most severe sanction against many individuals who have not yet been convicted of a crime. If detention was necessary—if there were no reasonable alternatives to the jailing of suspects—that situation would be understandable. But experience with alternatives to jail has indicated that many (but not all) people now incarcerated could be released safely and economically, pending disposition of the charges against them. Most of them would appear in court as required without being held in jail.

Some tentative conclusions can be drawn from the experience of existing programs as follows:

1. Pretrial alternatives generally cost much less than jail incarceration.
2. Persons released before trial seem to fare better in court than do those who are incarcerated.
3. Pretrial release alternatives appear to be as effective as jail in preventing recidivism and can reduce the size of criminal justice agency workloads.

Post-Occupancy Evaluations

The Post-Occupancy Evaluation (POE) Program, which was pioneered at the Contra Costa County Jail in California, has been developed to collect data on facility design and policy in an organized, systematic, and reliable manner and present the findings clearly. The National Institute of Corrections sponsored the development of the POE Program, using a ten-step model:

1. Establish initial contact and sign-on. First contacts usually come through personal referral or the PONI process. The POE is much easier to conduct, and the results are more likely to be used, if it is perceived as something that is being done with the institution rather than something done to or for it. Part of sign-on is assessing willingness to make a real commitment to the POE process.

2. Identify a liaison. It is necessary to identify one individual from the institution who will serve as the contact point and primary liaison for the study. This person will make early contact with administrators, staff representatives (union officials if present), and inmate groups to explain the POE process and get their input on what they see as the critical questions to be answered. Where possible, a facility POE committee should be created to work with the research team.

3. Complete an administration survey. Administrators are asked to complete a detailed survey providing information about things such as the facility's population, spaces, and philosophy. They are also asked to supply copies of plans and design programs.

4. Complete staff and inmate surveys. These are modified as needed to cover local issues and usually are administered by the liaison or a locally hired research assistant.

5. Input and analyze survey data. Data input has been auto-mated through the use of optical scanning. Standard procedures produce tabular and graphic data output.

6. Hold a team conference. With the results of the surveys as a starting point, the research team (NIC consultants and facility personnel) meet, possibly via teleconference, to review findings and identify questions, problems, successes, and any issues requiring further clarification. The previously conducted staff and inmate surveys should provide focus to the on-site interviews (to be conducted in Step 8), enabling the team to explain and understand issues, concerns, or problems that are important to staff and inmates.

7. Modify on-site data collection forms. Interview schedules and observational formats are modified to reflect specific local issues identified in Step 6.

8. Conduct on-site data observation and interviews. During on-site visits, managers, staff, and inmates are interviewed both individually and in groups, and observations of staff and inmate behavior are conducted. These can include informal observations, such as noting where staff and inmates "hang out," or more formal behavior tracking, such as coding the frequency, location, and quality of staff-inmate interactions.

9. Analyze data and write a report. The results of the on-site data collection are analyzed, reviewed along with survey findings, and summarized in a POE report.

10. Prepare a final report. A final report is presented to the institution and to NIC. ∎

SOURCE: Richard Wener, Jay Farbstein, and Carol Knapel, "Post-Occupancy Evaluations." Corrections Today 55; 6 (1993): 97–98.

4. Alternative programs can reduce jail populations and eliminate the need for expansion or new construction.[50]

Pretrial alternatives to detention run along a continuum of increasing controls or sanctions (Figure 9-1). Any community wishing to maximize the use of alternatives will provide a series of options that offer varying levels of supervision and services. That will permit the release of more persons with less waste of expensive resources.[51] Least interventionary and least costly options are used for low-risk cases. More expensive options and options involving greater interference in the life of the individual, such as house arrest and electronic monitoring, are reserved for cases in which those are the only alternatives to the even more costly option of jail incarceration.

Summary

Although improving jail facilities and upgrading jail personnel takes a great deal of time and money, many other helpful procedures can be initiated more simply. Some were recommended back in 1937 by the National Jail Committee of the American Correctional Association. The fact that so many of those suggestions would still benefit jails today, almost sixty years later, reflects most of our jail systems' general resistance to change. The 1970 Plan for Accreditation of the American Correctional Association has significantly improved jail practices in many jurisdictions,[52] as have standards of the American Correctional Association in the 1990s.

Jail administrators have an obligation to society to seek methods that can work in their own communities. Administrators are the practitioners who, with community involvement, must break the tradition of neglect and indifference that is the jail's legacy.[53] Unless vigorous and imaginative leadership is exhibited, even revitalized jails will soon regress to their squalid past.

The best policy is to search for ways to keep people out of jail, yet still protect the citizenry. Both goals can be met by providing security and staff training and meeting the standards suggested by the professional associations that oversee the staff. As a closing thought on jail systems, we include the recent remarks of Anthony Travisono, former executive director of the American Correctional Association:

> As we all know, security can be in the form of buildings and equipment, or programs for inmates, or training and aid programs for staff. All are components of a well-balanced institutional security program. The crowding problem really tests the staff's ability to be stable and innovative, so administrations need to provide programs for inmates and staff to cope with this enormously stressful environment.
>
> Staff training programs and employee help groups aimed at stress reduction have become more necessary to meet today's challenges. We are aware that when fighting alligators, there is no time to sit back and read about why the alligators are in the swamp in the first place, but training and stress-reduction programs are a vital part of dealing with the conditions in which correctional staff find themselves. Now is not the time to cut back on these vital programs, but instead to offer even more.

I recently visited an institution in which the entire staff was on holiday schedule, with all employees reporting, so that the majority of staff could spend eight hours in a variety of training and refresher programs—from baton training to conflict resolution. It appeared that staff and inmates were able to deal with the schedule without any hassles, and as one inmate said, "They need all the training they can get to handle us." There may not be any other way to accomplish ongoing training to meet minimal ACA standards.

Innovation will be the word most commonly used in the next several years to find ways to get the job done.[54]

We are reminded again that it is the fine people who keep the jails of America moving ahead, against tremendous problems, and keep them from slipping back into the horrors of the past. We shall now move on to a look at one of the major alternatives to going from jail to a prison after conviction: probation. In times of overcrowding and high levels of violence, probation has become a major player in correctional supervision in the 1990s and will probably grow in the twenty-first century.

Review Questions

1. Why has the fee system been such a detriment to jail progress?
2. What effects do the changing roles of corrections have on jail operations?
3. The community correctional center is a new concept. Does it differ much from the jails today? How?
4. What is the area of greatest weakness in the jails? Would more personnel be the answer? Why or why not?
5. What are the major alternatives to pretrial confinement? To the use of jail for postconviction sentencing?
6. Describe the operations of a third-(new)-generation jail.
7. What medical problems must jails address?
8. Draft a plan for reducing jail overcrowding.

Words to Remember

jail inmates	direct-supervision jails	price-tag justice
presumption of innocence	Big 505	weekender
first-generation jails	bullpen	pretrial alternatives
second-generation jails	drunk tank	
third-(new)-generation jails	fee system	

Endnotes

1. The New York City Department of Corrections floating detention facility held one hundred maximum security and seven hundred other inmates in fourteen fifty-inmate dormitories, built at a cost of $200,000 per bed. James Cottrell and John Shanahan, "A Jail That Floats," *Corrections Today* 54:2 (1992): 132–133. See also Norval Morris and David Rothman, eds., *The Oxford Dictionary of the Prison: The Practice of Punishment in Western Society* (Oxford: Oxford University Press, 1995).

2. For an excellent overview of involving the community in jail administration, see William Wood, "A Practical Guide to Community Relations," *American Jails* 6:5 (1992): 14–17, and Michael Lee, "Ohio Jail Advisory Board," *American Jails* 6:5 (1992): 49–51.

3. See in particular Dorothy Fox and Jane Pickett, "Frontier Jail," *American Jails* 5:3 (1992): 77–80, and Freida Kelly, *The History of Kilmainham Gaol* (Dublin: Mercier, 1988).

4. Jail inmates convicted of driving under the influence (DUI) are more likely to be white and older than other inmates and as likely to have prior arrests. Many have substantial histories of violent and property offenses. Ralph Weisheit and John Klofas, "Social Status of DUI Offenders in Jail," *International Journal of the Addictions* 27:4 (1992): 793–816.

5. Hans Mattick and Alexander Aikman, "The Cloacal Region of Corrections," *The Annals* 381 (January 1969): 109–118.

6. Richard Frey and Kim Allen, "Community-Based Correctional Alternatives: Jefferson County's Response to Jail Crowding," *American Jails* 1 (Summer 1987): 37–38.

7. Brian Reaves, *Pretrial Release of Felony Defendants, 1990* (Washington, D.C.: U.S. Department of Justice, 1992). See also Keith Cooprider, "Pretrial Bond Supervision: An Empirical Analysis with Policy Implications," *Federal Probation* 56:3 (1992): 411–449, and Thomas Bak, *Defendants Who Avoid Detention: A Good Risk?* (Washington, D.C.: Administrative Office of the U.S. Courts, 1994).

8. Charles Ares et al., "The Manhattan Bail Project: An Interim Report on the Use of Pretrial Parole," *New York University Law Review* 38 (1963): 67–83; Ann Rankin, "The Effect of Pretrial Detention," *New York University Law Review* 39 (1964): 651–659; and Christine Martin, *Cook County Pretrial Release Study* (Chicago: Criminal Justice Information Authority, 1992). Also see William Rhodes, Raymond Hyatt, and Paul Scheinman, *Protecting Pretrial Misconduct with Drug Tests of Arrestees* (Washington, D.C.: U.S. Department of Justice, 1996).

9. Bureau of Justice Statistics, *Felony Case-Processing Time: Special Report* (Washington, D.C.: U.S. Department of Justice, August 1986), p. 2.

10. Pheny Smith, *Felony Defendants in Large Urban Centers, 1990* (Washington, D.C.: U.S. Department of Justice, 1993), p. 13.

11. Cooprider, "Pretrial Bond Supervision," found that electronic-monitored pretrial defendants seldom missed a court date and most were returned to the community after case disposition.

12. John McLagan, "Sentencing to Service: A Project of the Minnesota Department of Corrections and the Minnesota Department of Natural Resources," *American Jails* 5:6 (1992): 28–32.

13. Laura Winterfield and Sally Hillsman, *The Staten Island Day-Fine Project* (Washington, D.C.: U.S. Department of Justice, 1993). See also John Matthais, Gwendolyn Lyford, and Paul Gomez, *Current Practices in Collecting Fines and Fees in State Courts* (Denver, CO: National Center for State Courts, 1995).

14. Bobbie Huskey, "The Expanding Use of Community Correctional Centers," *Corrections Today* 54:8 (1992): 70–73. See also Robert Langworthy and Edward Latessa, "Treatment of Chronic Drunk Drivers: The Turning Point Project," *Journal of Criminal Justice* 21:2 (1993): 265–267.

15. Lois Spears and Don Taylor, "Coping with Our Jam-Packed Jails," *Corrections Today* 52 (June 1990): 20. See also Mary Stohr, Nicholas Lovnick, and Ben Menke, "Staff Management in Correctional Institutions: Comparing Dilulio's 'Control Model' and 'Employee Investment Model' Outcomes in Five Jails," *Justice Quarterly* 11:3 (1994): 471–497.

16. Mary Stohr-Gillman, Linda Zupan, Craig Curtis, Ben Menke, and Nicholas Lourich, "The Development of a Behavioral-Based Performance Appraisal System," *American Jails* 5:2 (1992): 10–16.

17. Jeffrey Senese, Joe Wilson, Arthur Evans, Robert Aguirre, and David Kalinich, "Evaluating Jail Reform: Inmate Infraction and Disciplinary Response in a Traditional and a Podular/Direct Supervision Jail," *American Jails* 6:4 (1992): 14–24.

18. James Pea, "Lewis County, Washington: A Well-Run Small Jail," *American Jails* 1 (Summer 1987): 35–36. See also Larry Mays and Joel Thompson, "Mayberry Revisited: The Characteristics

and Operations of America's Small Jails," paper presented at the annual meeting of the Academy of Criminal Justice Sciences, St. Louis, March 17, 1987, and Tim Brennan and David Wells, "The Importance of Inmate Classification in Small Jails," *American Jails* 5:2 (1992): 49–52.

19. Craig Perkins, James Stephans, and Allen Beck." *Jails and Jail Inmates 1993–1994* (Washington, D.C.: U.S. Department of Justice, 1992). Most of the data in this section were drawn from this report.

20. In this report, a jail consists of a confinement facility administered by a local law enforcement agency, intended for adults but sometimes also holding juveniles and confining detained persons pending adjudication and/or persons committed after adjudication for sentences of usually a year or less. Temporary holding facilities, or lockups, that do not hold persons after being formally charged in court (usually within forty-eight hours of arraignment) are excluded.

21. Mark Mauer, "Americans Behind Bars," *Criminal Justice* 6:4 (1992): 12–18, 38–39.

22. While blacks are disproportionately involved in the criminal justice system, a long-standing criminological taboo exists against discussing the relationship between crime and race. There is no "black criminology" to tease out the data or theoretically interpret the observed overinvolvement. The three basic arguments are that there are more black offenders per 100,000 population, or that certain black offenders tend to commit very large numbers of crimes, or that criminal justice system personnel decision makers are biased against blacks in decision making. See the excellent critique by Kathleen Russell, "Development of a Black Criminology and the Role of the Black Criminologist," *Justice Quarterly* 9:4 (1992): 667–683. For an examination of the juvenile justice system issues, see Edmund McGarrell, "Trends in Racial Disproportionality in Juvenile Court Processing: 1985–1989," *Crime and Delinquency* 39:1 (1993): 29–48.

23. P. Taft, "Backed Up in Jail," *Corrections Magazine* 5 (June 1979): 28.

24. National Advisory Commission on Criminal Justice Standards and Goals, *Corrections* (Washington, D.C.: U.S. Government Printing Office, 1973), p. 276. See also Walter Busher, *Jail Overcrowding: Identifying Causes and Planning for Solutions* (Washington, D.C.: U.S. Department of Justice, 1983). See also Wayne Welsh, *Counties in Court: Jail Overcrowding and Court-Ordered Reform* (Philadelphia: Temple University Press, 1995).

25. Michael Shannon, "The Dayton Human Rehabilitation Center," *American Jails* 6:4 (1992): 69–73, and Charlotte Arnold, "The PROGRAM for Female Offenders, Inc.," *American Jails* 5:5 (1992): 36–40.

26. Louis Jankowski, *Jail Inmates 1991* (Washington, D.C.: U.S. Department of Justice, 1992), p.4.

27. On jail standards, see Bruce Olsen, "New York Jail Standards," *American Jails* 1:4 (1987): 19–21; Tom Reid, "Minnesota In-Service Training Methods: How to Exceed All Training Standards at a Low Cost," *American Jails* 1:3 (1987): 10–12; and Kathy Briscoe and Joyce Kuhrt, "How Accreditation Has Improved Correctional Health Care," *American Jails* 6:4 (1992): 48–52.

28. Jail designs and construction are undergoing rapid upgrading. See the excellent initial works by Charles DeWitt, all published in 1986: *Florida Sets Example with Use of Concrete Modules, New Construction Methods for Correctional Facilities,* and *California Tests New Construction Concepts* (Washington, D.C.: U.S. Department of Justice, 1986). See also the small jail design in Rod Miller and Bill Clark, *Maine Jails: Progress Through Partnerships* (Washington, D.C.: U.S. Department of Justice, 1987), p. 4. See also the special theme issue "Accreditation," *Corrections Today* 54:3 (1992), and Walter Sipple, "Direct Supervision," *American Jails* 5:3 (1992): 68–70. A review of the first two decades of third-generation jails can be found in Raymond Harris and David Russell, "Podular Direct Supervision: The First Twenty Years," *American Jails* 9:3: (1995): 11–12.

29. Jails are particularly vulnerable to fatal fires. See N. E. Schafer, "Fire Safety in Jails: Planning for Emergencies," *Federal Probation* 46 (1982): 41–45. See also Phillip Goldberg, "Avoiding Fatal Fires," *American Jails* 1 (Fall 1987): 46, 50, 53; William Archambeault and Betty Archambeault, *Correctional Supervisory Management* (Englewood Cliffs, NJ: Prentice Hall, 1982), pp. 382–386; and Jeffrey Zens, "Mockups Pinpoint Jail Design Flaws Before It's Too Late to Fix Them," *Corrections Today* 54:2 (1992): 112–118.

30. Kenneth Kerle and Francis Ford, *The State of Our Nation's Jails 1982* (Washington, D.C.: National Sheriffs Association, 1982).

31. QRC Research Corporation, *Study of Local Jails in West Virginia* (Lexington, KY: QRC Research Corporation, 1982).

32. Michael Haley, "Alabama Jail Assistance Project," *American Jails* 6:1 (1993): 36–39.

33. Mary Stohr, Ruth Self, and Nicholas Lovrich, "Staff Turnover in New Generation Jails: An Investigation of Its Causes and Prevention," *Journal of Criminal Justice* 26:5 (1992): 455–478.

34. L. Cary Bittick, *Jail Officer's Training Manual* (Alexandria, VA: National Sheriffs Association, 1984), p. iv.

35. Ted Heim, "The University Role in Training Jail Personnel: The Washburn Experience," *American Jails* 6:1 (1993): 18–22, and Ron Klein and Lon Stephenson, "Training Development," *American Jails* 5:3 (1992): 63–66.

36. Chris Eskridge, *Pretrial Release Programming: Issues and Trends* (New York: Clark Boardman, 1983). See also Keith Cooprider, "Pretrial Bond Supervision," and Janice Fernette, *Case Processing Time Standards and Goals* (Williamsburg, VA: National Center for State Courts, 1992).

37. Winterfield and Hillsman, *The Staten Island Day-Fine Project,* pp. 1–4. See also the policy statement of the National Council on Crime and Delinquency, *Criminal Justice Policy Statement* (San Francisco: National Council on Crime and Delinquency, 1992).

38. See Ronald Goldstock, "The Prosecutor as Problem Solver: Leading and Coordinating Anticrime Efforts," *Criminal Justice* 7:3 (1992): 3–9, 48–49.

39. Frederick Bennett, "After the Litigation: Part I," *American Jails* 6:3 (1992): 81–84; "After the Litigation: Part II," *American Jails* 6:4 (1992): 30–36; Matthew Lopes, "The Role of the Masters in Correctional Litigation," *American Jails* 6:4 (1993): 27–29; Daniel Pollack, "How to Find a Good Lawyer," *Corrections Today* 54:8 (1992): 114–118; and Heidi M. Murphy, "Supreme Court Ruling Changes the Standard on Inmate Abuse," *Corrections Today* 54:1 (1992): 195.

40. Thomas Siberia, "Helping Correctional Officers Recognize and Interact with Handicapped Offenders," *American Jails* 6:2 (1992): 31–34; Randall Atlas, "Is Accessibility a Disability? The Impact of ADA on Jails," *American Jails* 6:5 (1992): 53–59; and John Wass and Ron Marks, "The Young Offenders Acts," *Corrections Today* 54:8 (1992): 88–93.

41. Dennis Williams, "State Standards Programs: The Process in Florida," *American Jails* 6:1 (1992): 46–50; Dave Wells and Tim Brennan, "Jail Inmate Classification System: The Michigan Classification Project," *American Jails* 6:1 (1992): 59–62; Matthew Lopes, "The Role of the Masters in Correctional Litigation"; W. J. Bryan, "Jails and Courts," *American Jails* 6:3 (1992): 51–53; Tim Brennan and Dave Wells, "The Importance of Inmate Classification in Small Jails," *American Jails* 6:2 (1992): 49–57; and John Harlan and Patrick Mueller, "Legal Issues in Detention Officer Applicant Investigations," *American Jails* 6:2 (1992): 54–57.

42. Fuller Torrey, Joan Stieber, and Jonathan Ezekiel, *Criminalizing the Seriously Mentally Ill: The Abuse of Jails as Mental Hospitals* (Arlington, VA: National Alliance for the Mentally Ill, 1992); and Valerie Hildebeitel, "Addressing the Needs of the Mentally Ill Inmate," *American Jails* 5:4 (1992): pp. 60–61. See also Patrick Kirkade, Matthew Leone and Scott Semond, "The Consequences of Jail Crowding," *Crime and Delinquency.* 41:1, 1995: 150–161.

43. Jankowski, *Jail Inmates 1991,* p. 4.

44. Clifford Findeiss and Marta Prado, "Cost Effective Management of Correctional Health Care," *American Jails* 6:4 (1992): 57–60.

45. Diane Young, "A Preventive Health Care Event in a County Jail," *American Jails* 6:3 (1992): 47–49.

46. Parker Eales, "Tuberculosis Control: The New Disaster Plan for Jails," *American Jails* 6:2 (1992): 12–16; Robin Mueller, "Tuberculosis: The Deadly Disease Strikes Jail Populations," *American Jails* 6:2 (1992): 23–30; and Parker Eales, "MDR Tuberculosis: New TB Strain Demands Immediate Attention," *Corrections Today* 54:3 (1992): 64–67.

47. Mary Coplin, "Maryland Model: Forward Looking Program Tackles AIDS Crisis," *Corrections Today* 54:8 (1992): 104–107, and Howard Messing, "AIDS in Jails," *American Jails* 7:1 (1993): 40–46. Also see James Tesoriero and Malcom McCullough, "Correctional Health Care Now and Into the Twenty-first Century," R. Macraskin and A. Robertson (eds.), in *Vision for Change* (Englewood Cliffs, NJ: Prentice Hall, 1996), pp, 215–236.

48. Della Donaldson, "Health Education for Staff and Inmates: Can We Afford Not to Teach It?" *American Jails* 6:1 (1992): 18–20; Rhonda Manning, "The Inmate Fee for Medical Services Program," *American Jails* 6:1 (1992): 32–37; John Clark and Bertha Mackey, "Breaking Out of Tradition: Inmate Self-Medication," *American Jails* 6:1 (1992): 38–45; Briscoe and Kuhrt, "How Accreditation Has Improved Correctional Health Care"; and Findeiss and Prado, "Cost Effective Management of Correctional Health Care."

49. Patricia Satterfield, "Creating Strategies for Controlling Health Care Costs," *Corrections Today* 54:2 (1992): 190–194.

50. J. Galvin et al., *Instead of Jail: Pre- and Post-Trial Alternatives to Jail Incarceration,* Vol. 1 (Washington, D.C.: U.S. Government Printing Office, 1977), pp. 7–9.

51. National Council on Crime and Delinquency, *Criminal Justice Policy Statement.*

52. Wayne Higgins and Charles Kehoe, "Accreditation's Effects on Jails and Juvenile Facilities," *Corrections Today* 54:3 (1992): 40–43.

53. Dennis McCarthy, Henry Steadman, and Joseph Morrissey, "Issues in Planning Jail Mental Health Services," *Federal Probation* 46 (1982): 56–63; Paul Paquette, "The Nuts and Bolts of Implementing the Regional Jail Concept," *American Jails* 1 (Fall 1987): 42, 44–45; Francis Ford, "Politics and Jails, Part II," *American Jails* 7:1 (1993): 11–17; Wood, "A Practical Guide to Community Relations" and Nancy Bard and Dave Smith, "The Challenge: Community Involvement in Corrections," *American Jails* 6:5 (1992): 18–20.

54. Anthony Travisono, "Crowding in Our Jails: Overcoming Obstacles Through Security, Staff Training," *Corrections Today* 52 (June 1990): 4.

CHAPTER TEN

Probation

Overview

Our examination of the correctional process now turns to probation and probation supervision, the major alternative to incarceration as used by sentencing judges across America. Probation is a sentence, which does not include confinement, that imposes conditions governing the release of the offender into the community based on good behavior. The sentencing court retains authority to supervise, modify conditions, cancel the status and resentence, if the probationer violates the terms of his or her probation. Increasingly, across the nation, courts are using recent developments in technology to better monitor the behavior of the probationer. This chapter offers a brief history of probation and its developments up to the last few years of the 1990s.

Suspended Sentence and Sanctuary

Following a determination of guilt, the courts have a number of options for dealing with the offender. They include fines, probation, house arrest, restitution, intensive supervision, split sentences, community work orders, incarceration in jail, shock probation, imprisonment in state penal facilities, halfway house treatment, or combinations of these.[1] As you can see in Figure 9-1, the option most often selected today is probation; approximately 59 percent of convicted offenders were placed on **probation** in 1994. The percentage of offenders in the nation on probation supervision ranged from a high of 85 percent in Nevada to a low of 9.8 percent in Pennsylvania. Thirty percent of state felony offenders were sentenced to probation. There were 2,843,445 adults on probation at the end of 1994.[2]

> **H**umane treatment may raise up one in whom the divine image has long been obscured. It is with the unfortunate, above all, that humane conduct is necessary.
>
> —Fyodor Dostoyevski

Probation is a derivative of the suspended sentence, handed down to us somewhat indirectly by way of past judicial procedures. Both the **suspended sentence** and probation mitigate the punishment for an offender through a judicial procedure, and their earliest antecedent is found in the **right of sanctuary**,[3] frequently cited in the Bible. In many cultures, holy places and certain cities were traditionally set aside as places for sanctuary.

The right of sanctuary was written into Mosaic law.[4] To escape the blood vengeance of a victim's family, a killer could go to certain specified cities and find refuge. During the Middle Ages, many churches were able to offer sanctuary for those hiding from harsh secular law. The practice of sanctuary disappeared in England in the seventeenth century and was replaced with **benefit of clergy**. This practice, originally reserved for clerics, was eventually extended to those who could pass the Psalm 51 test—a test of the offender's ability to read the verse that begins "Have mercy upon me." The result was a form of suspended sentence that allowed the offender to move about in society.

Probation is increasingly being linked with a short sentence to jail or "boot camps" (see Chapter 11), followed by a period of probation. In California in 1995, such a sentence combination was the dominant sentence (61 percent) for felony offenders.[5]

The suspended sentence differs from probation, though the terms are sometimes used interchangeably. The suspended sentence does not require supervision and usually does not prescribe a specified set of goals for the offender to work toward. It is merely a form of quasi-freedom that can be revoked, with a prison sentence imposed at the instruction of the court. Sentence can be suspended in one of two ways:

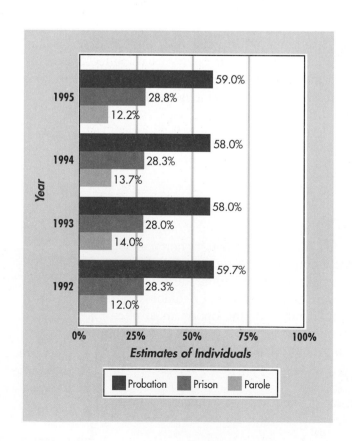

FIGURE

10.1

Percentage Estimates of Individuals on Probation, in Prison, and on Parole on January 1, 1992—1995

SOURCE: C. Camp and G. Camp, *The Corrections Yearbook 1995: Probation and Parole* (South Salem, NY: Criminal Justice Institute, 1995), p. 4. The numbers for 1995 are 1,018,899 in prison, 2,257,000 on probation, and 531,650 on parole.

1. The sentence is imposed, but its execution is suspended.
2. Both the imposition and execution of the sentence are suspended.

Of the two, the second is the more desirable because of the reduced stigma. However, the practice of suspending sentences, like sanctuary, has generally been replaced in America with supervised probation. Sentences may be vacated by the sentencing judge, and the offender may be placed at liberty in the community, but that is a relatively infrequent occurrence.

Under the European model of suspended sentence, or *sursis* (surcease), the offender has satisfactorily fulfilled the conditions if no further offense is committed during the established period. Little control or supervision is provided, with the result that most offenders with suspended sentences are denied the specialized or therapeutic services needed to prevent further criminal involvement.[6]

STIGMA
A mark of shame and disgrace assigned to an offender by virtue of his or her having committed the offense or conviction. Stigma also means the person is disvalued (from a previous status), and the social reaction is generally to avoid, punish, or isolate the disvalued person. Societal reaction is believed to create additional difficulties for ex-offenders who desire to become nonoffenders or to "go straight."

The History of Probation

Probation has undergone a number of changes since its informal beginnings in the nineteenth century. Let's take a brief look at just how the concept was born.

John Augustus,[7] a Boston shoemaker, is credited with being the father of probation. He liked to spend his spare moments observing what transpired in the courts, and he was disturbed that minor offenders and common drunks were often forced to remain in jail because they had no money to pay their fines. He convinced the authorities to allow him to pay their fines and offered them friendly supervision. Between 1841 and 1858, he bailed out almost two thousand men, women, and children. He was sharply criticized for his "strange" ideas, which were described by criminologist Sheldon Glueck:[8]

> His method was to bail the offender after conviction, to utilize this favor as an entering wedge to the convict's confidence and friendship, and through such evidence of friendliness as helping the offender to obtain a job and aiding his family in various ways, to drive the wedge home. When the defendant was later brought into court for sentence, Augustus would report on his progress toward reformation, and the judge would usually fine the convict one cent and costs, instead of committing him to an institution.[9]

Augustus's efforts encouraged his home state of Massachusetts to pass the first probation statute in 1878. Four more states had followed suit by 1900. Probation was established as a legitimate alternative to incarceration, and a strong impetus to employ it came with the creation of the first juvenile court in 1899:[10] the need to supervise young offenders and keep them out of adult prisons.

John Augustus (1785–1859) called the father of probation, was a Boston shoemaker interested particularly in the temperance crusade in the 1840s. As a member of the Washington Total Abstinence Society, he worked at getting men to give up alcohol. Part of his voluntary service in Boston was to visit courts and request temporary suspensions or postponements of sentence.

The Spread of Probation

Juvenile probation service developed with the growing movement for juvenile courts. By 1910, thirty-seven states and the District of Columbia had passed a children's court act, and forty had established some kind of probation service for juveniles. Every state had enacted juvenile probation service in some measure by 1927, as the practice became firmly entrenched.

Not until 1956, however, was probation available for adult offenders in every state. The variations in the organization and operation of probation services make it difficult to compare them by state, but the growth in the number of registered probation officers attests to the rapid acceptance of this area of corrections. In 1907, the first directory of probation officers identified 795 volunteers, welfare workers, court personnel, and part-time personnel serving as officers. Most of them were in the juvenile system. By 1937 the figure had grown to over 3,800, of which 80 percent were in full-time service. By 1995, probation officers numbered over 59,000. Fifty-two agencies, with 31,350 officers, reported adult probation services as one of their functions, with a total of 2,282,168 clients being supervised through an average client caseload of 117 probationers. (See Figure 10-2.) Probation is seen as one of the brightest hopes in the field of corrections, and the number of probation officers continues to grow.[11]

Probation at the End of the 1990s

Probation, often confused with the suspended sentence, is actually one form of a sentence in itself. The American Bar Association defines probation as follows:

> A sentence not involving confinement which imposes conditions and retains authority in the sentencing court to modify the conditions of the sentence or to resentence the offender if he [or she] violates the conditions. Such a sentence should not involve or require suspension of the imposition or execution of any other sentence. . . . A sentence to probation should be treated as a final judgment for purposes of appeal and similar procedural purposes.[12]

Across the nation, probation is administered by hundreds of separate agencies, with a wide variety of rules and structures within the states. Whereas one agency may be required to serve juvenile, misdemeanant, and felony offenders, another agency may handle only one type of offender. The term *probation* has multiple meanings within the multiple areas of corrections. As shown by Table 10-1, volumes and types of offenders on probation are quite large and varied.

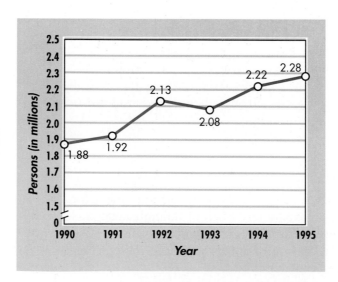

FIGURE

10.2

Number of Persons on Probation on January 1, 1990—1995

SOURCE: C. Camp and G. Camp, *The Corrections Yearbook 1995: Probation and Parole* (South Salem, NY: Criminal Justice Institute, 1995), p. 19.

Figures 10-3, 10-4, and 10-5 compare the types of sentences by the nature of the conviction, the average length of probation sentences for felons, and the types of offenses of felons sentenced to probation by sex. This gives the reader a somewhat clear view of the types of persons and how long a specific kind of probationer can expect to be under supervision. This snapshot of probation is the most recent data available and reflects the status of probation at the end of 1992. Indications are that this pattern would be similar today.

As a *disposition*, probation was first seen as a new type of suspended sentence. If convicted offenders could meet certain conditions established by the court, they were allowed to remain in their communities under limited freedom. Those conditions vary greatly from jurisdiction to jurisdiction and judge to judge, but they usually include prohibitions regarding drinking, travel, association with undesirable persons, restitution, community work orders, house arrest, electronic monitoring, and intensively supervised probation. Currently, probation is a sentence in its own right.

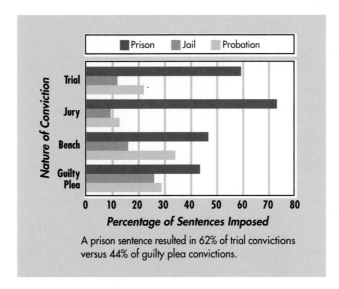

A prison sentence resulted in 62% of trial convictions versus 44% of guilty plea convictions.

FIGURE

10.3

Types of Sentences Imposed by State Courts, by Nature of Conviction, 1992

SOURCE: Patrick Langan and Robyn Cohen, *State Court Sentencing of Convicted Felons, 1992* (Washington, D.C.: U.S. Department of Justice, 1996), p. 41.

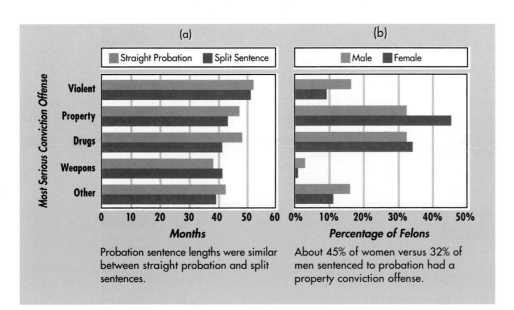

Probation sentence lengths were similar between straight probation and split sentences.

About 45% of women versus 32% of men sentenced to probation had a property conviction offense.

FIGURES

10.4 & 10.5

(a) Average Probation Sentence for Felons Convicted in State Courts, 1992

(b) Offenses of Felons Sentenced to Probation, by Sex, 1992

SOURCE: Patrick Langan and Robyn Cohen, *State Court Sentencing of Convicted Felons, 1992* (Washington, D.C.: U.S. Department of Justice, 1996), p. 29.

TABLE *10.1*

Types of Felony Sentences Imposed by State Courts, by Most Serious Offense, 1992

Conviction Offense	Percent of Felons Sentenced by Most Serious Incarceration			
	Total	Prison	Jail	Probation
All offenses	100%	44%	26%	30%
Violent offenses	100	60	21	19
Murder	100	93	4	3
Rape	100	68	19	13
Robbery	100	74	14	12
Aggravated assault	100	44	28	28
Other violent	100	39	29	32
Property offenses	100	42	24	34
Burglary	100	52	23	25
Larceny	100	38	27	35
Fraud	100	31	21	48
Drug offenses	100	42	28	30
Possession	100	33	29	38
Trafficking	100	48	27	25
Weapons offenses	100	40	26	34
Other offenses	100	35	30	35

SOURCE: Patrick Longan and Robyn Cohen, *State Court Sentencing of Convicted Felons, 1992* (Washington., D.C.: U.S. Department of Justice, 1996), p. 4.

As a *status*, probation has many advantages for offenders. Although their freedom is somewhat limited, their status is considered better than that of confined offenders. They are neither completely free nor totally restricted; they can work, keep their families off welfare, avoid the stigma of incarceration, and make restitution to their victims.

As a *subsystem* of the criminal justice system, probation has many different structures and organizations. In that context, it refers to the administrative agency that offers the probation service to juvenile or adult offenders.[13]

The set of functions, activities, and services that probation performs for its administrative agency and the offender is the probation *process*. The process model for probation service is usually seen as a series of interlinking activities among the courts, the offender, and the offender's community and its resources. The process includes the offender's *reporting* regularly to a probation officer; the *servicing* of the offender's needs through treatment, counseling, and so on; and the officer's *supervision* of the probationer to ensure that the rules of the probation order are observed.[14] Hence probation today is a process that gives the judge an alternative disposition, which results in an improved status for the offender within a subsystem of the criminal justice system.

Organization and Administration of Probation

The problems associated with a lack of organization in the criminal justice system are exemplified in probation services. Under the original concept, the judges themselves were to administer the probation services. For small jurisdictions this may still be the

Is Sentencing Affecting Probation?

The number of inmates in state and federal prisons jumped from 755,425 at the end of 1990 to 1,053,738 in 1995, or 39.5 percent. This is the highest number of inmates ever held in American prisons, and the percentage increase between 1990 and 1995 is the highest in modern history. The number of probationers also increased, however, in the same time frame. The totals rose from 2,670,234 to 2,843,455 between 1990 and 1994 (up 6 percent). We now have more than 1.5 percent of the adults in the nation on probation.

As we continue to escalate the incarceration of increasing numbers of dangerous and violent offenders in America's pris-

ons, who are the offenders now on probation? Some are higher-risk offenders who would be incarcerated in earlier years and would not have come to the attention of the courts as potential probationers. The increase in the prison and the probation populations suggests we continue to narrow the options for social control in America, a trend that seems to be picking up steam as we head for the year 2000. ■

SOURCE: Bureau of Justice Statistics, *Correctional Populations in the United States* (Washington, D.C.: U.S. Department of Justice, 1995), p. 1.

case in some instances, and those judges may be the best-informed decision makers in the criminal justice system. Most states, however, administer probation through a wide range of organizational and operational systems that are often unresponsive to one another's goals or efforts. The most common plan offers probation service at the state level.[15] Even in those states that have attempted to form a state-administered probation system, county participation has sometimes been maintained at the discretion of local officials. This concept of local autonomy is an American tradition, but it has hampered efforts to develop integrated probation services on a statewide basis.[16]

The means of administering probation programs are as varied as the types of organizations. Many are administered by judges, some by social workers, and a few by persons trained in public administration. In some states (such as Florida), the Salvation Army provides presentence investigation services, as well as probation case supervision for select offenders. The need for public administration training for probation personnel has been expressed in at least two major studies.[17] Because the methods of most probation officers reflect the background and training of their administrators, there is little uniformity in approaches. Different perspectives at different levels within the same agency can result in

Parole agent counsels a parolee

—COURTESY OF STATE OF CALIFORNIA DEPARTMENT OF CORRECTIONS

TABLE 10.2		
Percentage and Types of Persons on Probation: 1991, 1995		
	1/1/92	*1/1/95*
Percentage on probation	59.7%	59.3%
Average probationers per jurisdiction	40,994	43,888
Percentage female	19.9%	19.6%
Percentage nonwhite	33.6%	44.2%
Average agency caseload	113	117
Daily cost per probationer	$2.33	$2.49

SOURCE: C. Camp and G. Camp, *The Correction Yearbook: Probation and Parole 1993, 1995.* (South Salem, NY: Criminal Justice Institute, 1993, 1995), p. 5.

poorly defined goals and policies within the organization. The deeply rooted tradition of placing and keeping probation under court supervision, combined with rapid expansion of services, has undermined those agencies' effectiveness. That problem is especially critical in states that have not made an effort to train their administrators, especially at the executive and middle-management levels. Training probation officers in the field is a highly commendable goal, but change must begin at the management level to ensure maximum benefit from the officers' increased skills.

PROBATION SUBSIDY

A probation subsidy is a program run by a state. The subsidy provides money to counties and local jurisdictions for not committing offenders to prisons. The intents of subsidies are to bolster local probation services, encourage expansion of probation services, develop innovative probation strategies, and lessen the prison overcrowding problem.

Probation subsidies originated in California and, for a period before the resurgence of neoclassical ideology, forced sharp changes in an otherwise enlightened environment and reduced the proportion of felony offenders sentenced to California penal institutions. Increasing probation service strength also saved the California prison system millions of dollars in the interim. Coupled with intermediate punishments, particularly intensive supervised probation, such subsidies could form the backbone of a correctional reform in many states suffering from prison overcrowding.

Probation Services

As shown in Table 10-2, the probation officer has a heavy workload burden in most jurisdictions. The average probation officer suffers from the problem of serving two masters. The officer is usually required to meet with probationers to discuss their progress and troubles (casework)[18] and to give the court his or her reports and recommendations. The idea that the probation officer must often act as a social worker has had a profound effect on the development of probation services. Earlier, overemphasis on casework and the medical model of the probation officer as a "therapist" resulted in a narrow focus on the relationship between probationer and officer. As a consequence, many officers overlooked the social factors that might have contributed to the offender's criminal behavior, such as poverty, unemployment, poor housing, racism, poor health, and lack of education. The undesirability of the casework emphasis was expressed in a report by the National Advisory Commission on Criminal Justice Standards and Goals:

> The social task in corrections seems to call for social workers rather than for caseworkers or group workers. All social workers in corrections work with individuals, groups, and communities, with less emphasis on the use of one method than is characteristic of many social-work jobs.[19]

Casework

Casework generally refers to the social work model of offering services to the client based on an analysis of the case and diagnosis of client needs, problems, and designing a treatment plan to rehabilitate the offender. This approach reflects a medical model of corrections that raises the two questions of "Who are offenders?" and "What shall we do with them?" The answers are "They are sick, and corrections should heal them and make them well."

Faced with the realities that most federal probation officers are not well prepared to provide casework and that most clients do not require that approach, the Federal Probation Service has shifted emphasis to a Community Resource Management Team Model. Basically, this approach argues that the offender should be reintegrated in the community, using existing community resources. Team members, usually specializing in one aspect of client needs (such as employment, drug abuse problems, emotional counseling), serve as "brokers," referring clients to local facilities and services. This **team approach** is believed to be a more effective reintegration approach than an officer would provide through conducting classical casework therapy.

One inherent drawback in the casework model is the likelihood that the officer will try to exceed the limited function assigned to probation. Placing probationers in foster homes, operating shelters for them, and attempting to deal with such extreme problems as alcoholism, drug addiction, and mental illness should properly be the concern of the appropriate community agency, not the probation officer. Probation officers do not usually have the background required to handle all the problems of their probationers. But probation officers are expected to account for their probationers if they get into trouble again. One of the first questions asked by the court in this circumstance is usually "When did you last see your client?" In a system that demands accountability of that kind, probation officers often overextend themselves in an effort to prevent or justify their clients' failures.

A probation officer supervised an average of 117 probationers in 1995 and will probably handle more in 1998, hardly the ideal **caseload**. While the concept of an optimum, or ideal, caseload (such as thirty-five or fifty cases) is handy when calculating rough estimates of resources, the danger is that those figures seem to translate into the "standard" caseload that each officer should carry, even though different probationers require different kinds and degrees of service. A frequent response to the pressures resulting from highly mixed caseloads is the establishment of a standardized procedure for all cases, regardless of their complexity. A broad system of different treatments, assigning specific kinds of cases to specific types of probation officers, is a crucial need. Methods of providing the probation service are undergoing rapid change.

NEGATIVE SUBSIDY

In addition to the policy option of subsidizing probation services in counties that commit fewer than expected offenders to prison every year, or for meeting state requirements and standards, some states have decided that certain types of offenders ought to be kept in their local community under probation control. To encourage such retention, Oregon charges each county $3,000 for every committed offender whose crime falls in the "least severe" category. This means that a check for $3,000 must accompany the commitment papers when the least risky case offender is transported to prison. This is a "negative" subsidy, designed to encourage local communities to accept responsibility for providing correctional care and control for their own residents.

Prisoners learnng a trade at a work-release program

— *PHOTO BY RUSS KINNE, COURTESY OF COMSTOCK*

Restrictions and Conditions

Restrictions on and conditions of probation are usually a result of statutory requirements and the opinion of the sentencing court regarding the offender. Most states have a number of **statutory restrictions** for felony cases, usually related to the type of offense. Probation will often be denied to an offender with a prior record or one convicted of murder or sex crimes. Murder and rape are the most universally recognized offenses that do not permit probation. Otherwise, restrictive offenses and standards vary greatly among states. The most important aid in deciding to deny or grant probation is giving detailed and accurate pre-sentencing information to the judge. It is also important to ensure that the decision-making process focuses on the offender, not the offense, insofar as the statutes will allow. This is difficult when statutory limitations are extensive. Although many states are moving toward eliminating mandatory exclusions, others are expanding their list of exclusions. See Figure 10-6 for a probation order.

Rules or conditions for probation cannot be formulated as a set of standard operating procedures. The **conditions** for continuing probation should be tailored to the needs of the individual offender. Unfortunately, the court's frequent delegation of rule-making power to probation officers puts them in the almost impossible position of being lawmakers, enforcers, and confidants. The most effective way to ensure that rules are not established arbitrarily is to have them carefully reviewed by the court. In a situation in which probation officers are devising too many rules, their violations will soon overload the court.

It is generally conceded that probation rules should not extend to every kind of conduct. A number of courts require the probation officer who makes the pre-sentence investigation to recommend the conditions for the offender's probation, which are usually based on the officer's expectations regarding where the offender will be living, how he or she will make a living, and so on. The terms are discussed by the judge with the probation candidate, his or her counsel, and the probation officer. Decisions made in this manner will usually result in a few important restrictions, giving the probationer a clear idea of what constitutes acceptable behavior.

STATE OF NORTH CAROLINA

File No. _____

_____ County _____ Seat Of Court

In The General Court Of Justice
☐ District ☐ Superior Court Division

NOTE:
(This form is not to be used for multiple offenses unless they are consolidated for judgment.)

STATE VERSUS

Defendant _____

Race	Sex	DOB

JUDGMENT SUSPENDING SENTENCE
AND
COMMITMENT ON SPECIAL PROBATION
G.S. 15A-1341, 15A-1342, 15A-1343, 15A-1346

Attorney For State _____

Def. Found ☐ Not Indigent Def. Waived ☐ Attorney

Attorney For Defendant _____ ☐ Appointed ☐ Retained

The defendant ☐ pled guilty to: ☐ was found guilty by the Court of: ☐ was found guilty by a jury of: ☐ pled no contest to:

File No.(s) And Offense(s)	Date of Offense	G.S. No.	Fel./M.	Class	Max. Term	Presumptive

The Court has considered the aggravating and mitigating factors in G.S. 15A-1340.4(a) and
☐ makes no written findings because the prison term imposed does not require such findings.
☐ makes no written findings because the prison term imposed is pursuant to a plea arrangement as to sentence.
☐ makes the Findings Of Factors In Aggravation And Mitigation Of Punishment set forth on the attached AOC-CR-303.

The Court, having considered evidence, arguments of counsel and statement of defendant, finds that the defendant's plea was freely, voluntarily, and understandingly entered, and Orders the above offenses be consolidated for judgment and the defendant be imprisoned.

for a term of _____ in the custody of the
☐ N.C. Dept. of Correction
☐ Sheriff of _____ County

The defendant shall be given credit for _____ days spent in confinement prior to the date of this Judgment as a result of this charge, to be applied toward the ☐ sentence imposed above. ☐ imprisonment required for special probation below.

SUSPENSION OF SENTENCE

With the consent of the defendant and subject to the conditions set out below, the execution of this sentence is suspended and the defendant is placed on ☐ supervised probation for _____ years. ☐ unsupervised probation for _____ years.
☐ The above period of probation shall begin: ☐ when the defendant is paroled or otherwise released from incarceration in the case referred to below. ☐ at the expiration of the sentence in the case referred to below.
(**NOTE:** List Case Number, Date, County And Court In Which Prior Sentence Imposed.)

SPECIAL PROBATION – G.S. 15A-1351

☐ As a condition of special probation, the defendant shall ☐ serve an active term of _____ ☐ days ☐ months in the custody of the ☐ N.C. DOC. ☐ Sheriff of this County. ☐ submit to IMPACT imprisonment per attached CR-302, Page Two. ☐ pay jail fees.
(**NOTE:** This term shall NOT be reduced by good time, gain time or parole, or, unless provided above, by time in jail awaiting trial.)

The defendant shall report in a sober condition to begin serving his term on:

Day	Date	Hour	☐ AM ☐ PM

and shall remain in custody until:

Day	Date	Hour	☐ AM ☐ PM

☐ The defendant shall again report in a sober condition to continue serving this term on the same day of the week for the next _____ consecutive weeks, and shall remain in custody during the same hours each week.

MONETARY CONDITIONS

The defendant shall pay to the Clerk of Superior Court the "Total Amount Due" shown below, plus the probation supervision fee set by law ☐ pursuant to a schedule determined by the probation officer. ☐ at the rate of $ _____ per _____, beginning on _____ and continuing on the same day of each _____ thereafter until paid in full. ☐ Other:

Fine $	Costs $	Restitution* $	Attorney's Fee $	Community Service Fee $	Total Amount Due $

*The name(s) and address(es) and amount(s) due the person(s) to receive this restitution are:

☐ All payments received by the Clerk shall first be disbursed pro rata among the persons entitled to restitution.
☐ Upon payment of the "Total Amount Due", the probation officer may transfer the defendant to unsupervised probation.

AOC-CR-302, Rev. 7/91   Material opposite unmarked squares is to be disregarded as surplusage.

(Continued on page 194)

FIGURE
10.6

Probation Agreement Form

SOURCE: North Carolina Department of Correction, Division of Adult Probation and Parole. Reprinted with permission.

Even when probationers have a clear picture of what conditions are expected, many cannot conform to them due to multiple problems, drug dependency, rebelliousness, and a sense of "having gotten away with it" because the judge did not sentence them to a prison term. Under those conditions, judges increasingly engage in **tourniquet sentencing:** tightening the conditions of probation until the offender begins to constrain his or her behavior to avoid more punitive conditions. This is particularly seen in the intermediate punishments, those sentencing dispositions that fall between

FIGURE

10.6(Con't.)

Probation Agreement
Form

SOURCE: North Carolina Department of Correction, Division of Adult Probation and Parole. Reprinted with permission.

REGULAR CONDITIONS OF PROBATION – G.S. 15A-1343(b)

The defendant shall: 1. Commit no criminal offense in any jurisdiction. 2. Possess no firearm, explosive device or other deadly weapon listed in G.S. 14-269. 3. remain gainfully and suitably employed or faithfully pursue a course of study or of vocational training that will equip him for suitable employment. 4. Satisfy child support and family obligations, as required by the Court. If the defendant is on supervised probation, he shall also: 5. Remain within the jurisdiction of the Court unless granted written permission to leave by the Court or his probation officer. 6. Report as directed by the Court or his probation officer to the officer at reasonable times and places and in a reasonable manner, permit the officer to visit him at reasonable times, answer all reasonable inquiries by the officer and obtain prior approval from the officer for, and notify the officer of, any change in address or employment. 7. Notify the probation officer if he fails to obtain or retain satisfactory employment. 8. At a time to be designated by his probation officer, visit with his probation officer at a facility maintained by the Division of Prisons. If the defendant is to serve an active sentence as a condition of special probation, he shall also: 9. Obey the rules and regulations of the Department of Correction governing the conduct of inmates while imprisoned. 10. Report to a probation officer in the State of North Carolina within 72 hours of his discharge from the active term of imprisonment.

SPECIAL CONDITIONS OF PROBATION – G.S. 15A-1343(b1), 143B-262(c)

The defendant shall also comply with the following special conditions which the Court finds are reasonably related to his rehabilitation:

☐ 11. Surrender his driver's license to the Clerk of Superior Court for transmittal to the Division of Motor Vehicles and not operate a motor vehicle for a period of _____ or until relicensed by the Division of Motor Vehicles, whichever is later.

☐ 12. Submit at reasonable times to warrantless searches by a probation officer of his person, and of his vehicle and premises while he is present, for the following purposes which are reasonably related to his probation supervision:
☐ stolen goods ☐ controlled substances ☐ contraband ☐ _____

☐ 13. Not use, possess, or control any illegal drug or controlled substance unless it has been prescribed for him by a licensed physician and is in the original container with the prescription number affixed on it; not knowingly associate with any known or previously convicted users, possessors, or sellers of any illegal drugs or controlled substances; and not knowingly be present at or frequent any place where illegal drugs or controlled substances are sold, kept, or used.

☐ 14. Supply a breath, urine, and/or blood specimen for analysis of the possible presence of a prohibited drug or alcohol, when instructed by his probation officer.

☐ 15. Successfully pass the General Education Development Test (G.E.D.) during the first _____ months of the period of probation.

☐ 16. Complete _____ hours of community or reparation service during the first _____ days of the period of probation, as directed by the community service coordinator, and pay the fee prescribed by G.S. 143B-475.1(b) ☐ pursuant to the schedule set out under monetary conditions above. ☐ within _____ days of this Judgment and before beginning service.

☐ 17. Report for initial evaluation by _____,
participate in all further evaluation, counseling, treatment, or education programs recommended as a result of that evaluation, and comply with all other therapeutic requirements of those programs until discharged.

☐ 18. Other:

☐ 19. Comply with the Additional Conditions Of Probation which are set forth on AOC-CR-302, Page Two.

☐ A hearing was held in open court in the presence of the defendant at which time a fee, including expenses, was awarded the defendant's appointed counsel or assigned public defender.

ORDER OF COMMITMENT/APPEAL ENTRIES

☐ It is ORDERED that the Clerk deliver three certified copies of this Judgment and Commitment to the Sheriff or other qualified officer, and that the officer cause the defendant to be delivered with these copies to the custody of the agency named on the reverse to serve the sentence imposed or until he shall have complied with the conditions of release pending appeal.

☐ The defendant gives notice of appeal from the judgment of the District Court to the Superior Court. The current pretrial release order shall remain in effect. ☐ except that:

☐ The defendant gives notice of appeal from the judgment of the Superior Court to the Appellate Division. Appeal entries and any conditions of post conviction release are set forth on Form AOC-CR-350.

SIGNATURE OF JUDGE

Date	Name Of Presiding Judge (Type Or Print)	Signature Of Presiding Judge

CERTIFICATION

I certify that this Judgment and the attachment(s) marked below are true copies of the originals.
☐ Judgment Suspending Sentence, Page Two [Additional Conditions Of Probation (AOC-CR-302, Page Two)]
☐ Findings Of Factors In Aggravation And Mitigation Of Punishment (AOC-CR-303)

Date Of Certification	Date Certified Copies Delivered To Sheriff	Signature And Seal
		☐ Deputy CSC ☐ Assistant CSC ☐ Clerk Of Superior Court

NOTE: Defendant signs the following statement in all cases except unsupervised probation without community or reparation service.
I have received a copy of this Judgment which contains all of the conditions of my probation, and I agree to them. I understand that no person who supervises me or for whom I work while performing community or reparation service is liable to me for any loss or damage which I may sustain unless my injury is caused by that person's gross negligence or intentional wrongdoing.

Date Signed	Signature Of Defendant	Witnessed By:

AOC-CR-302, Side Two, Rev. 7/91   Material opposite unmarked squares is to be disregarded as surplusage.

---

probation and long-term incarceration. They include victim restitution, community work orders, house arrest, electronic monitoring and intensive supervised probation, and are sometimes known as "probation plus" programs. See Figure 10-7.

Felony Probation

The rapid growth of serious and violent crime in America has spurred a movement toward the increase in the use of *felony* probation. Probation, as we have seen, has traditionally been for misdemeanors and low-level nonviolent crime. Prison over-

Probation officer visits a client at home

—PHOTO BY M.K DENNY, *COURTESY OF PHOTOEDIT*

crowding and bulging jails have forced the correctional administrators to take a close look at some other categories of felons for relief of an overtaxed system. A major study was conducted to determine the results, in terms of recidivism, if the definition of "eligible for probation" was loosened a bit. The total recidivism rate for three years was interesting and promising, a combined total of 62 percent (40 percent of those with felony arrests or disciplinary hearings and 22 percent for other reasons), which compares rather favorably to other recidivism studies at the end of three years from either prison or parole.[20]

Because the cost of incarceration and building costs have become so high, and the institutions so crowded, **felony probation** seems to be a concept that has come to be a calculated risk worth taking. We need only look at the dismal results from incarceration to agree that it may be possible to increase this option when combined with a thorough and complete presentencing investigation and consideration of risk. Programs combined with probation services to protect the community are expanded upon in the next chapter.

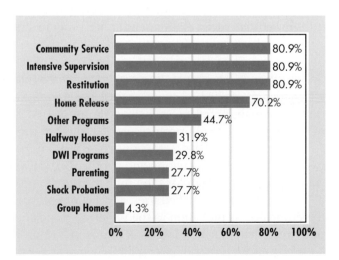

Program	Percentage
Community Service	80.9%
Intensive Supervision	80.9%
Restitution	80.9%
Home Release	70.2%
Other Programs	44.7%
Halfway Houses	31.9%
DWI Programs	29.8%
Parenting	27.7%
Shock Probation	27.7%
Group Homes	4.3%

FIGURE

10.7

Percentage of Jurisdictions Administering Specific Probation Programs (1994)

SOURCE: C. Camp and G. Camp, *The Corrections Yearbook 1995: Probation and Parole* (South Salem, NY: Criminal Justice Institute, 1995), p. 5.

Probationers Rearrested for a Felony Within Three Years

State courts in thirty-two counties across seventeen states sentenced 79,000 felons to probation in 1986. Within three years of sentencing, while still on probation, 43 percent were rearrested for a felony. An estimated 18 percent of the arrests were for a violent crime (murder, rape, robbery, or aggravated assault); 33 percent were for a drug offense (drug trafficking or drug possession).

Of each one hundred felony probationers tracked by this survey for three years

- twenty-six went to prison
- ten went to jail and
- ten absconded.

These findings are from a follow-up survey of felons on probation, using a sample that represented a fourth of the total 306,000 felons sentenced to probation in 1986. The survey used state criminal history files and probation files to obtain information. It was not based on a nationally representative sample; 39 percent of follow-up cases were from a single state.

Nevertheless, based on 12,370 sample cases representing 79,043 felons placed on probation in the counties and states studied, the follow-up represents the largest survey of its kind ever done. ∎

SOURCE: Bureau of Justice Statistics, *National Update*, Vol. 1, no. 4 (Washington, D.C.: U.S. Department of Justice, April 1992), p. 10.

Summary

Because of the prison population crisis across the nation, many states are exploring many strategies to reduce the overcrowding. Probation is one of the most popular of three types. The basic three strategies can be described as bricks and mortar, front-end solutions, and back-end solutions.

Bricks and mortar refers to attempts to construct new or renovate existing facilities to expand available beds. Even though there are literally billions of dollars in construction, renovation, expansion and ongoing retrofitting, no one with any understanding of the comprehensive nature of the problem holds much hope that the nation can build enough prisons to accommodate the influx of inmates (see Chapter 12).

Front-end solutions refers to those alternative sentences such as probation and intermediate punishments that include, among others, house arrest, deferred prosecution, electronic monitoring, shock probation, intensive supervised probation, intermittent jail incarceration, and other programs (see Chapter 11).

Back-end solutions refers to ways used to reduce prison populations after the offender arrives in prison. They can be viewed as "early-out" or "extended limits" options: parole, shock parole, emergency release (usually court ordered), expanded good-time credits to count against the minimum sentence, work and educational furlough, prerelease to halfway houses (used extensively by the U.S. Bureau of Prisons, the federal prison system), and other programs (see Chapter 13).

On the last day of 1992, there were 883,593 inmates in the prisons of the fifty-two jurisdictions of the nation and another 88,838 in other facilities and jails. This is another all-time high for the number incarcerated on a given day.[21]

Probation has established itself as a major component of corrections. It appears the emphasis on probation as the preferred disposition will keep it in the forefront of correctional reform. If the costs of prison and probation are compared, you will see a cost of $2.12 per day compared to an average of $50.22 per day in prison,[22] the taxpayer will rule in favor of probation. As the population grows, the number of offenders and variations on probation strategies will surely increase as well. Students of probation concur that the practice is approximately 75 percent effective on a national basis;[23] some states, particularly Nebraska, report a 90 percent success rate. An alternative to imprisonment that is about one-tenth as costly (and at least as effective) has great appeal and clearly answers the need for a sound and economical approach to corrections.

Review Questions

1. Explain the purpose of probation, and describe the methods by which it is usually administered.
2. What organizational system is best suited for probation? Why?
3. What are some of the restrictions often applied in probation? What kinds of offenders are usually denied probation?
4. Discuss the effectiveness of probation as compared with imprisonment.
5. Identify and define five "front-end" solutions to prison overcrowding.
6. What role conflicts are inherent in the nation's probation service, and how can they be reduced?
7. Why should probation be the sentence of choice?
8. Why have intensive supervision probation programs become so popular?

Words to Remember

probation	casework	conditions
suspended sentence	team approach	tourniquet sentencing
right of sanctuary	caseload	felony probation
benefit of clergy	statutory restrictions	

Endnotes

1. Combining alternatives at this level of the system is usually called "sanction stacking." See James Byrne, "The Future of Intensive Probation Supervision," *Crime and Delinquency* 36/1 (1990): 3-34.

2. George M. and Camille Graham Camp, *The Corrections Yearbook 1993: Probation and Parole* (South Salem, NY: Criminal Justice Institute, 1993), pp. 3–4.

3. Norman Johnston, *The Human Cage: A Brief History of Prison Architecture* (New York: Walker, 1973), p. 8: "The concept of imprisonment as a substitute for death or mutilation of the body was derived in part from a custom of the early Church of granting asylum or sanctuary to fugitives and criminals."

4. See Numbers 35:6 and Joshua 20:2–6.

5. Daniel E. Lundgren, *Crime and Delinquency in California: Advance Release* (Sacramento: California Department of Justice, May 1996), 2–3.

6. David Fogel, "Nordic Approaches to Crime and Justice," *CJ International* 3 (January–February 1987): 8–21. The importance of treatment is clearly delineated in Paul Gendreau and Robert Ross, "Revivication of Rehabilitation: Evidence from the 1980s," *Juvenile Justice Quarterly* 4 (1987): 349–408.

7. Alexander Smith and Louis Berlin, *Introduction to Probation and Parole* (St. Paul, MN: West, 1976), pp. 76–8.

8. Sheldon Glueck (1896–1980) was an American criminologist noted for his extensive long-range research on criminal careers. Those studies followed the history of many groups of young people; Glueck aimed to predict who might become delinquent. Glueck wrote many books with his wife, Eleanor, who was an equally famous criminologist and educator.

9. Harry Elmer Barnes and Negley K. Teeters, *New Horizons in Criminology,* 3rd ed. (Englewood Cliffs, NJ: Prentice Hall, 1959), p. 554.

10. Missouri (1897), Rhode Island (1899), New Jersey (1900), and Vermont (1900).

11. Camp and Camp, *The Corrections Yearbook 1993,* p. 7.

12. American Bar Association Project on Standards for Criminal Justice, *Standards Relating to Probation* (New York: Institute of Judicial Administration, 1970), p. 9.

13. Bureau of Justice Statistics, *Correctional Populations in the United States, 1994* (Washington, D.C.: U.S. Department of Justice, 1995).

14. Ibid.

15. Harry E. Allen et al., *Critical Issues in Adult Probation: Summary Report* (Washington, D.C.: U.S. Department of Justice, 1979), p. 43.

16. An exhaustive list of providers of probation services can be found in American Correctional Association, *ACA Directory of Juvenile and Adult Correctional Departments, Institutions, Agencies and Paroling Authorities* (Laurel, MD: American Correctional Association, 1996), pp. xiv–xv.

17. The two studies are *Joint Commission on Correctional Manpower and Training, Corrections 1968: A Climate for Change* (Washington, D.C.: JCCMT, 1968), p. 30, and Herman Piven and Abraham Alcabes, *The Crisis of Qualified Manpower for Criminal Justice: An Analytic Assessment with Guidelines for New Policy,* Vol. 1 (Washington, D.C.: U.S. Government Printing Office, 1969).

18. See John Whitehead, "Probation Mission Reform," *Criminal Justice Review* 9 (1984): 15–21, and "Job Burnout and Job Satisfaction Among Probation Managers," *Journal of Criminal Justice* 14 (1985): 29–40. For an examination of the impact of changing philosophies on probation officers, see Patricia Harris, Todd Clear, and Christopher Baird, "Have Community Supervision Officers Changed Their Attitudes Toward Their Work?" *Justice Quarterly* 6/2 (1989): pp. 233–246.

19. National Advisory Commission, *Corrections,* p. 319. See also R. Adams and H. J. Vetter, "Probation Caseload Size and Recidivism Rate," *British Journal of Criminology and Deviant Behavior* 11 11/4 (1971): 390-393. On classification, see the July 1987 issue of *Crime and Delinquency* 32 (1987): 251–390.

20. Patrick A. Langan and Mark A. Cunniff. *Recidivism of Felons on Probation 1986–89* (Washington, D.C.: U.S. Department of Justice, U.S. Government Printing Office, February 1992), p. 5.

21. Camp and Camp, *The Corrections Yearbook 1993,* pp. 3–4, and Darrell K. Gilliard, *Prisoners in 1992* (Washington, D.C.: U.S. Department of Justice, U.S. Government Printing Office, May 1993), p. 2.

22. Camp and Camp, *The Corrections Yearbook 1993: Probation and Parole,* pp. 3–4.

23. Allen et al., *Critical Issues in Adult Probation,* pp. 30–37.

CHAPTER ELEVEN

Intermediate Sanctions

Overview

Our investigation of the correctional process has focused thus far on the entry point of the overall process, jails, and probation as the major nonincarceration sanction in the minds of the sentencing judges. In this chapter we will explore the growing use of intermediate sanctions, the various and varied new correctional options used as adjuncts and part of probation, although some jurisdictions have not used these sanctions as adjuncts to probation.

The dominant characteristic of intermediate sanctions is the use of increased surveillance and tighter controls over offenders. Advocates for the offender object on the basis of these controls being increased *punishment* as a rationale for their objections to tighter controls. Others argue that prison construction is too expensive for most jurisdictions and intermediate sanctions permit cost avoidance of construction, staffing, and maintenance of incarceration facilities. Still other proponents note the reintegrative aspects of intermediate sanctions, and reduced recidivism among offenders assigned to such programs. Many are less expensive and more effective than incarceration. Although not fully integrated into the coordinated system of community corrections, these intermediate sanctions are rapidly being adopted across the nation into a wide system of local, county, state, and federal correctional systems. We first review the use of **intermediate sanctions** as an adjunct to probation.

As we saw in the previous chapter, probation has become the backbone of contemporary corrections, treating offenders and providing protection to the community through supervising probationers. In the last two decades, occasioned by crowding of jails and prisons as well as a shift in the philosophical assumptions about controlling offenders,[1] a broad range of different treatments and innovative technology have been developed. These innovative

This Nation's efforts to curb violence, drug trafficking, and other crimes have led to more convictions and longer sentences. Our prisons and jails are full, and large numbers of nonviolent offenders are being released to community supervision, primarily probation . . . .. [I]t is unlikely that this situation will change radically for the remainder of this decade.

—Michael Russell, Acting Director
National Institute of Justice (1993)

programs and control schemes are generally called *intermediate sanctions.*[2] The promise, practices, and protection of intermediate sanctions start with the overcrowding issue.

Overcrowding

As we observed earlier, street crime is a "young man's game," and national data consistently indicate that a large percentage of crimes are committed by young men ages fifteen to twenty-four. Initially as charges of the juvenile justice system, many continue their pattern of offending into adulthood and eventually enter the criminal justice system. Most persistent offenders receive increasingly severe punishments,[3] including sentences to jail and prison confinement. In the United States, there is a lag between onset of offending and eventual confinement as an adult of approximately ten years. In other words, persistent offenders are more likely to have been subject to correctional control (fines, **day attendance centers, restitution orders, house arrest,** and even **electronic monitoring**) while in the community before their incarceration.

Processing offenders in the justice system has become a risk management strategy, and persistent offenders are usually given increasingly restrictive alternatives while corrections tries to stop their criminal behavior ("desistance"). Many offenders are given a number of such opportunities and assistance before a sentencing judge resorts to incarceration, the most punitive arrow in the armory of corrections.

Before the 1970s, many if not most offenders were placed on probation, to achieve the ideal of rehabilitation.[4] Individualized treatment during that relatively progressive era became subject to strong attack by conservatives, researchers, and liberals of many stripes. The arguments were that corrections officials were abusing their discretion, rehabilitation did not work, strict law and order should be used to capture the streets, and offenders richly deserved punishment. This was seen as the only way to protect law-abiding citizens as well as to retain the social fabric. This philosophy was particularly evident in the nation's war on drugs, a war that has clearly not been won.

Coupled with the death of the medical model, politicians at both local and national levels used the issue of crime as a vehicle to demonstrate how getting tough would solve the problem.[5] Seeking reelection on the hard-line bandwagon

Intermediate Sanctions

Intermediate sanctions, ranging in severity from day fines to so-called boot camps, are interventions that are beginning to fill the sentencing gap between prison at one extreme and probation at the other. Lengthy prison terms may be inappropriate for some offenders; for others probation may be too inconsequential and may not provide the degree of public supervision necessary to ensure public safety.

By expanding sentencing options, intermediate sanctions enable the criminal justice system to tailor punishment more closely to the nature of the crime and the criminal. An appropriate range of punishments makes it possible for the system to hold offenders strictly accountable for their actions. ■

_____
SOURCE: Voncile Gowdy, *Intermediate Sanctions* (Washington, D.C.: U.S. Department of Justice, 1993), p. 2.

may have served narrow political ends. However, it also led to the enactment of a series of stringent policies ranging from a shift to determinate punishment, to mandatory minimum sentences to prison, and to the building of more supermaximum prisons.[6]

These events coincided with the 1945 to 1976 baby-boom population bulge, which entered the "high-commitment" years of ages twenty-nine to thirty-nine between 1975 and 1985. These three major forces (a larger number of persons at risk to commit crime and be incarcerated, the shift to conservative beliefs about how to deal with offenders and crime, and enactment of more stringent punishments) contributed to an ever-increasing stream of offenders being committed to prison (up from 448,264 to 1,053,000 in 1996).

By 1993, the combined number of prisoners in the nation and in jails exceeded any previous total. "America the Free" became the free world's leader in the rate of incarceration, surpassing South Africa and Singapore, and exceeded only by the Russian Republic (of the former Soviet Union). Prisons bulged, and the nation began a building binge, trying to construct sufficient numbers of jail and prison cells to accommodate the massive increase of incarcerated offenders. When it became evident that the bricks and mortar approach could not be met, correctional innovators turned to developing alternative punishment programs, variously known as intermediate sanctions/punishments. A study in 1993 clearly showed the comparison of rates of incarceration among the United States, South Africa, and the Russian Republic.[7] Figure 11-1 shows rates of 519, 368, and 558 per 100,000 population, respectively. What is even more interesting in this study was the comparison with the rest of the world's industrialized nations.

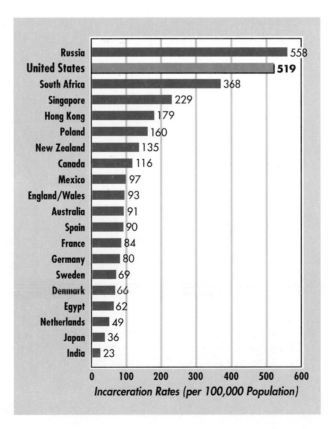

SOURCE: Mark Mauer, "The International Use of Incarceration," *The Prison Journal* 75:1 (1995): 113–123.

FIGURE 11.1

Incarceration Rates for Selected Nations (1994)

Intermediate sanctions provide midrange dispositions that better reflect the severity of the offense than do probation or imprisonment. While many if not most offenders can best be served by reintegration programming, some are thought to be too dangerous to be released to traditional probation supervision with infrequent face-to-face contacts. Thus a continuum of sanctions ranging from probation to imprisonment has been developed: restitution, fines, day fines, community service, intensive supervised probation, house arrest, electronic monitoring, and shock incarceration. The latter includes shock probation and shock parole, as well as boot camps. Figure 11-2 depicts the range of sentencing options. We begin our more detailed examination of these programs with **restitution**.

RESTITUTION PROGRAMS

A common condition for probation is the requirement that victims be compensated for their losses or injury. The emphasis given to the study of victimology in the last few years has resulted in some state compensation of crime victims by payment of medical costs and other financial reimbursement. Through the system of probation, however, the victim is often repaid by the offender. It is important that probation authorities link the amount of payment to the offender's ability to pay. Installment payment is usually the most realistic approach. In some cases a partial restitution may be all that is reasonably possible (for example, in the case of an arsonist who burns down a multimillion-dollar building). There are many reasons offered to support restitution programs. Obviously, restitution offsets the victim's loss when property is stolen; restitution can even be ordered for the deductible amount an insurance company might require an insured victim to pay before the insurance coverage would become effective. Time lost from work while being a witness in court and being hospitalized are subject to offender restitution. It appears that restitution may be ordered for any injury caused by the offense for which the offender was convicted. Other rationales are that restitution forces the offender to accept personal responsibility for the crime;

FIGURE

11.2

A Range of Sentencing Options, Ranked by the Level of Punishment

SOURCE: James Byrne, "The Future of Intensive Probation Supervision," *Crime and Delinquency* 36/1 (1990) pp.3-34.

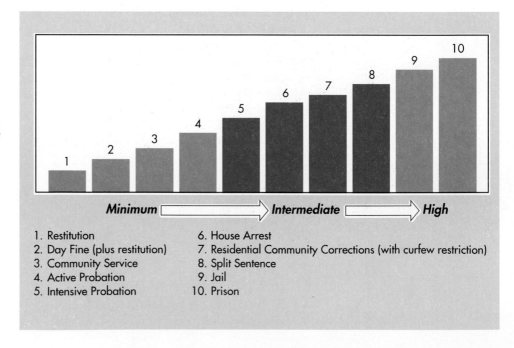

Minimum ⟹ Intermediate ⟹ High

1. Restitution
2. Day Fine (plus restitution)
3. Community Service
4. Active Probation
5. Intensive Probation
6. House Arrest
7. Residential Community Corrections (with curfew restriction)
8. Split Sentence
9. Jail
10. Prison

restitution can lead to reconciliation of offender and victim; and, finally, it provides one way the victim can become part of the otherwise impersonal processing of victims within the justice system. It appears that restitution programs are more numerous in the juvenile justice system than they are in the adult system.[8]

Although almost every state has restitution programs in operation (77.6 percent), Florida, Minnesota, and Michigan appear to be leaders in the development of American restitution programs. (Restitution programs have been extensively implemented and evaluated in Great Britain.) In Minnesota, parolees may also be required to reside in a residential center and pay part of their wages to victims. Other jurisdictions require victim-offender conferences to establish the amount of financial compensation to be given the victim.

DAY FINES

The fine is a common and widely accepted punishment[9] imposed on misdemeanors and some less serious felony offenses. A fine is a penalty imposed by a court that requires the offender to pay a specific amount of money. The fine is a cash payment of a dollar amount assessed by the judge on an individual basis or determined by a published schedule of penalties. Fines may be paid in installments in many jurisdictions or by use of the offender's credit card.

Monetary assessments are typically given to low-risk offenders, and the amount of this financial sanction tends to increase with the severity of the crime. Judges tend to employ rational discretion in these areas. Surprisingly, most fines are collected in large part if not in whole, and there is substantial evidence that the chance of further arrest and incarceration is significantly less for those assessed a fine than for those receiving a jail term, when the investigator controls for offender attributes and offense.[10]

Fines are an ancient and widely used penal measure, and noncustodial sanctions are not new in American sentencing. What is new is a variation on financial sanctions known as the **day fine**, so called because the amount of the fine is tied to an offender's daily earnings, a practice common in European and some South American countries. In the United States, this is not a common

RESTITUTION

Restitution is court-ordered condition of probation that requires the offender to repair the financial, emotional, or physical damage done (a reparative sentence) by making financial payment of money to the victim or, alternatively, to a fund to provide services to victims. In addition, restitution programs are frequently ordered in the absence of a sentence to probation.

How Day Fines Work

The general concept of day fines is simple: determining the amount of punishment to be administered to an offender is separated from a consideration of how much money that offender must pay. Judges determine how much punishment an offender deserves; this is then denominated into some unit other than money. These *punishment units* are then translated into monetary units based on how much money the offender makes per day.

Practically speaking, the day fine approach consists of a simple two-step process. First, the court uses a "unit scale" or "benchmark" to sentence the offender to a certain number of day fine units (for example, 15, 60, or 120 units) according

to the gravity of the offense and without regard to income. To guide the court's choices, benchmarks or unit scales are typically developed by a planning unit of judges, prosecutors, and defense counselors familiar with the disposition patterns of a court.

The value of each unit is then set at a percentage of the offender's daily income, and the total fine amount is determined by simple multiplication. ▪

SOURCE: Laura Winterfield and Sally Hillsman, *The Staten Island Day-Fine Project* (Washington, D.C.: U.S. Department of Justice, 1993), p. 1.

TOURNIQUET SENTENCING

James Byrne has identified the major sanction options that sentencing might impose, and ranked them by levels of punishment inherent in each. Restitution, for example, is seen as less punitive than community service; house arrest is a lower level of punishment than jail incarceration. You should remember that judges can and frequently do impose several sanctions simultaneously and retain authority to initiate *tourniquet sentencing*, a process that increases and tightens the numbers and conditions of punishments until the probationer is brought under the most effective control.

SOURCE: James Byrne, "The Future of Intensive Probation Supervision," *Crime and Delinquency*. 36/1 (1990), pp. 3-34

practice, for fines have traditionally been based on the offense rather than the individual offender's ability to pay. With the movement toward intermediate punishments, day fines have been enthusiastically incorporated into sentencing systems by judges who are increasingly interested in a graduated progression of intermediate penalties.

Sentencing judges will become more familiar and comfortable with the day fine, imposing financial penalties that can be adjusted to individual circumstances and cases. Day fines have the additional potential of raising total collected fine revenues and have been implemented not only in Staten Island, New York, but in numerous other jurisdictions across the country.[11]

INTENSIVE SUPERVISED PROBATION

Another alternative sanction program is **intensive supervised probation** (ISP), designed to provide increased surveillance of offenders deemed to be too serious for "routine" probation. The program is a management strategy for probation services, which might need to increase the level of surveillance for individuals who were not adjusting on probation. ISP is a program frequently found in "tourniquet sentencing."

Georgia is believed to be the first jurisdiction to impose a statewide system of ISP (starting in 1974) and, by 1995, forty-six states had implemented such programs. No doubt every state has at least one jurisdiction—city, county, or even the state—with the program.

There is no generic ISP. It is a form of release that emphasizes close monitoring of convicted offenders and requires rigorous conditions on that release. Most ISP programs call for the following:

- Some combination of multiple weekly contacts with a supervising officer;
- Random and unannounced drug testing;
- Stringent enforcement of probation or parole conditions;
- Required participation in relevant treatment programs, employment, and perhaps community service.[12]

Types of ISPs

ISPs are usually classified as prison diversion, enhanced probation, and enhanced parole. Each has a different goal. *Diversion* is commonly referred to as a "front door" program because its goal is to limit the number of offenders entering prison. Prison diversion programs generally identify incoming lower risk inmates to participate in an ISP in the community as a substitute for a prison term.

Enhancement programs generally select already sentenced probationers and parolees and subject them to closer supervision in the community than regular probation or parole. People placed in ISP-enhanced probation or enhanced parole programs show evidence of failure under routine supervision or have committed offenses deemed to be too serious for supervision on routine caseloads.

Treatment and service components in the ISPs included drug and alcohol counseling, employment, community service, and payment of restitution. On many of these measures, ISP offenders participated more than control members; participation in such programs was found to be correlated with a reduction in recidivism. ∎

SOURCE: Joan Petersilia and Susan Turner, *Evaluating Intensive Supervision of Probation/Parole: Results of a Nationwide Experiment* (Washington, D.C.: U.S. Department of Justice, 1993), pp. 2, 7.

Intensive supervision programs have become increasingly popular because they offer many attractive strategies: diversion of offenders from prison,[13] "getting tough" on crime (without the appearance of "being soft on criminals" because the offender is not incarcerated), increasing control over "marginal" offenders, avoiding the huge cash outlay for prison construction, surveillance enhancement, and lowering the overall cost of correctional supervision.

Persons placed on ISP usually have more frequent contacts with probation officers who are carrying smaller caseloads. In Georgia, for example, two officers might share a caseload of twenty-five probationers, or a team of three officers might supervise forty probationers.[14] Typically, ISP probationers make restitution payments, perform community work, work at legal employment, pay probation fees,[15] and undergo random alcohol-[16] and drug-use testing.

Intensive supervised probation programs have been implemented in almost every state and some counties, including Santa Clara, California, Washington, Ohio, Georgia, and Florida, to name a few. Initial evaluations and implications were favorable and later evaluations indicate more success with certain types of offenders.[17] This control sanction will be increasingly adopted and refined in future years.

COMMUNITY SERVICE PROGRAMS

Community service or work orders represent court-ordered voluntary work for specified numbers of hours that offenders perform, usually in the form of free labor to some charitable organization or in public service such as serving as a volunteer

Georgia's Experience with Intensive Probation Supervision

Although probation programs with varying degrees of supervision have been implemented throughout the country, Georgia's ISP is widely regarded as one of the most stringent in the nation. Standards include the following:

- Five face-to-face contacts per week
- 132 hours of mandatory community service
- Mandatory curfew
- Weekly checks of local arrest records
- Automatic notification of arrest elsewhere via the State Crime Information Network listing
- Routine and unannounced alcohol and drug testing.

The supervision standards are enforced by a team consisting of a probation officer and a surveillance officer. The team supervises twenty-five probationers. In some jurisdictions, a team of one probation officer and two surveillance officers supervises forty probationers. The standards are designed to help offenders direct their energies toward productive activities, to assume responsibilities, and to become law-abiding citizens. Most offenders chosen for the ISP program were already sentenced to prison, presented an acceptable risk to the community, and had not committed a violent offense. A risk assessment instrument was used to screen select offenders. While the majority of those selected fell into the category of nonviolent property offenders, a large number of individuals convicted of drug- and alcohol-related offenses were included as the program developed. Some of these offenses also involved violence.

Of the original 2,322 people in the program between 1982 and 1985, 370 (or 16 percent) absconded or had their probation revoked. The remaining 1,952 were successfully diverted from prison; many were still under some form of probationary supervision. The highest rate of success (87 percent) was seen in drug-related criminal offenders, and Georgia reduced the percentage of felons incarcerated from 37 to 27 percent. Georgia achieved a cost savings of nearly $6,000 per offender served. ■

SOURCE: Billie S. Erwin, *Evaluation of Intensive Probation Supervision in Georgia* (Atlanta: Georgia Department of Correction, 1987), pp. 2-3.

hospital orderly, doing street cleaning, performing maintenance or repair of public housing, or providing service to indigent groups. Some examples of the latter would be sentencing a dentist to perform one hundred hours of free dental service to welfare recipients or a physician to provide fifty hours of free medical attention to jail inmates on Saturdays.

Both **community work orders** and restitution programs have their critics.[18] Some argue that offenders committing crimes of violence should not be allowed a penalty less than incarceration for their offenses, and that the physical and psychological costs to victims of crimes of violence are almost impossible to calculate. There also seems to be some uncertainty over whether an offender sentenced to perform community work or restitution ought to be resentenced to incarceration for noncompliance. Despite the criticism, there appears to be consensus that offenders should repay their victims for losses, even if the repayment is as symbolic as community work.

HOME DETENTION

In the United States, house arrest, usually conjuring up images of political control and fascist repression, is court-ordered **home detention**, confining offenders to their households for the duration of sentence. Introduced in 1984 in Florida, home detention rapidly spread throughout a nation searching for punitive, safe, and secure alternatives to incarceration.[19] The sentence is usually in conjunction with probation but may be imposed by the court as a separate punishment (as it is in Florida). Florida's Community Control Program (FCCP) was designed to provide a safe diversion alternative and to help address the problem of prison population escalation and associated high costs.[20]

Participants may be required to make victim compensation, perform community work service, pay probation fees, undergo drug and alcohol testing and, in some instances, wear electronic monitoring equipment to verify their presence in the residence. (In some jurisdictions, house arrest is used on a pretrial basis, as an isolated sentence, in conjunction with probation or parole, or with a prerelease status such as education or work furlough.) House arrest allows the offender to leave his or her residence only for specific purposes and hours approved by the court or supervising officer, and being absent without leave is a technical violation

Florida Community Control Program (FCCP)

Although based in the community, not behind bars, the FCCP is in no way soft treatment for those sentenced to it; rather, it is punishment oriented, with stringent safeguards for the public's safety. Those offenders not actually undertaking an approved activity, such as drug treatment, are often under house arrest. Supervising officers visit them a minimum of twenty-eight times a month, and the state's sentencing guidelines list a term on community control as just below prison—and ahead of jail—in severity.

The National Council on Crime and Delinquency [evaluation] found that not only has the program helped alleviate prison crowding, but the offenders who complete the program demonstrate a lower new offense rate than those released from a prison term for similar offenses. ∎

SOURCE: Charles DeWitt, in Dennis Wagner and Christopher Baird, eds., Evaluation of the Florida Community Control Program (Washington, D.C.: U.S. Department of Justice, 1993), p. 2.

Electronic monitoring allows
house arrest to be more
effective

—PHOTO BY RICARDO DEARATANHA,
COURTESY OF LOS ANGELES TIMES PHOTO

of conditions that may result in resentencing to jail or prison.[21] Home detention
is a punitive sentence and was designed in most cases to relieve institutional overcrowding. For many offenders it is their last chance to escape from being committed to prison. In addition to surveillance of the offender, home detention is
viewed as a cost avoidance program, a front-end solution to prison overcrowding,
and a flexible alternative for certain offenders (such as a pregnant offender until
time of delivery). The use of telemonitoring devices, discussed later, can significantly increase the correctional surveillance of offenders.

The most significant critical argument against home detention is that, by
making a nonincarcerative control mechanism available to corrections, many
petty offenders are brought under correctional control who would best be handled by diversion, fines, or mental health services. In general, such inclusive
actions are viewed as "net widening," which occurs when offenders are sentenced to community control who might otherwise have received a lesser or
even no sentence.

The National Council on Crime and Delinquency conducted an evaluation
of the FCCP and concluded that the impact on prison crowding, offender behavior, and state correctional costs has been positive. With an estimated prison diversion rate of 54 percent, community control is cost effective despite the combined
effect of net widening and the punishments imposed on almost 10 percent of
FCCP participants for technical violations. Furthermore, the new offense rate for
community control offenders is lower than for similar offenders sentenced to
prison and released without supervision. For every one hundred cases diverted
from prison, Florida saved more than $250,000.[22]

Home detention is expected to receive increased endorsement in the remainder of this decade and may become the sentence of choice for many nonviolent
offenders in lieu of jail, prison, or even formal probation.

 FURLOUGH
Furloughing is a
prison release pro-
gram permitting the
inmate to pursue education,
vocational training, or employment in the community.
Another purpose is to achieve
closer surveillance of the
offender by requiring a transitional period of up to 120 days
in a community residential center (CRC). The Bureau of
Prisons requires almost every
offender nearing release from
confinement to reside in a CRC
as prerelease furloughees. In
most jurisdictions, furloughees
are legally inmates and can be
more easily returned to confinement if they commit technical violations or a new offense.

ELECTRONIC MONITORING

Home detention has a long history as a criminal penalty, but its new popularity with correctional authorities is due to the advent of electronic monitoring, a technological link thought to make the sanction both practical and affordable.

The concept of electronic monitoring is not new, having been proposed in 1964 by Schwitzgebel as **electronic parole**, and initially used to monitor the location of mental patients.[23] One of the first studies of home detention enforced by electronic monitoring began in 1986 and, by early 1992, there were at least 40,000 electronic monitors in use.[24]

Electronic monitoring can be active or passive. In active monitoring, a transmitter attached to the offender's wrist or ankle sends signals relayed by a home telephone to the supervising office during the hours the offender is required to be at home. Under passive monitoring, a computer program is used to call the offender randomly during the hours designated for home confinement. The offender inserts the wristlet or anklet into a verifier to confirm his or her presence in the residence. There does not appear to be any difference in recidivism between those on passive or active systems. (Only about one in three offenders on home detention wears monitoring devices.)[25]

National surveys indicate that electronic monitoring was initially (1987) used for property offenders on probation, but a much broader range of offenders was being monitored (1989) than in the past. Monitoring has been expanded to include not only probationers but also to follow up on persons after incarceration, to control those sentenced to community corrections, and to monitor persons before trial or sentencing. See Figure 11-3.

The 1989 survey on telemonitoring of offenders noted certain favorable findings:

- Most jurisdictions using electronic monitoring tested some offenders for drug use, and many routinely tested all. Some sites charged for the testing; more than 66 percent charged offenders for at least part of the cost of leasing the monitoring equipment.

- The average monitoring term in 1989 was seventy-nine days. The longer the period of monitoring, the higher the odds of success. The chances of termination do not vary by type of offense, except that those committing major traffic violations committed *fewer* technical violations and new offenses.

FIGURE

11.3

Percentage of Jurisdictions Administering Specific Probation Programs

SOURCE: C. Camp and G. Camp, *The Corrections Yearbook 1995: Probation and Parole* (South Salem, NY: Criminal Justice Institute, 1995), p. 32.

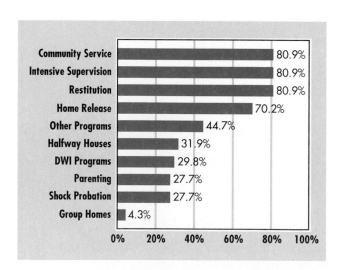

- There were no significant differences in successful terminations among probationers, offenders on parole, or those in community corrections. All had successful terminations rates ranging between 74 and 86 percent. (West Palm Beach, Florida, reported a 97 percent successful completion rate in 1992.)

- Rule violations resulted in reincarceration, brief confinement at a residential facility, intensified office reporting requirements, stricter curfews, or additional community sevice.[26]

Recent evaluations in Oklahoma, Florida, California (Los Angeles), England and Wales,[27] Illinois (Lake County),[28] and Texas[29] indicate continuing success of electronic monitoring of correctional offenders, a technology that no doubt will be improved and expanded in the coming years. There is strong public sentiment for the use of house arrest.

In evaluating a treatment program for adult offenders sentenced to probation, Latessa and Travis found that, in comparison with other similarly situated offenders, the members of their study group had less formal education and were far less likely to have married. They exhibited more prior involvement in alcohol and drug treatment and suffered from more psychiatric problems. Hence the study group was higher need and higher risk, and more likely to recidivate. The center's clients received more services and treatment in almost every area examined. Even though prior criminal histories would have predicted higher failure rates, the center's clients did as well as the comparison group in terms of reoffending. Employment services and enrolling in an educational program reduced recidivism. Clearly, for high-risk offenders, residential centers that provide specific client-needed services can be valuable assets in offender control and outcome,[30] particularly for community control clients whose technical violations are a result of high needs otherwise unaddressed within the community.

COMMUNITY RESIDENTIAL CENTERS

Formerly known as halfway houses, community residential treatment centers are a valuable adjunct to community control and treatment services. Originally designed as residences for homeless men, they are now seen as the possible nuclei of community-based correctional networks of residential centers, drug-free and alcohol-free living space, prerelease guidance centers, and private sector involvement with multiple-problem offenders in need of intensive services. They also serve as noninstitutional residence facilities for a number of different classes of offenders, most of whom are high-need and pose medium to high risk to community corrections.

Much of the contemporary evaluative work in the area of community residential centers has been conducted by University of Cincinnati investigators headed by Edward Latessa.

Inmates in boot camps learn
to handle criticism

—*PHOTO BY GERD LUDWIG, COURTESY
OF WOODFIN CAMP & ASSOCIATES*

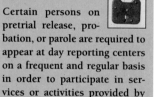

**DAY REPORTING
CENTERS**

Certain persons on
pretrial release, pro-
bation, or parole are required to
appear at day reporting centers
on a frequent and regular basis
in order to participate in services or activities provided by
the center or other community
agencies. Failure to report or
participate is a violation that
could cause revocation of conditional release or community
supervision.

Reports indicate that offenders in these programs must not
only physically report to their
centers daily but also provide a
schedule of planned activities,
and participate in designated
activities. In addition offenders
must call the centers by phone
throughout the day; they can
also expect random phone
checks by center staff both during the day and at home following curfew. In some programs,
offenders must contact their
respective centers an average of
60 times weekly and, in all but
one, take random drug tests.

$\mathcal{I}$ntermediate Sanctions and Shock Programs

The intermediate sanctions already discussed assume the offender can be contained and treated within existing community programs and technologies, and that tourniquet sentencing will serve to control behavior and prevent new crime. Intermediate punishments, however, also include two major alternatives for non-predatory offenders who are, in addition, not career criminals. We discuss two here: shock probation and boot camp programs. A third and related program is shock parole, discussed in more detail in Chapter 13. We begin with shock probation.

SHOCK PROBATION

In 1965, the Ohio legislature passed a law permitting sentencing judges to incarcerate offenders in state prisons for short periods of time and then recall the inmate to probation within the community. The assumption was that a short period of incarceration (90 to 130 days), followed by a period of probation, would "shock" the offender into abandoning criminal activity and into pursuit of law-abiding behavior. Clearly, this program was based on a specific deterrence model and was designed for a segment of the offender population for whom probation was insufficient punishment but long-term imprisonment was not necessary. The method would not be used for first-time offenders but for persons not yet committed to giving up predatory behavior.

This option, rapidly adopted by at least fourteen states,[31] puts decision making squarely in the hands of the judiciary. The sentencing judge is allowed to reconsider the original sentence to prison and, upon motion, to recall the inmate and place him or her on probation, under conditions deemed appropriate.

Evaluations of the effectiveness of shock probation in preventing recidivism and cost avoidance have focused on Ohio, Texas, and Kentucky. Vito[32] has conducted the most sophisticated evaluations and concluded the following:

1. The shock experience should not be limited to first-time offenders; eligibility should properly include those with prior records, as deemed eligible by the judge.

2. The length of incarceration necessary to secure the deterrent effect could be much shorter, probably thirty days or less.

3. Reincarceration rates have never exceeded 26 percent and, in Ohio, have been as low as 10 percent. The level of these rates clearly indicates that the program has potential for reintegration.

4 Shock probation has considerable potential to reduce institutional over-crowding characteristic of contemporary corrections.[33]

Shock probation can be seen as an alternative disposition for sentencing judges who wish to control probationer behavior through deterrence and tourniquet sentencing. It is one of the last ditch programs of prison avoidance available to judges faced with the difficult decision of how best to protect the public while maximizing offender reintegration.

BOOT CAMP PROGRAMS

Shock incarceration programs, or **boot camps** as they are more commonly called, appeared first in Georgia (1983) and Oklahoma (1984). The concept spread quickly and, since 1993, seventy-five boot camp prisons have opened in twenty-nine state correctional jurisdictions, in addition to many programs developed and being considered in cities and counties (Santa Clara, California, for example) for juveniles.[34] See Figure 11-4 for details on boot camps.

While labeled a recent innovation, the basic elements of boot camp were present in the Elmira Reformatory in 1876, designed by Zebulon Reed Brockway. In its form, boot camp combines elements of military basic training and traditional correctional philosophy, particularly rehabilitation. Although there is no generic boot camp because individual programs vary in form and objectives, the typical boot camp is targeted at young nonviolent offenders.[35] Once in the camp, the participant is subjected to a regimen of (1) military drills and discipline, (2) physical exercise, (3) hard physical labor, (4) specialized education and training, and (5) counseling and treatment for substance abuse and addiction.

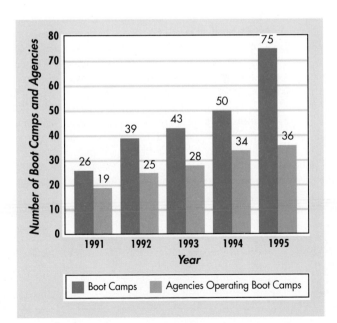

FIGURE

11.4

Boot Camps and the Number of Agencies Operating Them, 1991–1995

SOURCE: G. Camp and C. Camp, *The Corrections Yearbook 1995: Probation and Parole* (South Salem, NY: Criminal Justice Institute, 1995), p. 9.

Most boot camp programs require the inmates to volunteer, offering as an incentive an incarceration period of a few months, compared to the much longer periods they would have spent in prison or on probation. Generally, a state boot camp graduate is released to parole, intensive supervision, home confinement, or some type of community corrections.

The philosophy behind the prison boot camps is simple. Offenders who can be turned around before they commit a major crime can improve their own opportunities for living a successful life free of incarceration. Traditional prisons generally have not been viewed as successful in rehabilitating offenders. According to boot camp advocates, the population at greatest risk of entering prison is the young adult who is poorly educated, comes from a low-income background, has not had proper role models or discipline, has little or no work skills, and is subjected to an environment where drug use and trafficking are common. Because many misdirected young persons have become productive citizens after exposure to military training, the boot camp endeavors to provide this same discipline and direction to persons who still have a chance of being diverted from a life of crime and incarceration.

The boot camp concept appeals to diverse elements of the justice system. For the offender, it offers a second chance. He or she[36] generally will be returned to the community in a much shorter period without the stigma of having been in prison. For the judge, it is a sentencing option that provides sanctions more restrictive than probation but less restrictive than a conventional prison. For the correctional system, it allows the placement of individuals outside the traditional prison environment and reduces costs and crowding by moving the persons through the system in less time.

Boot camps also appeals to groups with diverse views on the objectives of corrections. For those who believe corrections should focus more on rehabilitation, the

Boot Camp Prisons

Boot camp programs, frequently called shock incarceration, require offenders to serve a short term in a prison or jail in a quasi-military program similar to military boot camps or basic training. Currently about thirty-six state, local, and federal agencies operate boot camps; another eight programs have been designed solely for juveniles. This brief focuses on state boot camp programs for adults.

Most state programs target young adult offenders convicted of nonviolent crimes who are serving their first prison terms. Offenders accepted into the programs must serve between 90 and 180 days in the heavily regimented programs. Both the number of states with shock incarceration programs and the capacities of these programs have continued to increase in the 1990s. New York has the largest capacity, with 1,500 beds, but programs in Georgia (800 beds), Oklahoma (400 beds), Michigan (600 beds), Texas (400 beds), and Maryland (440 beds) continue to grow in size. There are currently well over 7,000 beds devoted to boot camp programs. On average, offenders spend 107 days in the programs. Thus, more than 23,000 offenders could potentially complete programs in a one-year period.

Offenders who successfully complete shock incarceration programs are released to community supervision. Forty-two percent of the states intensively supervise offenders who are released from boot camp, 50 percent vary the supervision depending upon evaluated risk, and the remaining 8 percent require moderate or standard supervision. In some states a fairly large percentage of the inmates are dismissed from the program for one reason or another. These offenders must serve their sentences in traditional prisons or return to court for resentencing. ∎

SOURCE: Doris Layton MacKenzie, *NIJ Journal* 227 (Washington, D.C.: National Institute of Justice, November 1993), p. 21, and George M. and Camille G. Camp, *The Correctional Yearbook: Adult Corrections* (South Salem, NY: Criminal Justice Institute, 1995), p. 9.

Boot camp prison for first offenders stresses discipline

—*COURTESY OF NEW YORK CITY DEPARTMENT OF CORRECTIONS*

shorter sentence, structured environment, supervision after release, and emphasis on training and treatment can be found in the boot camp. For those who believe prisons should serve as punishment and a deterrent, the highly disciplined environment, military-style drills, physical exercise, and work within a correctional setting exist in the boot camp.

Data on effectiveness of boot camp programs are not numerous, and preliminary evaluations indicate extensive innovation going on within the programs. Recidivism after release was comparable to that of similar offenders who had served prison sentences. Some programs have abandoned the military-style training and incorporated educational, wilderness, job corps, and industrial components.[37] Preliminary findings from Louisiana suggest that offenders who completed shock incarceration had fewer arrests, convictions, and revocations for new crimes (although they had more revocations for technical violations) than comparison groups of parolees and probationers.[38] Additional evaluations of the Louisiana program indicate that prison beds were saved (fewer inmates spent time in prison due to the shock incarceration program) and that Louisiana saved almost $8,000 for each offender who completed boot camp shock incarceration instead of a traditional prison sentence. There are many indicators suggesting that shock incarceration or boot camps achieve many correctional objectives, especially if linked to drug treatment programs, but definitive answers will require more numerous and extensive evaluations of the various types of programs commonly known as boot camp programs.

Summary

Corrections is undergoing rapid change as innovators search for programs, technologies, strategies, and policies for coping with the increasing number and diversity of jail and prison populations, as well as the crush of overcrowding. Not only are institutions crowded; probation, parole, and community corrections are also impacted by the waves of offenders caught in the arms of the law.

Our review of intermediate sanctions provides both insight into the reasons for the volume of clients, but also describes promising programs and strategies for managing the risks posed by different types of offenders who need differing treatments and supervision. Change will continue. This is an exciting time for corrections as a field and for students wishing to have an impact on the futures of clients and the safety of communities.

In the next chapters we shall examine the use of incarceration, as those that make it through the correctional filter finally end up in the prisons of the nation. The use of incarceration has now placed over a million people into our prisons and the number grows every day. What is imprisonment and what is it like? The next chapter will seek some answers to these questions. We end this Part with the status of parole and its impact on the system of corrections.

*R*eview Questions

1. Explain the difference between fines and day fines.
2. Differentiate between shock probation and boot camp shock incarceration.
3. What roles do community residential centers play in corrections?
4. Did Florida's Community Control Program achieve its objectives?
5. Describe a boot camp program.

*W*ords to Remember

intermediate sanctions	electronic monitoring	community work orders
day attendance centers	restitution	home detention
restitution orders	day fine	electronic parole
house arrest	intensive supervised probation	boot camps

*E*ndnotes

1. Malcolm M. Feeley and Jonathan Simon, "The New Penology: Notes on the Emerging Strategy of Corrections and Its Implications," *Criminology* 30:4 (1992): 449–474. See also Steven Donziger, *The Real War on Crime* (New York: HarperCollins, 1996), pp. 55–62.

2. Voncile Gowdy, *Intermediate Sanctions* (Washington, D.C.: U.S. Department of Justice, 1993). See also the Theme Issue of *Corrections Today* 57:1 (1995).

3. Daniel Nagin and David Farrington, "The Onset and Persistence of Offending," *Criminology* 30:4 (1992): 501–524, and Lilana Pezzin, "Earnings Prospects, Matching Effects and the Decision to Terminate a Criminal Career," *Jodurnal of Qualitative Criminology* 11:1 (1995): 29–50.

4. Francis Cullen, Edward Latessa, Velmer Burton, and Lucien Lombardo, "The Correctional Orientation of Prison Wardens: Is the Rehabilitative Ideal Supported?" *Criminology* 31:1 (1993): 69–92.

5. Editors, "Alternatives to Prison: Cheaper Is Better," *The Economist,* November 19, 1994, p. 33, and Marla Sandys and Edmund McGarrell, "Attitudes Toward Capital Punishment," *Justice Quarterly* 11:4 (1994):651–677.

6. Michael Tonry, "Racial Politics, Racial Disparities, and the War on Crime," *Crime and Delinquency* 40:4 (1994): 475–494. See also J. Robert Lilly and Mathieu DeFlem, "Profit and Penalty: An Analysis of the Correctional-Commercial Complex," *Crime and Delinquency* 42:1 (1996):3–20.

7. Mark Mauer, "The International Use of Incarceration," *The Prison Journal* 75:1 (1995): 113–123.

8. Roy Sudipto, "Juvenile Restitution and Recidivism in a Midwestern County," *Federal Probation* 59:1 (1995): 55–62. See also Andrew Ashworth, Martin Killias, and Max Kommer, "Consistency in Sentencing," *European Journal on Criminal Policy and Research* 2:1 (1994): 5–118, particularly the excellent arguments of Josine Junger-Tas.

9. Sherwood Zimmerman, Beverly Rivera, and Mark Seis, An Indirect Assessment of Public Tolerance for Day Fines, paper presented at the annual meeting of the Academy of Criminal Justice Sciences, March 8, 1991, Nashville, Tennessee.

10. Margaret Gordon and Daniel Glaser, "The Use and Effects of Financial Penalties in Municipal Courts," *Criminology* 29:4 (1991): 651–676, and John Mathias, Gwendolyn Lyford, and Paul Gomez, *Current Practicess in Collecting Fines and Fees in State Courts* (Denver, CO: National Center for State Courts, 1995).

11. Day-fine sentences are being implemented in Maricopa County, Arizona, and in Oregon, Iowa, and Connecticut. See Josine Junger-Tas, *Alternatives to Prison Sentences: Experience and Developments* (Amsterdam: Kugler, 1994).

12. Joan Petersilia and Susan Turner, *Evaluating Intensive Supervised Probation/Parole Results of a Nationwide Experiment* (Washington, D.C.: U.S. Department of Justice, 1993). See also the Netherlands Ministry of Justice, *Dutch Penal Law and Policy: Alternative Sanctions for Juveniles in the Netherlands* (The Hague: Netherlands Ministry of Justice, 1993).

13. Kim English, *Colorado's Intensive Supervision Probation* (Denver: Colorado Division of Criminal Justice, 1994).

14. Billie S. Erwin, *Final Report: Evaluation of Intensive Probation Supervision in Georgia* (Atlanta: Georgia Department of Corrections, 1987).

15. Peter Finn and Dale Parent, *Making the Offender Foot the Bill* (Washington, D.C.: U.S. Department of Justice, 1992).

16. Edward Latessa and Dina Chirichella, "Intensive Supervision of Alcoholic Offenders: Outcomes and Prediction," paper presented at the annual meeting of the Academy of Criminal Justice Sciences, San Francisco, April 7, 1988. See also Joan Petersilia, Susan Turner, and Elizabeth Deschenes, "The Costs and Effectiveness of Intensive Supervision for Drug Offenders," *Federal Probation* 56:4 (1992): 12–17.

17. Petersilia, Turner, and Deschenes, "The Costs and Effectiveness of Intensive Supervision for Drug Offenders." See also Craig Fischer, "GAO Finds Some Merit in Intensive Probation," *Criminal Justice Newsletter* 24:14 (July 16, 1993): 4–5; Mark Jones, *Intensive Probation Supervision in Georgia, Massachusetts, and New Jersey* (Huntsville, TX: Sam Houston State University, 1991); and Jeffrey Senese, "Intensive Supervised Probation and Public Opinion: Perceptions of Community Correctional Policy and Practice," *American Journal of Criminal Justice* 16:2 (1992): 33–56.

18. Julie Martin, "Community Services: Are the Goals of This Alternative Sentencing Tool Being Met?" *Court Review* 28:4 (1991): 5–11.

19. Michael Maxfield and Terry Baumer, "Home Detention with Electronic Monitoring: Comparing Pretrial and Postconviction Programs," *Crime and Delinquency* 36:4 (1990): 521–536.

20. Leonard Flynn, "House Arrest," *Corrections Today* 48:5 (1986): 64–68.

21. U.S. Government Accounting Office, *Intermediate Sanctions* (Washington, D.C.: U.S. Government Accounting Office, 1990).

22. Dennis Wagner and Christopher Baird, *Evaluation of the Florida Community Control Program* (Washington, D.C.: U.S. Department of Justice, 1993), p. 5.

23. R. K. Schwitzgebel, R. L. Schwitzgebel, W. N. Pahnke, and W. S. Hurd, "A Program of Research in Behavioral Electronics," *Behavioral Scientist* 9:3 (1964): 233–238. See also R. K. Gable, "Application of Personal Telemonitoring to Current Problems in Corrections," *Journal of Criminal Justice* 14:2 (1986): 173–182; J. R. Lilly, R. Ball, and W. Lotz, "Electronic Jail Revisited," *Justice Quarterly* 3:3 (1986): 353–361; and J. R. Lilly, R. Ball, and D. Curry, eds., "Electronic Monitoring of the Drunk Driver," *Crime and Delinquency* 39:4 (1993): 462–484.

24. Gowdy, *Intermediate Sanctions,* p. 6.

25. Joan Petersilia, *Expanding Options for Criminal Sentencing* (Santa Monica, CA: Rand, 1987), p. 37.

26. Gowdy, *Intermediate Sanctions,* pp. 6–7.

27. George Mair, "Evaluating Electronic Monitoring in England and Wales," paper presented at the annual meeting of the American Society of Criminology, San Francisco, November 18, 1989. See also J. R. Lilly, "Tagging Revisited," *The Howard Journal* 29:4 (1990): 229–245, and National Association for the Care of Offenders and the Prevention of Crime, *The Electronic Monitoring of Offenders* (London: National Association for the Care of Offenders and the Prevention of Crime, 1989).

28. Michael Brown and Preston Elrod, "Electronic House Arrest: An Examination of Citizen Attitudes," *Crime and Delinquency* 41:3 (1995): 332–346.

29. Richard Enos, Clifford Block, James Quinn, et al., *Alternative Sentencing: Electronically Monitored Correctional Supervision* (Bristol, IN: Wyndham Hall, 1992).

30. Edward Latessa and Lawrence Travis, "Halfway Houses or Probation: A Comparison of Alternative Dispositions," *Journal of Crime and Justice* 14:1 (1991): 53–75.

31. Gennaro Vito and Harry Allen, "Shock Probation in Ohio: A Comparison of Outcomes," *International Journal of Offender Therapy and Comparative Criminology* 25:1 (181): 70–77. See also Michael Vaughan, "Listening to the Experts: A National Study of Correctional Administrators' Responses to Prison Overcrowding," *Criminal Justice Review* 18:1 (1993): 12–25.

32. Gennaro Vito, "Developments in Shock Probation: A Review of Research Findings and Policy Implications," *Federal Probation* 50:1 (1985): 22–27.

33. Ibid., pp. 23–25.

34. Doris MacKenzie, James Shaw, and Voncile Gowdy, *An Evaluation of Shock Incarceration in Louisiana* (Washington, D.C.: U.S. Department of Justice, 1993): 2. See also Blair Bourque, et al., *Boot Camps for Juvenile Offender* (Washington, D.C.:U.S. Department of Justice, 1996).

35. The bulk of the following section is drawn from the U.S. Government Accounting Office, *Prison Boot Camps* (Washington, D.C.: U.S. Department of Justice, 1993).

36. One boot camp program for female misdemeanants can be found in the Santa Clara (San Jose), California, Office of the Sheriff.

37. Gowdy, *Intermediate Sanctions,* p. 8.

38. MacKenzie, et al., *An Evaluation of Shock Incarceration in Louisiana.* See also Cherie Clark, D. Aziz, and D. MacKenzie, *Shock Incarceration in New York: Focus on Treatment* (Washington, D.C.: U.S. Department of Justice, 1994).

CHAPTER TWELVE

Imprisonment

*O*verview

Our examination of the correctional process has now spanned jails and detention facilities, explored probation, and looked at numerous intermediate sanctions used to control and supervise offenders short of long-term incarceration in a state, local, or federal prison. That option, the last in the queue of options that allows some retention of the offender in a community setting, is the most extreme and punitive process in corrections. Imprisonment isolates offenders who are so violent or unreliable that they must be placed in one of the numerous and varied facilities that have been built to protect society from incarcerated offenders.

Prisons are seldom seen as desirable places in which to live and, while prisons generally incapacitate their inhabitants during the time they are behind the bars, walls, and fences of these institutions, they are also places where offenders serve out the *punishment* meted out by the courts. Over the last few decades, in part due to the "War on Drugs," usage of incarceration has dramatically increased in a vague hope of keeping abreast of the huge surge of offenders sentenced to prisons. In the present chapter, we explore the prison process, the growth in prison populations, and the building binge that has been the result. We begin with an examination of the phenomenon of prison population growth, the human side of the equation.

*P*rison Populations
Continue to Climb

Since 1980, the United States has experienced unprecedented expansions of the incarceration of offenders and the building of prisons in its history as a nation, perhaps in the history of the free world. This increase is attributed to a number of factors explained in more detail in the paragraphs that follow, but includes increasing fear of crime

As he went through Cold-Bath Fields he saw
A solitary cell;
And the Devil was pleased, for it gave him a hint
For improving his prisons in Hell.

—Samuel Taylor Coleridge

217

The Iowa State Men's Reformatory in Anamosa is considered an architectural masterpiece

—*COURTESY OF IOWA DEPARTMENT OF CORRECTIONS*

and criminals by citizens, a perception of being victimized, increased media attention and coverage of **"get-tough" legislation**, the impact of the so-called **"War on Crime,"** and increased severity and length of new sentencing initiatives. More recent evidence suggests that violent offenders contributed 16 percent of the population increase and incarceration of drug offenders accounted for another 46 percent. Property offenses contributed the remaining 38 percent of the increase.[1] Since 1980 the number of prisoners has increased by over 300 percent! Hundreds of billions of dollars have been invested in building literally hundreds of prisons. At least 1.5 million adult citizens are behind the bars of jails and prisons in America. Over 4 million offenders are under supervision of probation or parole. Some 1 in 38 adults, 1 in 21 adult men, and 1 in 6 adult black men are under some form of correctional supervision. In total, blacks are incarcerated at a rate greater than six times that of whites (1,947 to 360 per 100,000, respectively), arguably because blacks are arrested at higher rates than are whites, for crimes that are differentially punished, and the criminal justice system processes them more severely.[2] The growth in the number of inmates by sex and race is shown in Figure 12-1.

The growth in prison populations can be seen in Figure 12-2; the nation had an estimated 1,092,660 inmates at the beginning of 1996, representing a 345 percent growth in prison population since 1980.[3] The 1996 numbers translate into a nationwide need for approximately 1,500 prison bed spaces and almost 300 new correctional officer positions *per week*.[4] To accommodate the surge in population, the state and federal governments have opened 305 new prisons since 1989.[5] Another 108 new prisons and 167 major prison renovation projects are currently underway to add over 124,962 new beds. On average, each bed will cost $79,958 for construction[6] and $20,000 per inmate per year.[7] The picture by region and state can be found in Table 12-1.

The trends of the past decade indicate that we are willing and ready to build more and more prisons and incarcerate an even larger percentage of the population.

PRISON

A state, federal, or local confinement facility having custodial authority and control over adult felons convicted and sentenced to confinement for more than one year.

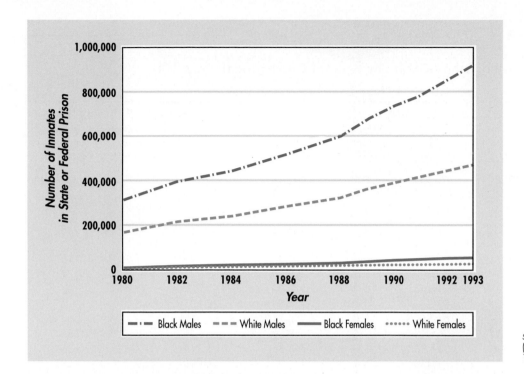

FIGURE

12.1

Number of White and
Black Inmates in State or
Federal Prison, by Sex,
1980–1983

SOURCE: J. Beck and D. Gilliard, *Prisoners in 1994*
(Washington, D.C.: U.S. Department of Justice,
1995), p. 9.

Efforts for prison improvement fly in the face of get-tough legislation, the population's epidemic fear of crime, and sentencing laws and procedures that put even more persons behind bars (see Chapter 7). Some of the ambivalence of the American public regarding prisons and imprisonment relate to a lack of clear understanding and mutual acceptance of the purpose for confinement.[8]

The consequent **overcrowding** of the system means that offenders are doubled up in cells meant for one; packed into makeshift dormitories; and bunked in the basements, corridors, converted hospital facilities, tents, trailers, warehouses, and program activity areas of the nation's prisons.[9] There are currently 387 Americans in prison for every 100,000 citizens—the highest rate for any

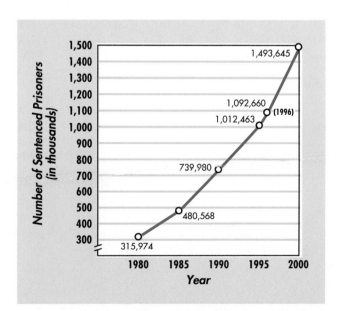

FIGURE

12.2

Number of Sentenced
Prisoners Under State
and Federal Jurisdiction,
1980–2000:
Straight-Line Projection
Based on 1993–1994
Increase

SOURCE: J. Beck and D. Gilliard, *Prisoners in 1994*
(Washington, D.C.: U.S. Department of Justice,
1995), p. 8.

TABLE *12.1*

Prisoners Under the Jurisdiction of State or Federal Correctional Authorities, by Region and Jurisdiction, Year-End 1993 and 1994

Region and Jurisdiction	Total			Sentenced to More Than 1 Year			
	Advance 1994	Final 1993	Percentage Change, 1993-94	Advance 1994	Final 1993	Percentage Change 1993-94	Incarceration Rate, 1994
U.S. total	1,053,738	970,444	8.6	1,012,463	932,266	8.6	387
Federal	95,034	89,587	6.1	79,795	74,399	7.3	30
State	958,704	880,857	8.8	932,668	857,867	8.7	356
Northeast	153,124	146,501	4.5	146,754	140,941	4.1	285
Connecticut	14,380	13,691	5.0	10,500	10,508	-.1	321
Maine	1,537	1,469	4.6	1,464	1,446	1.2	118
Massachusetts	11,282	11,100	1.6	10,340	10,145	1.9	171
New Hampshire	2,021	1,775	13.9	2,021	1,775	13.9	177
New Jersey	24,632	23,831	3.4	24,544	23,831	3.0	310
New York	66,750	64,569	3.4	66,750	64,569	3.4	367
Pennsylvania	28,302	26,060	8.6	28,301	26,055	8.6	235
Rhode Island	2,919	2,783	4.9	1,853	1,719	7.8	186
Vermont	1,301	1,223	6.4	981	893	9.9	168
Midwest	183,436	173,277	5.9	182,768	172,709	5.8	297
Illinois	36,531	34,495	5.9	36,531	34,495	5.9	310
Indiana	15,014	14,470	3.8	14,925	14,364	3.9	258
Iowa	5,437	4,898	11.0	5,437	4,898	11.0	192
Kansas	6,373	5,727	11.3	6,373	5,727	11.3	249
Michigan	40,775	39,318	3.7	40,775	39,318	3.7	428
Minnesota	4,572	4,200	8.9	4,572	4,200	8.9	100
Missouri	17,898	16,178	10.6	17,898	16,178	10.6	338
Nebraska	2,633	2,518	4.6	2,590	2,467	5.0	159
North Dakota	536	498	7.6	501	446	12.3	78
Ohio	41,913	40,641	3.1	41,913	40,641	3.1	377
South Dakota	1,734	1,553	11.7	1,734	1,553	11.7	240
Wisconsin	10,020	8,781	14.1	9,519	8,422	13.0	187
South	421,817	372,882	13.1	412,309	364,551	13.1	451
Alabama	19,573	18,624	5.1	19,074	18,169	5.0	450
Arkansas	8,836	8,625	2.4	8,711	7,984	9.1	353
Delaware	4,411	4,210	4.8	2,788	2,781	.3	393
Dist. of Col.	10,943	10,845	.9	8,962	8,908	.6	1,583
Florida	57,139	53,048	7.7	57,129	52,883	8.0	406
Georgia	33,425	27,783	20.3	32,523	27,079	20.1	456
Kentucky	11,066	10,440	6.0	11,066	10,440	6.0	288
Louisiana	24,092	22,468	7.2	22,956	22,468	2.2	530
Maryland	20,998	20,264	3.6	19,854	19,121	3.8	395
Mississippi	11,274	10,078	11.9	10,950	9,769	12.1	408
North Carolina	23,639	21,892	8.0	22,983	21,367	7.6	322
Oklahoma	16,631	16,409	1.4	16,631	16,409	1.4	508
South Carolina	18,999	18,704	1.6	18,168	17,896	1.5	494
Tennessee	14,474	12,824	12.9	14,474	12,824	12.9	277
Texas	118,195	92,013	28.5	118,094	92,013	28.3	636
Virginia	26,192	22,850	14.6	26,016	22,635	14.9	395
West Virginia	1,930	1,805	6.9	1,930	1,805	6.9	106
West	200,327	188,197	6.4	190,837	179,666	6.2	333
Alaska	3,292	3,068	7.3	1,934	1,954	-1.0	317
Arizona	19,746	17,811	10.9	19,005	17,160	10.8	459
California	125,605	119,951	4.7	121,084	115,573	4.8	384

TABLE *12.1* *(Con't)*

Region and Jurisdiction	Total				Sentenced to More Than 1 Year			
	Advance 1994	Final 1993	Percentage Change, 1993-94	Advance 1994	Final 1993	Percentage Change 1993-94	Incarceration Rate, 1994
West *(con't.)*	200,327	188,197	6.4	190,837	179,666	6.2	333
Colorado	10,717	9,462	13.3	10,717	9,462	13.3	289
Hawaii	3,333	3,129	6.5	2,392	2,330	2.7	202
Idaho	2,964	2,606	13.7	2,964	2,606	13.7	258
Montana	1,680	1,541	9.0	1,680	1,541	9.0	194
Nevada	7,122	6,138	16.0	6,877	6,138	12.0	460
New Mexico	3,866	3,498	10.5	3,679	3,373	9.1	220
Oregon	6,936	6,557	5.8	5,458	5,111	6.8	175
Utah	3,016	2,888	4.4	2,997	2,871	4.4	155
Washington	10,833	10,419	4.0	10,833	10,419	4.0	201
Wyoming	1,217	1,129	7.8	1,217	1,128	7.9	254

SOURCE: J. Beck and D. Gilliard, *Prisoners in 1994* (Washington, D.C.: U. S. Department of Justice, 1995), p. 3.

industrialized nation.[10] If present trends continue, there will be almost 1.5 million Americans in prisons by the end of 1999 (see Figure 12.2).

Although such a rapid increase in prison population is not easily explained, part of the reason for it may be traced to a hardening of public attitudes toward crime. These attitudes, in turn, produce more and more get-tough policies in the criminal justice system. The courts are under pressure to deter crime by giving longer sentences, and so they are using probation less often and are themselves pressing for better legislation in the area of probation. The legislators respond by

TABLE *12.2*
State and Federal Prison Populations, 1980–1994

Year	Number of Inmates	Annual Percentage Change	Total Percentage Change Since 1980
1980	329,821	—	—
1981	369,930	12.2	12.2
1982	413,806	11.9	25.5
1983	436,855	5.6	32.5
1984	462,002	5.8	40.1
1985	502,752	8.8	52.4
1986	545,378	8.5	65.4
1987	585,292	7.3	77.5
1988	631,990	8.0	91.6
1989	712,967	12.8	116.2
1990	773,124	8.4	134.4
1991	824,133	6.6	149.9
1992	883,593	7.2	167.9
1993	970,444	8.9	194.2
1994	1,053,738	8.1	219.4

SOURCE: *State and Federal Prison Populations 1980–1984* (Washington, D.C.: U.S. Department of Justice, 1955), p.4.

passing more mandatory sentencing laws, limiting the judges' latitude to grant probation or intermediate punishments, and increasing the minimum time.

The incidence of colds, infectious diseases, hepatitis, tuberculosis, sexually communicable diseases, psychological disturbances, and psychiatric crises also are related to overcrowding. The more overcrowded the institution, the higher the incidence of medical problems.

Overcrowded maximum security prisons appear to be most likely to have the worst impact on prisoner health and safety. Correctional administrators and elected officials must plan to reduce the negative impacts of imprisonment on offenders for parole consideration. The policymakers continue to ignore the evidence that an increased use of imprisonment is positively correlated with higher, rather than lower, levels of crime. Public safety is not enhanced by greater use of imprisonment.[11]

Another factor contributing to the increase of the prison population as a whole is the growth of the general population in the nineteen- to twenty-nine-year-old age group. This is seen as the population at risk, as crime is usually a young man's activity. That group is a direct result of the **baby boom** following World War II, which clogged the school systems of America in the 1950s and 1960s and has now affected yet another area—urban crime. That group is also the one with the highest unemployment rate and, in a time of general underemployment, will continue to commit crime out of proportion to its size.[12]

Classification: A Move Toward Corrections

The demoralizing influence of the early maximum security prisons and the enforced idleness they produced resulted in two movements in corrections over the last half century. One course of action has been to continually upgrade living conditions and humanitarian treatment within the security prisons. The second action has introduced **classification**, a concept borrowed from psychology, into the imprisonment process. Classification in prison usually refers to two actions:

Effects of Prison Overcrowding

Despite the fact that the nation has opened or expanded almost three hundred prisons in less than seven years, the average prison space available for inmates has dropped by over 10 percent. Prison overcrowding has gotten worse, especially as crime has become more violent, and drug-related crimes have more often resulted in confinement.

What effects does prison crowding have? One is that fewer programs can be made available for inmates on a relative basis; another is that recreational opportunities are fewer. But it is in the health and safety areas that the impact is felt most.

The rates of death, suicide, homicide, inmate assault, and disturbance increase as prison population density increases (population density is measured by square feet of floor space per inmate). This finding holds regardless of whether a prisoner is confined in maximum, medium, or minimum security. Such data are further exacerbated by the increasingly more violent persons being imprisoned. ∎

Minnesota Prison Time Served Among Longest

A national comparison completed during the biennium shows that Minnesota's prison sentences in terms of actual time served are among the toughest in the nation.

Penalties for dangerous, violent, repeat offenders have been increased dramatically since 1989.

The comparison, completed by the state Sentencing Guidelines Commission staff, shows that offenders in Minnesota serve more time in prison than they do in thirty-four states that responded to a national survey. The comparison includes murder, manslaughter, rape, robbery, assault, burglary, and drug crimes.

Also, prison good time for all felons was abolished in the 1992 crime bill. Inmates must serve the entire imprisonment sentence ordered by the court. Each offender is also sentenced to a period of community supervision and surveillance in addition to prison time.

Among other changes in law and state sentencing guidelines are: sentence lengths for more serious crimes were doubled in 1989, life sentences were increased from seventeen years to thirty years before parole consideration, life sentences without the possibility of parole were added, life sentences for certain repeat sex offenses became law, and penalties for drug offenders were increased.

As a result, the Sentencing Guidelines Commission indicates that the average Minnesota prison sentence is the highest ever. ■

SOURCE: Minnesota Department of Corrections, *1994-1995 Biennial Report* (St. Paul, Minnesota, 1995), P. 7.

1. A differentiation of the prisoner population into custodial or security groups, thus permitting a degree of planned custodial flexibility not previously possible

2. Opening of the prisons to the teacher, psychologist, social worker, psychiatrist, and others[13]

The advent of classification in the post–World War II era marks a substantial shift for imprisonment from punishment to correction as a goal. The timing was fortuitous because unionism and federal legislation of the 1930s severely restricted prison industries. The idleness that followed the restrictive federal laws would have been even more troublesome were it not for the Prison Industries Reorganization Administration. Operating between 1935 and 1940, that agency developed programs of constructive activities for prisons, contributing to the development of rehabilitation programs more characteristic of prisons between 1940 and 1973.

Modern correctional centers do not look like gothic castles

—*COURTESY OF OMAHA CORRECTIONAL CENTER*

The movement toward increased use of classification was accompanied by a great amount of rhetoric about "correctional treatment." Some of the more positive aspects of that strategy were outlined by the American Correctional Association:

> The offender was perceived as a person with social, intellectual, or emotional deficiencies which should be diagnosed carefully and his deficiencies "clinically" defined. Programs should be designed to correct these deficiencies to the point that would permit him to assume a productive, law-abiding place in the community. To achieve the goals of correctional treatment, it would be necessary only to maintain the pressure on the inmate for his participation in the treatment programs, to continue to humanize institutional living, to upgrade the educational level of the line officer, and to expand the complement of professional treatment and training personnel. The coordination of the variety of treatment and training programs would be assured by the establishment of a division of "classification, treatment, and training" or some similar designation, either in the central office, in the institution, or both. This model of the "progressive prison" continues to be advocated as the standard pattern of the contemporary prison.[14]

"Correctional treatment," however, defies definition, especially when attempted in a maximum security institution where the overriding emphasis is on custody. Current convention defines almost everything done to, for, with, or by the inmate as immediately covered by the umbrella categorization of **correctional treatment**.

Correctional treatment is generally assumed to begin with the classification process. Classification procedures are conducted in reception units located within the prisons or in the special reception and classification centers. They are sometimes carried out by classification committees, reception-diagnostic centers, or community classification teams. The purpose of classification varies among institutions, but basically it attempts to help with inmate management or treatment planning.

Management classification dates back to the earliest efforts to segregate prisoners by categories. The *European Standard Minimum Rules for the Treatment of Offenders* is a good example of a classification scheme that uses segregation as a management tool:

The Rise in Imprisonment

Two trends are responsible for the present rise in confinement. First, longer sentences are being imposed for such nonviolent felonies as larceny, theft, and motor vehicle theft. In 1992, these crimes accounted (according to the *Uniform Crime Report*) for 66 percent of crime in America. As James Q. Wilson, who has not in the past been averse to imprisonment, recently wrote: "Very large increases in the prison population can produce only very modest reductions in crime rates." "Judges," he observes, "already send the most serious offenders with the longest records to prison," and "the most serious offenders typically get the longest sentences."

Second, everyone who works in the criminal justice system recognizes that drugs have become its driving force. According to the Bureau of Justice Statistics (1992), more than half of all violent offenders in state prisons said they were under the influence of alcohol or drugs at the time of their offense. ■

SOURCE: Jerome H. Skolnick, "What Not to Do About Crime: The American Society of Criminology 1994 Presidential Address," *Criminology* 33:1 (1995): p. 9.

The different categories of prisoners shall be kept in separate institutions or parts of the institution, taking account of their sex, age, criminal record, the legal reasons for their detention, and the necessities of their treatment. Thus, (a) men and women shall so far as possible be detained in separate institutions. In an institution which receives both men and women, the whole of the premises allocated to women shall be entirely separate; (b) untried prisoners shall be kept separate from convicted prisoners; (c) persons imprisoned for debt and other civil prisoners shall be kept separate from persons imprisoned by reason of criminal offense; (d) young prisoners shall be kept separate from adults.[15]

Although management categories are valuable for the correctional administrator, continuing status evaluation and reclassification are critical. If treatment in the correctional setting is to be effective, the inmate must be reclassified and different treatments designed and applied from time to time. Unfortunately, many a well-conceived treatment plan has failed because of inaccurate or nonexistent reclassification.[16]

The usual purpose for classification, from the viewpoint of the staff, is to create a plan that will "correct" the prisoners and send them back to society as changed people. The prisoners, on the other hand, look upon the classification process as yet only another way to *get out*. They try to determine what they are supposed to do to prove they are ready for release and then do it. Because the emphasis on what they must do tends to shift in accordance with the convenience of the administration, the composition of the treatment staff, or "suggestions for improvement" from the paroling authority, this is not an easy task. An inmate may be classified as deficient in education, for example, and so he or she begins day classes. But because the inmate is a skilled baker, he or she is needed in the kitchen and must shift to that role to earn a "good attitude" rating for potential release. In the complex organization of the prison, institutional needs must be met, even at the expense of correcting the offenders.[17]

Classification was hailed as a revolution in corrections, moving the focus from the mass production tactics of the past to individualized treatment. The failure of classification and advanced social work techniques lies partly in the fact that the establishment is resistant to change and partly in the poor environment for change provided in the prisons themselves. Several states have abandoned classification reception-diagnostic centers as counterproductive because the centers raised inmate and staff aspirations above the level of possible achievement. The treatment model has a place somewhere in corrections but not, it seems, in maximum security prisons.

After classification, the offender may be sent to one of five security levels of institutions: maximum (11 percent), high/close (10 percent), medium (47 percent); minimum (27 percent), or community/other facilities (11 percent).[18] We start with the 109,275 male and female offenders housed in the nation's maximum security institutions.[19]

*M*aximum Security Prisons

The purposes of confinement are punishment, deterrence, quarantine, rehabilitation and, more recently, reintegration back into the community.[20] The specific goals and the settings for their achievement are dictated by the particular society's dominant orientation, whether toward individual rights or collective security. Because both orientations command a strong following in America, neither one has entirely superseded the other. The scales have tipped in favor of security more often than equity, however, and the battle continues. We are currently witnessing a swing toward using incarceration primarily for purposes of punishment and deterrence.

Prisons were originally built as places that stressed maximum security above all other concerns. Typically, they are surrounded by a wall, usually thirty to fifty feet high and several feet thick, topped with razor wire, equipped with towers staffed by armed guards trained and prepared to prevent possible escapes or riots, lit by floodlights after dark, and sometimes bounded by electrified wire fences to further discourage escape attempts. These stone fortresses are usually placed far out in the countryside, away from the mainstream of American life.

The walled prison was so popular, it was not until 1926 that the first unwalled prison appeared in the United States.[21] It is clear when one approaches a typical maximum security prison that it is designed for punishment. The fearsome and forbidding atmosphere of the Auburn style of prison exemplifies the penal philosophy that prisoners must not only do time for their misdeeds but also do so in an environment that emphasizes rejection, doubt, guilt, inferiority, diffusion, self-absorption, apathy, and despair.[22] It is small wonder that these kinds of prison usually release inmates who are emotionally less stable than they were when they entered.[23]

The Human Cage vividly describes the nineteenth-century maximum security prison:

> In 1825 prisoners arrived in leg shackles from Auburn at a site on the Hudson River, later to be known as Sing Sing, to construct a new prison. The plan was similar: tiny cells back to back on five tiers, with stairways on either end in the center of the very long range. Cell doors were iron with grillework in the upper portion, and they fastened with gang locks. Cells received small amounts of light coming through a tiny window located nine feet away in the outer wall opposite the cell door. These cells were extremely damp, dark, and poorly ventilated and, like those at Auburn, contained no toilet facilities except buckets. The East House, which alone contained 1,000 cells and continued in use until 1943, was to become the prototype for most American prison cellhouse construction, rather than the earlier Auburn prison from which the system took its name.[24]

Pelican Bay Prison in northwest California, the newest supermaximum institution

—COURTESY OF THE STATE OF CALIFORNIA DEPARTMENT OF CORRECTIONS

For the remainder of the nineteenth century in this country, the characteristic layout for nearly all prisons was to consist of a central building housing offices, mess hall, and chapel, usually flanked and joined on each side by a multitiered cell block. In the prison enclosure formed by the wall would be shops, hospital, and power plant. In 1834 Ohio opened a prison on this plan in Columbus. Five tiers of tiny cells back to back were built with convict labor. Wisconsin opened a similar type of prison at Waupun in 1851. The Illinois Penitentiary at Joliet (1856–1858), the Rhode Island Penitentiary at Cranston (1873–1878), the Tennessee Penitentiary at Nashville (1895), and a number of others were on this plan. The largest prison of this sort was the Western Penitentiary at Pittsburgh (1882) with eleven hundred cells on five tiers. A few such institutions were erected following the turn of the century—Cheshire, Connecticut, was opened in 1913 and Monroe, Washington, in 1908—but by that time nearly all the states had built maximum security prisons and little prison building would occur again until the 1930s.[25]

The great **Gothic-style**[26] **monoliths** had been built in the belief that that kind of architecture, as part of the total system, would aid in the restoration of prisoners. The idea was discredited by the beginning of the twentieth century, however, and both American and European penologists began to concentrate on treatment strategies. But because America was left with almost sixty of those monstrosities,[27] built before 1900 with only economy, security, and isolation in mind, the new programs had to be designed to fit the existing structures. Of course, it should have been the other way around—the physical plants should have been built to fit the programs and, although corrections philosophy has changed drastically in the past fifty years, America is still tied to the approaches of nearly two centuries ago by the outmoded architecture of most maximum security prisons.

INSIDE THE WALLS

After classification, offenders may be transported to another institution. If they are fortunate, they will be placed in one of the smaller institutions; if not, they will enter one of the giant walled cities. The offenders will pass through a double fence or stone wall surrounded by manned guard towers. As the large steel main gate

Prison Workloads

A recent national survey of wardens and state commissioners of corrections revealed considerable agreement on prison workload problems:

- More than half reported that their facilities were full, primarily because of drug offenders serving long sentences who occupied 75 percent of available cells;

- Identifying gang members and gang activities were major problems, and there was a need to develop programs that would discourage gang activities in prison;

- Three out of four wardens indicated a need for more pro-

gram staff, particularly to deal with alcohol and drug substance abuse as well as sex offenders;

One warden noted: "Lines for everything are longer: inmate canteen, inmate meds, meals . . . .. Sentence length and distant parole eligibility (if at all) build a central core population. This core population will probably quadruple in the next seven years." ∎

SOURCE: National Institute of Justice, NIJ Survey of Wardens and State Commissioners of Corrections (Washington, D.C.: U.S. Department of Justice, 1995), pp. 1–2.

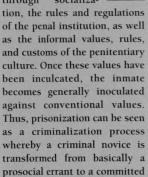

PRISONIZATION

The process by which the inmate learns, through socialization, the rules and regulations of the penal institution, as well as the informal values, rules, and customs of the penitentiary culture. Once these values have been inculcated, the inmate becomes generally inoculated against conventional values. Thus, prisonization can be seen as a criminalization process whereby a criminal novice is transformed from basically a prosocial errant to a committed predatory criminal.

It is important to remember that correctional staff can be prisonized as well, although the degree and extent of socialization is not as extensive, nor long lasting. Prisonization for the officer generally reflects the necessity of managing and interacting with inmates; the officer has to know and manipulate the inmate system to attain individual and institutional goals.

slams shut behind them, the process of **prisonization** begins. Donald Clemmer, the originator of this concept, described it best:

> Every man who enters the penitentiary undergoes prisonization to some extent. The first and most obvious integrative step concerns his status. He becomes at once an anonymous figure in a subordinate group. A number replaces a name. He wears the clothes of the other members of the subordinate group. He is questioned and admonished. He soon learns that the warden is all-powerful. He soon learns the ranks, titles, and authority of various officials. And whether he uses the prison slang and argot or not, he comes to know their meanings. Even though a new man may hold himself aloof from other inmates and remain a solitary figure, he finds himself within a few months referring to or thinking of keepers as "screws," the physician as the "croaker," and using the local nicknames to designate persons. He follows the examples already set in wearing his cap. He learns to eat in haste and in obtaining food he imitates the tricks of those near him.
>
> After the new arrival recovers from the effects of the swallowing-up process, he assigns a new meaning to conditions he had previously taken for granted. The fact that food, shelter, clothing, and a work activity had been given him originally made no special impression. It is only after some weeks or months that there comes to him a new interpretation of these necessities of life. This new conception results from mingling with other men and it places emphasis on the fact that the environment *should* administer to him. This point is intangible and difficult to describe insofar as it is only a subtle and minute change in attitude from the taken-for-granted perception. Exhaustive questioning of hundreds of men reveals that this slight change in attitude is a fundamental step in the process we are calling prisonization.[28]

The effort to depersonalize and routinize is seemingly without respite. The maximum security prison is geared to supervision, control, and surveillance of the inmate's every move. Every other human consideration is weighed against its possible effect on security.

The pragmatic penal leaders in the last half of the nineteenth century began to accept imprisonment as a valid end in itself, rather than as a means to reform. This attitude turned prisons into a dumping ground for America's poor and "different" masses. Immigrants, blacks, and people who did not fit the "all-American" image were likely candidates for these remote asylums.[29] The reformers' rhetoric spoke of rehabilitation, but the actions of corrections administrators belied that emphasis. Prisons were built to keep the prisoners in, but also to keep the public out. To justify the imprisonment of such a heterogeneous group of offenders under such rigid control required a theory of uniform treatment and uniform punishment, without regard to individual differences.

The tendency in the nineteenth century to incarcerate minorities out of proportion to their numbers in society remains with us in the last decade of the twentieth century. Whereas almost one-half of 1 percent of the adult American males were incarcerated in prisons in 1982, blacks were considerably overrepresented: they formed over 2 percent of the total adult male population. In 1993, adult black males in America were almost nine times more likely to be in prison than were adult white males. For females, the ratio is almost eight to one.[30] The reasons for the disparity are hotly debated.[31]

New inmates are reminded of that principle as they are processed into the prison. The buildings, policies, rules, regulations, and control procedures are designed to minimize prisoners' control over their environment. No privacy is allowed in their windowless and open cells. Even the toilets are open to view, and showers are taken under close visual supervision. Every consideration is given by the designers and operators to prevent intrusion or contact from the outside. Visits are usually closely supervised, and a visitor's contacts with the inmates are sometimes possible only by special communication devices[32] that allow conversation but no physical contact. A body search of the inmate, including visual inspection of all body cavities, is invariably conducted if contact has been made. Everything is locked, and all movements require short trips between locked doors.[33]

This description offers only a rough idea of a "typical" maximum security prison on the inside. Nothing can substitute for an actual visit to or confinement in one of these monuments to society's triumph of external control over internal reform. Some of these human cages are over 170 years old and some are relatively new, but the differences involve only minor construction refinements, not basic philosophical changes. Such prisons form the backbone of corrections because they house well over 100,000 inmates and because they are both expensive and durable.

Prisons vary so greatly from state to state that generalizations are dangerous, and the comments of Alexis de Tocqueville in that regard, though made over a century and a half ago, are still valid today.[34] He wrote in 1833 that "aside from common interests, the several states preserve their individual independence, and each of them is sovereign master to rule itself according to its own pleasure. . . . By the side of one state, the penitentiaries of which might serve as a model, we find another whose prisons present the example of everything which ought to be avoided."[35]

Medium and Minimum Security Institutions

In the twentieth century, a broad range of experimental alternatives to the maximum security approach was launched (see Figure 12.3). Much of the construction in corrections over the past half century has been for medium security institutions, in which are now housed about one-third of all state prisoners. Early medium security prisons were hard to distinguish from maximum security institutions; control still was a dominant concern. But even though security may be almost as tight in a medium security prison, the prisoners are not so aware that they are being watched. Also, medium security prisons are usually smaller, without the overwhelming impersonality of maximum security monoliths. There are more inmate programs, and the offender's routine is somewhat less regimented.

Some of the most recent medium security prisons are patterned after the so-called campus design, including attractive residence areas with single rooms (not cells) and dormitories for inmates. External fences and subtle features installed within buildings to maintain security and protect the inmates from one another are the only obvious signs that the prisoners are under observation. Sophisticated electronic and other surveillance equipment is used, but unobtrusively. Assisting in the effective design of those new correctional facilities are such organizations as the National Clearinghouse for Correctional Programming and Architecture.[36] If we continue to use imprisonment as a response to criminal behavior, the new medium security systems may well represent the first wave of the future for correctional prisons in America.

MEDIUM AND MINIMUM SECURITY PRISONS Medium security institutions are prisons designed, built, and operated to prevent escape, disturbances, and violence. Double fences topped with barbed or razor wire usually enclose such institutions. However, they have fewer restrictions on the movement and activities of prison inmates than those found in maximum security institutions. Minimum security prisons allow maximum inmate movement, freedom, and self-determination, while still following methods to avoid escape, violence, and disturbances. Most inmates prefer less secure settings, but usually such environments are viewed as privileges for inmates who are felt to be trustworthy or who have proven their ability to conform in less structured environments. Regular reclassification reviews will improve the match between lesser security and inmate trustworthiness.

An outside work gang in Georgia cleans up litter

—COURTESY OF GEORGIA DEPARTMENT OF CORRECTIONS

NEW PRISONS: 1989–1996

Since 1989, the prison construction boom has continued, if not accelerated. At least 309 new prison facilities were added (excluding renovations, expansions, and extensions of existing prisons, as well as prison camps, community work-release units, facilities for offenders convicted of driving under the influence of alcohol and drugs, etc.). Any new prison built in 1995 was more likely to be a medium security facility.[37]

One of the newer trends to emerge from overreliance on prisons for correcting offenders is the so-called bricks-and-mortar solution to prison overcrowding. Basically, states are attempting to solve a policy problem by constructing new buildings or renovating older facilities. Ordinarily, construction is time consuming, and prisons are "handcrafted" on site; the expected time from the decision to build to committing the first inmate to prison is almost five years. Innovations in prison construction have taken place in Oklahoma,[38] Florida,[39] California,[40] and Ohio.[41] These newer options in construction and financing

FIGURE

12.3

Security Levels of Beds in All Institutions, January 1, 1993

SOURCE: George Camp and Camille Graham Camp, *The Corrections Yearbook 1993: Adult Corrections* (South Salem, NY: Criminal Justice Institute, 1993), p. 39.

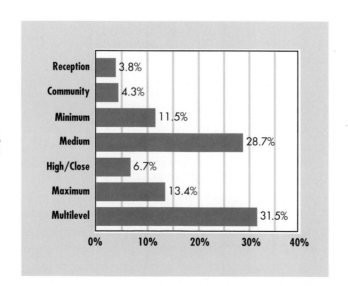

have allowed corrections to avoid more costly and time-consuming construction approaches and have somewhat eased prison overcrowding.

There are two other kinds of correctional institutions today: the minimum security and **open institutions,** designed to serve the needs of rural farm areas and public works rather than those of the offender. Prisoners with good security classifications are assigned to such programs, which range from plantation-style prison farms to small forestry, forest fire fighting, and road camps.

In many ways, the minimum security and open facilities are beneficial. They rescue relatively stable inmates from the oppressive rigors of confinement and from personal danger in the large stifling prisons. As long as we continue to give long prison terms to offenders who are little threat to themselves or the public, the open facilities are preferable to traditional prisons. On the other hand, if we develop more programs of education,[42] work, vocational training, and treatment[43] within the maximum and medium security institutions, inmates in the minimum security work-oriented camps may miss these opportunities. Also, as intermediate punishments and community-based corrections programs continue to drain off the least dangerous and more treatable offenders, the open facilities will lose their value—they are not suited to the hard-core offenders who will remain. Professionals in the corrections field will have to resist efforts to place offenders into minimum security or open facilities for economic reasons, rather than placing them into community-based programs for correctional treatment reasons.

The minimum security institution is a logical compromise between the medium security prison and community-based corrections. The abandonment of the fortress-style prisons of a bygone era is a necessary step in that direction, as a few very small maximum security facilities could be built or renovated to house the estimated 15 to 20 percent of the incarcerated felons who need that kind of protection and surveillance.

Alternatives to Prison Overcrowding

There are basically three correctional options for reducing prison populations and overcrowding, and you have already encountered two: the so-called brick-and-mortar building program and the front-end, or prison avoidance, program. The latter includes restitution programs, intensive supervised probation, house arrest, electronic monitoring, shock probation, boot camps,[44] intermittent imprisonment, and other innovative programs of intermediate sanctions. In the next chapter, dealing with parole, we discuss the back-end alternatives: early release, parole, increased good-time credits, home arrest under parole, halfway houses, prerelease centers, and other alternatives to prison overcrowding.

They are all viable options, but we need to stress three major points. First, the further the offender is carried into the prison-parole cycle, the more expensive corrections will become. Second, the brick-and-mortar solution tends to mortgage the future of corrections and taxpayers, saddling both with institutions that are not likely to be emptied in the near future. Finally, there is considerable evidence that the longer the offender remains in prison, the more likely incapacitation will lead to recidivism.

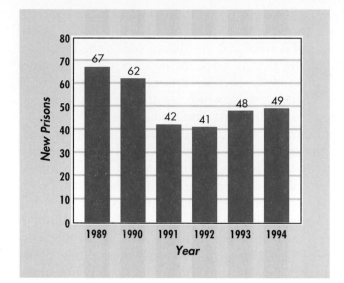

FIGURE

12.4

New Prisons Opened
in Each Year, 1989–1994

SOURCE: George Camp and Camille Graham
Camp, *The Corrections Yearbook 1995: Adult
Corrections* (South Salem, NY: Criminal Justice
Institute, 1995), p. 38.

An analysis of the nation's 1980 arrest data revealed that some 70 percent of the persons arrested for the eight most serious (Type I) offenses had prior adult arrests and 27 percent had a prior adult incarceration. By July 1982, 40 percent of the 1980 arrestees had been arrested again.[45] Greenfield found that an estimated 61 percent of those admitted to prison in 1979 were recidivists (had been incarcerated as juvenile or adult, or both). This rate increased to 94 percent in 1991.[46] Almost half of the prison releasees will return to prison in less than twenty years, usually by the first three years following initial release.[47] Prisons that are overcrowded do little to lower the recidivism rate.

The Future of Imprisonment

It has frequently been shown that the large adult prisons operated by the state provide the least effective means to rehabilitate and reintegrate offenders. Despite findings to that effect, in the 1920s,[48] 1930s,[49] 1960s,[50] 1970s,[51] and 1980s[52] and early 1990s, the building and filling of maximum security prisons continued (see Figure 12-3). The advent, and relative success, of community-based treatment of criminal offenders has begun to dent the armor of the diehards who advocate punitive prison as the ultimate correctional solution. It is the threat that these new programs pose to the old-line institutional staff that must be overcome before the present system, which exists primarily to perpetuate itself, can undergo any real change.[53]

There are other reasons the system is so slow to change, too. Long sentences are one problem: It is difficult to offer programs and promise of the future to an offender who will not be released for ten years or more. Also, laws and practices that restrict the employment of ex-offenders make a mockery of the vocational training programs in many prisons. And to expect a person who has been earning $500 a day as a drug pusher to return to the same environment and work cheerfully as a janitor for the minimum wage is totally unreasonable. The street conditions that make possible such high illegal earnings cannot be controlled by the correctional staff, but the conditions do influence the results of the programs' efforts.

Summary

The litany of cures for correctional ills may seem to be a replay of previous efforts. The significant difference today lies in the interest and assistance of the federal government in the form of funds, technical advice, and planning assistance through the efforts of the National Institute of Justice, Office of Juvenile Justice and Delinquency Programs, and the National Institute of Corrections.

The kind of patchwork effort recommended by the National Advisory Commission is a good beginning. Prison problems are relentless, however, and even the most humane reformers are subtly changed by the enormous problems that face them. They become cold, callous, and finally prisonized themselves. William Nagel, in *The New Red Barn*, quotes early twentieth-century scholar and penologist Frank Tannenbaum:

> We must destroy the prison, root and branch. That will not solve our problem, but it will be a good beginning. . . . Let us substitute something. Almost anything will be an improvement. It cannot be worse. It cannot be more brutal and useless.[54]

Although this is a laudable goal, the realities of prison population increases and the need to open fifteen hundred new beds for inmates *per week* in America will make the goal difficult to attain in the foreseeable future.

Review Questions

1. What are the main purposes of confinement?
2. Differentiate between classification for management and for treatment.
3. Describe a typical maximum security prison. Explain the main differences among maximum, medium, and minimum security institutions.
4. What are the front-end solutions to prison overcrowding? The bricks and mortar solution?
5. What are the impacts of prison overcrowding?
6. Develop an argument against imprisonment of offenders from the recidivism perspective.
7. Why is the nation's prison population so high?
8. Why have prison populations grown so rapidly?

Words to Remember

"get-tough" legislation	baby-boom classification	open institutions
"War on Crime"	correctional treatment	overcrowding
Gothic-style monoliths		

$\mathcal{E}$ndnotes

1. Marc Mauer, "The Institutional Use of Incarceration," *The Prison Journal* 75:1 (1995): 113–123.

2. Steven Donziger, *The Real War on Crime* (New York: HarperCollins, 1996), pp. 31, 42.

3. J. Beck and D. Gilliard, *Prisoners in 1994* (Washington, D.C.: U.S. Department of Justice, 1995).

4. Ibid., p. 5.

5. George Camp and Camille Camp, *The Corrections Yearbook 1995: Adult Corrections* (South Salem, NY: Criminal Justice Institute, 1996), p. 38.

6. Ibid., p. 45.

7. Calculated from budgeting data in American Correctional Association, *1996 Directory* (Lanham, MD.: American Correctional Association, 1996), pp. xiv–xv.

8. Public Agenda Foundation, *Punishing Criminals: Pennsylvanians Consider the Options* (New York: Public Agenda Foundation, 1993); Sandra Lee Brown and Liqun Cao, "The Impact of Race in Criminal Justice Ideology," *Justice Quarterly* 9:4 (1993): 685–701; and Francis Cullen, Edward Latessa, and Velmer Burton, "The Correctional Orientation of Prison Wardens: Is the Rehabilitative Ideal Supported?" *Criminology* 31:1 (1993): 69–92. Also see Donziger, *The Real War on Crime*.

9. Prison managers feel they can cope with accelerating prison populations by building new prisons, adding beds, increasing security staff, increasing security, renovating bed space, and so on. Far down their list of priorities are adding service and program staff. George Camp and Camille Camp, *Management of Crowded Prisons* (South Salem, NY: Criminal Justice Institute, 1989).

10. Beck and Gilliard, *Prisoners in 1994,* p. 2.

11. Jails and prisons are not effective in reducing recidivism. Shorter prison sentences deter criminals from recidivating. See Stephen Coleman and Katheryn Guthrie, *Sentencing Effectiveness in Preventing Crime* (St. Paul: Minnesota Criminal Justice Statistical Analysis Center, 1988). See also the excellent work by Michael Tonry, "Mandatory Penalties," in Michael Tonry, ed., *Crime and Justice: A Review of the Research*, Vol. 16 (Chicago: University of Chicago Press, 1993), pp. 243–273. And see Sandra Tunis, *Outcome Evaluation of Jail-Based Drug Treatment: Effects on Recidivism* (San Francisco: National Council on Crime and Delinquency, 1995).

12. See Ronald Simon and Phyllis Gray, "Perceived Blocked Opportunity as an Explanation of Delinquency Among Lower-Class Black Youth," *Journal of Research in Crime and Delinquency* 26 (1989): 90–101. But also see Joanne Belknap, "The Economics-Crime Link," *Criminal Justice Abstracts* 21 (1989): 140–157; Thomas Bernard, "Angry Aggression Among the 'Truly Disadvantaged,' " *Criminology* 28 (1990): 73–96; and Jerry Neopolitan, "Poverty, Race, and Population Concentrations: Interactive Associations to Violent Crime," *American Journal of Criminal Justice* 16:2 (1992): 143–153. See also Harry Allen, "The American Dream and Crime in the Twenty-First Century," *Justice Quarterly* 12:3 (1995), 427–445, and James Nelson, *Disparities in Processing Felony Arrests in New York State, 1990–92* (Albany, NY: State Division of Criminal Justice Services, 1995).

13. Benjamin Frank, "Basic Issues in Corrections," *Perspectives on Correctional Manpower and Training* (Washington, D.C.: American Correctional Association, 1970). See also the special topic volume devoted to classification, *Crime and Delinquency* 32 (1986): 317, and Christopher Baird, *Validating Risk Assessment Instruments Used in Community Corrections* (Madison, WI: National Council on Crime and Delinquency, 1992).

14. American Correctional Association, *Manual of Correctional Standards*, 3rd ed. (Washington, D.C.: American Correctional Association, 1966), pp. 2–3; Jack Alexander and James Austin, *Handbook of Evaluating Objective Prison Classification System* (Washington, D.C.: National Institute of Corrections, 1992); and Wayne Higgins et al., "Accreditation," *Corrections Today* 54:3 (1992): 40–62.

15. United Nations Department of Economic and Social Affairs, *Standard Minimum Rules for the Treatment of Prisoners and Related Recommendations* (New York: United Nations, 1958), p. B-16.

16. President's Commission on Law Enforcement and Administration of Justice, *Task Force Report: Corrections* (Washington, D.C.: U.S. Government Printing Office, 1967), p. 20.

17. Guidelines for developing, implementing, and testing objective prison classification instruments can be found in Robert Buchanan, Karen Whitlow, and James Austin, "National Evaluation of Objective Prison Classification Systems: The Current State of the Art," *Crime and Delinquency* 32 (1987): 272–290.

18. George Camp and Camille Camp, *The Corrections Yearbook 1995* (South Salem, NY: Criminal Justice Institute, 1995), p. 21.

19. American Correctional Association, *1996 Directory,* pp. xxx–xxxi.

20. William G. Nagel, *The New Red Barn: A Critical Look at the Modern American Prison* (New York: Walker, 1973), pp. 11–13.

21. The District of Columbia Reformatory, built at Lorton, Virginia, in 1926.

22. Howard B. Gill, "Correctional Philosophy and Architecture," *Journal of Criminal Law, Criminology, and Police Science* 53 (1962): 312–322. For a profile of Howard Gill, see Barbara Neff, "Celebrating 61 Years in Corrections," *Corrections Today* 49 (1987): 159–160.

23. Franco Ferracuti et al., *Mental Deterioration in Prison* (Columbus: Ohio State University Program for Study of Crime and Delinquency, 1978), p. 81. See also Hans Toch, Kenneth Adams, and Douglas Grant, *Coping: Maladaption in Prison* (New Brunswick, NJ: Transaction, 1989); Bonnie Carlson and Neil Cervera, *Inmates and Their Wives: Incarceration and Family Life* (Westport, CT: Greenwood, 1992); and Victor Hassine, *Life Without Parole: Living in Prison Today* (Los Angeles: Roxbury, 1996).

24. Norman Johnston, *The Human Cage: A Brief History of Prison Architecture.* (The American Foundation, Philadelphia, Pennsylvania, 1973), p.40.

25. Ibid, p. 41.

26. Gothic architecture was designed to overwhelm the person who entered such structures. The famous gothic churches of Europe were known to make people feel small and insignificant.

27. Number of maximum security prisons built in America are as follows: prior to 1830, 6; 1831 to 1870, 17; 1871 to 1900, 33; 1901 to 1930, 21; 1931 to 1960, 15; 1961 to 1975, 21; 1976 to 1986, 17; 1987 to 1995, 9; for a total of 149.

28. Donald Clemmer, "The Process of Prisonization," in Leon Radzinowicz and Marvin Wolfgang, eds., *The Criminal in Confinement* (New York: Basic Books, 1971), pp. 92–93. See also Hans Tock, John Seymour, Daniel Lockwood, et al., *Living in Prison: The Ecology of Survival* (Washington, D.C.: American Psychological Association, 1992). See Hassine, *Life Without Parole.*

29. Minorities are vastly overrepresented in prisons. Explanations of this disparity range from system discrimination to differential involvement in crime. For the differential involvement position, see Patrick Langan, "Racism on Trial: New Evidence to Explain the Racial Composition of Prisons in the United States," *Journal of Criminal Law and Criminology* 76 (1985): 666–683. For the discrimination perspective, see Cassia Spohn, John Gruhl, and Susan Welch, "The Impact of the Ethnicity and Gender of Defendants on the Decision to Reject or Dismiss Felony Charges," *Criminology* 25 (1987): 175–191; Katheryn Russell, "Development of a Black Criminology, and the Role of the Black Criminologist," *Justice Quarterly* 9:4 (1993): 667–683; and Donziger, *The Real War on Crime.*

30. Beck and Gilliard, *Prisoners in 1992,* p. 8.

31. See Carl Pope and William Feyerherm, "Minority Status and Juvenile Justice Processing: An Assessment of the Research Literature," *Criminal Justice Abstracts* 22 (June 1990): 327–335. See also Steward Tolnay, E. M. Beck, and James Massey, "Black Competition and White Vengeance: Legal Executions of Blacks as Social Control in the Cotton South: 1890–1929," *Social Science Quarterly* 73:3 (1992): 627–644, and Paula Johnson, "At the Intersection of Justice: Experiences of African–American Women in Crime and Sentencing," *American University Journal of Gender and the Law.* 4:1 (1995): 1–76.

32. Special devices for communicating include telephones on either side of bulletproof glass and booths with wire screen between inmates and visitors.

33. For discussion of architecture, construction, design, and innovations in jails and prisons, see the special theme issue of *Corrections Today* 55:2 (1993): 74–128.

34. Alexis de Tocqueville was one of the French commissioners who visited America in 1833. He wrote a treatise on what he observed in the American penitentiary system (see note 35).

35. Gustave de Beaumont and Alexis de Tocqueville, *On the Penitentiary System in the United States and Its Application in France* (Carbondale: Southern Illinois University Press, 1964), p. 48.

36. The National Clearinghouse for Correctional Programming and Architecture is located at the University of Illinois, Department of Architecture, Urbana, Illinois 61801. For more information on prison architecture, see Randy Atlas, "High Rise Confinement for the 'Innocent Until Proven Guilty,' " *Florida Architecture* 15 (May–June 1984): 29–30; Michael Cohn, "Tomorrow's Designs Today," *Corrections Today* 49 (1987): 32–34; American Institute of Architects, *1985 Architecture for Justice Exhibition* (Washington, D.C.: American Institute of Architects, 1985); and Dale Sechrest and Shelley Price, *Correctional Facility Design and Construction Management* (Washington, D.C.: U.S. Department of Justice, 1985). See also the special themes issues of *Corrections Today* 51 (April 1989), 52 (April 1990), and 55 (April 1993).

37. Camp and Camp, *The Corrections Yearbook*, 1995, pp. 38–39.

38. Charles DeWitt and Cindie Unger, *Oklahoma Prison Expansion Saves Time and Money* (Washington, D.C.: U.S. Department of Justice, 1987).

39. Charles DeWitt, *Florida Sets Example with Use of Concrete Modules* (Washington, D.C.: U.S. Department of Justice, 1986).

40. Charles DeWitt, *California Tests New Construction Concepts* (Washington, D.C.: U.S. Department of Justice, 1986), and Carole Sanchez Knopel, *Construction Options: A California Case Study* (Washington, D.C.: U.S. Department of Justice, 1992).

41. Charles DeWitt, *Ohio's New Approach to Prison and Jail Financing* (Washington, D.C.: U.S. Department of Justice, 1986).

42. Frank Porporino and David Robinson, *Can Educating Adult Offenders Counteract Recidivism?* (Ontario: Correctional Service of Canada, 1992), and Kaye McLaren, *Reducing Reoffending: What Works Now* (Wellington: Penal Division, New Zealand Department of Justice, 1992).

43. Gennaro Vito, "Putting Prisoners to Work: Policies and Problems," *Journal of Offender Counseling Services and Rehabilitation* 9 (1985): 21–34. See also Michael Vaughn, "Academic and Vocational Education for Incarcerated Adult and Juvenile Sex Offenders: A National Study," *Journal of Addictions and Offender Counseling* 12:2 (1992): 47–61; U.S. Government Accounting Office, *Federal Prisons: Inmate and Staff Views on Education and Work Training Programs* (Washington, D.C.: U.S. Government Accounting Office, 1993); and Caroline Wolf Harlow, *Drug Enforcement and Treatment in Prisons, 1990* (Washington, D.C.: U.S. Department of Justice, 1992).

44. J. Burns and G. Vito, "An Impact Analysis of the Alabama Boot Camp Program," *Federal Probation* 59:1 (1995): 63–67.

45. Cornelius Behan, "ROPE: Repeat Offender Project Experiment," *FBI Law Enforcement Bulletin* 56 (1987), pp. 1–5.

46. Allen Beck et al. *Survey of State Prison Inmates, 1991* (Washington, D.C.: U.S. Department of Justice, 1993), p. 11.

47. Lawrence Greenfield, *Examining Recidivism* (Washington, D.C.: U.S. Department of Justice, 1985), p. 340, and Cynthia Corbo, *Release Outcome—1984: Follow-up Study* (Trenton: New Jersey Department of Corrections, 1992).

48. National Commission on Law Observance and Enforcement (Wickersham Commission), *Report on Prisons* (Washington, D.C.: U.S. Government Printing Office, 1929).

49. *Attorney General's Survey of Release Procedures* (Washington, D.C.: U.S. Government Printing Office, 1939).

50. *The President's Commission on Law Enforcement and Administration of Justice* (Washington, D.C.: U.S. Government Printing Office, 1967).

51. National Advisory Commission on Criminal Justice Standards and Goals, Corrections (Washington, D.C.: U.S. Government Printing Office, 1973).

52. Marilyn McShane and Frank Williams, "Running on Empty: Creativity and the Correctional Agenda," *Crime and Delinquency* 35 (October 1989): 562–76.

53. John Hale, "Correctional Officers: The Forgotten Battalion in the War Against Crime," *Corrections Today* (December 1989): 168. See also the "Best in the Business" theme issue, *Corrections Today* 55:3 (1993).

54. Nagel, *The New Red Barn,* p.148.

CHAPTER THIRTEEN

Parole

Overview

The correctional process as described so far has followed offenders as they were filtered through the correctional system. We have seen how those who wind up in prison have both challenges and opportunities as they serve out their sentences and descend down the classification ladder until they are at minimum status and approach their release date. This chapter now brings our focus to parole, the most often used way to leave prison and reenter society in a graduated manner. Parole is a correctional process that now finds itself under attack as a method to gain early release from their sentence. The attitude sweeping the nation, as prison populations continue to rise, is to make sentencing even harsher and to make the inmates serve as much of their sentence in a prison as possible. The student needs to understand the fact that many other issues underlie the process of parole (or earned early release) in today's environment as we reexamine the use of this time-tested tool. We begin with a brief review of the background of parole.

Pardon and Parole: Two Ways Out of Prison

Most offenders who enter the prisons of America eventually end up back on the streets of the old neighborhoods. Unless prisoners die in prison (from natural or other causes), almost all will come out someday. The cruelly long sentences of the nineteenth century usually meant that the few offenders who did leave the prisons were bitter, broken, or both. Today the odds are heavy that offenders will leave prison on parole, usually long before the expiration of their maximum sentences. In recent years, the number and percentage of prisoners **released on parole** have climbed steadily. In 1966, the prisoners released on parole numbered 61 percent of the

> **P**robation, parole, and their descendent operations now borrow from the same continuum of program components, namely intensive supervision, restitution, electronic monitoring, and community service. In addition, these individual program components may serve as independent sanctions and as the means for diversion from the official criminal justice system.
>
> —*Marilyn McShane and Wesley Krause*

total, but that figure had jumped to over 70 percent by 1993. The U.S. total of persons under parole supervision increased by more than 2 percent from 1991 to the end of 1993, from 12 percent of those of the total under correctional supervision to 14 percent, respectively. There were 690,159 offenders under parole supervision at year-end 1995[1] (see Figure 13-1). The significance of parole is clear when we recognize that the only alternatives are clemency, completion of sentence, death, or probation (usually shock probation). Parole is the fastest-growing system in corrections.[2]

In the days of frequent capital punishment and life sentences, death in prison was a strong possibility. The prisoner might die as a result of natural causes, an accident, or homicide inside the walls. Another way out—sometimes not much better, from the offender's viewpoint—is to be forced to serve the entire maximum sentence before release (to **max out**). Infinitely better, but rare, is *executive clemency*, in the form of a pardon or similar action by the governor. A full pardon usually means complete exoneration of blame for the offense and relieves the prisoner of the stigma of guilt. One version of the pardon is **amnesty**, which may be granted to a group or class of offenders. The United States has a long tradition of granting amnesty to soldiers who deserted or avoided service in major wars. And in countries where it is customary to imprison any and all political dissidents, the government may use mass amnesty to gain public favor. Executive power can also be used to grant a **reprieve**, usually in the case of the death penalty (a well-used plot line in grade B movies of the 1930s and 1940s, in which the star is granted a last-minute reprieve while being strapped into the electric chair). A reprieve does not usually result in a release, but merely a reduction in the severity of the punishment. Punishment can also be lessened by **commutation**, a shortening of the sentence by executive order. Usually, the commutation is based on time already spent in jail and prison, and results in almost immediate release of the petitioner. Another form of release, discussed in Chapter 8, results from some sort of appellate review action. These procedures, along with parole (and, of course, escape and natural death) cover the major ways a prisoner can expect to leave prison.

The classic definition of parole is "release of an offender from a penal or correctional institution, after he has served a portion of his sentence, under the continued custody of the state and under conditions that permit his reincarceration in the event of misbehavior."[3] The term *parole* is attributed to Dr. S. G. Howe of Boston,[4] who used it in a letter to the Prison Association of New York in 1846. It is the amount of supervision exercised over the parolee that distinguishes American parole procedures from those of other countries. As the state parole systems developed in

	1/1/92	1/1/95
Percentage Sentenced on Parole	**12.0%**	12.2%
Average Parolees per Jurisdicion	**9,144**	12,777
	1/1/92	1/1/95
Percentage Female	**8.8%**	11.1%
Percentage Nonwhite	**44.4%**	58.5%
	1991	1994
Average Agency Caseload	**75**	84
Average Daily Cost per Parolee	**$2.89**	$2.67

FIGURE

13.1

Parole Caseloads

SOURCE: C. Camp and G. Camp, *The Corrections Yearbook 1995: Probation and Parole* (South Salem, NY: Criminal Justice Institute, 1995), p. 34 and *1993: Probation and Parole*, p. 33 .

America, the reliance on rules and supervision became a crucial element. As the United States entered the twentieth century, parole had gained a strong foothold as a way for prisoners to return to the free world. Today, all but two states have some system of parole supervision for released offenders, even though some nineteen states are now in the process of reducing or eliminating its use. In 1995, Virginia became the most recent state to abolish supervision or aftercare as a method of release from prison.

Parole Administraton

If prisoners want to be released on parole, they must be recommended and reviewed by some procedure that will select them for that option. For this reason, how parole is administered and by whom is of vital concern to the prison population, as well as to the rest of society.

THE PAROLE BOARD

When parole selection procedures were first instituted, many states had a single commissioner of parole, appointed by the governor. That kind of political patronage soon led to corruption and controversy and was generally abandoned after World War II. Two models for parole recommendation have replaced it: (1) **parole boards** that are linked to, or actually part of, the correctional system staff and (2) parole boards that are independent of correctional institutions and the administrators of the system. A third model, a consolidation of all correctional and parole services, incorporates the most desirable aspects of the first two models.

The correctional system model tends to perceive the parole decision as merely another in a series of decisions regarding the offender. The institutional staff feels it is best suited, because of its close contact with the offender, to make the parole decision. That argument, however, is based on the false assumption that strict obedience to the conditions and rules dominating prison life somehow is linked to a healthy adjustment on the outside. In other words, the kind of behavior that might lead the staff to conclude an inmate was ready for parole could in fact cripple his or her efforts to cope on the outside.

Complete subordination to rules and regulations and suppression of individuality—the desired behavior in institutions to ensure a smooth operation—are hardly the requisite skills for survival in the free world. Another potential problem with parole decisions made by the institutional staff could be a twisted use of that procedure to get rid of prison troublemakers. Institutional decision making can be buried too readily in the invisible activity behind the walls. Removed from public scrutiny or control, the parole decision soon becomes just another mechanical process that treats offenders, vitally concerned with the decision, as only incidental to the outcome.

In time, the independently authorized parole-releasing authority became the most widely used model in adult corrections. As a matter of fact, today no adult parole authority is controlled directly by the staff of a penal institution.[5] The obvious purpose of this independent authority was to remove the decision-making procedure from the atmosphere we just described. It was felt that the institutional parole authorities were too easily swayed by the subjective input of the staff.

Although an independent board may well be more objective than the correctional bureaucracy in making parole recommendations, it does not provide the perfect system. Board members' lack of knowledge about the programs, policies, and conditions within the prisons creates an organizational gap, critics have argued, that causes unnecessary conflict between prison authorities and the boards.

First, the claim is made that such boards tend to be insensitive to institutional programs and fail to give them the support they require. Second, independent boards are accused of basing their decisions on inappropriate considerations, such as the feelings of a local police chief. Third, their remoteness from the institutional program gives independent boards little appreciation of the dynamics in a given case; their work tends to be cursory, with the result that too often persons who should be paroled are not, and those who should not be paroled are released. Fourth, the argument is made that independent systems tend to place on parole boards persons who have little training or experience in corrections.[6]

An attempt to solve the problems that have plagued the institutional and independent systems has resulted in a hybrid and most popular model, the **consolidated board**. The consolidated model places the authority for parole decisions in the department of corrections but includes independent powers in the decision-making process. This arrangement reflects the general move toward the consolidation of all correctional services, such as institutional programs, community-based programs, and parole and aftercare programs, under state departments of correction. The consolidation model views the treatment of offenders as they pass through the correctional system as a continuum, rather than a series of separate, unrelated experiences. It is claimed that removal of the decision-making authority to a level above the institutions, but still within the system, tends to foster objectivity while maintaining a sensitivity to the programs and problems of the prison administrators. This approach is gaining wide acceptance, and a large percentage of the state parole boards responsible for releasing adult offenders now function as part of an administrative structure that includes other agencies for offenders.[7] Although this system is preferable to the alternatives outlined earlier, its advocates still must struggle to maintain its autonomy through careful selection of board members and avoidance of automatic tenure, with explicit delineation of parole board tasks and responsibilities.

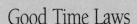

Good Time Laws

The term *good time* did not refer to having fun within the walls. Instead, it involved taking days off the offender's sentence as a result of conduct and behavior in accordance with the institutional rules. In 1817, New York was the first state to pass a good-time statute. The rules throughout the nation were firm and fairly straightforward, even though they varied from state to state. New York's statute enabled the correctional administrator to reduce by one-fourth the time of any prisoner sentenced to imprisonment for not less than five years, upon certificate of the principal keeper and other satisfactory evidence that such prisoner had behaved well and had acquired, on the whole, the net sum of $15 or more per annum. Every state in the union and the District of Columbia had passed some kind of good-time law by 1916. California awarded good time in 1990 at a "1-for-2" ratio: one day of reduction for every two days of good time. ∎

A modern, more relaxed parole hearing

THE PAROLE SELECTION PROCESS

How is an offender selected for parole? This question has been asked by many researchers and, until recently, little concrete evidence was found that any reasonably objective criteria were used. Earlier studies showed that the main factor considered in the selection process was the seriousness of the crime for which the offender was originally convicted.[8] In 1979, however, a national study of parole boards determined that specific factors were considered evidence of parole readiness. The five most important factors were participation in prison programs, good prison behavior, change in attitudes, increased maturity, and development of insight.[9] Perhaps a good way to analyze this process is to follow a typical parole review and selection effort.

Most parole boards operate by assigning cases to individual board members, who review the cases in detail and then make recommendations to the board as a whole. In most cases the recommendation of the individual member is accepted, but sometimes the assembled board will request more information. At this point, the prisoner will often be asked to appear. Some states send individual board members to the institutions to interview the inmate and the prison staff; others convene the entire board at the various institutions on a regular schedule. If inmates do not meet whatever mysterious standards the board has established for parole, their sentences are continued and they are **flopped.** But if they are accepted, they are prepared for turnover to the adult parole authority for a period of supervision determined by the parole board.

One problem in making parole decisions is the tendency of most boards to disregard the right of offenders to know what standards they are expected to meet (and, if they fail, the reasons for it):

It is an essential element of justice that the role and processes for measuring parole readiness be made known to the inmate. This knowledge can greatly facilitate the earnest inmate toward his or her own rehabilitation. It is just as important for inmates to know the rules and basis of the judgment upon which they will be granted or denied parole as it was important for them to know the basis of the charge against them and the evidence upon which they

FLOPPED

Flopped is inmate slang for failing to meet parole board standards for release. A flop usually means the inmate will not be eligible to be considered anew by the board until another six months or more of incarceration, treatment, or observation in the institution.

were convicted. One can imagine nothing more cruel, inhumane, and frustrating than serving a prison term without knowledge of what will be measured and the rules determining whether one is ready for release. Justice can never be a product of unreasoned judgment.[10] This criteria problem also affects the correctional staff, who should know the rules of the game so they can guide inmates in the direction desired by the parole board.

Another problem facing potential parolees is the lack of an appeal process. Because criteria for granting parole and reasons for denying it are not specified, inmates—and concerned citizens—have often questioned the validity of board decisions. Future parole selection processes must include self-regulating internal appeal procedures, or the courts will be deluged with relevant cases until the Supreme Court finally establishes a basis for rules and procedures under the rubric of the Fourteenth Amendment. Some states, recognizing the handwriting on the wall, have begun to establish criteria and develop appeal procedures before they are forced to do so by court decisions based on class action suits.

Inmates, correctional critics, scholars, parole board members, study panels, and prison writers have commented on the release decision, characterizing it as arbitrary, capricious, prejudiced, lawless, and offering no meaningful future directions for inmates who have not been released. One response to those criticisms has been the development of parole guidelines; the U.S. Parole Commission has been in the forefront of that movement,[11] although twenty-two other jurisdictions (such as New York and Florida) have structured discretionary decision factors into their parole guidelines.

The federal guidelines used characteristics of the offense and the traits and previous criminal behaviors the inmate brings to the current offense to construct a matrix that specifies the amount of time (within narrow bounds) an inmate would have to serve before release. Good-time and earned-time credits can reduce the anticipated prison sentence. Such an approach permits the offender to know immediately how long the sentence will be and what must be done to shorten it. The approach also reduces the anxiety and hostility of the on-the-spot decision-making process frequently found in other jurisdictions. If the parole commission deviates more than 20 percent from the guidelines, the rationale for deviation must be explained in writing, and an appeal procedure permits legal review. More states should consider this promising approach.

PAROLE REVOCATION

The rules for conditional release, developed under Crofton's **Irish system,** form the basis for most parole stipulations, even today. The conditions for parole should be related to the objectives of a parole system, as follows:

1. Release of each person from confinement at the most favorable time, with appropriate consideration to requirements of justice, expectations of subsequent behavior, and cost.
2. The largest possible number of successful parole completions.
3. The smallest possible number of new crimes committed by released offenders.
4. The smallest possible number of violent acts committed by released offenders.
5. An increase of general community confidence in parole administration.[12]

The methods by which those objectives can be carried out include the following:

DISCRETIONARY RELEASE Parole of an inmate from prison prior to the expiration of maximum sentence, according to the boundaries set by the sentence and the legislature. Discretionary release usually functions under the indeterminate sentence and implies the inmate is ready to undergo community treatment and supervision.

MANDATORY RELEASE The required release of an inmate from incarceration because the statutes mandate the release of any inmate having served the equivalent of the maximum term. Mandatory release means the parole board refused to release the inmate prior to attainment of the equivalent of the maximum time imposed by the court. Mandatory release reflects the impacts of good-time, jail-time, and program-time credits on the actual length of time an offender can be held on a sentence of incarceration. More than 30 percent of prison releasees are by mandatory release.

Alexander Maconochie (1787–1860), the head of the British penal colony on Norfolk Island close to Australia, established an early form of parole in 1840. The "mark" system allowed inmates to earn credits toward a conditional release called ticket-of-leave. Crofton included revocation of the ticket-of-leave if previously established conditions were violated. His system also provided for supervision by police officials, the first parole officers. He believed that punishment should be geared toward reform. On return to England, he was dismissed as governor of the Birmingham Borough for being too lenient in 1851.

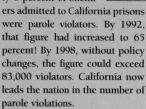
1. A process for selecting persons who should be given parole and for determining the time of release.

2. A system for prerelease planning both inside the institution with the offender and outside the institution with others in the community at large.

3. A system for supervision and assistance in the community.

4. A set of policies, procedures, and guidelines for situations in which the question of reimprisonment must be decided.[13]

Designed in the belief that those conditions should be followed to the letter, and in the awareness the public saw the paroled offender as a "**convict bogey**," many early programs were based on unreasonable restrictions. Many of the rules were no more than convenient techniques for ensuring the quick return of parolees to prison if they created even a slight stir for the parole supervisors. More recently, the rules were replaced with simpler and common-sense statements such as presented in Figure 13-2.

One can imagine that conforming to the early rule requiring the parolee to "only associate with persons of good reputation" would be difficult for a man whose wife was a prostitute or whose father was an ex-convict. The emphasis on such rules gave parole officers great discretionary power over parolees. The parolees knew they could be returned to prison for a technical violation of their parole conditions at almost any time the parole officer desired, a situation hardly conducive to reform and respect for the law. Parolees who had committed some minor violation might decide, "If I'm going to get busted for a technical violation, I might as well do something *really* wrong." The revised nonrestrictive rules in the 1973 statement are aimed at eliminating the need for that kind of rationale.

Even with the new and simpler rules, of course, technical violations are possible, and Ohio took special steps to handle them. If parolees have violated one of the simple conditions but did not commit another convictable offense, they would be sent to a community reintegration center.[14] There they were given guidance to help them deal with complete freedom in the community without the need to return to a penal institution. Ohio's reintegration centers, located in three communities, give parolees a chance to continue their employment and other community contacts while proving to the parole authorities that they can adjust to their problems without further incarceration. The centers represent a hopeful model for handling technical violations by parolees. A combination of rules that are easy to grasp and follow, plus an alternative to reincarceration for those who slip up occasionally, are more humane, less expensive, and less damaging solutions than is a return to prison.[15]

PAROLEE RIGHTS AT REVOCATION

Because of arbitrary procedures used in earlier parole revocation hearings, the U.S. Supreme Court in 1971 defined the basic rights of parolees at a parole revocation hearing in *Morrissey* v. *Brewer*, 408 U.S. 271. Parolees must be notified in writing of the charges they face at least twenty-four hours before the preliminary hearing ("probable cause"). Revocation candidates have a right to hear the evidence against them, to cross-examine, and to refute the testimony. Furthermore, they can present their own evidence, and they have the right to a written report from the hearing that must be held before a neutral third party. Some states mandate legal counsel at this stage. At the second hearing, usually before a representative or member(s) of a parole board, the same rights are continued.

The Members of the Parole Board have agreed that you have earned the opportunity of parole and eventually a final release from your present conviction. The Parole Board is therefore ordering a Parole Release in your case.

Parole Status has a two-fold meaning: One is a trust status in which the Parole Board accepts your word you will do your best to abide by the Conditions of Parole that are set down in your case; the other, by state law, means the Adult Parole Authority has the legal duty to enforce the Conditions of Parole even to the extent of arrest and return to the institution should that become necessary.

1. Upon release from the institution, report as instructed to your Parole Officer (or any other person designated) and thereafter report as often as directed.
2. Secure written permission of the Adult Parole Authority before leaving the [said] state.
3. Obey all municipal ordinances, state and federal laws, and at all times conduct yourself as a responsible law-abiding citizen.
4. Never purchase, own, possess, use or have under your control, a deadly weapon or firearm.
5. Follow all instructions given you by your Parole Officer or other officials of the Adult Parole Authority and abide by any special conditions imposed by the Adult Authority.
6. If you feel any of the Conditions or instructions are causing problems, you may request a meeting with your Parole Officer's supervisor. The request stating your reasons for the conference should be in writing when possible.
7. Special Conditions: (as determined). I have read, or have had read to me, the foregoing Conditions of my Parole. I fully understand them and I agree to observe and abide by my Parole Conditions.

Witness _____   Parole Candidate _____

Date _____

Sir Walter Crofton (1815–1897) director of the Irish prison system in 1846, improved on the ticket-of-leave system developed by Alexander Maconochie. Crofton included revocation of the ticket-of-leave if previously established conditions were violated. His system also had provisions for supervision by police officials, the first parole officers.

FIGURE

13.2

Statement of Parole Agreement

SOURCE: State of Ohio, Department of Rehabilitation and Correction, Adult Parole Authority, Statement of Parole Agreement APA-271 (Columbus: State of Ohio).

Innovations in Parole Supervision

In addition to trying the casework approach of traditional parole field supervision, many jurisdictions are developing alternative techniques for supervising clients more intensively or providing a different parole service delivery mechanism. Some states

BPT hearings: Deputy Commissioners with inmate

—PHOTO BY FOLSOM, COURTESY OF THE STATE OF CALIFORNIA DEPARTMENT OF CORRECTIONS have also begun to shift the focus of parole away from service delivery to supervision. Those efforts are seen in house arrest, electronic monitoring of parolees, and intensive supervised parole. (See Figure 13-3.) The three strategies were explored in Chapter 11 as **front-end solutions** used *before* long-term incarceration. Our focus here is on two special early release programs: shock parole and shock incarceration.

SHOCK PAROLE

Twenty years ago, the Ohio legislature pioneered a bill that would provide for the early parole of inmates after just six months of incarceration. Limited to first offenders, the theoretical underpinning is specific deterrence. It was assumed the offender would be so "shocked" by the realities of the prison experience and punishment that he or she would be motivated to avoid further incarceration after release to regular parole supervision. Shock parole also releases the inmate before he or she becomes prisonized and begins to identify with more dangerous, violent, and predatory offenders. Shock parolees can be released from prison if the following criteria are met:

1. The offense for which the prisoner is incarcerated was not murder or aggravated assault.
2. The prisoner has not served at least thirty days for a prior felony conviction in any federal or state reformatory or prison.
3. The prisoner is not a psychopathic offender.
4. Further confinement for purposes of rehabilitation or correction is not needed.
5. There is a strong possibility that the offender will respond positively to early parole and is not likely to commit another crime.[16]

This discretionary release program is generally vested with the parole board, which conducts hearings on eligibility in the same fashion as for other parole considerations. Persons who have received **shock probation**, and failed or reoffended, usually are not eligible for shock parole. Research[17] indicates less recidivism and parole violations for shock parolees than for other parolees. At least nine states have shock parole procedures. In a period of serious prison overcrowding, this

FIGURE

13.3

Percentage of Parole Jurisdictions Administering Specific Programs (1994)

SOURCE: C. Camp and G. Camp, *The Correction Yearbook 1995: Probation and Parole* (South Salem, NY: Criminal Justice Institute, 1995), p. 62.

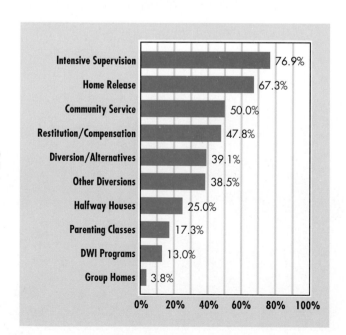

innovative program can still send a clear deterrent message to naive inmates, lessen overcrowding, and reduce the staggering costs of imprisonment. The problems with overcrowded correctional institutions and a continuous rise in the number of incarcerated offenders who are dangerous and violent, however, make it more difficult to find candidates for shock probation. Most of those who would qualify for shock parole are now considered candidates for the boot camp programs we outlined in Chapter 11.

SHOCK INCARCERATION

Shock incarceration, also known as **boot camp programs,** has enjoyed widespread acceptance by legislators, the public, and correctional leaders. Some are managed in jail-linked programs. Others are linked to probation conditions and require a brief period of incarceration combined with boot camp programming before return to the community under probation supervision. Our focus here is on shock incarceration that leads to *parole* and highlights the state of New York, which requires treatment as an integral part of the overall program.[18]

Shock incarceration facilities, or boot camp prisons, for young adults have been developed in city, county, state, and federal jurisdictions. These facilities provide for shorter periods of incarceration than the youthful offenders would normally receive, but the regime involves strict, military-style discipline, unquestioning obedience to orders, and highly structured days filled with drill and hard work. New York State's boot camps add a new dimension to this typical regimen. In New York, the program is designed to provide a total learning environment that fosters involvement, self-direction, and individual responsibility.

New York State's shock incarceration program for young adults provides a therapeutic environment where young non-violent offenders receive substance abuse treatment, academic education, and other help to promote their reintegration into the community. All aspects of the boot camp regimen have as their goal

Shock Incarceration in New York

Shock incarceration facilities, or boot camp prisons for young female adults, have been developed in city, county, and state jurisdictions. These include the New York State Program for youthful female offenders. A typical case is discussed below. Rita is an example of the type of offenders that might best benefit from boot camp programs. Her case is described in some detail to indicate how boot camps interface with parole.

WOMEN IN SHOCK INCARCERATION

Rita finishes fifty sit-ups and springs to her feet. At 6 A.M. her platoon begins a five-mile run, the last portion of this morning's physical training. After five months in New York's Lakeview Shock Incarceration Correctional Facility, the morning workout is easy. Rita even enjoys it, taking pride in her physical conditioning.

When Rita graduates and returns to New York City, she will face six months of intensive supervision before moving to regular parole. More than two-fifths of Rita's platoon did not make it this far; some withdrew voluntarily, and the rest were removed for misconduct or failure to participate satisfactorily. By completing shock incarceration, she will enter parole eleven months before her minimum release date.

The requirements for completing shock incarceration are the same for male and female inmates. The women live in a separate housing area of Lakeview. Otherwise, men and women participate in the same education, physical training, drill and ceremony, drug education, and counseling programs. Men and women are assigned to separate work details and attend "Network" group meetings held in inmates' living units. ∎

the development of law-abiding citizens. The therapeutic approach adopted by New York State for shock incarceration facilities has an added heavy emphasis on substance abuse education and treatment and the development of personal responsibility. A program called "Network," in which staff receive special training, integrates all these components into a single treatment environment.

The New York State Shock Incarceration program has had the following outcomes:

1. Substantial savings in operational and capital costs. This has been accomplished by reducing to six months the time these offenders would ordinarily have spent in prison;

2. Improvements in educational achievement. On average, graduates of Shock Incarceration in New York have improved their reading and math scores by one grade level;

3. Comparable or better return-to-prison rates. When return-to-prison rates of shock incarceration program graduates are compared to those of other inmates, the graduates did as well as (or in some situations better than) parolees who did not participate or complete the program.

Evaluations of shock incarceration to date[19] suggest that prison-bound offenders benefit from the specific deterrence and treatment of boot camp programs, but that some jurisdictions may be committing less risky and lower need offenders to shock incarceration (**net-widening**) to punish rather than to rehabilitate. When more detailed results are measured, it is likely that well-focused and treatment-inclusive programs will be found effective as a correctional mechanism to treat and release selected prisoners earlier than their court-mandated minimum period of incarceration without endangering public safety. Research results will also probably validate this approach as an effective way to avoid higher costs of incarceration and providing prison bed space for more intractable inmates.

Personnel and Caseload Problems in Parole

As one of the busiest parts of corrections, the field of parole offers great opportunities and challenges for professionals in criminal justice. It is reported that 690,159 offenders were under parole supervision in America in 1994.[20] The number of parole employees will have to increase dramatically to match further increases, although the number of employees involved in parole (many of whom also handle probationers) has increased by 17 percent since 1991.[21] It is essential that well-qualified individuals seek careers in parole supervision. In the past, a lack of such qualified personnel forced the recruitment of parole officers whose basic orientation came from other disciplines (for example, law enforcement officers, teachers, investigators, and custodial personnel from prisons). Those officers often favored the "watchdog" or "control" model of parole supervision, whereby the officer's constant expectation that the parolee would fail did indeed produce such failure (a *self-fulfilling prophecy*).[22] The expansion of parole services in the last two decades has attracted more professionals from the social sciences, especially social workers. That trend assists in the overall goal of professionalization for corrections as a whole.[23]

Because social workers have become prominent in the field of parole supervision, the old caseload issue has arisen as a persistent and continuing problem. Caseloads for parole had a downward or, at best, a "flat" trend from 1988 to 1990. Beginning in 1991, however, the trend began to climb to a high of 84 in 1994.[24] This is most likely due to a larger number of inmates who are being released to reduce overcrowding. Despite increased workloads, the rate of successful termination from parole is still at least 51 percent nationwide.[25]

Actually, research has shown it is not the number of cases each parole officer handles that makes the biggest difference in outcome. Rather, the type of case as it relates to the background and experience of the parole officer and the agency's orientation are the keys to the officer's effectiveness. Some officers can handle as many as one hundred fairly simple low-risk cases in which parolees require little assistance to lead a crime-free existence in the community, whereas the same officers can barely handle a caseload of ten to fifteen high-risk cases. The message is clear. Administrators must emphasize a differential assignment of cases, keeping in mind such factors as the complexity of the cases, the needs and risks of offenders, and the background and ability of the parole officer. A proper assignment would match parolees who need minimal attention and reporting with officers whose background stresses control and custody, and parolees whose problems are more extensive with officers who have had social work experience. Clearly, the rising number of parolees creates a fertile field for the criminal justice professional.

Emerging Issues in Parole

Although parole retains its place as one of the most important areas of the correctional spectrum, it still presents some problems for administrators, and it has its share of enemies. Parole is under attack all across America. One of the problems is the selection of parole authority personnel. It is difficult to decide between candidates from within the department, who might be hesitant to challenge a system that gave them their chance, and candidates from outside the system, who might be uninformed and politically motivated individuals willing to use the position for personal gain. Standards have been suggested for the selection of parole authority personnel, but they do not guarantee that boards will display the required expertise and skills. The only really effective way to ensure qualified boards is to make the standards part of the statutes, thus removing the selection process from the political arena. Among other considerations, these statutory measures should permit qualified ex-offenders to serve, especially as hearing examiners.[26] No one could be as sensitive as an ex-offender to an inmate's tension and uncertainty when trying to present his or her case to the parole board. In addition to the careful selection of board members based on statutory criteria, administrators must require that parole personnel undergo extensive training in recent legal decisions, advances in technology, and current correctional practices in the institutions they will serve. The government's Standards and Goals Commission has recommended that such training be provided on a national scale.[27]

The trend today is toward the determinate sentence or **just deserts model** for sentencing in more and more states. Hussey and Lagoy studied the process and its impact in eight of the determinate sentencing states, and a summary of the provisions have far-reaching implications for the future of parole as we know it.

After examining the determinate sentencing schemes in the eight states reviewed . . . it is difficult to escape the conclusion that they are inconsistent structurally and philosophically. It is equally clear that the parole system has been significantly altered in all seven states. Arizona is the only system that retains both discretionary parole release and parole supervision until the expiration of the sentence imposed.

It appears that the influence of politics can be most closely observed in the prescription of potentially severe sentence lengths (i.e., twenty to fifty years) and in the magnitude of the range of sentences within a particular crime class. This suggests that legislatures are uncomfortable with the basic tenets of just deserts-limited incarcerative terms uniformly imposed. Apparently, they perceive that the public demands that they be tough on crime and being tough does not allow for shorter prison terms, even if they are imposed more uniformly on a greater number of offenders.[28]

It is clear that the movement toward determinate sentencing and away from the so-called treatment model presents, in more and more jurisdictions, a clouded future for parole, parole boards, and parole supervision. The public may finally find that prisoners who return to society with no guidance or supervision after a long incarceration are even more in need of parole than the graduates of past practices. The results will be difficult to determine because it will be many years until the effects of determinate sentencing are better understood.[29]

Parole Remains a Major Segment of Corrections

Despite growing pressures for the determinate sentence and the elimination of supervision upon release, parole is still a growing segment of community corrections and increased by 30 percent in the five years between 1990 and 1994.[30] Although many prisoners now are released unconditionally directly back to the community, approximately 70 percent are still released to community supervision. In some states the title of *parole officer* has been changed to *community corrections officer* to reflect a custodial leaning, but the inmates remain under essentially the same controls as before.

Pardon

An act of executive clemency that absolves the party in part or in full from the legal consequences of the crime and conviction. For the accused, pardon stops further criminal justice proceedings.

Pardons can be full or conditional; the former generally applies to both the punishment and the guilt of the offender and blots out the existence of guilt in the eyes of the law. It also removes an offender's disabilities and restores civil rights. The conditional pardon usually falls short of the remedies available in the full pardon, is an expression of guilt, and does not obliterate the conviction but may restore civil rights.

The U.S. Supreme Court decisions on pardons and their effects are directly contradictory, and thus state laws usually govern pardons. While pardons are not frequent in the nation at this time, it is reasonable to expect they may become more frequent as prison overcrowding becomes more critical. ∎

Parolee on work release program

—*COURTESY OF CHURCHILL AND KLEHR*

Both parole and probation have a similar history and, even though they occur at opposite ends of the correctional process, their clients are supervised in much the same way. Thirty-four states have combined the administration of probation and parole into a single agency. Even probation, which had traditionally been a preincarceration option, now takes place in many cases after a brief period of jail or prison time. The main difference remains the method by which the offender is placed under either option. Probation remains a direct sentence by the court, whereas parole is a function of the executive branch, with discretionary parole being granted by the parole board and mandatory parole by corrections agencies under the governor. These parole agencies provide a variety of services. (See Figure 13-4.)

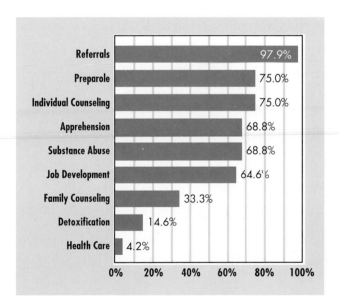

FIGURE

13.4

Percentage of Parole Agencies Providing Specific Services (1994)

SOURCE: C. Camp and G. Camp, *The Corrections Yearbook 1995: Probation and Parole* (South Salem, NY: Criminal Justice Institute, 1995), p. 61.

PAROLE BOARD MEMBERS

Governors appoint parole board members in forty-one jurisdictions, most often with the advice and consent of the state legislature. The most frequent term of service is four years, and forty-one states have staggered terms of office for members, thus assuring continuity of parole boards regardless of changes in the governor's mansion.

There are no statutory qualifications for being a parole board member in twenty-nine jurisdictions, and the other twenty-two jurisdictions have qualifications that speak to length of time and experience in corrections (or a related field). In addition, seven jurisdictions have an education requirement of at least a bachelor's degree.

Pardons and Parole Boards

Across the nation, parole boards are often directly involved in the consideration for a pardon, recommending this act of clemency to the state's governor. Although pardons are relatively rare,[31] they can lessen social stigma and restore rights.[32] No mention of parole boards would be complete without mentioning their role in pardons. Some states restore civil rights when parole is granted; others when the offender is released from parole. In still others, it is necessary for a governor to restore all rights, usually through a pardon.

California's **procedures for pardon** illustrate the latter. What is required for a pardon in California? Generally, the offender must have led a crime-free existence for ten years following release from parole. The offender must initiate a petition for pardon in a superior court (also called a court of common pleas in other jurisdictions). A formal hearing is held, and the officiating judge solicits opinions from the local district attorney and chief law enforcement officer in the jurisdiction. A computer search is made for any arrests and convictions. The local probation department prepares a pre-pardon hearing report. If the preponderance of evidence is favorable and no arrest or conviction record is found, the petition is approved by the superior court and is forwarded to the governor's office. The governor may then order the equivalent of a parole board (Board of Prison Terms) to prepare an investigation that would contain a recommendation for pardon. If the report is favorable, the governor may pardon the petitioner, thereby restoring to him or her all of the rights and immunities of an ordinary citizen. It is evident that most ex-offenders, though no doubt preferring a pardon, may favor even more having the crime and conviction put as far behind them as possible. They may also not have the perseverance to endure such an involved and expensive procedure. Finally, statistics show that almost all ex-offenders are rearrested within the ten-year time period, even if there is no further action by criminal justice system officials. No wonder so few ex-offenders seek and receive pardons!

Summary

We have seen that nearly every offender who enters prison is eventually released in some fashion. The question to ask is not "When?" but "How?" And the answer today is most often through parole. Two functions are involved in parole: the surveillance

Crime and Fear

Recently, during an election year, residents of a tranquil town in rural Virginia were polled on their most important concerns. At the time, one of the leading candidates was attracting media interest with his proposal that parole be abolished for all violent offenders. There had not been a homicide for over two decades in the town. There was virtually no violent street crime. Yet the majority of citizens listed fear of violent crime as their most pressing concern.

What happened in this town is a metaphor for what is happening in much of America. Crime is a real threat, but at least some of the tremendous fear Americans have is the product of a variety of factors that have little or nothing to do with crime itself. These factors include media reporting on crime issues and the role of government and private industry in stoking citizen fear. ■

SOURCE: Steven R. Donziger, (ed.), *The Real War on Crime* (New York: HarperCollins, 1996), p. 63.

function, ensuring adequate supervision and control (in the form of a parole officer) to prevent future criminal activity, and the helping function, marshaling community resources to support the parolee in establishing noncriminal behavior patterns.

The parole process is a series of steps that frequently includes an appearance before a parole authority, establishment of a set of conditions to be met by the parolee, the assignment to a parole officer followed by regular meetings with the officer, appearance at a revocation hearing if parole is violated, and the eventual release from conditional supervision. That process has sometimes been changed or modified by the heat of public opinion and court decisions.

Although the parole process is a valuable aid to the corrections system, it is far from perfect.[33] A major benefit for parole, as with probation, is the relatively low cost per day for these services. The quality of personnel, at both the parole authority and parole officer levels, has been greatly improved. Salary levels, tenure regulations, and professional standards are still being recommended, despite the tight economics of the late 1990s. As these standards are met, parole officers will become true professionals.

Now that we have completed our review of Part III, the correctional process, it is time to take a look at the kinds, numbers, and characteristics of those persons who populate the programs and facilities of the correctional system. Part IV will introduce the student to the differences and similarities between and among those offenders, regardless of sex, race, age, or ethnic origin, and their impact on the processes which constitute the correction process.

Review Questions

1. Differentiate between determinate and indefinite sentences.
2. What are the three main models of parole boards?
3. What are the main differences between parole and probation?
4. Why should parole boards be independent of institutions?
5. What are four promising new strategies for parole?
6. Should parole supervision be abolished?
7. How do most inmates exit prison?
8. How are boot camps useful to corrections?
9. How can parole caseloads be made smaller and more manageable?
10. What is your evaluation of the qualifications for parole board members?

Words to Remember

released on parole	parole boards	shock probation
"max out"	consolidated board	boot camp programs
amnesty	flopped	just deserts model
reprieve	Irish system	procedures for pardon
commutation	convict bogey	front-end solutions
net-widening		

€ndnotes

1. D. Gilliard and A. Beck, *The Nation's Correctional Population Tops 5 Million* (Washington, D.C.: U.S. Department of Justice, 1995), p. 6.

2. Edward Latessa and Harry Allen, *Corrections in the Community* (Cincinnati: Anderson, 1997), pp. 205–206.

3. Wayne Morse, *The Attorney General's Survey of Release Procedures* (Washington, D.C.: U.S. Government Printing Office, 1939), p. 23.

4. Dr. Samuel G. Howe, husband of famed suffragist and reformer Julia Ward Howe, is credited with the first use of the word *parole* in its present sense. It originally meant "word" (of honor) not to commit further crimes.

5. National Advisory Commission, *Corrections* (Washington, D.C.: U.S. Government Printing Office, 1973) p. 396. In 1979, thirty-nine of the fifty-three paroling authorities in the United States were autonomous agencies. See Eric Carlson, *Contemporary United States Parole Board Practices* (San Jose, CA: San Jose State University Foundation, 1979), p. 11.

6. National Advisory Commission, *Corrections*, p. 396.

7. Ibid., p. 397.

8. Joseph E. Scott, "An Examination of the Factors Utilized by Parole Boards in Determining the Severity of Punishment," Ph.D. dissertation, Indiana University, 1972, pp. 57–59. See also Eric Metchik, "Judicial Views of Parole Decision Processes: A Social Science Perspective," *Journal of Offender Rehabilitation* 18:1/2 (1992): 135–157.

9. Carlson, *Contemporary United States Parole Board Practices*, p. 105. Over half of the states permit victims to be present and offer oral or written statements to the board. Victim statements are believed to be given as much weight as institutional behavior, although there is agreement that personal appearances have more impact on decisions. See Maureen McLeod, "Getting Free: Victim Participation in Parole Board Decisions," *Criminal Justice* 4/1 (1989): 12-15, 41–43.

10. Everette M. Porter, "Criteria for Parole Selection," in *Proceedings of the American Correctional Association* (New York: American Correctional Association, 1958), p. 227.

11. Peter Hoffman, "Twenty Years of the Use of a Risk Prediction Instrument: The United States Parole Commission's Salient Factor Score," *Journal of Criminal Justice* 22:6 (1994): 477–494.

12. President's Commission on Law Enforcement and Administration of Justice, *Task Force Report: Corrections* (Washington, D.C.: U.S. Government Printing Office, 1967), p. 184.

13. Ibid., p. 185.

14. Reintegration centers are located in Columbus, Cleveland, and Cincinnati. They are designed to house technical parole violators for sixty to ninety days and to treat their immediate problems through programmed learning techniques and concerned supervision.

15. In 1988, it cost California an average of $9,582 per offender ($242 million) to maintain a "use drugs—go back to prison" parole revocation policy. See James Austin, *Parole Outcomes of Determinate Sentencing* (Madison, WI: National Council on Crime and Delinquency, 1989).

16. Diane Vaughan, "Shock Probation and Shock Parole: The Impact of Changing Correctional Ideology," in D. Petersen and C. Thomas, eds., *Corrections: Problems and Prospects* (Englewood Cliffs, NJ: Prentice Hall, 1980), pp. 216–237.

17. Diane Vaughan et al., "Shock Parole: A Preliminary Evaluation," *International Journal of Criminology and Penology* 4 (1976): 271–284. See also New York State Department of Correctional Services, *The Seventh Annual State Legislation Report 1995* (Albany: New York State Department of Correctional Services, 1995).

18. This section is drawn from C. Clark, D. Aziz, and D. MacKenzie, *Shock Incarceration in New York: Focus on Treatment* (Washington, D.C.: U.S. Department of Justice, 1994).

19. Doris MacKenzie, R. Brame, and David McDowall, "Boot Camp Prisons and Recidivism in Eight States," *Criminology* 33:3 (1995): 327–357.

20. George Camp and Camille Graham Camp, *The Corrections Yearbook: Probation and Parole 1995* (South Salem, NY: Criminal Justice Institute, 1995), pp. 47–48.

21. Calculated from ibid, p.38.

22. Robert K. Merton is credited with elucidating the concept of the self-fulfilling prophecy: if those around a prison expect an inmate to behave in a certain way—to be stupid or brilliant, successful or a failure—their expectations will tend to shape his or her behavior. Robert K. Merton, *Social Theory and Social Structure* (Glencoe, IL.: Free Press, 1949), pp. 136–140.

23. Peter Lejins, "ACA Education Council Proposes Correctional Officer Entry Tests," *Corrections Today* 52 (February 1990): 56, 58, 60. See also William Smith, Edward Rhine, and Ronald Jackson, "Parole Practices in the United States," *Corrections Today* 51 (October 1989): 22–28. And see P. Greenwood, E. Deschenes, and J. Adams, *Chronic Juvenile Offenders* (Santa Monica, CA: Rand, 1993).

24. Camp and Camp, *The Corrections Yearbook: Probation and Parole 1995*, p. 52.

25. K. Macguire and Ann Pastore, eds., *Sourcebook of Criminal Justice Statistics 1994* (Washington, D.C.: U.S. Department of Justice, 1995), p. 580.

26. See P. McAnany and E. Tromanhauser, "Organizing the Convicted: Self-Help for Prisoners and Ex-cons," *Crime and Delinquency* 23 (January 1977): 68–74.

27. National Advisory Commission, *Corrections*, p. 414.

28. Frederick A. Hussey and Stephen P. Lagoy, "The Determinate Sentence and Its Impact on Parole," *Criminal Law Bulletin* 19 (March–April 1983): 101–130.

29. For a discussion of political influence in determinate sentencing controversies, see P. Griset, "Determinate Sentencing and Agenda Building: A Case Study of the Failure of a Reform," *Journal of Criminal Justice* 23:4 (1995): 349–362. See also John Wooldredge, "A State-Level Analysis of Sentencing Policies and Inmate Crowding in State Prisons," *Crime and Delinquency* 42:3 (1996): 456–466.

30. Gilliard and Beck, *The Nation's Correctional Population Tops 5 Million*, p. 6.

31. No presidential pardon (or commutation) was awarded in 1994. Macguire and Pastore, *Sourcebook of Criminal Justice Statistics* 1994, p. 507.

32. Office of the Pardon Attorney, *Civil Disabilities of Convicted Felons: A State-by-State Survey* (Washington, D.C.: U.S. Office of the Pardon Attorney, 1992).

33. For a critique, see John R. Manson. "Determinate Sentencing" *Crime and Delinquency* 23 (April 1977): pp. 204-207. See also the "Comments" that follow, pp. 207-214; and Grover Trask. *Blue Ribbon Commission on Inmate Population Management: Final Report* (Sacramento, CA: Prison Industry Authority, 1990), pp. 83-92.

*R*ecommended Readings: Part III

Ashford, Jose B., and Craig LeCroy, "Juvenile Parole Policy in the United States: Determinate versus Indeterminate Models," *Justice Quarterly* 10:2 (June 1993): 179–195.

Austin, James. *Parole Outcome in California: The Consequences of Determinate Sentencing, Punishment, and Incapacitation on Parole Performance*. Madison, WI: National Council on Crime and Delinquency, 1989.

Bondi, Connie B. "When Policies Conflict: Can Retributive State Policy Goals Be Met Effectively by Rehabilitative Alternative Sentencing Strategies?" *Criminal Justice Policy Review* 2:2 (1991): 121–132.

Burke, Peggy. *Abolishing Parole: Why the Emperor Has No Clothes*. American Probation and Parole Association, Chicago, Illinois, 1995.

Camp, George, and Camille Graham Camp, *Management of Crowded Prisons*. South Salem, NY: Criminal Justice Institute, 1989.

Champion, Dean. *Probation, Parole and Community Corrections*. Upper Saddle River, NJ: Prentice Hall, 1996.

Cushman, Robert C., and Dale K. Sechrest. "Variations in the Administration of Probation Supervision," *Federal Probation* 56:3 (1992): 19–29.

Donziger, Steven, ed. *The Real War on Crime*. New York: HarperCollins, 1996.

Enos, Richard, Clifford M. Block, James F. Quinn, et al. *Alternative Sentencing: Electronically Monitored Correctional Supervision*. Bristol, IN: Wyndham Hall Press, 1992.

Erwin, Billie. *Intensive Probation Supervision with Electronic Monitoring*. Atlanta: Georgia Department of Corrections, 1989.

Irwin, John, and James Austin. *It's About Time*. San Francisco: National Council on Crime and Delinquency, 1987.

Kercher, Glen A., and Lydia Long. *Supervision and Treatment of Sex Offenders*. Huntsville, TX: Sam Houston Press, 1991, 295 pp.

Latessa, Edward, and Harry Allen. *Corrections in the Community*. Cincinnati: Anderson, 1997.

Liberton, Michael, Mitchell Silverman, and William Blount. "Predicting Probation Success for the First-Time Offender." *International Journal of Offender Therapy and Comparative Criminology* 36:4 (1992): 335–347.

Linder, Charles. "The Probation Field Visit and Office Report in New York State: Yesterday, Today, and Tomorrow." *Criminal Justice Review* 17:1 (1992): 44–60.

Metchik, Eric. "Judicial Views of Parole Decision Processes: A Social Science Perspective." *Journal of Offender Rehabilitation* 18:1/2 (1992): 135–157.

Minor, Kevin, and David J. Hartmann. "An Evaluation of the Kalamazoo Probation Enhancement Program." *Federal Probation* 56:3 (1992): 30–35.

Minor-Harper, Stephanie, and Christopher Innes. *Time Served in Prison and on Parole 1984*. Washington, D.C.: U.S. Department of Justice, 1987.

Mullany, Fahy. *Economic Sanctions in Community Corrections*. Washington, D.C.: National Institute of Justice, 1988.

National Advisory Commission on Criminal Justice Standards and Goals. *Courts*. Washington, D.C.: U.S. Department of Justice, 1973.

Packer, Herbert L. *The Limits of the Criminal Sanction*. Stanford, CA: Stanford University Press, 1968.

Petersilia, Joan. "Debating Crime and Punishment in California." *Evaluation and Program Planning* 17:2 (1995): 165–177.

Rhine, Edward E., ed. *Reclaiming Offender Accountability: Intermediate Sanctions for Probation and Parole Violators*. Laurel, MD: American Correctional Association, 1993.

Trask, Grover. *Blue Ribbon Commission on Inmate Population Management: Final Report*. Sacramento, CA: Prison Industry Authority, 1990.

The
Correctional
Client

CHAPTER FOURTEEN

Jail Inmates

Overview

As described by Frank Schmalleger in the quote below, it is a small wonder that there is great concern for the treatment and care of persons who are processed in these facilities, large or small, old or new, and with as many as three thousand or as few as ten residents. The student has been given a preliminary feel of this vast network of facilities and legal and operational processes that we call "corrections." The up and down history of corrections has been impacted by vagaries and indecision as to what philosophy to apply at different times, as a pendulum swings, in dealing with the law violators in American society. Legal processes and vacillating laws examined so far have shown how a wide variety of sentences and alternatives can be applied in the name of "justice." The various correctional supervision processes designed to deal with the numerous sentencing options are characterized by both exclusivity and frequent overlap in meeting the shifting demands of society and the public's perception of the "crime problem." As has been shown, these have ranged from treatment and rehabilitation of offenders to punishment and programs designed to "get tough on crime" over the last few decades.

Part IV will now examine those human beings who make up the offender clientele of these justice-related activities and comprise the raw material for the sometime arcane practices called corrections system. The first group of clients we shall examine in this opening chapter of the correctional system are those at the beginning of the system: at the booking desk of the county or local jail.

As we learned in Chapter 9, of all the institutions through which offenders pass in the correctional funnel, none has a more diverse population (or a more sordid past) than the jails. *Jails* are confinement facilities usually operated by a local law enforcement agency, holding detained persons pending adjudication and/or persons committed after adjudication. The jail is the first institutional contact within the criminal justice system that accused adult males and females (and many juveniles) experience.

> Jails have been called the "shame of the criminal justice system." Many are old, overcrowded, poorly funded, scantily staffed by underpaid and poorly trained employees, and given low priority on local budgets.
>
> —Frank Schmalleger

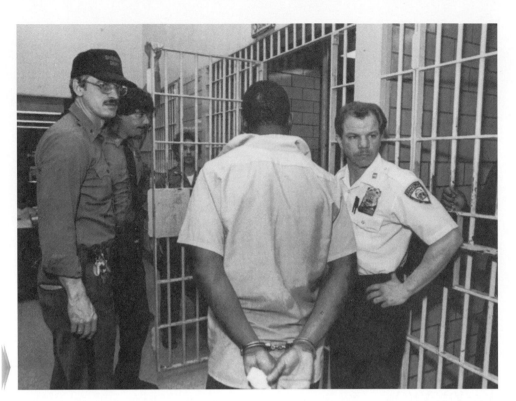

Security measures in jails
are carefully considered

—*PHOTO BY SPENCER A. BURNETT,
COURTESY OF THE NEW YORK CITY
DEPARTMENT OF CORRECTIONS*

Jail Clients Vary Widely

Jails are primarily detention or confinement facilities intended for holding **arrested adults,** but sometimes (sometimes too often), they also house juvenile offenders. They hold detained persons pending disposition or adjudication and/or persons committed after adjudication to serve sentences generally of a year or less. Jails are usually supported by local tax revenues and, as such, are particularly vulnerable to resource reductions.

Additional categories of jail inmates include mentally ill persons for whom there are no other facilities, parolees and probationers awaiting hearings, federal prisoners awaiting pickup by marshals, and offenders sentenced to departments of corrections for whom there is not yet prison bed space but who cannot be released. This amalgam of residents in the nation's jails and **detention centers** make describing that population difficult.

Not only are jails important as the intake point of the justice system, they are significant to the lives of the persons who pass through them. It is at the level of the jail that important decisions are made about the accused's present and future freedom. Experiences encountered in the jail impact and color the future lives of those persons booked, processed and housed there, as few of them are being held for serious crimes. Rather, they are usually the lower rung on the ladder of the local social system, local community members who are impoverished on many dimensions, and those in need of other social services that are generally inadequate or unavailable.

Although jails keep alleged offenders off the streets, they also keep those same individuals away from their work, family, friends, and business (even if crime might be their business). Already tenuous ties to the community may be further strained by the jail experience. Moreover, other disreputable members of society (derelicts, homeless people, drug abusers, hustlers, drunks, etc.) may vandalize

DETENTION

The legally authorized confinement of a person subject to criminal or juvenile court proceedings until commitment to a correctional facility or release. Detention describes the custodial status (reason for custody) of persons held in confinement after arrest or while awaiting the completion of judicial proceedings. Release from detention can occur either prior to or after trial or adjudication, as a dismissal of the case, an acquittal, or sentencing disposition that does not require confinement.

CIVIL DISABILITIES

Rights or privileges denied a person as a result of conviction or a guilty plea, in addition to other than the imposed legal penalty.

and/or burglarize their residence, which may have been left unattended and unguarded for even the brief time of jail detention. Data from a 1995 survey of 145 jail systems disclose that the average length of stay in jails nationwide (both pretrial and sentenced) increased in 1995 to a combined average of almost eighty-six days (see Figure 14-1).

Finally, jails are important because of what happens to the inmates there: the shock of incarceration, loss of control over their environment, danger from violent inmates, absence of meaningful activity, and dead time. Psychological problems already affecting behavior may be exacerbated: self-mutilation[1] and suicide[2] occasionally occur. Sometimes it is difficult to rebut those, like Flemming, who argue that the purpose of **pretrial jail incarceration** is punishment.[3]

Who are the "rabble" that the jail accepts at entry to the justice system and will probably discharge after a brief stay?[4] Are they dangerous predators? Or are they just marginal people[5] who pose some threat to the community and must be controlled? The answer may be both. We turn first to an examination of the make-up of these residents of the nation's jails.

CHARACTERISTICS OF THE JAIL POPULATION

The felon and the misdemeanant, the first-time and the repeat offender, the adult (male and female) and the juvenile, the accused and the convicted, not to mention the guilty and the innocent, are housed in America's jails. Jails house individuals pending arraignment as well as those awaiting trial, conviction, and sentencing; probation, parole, and bail bond violators and absconders; juveniles pending transfer to juvenile facilities; mentally ill persons awaiting transfer to appropriate facilities in the mental health system, and chronic alcoholics.[6] Those individuals include persons being held for the military or in protective custody; witnesses; persons found in contempt of court; persons awaiting transfer to state, federal, or other local authorities;

COCAINE

A drug that naturally occurs in the leaves of the coca plant, *Erythroxlon coca*, which is native to Colombia, Peru, and Boliva. Euphoric excitement is produced when it is snorted and absorbed by the soft tissues in the nose. Crack cocaine is a crystallized version of the drug that was developed in the Caribbean. Crack is smoked or injected and produces a much stronger effect on the user than when snorted.

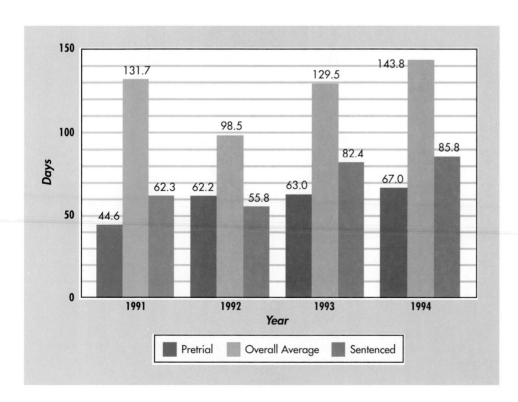

FIGURE

14.1

Average Length of Stay of Prisoners in U.S. Jail Systems, 1991–1994

SOURCE: George Camp and Camille Graham Camp, *The Corrections Yearbook 1995: Jail Systems* (South Salem, NY: Criminal Justice Institute, 1995), p. 60.

and temporarily detained persons.[7] About 53 percent of the nation's jailed are pretrial, 9 percent **unsentenced**, and 38 percent actually serving sentences, although this last number is rising as local jurisdictions "crack down"[8] on those who drive while intoxicated (DWI) and on those involved in domestic disturbance[9] crimes.

Some 93 percent of the jail population is male. Statistics on jails are difficult to obtain, however, and national surveys are infrequent and often suspect.[10] Data are fairly consistent in most surveys, and those used here should be used as a "rule of thumb" for describing the jail population. There are estimated to be 490,442 men, women, and children in the nation's approximately thirty-three hundred jails on any given day.[11] Men held in jails are in many ways the so-called losers of society in terms of economic and social status, occupation, marital status, education, and almost any other factor you wish to consider. The dimensions of the jail population are graphically summarized in Figures 14-2 and 14-3. The latest national picture is seen in Table 14-1.

Two important conclusions may be drawn from these data. First, the number of jail inmates has increased sharply since the 1983 jail census (up 106 percent and projected to exceed 500,000 in 1995). At 270 jail inmates per 100,000

FIGURE
14.2

Jail Inmates, 1983–1995

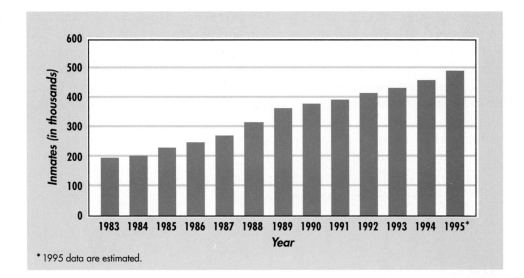

* 1995 data are estimated.

FIGURE
14.3

Jail Incarceration Rate per 100,000 Residents Age Eighteen and Older, 1983–1995

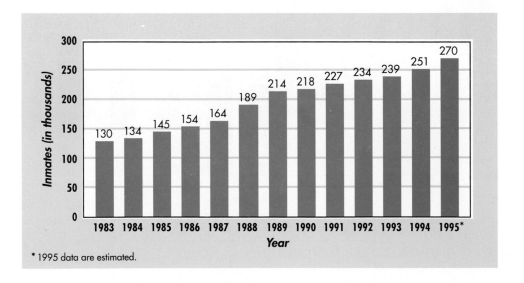

* 1995 data are estimated.

TABLE *14.1*

Local Jail Facilities, Inmates, and the Number of Inmates per 100,000 Population, by Region and State, June 30, 1983, 1988, and 1993

Region and State	Number of Inmates 1983	Number of Inmates 1988	Number of Inmates 1993	Percentage Change in Number of Inmates, 1983–93	Inmates per 100,000 Population, 1993
United States total	223,551	343,569	459,804	106	178
Northeast	36,634	57,613	73,871	102	144
Maine	560	669	704	26	57
Massachusetts	3,304	5,454	7,878	138	131
New Hampshire	475	789	1,127	137	100
New Jersey	5,971	11,124	15,122	153	192
New York	16,154	25,928	29,809	85	164
Pennsylvania	10,170	13,649	19,231	89	160
Midwest	39,538	50,646	70,646	79	116
Illinois	8,849	9,891	14,549	64	124
Indiana	3,599	5,235	8,297	131	145
Iowa	839	1,036	1,602	91	57
Kansas	1,328	1,906	2,797	111	111
Michigan	7,637	9,404	12,479	63	132
Minnesota	1,954	3,227	3,654	87	81
Missouri	3,783	4,154	5,030	33	96
Nebraska	844	1,156	1,680	99	105
North Dakota	243	288	361	49	57
Ohio	7,116	9,160	11,695	64	105
South Dakota	316	522	623	97	87
Wisconsin	3,030	4,667	7,879	160	156
South	89,479	143,751	210,599	135	235
Alabama	4,464	4,819	7,072	58	169
Arkansas	1,602	1,994	2,846	78	117
District of Columbia	2,843	1,693	1,687	–	292
Florida	14,668	28,236	34,183	133	250
Georgia	10,214	17,482	22,663	122	328
Kentucky	3,711	4,695	6,813	84	180
Louisiana	8,507	11,222	16,208	91	377
Maryland	4,608	7,486	9,358	103	188
Mississippi	2,498	3,501	4,851	94	184
North Carolina	3,496	5,469	8,939	156	129
Oklahoma	2,215	2,595	4,102	85	127
South Carolina	2,690	3,497	5,713	112	157
Tennessee	6,005	10,858	14,375	139	282
Texas	15,224	29,439	55,395	264	307
Virginia	5,719	9,372	14,623	156	225
West Virginia	1,015	1,393	1,771	74	97
West	57,900	91,559	104,688	81	187
Alaska	37	27	31	–	–
Arizona	2,940	6,006	7,231	146	184
California	41,720	64,216	69,298	66	222

(Continued on page 264)

TABLE *14.1 (Con't)*

Region and State	Number of Inmates			Percentage Change in Number of Inmates, 1983–93	Inmates per 100,000 Population, 1993
	1983	1988	1993		
<u>West (Con't.)</u>					
Colorado	2,747	4,882	6,316	130	177
Idaho	604	810	1,485	146	135
Montana	405	616	680	68	81
Nevada	940	2,343	2,987	218	215
New Mexico	1,346	2,188	3,058	127	189
Oregon	2,304	2,819	3,777	64	125
Utah	906	1,261	1,895	109	102
Washington	3,610	5,934	7,435	106	141
Wyoming	341	457	495	45	105

SOURCE: Craig Perkins, James Stephan, and Allen Beck, *Jails and Jail Inmates, 1993–1994* (Washington, D.C.: U.S. Department of Justice, 1995), p. 4.

CRISIS INTERVENTION CENTER

A service designed to give immediate help to people with serious emotional problems. Many large cities have "crisis hot lines" to persons who can help those who are considering suicide or have other problems that require immediate counseling and referral.

adults in the United States in 1994, this rate was 93 percent higher than 1983 and is projected to be even higher in 1995. Second, it should be noted that the rate of jail incarceration varies significantly by state, ranging from a low of 57 per 100,000 residents in Maine, North Dakota, and Iowa to a high of 377 per 100,000 residents in Louisiana.[12] Parenthetically, while most of the jail inmates were adult males, the *number* of jail inmates who were female increased *182 percent* from 15,600 in 1983 to 44,000 in 1994.[13]

Why Are They in Jail?

Persons held in jails in the United States fall into several categories:

1. Accused
   a. Pending arraignment
   b. Awaiting trial
   c. Awaiting conviction
   d. Awaiting sentencing
2. Readmitted
   a. Probation violations
   b. Parole violations
   c. Bail/bond violations
3. Absconders
4. Detained juveniles
5. Transferees to
   a. State institutions
   b. Other local institutions
   c. Federal institutions
   d. Deportation authorities

Who Is a Juvenile?

Most, but not all, states define a juvenile as a person under age eighteen who is subject to juvenile court jurisdiction. Exceptions usually depend on offense severity or an offender's adjudication history.

In the 1994 survey, to achieve reporting uniformity, jail authorities were asked to report the number of inmates under age eighteen. Of the 6,725 total in 1994, 76 percent were identified as juveniles tried or scheduled to be tried as adults.

Statutes and judicial practices sometimes allow youths to be held in adult jails. Often, juveniles accused of acts that are crimes for adults may be held in local jails or police lockups, given certain conditions:

- separated by sight and sound from the general population,
- held for a limited time, typically fewer than six hours.

Most confined juveniles are housed in institutions specified for them. In 1993 about ninety-six thousand were in public and private juvenile detention and correctional facilities. ▪

SOURCE: Craig Perkins, James Stephen, and Allen Beck, *Jails and Jail Inmates 1993–94* (Washington, D.C.: U.S. Department of Justice, 1995). [See Chapter 17.]

About one in every eight jail inmates is being held for other correctional authorities and approximately fifty-four thousand inmates (about 12 percent of the total inmates projected to be in large jails in 1995—a constant figure for the past several years) were being held back for state and federal prison systems, as well as other local correctional agencies. Almost all the **"holdback" jail inmates** were being delayed due to overcrowding in state institutions, particularly adult prisons for felony offenders. A small percentage were federal prisoners being held for transfer to Bureau of Prisons institutions. The Federal Bureau of Prisons has recently developed jail facilities in its own system and therefore reduced its population of holdbacks drastically. Holdbacks were found in about half of all jails in 1994. Most jails charge fees for holding inmates for other jurisdictions, ranging from $35 per day for state prisoners to about $70 per day for federal holdbacks. Those holdbacks contribute to jail overcrowding in many large local jail jurisdictions.

The proportion of jail inmates who are minority members is shown by the pie chart in Figure 14-4. Minorities (particularly blacks and Hispanics) outnumbered whites almost three to two. Of all jail inmates in 1994 (the last date for which overall inmate characteristics are available), more than one in three were under the age of twenty-four, and only 19 percent were married. More than half

A women's section of a local jail

—PHOTO BY MICHAEL HAYMAN, COURTESY OF STOCK BOSTON

TABLE *14.2*

Prisoners Housed in Jails Because of Crowded State Facilities, by Sex, Region, and Jurisdiction, December 31, 1992 and 1993

Region and Jurisdiction	Number of Prisoners Housed in Jails						Prisoners in Jail as a Percentage of all Prisoners Dec. 31, 1993
	Total		Male		Female		
	1992	1993	1992	1993	1992	1993	
United States, total	18,428	52,721	17,009	51,056	1,419	1,665	5.4%
Northeast	4,450	4,477	4,289	4,313	161	164	3.1
Massachusetts	916	876	908	876	8	0	8.0
New Jersey	3,523	3,594	3,370	3,430	153	164	15.1
Vermont	11	7	11	7	0	0	0.6
Midwest	1,017	1,449	984	1,377	33	72	0.8
Indiana	779	1,005	761	981	18	24	6.9
Minnesota	0	134	0	134	0	0	3.2
Wisconsin	238	310	223	262	15	48	3.5
South	11,981	45,743	10,834	44,406	1,147	1,337	12.0
Alabama	966	1,204	923	1,156	43	48	6.5
Arkansas	496	667	446	667	50	0	7.7
Kentucky	574	396	489	378	85	18	3.8
Louisiana	4,663	6,390	4,180	5,817	483	573	28.4
Mississippi	907	1,543	841	1,424	66	119	15.6
Oklahoma	471	380	442	332	29	48	2.3
South Carolina	420	416	408	412	12	4	2.2
Tennessee	1,120	1,329	970	1,210	150	119	10.4
Texas	NA	29,546	NA	NA	NA	NA	29.6
Virginia	1,983	3,610	1,773	3,223	210	387	15.8
West Virginia	381	262	362	241	19	21	12.7
West	980	1,052	902	960	78	92	0.6
Arizona	95	157	95	157	0	0	0.9
Colorado	537	560	513	508	24	52	5.9
Idaho	240	213	202	192	38	21	8.2
Utah	108	122	92	103	16	19	4.2

SOURCE: U.S. Department of Justice, Bureau of Justice Statistics, *Correctional Populations in the United States, 1993* (Washington, D.C.: U.S. Department of Justice, 1995), Table 5.5.

FIGURE
14.4

Ethnicity of Jail Inmates, 1994

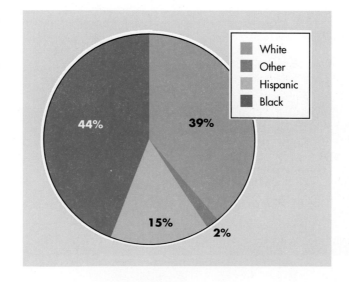

had less than a high school education, and only one in six had ever served in the military.

On a prearrest basis, about one-half had been employed full time, 11 percent were working part time, and 36 percent were unemployed. An astounding 78 percent of jail inmates had used drugs[14] sometime in their lives (see Figure 14-5), and more than four in ten had been drinking just before their offense, almost half being drunk or very drunk at the time of their offense.

This pattern of drug abuse is even more pronounced among convicted jail inmates. More than half said they were under the influence of drugs or alcohol (or both) at the time of their current offense, particularly for homicides, aggravated assault, burglary, drug possession, and most public order offenses (such as obstruction of justice, driving while intoxicated, and morals charges). About a quarter of the jail inmates had participated in a drug treatment program and nearly a sixth in an alcohol abuse treatment program.[15]

More than half of all jail inmates had grown up in a household without the presence of both parents, and almost four in ten had lived in a single-parent household. More than a third had family members (usually a brother or sister) who had also been incarcerated. More than a fourth had a parent or guardian who abused alcohol while the inmate was growing up. Some one in six male inmates reported sexual or physical abuse (or both) by an adult before the current incarceration, and one in eight had taken medication prescribed by a psychiatrist or other doctor for an emotional or mental problem. Characteristics of female jail inmates are explored in greater detail in Chapter 16, and the patterns just

DETOXIFICATION CENTER

A public or private facility for the short-term treatment of either acutely intoxicated persons or drug or alcohol abusers. Such a center functions as an alternative to jail for persons in an intoxicated condition who have been taken into custody.

Jail Provides Mental Health and Substance Abuse Services

"I would like to invite you to come visit my neighborhood. It has a higher concentration of substance abusers and chronically mentally ill people than any other area of the city."

Several years ago, Sheriff James H. Dunning of Alexandria, Va., gave this invitation to city council members and various department heads at the council's annual budget meeting. At first, people were taken aback that a distinguished politician could have such a "neighborhood"—until he identified it as the city's adult detention center.

Sheriff Dunning went on to say that a high percentage of the nearly 500 residents of his neighborhood was sure to move into the council members' neighborhoods once released from jail. That night Sheriff Dunning brought home to the city's decisionmakers the very real message that a jail is not an institution which can be ostracized from the natural flow of city resources. Members of his neighborhood, he said, are citizens of Alexandria and therefore have every right to the same services—particularly mental health and substance abuse services—available to other citizens.

Jail officials work closely with the Alexandria Department of Mental Health, Mental Retardation and Substance Abuse to provide services to inmates in need of mental health treatment. Through a cost-sharing approach, 7.5 full-time staff

members from the mental health and substance abuse department are assigned to the detention center. In addition, a host of specialists from the department provide a variety of services such as case management, training and research when needed.

Central to the success of the jail's mental health and substance abuse programming is the effective use of jail staff. The jail has designated "special management deputies" and unit counselors who receive ongoing mental health training. These individuals provide most of the first-line psychological intervention and triage, leaving only high priority cases for evaluation and treatment by the mental health department specialists.

The jail also has a Behavior Management Team composed of deputies, mental health, medical and classification staff that meets weekly. Team members must distinguish between inmates with traditional behavior problems and those who may be mentally ill, and then develop a coordinated adjustment plan among the various disciplines. ■

SOURCE: Connie Fortin, "Jail Provides Mental Health and Substance Abuse Services," *Corrections Today* 55:6 (1993): 105–106.

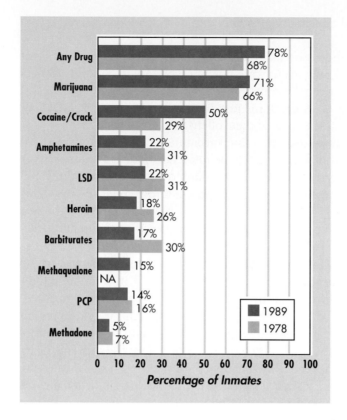

FIGURE

14.5

Percentage of Jail Inmates
Ever Using Drugs, 1978
and 1989

SOURCES: P. Banauch, *Jail Inmates 1983* (Washington,
D.C.: U.S. Department of Justice, 1985,), p. 6, and
A. Beck, *Profile of Jail Inmates 1989* (Washington,
D.C.: U.S. Department of Justice, 1991), p. 8.

described are generally more egregious for female than male jail inmates. These self-reports on drug abuse by jail inmates, sometimes known for their self-serving and deceptive purposes, are in part verified through urinalysis testing conducted at jail sites across the nation. Results for arrestees and across different charges at arrest indicate even more extensive drug use than previously self-

Inmates in a vocational
training program learn about
all aspects of auto repair,
including automotive
electrical systems

—*PHOTO BY MIKE DAVIES, COURTESY
OF THE ORANGE COUNTY CORRECTIONS
DIVISION, ORLANDO, FL*

Doing community service by helping renovate an abandoned neighborhood

—PHOTO BY JIM MAHONEY, *COURTESY OF THE IMAGE WORKS*

reported, particularly by robbery and burglary arrestees. (Alcohol abuse is *not* reflected in Figure 14-6 data.)

As for their criminal activities, almost one in four (23 percent) had been arrested for a crime of violence (particularly robbery), and another 38 percent had been arrested for crimes against property (particularly assault). The proportion of jail inmates committing crimes of violence *decreased* 27 percent from 1983 levels. Another 23 percent were charged with drug violations, an increase of 147 percent over 1983 levels. Some 80 percent of jail inmates (1989) had been previously sentenced to incarceration (42 percent) or probation (37 percent) prior to their instant offense. The proportion of inmates with mental illness was high.[16] (See Table 14-3 for inmate deaths in custody.)

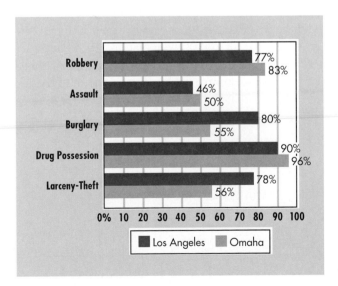

FIGURE

14.6

Drug Use by Male Arrestees: Percentage of Arrestees Testing Positive for Any Drug in 1994

SOURCE: T. Feucht, *Drug Use Forecasting* (Washington, D.C.: U.S. Department of Justice, 1995), pp. 16, 20.

Inmate Deaths in Local Jails During the Twelve Months Ending June 28, 1993

Cause of Death	Total	Percentage
Total	647	100%
Natural Causes*	290	45
AIDS	63	10
Suicide	234	36
Injury by Others	19	3
Other	41	6

*Excludes AIDS-related deaths

SOURCE: Louis Jankowski, *Jail Inmates 1991* (Washington, D.C.: U.S. Department of Justice, 1995), p. 11; reprinted in Craig Perkins, James Stephan, and Allen Beck, *Jails and Jail Inmates, 1993–94* (Washington, D.C.: U.S. Department of Justice, 1995), p. 6.

JOHN HOWARD ASSOCIATION

Named after the jail reformer, this association was formed in 1901 and is devoted to prison and jail reform and the prevention and control of crime and delinquency. It provides professional consultation and survey services in crime and delinquency and publishes a bimonthly newsletter.

Those sociodemographic and **criminal history data** suggest a marginal group of mostly male offenders who have had a lengthy but not necessarily serious[17] involvement in criminal activity. They could best be seen as a group of high-need disadvantaged urban dwellers whose needs have not been adequately addressed by the social services agencies in their local communities. Their needs are further described by the number of inmates of the largest jails who died[18] in 1994, as shown in Table 14-3. Of the 647 inmates who died in jails, more than one in three died at their own hands (suicide), up from the previous edition. Some 45 percent died of natural causes (excluding AIDS). The fact that one out of ten inmate deaths in jails were attributed to causes related to AIDS suggests that compassionate release of the fatally ill is a concept that has still to be fully embraced by local correctional facilities. Data on jail inmates with AIDS in large and **small jail facilities** can also be found in Figure 14-7.[19]

JAIL ADMISSION

There were approximately 14 million **admissions to jails** during 1993. Across the nation, that represents about almost 4 jail admissions per 1,000 residents, or 364 per 100,000 people in the nation. Ranking the regions of the nation by jail inmates would yield the South and West as number one (235 per 100,000 population), followed by the West (187 per 100,000 population), the Northeast (144 per 100,000 population), and the Midwest (116 per 100,000 population). No other major Western democracy has rates per thousand citizens that compare to these distressing numbers.

F I G U R E

14.7

Jail Inmates with AIDS

SOURCE: K. Maguire and A. Pastore, *Sourcebook of Criminal Justice Statistics* (Washington, D.C.: U.S. Department of Justice, 1995), p. 536.

Jail Size	Number with AIDS
50 largest jails	929
500+ inmates	487
250–499 inmates	146
100–249 inmates	144
Fewer than 100 inmates	182

Summary

The jail system and its operational problems were discussed in Chapter 9, including the innovations and futures of jail systems. This chapter provided a snapshot and characteristics overview of the kinds of people and their behaviors who make up the clients of the nation's jails. The data, as difficult as they are to gather, suggest that these "clients" are a group of the American society's so-called losers. The best way to solve the long-term problems of the millions of residents who rotate through America's jails is to address the underlying problems faced by jail inmates.[20] The jail system, which deals with problems ranging from DWI and petty theft to aggravated murder, evokes terror in some involuntary residents of these facilities and a "business as usual" attitude in others who have experienced it before. These residents are trying to cope with drug and alcohol abuse, unemployment, domestic problems, medical and **mental health issues** and needs, inadequate education and illiteracy, and failure to adapt to an urban environment. Such treatments are discussed in Chapters 21 and 27. Students interested in making an impact on corrections and finding creative solutions to persistent problems can fulfill that desire by working with the local jails and community corrections.

What becomes of this varied population of offenders passing through the jails of America? Most are convicted and become labeled as "offenders," then move on to the many options discussed in Part III. The four categories of persons that move on to other venues of the correctional system are male offenders, female offenders, juvenile offenders, and a particular set of clients known as "special category" offenders. In the next chapters, we examine each of those categories and discuss

Offender Care in Orange County

Here at the Orange County Corrections Division in Florida, we have established an extensive inmate management system to effectively manage inmates housed in our facilities and community corrections programs. The system, which uses a stair-stepped classification system, defines the parameters within which inmates must function and places them in control of their status and placement.

To give inmates the opportunity to make positive changes and acquire the tools necessary to become responsible citizens, we developed a continuum of care that begins during booking. After 10 days of incarceration, inmates undergo a needs assessment evaluation to identify educational and vocational levels and any psychological and substance abuse problems.

Orange County also provides an orientation; upon completion, inmates must either sign up for appropriate programming or be housed in an area that provides only minimum services required by Florida statute. Currently, inmates are housed in the following categories: booking (15 percent), assessment center (10 percent), special housing and maximum security units (24 percent) and programming (51 percent).

The ultimate aim of this continuum of care is to provide a dual sentencing system that allows the judiciary to sentence a defendant to either serve a period of traditional incarceration or to take responsibility and be held accountable to change his or her life. Offenders who choose to change are expected to complete habilitative programming and demonstrate positive behavioral changes. Those who choose not to be responsible have determined through their actions the appropriate housing and consequences.

The continuum of care allows offenders, through their behavior, to chart their course for the future. This is not a vision of ease or harshness but one based on the notion that offenders should be held accountable to change or be warehoused with no rewards.

In the continuum of care, individuals define and attain their needs by acting responsibly. If inmates choose not to accept responsibility for changing their lives, they are determining how the system should hold them accountable and what type of confinement is required. These inmates should be incarcerated in legal but Spartan settings, for as long as the law provides. ∎

SOURCE: Tom Allison, "Making Offenders More Accountable and Offering Opportunity for Change," *Corrections Today* 55:(6) (1993): 93—94.

Federal Jails

In 1993 the Federal Bureau of Prisons maintained a small number of detention facilities that functioned as jails. These were not counted among the city, county, or regional adult detention facilities called local jails in this report. Local facilities, however, did hold about 12,000 persons for Federal authorities, according to data reported by 90% of all facilities.

At midyear 1993 the Bureau of Prisons operated 7 jails, holding 5,899 persons who were awaiting adjudication or serving a sentence, usually of a year or less.

INMATE DEMOGRAPHICS

Ninety-three percent of Federal jail inmates were men, a slightly higher proportion than in local jails (90%). Seventy-two percent were white, 25% were black, and 3% were Asians, Pacific Islanders, American Indians, or Alaskan Natives.

CONVICTION STATUS

Slightly more than half of the Federal inmates were unconvicted and were awaiting arraignment, trial, or the completion of their trial.

FACILITY CAPACITY

The 7 Federal jails had a combined rated capacity of 3,810—the population being 155% of that capacity. The percentage occupied was about 50% higher than that of local jails of comparable size.

INMATE DEATHS

Eight inmates died while under the jurisdiction of Federal jail authorities during the annual period ending June 30, 1993. Four deaths resulted from illness or natural causes, two were suicides, and two were drug overdoses.

STAFF

Seventy-five percent of Federal jail employees were male, a higher percentage than the 70% of employees for local facilities. A majority of the Federal jail employees were correctional officers.

Overall, there were 2.9 inmates per staff member in Federal jails, about the same as in local facilities where the ratio was 2.8 inmates per employee. However, the number of inmates per correctional officer (5.5) was higher than in local jails with 500 to 999 inmates (4.4).

EXPENDITURES

Federal jail expenditures totaled slightly more than $166 million during the annual period ending June 30, 1993, excluding those at the Guaynabo, Puerto Rico, facility, in operation only a few months at the time of the census. Gross salaries and wages, employer contributions to employee benefits, purchases of food, supplies, contractual services, and other current operating costs accounted for 76% of expenditures. Construction costs, major repairs, equipment, improvements, land purchases, and other capital outlays made up the remaining 24%.

The average cost to house one Federal jail inmate during the year ending June 30, 1993, exclusive of capital expenditures, was $22,773, compared to $14,667 among local jails.

Characteristic	
Number of facilities	7
Number of inmates	5,899
Male	5,490
Female	409
White	4,271
Black	1,462
Other	166
Status of inmates	
Convicted	47%
Unconvicted	53%
Rated capacity	3,810
Percent of capacity occupied	155%
Inmate deaths during annual period ending June 30, 1993	8
Cause	
Illness/natural cause	4
AIDS	0
Suicide	2
Homicide	0
Other	2
Number of employees	2,009
Male	1,499
Female	510
Administrators	89
Correctional officers	1,080
Clerical and maintenance	263
Educational	26
Other	551
Number of inmates per employee	
All employees	2.9
Correctional officers	5.5
Annual expenditures	
Total	$166,297,143
Capital	39,360,670
Operating	126,936,473
Operating cost per inmate	$22,773

SOURCE: Perkins et al. (1995). *Jail and Jail Inmates 1993-94* (Washington, DC: USDJ): 12.

their impact and special characteristics as applied to corrections. As shown in the article above, the Federal Bureau of Prisons also operates seven jails with a population of nearly 6,000 and a wide variety of characteristics. The federal system also held about 12,000 prisoners in local jails under contract to them. As mentioned at the beginning of this chapter, these discussions deal with developing a better understanding of the people in the system and using such knowledge to improve the ways to deal with them in the various systems of corrections.

STALKING

A crime involving repeated following, spying upon, or otherwise harassing someone so that the victim experiences a "credible threat" of bodily harm. California passed the first antistalking law in the United States in 1990. By May 1993, thirty-seven states had adopted antistalking laws.

Review Questions

1. Why is the jail so important in the correctional system?
2. What is meant when we describe the jail population as "rabble"?
3. Identify five major problems that jail inmates bring to the institution.
4. What describes a juvenile and why should juveniles be removed from jails?
5. Why are so many prison-bound inmates held back in jails?
6. Describe the diversity of the jail inmate population.
7. What special problems do inmates bring to the jail setting?

Words to Remember

arrested adults

detention centers

pretrial jail incarceration

unsentenced

"holdback" jail inmates

criminal history data

small jail facilities

admissions to jails

mental health issues

Endnotes

1. Jeremy Coid, John Wilkins, Bina Coid, et al., "Self-Mutilation in Female Remanded Prisoners," *Criminal Behavior and Mental Health* 2:1 (1992): 1–14. See also Janet Haines, et al., "The Psychophysiology of Self-Mutilation," *Journal of Abnormal Psychology* 104:3 (1995): 471–489.

2. Joel Haycock, "Capital Crimes: Suicide in Jail," *Death Studies* 15:4 (1991): 417–433, and Heather Holly, Julio Arboleda, Florez Love, and Edgar Love, "Lifetime Prevalence of Prior Suicide Attempts in a Remanded Population and Relationship to Current Mental Illness," *International Journal of Offender Therapy and Comparative Criminology* 39:3 (1995): 191–220.

3. Roy Flemming, *Punishment Before Trial: An Organizational Perspective of Felony Bail Processes* (New York: Longman, 1982).

4. John Irwin, *The Jail: Managing the Underclass in American Society* (Berkeley: University of California Press, 1985). See also John Backstrand, Don Gibbons, and Joseph Jones, "Who Is in Jail? An Examination of the Rabble Hypothesis," *Crime and Delinquency* 38:2 (1992): 219–229.

5. Louis Jankowski, *Jail Inmates 1991* (Washington, D.C.: U.S. Bureau of Justice Statistics, 1992), p. 5.

6. Robyn Cohen, *Drunk Driving* (Washington, D.C.: U.S. Department of Justice, 1992). See also Allen Rodgers, "Effect of Minnesota's License Plate Impoundment on Recidivism of Multiple DWI Violators," *Alcohol, Drugs and Driving* 10:2 (1995): 127–134.

7. Jankowski, *Jail Inmates,* p. 5, and Craig Perkins, James Stephan, and Allen Beck, *Jails and Jail Inmates 1993–1994* (Washington, D.C.: U.S. Department of Justice, 1995), p. 5.

8. Patrick Kincaide and Matthew Leone, "The Effects of 'Tough' Drunk Driving Laws on Policing: A Case Study," *Crime and Delinquency* 38:2 (1992): 239–257. See also Brandon Applegate, et al., "Public Support for Drunk Driving Countermeasures: Social Policy for Saving Lives," *Crime and Delinquency* 41:2 (1995): 171–190.

9. Richard Berk and others found the deterrent effect of arrest in incidence of spouse abuse was no greater than other police interventions (temporarily separating spouses or referral to

counseling). Arrest appears to be a greater deterrent for middle-class and first-time arrestees, depending on backgrounds of the offenders. Richard Berk, Alec Campbell, Ruth Klap, et al., "The Deterrent Effect of Arrest in Incidents of Domestic Violence," *American Sociological Review* 57:5 (1992): 698–708. See also Richard Tolman and Arlene Weisz, "Coordinated Community Intervention for Domestic Violence," *Crime and Delinquency* 41:4 (1995): 481–495.

10. Every five years, since 1970, the U.S. Department of Justice has conducted a census of all jails in the nation. Data on the 1993 census will be available in 1995.

11. Perkins, et al., *Jails and Jail Inmates*, p. 1.

12. Ibid. p. 3.

13. Ibid, p. 5.

14. Ibid., p. 8. See also Roger Peters, William Kearns, Mary Murrin, and Addis Dolente, "Effectiveness of In-Jail Substance Abuse Treatment," *American Jails* 6:1 (1992): 98–104. *American Jails* is published by the American Jail Association, 1000 Day Road, Suite 100, Hagerstown, Maryland 21740, (301) 790-3930.

15. Allen Beck, *Profiles of Jail Inmates,1989* (Washington, D.C. US Bureau of Justice Statistics, 1991): 8–9.

16. Ibid., p 10. See also George Palermo, Edward Gumz, and Frank Liska, "Mental Illness and Criminal Behavior Revisited," *International Journal of Offender Therapy and Comparative Criminology* 36:1 (1992): 53–61, and U.S. Government Accounting Office, *Mentally Ill Inmates: BOP Plans to Improve Screening and Care in Federal Prisons and Jails* (Washington, D.C.: U.S. Government Printing Office, 1991).

17. Belinda McCarthy, "The Use of Jail Confinement in the Disposition of Felony Arrests," *Journal of Criminal Justice* 17 (1989): 241–251.

18. Perkins, et al., *Jails and Jail Inmates*, p. 11.

19. Kathleen Macguire and Ann Pastore, *Sourcebook of Criminal Justice Statistics* (Washington, D.C.: U.S. Department of Justice, 1995), p. 536.

20. See recommendation of Steven Donziger, *The Real War on Crime* (New York: HarperCollins, 1995), pp. 215–217, and Harry Allen, "The American Dream and Crime in the Twenty-First Century," *Justice Quarterly* 12:3 (1995): 427–445.

CHAPTER FIFTEEN

Male Offenders

Overview

In the last chapter, we acquired an understanding of the variety of offenders who are dealt with as "clients" of the jail and detention systems of America. As we saw in Part I, until very recently, incarceration practices were not intended to "correct" the behavior of inmates. Consequently, the young and the old, the sick and the well, the women and the men, and the dangerous and the naive were placed indiscriminately in one facility. As the concepts of penitence and corrections were developed, men and women were segregated in separate institutions. Later, institutions were further specialized, with different kinds of institutions for the younger inmates, who were separated from the more hardened felons (though these groups are still sometimes hard to tell apart), and juveniles were directed to a separate system (see Chapter 17).

In this chapter we shall examine the processes and conditions that are provided those men who are convicted and sentenced to the adult prisons of America, and placed there following their exposure to the conditions of jail life. If corrections and prisons can be thought of as businesses, we shall continue the analogy and consider adult male inmate groups as *clients* with different needs, problems, and demands. Using a business analogy, we can describe the growth of corrections in all areas as a growth industry.

As we pointed out in Part I, the prison was one of America's major contributions to the Western world. Whereas accused offenders were once housed in detention facilities only until their trial and punishment (which was usually severe), the Walnut Street Jail of 1790 and its successors provided a new kind of facility for punishment, penitence, treatment, and reformation.

In the nineteenth and early twentieth centuries, America built dozens of massive **bastionlike prisons**, capable of warehousing literally thousands of inmates in their multitiered cellblocks. Offering few treatment services, these castles for the more impoverished of

We know how hard it is to help prisoners become better men, and many penal authorities have given up too easily on that task. But whatever prisons do, they must not make men needlessly worse.

—John P. Conrad

Effect of the Baby Boom

After World War II, returning soldiers tended to marry young and begin families. The result was a large number of offspring born between 1945 and 1964, some 200 percent larger than would have been expected had the war not created delays in family formation and childbearing.

The large numbers of children worked their way through the school system, and the children matured, creating overcrowding first in grade school and then in high school populations. Many baby boomers entered college, creating another service delivery crisis.

The significance of the baby boom for corrections lay in the high crime rate years of ages nineteen to twenty-nine,

when offenders were most likely to commit crime. Thus the baby boom struck the correctional system from about 1970 to 1985. Because there is a "commitment lag" (generally ten years) between early onset of criminal behavior and being sent to prison, correctional overcrowding in the late 1980s can be seen as caused in part by World War II.

Baby boomers have themselves begun families, and there is an "echo boom" in the offing that will affect the criminal justice system in the late 1990s; it will particularly cause crises in corrections in the first part of the twenty-first century. ■

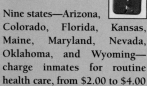

CHARGES FOR INMATE MEDICAL SERVICE

Nine states—Arizona, Colorado, Florida, Kansas, Maine, Maryland, Nevada, Oklahoma, and Wyoming—charge inmates for routine health care, from $2.00 to $4.00 per service.

society[1] were rapidly filled with offenders, and they remained full until the late 1960s and early 1970s, when prison populations began to drop. That drop, in part due to the increased use of community-based corrections, particularly probation, has now come to a halt, and the prison populations have achieved new heights. It appears that a variation of Murphy's law is operating in corrections: as rapidly as prisons are built, court commitments expand to fill all available cells, a tendency sometimes known as the **Iron Law of Prison Commitments**. The proliferation of prisons and the almost instant overcrowding of the new institutions seem to doom the men within to no help at best and to too much help (punishment) at worst.

This chapter deals with several questions. Who are the male prison inmates? What are their needs, and what programs should be devised to address those needs? What should we know about their backgrounds? What happens to the men in the prisons of America?

Prison Populations Continue to Soar

Keeping track of the rapidly fluctuating adult prison population is like trying to paint a moving bus. The number of male offenders housed in America's prisons is rising at an alarming rate, along with the total prison population. Between 1979 and 1996, the total prison population increased by a whopping 323 percent! In the previous edition of this text, your authors predicted the total adult prison population to top a million by the year 2000. Boy, were we wrong! The population rose from 883,500 in 1993 to the staggering figure of 1,042,636 in 1995. This did not include 54,132 male and female inmates sentenced to state prisons by the courts but who were, at the time, "holdbacks" (being held in county jail facilities because of prison overcrowding). Of the total number, 84,903 (8 percent) were incarcerated in federal facilities under the Bureau of Prisons (see Chapter 26), and 860,632 (91 percent) were in state prisons. Another 43,022 inmates were being held in other adult long-term institutions (e.g., the Cook County Department of Corrections, the New York City Department of Corrections, the Washington, D.C., Department of Corrections, and the Philadelphia Prison System). In total, there are approximately 378 inmates in adult prisons for every 100,000 residents, an increase of 14 percent over 1993.[2]

TABLE 15.1

Total Arrests, Distribution by Sex Offense (estimated population 207,624,000), 1994*

Offense Charged	Number of Persons Arrested Total	Male	Percentage Male	Percentage Distribution
Total	11,877,188	9,504,762	80.0%	100.0%
Murder and nonnegligent manslaughter	18,497	16,658	90.1	0.2
Forcible rape	29,791	29,460	98.9	0.3
Robbery	146,979	133,388	90.8	1.4
Aggravated assault	449,716	375,020	83.4	3.9
Burglary	319,926	286,502	89.6	3.0
Larceny-theft	1,236,311	824,980	66.7	8.7
Motor vehicle theft	166,260	145,701	87.6	1.5
Arson	16,764	14,304	85.3	0.2
Violent crime	644,983	554,526	86.0	5.8
Property crime	1,739,261	1,271,487	73.1	13.4
Crime index total	2,384,244	1,826,013	76.6	19.2

*Taken from 10,654 reporting agencies; 1994 estimated population of 207,624,000.

SOURCE: Federal Bureau of Investigation, *Crime in the United States 1994: Uniform Crime Report* (Washington, D.C.: U.S. Department of Justice, 1995), p. 234.

As shown in Table 15.1 above, there were almost 10 million arrests of males at the end of 1994. The most common offenses in 1995 for which sentences are being served in state correctional facilities include robbery, homicide, burglary, major drug offenses (excluding possession), minor drug offenses (including possession), assault, sexual assault, forgery, fraud, and embezzlement. Forty-seven percent of al state prisoners serve time against the person (including armed robbery), and 25 percent are imprisoned for crimes against property.

We must remember that those sentenced and actually incarcerated in adult prisons are at the bottom of the correctional filter. As a group, men in prisons are undereducated and underemployed, primarily because of their social class and lack of opportunity. Those men are often beset with medical and psychological problems. Two-thirds are from minority racial and ethnic groups (65 percent in 1995, see Figure15-1), are poor, and have been unable to cope with the complexities of urban life. Often recent arrivals, they have limited job skills and do not know how to use available social services in the community. Many come from broken homes with low annual incomes, and a large number are drug and alcohol abusers. These characteristics suggest the number of treatment challenges faced by correctional administrators.

SEGREGATION AND PROTECTIVE CUSTODY

More than 5 percent of the nation's prison inmates were being held in administrative or disciplinary segregation, or in protective custody in 1994.

	White	Black	Hispanic	Other	TOTAL*	Holdbacks	
State	284,288	396,148	115,366	17,128	**812,930**	48,617	
Federal	29,810	26,329	20,479	2,150	**78,768**	2	TOTAL + Holdbacks
Other	2,885	29,478	7,363	287	**40,013**	—	
Total	**316,983**	**451,955**	**143,208**	**19,565**	**931,711**	**48,619**	**980,330**

* Holdbacks not included in TOTAL.

FIGURE

15.1

Male Inmates in Adult Facilities, Year-end 1994

SOURCE: American Correctional Association, *1996 Directory: Juvenile and Adult Correctional Departments, Institutions, Agencies, and Paroling Authorities* (Lanham, MD: American Correctional Association, 1996), p. xxvi.

As you will see in Chapter 16, which addresses female inmates, the increase in male inmates in prison has been heavily impacted by the war on drugs, which was discussed in Chapter 4 in terms of the pendulum swing toward very strong enforcement and opening the floodgates into adult male prisons. The war on drugs accounted for a large part of the increase in prison populations from 1980; 46 percent of the increase in court commitments were due to drug offenses. More than one in four male state prison inmates, and six out of ten federal prison inmates, are serving time for a drug law violation or drug-related crime.[3]

Males have historically and overwhelmingly predominated in the prison population. Although the number of females sentenced to prison is increasing rapidly, males still represent over 93 percent of the total number of inmates in prison.

These conditions create problems for those whose mandate it is to provide reasonable and effective reintegration services while protecting society from the offenders. The problems in meeting this mission are exacerbated by a hardening of public attitudes toward and opinions about the male felon.

Adult male prisons (and almost all other detention facilities) are overcrowded to the danger point,[4] and it is obvious that the present systems will be unable to meet the increasing demands. Not only must we reexamine all of our institutions that hold male offenders, but we must also seriously consider alternatives to incarceration. (See Chapter 11.) Some male offenders are extremely dangerous and must be isolated from others. In the 1970s it was estimated that only some 15 to 25 percent of the male population in prison fell into this category. That situation, however, has changed; overcrowding and a higher level of violence in the community has tended to force correctional administrators to find ways to release those men considered least dangerous back into the community. This has left an increasingly greater percentage of violent offenders smoldering in a potential tinderbox. In some states, the number of violent offenders in maximum security prisons who committed crimes against the person is closer to 62 percent and growing, as property offenders are given alternatives to incarceration.[5]

As stated earlier, male offenders tend to be heavy users of alcohol and drugs. In 1991, for example, almost one-third of the men in prison had been drinking at the time of their current offense, and another one-third were under the influence of drugs. That pattern has changed only in the acquisition of a broader catalog of ever more powerful **"designer"** **drugs**—many of which induce violent behavior.

Tests of inmates at male adult prisons and correctional facilities continue to find ongoing drug use. Of all inmates tested, at least 1 percent tested positive for cocaine and heroin. Another 2 percent were positive for methamphetamines, and almost 6 percent were positive for marijuana. These statistics indicate that drug and alcohol abuse are serious problems that contribute negatively to the offenders' behavior, both in the community and in the institution. Drug and alcohol treatment programs both in and out of prison are no longer a luxury—they are a necessity.[6]

Education is an important factor in American society; it is viewed by many as an essential prerequisite for economic stability and success. In a high-tech society such as that of the United States, education is crucial for getting a job and earning an adequate income. Despite this need for education, the most recent national survey found that one in five Americans can be considered **functionally illiterate**.[7] As a group, male state prison inmates are less educated than their counterparts in the civilian population. Sixty-three percent of the inmates have not received a high school diploma, in contrast to 36 percent of the general population eighteen years of age or older. This sad situation is becoming even worse as more and more youths pass through our public school systems without being properly prepared to function with developed problem-solving skills in an urban environment. It is not too surprising that crime is often chosen as one alternative for survival under those circumstances. It is not enough that many inmates are now given a chance to earn a high school education in prison; the nation as a whole must insist that the education provided by our public school systems supply the skills needed to keep these men out of prison.

Finally, almost one in four imprisoned men are eligible to be furloughed into an early-release procedure, but fewer than half of those eligible are given the opportunity to take such a furlough. Most inmates (69 percent) have some kind of **institutional work assignment**, but the average pay is less than 60 cents per hour for their work. It is hard to motivate an incarcerated man to make a serious effort

CONJUGAL VISITS

Conjugal (or so-called family) visits were allowed in only seven states in 1994: California, Connecticut, Mississippi, New Mexico, New York, Washington, and Wyoming.

to learn a trade while he is working in prison for such low wages, when the same man has made up to $500 a day illegally in his community—and knows it can be done again.

Prisonization Plays a Big Role

Every venture intended to elevate humanity (or at least to encourage improvement) has as many unplanned and unwanted effects as it has desired effects. Efforts to give male offenders a setting in which to do penance and be "reformed" have resulted in a number of unwanted side effects, ranging from the mental and physical deterioration caused by extreme solitary confinement at Sing Sing to a more contemporary unwanted phenomenon called **prisonization**. The originator of the term, Donald Clemmer, described this process as "the taking on in greater or less degree of the folkways, mores, customs, and general culture of the penitentiary."[8] Clemmer observed that the acculturation into the prison community subjects the inmate to certain influences that either breed or deepen criminal behaviors, causing the prisoner to learn the criminal ideology of the prison—to become "prisonized." Prisonization is a process that includes accepting the subordinate role into which one is thrust as an inmate; developing new habits of sleeping, dressing, eating, and working; undergoing status degradation; adopting a new language; and learning that one is dependent on others (including one's fellow inmates) for the scarce pleasures found in incarceration, including food, work assignment, freedom from assault, and privileges. Students of prisonization believe that this process not only leads the inmate to further identify with criminal codes, goals, and behaviors but also serves to undercut reintegration programs and to lessen the offender's ability to adjust to society after release.[9]

The phenomenon of prisonization appears to exist in all prisons, not just the large gothic bastions that testify to archaic prison philosophies. It can be brought into the prison by older inmates but, even in new prisons that receive first-time offenders, the inmates' pains of imprisonment can generate the prisonization process.

A special cellblock for elderly inmates

—GREG MELLIS

Because prisonization occurs in every institution, although to varying degrees, it is necessary to understand the benefits that accrue to the men who adhere to the inmate codes. The future correctional administrator must also understand the pains of imprisonment that encourage socialization into the inmate subculture. Those pains are status deprivation, sexual deprivation, material deprivation, and enforced intimacy with other deviants.

The inmate subculture reduces the pains of imprisonment by encouraging the sharing of the few benefits and pleasures inside prisons, by helping prevent naked aggression by inmates against other inmates, and by providing a circle of friends who can and will come to an inmate's assistance if he is attacked. It also offers alternative sexual outlets,[10] defines appropriate roles for getting along with other inmates, and supplies companions with whom an inmate can share confidences and interact comfortably. In addition, this process makes available contraband drugs (including glue, "pruno,"[11] and prescription drugs stolen from prison dispensaries) on which an inmate can get high. There are also many other, less tangible benefits.

Fortunately, recent research suggests that the extent, and thus the negative impact, of prisonization may be reduced through the staff's institutional administration and orientation.

We would expect to find more solidarity (of the inmate code) and more traditional inmate types in a correctional system with only one institution for adult felons and where that institution is characterized by more severe material and sociopsychological deprivations.[12]

Others have suggested that the nature and extent of endorsement of prisoner norms ("be a **stand-up guy**," don't rat on another inmate," "mind your own business," "never exploit another inmate," "never cooperate with correctional officers," "do your own time," "be a man," "don't whine") can be significantly reduced.

In addition to the problems of prisonization, institutional populations are increasingly divided along ethnic and racial lines. The resulting groups frequently engage in power struggles for control of the institution, fighting among themselves and attacking prison officials and correctional officers. The fracturing of the inmate population into racial and ethnic groups (primarily a white/black/Mexican-American gang phenomenon in maximum security prisons) poses serious new problems for prison administrators, raises the level of anxiety among inmates, works against reintegration, and creates an atmosphere of perceived danger among the prison staff,[13] and a recent survey found that the vast majority of prison wardens of adult male correctional institutions believe that gang problems dramatically increase behind the walls.[14] Prison administrators will need to develop new techniques for coping with inmate division into white, black and brown, major groups and prison gangs so as to bring order to the prison setting and make reintegration programs more effective.

If the institutional administrator and staff emphasize individual and group treatment rather than custody and discipline, if a pattern of cooperation can be developed between informal inmate leaders and institutional authorities, if a medium or minimum custody level can be achieved, and if violators of rules governing the use of force by the correctional staff are consistently reprimanded, then the prison culture and the prisonization process can be markedly reduced. Some researchers have suggested that shorter prison terms tend to undercut the power of the prison culture, as inmates can and do participate in "anticipatory socialization" as they near the end of their prison sentences and begin to prepare for their participation in the activities of the free world. Therefore it is reasonable to assume that short fixed periods of incarceration would help reduce the negative effects of prisonization.

PRISON INDUSTRY PAY

Inmates are paid from $1.67 to $8.39 per day for work in institutional prison industries, while private prison industries, contracting for work done in prison facilities, using inmate labor, pays from $23.00 to $28.00 per day.

Inmate Slang

Male prisons are a society unto themselves, separated almost totally from the free society. Under these conditions prison slang, a form of a dialect in other language, is developed. Slang has emerged partly as an expression of community for the inmates, and also as an effort to confuse the correctional staff. We include some examples of inmate slang terminology, which may or may not be found to be in use in every institution:

1. Barn: a large open dorm
2. Box: radio
3. Brown shirt: correctional officer
4. Dead man walking: inmate on way to execution
5. Duck: a new guard.
6. Fire in the hole: correctional officer approaching
7. Fish: a new inmate
8. Hack: guard
9. Home boy: someone from the same city
10. Keester it: hide object in rectum
11. The Man: Usually the warden, can be a captain
12. One time: stash the drugs, guard on floor
13. Pack the rabbit: secrete object in rectum
14. Pruno: homemade alcohol
15. Range queen: inmate who takes woman's role
16. Shank: homemade knife
17. Snitch: informant
18. Stinger: homemade electric apparatus for heating water
19. Tailor-mades: factory-made cigarettes
20. Thump: to fight

The Continuing Prison Population Boom

As has been shown, in the years between 1979 and 1996 prison populations sharply increased, much to the dismay of both prisoners and concerned correctional administrators. There is little agreement on the exact reasons for the population boom, although some correctional personnel are quick to note that the police and courts may have become more efficient more quickly than the correctional subsystem did. As one administrator observed, "The police tooled up, the prosecutor's office has expanded along with the use of plea bargaining, and the courts finally stepped into the twentieth century. We in corrections have received the benefits of efficiency through sharply increased commitments."

Others have identified the hardening of public opinion as a factor, pointing out that judges are perceiving considerable local pressure to commit offenders rather than use probation. It could be that the reaction to crime in America has exceeded the threshold of fear[15] and reached panic proportions, with widespread public clamor for commitments contributing to prison overpopulation. This is particularly probable in the drug abuse area.[16]

It is more likely, however, that a principal cause is the increase in the **population at risk**,[17] those males in the age range of eighteen to twenty-nine. Inasmuch as crime is a young person's occupation and considering the fact that the number of persons in the high crime rate ages doubled between 1965 and 1985, one would expect the factor of age to contribute heavily to the overpopulation of American prisons. The **age at risk** problem was made worse by a population shift over the last fifteen years, during which families with young sons moved to urban areas from rural environments. The rural settings had

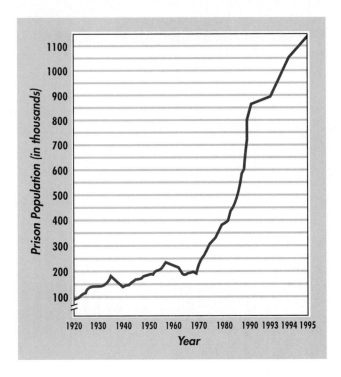

F I G U R E

15.2

Prison Population Counts
to 1995

SOURCE: Allen Beck, *Probation and Parole Population Reaches Almost 3.8 Million* (Washington, D.C.: U.S. Department of Justice, 1996), p. 7.

provided more control and more wholesome outlets for young men. Historically, such population shifts—regardless of the population group in motion—meant that the second generation engaged in more frequent criminal behavior. In that case, recent population shifts coincided with an increase in the population at risk, and we can therefore expect the committed population to rise for several more years.

America seems determined to resolve its crime problems with a "lock 'em up and throw away the key" philosophy.[18] Although incapacitation may be an effective way temporarily to prevent crime, helping offenders expand their opportunities and enter the mainstream of American society might be a more permanent way of lowering crime rates and the collateral national costs of incarceration.

A modern maximum security prison in Georgia

—COURTESY OF THE GEORGIA DEPARTMENT OF CORRECTIONS

New Inmates Reflect Surge in Heroin Use

NEW YORK, Dec. 2–The number of inmates arriving on Rikers Island who are addicted to heroin has increased by 23 percent this year, providing substance abuse experts with some of the most solid evidence yet of the resurgence of heroin use.

The addiction statistics from New York City's jails reflect a plentiful supply of relatively inexpensive but highly potent heroin that has become available in the United States in the last few years, substance abuse experts say.

"I'm able to verify the sense of people on the street that heroin use is going up and going up significantly," said Dr. Eran Bellin, the director of the Rikers Island Health Service, which is run by the Montefiore Medical Center.

Substance abuse officials say the sharp increase in heroin use detected among incoming inmates is particularly unsettling because the jail population in the past has proven to be an accurate predictor of other public health problems, from tuberculosis to sexually transmitted diseases.

On Rikers Island, officials have had to expand wards for heroin addicts as the number of inmates undergoing methadone detoxification has jumped to 1,392 in June 1995 from 879 in October 1993. Detoxification lasts from one to three weeks, and continuing treatment such as methadone maintenance can go on much longer.

Dr. Robert G. Newman, the president of Beth Israel Medical Center, which runs a network of 23 methadone clinics in the city, said the Rikers information is "the clearest quantifiable evidence" of the increase in heroin use in the general population.

Although New York City has long been considered the city with the worst heroin problem, there is evidence of increased heroin use throughout the country.

From 1988 to 1994, the number of emergency room visits in which heroin was a contributing factor rose nationwide to 64,221 from 38,063, according to the Federal Substance Abuse and Mental Health Services Administration. In the New York metropolitan region, heroin-related emergency room visits more than doubled during that period, to 10,892 from 5,394.

A spokeswoman at Daytop Village Inc., which operates 28 rehabilitation clinics nationwide, said the number of patients reporting that they had tried heroin rose to 37 percent in 1994 from 16 percent in 1993. "It's fast-addicting, it's very powerful and it's cheap," said a spokeswoman for Daytop Village, Joan Rizzo.

Heroin use declined in the early 1980's when the link between intravenous drug use and AIDS was established and it declined further when crack cocaine flooded the drug market in the mid-80's, law enforcement and substance abuse experts say. They say the surge in heroin use is partly attributable to the powerful strains of heroin now available that allow users to get high by sniffing the drug and avoiding the dangers of injection. But they add that cocaine use is hardly

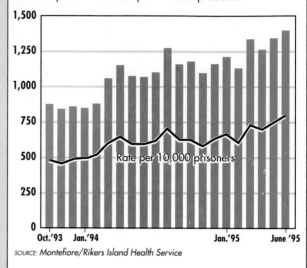

The number of inmates arriving at Rikers Island requiring detoxification from heroin addiction has been increasing rapidly. Health officials say the inmate population has been an accurate predictor of other public health problems.

SOURCE: *Montefiore/Rikers Island Health Service*

Courtesy of *The New York Times*

dwindling and that the two drugs are increasingly being used in combination.

Dr. Bellin said the increase in heroin dependency has been noticed during physical examinations performed on all new detainees coming into the city jail system.

From May through October of this year, 8,379 inmates arriving on Rikers Island showed signs of withdrawal from heroin and required detoxification, compared with 6,819 inmates for the same six months in 1994.

Although the number of people coming into Rikers has increased in recent years, that alone does not account for the increase in the number of new inmates addicted to heroin, Dr. Bellin said. He said the percentage of heroin-dependent inmates had risen to 7.6 percent in June, 1995 from 4.76 percent in October, 1993.

To contend with the heroin addicts and other inmates with drug problems, the Giuliani administration is restoring 600 drug treatment beds in the city jails that had been eliminated to save money.

Dr. Newman said the information from Rikers Island, coupled with similar reports from around the country, shows "a terrible, societally costly problem is getting even worse." He said that even as the crack epidemic captured the public attention in the 80's, heroin remained the drug of choice for a significant core of addicts.

He said the increase in heroin use would again reveal the tremendous shortage of treatment facilities for addicts. He said that there are an estimated 250,000 heroin users in New York City, but that methadone clinics in the city have a total capacity of 35,000 patients. Even with other rehabilitation

(Continued from page 284)

New Inmates Reflect Surge in Heroin Use

programs that do not prescribe methadone, there is a shortage of treatment slots, he said.

The public health problem caused by heroin could well be compounded, Dr. Newman said, if the price of heroin increases or the purity declines.

Robin Waugh, a spokeswoman for the Federal Drug Enforcement Agency in New York, said drug agents report that while the heroin now on the street is 60 to 70 percent pure, and much more powerful than the heroin available a few years ago, the price has remained stable. ∎

Rape in All-Male Institutions

In a detailed study of aggression among men behind prison walls, Anthony Scacco boasted that sex is a vehicle for exploitation rather than an expression of pathological personality or situational frustration.[19] The sexual assaults that occur within prisons and jails cannot be categorized solely as **homosexual attacks**;[20] rather they often are assaults made by heterosexually oriented males for political reasons—that is, to show power and dominance over other human beings. It is a depressing fact that victimization, degradation, racism, and humiliation of victims are the foremost reasons that sexual assaults are perpetrated on men in this setting.

Scacco also addressed a topic seldom openly discussed by correctional administrators: the polarization of inmates in prison, a phenomenon that has accelerated in recent years. Younger and more aggressive inmates appear to be polarizing into racial and ethnic groups, and the conflict between those groups—and with the correctional staff—has led to greater tension behind the walls.[21] As prison populations continue to grow, that polarization will probably also increase.

To reduce the potential for further disturbances among men in prison, Scacco proposed several steps:

1. The staff of a correctional institution should openly admit that they must meet together as a body and discuss their views on sexuality if they are to render assistance to the inmates in their care.

2. Masturbation for relief of sexual tension should be allowed within an institution, not denied to men within prison walls.

3. Classification at reception and orientation centers should keep sexually different and sexually attractive men from mixing with the rest of the inmate population, to keep the weaker and often younger inmates apart from other inmates with sexual desires which they would fulfill through sexual assault.

4. Conjugal visits, which reduce recidivism and homosexuality, are a more socially acceptable solution than rape.

5. Furlough programs should be implemented to maintain normal sexual relations.

6. Coeducational correctional institutions should be expanded, rather than prisons, and populations reduced to the remaining 30 percent of the inmate population that requires confinement.[22]

In institutions for only male felons, homosexual behavior between consenting adults has been a recurrent phenomenon, as in other such unisexual settings as naval ships and religious monasteries. It is unreasonable to expect inmates to abandon sexual behavior in prison, particularly when they face increasingly long sentences. As Peter Buffum noted,

> [The present pattern of homosexuality in prisons] means that as long as the prison is an environment which is largely devoid of situations where legitimate affectional ties can be established, there will be a tendency for the formation of homosexual relationships, especially among those persons serving long sentences who have concomitantly lost contact with meaningful persons in the free community. If, in addition, the prison does not allow legitimate attempts of the inmates to control their own lives and does not give an opportunity for expressions of masculinity and self-assertion that are meaningful among men at this social level, there will be homosexual relationships created to fulfill this need.[23]

Especially among younger inmates and those who accept passive roles, homosexual behaviors and relationships could impair future commitments to heterosexuality as well as create exploitative situations. When such relationships create jealousy among inmates, the potential for serious violence and administrative problems increases. If a third inmate becomes involved in a dyadic relationship or there is a transfer of affection, extreme violence can occur. The once-frequent pattern of transferring the passive partner to another institution is no longer an adequate or constitutional response by prison management. Segregating passive partners may cause the active inmates to coerce others into sexual behavior, as well as to raise legal issues of inmate rights and to create the potential for lawsuits arising from such isolation.

Prison administrators will need to consider and implement home visits at known intervals for those under long sentences, as well as provide activities and programs that will attack the real problems. At the beginning of 1993, however, only seventeen states reported permitting inmates to have family (**conjugal or private family**) visits.[24] This allowed inmates to have some control over their own lives and maintain affectionate relationships and stable interpersonal interaction. What will emerge will include opportunities for inmates to participate in inmate organizations; effective vocational, educational, and recreational programs; and co-correctional institutions.[25] Encouraging correspondence with and visits from relatives and employment of female correctional officers will also help reduce homosexual behavior, as will more involvement by volunteers in corrections.

The Graying of America's Male Prisoners

The proportion of prisoners in the nation's institutions who are elderly is rapidly increasing, in part due to the tougher long-term sentences inherent in the current "get tough on crime" stance, but also in part due to the general aging of the general population in America. It has been estimated that by the twenty-first century, at least one in ten (about 125,000 inmates) will be age fifty or over.[26] The growth rate of older inmates (age fifty or above) in Florida already exceeds the growth rate of younger offenders.

Elderly inmates are more likely to have committed crimes such as homicide and manslaughter, as well as sexual offenses. They are less likely to be imprisoned for robbery and burglary. Because of their significantly longer sentences, elderly inmates may be concentrated in prisons well beyond their proportions in the civilian population, which will pose problems for them as well as prison administrators. First, they will have health care problem concerns and need preventive health care programs that, if not provided, could be a source of considerable and, for correctional administrators, substantial litigation costs. At the least, they will suffer from depression and differing nutritional needs (less protein, fewer calories, and more soft food and fiber). Because taste sensations decline with aging, the elderly will request food richer in seasonings and will have a decrease in gastric acid and increase in gas production and constipation. Special diets will be needed.

In addition, growing old in prison will mean having to avoid exploitation and violence by younger inmates,[27] having to adjust new personal needs to prison life, and not having suitable programs (recreational, educational, or housing). Vulnerability to victimization, frailty, and isolation from outside relatives and friends will take their toll, as will fear of death, hopelessness, and being unable to cope when released.

Health care costs will increase significantly for hypertension, diabetes, stroke, cancer, and emphysema. Glasses, dentures, kidney dialysis, and heart surgery will be required. It has been estimated that by the year 2005, health care costs for elderly inmates will increase by fourteenfold.[28] Many prisons will become geriatric centers,[29] and special staff as well as staff training will be necessary to treat this special problem segment of the nation's offenders. Perhaps a nation that can explore space can find the necessary compassion to care for that small but increasing group as we enter the next century. Executive clemency, including pardons, may become a frequent act.

$\mathcal{S}$ummary

Male offenders who are not dangerous men can be diverted into such programs as deferred prosecution, house arrest, probation, weekend confinement, intensive supervised probation, shock incarceration, electronic monitoring, restitution and community work-release programs, and community reintegration centers. The last two of these programs are at least as effective as prisons are, and cost much less than the outrageous $100,000 per cell and up to $48,650 annual average per prisoner cost.[30] Community programs, rather than the prisons, should be expanded.[31] Indeed, intermediate punishments, along with tourniquet sentencing, should be the sentences of choice for all but the most callous, recalcitrant, and predatory offenders.

Prisons, however, seem to be almost impossible to get rid of, although they require enormous annual outlays for upkeep, and can corrupt both the keeper and the kept. These monuments to an age gone by do not and cannot achieve their stated mission unless correctional administrators are trained and dedicated, have sufficient resources, abide by the Constitution, and understand the effects of inaction and indecisiveness.

Expanding the alternatives for male offenders has another benefit: to the extent that male offenders are integrated into the community, their future criminal behavior will be sharply reduced, if not eliminated. Community-based corrections can reduce the crime problem in the United States to a far greater extent than can the current prison operations, by actually making offenders useful citizens.

Although a large number of prisons are under construction and there will be men in prisons for a long time to come, the more cost-effective and cost-beneficial community programs may eventually reduce the number of inmates under lock and key to only those who are too dangerous to be released. Corrections must and will divert its resources into those programs that offer humane treatment without sacrificing the protection of society. Warehousing male offenders in prison may temporarily achieve selective incapacitation, but it does little to resolve the causes of crime that contributed to incarceration. Indeed, whatever good is done to men through imprisonment is hard to detect, but the long-term harms are evident.

Never have so many Americans, and American men especially, been incarcerated in prisons and jails in the numbers and rates per one million as they are as we approach the twenty-first century. Yet the incarceration rate does not appear to be a function of the crime rate. It is most clearly a political response to a heightened fear of crime. It is also a "great experiment" designed to do what Prohibition attempted to do—deny to citizens a desired product: drugs. In a few decades, historians will no doubt label the current era as "The Second Great Prohibition Experiment."

In the interim, American prisons will remain overpopulated with offenders, most of whom are not dangerous and could be handled in community settings. The challenge facing correctional students and administrators is how to change America's penchant for solving basic social problems by resorting to a "lock 'em up and throw away the key" policy that has been used again in the presidential and congressional campaigns. Surely a nation that can develop computers, explore space, and harness nuclear power ought to be able to design programs and alternatives that can provide humane treatment and at the same time ensure public protection.

In the next chapter, we examine the situation faced by a growing percentage of incarcerated offenders who are female.

Review Questions

1. Why have prison populations increased recently? What short-term effects will result from that increase?
2. What is meant by the "population at risk"? How does it contribute to the population problem in male prisons?
3. Explain the dynamics of rape in a male prison.
4. What factors contribute to prisonization?
5. What can be done to reduce homosexuality in prisons?
6. What problems do elderly inmates pose or face?
7. How should male inmates be sentenced?
8. Why are so many prisoners members of minority groups?

$\mathcal{W}$ords to Remember

bastionlike prisons

court commitments

racial and ethnic groups

"designer" drugs

Iron Law of Prison
   Commitments

functionally illiterate

prisonization

stand-up guy

population at risk

conjugal or private
   family visits

age at risk

homosexual attacks

elderly inmates

institutional work
   assignment

$\mathcal{E}$ndnotes

1. Arguing for community surveillance and supervision of offenders, Orville Pung, director of the Minnesota Department of Corrections, asserts that prison is the ultimate welfare state. When the public understands this, there will be significantly less dependence on prisons. Orville Pung, "Let's Abolish 'Probation' and 'Treatment,' " *Overcrowded Times* 4:2 (1993): 3. For an international perspective in prisons, see Norval Morris and D. Rothman, *The Oxford History of the Prison: The Practice of Punishment in Western Society* (Oxford: Oxford University Press, 1995).

2. American Correctional Association, *1996 Directory: Juvenile & Adult Correctional Departments, Institutions, Agencies & Paroling Authorities* (Lanham, MD: American Correctional Association, 1996), p. xxxvi.

3. Allen Beck and D. Gilliard, *Prisoners in 1994* (Washington, D.C.: U.S. Department of Justice, 1995), p. 10, and Marc Mauer, "International Use of Incarceration," *The Prison Journal* 75:1 (1995): 113–123.

4. Prison administrators argue that reserve capacity is needed to operate a prison effectively. Prison dormitories and cells need to be repaired and maintained periodically. Additional space may be needed for emergencies. Special housing (such as protective custody and punitive segregation) and administrative units (such as prison recreation, intake, and program space) are required. The federal prison system is running at 137 percent of capacity, and forty-three states are over at least their lowest capacity, some (such as California) are as much as 191 percent of capacity. A total of 803,334 are in 1,239 state prison units. See Beck and Gilliard, *Prisoners in 1994,* p.4.

5. Allen Beck, *Survey of State Prison Inmates* (Washington, D.C.: U.S. Government Printing Office, 1991), p. 28.

6. Caroline Wolf Beck, *Drug Enforcement and Treatment in Prison, 1990* (Washington, D.C.: U.S. Department of Justice, 1992), p. 1. See also Henry Wexler, "The Success of Therapeutic Communities for Substance Abuse in American Prisons," *The Prison Journal* 75:1 (1995): 57–66.

7. Charles Bailey, "Prison Populations Surging, and Not Just Because of the Nation's Economic Slowdown," *Corrections Digest* 7 (February 1976): 9. See also Miriam Williford, *Higher Education in Prison: A Contradiction in Terms?* (Phoenix: Oryx Press, 1994).

8. Donald Clemmer, *The Prison Community* (New York: Rinehart, 1940), p. 8. See also Barbara Peat and Thomas Winfree, "Reducing the Intra-Institutional Effects of 'Prisonization': A Study of a Therapeutic Community for Drug-Using Inmates," *Criminal Justice Behavior* 19:2 (1992): 206–225. Also Hans Toch, "Inmate Involvement in Prison Governance," *Federal Probation* 59:2 (1995): 34–39.

9. Kenneth Adams, "Adjusting to Prison Life," in Michael Tonry, ed., *Crime and Justice: A Review of Research*, Vol. 16 (Chicago: University of Chicago Press, 1993), pp. 275–359.

10. Christine Saum, Hilary Surratt, and James Inciardi, "Sex in Prison: Exploring the Myth and Realities," *The Prison Journal* 75:4 (1995): 413–430. But see Richard Tewksbury, "Measures of Sexual Behavior in an Ohio Prison," *Sociology and Social Research* 74 (1989): 34–39. See also Bonnie Carlson and Neil Cervera, *Inmates and Their Wives: Incarceration and Family Life* (Westport, CT: Greenwood, 1992).

11. Pruno is alcohol made from fruit scraps, potato peelings, raisins, or any other biodegradable fruit and sugar; also known as raisin jack, orange sunshine, apple buck, white lightning, and so on.

12. Gene Kassebaum, David Ward, and Daniel Wilner, *Prison Treatment and Parole Survival: An Empirical Assessment* (New York: John Wiley, 1971), p. 301.

13. Robert Fong, "The Organizational Structure of Prison Gangs: A Texas Case Study," *Federal Probation* 54 (March 1990): 36–43. See also Robert Fong, Ronald Vogel, and Salvador Duentello, "Blood-in, Blood-out," *Journal of Gang Research* 2:4 (1995): 45–51.

14. National Gang Crime Research Center, "Preliminary Results of the 1995 Adult Corrections Survey," *Journal of Gang Research* 3:2 (1996): 27–63.

15. Ron Akers et al., "Fear of Crime and Victimization Among the Elderly in Different Types of Communities," *Criminology* 25 (1987): 487–505. See also Ronet Bachman, *Elderly Victims* (Washington, D.C.: U.S. Department of Justice, 1992).

16. Steven Donziger, *The Real War on Crime* (New York: HarperCollins, 1996), pp. 99–129.

17. Rob Wilson, "U.S. Prison Population Sets Another Record," *Corrections Magazine* 4 (June 1980): 5.

18. A term developed in the 1930s. See also Joan Petersilia, "California's Prison Policy: Causes, Costs, and Consequences," *The Prison Journal* 72:1,2 (1992): 8–36, and Theodore Sasson, *Crime Talk: How Citizens Construct a Social Problem* (Hawthorne, NY: Aldine, 1995).

19. Anthony Scacco, *Rape in Prison* (Springfield, IL: Charles C. Thomas, 1975).

20. Helen Eigenberg, "Homosexuality in Male Prisons: Demonstrating the Need for a Social Constructionist Approach," *Criminal Justice Review* 17:2 (1992): 219–234.

21. John Ramirez, "Race and the Apprehension of Inmate Misconduct," *Journal of Criminal Justice* 11 (1983): 413–427.

22. Scacco, *Rape in Prison*, pp. 99–116.

23. Peter Buffum, *Homosexuality in Prisons* (Washington, D.C.: U.S. Government Printing Office, 1972), p. 28. See also James Stephan, *Prison Rule Violators* (Washington, D.C.: Bureau of Justice Statistics, 1989), and David Heilpren, "Sexual Assault of New South Wales Prisoners," *Current Issues in Criminal Justice* 6:3 (1995): 327–334.

24. American Correctional Association, *1993 Directory* (Laurel, MD: American Correctional Association, 1993).

25. John Smykla, *Probation and Parole* (New York: Macmillan, 1984).

26. Sarah Bradley, "Graying of Inmate Population Spurs Corrections Challenges," *On the Line* 13 (March 1990): 5.

27. Richard Dugger, "The Graying of America's Prisons," *Corrections Today* 50 (June 1988): 26–34.

28. Bradley, "Graying of Inmate Population Spurs Corrections Challenges." See also Edith Flynn, "The Graying of America's Prison Population," *The Prison Journal* 72:1, 2 (1992): 77–98, and Philip Zimbardo. *Transforming California's Prisons Into Expensive Old Age Homes for Felons* (San Francisco: Center on Juvenile and Criminal Justice, 1994).

29. Gennaro Vito and Deborah Wilson, "Forgotten People: Elderly Inmates," *Federal Probation* 49 (March 1985): 18–24. See also Deborah Wilson and Gennaro Vito, "Long-Term Inmates: Special Need and Management Considerations," *Federal Probation* 52 (1988): 21–26. Illinois, Kentucky, Minnesota, North Carolina, Ohio, and Virginia already have special geriatric prison wings or housing units for their older inmates.

30. Per year cost of care at Minnesota Correctional facility, Sauk Centre, Minnesota. See American Correctional Association (1996), p. 240.

31. Pung, "Let's Abolish 'Probation' and 'Treatment.'"

CHAPTER SIXTEEN

Female Offenders

Overview

Although the male offender was shown in the previous chapter to provide the lion's share of adult prisoners (93 percent), the female inmate population is increasing at a faster rate of growth. In this chapter we will examine that phenomenon, as well as those similar processes and condition with which females must contend. We will look at the kinds of women and the crimes which placed them in state, federal, and other adult female prisons and correctional institutions. You will find that female offenders are moving away from "woman crime" and becoming more mainstream in their criminal behaviors and levels of violence, posing new challenges to old approaches.

In order to compare the relative levels of incarceration between female and male prisoners, we shall examine the crime rates for both categories and see the differing patterns of conviction and sentencing rates for those crimes. While the "steel ceiling" that has traditionally tended to divert women from long-term incarceration in correctional facilities seems to have cracked somewhat recently, particular trends are emerging for female prisoners. The student will be presented some of the problems specific to female offenders that cause them to need special treatment in many cases. We will ask, as we did in the last chapter, what happens to female offenders in the prisons of America?

Female Crime and Incarceration Rates Climbing

As shown by Figure 16-1, the number of female prisoners in adult facilities continued to grow rapidly—reaching an all-time high of 56,831, excluding the 5,415 holdbacks still in jail due to lack of space in state, federal, and other institutions. While this grand total represents only about 7 percent of the prison populations

No one has really known what to do with the few women that are condemned to prison, least of all the federal government.

—James V. Bennett, former director, Federal Bureau of Prisons

FIGURE

16.1

Female Inmates in Adult
Facilities, 1995

SOURCE: ACA 1996 Directory: Juvenile and Adult
Correctional Departments, Institutions, Agencies &
Paroling Authorities (ACA, Lanham, Maryland,
1996, p. xxvi.)

	White	Black	Hispanic	Other	TOTAL*	Holdbacks	
State	17,642	23,561	5,315	1,169	**47,687**	5,415	
Federal	2,114	2,410	1,472	139	**6,135**	—	**TOTAL +** Holdbacks
Other	231	2,204	554	20	**3,009**	—	
Total	**19,987**	**28,175**	**7,341**	**1,328**	**56,831**	**5,415**	**62,246**

* Holdbacks not included in TOTAL.

overall, it is a significant and worrisome trend. The rate of increase of female prisoners under jurisdiction of state, federal, or other correctional authorities was 10.6 percent from 1993 to 1994,[1] continuing a long trend of 11–12 percent growth each year. Projecting forward on this basis and starting at 1994 population levels, the United States will need over 106,000 beds for female prisoners as we enter the twenty-first century. This would equal one-third of the adult male prisoner population of 1980.

The incarceration rate for female prisoners in state institutions nationwide is 40 per 100,000.[2] The comparable male rate in the same category is almost nine times higher at 346 per 100,000.[3] The highest rate for female prisoners was the District of Columbia at 159 per 100,000; the lowest was the state of Maine at 9 per 100,000.[4] Regional jurisdictional highs were recorded by the South at an average of 54 per 100,000, followed in descending order by average regional rates for the West (40 per 100,000), the Midwest (31 per 100,000), and the lowest, the Northeast (24 per 100,000).[5] To get a better feel for who these prisoners are and why the rate and numbers are increasing, one has to look closer at the kinds of crimes, regionally and nationally, being committed by women.

Crime Statistics for Females

The period from 1970 through the 1990s were the years when women's equality and rights were asserted, if not established, on almost every front. Yet only recently has there been a movement to push for the rights of female prisoners in corrections. In a way, women still receive differential, even preferential, treatment at almost every station of the criminal justice system, partly in deference to traditional female sex roles. We now examine the more common kinds of "crime index" (see Chapter 5) offenses committed by women and compare some of the sentencing to institutions for women in a rapidly changing environment.

Although the criminal statistics contained in the FBI's *Uniform Crime Reports* are somewhat limited and "soft," especially for crimes involving women, they are the best available and can at least be accepted as indicators of trends. First, it should be noted that the total volume of crime for 1994 actually *decreased* by 3.3 percent over the 1993 crime total, continuing a trend from 1992–93 (-2.3 percent), and 1991–92 (-0.3 percent).[6] Much of the decrease was no doubt due to the "get-tough" attitudes on crime and selective incarceration for life of career criminals under "three-strikes" laws. These crime rate indicators are slowly beginning to return to previous levels of the mid-1980s.

A comparison of total **arrests by gender** in 1994 for the eight major (index) crimes can be found in Table 16-1. Two major conclusions are evident from examination of these data. First, women were arrested for 23 percent of all index

TABLE *16.1*

Total Arrests, Distribution by Sex Offenses, 1994[*]

| Offense Charged | Number of Persons Arrested | | Percentage Female | Percentage Distribution Female |
	Total	Female		
Total	11,877,188	2,372,426	20.0%	100.0%
Murder and nonnegligent manslaughter	18,497	1,839	9.9	0.1
Forcible rape	29,791	331	1.1	0.2
Robbery	146,979	13,591	9.2	0.6
Aggravated assault	449,716	74,696	16.6	3.1
Burglary	319,926	33,424	10.4	1.4
Larceny-theft	1,236,311	411,331	33.3	17.3
Motor vehicle theft	166,260	20,559	12.4	0.9
Arson	16,764	2,460	14.7	0.1
Violent crime	644,983	90,457	14.0	3.8
Property crime	1,739,261	467,774	26.9	19.7
Crime Index total	2,384,244	558,231	23.4	23.5

[*]Taken from 10,654 reporting agencies; 1994 estimated population of 207,624,000.
SOURCE: Federal Bureau of Investigation, *Crime in the United States 1994: Uniform Crime Report* (Washington, D.C.: U.S. Department of Justice, 1995), p. 7.

crimes. Second, they represent a large portion (33 percent) of persons arrested for larceny-theft, which accounts for a whopping 74 percent of all arrests for females. Addicted (not shown at Table 16-1) women are increasingly committing crimes of violence, up almost 8 percent over 1993) when compared to men, up less than 1/3 of a percent.[7] These figures clearly indicate the growing role of the female offender in the entire criminal justice system. As we note later, **preferential treatment** of women seems to be disappearing for those females arrested for nontraditional crimes (crimes of violence and crimes committed with one or more other female offenders). We may have to take a new look at the **"traditional" female crimes** as we continue to examine the "new" female offender of the late-1990s.

*P*rostitution: Old and New

The general increase in female criminality can also be seen as reflecting the changing patterns of criminal opportunity for women. It is interesting that arrests for prostitution, the crime Freda Adler calls "the oldest and newest profession,"[8] *decreased* –5.1 percent between 1993 and 1994. But the rate of decrease in prostitution among females under eighteen, which dropped over –67.4 percent between 1982 and 1991, dropped another –6.9 percent in 1994. (Arrests of males for similar crimes increased by 6.5 percent from 1993 to 1994.)[9] Whether this increase has to do with more jobs and better jobs for women, the growth of AIDS awareness, or a changing moral climate we leave for others to determine. We simply see it as a positive trend for females in that one area, but it may be offset by a trend for more violent crime by females.

The arrest figures for prostitution, however, are only the tip of the iceberg. Because prostitution is one of the so-called **"victimless" crimes**, and clients seldom complain because they would be implicating themselves, the number of arrests for prostitution usually reflects only cases of flagrant solicitation, rampant disease, or a local cleanup campaign.[10] Considerable folklore surrounds prostitution, most of it with no basis in fact. Those who profit from prostitution (almost never the prostitutes themselves) are not about to compile statistics or seek publicity. It is a business that thrives on sexual appetite, with the ultimate motive being simple profit.

Careers in prostitution range from the corner hooker to the jet-set courtesan, the main difference being the age, beauty, and price of the merchandise. The business of organized vice is not a simple question of boy meets girl; many levels of profit taking and payoff winnow down the prostitute's *nightly* earnings of, say, $350, to a *weekly* figure of less than $100. The pimp, the madam, the landlord, the crooked vice cop, and others all take their cuts. The real victims of this supposedly victimless crime are often the prostitutes themselves.

Other non–crime-index offenses for which females were arrested in 1994 are listed in Table 16-2. These high-volume crimes indicate a range of illegal behaviors, including driving under the influence (DUI), assaults, and drug abuse violations. In fact, if all the drug- and alcohol-related offenses were aggregated, they would account for 57 percent of the arrests of females under eighteen and 49 percent of the total females arrested for drug and alcohol-related crimes in 1994.[11] That is evidence of the marginality of females in American society,[12] a recurring point that many who study female criminals make in their explanations of causes of crime among females.[13]

TABLE 16.2

Types of Sentences Imposed by State Courts, Female Felons, 1992

Most Serious Conviction Offense	Total	Percent of Felons Sentenced to					
		Incarceration			Nonincarceration		
		Total	Prison	Jail	Total	Probation	Other
All offenses	100%	56%	30%	27%	44%	43%	1%
Violent offenses	100	69	42	27	31	31	1
Murder	100	92	84	8	8	8	0
Rape	100	78	42	36	22	22	0
Robbery	100	77	54	23	23	23	1
Aggravated assault	100	60	30	31	40	39	1
Other violent	100	66	29	37	34	33	–
Property offenses	100	50	27	23	50	49	2
Burglary	100	67	37	30	33	33	–
Larceny	100	53	27	26	47	46	2
Fraud	100	43	23	20	57	55	2
Drug offenses	100	61	31	30	39	38	1
Possession	100	58	27	31	42	41	1
Trafficking	100	64	34	30	36	36	
Weapons offenses	100	51	27	25	49	48	1
Other offenses	100	54	26	28	46	44	2

SOURCE: Patrick Longan and Robyn Cohen, *State Court Sentencing of Convicted Felons, 1992* (Washington, D.C.: U.S. Department of Justice, 1996), p. 18.

A Differential Justice System for Women?

The previous scarcity of research in the area of women's equality in general, and their role in the criminal justice system in particular, makes this area the current gold mine for researchers and writers.[14] It is unfortunate that much of the earlier literature was a warmed-over repetition of the old myths and inaccuracies of the 1940s and 1950s. In the rapidly changing 1970s, there began a knowledge explosion regarding female crime.

The first point at which the female offender comes into contact with the criminal justice system is the point of arrest. Although arrest may be a traumatic experience for the male offender, it has special problems for the female. It is estimated that 80 percent of the female offenders in America have dependent children at home and that a great percentage of those children have no one else to care for them.[15] Concern for the children and a tendency among officers to identify female offenders with their mothers or sisters cause arresting officers to be more discreet than they might be with a male in the same situation. A recognition of the need to provide more pretrial services for female offenders has prompted many communities to develop volunteer programs to assist with the women's problems at home. It is important to remember that the children of female offenders often become residents of juvenile institutions as a result of their mothers' actions. To the juveniles who are removed from the community and placed in what they perceive as a facility for other juveniles that have committed offenses, it becomes hard to accept that protection, not punishment, is the state's motivation (see Chapter 17).

An officer's reluctance to arrest for the traditional crimes that the female offender may commit is also the result of age-old customs, mores, and laws that have created great distinctions between men and women under apprehension.[16] Although police officers seldom hesitate to place a male offender "up against the wall" and to respond to force with equal force, they are often loath to do so with a female. Most police departments have strict rules and regulations regarding the apprehension, search, and detention of women. In most cases, a female officer or matron is assigned to detain women and conduct searches of their persons. The female offender is sometimes treated more like someone from a far-off planet rather than a person who has committed a criminal act.

The female offender seldom spends much time in detention before trial. Concern for the family and the lack of adequate female detention facilities or female personnel in the police department almost demand pretrial release for women.[17] Also, until quite recently, female offenders usually committed less serious offenses and could therefore be released on bail or on their own recognizance. In more recent years (1982 to 1994), women have been committing more serious crimes and, perhaps owing to the move to equalize punishments for co-defendants, have been receiving more severe sentences.

The view of the female offender's possible preferential treatment in the criminal justice system is not shared by all, however, as noted by Rita Simon:

> Others believe that judges are more punitive toward women. They are more likely to throw the book at the female defendant because they believe there is a greater discrepancy between her behavior and the behavior expected of women than there is between the behavior of the male defendant and the behavior expected of men. In other words, women defendants pay for the judges' belief that it is more in man's nature to commit crimes than it is in

FIRST FEDERAL INSTITUTION FOR WOMEN The first institution in the Federal Bureau of Prisons exclusively for women was the Federal Correctional Institution at Alderson, West Virginia, in 1925.

TABLE *16.3*

Arrests of Females for Type II (Non-Index) Crime, 1993–1994

Offense Charge	Total			Under Age Eighteen		
	1993	1994	Change	1993	1994	Change
Other assaults	160,820	178,284	+10.9%	37,950	43,612	+14.9%
Forgery and counterfeiting	28,472	31,444	+10.4	2,105	2,436	+15.7
Fraud	125,365	124,598	–.6	3,658	4,751	+29.9
Embezzlement	4,230	4,632	+9.5	243	282	+16.0
Stolen property; buying, receiving, possessing	16,026	17,216	+7.4	3,800	3,913	+3.0
Vandalism	29,687	31,911	+7.5	10,738	12,033	+12.1
Weapons; carrying, possessing, etc.	16,107	16,666	+3.5	3,941	4,062	+3.1
Prostitution and commercialized vice	55,478	52,652	–5.1	523	487	–6.9
Sex offenses (except forcible rape and prostitution)	7,289	6,738	–7.6	1,408	1,063	–24.5
Drug abuse violations	150,070	179,348	+19.5	9,924	14,898	+50.1
Gambling	2,029	2,284	+12.6	50	73	+46.0
Offenses against family and children	15,620	17,915	+14.7	1,216	1,373	+12.9
Driving under the influence	149,057	143,795	–3.5	1,310	1,407	+7.4
Liquor laws	72,744	78,276	+7.6	23,326	25,421	+9.0
Drunkenness	62,198	62,145	–.1	2,146	2,290	+6.7
Disorderly conduct	114,723	118,331	+3.1	25,411	30,274	+19.1
Vagrancy	2,921	4,371	+49.6	504	672	+33.3
All other offenses (except traffic)	465,638	527,354	+13.3	62,214	72,619	+16.7
Suspicion (not included in totals)	1,622	1,365	–15.8	221	297	+34.4
Curfew and loitering law violations	22,098	29,434	+33.2	22,098	29,434	+33.2
Runaways	81,400	86,706	+6.5	81,400	86,706	+6.5

SOURCE: Federal Bureau of Investigation, *Crime in the United States 1994: Uniform Crime Report* (Washington, D.C.: U.S. Department of Justice, 1995), p. 18.

woman's. Thus, when a judge is convinced that the woman before him has committed a crime, he is more likely to overact and punish her, not only for the specific offense but also for transgressing against his expectations of womanly behavior.

The existence of such statutes as the indeterminate sentence for women, or the sanctioning of a procedure whereby only convicted male defendants have their minimum sentences determined by a judge at an open hearing and in the presence of counsel, while the woman's minimum sentence is decided by a parole board in a closed session in which she is not represented by counsel, are cited as evidence of the unfair, punitive treatment that is accorded to women in the court.[18]

However, as women are arrested in greater numbers for crimes now committed mainly by men, they can expect the **paternalistic attitude of judges**—if such an attitude now exists—to diminish rapidly.[19]

The differential treatment accorded to women in many cases does not automatically mean better treatment or consideration. Moreover, as an alternative to differential treatment, the model of the male prison is sometimes copied, even to the point of ignoring the female inmates' obvious physical differences. At the other extreme, the best programs of differential treatment,[20] filled with compassionate understanding for the female residents, could serve as models for institutions housing either sex—or both:

> Built around multilevel and beautifully landscaped courtyards, the attractive buildings provide security without fences. Small housing units with pleasant living rooms provide space for normal interaction between presumably normal women. The expectation that the women will behave like human beings pervades the place. Education, recreation, and training areas are uncramped and well [designed]. Opportunity for interaction between staff and inmates is present everywhere.

> About 200 yards away from the other buildings are attractive apartments, each containing a living room, dining space, kitchen, two bedrooms, and a bath. Women approaching release live in them while working or attending school in the city. These apartments normally are out of bounds to staff except on invitation.[21]

This kind of model seems to reflect the relatively humane feeling toward the offender that continues to motivate the male-dominated criminal justice system to send very few women to prison.[22] It is true that men are also being filtered out of the correctional funnel in greater numbers, but it appears that women can be returned to society with less chance of further criminal activity that might endanger society.[23]

For those and other reasons, the female offender has traditionally received discretionary treatment by police and prosecutors, with only those women who

A solitary confinement section of a women's prison

—*PHOTO BY GALE ZUCKER, COURTESY OF STOCK BOSTON*

Computerized Mapping Service Offered by Ferguson Facility

Texas Correctional Industries has long provided technical services to government agencies through its records conversion facilities, but over the last year the Ferguson Mapping and Data Entry Facility has taken a giant step further into the Information Age by providing the service of Geographic Information Systems (GIS), a computerized mapping system, to various tax supported entities.

GIS is, basically, a system of converting the traditional forms of spatial data, such as paper maps, waterproof mylar maps, and aerial photos, to digital, or computerized, format and then tying a database of non-graphical information, or text, to the graphics of that computerized map, thereby creating "smart maps" with "intelligent graphics."

GIS is used by entities such as state agencies, county appraisal and water districts, municipalities, and universities for such purposes as regional planning, environmental studies, increasing the accuracy of appraisals, etc.

These entities' high demand for GIS service combined with its prohibitive cost led the Texas GIS Planning Council, in 1993, to recommend TDCJ's involvement.

Since entry into the field, the Ferguson facility has quickly established a name on the street for high quality, high volume GIS output at a fraction of the cost at which the same can be obtained from private industry, and has even gained favorable attention through national and European magazine articles.

The Mapping Facility's projects involve several technical processes. First, a customer's analog spatial data, or traditional forms of maps as described above, are scanned into the computer creating what's known as a "raster" image, which is simply a digital image which can be viewed on computer screen. Then working at one of 18 desktop computer equipped workstations, an inmate operator will trace over the raster image in a process known as vectorization or digitization. Next, using conventional data entry equipment, a database of information relating to the graphical features of the digitized map is entered into the computer. Upon completion, the project is output to magnetic tape, which the customer receives as the finished product.

The potential of GIS to enhance the productivity of projects such as large scale regional planning by allowing instant access to large quantities of information may be conveyed through the following relatively simple example.

If, say, the customer was a TDCJ unit maintenance department, they could supply the Ferguson Mapping Facility with blueprints of the unit's gas, water, and sewage lines, electrical schematics, etc. The Ferguson facility would scan the blueprints into computer, then trace over the images, denoting gas lines in yellow, water lines in green, etc., and then add text data. After receiving the finished product on magnetic tape, the maintenance department could, through computer access, click on what may have been designated as Level I and view only the gas lines, or click on Level II and view all the water lines, etc. Furthermore, the customer may click on the image of a specific gas or water valve and view text related to that valve, such as type of valve, date of installation, work order related information, etc. Hence the terms "smart map" and "intelligent graphics."

So far, customers to which the Ferguson Mapping and Data Entry Facility has provided service includes the Texas Department of Transportation, and the Williamson, Van Zandt, and Grayson Counties Appraisal Districts, among others. One of the more notable beneficiaries of the Mapping Facility's capabilities has been the nation of England which, after being unable to find an adequate GIS provider in Europe, contracted with TCI for the Ferguson Facility to provide environmental mapping.

Projects are pending with at least one other foreign nation, and with a Dallas-Ft. Worth area GIS consortium. Successful completion of these projects will solidify the Ferguson facility's position to provide service to other agencies.

TCI is on the ground floor of a massive conversion to GIS by the State of Texas. In preparation, the Ferguson facility is about to expand to three shifts employing a total of 150 inmates. Also a second Mapping Facility is tentatively planned.

Through its GIS program, TCI can provide valuable job skills to inmates, generate revenue to underwrite the cost of housing inmates, and provide this technology at a significant cost savings to tax supported entities. ∎

SOURCE: Marlyn Beckham and Neil Rayford, *Ferguson Records and GIS Services, Texas Correctional Industries.* (Texas Department of Criminal Justice, 1995.)

are considered particularly *hard cases* finally coming before a judge. It is also a fact that no politically minded prosecutor can enjoy bringing a mother with three small children to trial.[24] Thus, such trials seldom occur unless the case is both serious and airtight. As a result, cases against women are often released before trial, and the correctional funnel for them narrows sharply. Those women brought to court are still apt to receive consideration for probation, fines, and suspended sentences more often than men who commit comparable crimes. Finally, the few who are sentenced to prison are more likely to receive alternative dispositions.

As was noted earlier, despite the earlier preferential treatment of female offenders, the number of incarcerated females in the United States continues to rise. California alone held 15 percent of the incarcerated female offenders. If preferential treatment were not offered, the number of female prisoners in the nation could reach above 106,330 for the year 2000.

Why has the women's prison population increased so sharply? No one knows for certain, but some of the reasons given are that women are committing more crime and being arrested more often, and they are committing more serious crimes and are being sentenced more severely by judges. Other theories are that presentence investigators and the judiciary, influenced by the **women's liberation movement**, are less likely to give favorable sentencing considerations than they were in the past, that parole boards are using uniform sentencing guidelines that force female inmates to serve more time, and that women are getting their "just deserts" under the conservative backlash to treat all offenders more severely. Others argue that the war on drugs has dragged more female drug addicts into prisons than in the past. There are many theories, but not much data to support any one theory in particular.

WOMEN PRESIDENTS OF THE ACA

There have been five distinguished female presidents of the American Correctional Association:

Blanche LaDu, 1935
Martha Wheeler, 1972
Su Cunningham, 1986–1988
Helen Corruthers, 1990–1992
Bobbie Huskey, 1994–1996

The War on Drugs Creates Female Casualties, Too

As mentioned in Chapter 4, the war on drugs is a crime prevention strategy that rose in the late 1980s from politicians espousing a conservative ideology. It is predicated on protecting the moral fiber of the nation, and particularly American youth, by drying up drugs at their sources, interdicting drug traffic, increasing penalties for drug trafficking and possession, selectively incapacitating drug sellers and users, initiating asset seizure and forfeiture, and taking the profit out of drugs.

Three important effects have been the increase in the number of women (and men) sent to prison for drug possession and law violations, massive prison construction efforts, and increasing incarceration rates of minorities, particularly Hispanics and blacks dealing crack, the drug of choice among the minorities who are sometimes called the *underclass*. Notably absent is a reduction in drug availability, large amounts of interdicted drugs, a drop in drug use across the nation, or increased numbers of prevention and abuser treatment programs.

Billions of dollars have been spent in an effort that has led to widespread violence and corruption and has undermined governments throughout the world without achieving its goals of reducing crime and drug abuse. This war has incarcerated disproportionate numbers of minorities (particularly blacks) and spawned both a destructive fear of and hostility to police. The drug war hysteria has blocked medical research of drugs to prevent pain and blocked the development of programs to provide sterile needles and help prevent the spread of AIDS. The drug war has resulted in America now incarcerating more people per capita than any other country in the free world, including South Africa—even the police are put into a situation they cannot win.

There were more drug arrests of females in 1994 for drug offenses (including drug trafficking) than for *any single crime index category except larceny-theft*, an

Characteristics of Drug-Abusing Women Offenders

To gain a picture of the special needs of drug-abusing women offenders, information was taken from several sources covering women arrestees, women incarcerated in jails and prisons, women offenders diverted into community-based treatment instead of incarceration or as a condition of probation or parole, and women in publicly supported drug and treatment programs. Provided below are characteristics of these women:

- **Health problems.** Many drug-abusing women are physically or mentally ill. All drug users, and cocaine users in particular, are at increased risk for extreme weight loss, dehydration, digestive disorders, skin problems, dental problems, gynecological and venereal infections. tuberculosis, hepatitis B, hypertension, seizures, respiratory arrest, and cardiac failure.

- **Educational/vocational background.** Most of the women are unemployed or work at low-paying jobs. Most have not completed high school, have inadequate vocational skills, and lack many of the skills and knowledge needed to function productively in society.

- **Psychosocial problems.** Drug-addicted women tend to come from families with a high incidence of mental illness, suicide, alcohol or drug dependence, violence, or are victims of incest, rape, or physical or sexual abuse.

- **Responsibility for parenting.** Most drug-abusing women offenders are of child-bearing age, already have children, and are single mothers. Many of them receive little or no help from the children's father(s), lack supportive family and social networks, and have limited or no financial resources. Often their children become drug abusers themselves, thereby perpetuating both drug abuse and dysfunctional parenting across generations.

- **Drug use and treatment.** Most drug-abusing women offenders started abusing drugs and alcohol at an early age, and many used drugs, especially cocaine, on a daily basis prior to incarceration. In one survey of women in prison, 46 percent of respondents reported they had used drugs and/or alcohol at the time of their offense. Approximately 25 percent of adult women offenders have spent some time in a drug/alcohol treatment program which, however, has most likely been of limited duration and intensity.

- **Criminal justice and child protective services involvement.** A large percentage of drug-abusing women who seek treatment have had some involvement with the criminal justice system or with child protective services. One study reported that an estimated 60 to 80 percent of child abuse and neglect cases were from substance-abusing families.

- Although these characteristics have been found to typify the population of drug-abusing women offenders, they have different implications for programs. Individual women will differ in the manifestations and severity of these characteristics and attendant problems. Such diversity calls for an assessment of specific clients' needs and the provision of services designed to meet those needs. If a program lacks a well-developed assessment procedure, clients are less likely to receive appropriate services, such as treatment in a style matched to cultural identity and cognitive level and of adequate intensity and duration. ∎

SOURCE: Jean Wellisch, Michael Prendergast, and Douglas Anglin. "Drug-Abusing Women Offenders: Results of a National Survey," (Washington, D.C.: National Institute of Justice, 1994).

increase of 20 percent over one year, and a 50 percent increase for females under eighteen.[25] Since 1984, the number of adult female arrests for drug law violations has doubled, and the probability of imprisonment for those arrests has tripled. More than half of the increase of prisoners admitted to the states' prisons can be accounted for by drug offenses. If present trends continue, the nation will need to increase correctional prison staffs by over 62,000 officers in the next five years, as well as building 1,500 new prison beds *per week* nationwide.[26]

The plight of the woman behind jail or prison bars is often a difficult one. In terms of institutions, the male-oriented criminal justice system may totally ignore the special requirements of the female offender.[27] The nature of punishment for female offenders has come a long way from the time when they were thrown into the gaols as diversions for the incarcerated male felons, but more needs to be done before treatment of the female offender can be said to be an integrated part of corrections.

Women in Jail

Women have never been a large portion of the inmates of jails in the nation, but the war on drugs has contributed significantly to the number arrested and placed in jails and detention centers, as well as increased the proportion of all inmates who are female. In 1994, there were 48,879 female inmates in the jails in America. Those 48,879 females were more than 10 percent of the nation's *jail* inmates, up from 7 percent in 1983. That increase more than *tripled* (up 312 percent) the number of jailed inmates during this eleven-year period, and up 62 percent since 1988.[28]

The characteristics of female jail inmates are generally the same, except for drug-related crime increases, as those found in the 1989 survey of jails. More than half of the convicted inmates had used drugs in the month prior to the current offense that brought them to jail; almost 40 percent had used drugs daily. Some 39 percent of the female jail inmates had used cocaine or crack in the month before their current incarceration. About one in four convicted women in jail reported they had committed their current offense for money to buy drugs. Another one in five convicted female inmates reported being under the influence of alcohol at the time of their offense.

Other important demographic and criminal characteristics of females in jails included the following:

- About 13 percent of the female inmates were in jail for a violent offense, down from 21 percent in 1983.

- About half of the female inmates in 1989 who were convicted of a violent crime had victimized a female; a third had victimized a relative or intimate, and one in eight had victimized a minor.[29]

- Nearly one in three women were first-time offenders, compared to one in five men.

- Some 47 percent of women in local jails were on some criminal justice status (such as probation, parole, or pretrial release) when arrested for their current offense;

- More than two-thirds of the women in jail had children under the age of eighteen, and about half reported that their children were living with grandparents, but less than one in four said their children were living with the father.

- Broken homes were the obvious setting of their childhood, with some 40 percent reporting they had grown up in a single-parent household and 17 percent saying they had lived in a household without either parent.

- Almost a third of all women in jail had a parent or guardian who abused drugs or alcohol.

- More than four in every ten women in jail reported another family member, more frequently a brother or sister, had served time in jail or prison.

- Almost 44 percent reported they had been either sexually (37 percent) or physically abused (one in three), or both, at some time in their lives before their current incarceration.

- More than 65 percent of the female jail inmates were minority group members (50 percent black, 13 percent Hispanic, 2 percent other).

- Only 19 percent of the female jail inmates were currently married, although some 62 percent were at least twenty-five years of age.

This brief overview of female jail inmates suggests that they generally are not drawn from mainstream America; come from deprived and unstable backgrounds; have been extensively abused over time; and face significant employment, financial, psychological, emotional, and social barriers in their efforts to live in and seek reintegration into their local communities.[30] Most of these jail inmates are not dangerous but need assistance in existence and living. Incarceration in jail or prison may achieve punishment; societal goals would probably be better achieved if these high-problem female offenders were sentenced to community alternatives and received extensive treatment and service delivery. This is particularly true of **abused women** who enter the correctional system.[31]

Women in Prison

Female *prison* inmates totaled 56,245 (with 5,415 holdbacks for lack of beds) at year-end 1994, increasing at a faster rate during 1993 than did male inmates. Overall, the rate of growth for female prison inmates exceeded that for males for each of the last eleven years. From 1983 to 1994, the male population increased by 210 percent, and the female population gained by 312 percent. The rate of incarceration for women (45 per 100,000 females in the nation) was only one-eighth the rate for sentenced males (378 per 100,000 males in the nation). Despite the fact that the female prisoner population growth outpaced that of males, females only comprise about 6 percent of the imprisoned offenders.[32]

Changes in Female Inmates

The number is growing, and the characteristics of women prison inmates are changing rapidly over time. The racial composition of female prison inmates is shown in Table 16-4. While the proportion of Hispanic inmates has increased 20 percent since 1979, the modal female prisoner continues to be black, non-Hispanic, age twenty-five to thirty-four, never married, with some high school education, and not employed at the time of arrest. She has been likely sentenced for a nonviolent crime and is a recidivist (either been sentenced to probation or previously incarcerated as a juvenile or adult).

A huge increase has occurred in the percentage of women admitted to prison for drug offenses as well. A third of all female inmates reported they were under

TABLE *16.4*

Composition of Female Prisoners in 1994*

Group	Number	Percentage of Total
White	19,896	35.9%
Black	27,442	49.5
Hispanic	6,889	12.5
Other	1,186	2.1
Totals**	55,413	100.0%

*Excludes 5,415 female offenders pending in county jails.
**Some jurisdictions did not report genders.
SOURCE: American Correctional Association, *ACA Directory, 1996* (Lanham, Md. ACA, 1996), p. xxvi.

the influence of a drug at the time of their offenses. About 40 percent said they were using drugs daily in the month before their offenses, and 24 percent reported daily use of a major drug such as cocaine, heroin, methadone, LSD, or PCP. Overall, just under half of the women in prison (46 percent) had been using drugs or alcohol or both at the time the imprisonment offense occurred. An estimated 72 percent of the women in state prisons had used drugs at some time in their lives prior to admission, in contrast to 80 percent of the men. Almost one-third of the women inmates had participated in a drug treatment program at some point in their lives. Federal confinement facilities reported they could provide drug treatment for an estimated 7,800 inmates, as compared with 114,000 at state facilities.[33] Drug treatment programs within prison facilities[34] are inadequate for the number of inmates troubled by drug and alcohol abuse.

Over four in ten female prisoners reported they had been either physically or sexually abused some times in their lives; about half of these said the sexual abuse occurred before age eighteen. About half the women serving time for a violent offense had been abused and were more likely to be serving time for violence against a relative or intimate. Women who had not been abused were far less likely to have been convicted of a crime of violence.

Issues and Findings: Drug-Abusing Women Offenders

DISCUSSED IN THIS BRIEF
A national survey in 1992–1993 of drug abuse treatment programs for women offenders was funded by NIJ. The survey focused on issues of assessing drug-abusing women offenders' needs and services in community and custodial treatment programs.

KEY ISSUES
Drug-abusing women offenders constitute one of the fastest growing segments within the criminal justice system. Little is known regarding their specific needs since very few drug-abusing women offenders receive treatment in custody or in the community, and little is known about how treatment programs assess needs and conduct treatment services.

KEY FINDINGS
Highlights of survey results include:

- More treatment programs are available than in the past, but they have not reduced the difference between those women who need and those who receive drug treatment services.

- Many programs do not assess the multiple problems of the drug-abusing women offender population and fail to address them with suitable services.

- Treatment provided by the programs surveyed is usually limited in intensity and duration.

- Services offered for women drug abusers are mostly found in women-only programs rather than both-sex pro-

grams. Implications of these findings for changes in policy and practice include:

- More coordinated efforts among Federal, State, and local agencies are needed to research and implement improved treatment and related services for drug-abusing women offenders.

- More programs that provide continuing support for women are needed to enable a transition from treatment to independent living in the community; such support includes training in personal empowerment, as well as vocational training.

- More family services are needed, especially since few programs provide accommodations for infants and children; this deters drug-abusing women offenders from entering and continuing treatment.

TARGET AUDIENCE
Local, State, and Federal legislators and agencies; policymakers; drug treatment program staff; law enforcement officials; community leaders; health care organizations; child protective services constitute the audience. ▪

SOURCE: Jean Wellisch, Michael Prendergast, and Douglas Anglin. "Drug-Abusing Women Offenders: Results of a National Survey." (Washington, D.C.: National Institute of Justice, 1994).

More than 75 percent of the female prisoners were mothers, and two in three had children under age eighteen. More than 80 percent of their children under age eighteen were reported as living with a relative, usually the maternal grandmoth-er. For male prison inmates, almost 90 percent of their children under age eigh-teen are living with the children's mothers.

Women inmates are housed in a variety of facilities. About half of these facil-ities are penal institutions, known by a variety of names: prisons, reformatories, penitentiaries, correctional facilities, and prison camps. Most are housed in mini-mum to low security units.

This profile of the imprisoned female inmate hardly reflects a dangerous offender for whom incarceration in prison is required. Instead, such offenders could probably be handled more effectively, less expensively, and more humanely in alternatives to prison. Unfortunately, this situation most likely reflects probable national practice throughout the country for the next decade.

Women's Prisons

The 1993 American Correctional Association's directory lists only 26 training schools and 127 coed programs for female juvenile delinquents and 75 institu-tions for women and 64 coeducational facilities in that year.[35] But the administra-tion of these women's prisons has changed greatly in recent years. In 1966, only 10 of the nation's institutions for women were headed by female correctional administrators. The 1993 directory showed that 237 of the 1,653 correctional administrators of institutions were females.[36] As a matter of fact, the president of the prestigious American Correctional Association from 1994 to 1996 was the fifth president female of that organization.[37]

Because the conditions in the women's institutions vary greatly, it would be fruitless to attempt to describe them individually. They are not all horror stories; it is sufficient to state that the best and the worst aspects of the male institution are also in evidence in the women's prison, the only major differences being the variations based on the traits unique to each sex and the more numerous and var-ied training and education programs available to males.

Special Problems of Incarcerated Females

Among the many problems women face when in prison are pregnancy, loss of fam-ily ties, and aging behind the walls. We start this discussion with the pregnant inmate entering prison.

Earlier studies suggest that one in four adult women entering prison either was pregnant or had given birth to an infant within the previous twelve months.[38] Medical care, resources, and programs, while varying across institutions, are thought to be inadequate for such inmates. A primary explanation for the lack of programs has been the relatively small size of the female offender population and the expense involved in special programming for the small segment of prisoners that female inmates represent. The size argument, however valid in past decades, does not hold in current correctional scenes. While female inmates remain a small portion of the total prison populations, their numbers have increased to the point where new policies are needed.

Pregnant inmates need special diets, lighter work assignments, supportive programs, and a less stressful environment. Programs and resources are needed for miscarriages, premature birth, and deliveries. Until recently,[39] the major options were abortion, placing children with relatives, putting the children up for adoption, or foster care. Not only do such policy options pose severe emotional anguish and problems for mothers, separation of the newborn child from the mother can create severe emotional and developmental problems for the infant. Prisons should routinely provide counseling and prenatal care for pregnant inmates as well as full-time medical professionals (nurses, midwives, and physicians) during the term of pregnancy. Additional programs would include prenatal and postnatal counseling, outplacement assistance and counseling,[40] workload adjustments, and separate living quarters. Other family service programs that should be made available for all female inmates include classes in child development and parenting, infant mental health and family counseling, and stress management. While such programs have been introduced in a minority of prisons over time, few prisons are believed to have adequate policies and services. For pregnant offenders, perhaps the ideal setting might be the halfway house.

In addition, research on female inmates document that women are more family oriented than are male inmates and that as many as 80 percent of imprisoned women are mothers.[41] Evidence of the significance children play in the life of female inmates can be seen in pictures displayed on desks or taped behind prison identification badges, articles in prison newspapers, the frequency with which children are discussed, and general concern about the well-being of their individual children.[42] Many women feel their families and friends have abandoned them when they are sent to prison, just when their needs for support and friendship are highest and inmates are at the lowest point of their lives: ashamed, incarcerated, lonely, depressed, guilt-ridden, acutely worried about their children, scared, and with tarnished self-esteem. Family members are particularly central at this time, since they can care for the inmate's children and bring them to visit, send money and special foods, write and call, guard their property, and take up their

Female inmates learn useful skills in modern prisons

—PHOTO BY GALE ZUCKER, COURTESY OF STOCK BOSTON

cause if mistreated by institutional staff. Thus visiting is of crucial importance to female inmates who sense if not know that their role as mother is weak and their incarceration and absence can lead to a child's behavioral problems (obsessive crying, deterioration in relations with peers and school work, withdrawal from relatives and reality, and so on).

Although failure of relatives to visit is a great hardship for most incarcerated mothers, often it results more from physical and institutional barriers than lack of care and concern of relatives. Many institutions are located far away from the urban centers from which most female inmates originate, and travel and related expenses are hurdles to be overcome. Many relatives do not own cars and must depend on the kindness of neighbors for travel. Other discouraging factors include having to submit to searches before visiting, being too poor to afford overnight accommodations, or having work schedules too tight to permit frequent or lengthy visits. Some institutions are not "visitor friendly," with visits limited in frequency to only once a month, providing only one large room for visitations of all families, having no children's toys or playground, and presenting an unfriendly and hostile setting. Better managed institutions have children's play areas and equipment; allow conjugal and family visits; and provide accommodations for mothers to plan, cook for, and feed their children in separate visiting rooms and trailers. Weekend passes, home visits, home furloughs, halfway house placements, and frequent visiting privileges not only ease parenting problems, they also lessen the probability that the children will become innocent victims. Many institutions need to establish policies that encourage **family cohesion** and strengthen ties for the mother when she is eventually released.

The third major problem is aging in prison. The graying of America is reflected in prison populations, as seen in Table 16-5. This is particularly a problem with the older female inmate undergoing social, psychological, emotional, and physical changes within the institutional walls. Women in America tend to live longer than men (about seven or eight years) and make up about 60 percent of older Americans. In prison, they are "forgotten" inmates and have been little studied or recognized. Incarceration encourages dependency and passivity, factors that tend to shorten life expectancy under any circumstance. Visual, physical, and muscular impairments pose particular problems for elderly female inmates. Not only will staff have to be specifically trained and programs individualized, but also gerontology consultants and medical programs will be required that address issues such as dealing with menopause; breast cancer; hysterectomies; cataracts; and hip, spine, and back impairments. As the elderly female inmates swell in numbers, physical plants will need to be retrofitted, including color coding of floors and buildings, adding wall handrails and wheelchair ramps, widening door frames and entries, providing rest areas for more challenged inmates, and revamping space to include nursing and convalescent rooms and services. Special diets, medications, nursing patterns, and physical therapy will need to be initiated and expanded. It is clear a correctional crisis is in the making and that prisons are not conducive to caring for the elderly (age sixty-five and over), aged (age seventy-five plus), or very old (age eighty-five and over). Alternative sentencing, timely and compassionate release, and community correctional centers are more realistic options for those who pose no threat to the community or self. Correctional action now may avoid costly programming and extensive legal issues and lawsuits in the decades to come. Deliberate indifference to medical need has been declared a violation of constitutionally guaranteed rights (Eighth Amendment).[43]

TABLE 16.5

Inmate Population Over Age Fifty-five, 1988–1994

	Inmates		
Comparison Years	Males	Females	Percentage Gain
1988/1987	13,955	511	5
1990/1989	17,244	709	24
1992/1991	21,564	875	25
1994/1993	25,832	1,141	20
Change	+85%	+123%	

SOURCE: American Correctional Association, *ACA Directory, 1996* (Lanham, MD: American Correctional Association, 1996), p. xxxii.

The Co-correctional Institution

The **single-sex experience** and long-term deprivation of heterosexual outlets creates the same kinds of problems in female institutions that are found in male prisons. The recommendations for coeducational institutions may seem extreme to the uninitiated, but the leavening effect of a system that allows at least nonsexual social contact in daily activity with members of the opposite sex is considerable. Excessive administrative concern about overt signs of friendship as indicative of possible homosexual activity conflicts with many standard practices for women outside the walls. If two males were observed holding hands as they walked down the street, they would be suspected of deviant behavior. That same behavior, though not considered strange for women (and particularly girls) on the outside, is viewed with great suspicion inside the walls, for girls and women alike. The situation is graphically described by an inmate:

> It's tough to be natural. The thing that most of us are trying to accomplish here, we're trying to get our minds at a point to where we can handle whatever comes our way, to get our emotions balanced, to maybe straighten up our way of thinking. You know, it just makes it hard when you're trying to be a natural person—to react to things normally—when the staff won't let you be normal—when you do a normal thing that being a woman makes it normal, and then have them say no, you can't do that because if you do, that's personal contact and that's homosexuality. So there's our mental hassle.

> I know that when women are thrown together without men or without the companionship of men it makes it pretty rough on them—women being the emotional people that they are. They have to have a certain amount of affection and close companionship. You know, a woman, if she's with a man she'll put her hand on him or maybe she'll reach up and touch him. This is something that a woman does naturally without thinking, and so if a woman has a good friend, or an affair, she does the same thing because this is her nature. The thing of it is—like I have a friend at the cottage—neither one of us have ever played. We're never gonna play. And if somebody tried to force us into it, we couldn't, wouldn't, or what have you. But being a woman and after being here for quite a while, we put our arms around each other, we don't think there's anything the matter with it, because there's nothing there—it's

a friendship. We're walking down the hall, our records are both spotless, she's a council girl, I'm Minimum A [minimum custody classification]. I've never had anything on my record that was bad and my god, the supervisor comes out and says, "Now, now girls, you know we don't allow that sort of thing here." And we look at her and say, "What sort of thing?" "This personal contact." And yet this same supervisor, we saw her up at the corner putting her arm around another supervisor the same way we were doing. So this is where part of our mental hassle comes in.[44]

The redefinition of the natural acts just described into something considered evil and proscribed is another reason that institutionalization is so crippling to the long-term female prisoner. As inmates, male or female, learn that simple signs of friendship are prohibited, they learn to repress their impulses toward interpersonal warmth when they get out. The kind of behavior that makes them acceptable on the inside makes them appear *hard case* (unfeeling, unresponsive) on the outside. In the male this kind of coldness can be viewed as "tough" or "macho," but is sometimes considered unattractive.

Very few studies have been conducted on the homosexuality of female prisoners. A lot of conjecture is found in the literature, but true scientific research is rare. Even the monumental effort to compile statistics on female offenders in Sheldon and Eleanor Glueck's *500 Delinquent Women*[45] did not consider homosexuality, but gender and sex role research is increasing.[46]

The demands of institutional management make it difficult to prevent homosexual activity. There are never enough personnel to watch all of the inmates, and so lovers get together despite the staff's efforts. In many institutions the staff adopts the attitude of "looking the other way" in regard to the female inmates' sexual activity. (The same is true in many men's institutions; see Chapter 15.) It is possible homosexuality and homosociality is even more prevalent in the women's institutions than it is in men's, because a high percentage of the inmates have been so misused by men[47] that they have already turned to other females to fulfill their emotional needs on the outside. It is also quite possible that the impact of imprisonment is significantly different for women, tending to encourage a homosexual response. Women appear more likely to view arrest, jailing, the court trial, and commitment to prison in highly personal terms. This personalized reaction could

A drafting training program provides marketable skills at a female institution

—COURTESY OF WASHINGTON STATE DEPARTMENT OF CORRECTIONS

Girl Scouts Beyond Bars

Children of prison inmates are the hidden victims of their parents' crimes. Like children of divorced or deceased parents, they often show signs of distress caused by the lack of a stable home life and parental separation, such as depression, aggression, poor school performance, and truancy. Many times they also follow their parents' criminal behavior patterns. To keep mothers and daughters connected and to enhance parenting skills, Girl Scouts Beyond Bars involves mothers in their daughters' lives through a unique partnership between a youth services organization and state and local corrections departments.

Girl Scouts Beyond Bars programs have been implemented in the following states:

MARYLAND. In 1992 the pilot program began at the Maryland Correctional Institution for Women. More than 30 girls now visit their mothers two Saturdays each month. On alternate Saturdays, they attend meetings at a community church, just as girls in other troops would. Before the Girl Scout program started, many of these girls rarely visited their incarcerated mothers.

FLORIDA. Its first program started at the Jefferson Correctional Institution near Tallahassee in early 1994, and a second program soon followed in Fort Lauderdale. The Florida Department of Corrections hopes to expand the program to correctional facilities throughout the state. The program includes formal parenting instruction and transitional services for the mothers and monitoring of the children's school performance, and collaboration with mental health care providers.

OHIO. The Seal of Ohio Girl Scout Council launched the first program in a prerelease center, the Franklin Pre-Release Center in Columbus. When the Girl Scout council expanded the program to the Ohio Reformatory for Women in 1994, Ohio became the first to connect the inprison program with the transition to home.

ARIZONA. Maricopa County (Phoenix) is the first jail site in the country to form a Girl Scouts Beyond Bars partnership. Parents Anonymous and Big Brothers/Big Sisters have also joined the effort.

Girl Scout councils in four other states have also begun Girl Scouts Beyond Bars programs with their corrections partners. While the partnership has demonstrated its ability to increase mother-daughter visitation time, the long-term effect of breaking the cycle of criminal behavior will require a more comprehensive approach on the part of the correctional institution, the Girl Scout council, and the mothers involved.

The program, however, may be used as a model to involve more youth service organizations in crime prevention. Partnerships should include many community service organizations that can provide the range of support services for incarcerated parents and their children to stop negative social behaviors and to break intergenerational cycles of involvement in crime. ∎

SOURCE: Marilyn C. Moses. "Keeping Incarcerated Mothers and Their Daughters Together: Girl Scouts Beyond Bars." *Program Focus* (Washington, D.C.: National Institute of Justice, 1994), p. 2.

---

harden antisocial attitudes and lead to further illegal behavior. One study has identified three **psychological deprivations** that might contribute to homosexual behavior:

1. Affection starvation and need for understanding
2. Isolation from previous symbiotic interpersonal relations
3. Need for continued intimate relationships with a person.[48]

It would be hard to imagine an incarcerated felon (male or female) who does not suffer those deprivations to some degree.

The coeducational prison is a very new development in corrections. The first two were opened in 1971, in the Federal Bureau of Prisons system; by 1993, coed adult state and federal facilities totaled fifty-four. [49]

J. O. Smykla defined adult co-corrections as adult institutions, the major purpose of which is the institutional confinement of felons. Each is managed by one institutional administration and has regular programs or areas in which female and male inmates have daily opportunities for interaction.[50]

The general concept of co-correctional institutions is expected:

1. To reduce the dehumanizing and destructive aspects of confinement by allowing continuity or resumption of heterosexual relationships;

2. To reduce the institutional control problems through the weakening of disruptive homosexual systems, reduction of predatory homosexual activity, lessening of assaultive behavior, and the diversion of inmate interests and activities;

3. To protect inmates likely to be involved in "trouble" were they in a same-sex institution;

4. To provide an additional tool for creating a more normal, less institutionalized atmosphere;

5. To cushion the shock of adjustment for releasees by reducing the number and intensity of adjustments to be made;

6. To realize economies of scale in terms of more efficient utilization of available space, staff, and programs;

7. To provide relief of immediate or anticipated overcrowding, sometimes of emergency proportions;

8. To reduce the need for civilian labor, by provision of both light and heavy inmate work forces;

9. To increase diversification and flexibility of program offerings, and equal access for males and females;

10. To expand treatment potentials for working with inmates having "sexual problems," and development of positive heterosexual relationships and coping skills;

11. To provide relief of immediate or anticipated legal pressures to provide equal access to programs and services to both sexes; and

12. To expand career opportunities for women, previously often "boxed into" the single state women's institutions, as co-correctional staff.[51]

The question of whether those objectives have been met cannot yet be answered, primarily because evaluations of their effectiveness continue to be weak at best. The recidivism research studies to date, however, indicate probable success.[52]

Intermediate Punishments for Females

Our review of the problems posed by female offenders as well as the problems female inmates face due to incarceration suggests that most female offenders pose little danger to public safety, that substance abuse underlies much of their criminal behavior, and that much damage to inmates and their families may be done through incarcerating women whose basic problem is alcohol and/or drug abuse.

Institutions for women are not known for the long-term effectiveness of their "inside the walls" treatment programs, which tend to be limited in number and to occur in an artificial environment that stresses more than rehabilitates, that impedes more than helps. What is needed is a more reasonable public safety-oriented program that speaks to the underlying problems that have led to criminal behavior and incarceration. There are, of course, the intermediate punishments discussed in more detail in the chapters on probation and parole (Chapters 10 and 13): house arrest, restitution, community service, electronic monitoring, community-based residences, intensive supervised probation, and substance abuse treatment programs in the community. Such programs have long been recommended, and were reiterated by the Alliance of Non-Governmental Organizations of Crime Prevention and Criminal Justice in 1987.[53]

Thus, we offer two prescriptions for handling female offenders. First, because female offenders seldom pose much threat to public safety, they should be handled in a communitywide and coordinated correctional system with graduated degrees of supervision in the community, including the intermediate punishments just listed.[54] Tourniquet sentencing may be an adjunct to that effort.

Second, if it becomes necessary to incarcerate female offenders because they pose an unacceptable degree of danger to the community, they should be located in environments that permit coeducational corrections. They should keep their children with them, either in the prison dormitories, in separate rooms, or outside but adjacent to the prison so the children can benefit from community activities as well as continued bonding with their mothers. Female offenders should have maximum contact with the outside world, including more frequent visitation privileges, uncensored mail, home visitations, family (conjugal) visits, and home furloughs. Prerelease programs should be mandatory for all incarcerated female offenders, and such programming should include detailed information on community options and programs for continued treatment of drug and alcohol abuse problems, a reasonable condition related to a correctional goal and one that parole boards could impose and require.

Further examination, too, is needed regarding the approximately twenty-four out of every twenty-five convicted female offenders who are not imprisoned. The diversion model we identified with the non-incarcerated female offenders may well be a model for the rest of the criminal justice system.

Summary

This review of the rising role of the female offender on the correctional scene reveals the overuse of imprisonment as a correctional alternative in sentencing. This policy does not reflect contemporary correctional thought or recommended practice.

The philosophy of the reintegration model is to handle as many causes of criminal behavior as possible in the environment in which it arises—that is, in the local community. Sentencing low-danger, low-risk female offenders to prisons run by state authorities does little to deal with the causes that have contributed to the criminal events that bring the female offender before a sentencing court. Indeed, imprisonment itself is likely to lessen the ability of the female offender to function when released on parole, as imprisonment ruptures familial, economic, social, and parental ties. Separation from children due to incarceration is a major problem returning mothers face.

Local communities and counties, working in conjunction with volunteer and professional organizations (such as the National Council on Crime and Delinquency, the John Howard Society, and the National Center on Institutions and Alternatives), should develop and maintain a coordinated community corrections program that allows the female offender to remain in the local community

Women and Crime Fighting

One of the more overlooked facts about the criminal justice system is that women suffer significantly from the failings of crime-fighting policy. Though men dominate prison populations in raw numbers, women are the fastest-growing category of prisoners nationwide. In the 1980s, taxpayers financed the construction of thirty-four prisons for women, compared to only seven in the 1960s. In a 1990 survey, the American Correctional Association found that nearly half of the jurisdictions nationwide were planning to build additional jails for women. Women offenders have been affected harshly by changes in sentencing laws, by the impact of the war on drugs, and by laws that allow for the termination of child custody if parents are imprisoned.

The imbalances of our crime-fighting policies are even more critical to women. None of our current strategies have stemmed the single greatest threat to the safety of women: domestic violence. The Federal Centers for Disease Control reports that more women seek treatment in hospitals for injuries from domestic violence than from all muggings, car accidents, and rapes *combined*. ∎

SOURCE: Steven R. Donziger, (ed.), *The Real War on Crime* (New York: HarperCollins, 1996), p. 146.

and supports the process of reintegrating offenders by involvement with local agencies.[55] Reintegration is the direction of the future for female offenders.

Now that we have examined two kinds of clients that are sent on different paths from the jail environment, we shall move on to a more controversial problem—the juveniles and what do with them in a society that has grown alarmed over and hardened to the violence on the street that makes headlines. How we have dealt, are dealing, and should deal with juvenile criminals are the questions for the next chapter.

Review Questions

1. What are the major crimes for which women are convicted? Explain why.
2. What are some reasons women have been treated so differently in the correctional system?
3. What impact does incarceration have on "mothering" of children?
4. Develop a model for handling the female offender that would have differing degrees of social control and offer female criminals an opportunity to stop criminal activity.
5. Describe the typical female inmate.
6. Identify three groups of special-problem female offenders and their specific needs.
7. Why did most correctional innovations begin in women's prisons?

Words to Remember

arrests by gender	careers in prostitution	pregnant inmates
preferential treatment	paternalistic attitude of judges	family cohesion
"traditional" female crimes	women's liberation movement	single-sex experience
"victimless" crimes	abused women	psychological deprivations

Endnotes

1. Allen Beck and G. Gilliard, *Prisoners in 1994* (Washington, D.C.: Bureau of Justice Statistics Bulletin, 1995), p. 5.

2. Ibid., p. 6.

3. Ibid., p. 1.

4. Ibid. *(calculated from)*

5. Ibid., p. 6.

6. Federal Bureau of Investigation, *Crime in the United States 1994: Uniform Crime Reports* (Washington, D.C.: U.S. Department of Justice, November 1995), p. 7.

7. Ibid.

8. Freda Adler, *Sisters in Crime* (New York: McGraw-Hill, 1975).

9. Federal Bureau of Investigation, *Crime in the United States 1994*, p. 7

10. David Langum, *Crossing Over the Line: Legislating Morality and the Mann Act* (Chicago: The University of Chicago Press, 1994), and Catherine Beason and Roger Matthews, "Street Prostitution: Ten Facts in Search of a Policy," *International Journal of the Sociology of Law* 23:4 (1995): 395–415. See also Richard Tewksbury, "Cruising for Sex in Public Places," *Deviant Behavior* 17:1 (1996): 1–19.

11. Federal Bureau of Investigation, *Crime in the United States 1994*, p. 7.

12. See Jean Harris, *They Always Call Us 'Ladies': Stories from Prison* (New York: Scribners, 1988). See Lindsay Hayes et al., *The Female Offender in Delaware: Population Analysis and Assessment* (Alexandria, VA: National Center on Institutions and Alternatives, 1989), and Center for Women Policy Studies, *Violence Against Women as Bias Motivated Hate Crime* (Washington, D.C.: Center for Women Policy Studies, 1991).

13. Janet Rifkin, "Mediation in the Justice System: A Paradox for Women," *Women and Criminal Justice* 1 (1989): 41–54, and Henry Brownstein, Barry Spunt, and Susan Crimmins, "Women Who Kill in Drug Market Situations," *Justice Quarterly* 12:3 (1995): 473–498.

14. See Sally Simpson, "Feminist Theory, Crime and Justice," *Criminology* 27 (1989): 605–631, and the excellent work by Kathleen Daly, "Gender and Varieties of White-Collar Crime," *Criminology* 27 (1989): 769–793. See also Barry Flowers, *Female Crime, Criminals, and Cellmates* (Jefferson, NC: McFarland, 1995).

15. See Elaine DeCostanzo and Helen Scholes, "Women Behind Bars: Their Numbers Increase," *Corrections Today* 50 (June 1988): 104–108. See also Olga Kropova, "Life Behind Bars: The Soviet Experience," *Corrections Today* 51 (July 1990): 133–137; George Kiser, "Female Inmates and Their Families," *Federal Probation* 55:3 (1991): 56–63; and Marilyn Moses, "Girl Scouts Behind Bars: A Synergistic Solution for Children of Incarcerated Parents," *Corrections Today* 57:7 (1995): 124–126, 143.

16. Marvin Krohn, James Curry, and Shirley Nelson-Kilger, "Is Chivalry Dead? An Analysis of Changes in Police Dispositions of Males and Females," *Criminology* 21 (1983): 228–244. See also Anne Edwards, "Sex/Gender, Sexism and Criminal Justice: Some Theoretical Considerations," *International Journal of Sociology of the Law* 17 (1989): 165–184. For a contrasting view, see William Reese and Russell Curtis, "Paternalism and the Female Status Offender: Remanding the Juvenile Justice Double Standard for Desexualization," *Social Science Journal* 28:1 (1991): 63–83. For female offenders committing crimes of violence, such as assault and robbery, there is little contemporary evidence of preferential treatment. See Larry Mays and Mary Stohr, "The Characteristics and Attitudes of Staff in Exclusively Women's Jails," paper presented at the annual meeting of the Academy of Criminal Justice Sciences, Kansas City, March 18, 1993.

17. For information on jailed women, see Tracy Snell, *Women in Jail 1989* (Washington, D.C.: U.S. Department of Justice, 1992). For data on pretrial release, see Brian Reaves, *Pretrial Release of Felony Defendants, 1990* (Washington, D.C.: U.S. Department of Justice, 1994).

18. Rita Simon, *The Contemporary Woman and Crime* (Washington, D.C.: U.S. Department of Health, Education and Welfare, 1976), p. 50.

19. B. Farnsworth and R. Teske, "Gender Differences in Felony Court Processing," *Women and Criminal Justice* 6:2 (1995): 23–44.

20. Faye Sultan and Gary Long, "Treatment of Sexually/Physically Abused Female Inmates: Evaluation of an Intensive Short-Term Intervention Program," *Journal of Offender Counseling, Services and Rehabilitation* 12 (1988): 131–143. See also Charlotte Arnold, "The Program for Female Offenders, Inc.—A Community Corrections Answer to Jail Crowding," *American Jails* 5:6 (1992): 36–40.

21. National Advisory Commission on Criminal Justice Standards and Goals, *Corrections* (Washington, D.C.: U.S. Department of Justice, 1976), p. 346. This was a description of the Women's Treatment Center, Purdy, Washington.

22. Supreme Judicial Court of Massachusetts, *Gender Bias of the Court System in Massachusetts* (Boston: Supreme Judicial Court of Massachusetts, 1989).

23. Immarigeon and Chesney-Lind argue that the current level of incarceration of female offenders in the United States is disproportionate to the need to protect the general public. Criminal sanctions should be based on the least restrictive alternative consistent with public safety. Russ Immarigeon and Meda Chesney-Lind, *Women's Prisons: Overcrowded and Overused* (San Francisco: National Council on Crime and Delinquency, 1992). See also Steven Donziger, *The Real War on Crime* (New York: HarperCollins, 1995), especially pp. 146–158.

24. For a statement of the importance of child-parent bonds, see Creasie Finney Hairston and Peg McCartt Hess, "Family Ties: Maintaining Child-Parent Bonds Is Important," *Corrections Today* 51 (April 1989): 102–106. See also Robert Sampson, "Family Management and Child Development: Insights from Social Disorganization Theory," in Joan McCord, ed., *Advances in Criminological Theory* (Brunswick, NJ: Transaction, 1992), pp. 95–114, and Robert Sweet, "Strengthening Our Families, Fortifying Our Nation," *Juvenile and Family Court Journal* 42:3 (1991): 1–11.

25. Federal Bureau of Investigation, *Crime in the United States 1994* (Washington, D.C.: U.S. Department of Justice, November 1995), p. 226

26. Beck and Gilliard, *Prisoners in 1994*, p. 5.

27. Nicole Hahn Rafter, "Equality or Difference?" *Federal Prison Journal* 3:1 (1991): 16–19.

28. Beck and Gilliard, *Prisoners in 1994*, p. 3, 5.

29. Tracy Snell, *Women in Jail 1989* (Washington, D.C.: U.S. Department of Justice, 1992), pp. 1–11.

30. Virginia McCoy, J. Inciardi, and Lisa Metch, "Women, Crack and Crime," *Contemporary Drug Issues* 22:3 (1995): 435–451.

31. See Catherine Ingram-Fogel, "Health Problems and Needs of Incarcerated Women," *Journal of Prison and Jail Health* 10:1 (1991): 43–57; Sue Osthoff, Leigh Dingerson, Robert David, et al., "Focus on Abused Women and the Correctional System," *Response to Victimization of Women and Children* 14:79 (1991): 2–23; and Thomas Tiberia, "Helping Correctional Officers Recognize and Interact with Handicapped Offenders," *American Jails* 6:1 (1992): 31–34.

32. Beck and Gilliard, *Prisoners in 1994*, p. 3.

33. Carole Wolf-Harlow, *Drug Enforcement and Treatment in Prisons* (Washington, D.C.: U.S. Department of Justice, 1992), p. 1.

34. L.I.S., Inc., *Profiles of Correctional Substance Abuse Treatment Programs* (Longmont, CO: National Institute of Correction, 1994).

35. American Correctional Association, *ACA Directory 1993* (Laurel, MD: American Correctional Association, 1993), p. xvii.

36. Ibid., p. xlvi.

37. These were Blanche La Du, Martha Wheeler, Su Cunningham, Helen Corruthers, and Bobbie Huskey. See Joann Morton, "The Agency of Women: Women and the ACA," *Corrections Today* 57:5 (1995): 74–76, 78, 80, 82, 84.

38. George Church, "The View from Behind Bars," *Time,* September 22, 1990, pp. 20–22.

39. John Wooldredge and Kimberly Masters, "Confronting Problems Faced by Pregnant Inmates in State Prisons," *Crime and Delinquency* 39:2 (1993): 195–203.

40. Lance Couturier, "Inmates Benefit from Family Services Programs," *Corrections Today* 57:5 (1995): 100–107.

41. R. Kiser, "Female Inmates and Their Families," *Federal Probation*. 55:3 (1991): 56–63. Also see Peter Breen, "Bridging the Barriers," *Corrections Today* 57:7 (1995): 98–99.

42. Ibid (Kiser). See also Linda Acorn, "California Program Helps Women Offenders Make Smooth Transition," *Corrections Today* 54:4 (1992): 102–104, and Barbara Smith, Anna Laszlo, and Mike Akimoto, "Children on Hold," in *Improving the Responses to Children Whose Parents Are Arrested and Incarcerated* (Washington, D.C.: American Bar Association, 1994).

43. *Estelle v. Gamble*, 97 S. Ct. 285 (1976).

44. David Ward and Gene Kassebaum, "Sexual Tension in a Women's Prison," in M. Wolfgang and L. Savitz, eds., *The Criminal in Confinement* (New York: Basic Books, 1971), pp. 149–150. See also Candace Kruttschnitt, "Race Relations and the Female Inmate," *Crime and Delinquency* 29:4 (1983): 577–592.

45. Sheldon and Eleanor Glueck, *500 Delinquent Women* (New York: Alfred A. Knopf, 1934).

46. J.O. Smykla, *Co-Corrections: A Case Study of a Co-ed Federal Prison* (Washington, D.C.: University Press of America, 1979). See also Doris Mackenzie, James Robinson, and Carol Campbell, "Long-Term Incarceration of Female Offenders: Prison Adjustment and Coping," *Criminal Justice and Behavior* 16:3 (1989): 223–238.

47. Lenore Walker, *Terrifying Love: Why Battered Women Kill and How Society Responds* (New York: Harper & Row, 1989). See also Sultan and Long, "Treatment of Sexually/Physically Abused Female Inmates." See also the excellent special issue edited by Sue Osthoff, Leigh Dingerson, Robert David, et al., "Focus on Abused Women and the Correctional System," *Response to the Victimization of Women and Children* 14:79 (1991): 2–23.

48. David Ward and Gene Kassebaum, *Women's Prison: Sex and Social Structure* (Chicago: Aldine, 1965), pp. 9–10. For male inmates, see Glenn Walters and Thomas White, "Attachment and Social Bonding in Maximum and Minimum Security Prison Inmates," *American Journal of Criminal Justice* 16:1 (1991): 1–15. A Canadian program to prevent sexual abuse among male inmates can be found in Garry Perry, Bob Wilson, and Steve Boecheler, "Development of Sexual Abuse Programming Within a Correctional Centre," *American Jails* 6:2 (1992): 79–83.

49. American Correctional Association, *ACA Directory 1993*, p. xlvi.

50. J.O. Smykla, "The Impact of Co-corrections," paper presented at the Academy of Criminal Justice Sciences meeting (Cincinnati, March 1979). See also J. Ross et al., *Assessment of Coeducational Corrections* (Washington, D.C.: U.S. Government Printing Office, 1978), pp. 3–4.

51. Ross et al., *Assessment of Coeducational Corrections*, pp. 1–2.

52. Smykla, "The Impact of Co-corrections," pp. 12–16. See also *Newsweek*, January 11, 1982, p. 66.

53. Alliance of Non-Governmental Organizations on Crime Prevention and Criminal Justice, *Children with Their Mothers* (New York: Alliance of Non-Governmental Organizations on Crime Prevention and Criminal Justice, 1987).

54. Paul Gendreau, Nancy Shilton, and Patrick Clark. "Intermediate Sanctions: Making the Right Move." *Corrections Today* 57:1 (1995): 28–65 (special section of that issue).

55. Jerome Miller, *Last One over the Wall: The Massachusetts Experiment in Closing Reform Schools* (Columbus: Ohio State University Press, 1991). See also Jane Miller-Ashton, "Canada's Female Offenders: New Options in the Federal System," *Federal Prisons Journal* 3:1 (1992): 63–68.

CHAPTER SEVENTEEN

Juvenile Offenders

Overview

The last three chapters have dealt with the hodgepodge of "clients" who usually form separate groups for sentencing and incarceration following arrest and detention. In our early history the distinctions of sex, age, or personal infirmities were given little thought, and "offenders" were lumped into a single category—*prisoners*. Institutional inmates needed only to be classified as *convicted*, and even that distinction was often overlooked in society's haste to punish actual or alleged miscreants. As time passed, and many different paths were developed for various categories of offenders, jails were separated into male and female sections with those convicted sent to different, specialized kinds of institutions to serve out their sentences. But what about those offenders classified, by age, as juveniles? What became of them in the adult systems?

This chapter digresses slightly from the general pattern of the text, because the process of handling juvenile offenders has grown to an entirely separate *system* of justice. Therefore, we shall develop the history of juvenile justice in more detail than was provided in Part I, to show how juvenile procedures developed almost independently from adult justice and how their processing has grown into an entirely separate "industry." This is especially timely as we follow the activities of street gangs, children who kill children, and all the neoclassical efforts to again try juveniles in adult courts. It is our hope to provide the student, in this single chapter, with a basic understanding of juvenile justice in relationship to the other "clients" of corrections. Other texts and other courses have been written and presented on this single client group. This is not meant to be an exhaustive or complete treatise on juvenile justice, but simply a base upon which to build.

> At this stage [1995], public officials seem reluctant to spend taxpayers' dollars to reform juvenile corrections—even as they pour billions of dollars into adult prisons.
>
> —Barry Krisberg, NCCD

Where Does the Juvenile Fit In?

Like most of America's criminal justice system, our juvenile justice system derives from the **common law** of England. In regard to criminal responsibility, the English common law made three assumptions concerning age and criminal responsibility:

1. Children under the age of seven were presumed to be incapable of holding criminal intent.

2. From the ages of eight to fourteen, offenders were not held responsible unless the state could prove they could clearly distinguish between right and wrong.

3. If offenders were over the age of fourteen, they were assumed to be responsible for their acts and therefore deserving of punishment. In this case, the burden was on the defendants to prove they were not responsible.

In English common law, the king was considered the father of his country (**parens patriae**), who assumed responsibility for protecting all dependent children. And in England, that responsibility was fulfilled by the chancery court,[1] in which the needful child became a **ward** of the state under the protection of *parens patriae*. The **chancery court** was designed to act more flexibly than the more rigid criminal courts. The main concern was for the welfare of the child; legal procedures that might hamper the court in its beneficial actions were either circumvented or ignored. Thus there were two concepts under the common law: that children under certain ages were not responsible for their actions and that a certain category of children was in need of protection by the state. It was not until the ages of possible responsibility were raised to sixteen and eighteen that those two concepts merged into the concept of **juvenile delinquency**.

Measuring Juvenile Crime in America

Measuring the extent of juvenile crime among the sixty-nine million persons under the age of eighteen is a problem that has vexed researchers from the beginning of their attempts to study delinquency and juvenile crime. More than one in every four Americans in 1995 fits into this category and that number is expected to increase to seventy-nine million by the year 2010.[2] Because juvenile crime has been the domain of a highly splintered system, the only valid crime data have tended to come from local areas. The currency of data is also a problem: most information on juvenile justice is older than investigators would want it to be. Most indicators of juvenile crime are, of course, from either official or unofficial sources, and these numbers can vary greatly, depending on the era, the time being investigated, and the scope of the database. Most official figures come from the FBI's *Uniform Crime Reports* (*UCRs*), reports from the National Criminal Justice Reference Service (NCJRS), the annual *Sourcebook* of the Bureau of Justice Statistics (BJS), reports of the Office of Juvenile Justice and Delinquency Prevention (**OJJDP**), juvenile court statistics, and institutional and aftercare records. Unofficial figures come from self-reporting studies, the National Crime Victimization Surveys, cohort studies, and various academic studies conducted at universities and by private research organizations.

At best, all criminal justice statistics can do is show us the important trends in the various crime or offender categories under question. At worst, they can confuse and compound analysis to the point of uselessness. Most of the data used in this text come from official sources, primarily from the *UCRs* and reports from the NCJRS and OJJDP. Some of the more revealing data are analyzed here, but we encourage you to subscribe to the National Institute of Justice's *NIJ Catalog,* and to study the *UCR* as it is published each year.

Statistics are the baseline for analysis of juvenile crime. This analysis of the data identifies trends found among juvenile offenders and presents some profiles of them in order to better understand the scope and range of the juvenile justice problem. Statistics are often dry and difficult unless you keep in mind that the numbers represent real children and real victims.

The Juvenile Crime Problem

It has been estimated that approximately one out of every six boys and one out of every nine children in the United States will be referred to a juvenile court before their eighteenth birthday. The rise in juvenile crime has been considered the most serious aspect of the crime problem in the nation. In 1983, 30 percent of the serious index crimes and 16 percent of all violent crimes cleared by arrest were committed by persons under eighteen years of age. In 1994, those figures grew to 33 percent and 18 percent, respectively. These data, which only represent a small percentage of the actual crimes by those under eighteen, seem to validate that the rising trend in violent crime may in part be attributed to this pattern. The stable percentage in crimes against property committed by juveniles, despite the 9 percent decrease in property crime (1990–1994), again points to violent behavior as the crucial issue. The total combined change in index crimes from 1983 to 1992 for juveniles was 17.4 percent.[3]

Juveniles today are handled differently and separately from adults in almost every phase of the criminal justice system. Differential treatment and discretion by officials at various stages of the criminal process cloud the juvenile crime picture. There have been major adjustments in the juvenile justice system in the past few years, and many more will probably be initiated as we enter the next century.

Juvenile Violence: A Growing Problem

As we already noted, across the nation the amount of violent crime involving juveniles as offenders or victims is on the rise. From about the time of the emergence of **crack cocaine**, the use of violence has become a part of the gang culture, and these crimes seem to have also spread to many youths who are not gang members. The charts and tables in this chapter show the sad statistics of the rise of juvenile violence. Teens today are much more likely than adults to commit crimes of violence, based on their percentage in the population. These chilling statistics have caused the society as a whole, and the juvenile courts as well, to develop a "get-tough" attitude toward violent crime by juveniles. Examples of the growing problem of violence are as follows:

- Between 1990 and 1994, the number of Violent Crime Index arrests of juveniles increased by 26 percent, while the increase for adults (persons eighteen years of age or older) actually declined to a zero rate of increase.[4] Most alarming, juvenile arrests for murder increased by 15 percent, compared with 9 percent *decrease* for adults.

- The violent crime index arrests of juveniles in 1994 was the highest number in history, totaling 10 percent of those arrests for murder, 14 percent for forcible rape, 20 percent for robbery, and 13 percent for aggravated assault.

- Juveniles accounted for 14 percent of all violent crimes cleared by arrests in 1994 and 25 percent of the property crimes.

- Two of every ten juvenile murder arrests involved a victim under age eighteen, with an amazing 88 percent of those under fourteen years of age.

- Juveniles' use of guns in homicides was 65 percent of the time, during which time juvenile arrests for weapons violations grew at the same rate.

- In 1994 the nearly 63,400 juvenile weapons arrests had increased 103 percent since 1985.

- Eleven large cities in 1994 reported that 40 percent of juvenile males were in possession of a weapon at some time. Over one-third reported owning a firearm. Twenty-two percent reported that they carried a gun most of the time, and 50 percent reported a gun had been shot at them, with 11 percent injured by gunshot.

- Among students who carried a weapon, knives and razors were more likely to be carried (55 percent) than were firearms (20 percent). More than half of the black males who carried a weapon carried a gun.[5]

Table 17-1, and 17.2 and Figure 17.1 demonstrate the proportions of crime committed by juveniles under the age of fifteen, and the relationship of all juvenile crimes

TABLE *17.1*

Distribution of Juvenile (Under Age Fifteen) Arrests, 1985 versus 1994

Offense	Proportion of Juvenile Arrests Under Age Fifteen in Adult Arrests	
	1985	1994
Total	33%	35%
Violent Crime Index	29	31
Murder	13	12
Forcible rape	35	38
Robbery	26	29

Continued on page 320

TABLE *17.1*

Distribution of Juvenile (Under Age Fifteen) Arrests, 1985 Versus 1994 *(Con't)*

	Proportion of Juvenile Arrests Under Age Fifteen in Adult Arrests	
Offense	1985	1994
Aggravated assault	31%	33%
Property Crime Index	41	43
Burglary	37	41
Larceny-theft	43	45
Motor vehicle theft	25	30
Arson	64	68
Simple assault	38	42
Vandalism	52	49
Weapons	28	32
Prostitution	10	12
Drug abuse	16	17
Liquor laws	8	11
Curfew	28	30
Runaway	43	45

SOURCE: Federal Bureau of Investigation, *Crime in the United States 1985* (Washington, D.C.: U.S. Department of Justice, 1986), and *Crime in the United States 1994* (Washington, D.C.: U.S. Department of Justice, 1995).

TABLE *17.2*

Percentage Growth in Juvenile Arrests by Crime, 1985–1994

Between 1985 and 1994 the percentage growth in juvenile arrests for murder, robbery, weapons law violations, and motor vehicle theft far surpassed the growth in adult arrests

	Percent Change in Arrests					
	1993–1994		1990–1994		1985–1994	
	Juvenile	Adult	Juvenile	Adult	Juvenile	Adult
Total	11%	5%	21%	−2%	28%	19%
Crime Index Total	6	−1	9	−8	18	17
Violent Crime Index	7	0	26	0	75	48
Murder	−3	−6	15	−9	150	11
Forcible rape	−8	−6	0	−12	6	−5
Robbery	11	−7	32	−14	57	12
Aggravated assault	5	3	25	6	97	71
Property Crime Index	5	−2	6	−11	−11	6
Burglary	1	−6	−1	−17	19	−11
Larceny-theft	8	−1	10	−9	14	10
Motor vehicle theft	−2	0	−8	−11	74	33
Arson	18	−7	39	−17	39	−22
Nonindex offenses	14	6	29	−1	34	19
Other assaults	13	6	42	18	114	87
Forgery	12	7	13	19	−4	33
Fraud	36	2	95	11	5	23
Embezzlement	33	6	−22	−9	24	25
Stolen property	1	3	0	−7	32	21
Vandalism	6	0	20	−9	29	20
Weapons	2	−2	56	7	103	26
Prostitution	5	−1	−26	−13	−59	−15
Sex offense	−11	−4	3	−11	−1	-3
Drug abuse	42	16	89	14	66	60

Continued on page 321

TABLE *17.2*

Percentage Growth in Juvenile Arrests by Crime, 1985–1994

(Con't)

	Percent Change in Arrests					
	1993–1994		1990–1994		1985–1994	
	Juvenile	Adult	Juvenile	Adult	Juvenile	Adult
Nonindex offenses (con't)						
Gambling	34	6	92	-6	98	–44
Against the family	11	5	64	35	72	101
Driving under influence	10	–4	–31	–24	–42	–22
Liquor law violations	8	6	–19	–23	–12	4
Drunkenness	7	–4	–26	–24	–37	–30
Disorderly conduct	16	–1	42	–9	73	–4
Vagrancy	18	–18	38	–39	39	–35
All other offenses (except traffic)	14	13	32	11	23	51
Curfew	28	*	64	*	54	*
Runaways	7	*	19	*	19	*

NOTE: Because the absolute number of juvenile arrests is far below the adult level, a larger percentage increase in juvenile arrests does not necessarily imply a larger increase in the actual number of arrests. For example, while the *percentage* increase in juvenile arrests for a weapons law violation was much greater than the adult increase between 1985 and 1994, the increase in the *number* of arrests was actually 27 percent greater for adults.

* Not applicable to adults.

SOURCE: Federal Bureau of Investigation, *Crime in the United States 1994* (Washington, D.C.: U.S. Department of Justice, 1995).

in regard to the ratio of property crime and violent crimes and drugs. It is clear that these age groups are committing crimes disproportionate to their populations and age.

*J*uvenile Victims of Violence

Contrary to popular perceptions of the risk of violent crime, teenagers are victimized at higher rates than adults. The following shows some of the problems with victimization:

- Teen victimizations generally occur in or around school—12 percent of the violent crime victimizations of youth between grades 6 and 12 occurred at school.

Special education can help youths become self-sufficient

—*COURTESY OF OHIO DEPARTMENT OF YOUTH SERVICES*

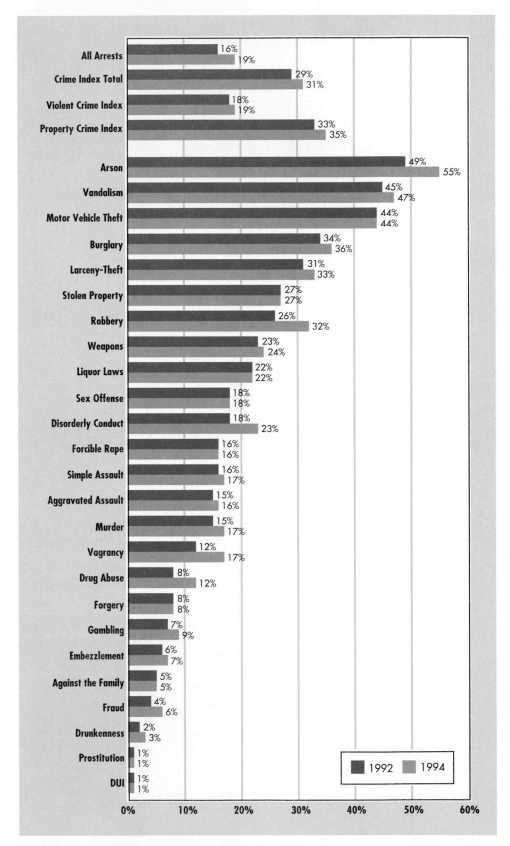

FIGURE

17.1

Juveniles' Proportion
of Property Crime Arrests
and Violent Crime
and Drug Arrests:
1992 and 1994

SOURCE: FBI, *Uniform Crime Reports* (Washington, D.C.: U.S. Department of Justice, 1993, 1995, taken from several locations.

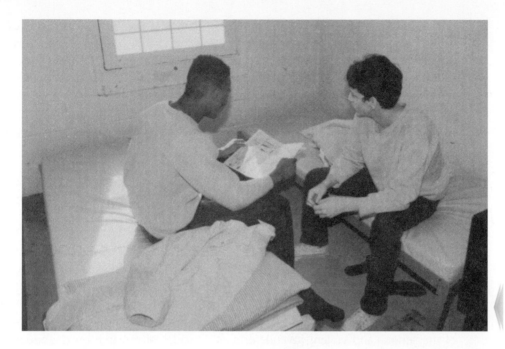

A typical room in a detention center

—*COURTESY OF OHIO DEPARTMENT OF YOUTH SERVICES*

- Schools with gangs had higher victimization rates. Eighteen percent of the students reporting gangs at school were victimized compared with 11 percent of those who reported no gang presence.[6]

- Data show that in 1994 more than twenty-seven hundred youth under age eighteen were murdered in the United States—an average of more than seven youth homicides each day.[7]

- Although the prevalence of homicides of children age thirteen and under has been relatively stable, teen homicides (ages fourteen through seventeen) have almost tripled—from 4 per 100,000 in 1984 to 11 per 100,000 in 1994.

- The 1994 homicide victimization rate among black youth was more than six times the rate for white youth.

- Adolescent homicide victims, those aged ten to seventeen, were most often killed by a friend or other acquaintance (61 percent), but murder by a stranger increased by 51 percent and more black than white juveniles were killed.

- More than 70 percent of teenage homicide victims were shot to death. The overwhelming majority of youth homicide victims in the ten to seventeen age range were male (73 percent).

- In 1994 more than 76 percent of murder victims between ages 15 and seventeen were killed with firearms, compared with 24 percent of all murder victims.[8]

- Courts were more likely to file petitions in cases involving violent offenses than in other delinquency cases. In 1993, 76 percent of violent offense cases were petitioned, compared with 50 percent of delinquency cases that did not involve violent offenses.

- Juveniles were detained in 49 percent of cases involving violent offenses in 1993, compared with 25 percent in other delinquency cases.

- In 1993 juvenile courts waived four out of ten violent offense cases to criminal court.[9]

It is important to note that the juveniles who are charged with violent crimes represent 19 percent of the total crimes committed by juveniles. Despite these relatively small numbers, such crimes of violence as drive-by shootings, casual murder, and senseless abuse of other children create a hard-line attitude in the American public. The courts recognize this perception and are responding with more severe dispositions, including referring those who commit such violent crimes to stand trial as adults. The administrator of the OJJDP points out the problem clearly:

> Youthful violence presents a serious challenge to our Nation. As such, it demands a serious response. If that response is to be effective—one that rehabilitates offenders, deters offenses, and protects the public—it must be well considered.[10]

The problem of violent crime will remain a problem well into the twenty-first century. Another recent OJJDP publication describes a comprehensive strategy for attempting to deal with serious and violent juvenile crime:

> Evidence continues to mount that a small proportion of offenders commit most of the serious and violent juvenile crimes. Decades of research on delinquent

Upper Age of Juvenile Court Jurisdiction

Oldest Age for Original Juvenile Court Jurisdiction in Delinquency Matters

15	16	17		
Connecticut	Georgia	Alabama	Kansas	Ohio
New York	Illinois	Alaska	Kentucky	Oklahoma
North Carolina	Louisiana	Arizona	Maine	Oregon
	Massachusetts	Arkansas	Maryland	Pennsylvania
	Michigan	California	Minnesota	Rhode Island
	Missouri	Colorado	Mississippi	South Dakota
	South Carolina	Delaware	Montana	Tennessee
	Texas	District of Columbia	Nebraska	Utah
		Florida	Nevada	Vermont*
		Hawaii	New Hampshire	Virginia
		Idaho	New Jersey	Washington
		Indiana	New Mexico	West Virginia
		Iowa	North Dakota	Wisconsin
				Wyoming

*In Vermont the juvenile and criminal courts have concurrent jurisdiction over all sixteen- and seventeen-year-olds.

- Many states have higher upper ages of juvenile court jurisdiction in status offense, abuse, neglect, or dependency matters—often through age 20.
- In many states the juvenile court has jurisdiction over young adults who committed offenses while juveniles.
- Several states also have minimum ages of juvenile court jurisdiction in delinquency matters—ranging from 6 to 12.

- Many states exclude married or otherwise emancipated juveniles from juvenile court jurisdiction.

SOURCE: L. Szymanski, *Upper Age of Juvenile Court Jurisdiction Statutes Analyses* (1994 update); L. Szymanski. *Lower Age of Juvenile Court Jurisdiction* (1994 update) (Washington, D.C.: U.S. Department of Justice, 1995).

careers and prevention have identified the following risk factors as contributing to serious, violent and chronic juvenile crime:

- Weak family attachments
- Lack of consistent discipline
- Physical abuse and neglect
- Poor school performance
- Delinquent peer groups
- High-crime neighborhoods

Building on a strong foundation of basic research and on promising approaches for delinquency prevention, intervention, and treatment, OJJDP has developed what it calls a "Comprehensive Strategy for Serious, Violent, and Chronic Offenders." Key principles for preventing and reducing at-risk behavior and juvenile delinquency include the following:

- Strengthen families in their role of providing guidance, discipline, and strong values as their children's first teacher.

- Support core social institutions, including schools, churches, and other local community-based organizations to alleviate risk factors and help children develop to their full potential.

- Promote prevention strategies that reduce the impact of negative risk factors and enhance protective factors.

- Intervene immediately when delinquent behavior first occurs.

- Establish a broad range of graduated sanctions that provides both accountability and a continuum of services to respond appropriately to the needs of each delinquent offender.

- Identify and control the small percentage of juvenile offenders who are serious, violent, and chronic offenders.[11]

The offending of juveniles is not the only concern. As has been shown, young people are disproportionately the victims of violence as well. Violence impacts the quality of life for these children in their developing years and must be addressed.

$\mathcal{G}$angs: At the Heart of Increasing Juvenile Crime

In October 1994, OJJDP offered some designs and models for communities to begin to deal with **juvenile gangs**. The presence of youth gangs and gang problems must be recognized before anything meaningful can be done to address it. Identifying the manifest and underlying factors contributing to the problem is also very important. Promising approaches are:

1. Targeting, arresting, and incarcerating gang leaders and repeat gang offenders

2. Referring fringe members ["wannabees"] and their parents to youth services for counseling and guidance

3. Providing preventive services for youth who are clearly at risk

Edwin H. Sutherland (1883–1950) was the developer of the best-known theory aimed at explaining delinquent behavior. It is called "differential association" and it first appeared in 1939 in his *Principles of Criminology* (third edition). Basically, it says that criminal behavior is learned in interaction with others. Sutherland's theory has been heavily criticized but it still acts as a cornerstone for many others. The highest award of the American Society of Criminology is in his name.

JUVENILE
A person subject to juvenile court proceedings because a statutorily defined event was alleged to have occurred while his or her age was below the statutorily specified limit of original jurisdiction of a juvenile court. A juvenile delinquent, then, has been adjudicated by an officer of a juvenile court for law violations that would be crimes if they had been committed by an adult.

4. Crisis intervention or mediation of gang fights

5. Patrols of community "hot spots"

6. Close supervision of gang offenders by criminal justice and community-based agencies

7. Remedial education for targeted youth gang members, especially in middle school: job orientation, training, placement, and monitoring for older youth gang members;

8. Safe zones around schools, and

9. Vertical prosecution, close supervision, and enhanced sentences for hard-core youth gang members (Vertical or hard-core prosecution puts the same prosecutor in charge of all aspects of a case from charging to sentencing.)[12]

Only one of twelve different models for gang suppression offered by the OJJDP, this one may best outline the steps to take. Lack of social opportunity is seen a primary factor in gang membership and gang crime. Not until the underlying reasons for belonging to a gang are found will appropriate solutions be developed. Gangs have been with the urban scene for decades, but it took the advent of cocaine, especially crack cocaine, to create gangs whose only real "color" motivation is *green*—the color of money.

Criminal Behavior Declines with Aging

Data on the relationship between crime and age indicate that crime is a young person's game. It seems to peak at age seventeen, before rapidly dropping down. Younger people may be more likely to be arrested because of inexperience and ineptness in crime. Young people also commit crimes that more easily result in arrest, such as purse snatching and drug selling. Also, youths tend to commit crimes in groups, and the resolution of a single crime (such as a car theft) may result in several arrests. The decline by age could also be an artifact of incapacitating repeat offenders by imposing longer sentences; such offenders then grow older in prison. Habitual offenders also seem to become less likely to be caught and arrested. Therefore, older prisoners who do return to crime tend to have longer periods before rearrest and enjoy longer periods of freedom between incarcerations.

Although the percentages of arrests remained rather consistent between 1983 and 1992, they fell slightly in absolute numbers, even as the overall population grew. This could be another indication of the shrinking of the population at risk (twelve- to eighteen-year-old youths), or it could mean that real progress is being made in the juvenile justice system. But, as we have shown, juveniles contribute to a significant and alarming portion of the crime problem.

Because a very large percentage of incarcerated felons were first incarcerated as juveniles in training institutions and schools for delinquents, we look briefly at the development and function of the juvenile court and the juvenile justice system, starting with the philosophy that produced them.

Despite concern for their children's welfare, most communities have a tolerance point for juveniles' disruptive behavior. When children go beyond that point, they can be taken into custody and recorded as delinquents. The mixing

Terms Used in Juvenile Proceedings

The principal features that distinguish current juvenile delinquency proceedings from adult criminal proceedings can be summarized as follows:

1. *Absence of legal guilt.* Legally, juveniles are not found guilty of crimes but are "found to be delinquent." Juveniles are not held legally responsible for their acts. Juvenile status, like insanity, is a defense against criminal responsibility. It is not, however, an absolute defense because of the possibility of waiver to criminal court.

2. *Treatment rather than punishment.* Whatever action the court takes following a finding of delinquency is done in the name of treatment or community protection, not punishment, as is the case for adult felony offenders.

3. *Absence of public scrutiny.* Juvenile proceedings and records are generally closed to the public. What goes on in court is presumed to be the business only of juveniles and their families. This position clearly has its roots in the early child-saving mission of the court. Hearings for serious juvenile offenders are now being opened to the public.

4. *Importance of a juvenile's background.* Juveniles' needs and amenability to treatment can, it is widely presumed, be deduced from their social history, prior behavior, and clinical diagnosis. This presumption is used to justify the wide discretionary powers granted to probation officers in screening petitions, to the court in deciding fitness and making dispositions, and to youth correction agencies in deciding when a ward should be released.

5. *No long-term incarceration.* Terms of confinement for juveniles are considerably shorter than those for adults.

6. *Separateness.* The juvenile system is kept separate from the adult criminal justice system at every point, from detention at arrest to the identities of the officials who handle the case in court, and in subsequent placements as well.

7. *Speed and flexibility.* Delinquency cases are disposed of more quickly than comparable adult criminal cases, and the juvenile court judge has a broader range of disposition alternatives. ∎

of juvenile offenders and adult felons was a practice that had existed for centuries, but in America's early history was looked on as repugnant. It was not until 1899 that the **delinquent juvenile** began to receive differential attention in the courts. The first juvenile court was established in that year in Chicago, and the delinquent joined the dependent and neglected child as a ward of the state. When the juvenile delinquent was thus placed under the cloak of *parens patriae,* he or she was removed entirely from the formal criminal justice system. The general procedures for the handling of juvenile offenders today are shown in Figure 17-2, where the correctional funnel for juveniles can be seen at work. Table 17-3 shows the similarities and differences between the adult and juvenile processing systems.

Categories of Juvenile Offenders

Essentially three kinds of children come into contact with the juvenile court system—a significant event in their lives. The children in two of those categories have committed no offense: they are either **dependent** (without family or support) or **neglected** (having a family situation that is harmful to them). The only category that involves an offense is the delinquent juvenile.

The care of neglected and dependent children is important, of course, but the juvenile courts were established primarily to handle delinquent juveniles. For judicial purposes, delinquents are divided into three categories:

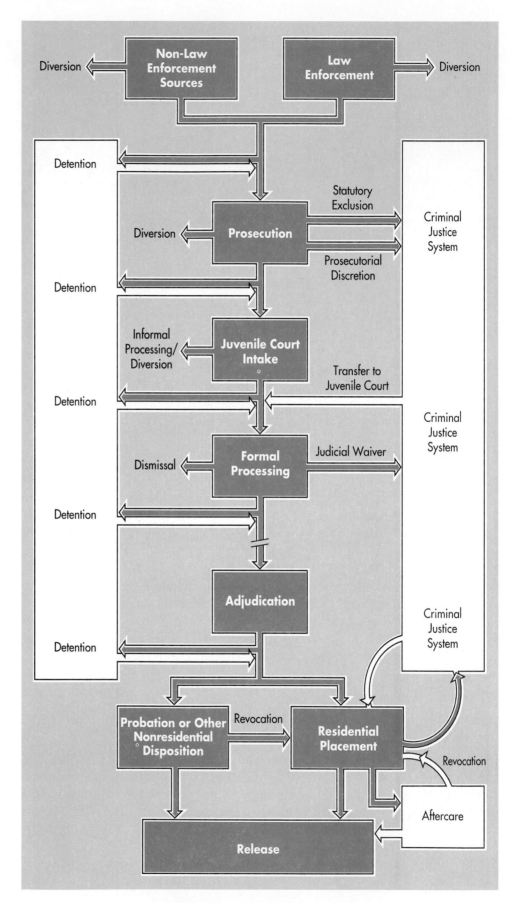

FIGURE

17.2

The Stages of Delinquency Case Processing in the Juvenile Justice System

NOTE: This chart gives a simplified view of case-flow through the juvenile justice system. Procedures vary among jurisdictions. The weights of the lines are not intended to show the actual size of caseloads.

SOURCE: Howard Snyder, et al. *Juvenile Offenders and Victims: 1996 Update on Violence* (Washington, D.C.: U.S. Department of Justice, 1996), p. 76.

TABLE *17.3*

Similarities and Differences Between the Juvenile and Criminal Justice Systems in the Handling of Offenders

Juvenile Justice System	Common Ground	Criminal Justice System
	Operating Assumptions	
• Youth behavior is malleable • Rehabilitation is usually a viable goal • Youth are in families and not independent	• Community protection is a primary goal • Law violators must be held accountable • Constitutional rights apply	• Sanctions proportional to the offense • General deterrence works • Rehabilitation is not a primary goal
	Prevention	
• Many specific delinquency prevention activities (e.g., school, church, recreation) • Prevention intended to change individual behavior—often family focused	• Educational approaches to specific behaviors (drunk driving, drug use)	• Generalized prevention activities aimed at deterrence (e.g., a Crime Watch)
	Law Enforcement	
• Specialized "juvenile" units • Some additional behaviors prohibited (truancy, running away, curfew violations) • Limitations on public access to information	• Jurisdiction involves full range of criminal behavior • Constitutional and procedural safeguards exist • Both reactive and proactive (targeted at offense types, neighborhoods, etc.)	• Open public access to all information
Diversion A significant number of youth are diverted away from the juvenile justice system —often *into* alternative programs		*Discretion* Law enforcement exercises discretion to divert offenders *out of* the criminal justice system
	Intake—Prosecution	
• In many instances, juvenile court intake, not the prosecutor, decides what cases to file • Decision to file a petition for court action is based on both social and legal factors • A significant portion of cases are diverted from formal case processing	• Probable cause must be established • Prosecutor acts on behalf of the state	• Plea bargaining is common • Prosecution decision based largely on legal facts • Prosecution is valuable in building history for subsequent offenses
Diversion Intake diverts cases from formal processing to services operated by the juvenile court or outside agencies		*Discretion* Prosecution exercises discretion to withhold charges or divert offenders out of the criminal justice system
	Detention—Jail/Lockup	
• Juveniles may be detained for their own or the community's protection • Juveniles may not be confined with adults without "sight and sound separation"	• Accused offenders may be held in custody to ensure their appearance in court	• Right to apply for bond
	Adjudication—Conviction	
• Juvenile court proceedings are "quasi-civil" —not criminal—may be confidential • If guilt is established, the youth is adjudicated delinquent regardless of offense. • Right to jury trial not afforded in all states	• Standard of "proof beyond a reasonable doubt" is required • Rights to a defense attorney, confrontation of witnesses, remain silent are afforded • Appeals to a higher court are allowed	• Constitutional right to a jury trial is afforded • Guilt must be established on individual offenses charged for conviction • All proceedings are open

Continued on page 330

TABLE 17.3

Similarities and Differences Between the Juvenile and Criminal Justice Systems in the Handling of Offenders *(Con't)*

Juvenile Justice System	Common Ground	Criminal Justice System
	Disposition—Sentencing	
• Disposition decisions are based on individual and social factors, offense severity, and youths' offense history • Dispositional philosophy includes a significant rehabilitation component • Many dispositional alternatives are operated by the juvenile court • Dispositions cover a wide range of community-based and residential services • Disposition orders may be directed to people other than the offender (e.g., parents) • Disposition may be indeterminate —based on progress	• Decision is influenced by current offense, offending history, and social factors • Decision made to hold offender accountable • Victim considered for restitution and "no contact" orders • Decision may not be cruel or unusual	• Sentencing decision is primarily bound by the severity of the current offense and offender's criminal history • Sentencing philosophy is based largely on proportionality and punishment • Sentence is often between determinate based on offense
	Aftercare—Parole	
• A function that combines surveillance and reintegration activities (e.g., family, school, work)	• A system of monitoring behavior upon release from a correctional setting • Violation of conditions can result in reincarceration	• Primarily a surveillance and reporting function to monitor illicit behavior

SOURCE: Editors. *Juvenile Offenders and Victims: A National Report.* (Washington, D.C.: Office of Juvenile Justice and Delinquency Prevention, 1995), pp. 74-75.

1. The first is composed of children who have allegedly committed an offense that would be a crime if it had been committed by an adult. That group makes up about 75 percent of the population of the state institutions for delinquent juveniles.

2. The second category of delinquents consists of those status offenders who have allegedly violated regulations that apply only to juveniles: curfew restrictions, required school attendance, and similar rules and ordinances.

3. The third and last group is labeled the "incorrigible juveniles" (those who have been declared unmanageable by their parents and the court). The second and third groups are often referred to as PINS (persons in need of supervision) or MINS (minors in need of supervision). Most concerned juvenile correctional officials would like to remove children in the PINS and MINS classifications (as well as status offenders) from the facilities designed primarily for the first category of delinquent juveniles.[13]

A juvenile institution is intended to provide specialized programs for children who must be under some form of restraint to be treated. Accordingly, it normally houses the more hardened, unstable, or nontreatable youths who fail to meet even the liberal standards for juvenile probation. The institution program attempts to prepare the youth for return to the community.

Despite the vast expansion and growth of community-based facilities, there has been no major decline in the use of juvenile institutions. Spending months or years in confinement away from family, friends, and familiar circumstances, however, is an odious prospect for a person of any age. For a young person, the prospect is especially frightening. Compared to the juvenile court's other dispositional options, institutional placement of a juvenile in a residential facility is the court's ultimate dispositional power. It is the court's most severe and only really feared disposition.

Juveniles Held in Institutional Environments

In the *Gault* decision, the Supreme Court emphasized the reality of institutionalization for a juvenile:

> Ultimately, however, we confront the reality . . .. A boy is charged with misconduct. The boy is committed to an institution where he may be restrained of liberty for years. It is of no constitutional consequence . . . and of limited practical meaning . . . that the institution to which he is committed is called an Industrial School. The fact of the matter is that, however euphemistic the title, a "receiving home" or an "industrial school" for juveniles is an institution of confinement in which the child is incarcerated for a greater or lesser time. His world becomes "a building with whitewashed walls, regimented routine and institutional hours. . .." Instead of mother and father and sisters and brothers and friends and classmates, his world is peopled by guards, custodians, state employees, and delinquents confined with him for anything from waywardness to rape and homicide.[14]

There were 102,582 juveniles in correctional programs at year-end 1994.[15] The ratio of male/female and ethnic composition of juveniles in residential facilities are shown in Figures 17-3 and 17-4.

Facilities designated exclusively for juvenile detention are usually not the best examples of how an ideal juvenile correctional facility should be designed and operated. Most of the structures were originally built for some other purpose and converted to their present use with as little expense as possible. Most are overcrowded before they reach their rated capacities. In adult institutions, the emphasis is on custody, and the same preoccupation with security shapes the programs

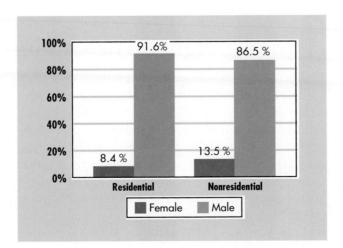

FIGURE

17.3

Percentage of Male and Female Juveniles in Residential Programs Compared with Nonresidential Programs, 1995

SOURCE: C. Camp and G. Camp, *The Corrections Yearbook 1995: Juvenile Corrections* (South Salem, NY: Criminal Justice Institute, 1995), p. 9.

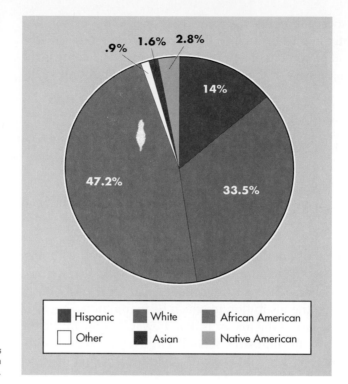

FIGURE

17.4

Ethnic Composition
of Agency Residential
Populations, 1995

SOURCE: : C. Camp and G. Camp, *The Corrections
Yearbook 1995: Juvenile Corrections* (South
Salem, NY: Criminal Justice Institute, 1995), p. 9.

Jerome Miller served
as the Commissioner
of the Department of
Youth Services, a
pioneer in
deinstitutionalization, and in that
post convinced the
governor of Massachusetts to
approve the closing of all but one
juvenile correctional institution (the
Shirley Training School, which
served a few remaining girls) and
placing all other adjudicated
juveniles into community-based
programs. This bold move,
supported by the media and
politicians, has been copied in
many states since that time and
proved that the large majority of
adjudicated juveniles could be
better dealt with in the community.

and general environment in juvenile facilities. Most are located in urban areas and are virtually sealed off from the community by their physical structure and other security measures. The youth are placed in dormitory-style housing, or single cells in some cases, often with the fixed furniture and dreary interiors that are typical of adult institutions. Most juvenile detention centers lack services and programs that might improve the residents' chances of staying away from crime. These juveniles are denied most of the good aspects of adult programs and are subject to the worst aspects of institutional programs. The average cost for juvenile institutional confinement is about $100 per resident per day.

Institutions are the most expensive and least successful method of handling juvenile offenders. But until the services needed for supervision and treatment in the community are forthcoming, judges often have no other choice but to commit offenders. The junior prisons are not all bad, but the **custody philosophy** is the prevailing model, which creates the same problem as that at the adult level.

Juvenile Rights: The Landmark Cases

Figure 17-5 is a schematic and brief explanation of the landmark Supreme Court cases that established many juvenile rights. In the landmark opinions in *Kent* v. *United States*, 383 U.S. 541 (1966), and *In re Gault*, 387 U.S. 1 (1967), the Supreme Court at long last evaluated juvenile court proceedings and children's constitutionally guaranteed rights. In *Kent* v. *United States*, the Court noted that the child involved in certain juvenile court proceedings was deprived of constitutional rights and at the same time not given the rehabilitation promised under earlier juvenile court philosophy and statutes. It pointed out that "there may be grounds for concern that the child receives the worst of both worlds."[16] On May 15, 1967, the Supreme Court rendered its first decision in the area of juvenile delinquency procedure. In the decision, Justice Abraham Fortas ruled that a child alleged to be a juvenile delinquent had at least the following rights:

1. Right to notice of the charges in time to prepare for trial;
2. Right to counsel;
3. Right to confrontation and cross-examination of his or her accusers; and
4. Privilege against self-incrimination, at least in court.

The *Gault* decision ended the presumption that the juvenile courts were beyond the scope or purview of due process protection. With *In re Winship*, 397 U.S. 358 (1970), the Supreme Court held that to justify a court finding of delinquency against a juvenile, the proof must be beyond a reasonable doubt that the juvenile committed the alleged delinquent act. *McKeiver* v. *Pennsylvania*, 403 U.S. 528 (1971) implied that the due process standard of "fundamental fairness" applied, and the Court rejected the concept of trial by jury for juveniles. The Court contended that the "juvenile proceeding has not yet been held to be a 'criminal prosecution' within the meaning and reach of the Sixth Amendment . . . ."[17] The cases shown in Figure 17-5, following *McKeiver*, have slowly added more and more rights to juvenile process, while still trying to keep it separate.

The Supreme Court has not been the only source of change in the area of juvenile rights, however. Federal acts and legislation have also played an important role. Until the *Uniform Juvenile Court Act of 1968*, a child could still be taken into custody by police or others in a situation in which the Fourth Amendment would have exempted an adult. In 1974, the U.S. Congress passed the *Juvenile Justice and Delinquency Prevention Act* (Public Law 93-415). This act requires a comprehensive assessment regarding the effectiveness of the existing juvenile justice system. The intent of the act is to clearly identify those youth who are victimized or otherwise troubled but have not committed criminal offenses, and to divert such youth from institutionalization. Simultaneously, the act would promote the utilization of resources within the juvenile justice system to more effectively deal with youthful criminal offenders.[18]

Thus far, the procedural rights guaranteed to a juvenile in court proceedings are as follows:

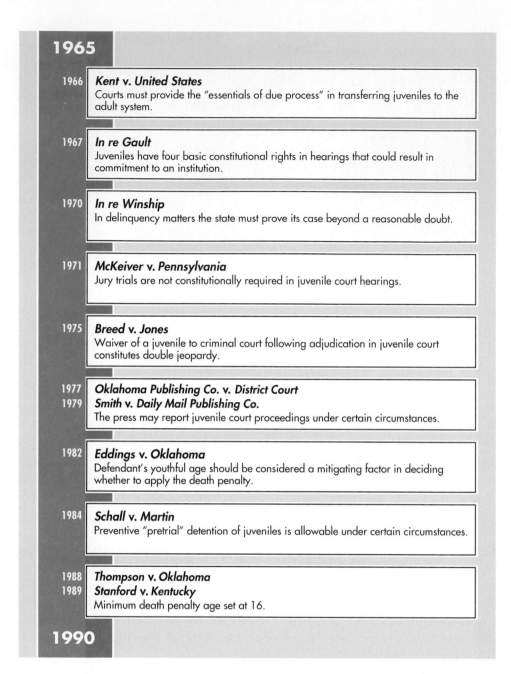

1965

1966
Kent v. United States
Courts must provide the "essentials of due process" in transferring juveniles to the adult system.

1967
In re Gault
Juveniles have four basic constitutional rights in hearings that could result in commitment to an institution.

1970
In re Winship
In delinquency matters the state must prove its case beyond a reasonable doubt.

1971
McKeiver v. Pennsylvania
Jury trials are not constitutionally required in juvenile court hearings.

1975
Breed v. Jones
Waiver of a juvenile to criminal court following adjudication in juvenile court constitutes double jeopardy.

1977
Oklahoma Publishing Co. v. District Court
1979
Smith v. Daily Mail Publishing Co.
The press may report juvenile court proceedings under certain circumstances.

1982
Eddings v. Oklahoma
Defendant's youthful age should be considered a mitigating factor in deciding whether to apply the death penalty.

1984
Schall v. Martin
Preventive "pretrial" detention of juveniles is allowable under certain circumstances.

1988
Thompson v. Oklahoma
1989
Stanford v. Kentucky
Minimum death penalty age set at 16.

1990

FIGURE

17.5

A Series of U.S. Supreme Court Decisions Made JuvenileCourts More Like Criminal Courts but Maintained Some Importance Differences

1. The right to adequate notice of charges against him or her;
2. The right to counsel and to have counsel provided if the child is indigent;
3. The right to confrontation and cross-examination of witnesses;
4. The right to refuse to do anything that would be self-incriminatory;
5. The right to a judicial hearing, with counsel, prior to the transfer of a juvenile to an adult court; and
6. The right to be considered innocent until proven guilty beyond a reasonable doubt.

The major decisions of the U.S. Supreme Court have led to four major trends in the handling of juveniles: diversion, decriminalization, removal of status offenders, and **decarceration**.

Juveniles at Texas
Department of Corrections
(Clemons Unit)

—*PHOTO BY ALAN POGUE, COURTESY
OF TEXASTOCK, INC.*

Diversion is the official halting or suspension, at any legally prescribed processing point after a recorded justice system entry, of formal juvenile (or criminal) proceedings against an alleged offender and referral of that person to a treatment or care program administered by a nonjustice agency or private agency. Sometimes no referral is given. Diversion programs function to divert juveniles out of the juvenile justice system, encourage the use of existing private correctional agencies and facilities for such youths, and avoid formal contact with the juvenile court. Those programs include remedial education programs, foster homes, group homes, and local counseling facilities and centers. The effectiveness of such programs has not yet been demonstrated, but they are being closely evaluated.

Decriminalization does just what it sounds like—makes the act not criminal anymore. The principal aim in the juvenile and criminal justice systems is to remove from the scope of law and social control certain types of currently proscribed behaviors that pose little perceived danger to society. Those behaviors are frequently seen as "deviant" rather than illegal and thus "not the law's business." The decriminalization movement, then, would delete deviant behavior from juvenile laws and proceedings and leave to social agencies the task of providing assistance if and when requested.[19]

One category of juveniles that falls under the aegis of the juvenile court is the "status" offender. These youths commit offenses that are based only on the offender's status as a juvenile. These offenses include ungovernability, running away, unruliness, school truancy, disregard for or abuse of lawful parental authority, repeated use of alcoholic beverages, and so on. The Institute of Juvenile Administration of the American Bar Association, a national standards-setting organization, recommended the following:

1. A juvenile's acts of misbehavior, ungovernability, or unruliness which do not violate the criminal law should not constitute a ground for asserting juvenile court jurisdiction over the juvenile committing them.

2. Any law enforcement officer who reasonably determines that a juvenile is in circumstances which constitute a substantial and immediate danger to the juvenile's physical safety may, if the juvenile's physical safety requires such action, take the juvenile into limited custody (subject to the limitations of this part).[20]

Decarceration removes as many juveniles from custody as possible and treats them in an open environment. This option, given the violent nature of juveniles incarcerated, seems to still be waiting for its time to come. These recommendations reflect the earlier intent of the *Juvenile Justice and Delinquency Prevention Act* (JJDPA) to divert status offenders to shelter facilities rather than juvenile detention centers or jails, as well as not to detain or confine status offenders in any institution in which they would have regular contact with adult offenders.

Today's Approach to Juvenile Institutions

Directors of early juvenile institutions were concerned chiefly with the protection of society. Youths confined within institutional walls were judged enemies of society, and their custody was looked upon as a disciplinary measure. How far have things advanced since then? Has there been measurable progress in the search for an answer to the problem of juvenile delinquency? For the past several decades, juvenile institutions have been subscribing, at least superficially, to a philosophy of social responsibility for the rehabilitation of deviant youth. As a consequence, today's institutions call for greater emphasis on education, vocational, and personality training and the inculcation of socially accepted living habits.

Society has a way of placing its concerns in an order of priority, concerns that are social and technological. One often hears the inquiry, "If we can put a man on the moon, why can't something be done about crime?" In the meantime, juvenile crime increases, public schools cease to function, and organized and armed youth gangs reemerge as a deadly menace in communities nationwide. A return to the extensive use of incarceration, which stigmatizes youthful criminals as the enemies of society, may well be the future for juvenile corrections. Although not all youths belong in juvenile correctional institutions, economic pressures may force a line to be drawn. The proponents of community-based programs and treatment for troubled youth may argue against it, but a return to old-fashioned discipline, large congregate institutions, and the reform school-style institutions may be unavoidable.

Detention

The National Council on Crime and Delinquency (NCCD) provides a clear, simple definition for detention care: "The temporary care of children in physically restricted facilities pending court disposition or transfer to another jurisdiction or agency."[21] To provide the child with a constructive experience, NCCD notes further that detention should meet four basic objectives:

1. Secure custody with good physical care in a manner that will offset the damaging effects of confinement,

2. A constructive and satisfying program of activities to provide the child with an opportunity to develop and recognize strengths and to help him find socially acceptable ways of gaining satisfaction,

Juveniles Tried As Adults

All states allow juveniles to be tried as adults in criminal court under certain circumstances.

There is more than one path to criminal court. A juvenile's delinquency case can be transferred to criminal court for trial as an adult in one of three ways:

- Judicial waiver.
- Prosecutorial discretion.

- Statutory exclusion.

In a given State, one, two, or all three transfer mechanisms may be in place.   ■

SOURCE: National Institute of Justice, *Juvenile Offenders and Victims: A National Report* (Washington, D.C., 1995), p. 85.

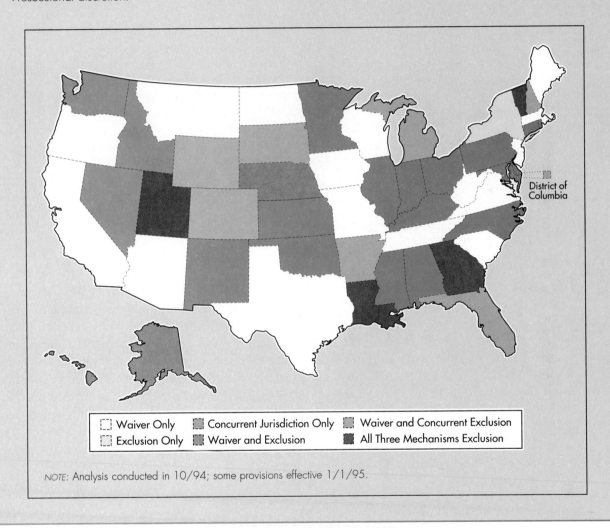

District of Columbia

☐ Waiver Only	▦ Concurrent Jurisdiction Only	▦ Waiver and Concurrent Exclusion
☐ Exclusion Only	▦ Waiver and Exclusion	▦ All Three Mechanisms Exclusion

NOTE: Analysis conducted in 10/94; some provisions effective 1/1/95.

3. Individual and group guidance to help the child use his detention experience positively, and

4. Observation and study to provide screening for undetected mental or emotional illness as well as a diagnosis upon which to develop an appropriate treatment plan.[22]

Authorities generally agree that only certain youths should be detained involuntarily. They include those who would probably disappear prior to their hearing,

Impact of Youthful Offenders in Texas Prisons

The total impact of youthful offenders being tried and sentenced as adults has not been fully realized by the TDCJ since new legislation expanding certification and determinate sentencing possibilities did not become effective until January 1, 1996. TDCJ does, however, expect a steady increase in the number of offenders under age 18 being sentenced as adults. (During 1994, 177 youthful offenders were received by TDCJ; and by 1995, a total of 502 were received. As of May 31, 1996—there were 416. This includes both adult certifications and determinate sentences.)

Since January, 1995, TDCJ-ID began preparing for the impact of the juvenile justice reforms by identifying major issues in dealing with these offenders through coordinated efforts with TYC, juvenile probation, and adult parole. Since that time, special programming has been developed to encourage their successful reintegration upon release as well as to provide security and protection to staff and the offenders while incarcerated.

Some of the most crucial issues and problems experienced by TDCJ-ID associated with the youthful offenders include:

- Gang activity within the institution;
- Increased aggression and violence including assaults on staff as well as offenders (both gang and racially motivated);
- Large representation of minority offenders (As of May 31st, there were 176 black, 126 hispanic, and 36 white male youthful offenders.);
- Recognized need for ongoing staff development and training associated with special issues of violent youth to include effective management tools. (Prior to the implementation of the youthful offender programs and special housing area, TDCJ staff had very little knowledge, experience, or training in dealing with this age of offender).

SOURCE: Janice Willett (personal correspondence), *Programs and Services,* Texas Department of Criminal Justice, June 1996.

those with a high probability of committing a dangerous offense while awaiting court disposition, and those who must be held for another jurisdiction.

Of all facilities being used in the United States to incarcerate youth, the detention facility is the most common, and may include jails, centers located above the juvenile court, converted mental wards, or any place in which youth can be imprisoned, pending a hearing or transfer. Since five out of every six children held in all juvenile facilities are in detention, the chance of leaving a detention facility to return to a nondelinquent life-style is remote, especially when we consider the lack of services and programs for youths in detention. They are denied most of the good in the adult programs and are subjected to the worst aspects of institutional living.

$\mathcal{I}$nstitutional Treatment and Rehabilitation

Twenty-five years ago, the Commission on Criminal Justice Standards and Goals offered extensive guidelines and standards to assist the juvenile institutions in their reexamination of educational and vocational training programs. Unfortunately, in spite of those standards and guidelines, actual experience has shown that most youths committed to juvenile institutions are just "doing time." Their release is more often based on such nontreatment-related factors as overcrowding, administrative decisions and, incredibly, nontreatability. Instead of being a constructive and maturing experience, incarceration in a juvenile institution is as likely to be harmful for the juvenile.

Services in Institutions

Institutionalized juveniles, for whatever reason they are in institutions, must be provided access to services required for individual growth and development. Those services include meaningful quality education and adequate vocational training programs.

Irving Kaufman suggests that to accomplish that end, all sentences should be fixed terms. Any subsequent change should be imposed by the court upon show of good cause.

Indeterminate sentences have been rejected by the commission as a game of chance based on arbitrary decisions. Frequently in the past the most violent juveniles were released from institutions because they were, ironically, difficult to control. Power to determine the actual length of stay of a juvenile is thus removed from the hands of correctional authorities. To encourage good behavior, correctional administrators are allowed to reduce a youth's sentence by no more than 5 percent. The maximum term of incarceration should not exceed two years for any offense.[23]

Currently, even when the treatment staffs do plan a potentially meaningful program, they can seldom be assured of how long they have with their clients. As long as release is possible at any time, training programs are practically worthless. We must keep in mind, however, that the length of time a youth spends in an institution and the degree to which he or she is rehabilitated are not always related. To assume, for example, that the longer a youth spends incarcerated the more he or she will be rehabilitated, and vice versa, is not always true. To justify the use of fixed-length sentences, therefore, on the basis of allowing enough time for the

Teens and Violence

If the criminal justice system has largely been driven by the need to protect society by punishing offenders, the hallmark of the juvenile justice system is the quite different presumption that young people who commit crimes can learn to do better if placed in the right setting and given the right care. Yet most juvenile correctional facilities in the United States are designed to hold large numbers of youths in primitive conditions. Many of these juvenile facilities are overcrowded, rely on leg shackles and handcuffs to control behavior, and "graduate" youths who often go on to commit more serious crimes as they get older. Each year about 11,000 out of the 65,000 incarcerated juveniles commit suicidal acts, yet most facilities have inadequate suicide prevention programs.

In recent years, as stories of teen violence have become regular features of our newspapers and television news programs, we have lost sight of the crucial distinction between adult and juvenile facilities. Until the 1980s, the biggest threats to young people were car accidents and suicide. In that decade, according to the National Center for Health Statistics, teenage males in all racial and ethnic groups became more likely to die from a bullet than from all natural causes.   ◾

SOURCE: Steven R. Donziger, (ed.), *The Real War on Crime* (New York: HarperCollins, 1996), p. 130.

Culver City street gang

completion of adequate training programs, and then fail to provide those programs, would be in violation of the principle of right to treatment.

Summary

It is reasonable to consider that the relatively high proportion of adult felons who were processed through the juvenile treatment delivery systems and training institutions as youths might decrease sharply as alternatives to formal processing, institutionalization, and labeling are developed for juveniles. Unfortunately, those youths who are left to go through the ever-hardening juvenile institutions are being labeled more and more like their adult counterparts. More and more are being referred directly to the adult justice system.[24]

Although there are occasional examples of programs for our youth that seem to be breaking the patterns of delinquent and criminal behavior, the public seems to have little patience with wayward youth. Gangs and violent acts reinforce that attitude. The number of community-based beds for juvenile programs is shrinking. It is essential that the impacts of poor programming and systems that punish instead of treat our children become known to the general public. Only with informed public support can the patterns of "crime schools" and neglect be broken, so that juveniles will be able to escape the further impact of the adult system. The public seems to be responding to that kind of logic by attempts at lowering the age of responsibility for criminal remand to adult courts.

It seems that juvenile justice in America will continue at least to give lip service to the ideals of *parens patriae,* but with the Supreme Court watching closely to see that the rights of young citizens are not abused. If we abandon our young people and begin to assume their behavior is adult because it is repugnant or violent, the jails and prisons of the late 1990s will continue to be overcrowded to the extreme, and we will have two million adults behind bars.

Review Questions

1. Explain the concept of *parens patriae.* How does it apply today?
2. Describe and differentiate between the three kinds of children who come into contact with the juvenile courts.
3. What were the major findings in the case of *In re Gault*?
4. What effect does differential treatment have on juvenile justice? Explain.
5. What are the major trends in the juvenile justice system?

Words to Remember

common law	OJJDP	neglected
parens patriae	crack cocaine	custody philosophy
ward	juvenile gangs	decarceration
chancery court	delinquent juvenile	decriminalization
juvenile delinquency	dependent	

Endnotes

1. Chancery courts date back to England's feudal era. They traditionally had broad power over the welfare of children but exercised that authority almost exclusively on behalf of minors whose property rights were in jeopardy. In America, this authority was extended to minors in danger of personal as well as property attacks.

2. Howard N. Snyder, Melissa Sickman, and E. Poc Yamagata, *Juvenile Offenders and Victims: 1996 Update on Violence* (Washington, D.C.: Office of Juvenile Justice and Delinquency Prevention, February 1996).

3. Ibid.

4. Ibid.

5. Ibid.

6. Ibid.

7. Ibid.

8. Office of Juvenile Justice and Delinquency Prevention (OJJDP), *Juveniles and Violence: Juvenile Offending and Victimization* (Washington, D.C.: U.S. Department of Justice, July 1993), pp. 3–5.

9. Snyder, Sickman, and Yamagata, *Juvenile Offenders and Victims: 1996 Update on Violence* (Washington, D.C.: Office of Juvenile Justice and Delinquency Prevention, February 1996).

10. Jeffrey Butts and D. J. Conners, *The Juvenile Court's Response to Violent Offenders: 1985–1989* (Washington, D.C.: Office of Juvenile Justice and Delinquency Prevention, April 1993), pp. 14–15.

11. Barbara Allen-Hagen and Melissa Sickmund, *Juveniles and Violence: Juvenile Offending and Victimization* (Washington, D.C.: Office of Juvenile Justice and Delinquency Prevention,

and Victimization (Washington, D.C.: Office of Juvenile Justice and Delinquency Prevention, July 1993), p. 4.

12. Irving Spergel, et al., *Gang Suppression and Intervention: Community Models* (Washington, D.C.: Department of Justice, October 1994), pp. 3–4.

13. Marc LeBlanc and Louise Biron, "Status Offenses: A Legal Term Without Meaning," *Journal of Research in Crime and Delinquency* 17:1 (January 1980): 114–125. See also Charles Logan and Sharla Rausch, "Why Deinstitutionalizing Status Offenders Is Pointless," *Crime and Delinquency* 31:4 (1985): 501–517, and Jerome Miller, *Last One Over the Wall: The Massachusetts Experiment in Closing Reform Schools* (Columbus: Ohio State University Press, 1991). Also see William Hogan, ed., "Symposium: Juvenile Justice in Massachusetts," *New England Journal on Criminal and Civil Confinement* 21:3 (1995): 317–435 (theme issue).

14. *In re Gault*, 387 U.S. 1, 27 (1967).

15. C. Camp and G. Camp, *The Corrections Yearbook 1995: Juvenile Corrections* (South Salem, NY: Criminal Justice Institute, 1995), p. 1.

16. *Kent v. U.S.*, 383, U.S. 541 (1966).

17. *McKeiver v. Pennsylvania*, 403 U.S. 541 (1971).

18. *Juvenile Justice and Delinquency Act of 1975, P.L. 93-415*, signed into law on September 7, 1994.

19. Lamar Empey, "The Social Construction of Childhood, Delinquency and Social Reform," in Malcolm Klein, ed., *The Juvenile Justice System* (Beverly Hills, CA: Sage, 1976), pp. 27–54. See also Ralph Weisheit and Katherine Johnson, "Exploring the Dimensions of Support for Decriminalizing Drugs," *Journal of Drug Issues* 22:1 (1992): 53–73.

20. Institute of Judicial Administration, American Bar Association, *Standards Relating to Interim Status: Release, Control and Detention of Accused Juvenile Offenders Between Arrest and Disposition* (Cambridge, MA: Ballinger, 1980).

21. *Standards and Guidelines for Detention of Children and Youth* (Paramus, NJ: National Council on Crime and Delinquency, 1961), p. 3. See also their *Juvenile Justice Policy Statement* (San Francisco: National Council on Crime and Delinquency, 1991).

22. Ibid.

22. Ibid.

23. Irving Kaufman. "Juvenile Justice and Injustice," *American Bar Association Journal* 62 (1976): 730-734.

24. Steven Donziger, *The Real War on Crime* (New York: HarperCollins, 1996), pp. 134–140.

Special Category Offenders

Overview

Now we come to the chapter that deals with those offenders who have many more problems than other offenders in the mainstream of criminal behavior. We shall examine some of the so-called rejects of society who are too often found in America's jails and correctional facilities.[1] Many of those individuals are handicapped by their mental processes, and others are labeled by their specific problems, extreme behavior, or personal background.

Of the many categories that could be examined, we have chosen to discuss the *mentally disordered offender*, the *developmentally challenged offender*, the *sex offender*, *geriatric inmates* and *offenders*, and *inmates with AIDS*. Although those categories do not exhaust the possible types of special category offenders, they offer a spectrum of the problems faced by correctional administrators and individual offenders in their custody and treatment. Little meaningful programming was done in the area of special category inmates until the last few years. We will delve a little into the history and development of categories of mentally disturbed and mentally ill offenders to provide a proper framework for examination of these special people.

The funding crunch of the early 1990s, combined with increasing overcrowding, continues to place these stigmatized offenders into the correctional bureaucratic system, where their special needs are more often ignored than met. What their needs are and how they are met will be discussed in this chapter. We shall also assess the growing numbers of these special categories and how our systems are coping with this problem. The student has now been exposed to most of the "clients" found in the criminal justice and juvenile justice systems. Part V will delve into the rights of all of these offenders, in or out of the confinement facilities in America, as well as their right to life itself.

> Social groups create deviance by making the rules whose infraction constitutes deviance and by applying those rules to particular people and labeling them as outsiders.
>
> —H. S. Becker

The Mentally Disordered Offender

What kind of illness would civilized people find so repulsive that they would reject the sufferers in the most barbaric fashion and brand them with a stigma that would remain, even if a cure were achieved? These unfortunates—the mentally disordered—used to be scorned and burned but, in more enlightened times, we built backwoods fortresses for them, presumably to protect ourselves from contagion. They have been executed as witches, subjected to exorcisms, chained, or thrown into gatehouses and prisons to furnish a horrible diversion for the other prisoners.[2] The methods recommended by Celus, a first-century Roman scholar, established the pattern of treatment for the years to come: "When he [the mentally disordered person] has said or done anything wrong, he must be chastised by hunger, chains, and fetters."[3] In line with that approach, throughout human history the mentally disordered have been subjected to misguided, cruel, sadistic, and fear-based treatment, ranging from burning at the stake to banishment from society.

Before the Middle Ages, the **mentally disturbed** were generally tolerated. They were usually cared for locally by members of their own family, tribal system, or primitive society. However, the advent of widespread poverty, disease, and religious fanaticism seemed to trigger intolerance for any deviation. The mentally disturbed were thought to be possessed by devils and demons and were punished harshly because of it. At that time, the insane were driven out of society; later, they were confined—another form of isolation from society.

The first insane asylum was constructed in Europe in 1408.[4] From that date until recently, the asylum was a dumping ground for all the mentally disordered people we could neither understand nor cure. The states, one after another, responded to that compelling method of ridding society of misfits, and built numerous institutions during the mid-1800s. The inflated claims of cures for mental illness could not stand up against the process of institutionalization, however, and long-term commitments, not cures, became the rule of the day.

Asylums became yet another "invisible empire" in America, with the punitive excesses and lack of care or caring ignored by society. With the discovery of tranquilizing drugs, they became places where patients were put into a controllable stupor, until the "magic cure" for mental illness could be found. Longer and longer periods of institutionalization, often ordered at the request of family members, finally got the attention of the courts. In the 1960s the rights of all citizens, to include the mentally ill and the convict, were reexamined at every level. The abuses of the asylums were brought to light and the counterreaction was extreme. In the early 1970s, state after state adopted policies under the Community Mental Health Act that swept the country. The essential goal was to release (**deinstitutionalize**) all inmates of the asylums who were not a "clear and present danger" to themselves and others.

Although benign in their intents, these acts flooded the central cities of America with tens of thousands of mentally impaired street people. The response by most jurisdictions has been to transfer the problem into the jails and correctional institutions of America, a process known as "transinstitutionalization."[5] In Seattle, Washington, the former King County executive was fond of saying that the King County Jail was the "third largest mental health facility in the state. The first being the Western State Hospital, the second the section of I-5 *between* the jail and the hospital."[6]

Mental Illness and Corrections

Most persons familiar with the justice system will understand that the courts are concerned with the three major types of pleas that could be entered in the preadjudication phases: "incompetent to stand trial," "not guilty by reason of insanity," and "guilty but mentally ill." The special issues in determining guilt are described in this chapter. In addition, there are two categories of postadjudication offenders whose special psychological needs pose problems for institutional corrections: inmates whose mental health deteriorates to episodic crises and those sentenced to death who become mentally disturbed.

For some inmates, the impacts of prison life overwhelm their usual coping patterns. Some factors that lead to "prison psychosis" include the routine of the prison, fear of other inmates, forced homosexual behavior, assault and fear of assault, deterioration in affairs and circumstances of family on the outside of prison, depression, and so on. When the psychological crisis comes, correctional administrators frequently transfer affected inmates to prison infirmaries or psychological treatment wards, or initiate inmate transfer to a mental health system. Long-term and intensive psychotherapy for "mentally ill" inmates, however, is believed to be rare. Treatment for episodic mental crisis tends to remain at the first aid level in many states.

Death rows do not usually contain a large proportion of a prison's population but subsume a disproportionate share of the per inmate cost due to the demands of observing, caring, and maintaining death row. That includes a lower staff-inmate ratio, mail processing, death-watch officer workload, closer custody during recreational periods, and so on. Some inmates on death row become mentally ill and, as such, cannot be executed (*Ford* v. *Wainright*, 106 S. Ct. 2595, 1986). The state has an additional burden of determining if the death-row inmate is insane, establishing some procedure to restore the inmate to sanity, and then certifying the sanity of the patient-inmate. Because this would be tantamount to a "death sentence" and thus not a favor for the inmate, it is unlikely mental health physicians would undertake that process alone or with great enthusiasm. It remains for the states to develop procedures for identifying, diagnosing, treating, and certifying the sanity of death-row inmates who claim to be insane.

For the extreme behavior cases, there are special units for more intensive treatment, such as the one in Washington state. That unit is a model of how to deal with extreme mentally and behaviorally disordered prisoners. Unfortunately, that fine facility can handle only 144 inmates. Though commendable, the figure is only about one-tenth of the commonly recognized population of inmates who could use more intensive mental health services. One quickly finds that only the really severe cases are able to be referred to the Special Offender Center.

Is the mentally disordered person more prone to criminal behavior? Or does the criminal justice system respond to such misfits in a legal manner only because the mental health system has been rendered helpless to deal with most of them? Steadman and Monahan have studied that relationship and have made some rather interesting discoveries:

- The correlates of crime among the mentally disordered appear to be the same as the correlates of crime among any other group: age, gender, race, social class, and prior criminality.
- Likewise, the correlates of mental disorder among criminal offenders appear to be the same as those in other populations: age, social class, and previous disorder. Populations characterized by the correlates of both crime and mental disorder (e.g., low social class) can be expected to show high rates of both, and they do. ∎

SOURCE: Henry J. Steadman and John Monahan, *Crime and Mental Disorder* (Washington, D.C.: U.S. Department of Justice, 1984), p. 5.

Mentally Ill Inmates

From the 1960s to the 1980s, the deinstitutionalization movement demanded that the mentally ill be treated in the community, using new drug therapies that appeared to control even the most extreme behaviors of the mentally ill. This liberation of psychiatric patients was reinforced by court decisions that awarded certain legal rights to the emotionally ill. Yet few community programs were developed to treat psychiatric patients effectively. Released to the community without adequate support and treatment services, the mentally ill gravitated to confinement facilities for offenders, particularly the jail but also the prison.

It is estimated that about 10 percent of prisoners have severe or significant psychiatric disabilities. The greater the level of disability, the more likely the

DEINSTITUTIONAL-IZATION

This concept contains the transfer of the mentally ill from confinement facilities for criminal actions (rather than underlying mental health problems). Prison overcrowding, acute shortage of funds for treatment services, deleterious effects of confinement, and lengthier sentences to prison have meant that prison mental health services are generally found to be inadequate.

inmate to receive mental health services. In practice, proportionately more female prisoners use mental health services than do males, and whites are more likely to seek or secure prison mental health services. Perhaps one-half of the inmates (at least in New York) who need such treatment go untended.

While the U.S. Supreme Court has not found that inmates have a constitutional right to treatment, it has ruled an inmate's constitutional right to medical treatment includes the right to treatment for serious emotional illness. Corrections is caught in the middle. Institutions are not required to provide services simply because their clients are criminals, and thus have shifted critical funds to other uses (such as increased security staffing). On the other hand, the threat of potential litigation has meant that some revision and provision of mental health services for seriously ill inmates is necessary.[7]

As the mentally ill became a larger segment of the population in jails and prisons, professionals in the mental health field became essential to the correctional administrators. Although the ratio of mental health practitioners to clients remains much too low, there has been some progress. Because many institutions must deal with mental health issues on a priority basis, little to no services are provided for the majority who do not exhibit violent or bizarre behavior. It is a practical fact in corrections that "the squeaky wheel gets the oil."

It appears that the relationship between crime and mental disorder (at least in *groups*, as shown in this study) has no real causal effect.[8] It is essential that we learn more about distinguishing between different kinds of mental illness and their impacts on correctional administration. It is important to remember that the real link to look for is one that indicates the potential harm

Mentally Ill Prison Inmates

In the 1960s and 1970s, the deinstitutionalization movement demanded that the mentally ill be treated in the community, using new drug therapies that appeared to control even the most extreme behaviors of the mentally ill. This liberation of psychiatric patients was reinforced by court decisions that recognized certain legal rights of the emotionally ill. Yet few community programs were developed to treat psychiatric patients effectively. Released to the community without adequate support and treatment services, the mentally ill gravitated to confinement facilities for offenders, particularly the jail but also the prison.

It is estimated that about 10 percent of prisoners have severe or significant psychiatric disabilities. The greater the level of disability, the more likely the inmate to receive mental health services. In practice, proportionately more female prisoners use mental health services than do males, and whites are more likely to seek or secure prison mental health services. Perhaps one-half of the inmates (at least in New York) who need such treatment go untended.

About 8 percent of the federal Canadian inmates are estimated to become psychotic during their lifetimes, and another 22 percent would be depressive. Sex offenders are particularly prone to depression and anxiety.

Deinstutionalization, transfer of the mentally ill to confinement facilities for criminal actions (rather than underlying mental health problems), prison overcrowding, acute shortage of funds for treatment services, deleterious effects of confinement, and lengthier sentences to prison have meant that prison mental health services are inadequate.

While the U.S. Supreme Court has not found that inmates have a constitutional right to treatment, it has ruled an inmate's constitutional right to medical treatment includes the right to treatment for serious emotional illness. Corrections is caught in the middle. Institutions are not required to provide services simply because their clients are criminals, and thus have shifted critical funds to other uses (such as increased security staffing). On the other hand, the threat of potential litigation has meant that some revision and provision of mental health services for seriously ill inmates is necessary. ∎

SOURCES: Henry Steadman et al., "Estimating Mental Health Needs and Service Utilization Among Prison Inmates," *Bulletin of the American Academy of Psychiatry and the Law* 19:3 (1991): 297–307. Canadian data from Laurence Motiuk and Frank Porporino, *The Prevalence, Nature and Severity of Mental Health Problems Among Federal Inmates in Canadian Penitentiaries* (Ontario: Correctional Service Canada, 1992).

to the mentally ill person and others. It may be a long time before such options are available to corrections.

Two Ways to Escape Criminal Responsibility

There are two justifications that defendants can invoke in an attempt to relieve themselves of criminal responsibility for a criminal act. The first is "**not guilty by reason of insanity**"; the second is "**incompetent to stand trial**." In the first instance, offenders do not deny the commission of the act but assert that they did not have the capacity to understand the nature of the act or that it was wrong. The second instance is based on the common-law criterion that defendants must be able to understand the charges against them and to cooperate with their counsel in the preparation of their own defense. The procedures for determining competency vary considerably from jurisdiction to jurisdiction, but most make it a court decision based on psychiatric testimony. If defendants are found incompetent to stand trial, they are usually committed to a mental institution until declared competent.

The Criminally Insane

With the advent of legal insanity and legal incompetence as defenses against criminal conviction came the development of special asylums for the **criminally insane**, in most cases just another form of prison without due process protections. These institutions are usually reserved for the following categories of offenders:

1. Persons adjudicated incompetent to enter a plea or stand trial;
2. Defendants found not guilty by reason of insanity;
3. Persons adjudicated under special statutes, for example, "sexually dangerous persons," "defective delinquents," "sexual psychopaths," among others;
4. Convicted and sentenced offenders who have become mentally disturbed while serving a prison sentence and have been transferred to a mental health facility; and
5. Other potentially hazardous mentally ill persons requiring special security during the course of their evaluation and treatment.[9]

In more recent years, those claiming to be not guilty by reason of insanity (NGRI) have been the subject of considerable debate.[10] President Richard M. Nixon persistently sought to have the NGRI defense abolished. More informed criminologists point to such problems with the insanity defense as excessive media coverage, suspicion of malingering by the defendant, and conflicting and suspicious testimony by professional colleagues testifying for either the defense or the prosecution.

The insanity defense is used in only about 1 percent of all felony cases, and, of those, only one in four are found to be NGRI. One study found only the most emotionally disturbed defendants to be successful in their plea and that successful persons had committed more serious offenses. The decision to acquit is more frequently made in court by prosecutors, defense attorneys, and the judge, and less frequently by jury members.[11] Insanity aquittees are generally found less likely than their cohort of convicted offenders to commit crimes after release.[12]

John Wayne Gacy killed no fewer than 33 young men between 1972 and 1977 by luring them to his home for sex, making him the man who committed more confirmed murders than anyone in America. He was a prominent Chicago contractor and was known for playing a clown at children's hospitals. He died in 1996.

Prosecutors often hope that those accused offenders acquitted[13] through the plea of NGRI will be institutionalized for a period sufficient to reduce their dangerousness, and to provide both public safety and retribution. The debate continues. Perhaps the best solution would be to determine guilt and then shift the issue of diminished capacity (insanity, in this case) to the sentencing or case disposition stage. That position was recognized by the American Psychiatric Association following the attack of John Hinckley on the life of President Ronald Reagan.

As a response, by 1986 twelve states abolished the insanity defense entirely, then created "guilty but mentally ill" (GBMI) statutes in its place.[14] Under these statutes, an offender's mental illness is acknowledged but not seen as sufficient reason to allow him or her to escape criminal responsibility. If convicted, offenders are committed to prison. Some states will provide mental health treatment in the prison setting, but others may transfer the offender to a mental health facility for treatment. In Georgia, defendants who entered insanity pleas but were determined GBMI received harsher sentences than their counterparts whose guilt was determined in trial, suggesting increased punishment for the disturbed offender.[15]

The position of the American Psychiatric Association is that significant changes in the legislation should be made to deal with the disposition of violent insanity acquittees:

1. Special legislation should be designed for those persons charged with violent offenses who have been found not guilty by reason of insanity.

2. Confinement and release decisions should be made by a board including both psychiatrists and other professionals representing the criminal justice system and akin to a parole board.

3. Release should be conditional on having a treatment supervision plan in place, with the necessary resources available to implement it.

4. The board having jurisdiction over the released insanity acquittees should also have the authority to reconfine them.

5. When psychiatric treatment in a hospital setting has obtained the maximal treatment benefit possible, but the board believes that for other reasons confinement is still necessary, the insanity acquittee should be transferred to the most appropriate nonhospital facility (prison).[16]

While the public remains upset by a seeming loophole in the net of justice, the courts continue to try to find equitable ways to deal with the offender who has diminished mental capacity.

The Problems of Prediction

It is unfortunate that the long indeterminate sentences often given to mentally disordered offenders reflect a fear that those committed might be a problem in the future. Lewis Carroll presented the problem effectively in *Through the Looking Glass*:

> "[T]here's the King's Messenger," said the Queen. "He's in prison now, being punished; and the trial doesn't even begin till next Wednesday; and of course the crime comes last of all."
>
> "Suppose he never commits the crime?" said Alice.

"That would be all the better, wouldn't it?" the Queen said, as she turned the plaster round her finger with a bit of ribbon.

Alice felt there was no denying *that*. "Of course it would be all the better," she said, "but it wouldn't be all the better his being punished."

"You're wrong *there*, at any rate," said the Queen. "Were you ever punished?"

"Only for faults," said Alice.

"And you were all the better for it, I know!" the Queen said triumphantly.

"Yes, but then I *had* done the things I was punished for," said Alice. "That makes all the difference."

"But if you hadn't done them," the Queen said, "that would have been better still; better, and better, and better!"[17]

It is the expectation that someone is capable of predicting criminal inclination that makes so questionable the programs for treating the mentally disordered. Who can **predict potential dangerousness** with any degree of accuracy? The noted psychiatrist Bernard Rubin stated, "The belief in the psychiatrist's ability to predict the likely dangerousness of a patient's future behavior is almost universally held, yet it lacks empirical support." And he added, "Labeling of deviancy as mental illness or predicting dangerousness is just a convention to get someone to treatment. Once in treatment, the concept of dangerousness is forgotten."[18]

So we see the paradox of requiring psychiatrists to predict behavior and to attach a label to offenders, when that might result in an indefinite, or even lifelong, commitment to a mental institution for someone who is not really dangerous (a "false positive" prediction). Further, the individual is then labeled for custody and treatment in a special area within that institution. When we consider the wealth of folklore surrounding mental institutions, it becomes clear that a dreadful stigma accompanies the label of "criminally insane."

The Developmentally Challenged Offender

Within the correctional system there are offenders who, though considered legally sane and competent to stand trial, are **developmentally challenged**. (An IQ score of 69 or below on a standardized test is the generally accepted measure for identifying the developmentally challenged, but there are exceptions.) Their intellectual level and social adaptability measure well below average; yet they are adjudged legally responsible for their actions.

In their guidelines for incarcerated developmentally challenged offenders, Santamour and West address the problems encountered:

1. In prison, the retarded [developmentally challenged] offender is slower to adjust to routine, has more difficulty in learning regulations, and accumulates more rule infractions, which, in turn, affect housing, parole, and other related matters.
2. Retarded [developmentally challenged] inmates rarely take part in rehabilitation programs because of their desire to mask their deficiencies.

3. They often suffer the brunt of practical jokes and sexual harassment.

4. Such inmates are more often denied parole, serving on the average two or three years longer than other prisoners for the same offense.[19]

Administrators in both fields (corrections and mental health) have a tendency to regard the developmentally challenged offender as a misfit in their system of services. (Developmentally challenged tend to have higher rates of involvement in violent incidents in prison.[20]) They look to one another to assume responsibility for programming and funding. Because of the few resources available to each system and even more pressing concerns, the result is often very limited programming.

The special needs of the developmentally challenged offender are unique, and the program models are few. Those models that do exist are limited primarily to special education programs geared more to the needs of the individual with learning disabilities other than those of the "retarded" person. One promising model concerned with the developmentally challenged offender on a county level focuses on substance abuse, psychological needs, and both vocational and educational improvement.[21]

Developmentally Disabled Prisoners: Findings

Few jails or prisons have sufficient facilities and programs to handle the special needs of developmentally disabled offenders, and hospitals and other health facilities are seldom capable of administering correctional programs with sufficient security to protect society's rights. Without alternatives, judges are left with no other choice than to sentence those individuals to prison.

- Some mentally retarded offenders require incarceration because of the seriousness of their crimes or their records as repeat offenders, but most other mentally retarded offenders could be diverted from prison to community treatment programs while still ensuring the safety of the community.

- There is tremendous variation in estimates of the number of mentally retarded persons incarcerated in prison: earlier research indicates that the percentage of those offenders is higher than the percentage within the general population, while the most recent studies place the percentage at about the same level as that within the general population.

- Mentally retarded offenders are often used by their peers, reflecting their great need for approval and acceptance. They have no long-term perspective and little ability to think in a causal way to understand the consequences of their actions.

- Retarded persons are often victimized or abused by other inmates.

- Identifying the offenders who have special needs is essential for planning individualized programs. Due process and functional diagnosis and evaluation performed by specially trained staff utilizing sophisticated assessment tools and procedures are essential.

- Because mental retardation is usually undetected, violation of the legal rights of such persons is frequent.

- Criminal justice and corrections personnel are not presently trained to handle the special problems and needs of such offenders.

- Matters of competency relating to diminished mental capacity should be considered at the first point of contact with the criminal justice system and at each decision point in the continuum.

- Developmentally disabled offenders should be assigned to programs that meet their individual needs: some may be mixed in with the regular prison population; some need a segregated environment; some would benefit most from a community setting; and others might be placed in a regular mental retardation group home or guardianship arrangement.

- The survey of local jurisdictions revealed the need for training about mental retardation for criminal justice personnel who normally do not distinguish between mental retardation and mental illness; the need for early identification of mentally retarded persons once they come in contact with the criminal justice system; and the need for more community resources, particularly residential programs, to serve mentally retarded offenders. ■

Working with learning-disabled inmates

—PHOTO BY STEPHEN STEURER, COURTESY OF AMERICAN CORRECTIONAL ASSOCIATION

It should be emphasized that all offenders within the correctional system, whether or not they are developmentally challenged, demand our attention. Abuses are all too frequent, and few inmates are spared from the pervasively negative impact of the correctional system itself. The consideration given here to the special needs of the developmentally challenged offender is not meant in any way to endorse the conditions under which prisoners in general are treated but, rather, to draw attention to that group's special needs.

AN HISTORIC PERSPECTIVE

In reviewing historical and philosophical trends in the study of the developmentally challenged offender, it is noteworthy that before the late nineteenth century, there was little attempt to differentiate between the developmentally challenged individual and one who commits a crime. Farber, tracing the development of theories with respect to mental retardation and criminality found that, for the majority of theorists, there was a general equation between criminality and subnormal intelligence.[22] Brown and Courtless outlined three phases that characterized the late nineteenth and early twentieth centuries in the development of theories concerning the developmentally challenged person and criminal behavior.[23] From 1890 to 1920, theorists felt that mental retardation predisposed a person to commit criminal acts—linking mental retardation and criminality with poverty, insanity, and moral and physical degradation. The second period to which Brown and Courtless referred—1921 to 1960—has been called the time of "denial and neglect." Theorists questioned whether in fact mental retardation predisposed one to commit criminal acts.

Currently there is less reluctance to associate retardation directly with delinquency. Much of the revived interest from the 1960s to date has been generated by the legal community and not by criminologists. Such a phenomenon stems from a growing awareness that the preponderance of developmentally challenged individuals in the criminal justice system may be more an administrative and legal artifact than evidence for a causal relationship between mental retardation and criminality.

Texas Has Recommendations

1. All criminal justice personnel should receive basic training in regard to mental retardation.

2. Every effort should be made to identify offenders who are mentally retarded at each stage of the criminal justice process, especially in the earlier stages.

3. Funding should be increased, both for adult probation and for parole, for the purchase of community services for the mentally retarded probationer and parolee.

4. In all appropriate cases the mentally retarded offender should be diverted to community programs.

5. For those mentally retarded offenders who are sentenced to prison, great care should be taken to protect them from abuse and manipulation by other inmates, and special program activities should be provided that take into consideration their handicap of mental retardation.

6. Experts in the field of mental retardation in Texas should direct some of their efforts to development of prevention programs to keep mentally retarded persons from becoming offenders.

7. Mentally retarded offenders should be accepted by all programs designed for mentally retarded persons.

8. The Texas Code of Criminal Procedures should be amended to allow for the transfer of mentally retarded offenders from Texas Department of Corrections to an appropriate Texas Department of Mental Health and Mental Retardation (TDMHMR) program where the prisoner may, in fact, serve out the full prison term.

9. The question of competency should be considered at the first possible stage in the criminal justice system.

10. Mental retardation should be considered in the law as a mitigating circumstance and therefore be taken into consideration at the time of sentencing if, in fact, the offender has been found competent but mentally retarded.

11. The standards of Texas Commission on Jail Standards should include specific references to mentally retarded inmates and their needs.

12. Ultimately, the TDMHMR should provide services to all mentally retarded adult offenders.

13. In Texas IQ tests should be developed that are less culturally biased against blacks and minorities.

The landmark *Ruiz* decision has also set the tone for judicial consideration of the developmentally challenged inmate.[24] This class action suit involved issues of overcrowding, medical care, inmate trustees as guards, and other conditions; the federal court declared the Texas prison system to be unconstitutional. Judge Justice found that between 10 and 15 percent of the Texas Department of Corrections inmates were retarded and that they were distributed throughout the system. The judge echoed Santamour and West concerning the retarded inmates' special problems and added the following:

1. They are abnormally prone to injuries, many of which are job related.

2. They are decidedly disadvantaged when appearing before a disciplinary committee. This raises basic problems of fairness and the special need for assistance.[25]

It seems obvious that the issue of the developmentally challenged inmate is slowly coming to the forefront, led by the efforts of the courts.

Retarded offenders are often individuals who have never been accepted by society at large. Becoming a part of the "society of captives" is often their first experience of acceptance and thus has a pervasive impact. At Bridgewater State Hospital and Prison in Massachusetts, personnel commenting on the strengths of the association between retarded inmates and the prison culture noted that it was only the retarded inmates who returned to prison for social visits. Are developmentally challenged offenders in need of special consideration in regard to criminal responsibility? As noted by Richard C. Allen:

Historically, society has pursued three alternative courses with the developmentally challenged offender: we have ignored his limitations and special needs; or we have sought to tailor traditional criminal law processes to fit them; we have grouped him with psychopaths, sociopaths, and sex deviates in a kind of society of the outcast and hopeless.[26]

One way to accomplish such consideration would be with a special court, similar to a juvenile court, where the developmentally challenged offender is handled both for the crime and for his or her condition.

THE COMMON SEX OFFENSES

Any analysis of sex offenses is complicated because state legislatures are often too inhibited to describe specifically the acts they are seeking to punish. Thus, punishment may be decreed for "lewd and lascivious conduct," "acts against nature," "carnal knowledge," "imperiling the morals of a minor," and so on. Almost any sexual activity may be prosecuted under one or another of those vague and broad rubrics. The same term, moreover, means different things in different states. Thus, *sodomy*, which in many states refers primarily to male homosexual acts, may or may not also be applied to heterosexual oral or anal intercourse or to sexual contacts with animals.

Highly misleading terms may be used, such as *statutory rape* for an offense that is not rape at all but sexual intercourse with a fully consenting female who has not yet reached the age of legal consent (eighteen in some states).[27]

Discussions of **sex offenses** (as shown by recent trends in Figure 18.1), are further complicated by the fact that a man charged with a serious offense such as rape may be permitted, in the course of plea bargaining, to plead guilty to a lesser offense; hence men who are in fact rapists may be lodged in correctional institutions for such apparently nonsexual offenses as breaking and entering or assault. In the following discussion we consider the actual offenses committed, rather than the vague legal terminology often used or the lesser offenses to which an offender may plead.

Until the past few years, the term *sex offense* commonly called to mind a lust-murder of the most irrational and heinous type. More recently, the intense and

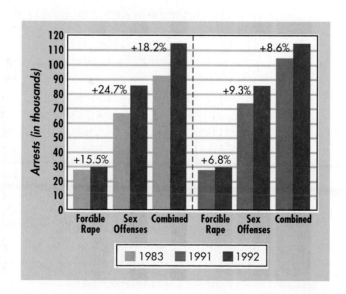

FIGURE

18.1

Sex Offenses Cleared by Arrest, 1983–1992 and 1991–1992

SOURCE: Federal Bureau of Investigation, *Uniform Crime Reports 1992* (Washington, D.C.: U.S. Department of Justice, 1993), pp. 222, 225.

proper concern of the women's movement with rape and related crimes, such as assault with intent to commit rape, has tended to make rape the predominant sex offense in the minds of many people. Certainly, rape is among the most important of the sex offenses, and it is an offense with which the public will be continually concerned. Many experts feel that rape, in its more violent forms, is not a sex crime at all but a crime of power and dominance over women.[28]

By far the most common sex offenses, however, are three that are rarely prosecuted: fornication, adultery, and male homosexual contact:

Fornication, which is sexual intercourse between persons not married to each other, remains a crime in most states but is generally ignored by the law enforcement and criminal justice systems.

Adultery is sexual intercourse between two persons, at least one of whom is married to someone else. It also remains a crime in most states, rarely punished and almost never leading to participation in a treatment program.

Male homosexual conduct and other acts classed as *sodomy* are the most common of all sex offenses; the Kinsey reports and more recent data indicate that millions of such sexual contacts are committed each week.

Such offenses were not lightly punished during past eras of American history. In the 1640s in Massachusetts, for example, **buggery**—anal intercourse with man, woman, or beast—was punishable by death for both parties. In 1648, rape also became punishable by death. Rapists whose lives were spared might be sentenced to have their nostrils slit and to wear halters around their necks. Adultery with a married or engaged woman was punishable by death for both parties, but adultery between a married man and a single unbetrothed woman was considered mere fornication, punishable by a public whipping. Also punishable by public whipping was sexual intercourse between unmarried persons and pregnancy of unmarried women.

Times have changed, however. Many states have repealed their laws against sodomy—including both male homosexual acts and heterosexual oral and anal

AIDS is also found in confinement and requires special care

—PHOTO BY JEFFREY D. SCOTT, COURTESY OF IMPACT VISUALS

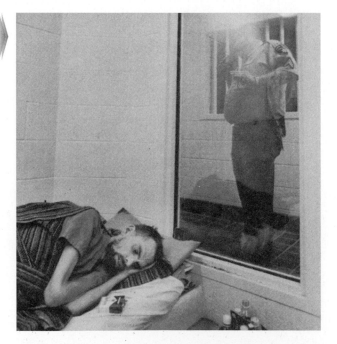

acts. Most states that have repealed their sodomy laws have similarly decriminalized fornication, adultery, and other sexual activities engaged in by consenting adults in private.[29] Similar repeals are under consideration in other states. Even in states in which such laws remain on the books, they are rarely enforced, and even more rarely do they lead to the person's participation in a treatment program for sex offenders.

Laws governing public indecency and solicitation—solicitation for both prostitution and male homosexual contact—are still enforced in many jurisdictions. But they commonly lead to fines, probation, or short sentences in local correctional institutions. Rarely if ever do they lead to participation in a sex offender treatment program.

With enormous categories of offenses eliminated or almost eliminated and with the very small number of rape-murders, sex-torture cases, and sex dismemberments similarly eliminated as grounds for providing treatment, there remain five categories of sex offenses that account for the overwhelming majority of treatment program participants:

1. rape, attempted rape, assault with intent to rape, and the like,[30]
2. child molestation,[31]
3. incest,[32]
4. exhibitionism and voyeurism, and
5. miscellaneous offenses (breaking and entering, arson, and the like) in cases in which there is a sexual motivation.

The great majority of sex offenders currently participating in treatment programs are predominantly heterosexual and are there for heterosexual offenses— though some of them, like some heterosexual nonoffenders, have had occasional or incidental homosexual contacts. Most homosexual participants in treatment programs are there for sexual contacts, rarely violent, with male children or adolescents. Some are homosexual incest offenders. A few have committed homosexual rape or rape-related offenses.

Almost all sex offenses prosecuted in the United States today (except for prostitution-related offenses and offenses involving indecent stage performances) are committed by men. The only significant exceptions are the rare cases of child molestation in which a woman is prosecuted along with a man, often her husband. As a rough estimate, two or three hundred males are prosecuted for sex offenses

Child Abusers and Molesters

Any act of commission or omission that endangers or impairs a child's physical or emotional health and development. The major forms are physical (such as neglect), emotional (deprivation and abandonment), and sexual. Child abusers are found among all ethnic, racial, class, and religious groups. A child abuser is typically a person closely related by blood, kinship, or marriage, such as a parent, stepparent, guardian, other relative, or even a neighbor engaged in a repeated pattern of abuse.

A child molester is one who injures or has questionable sexual relations or dealings with a person under the age of puberty or legal age. Victims may be subject to rape, fondling, indecent exposure, sodomy, or murder.

In correctional facilities, child abusers and molesters rank low in the social system and are themselves frequently targets of prejudicial or lethal acts by other inmates.　■

SOURCE: George Rush, *The Dictionary of Criminal Justice* (Guilford, CT: Dushkin, 1991), p. 44.

for every female prosecuted. It is probable, of course, that the ratio of offenses committed by females is much higher than the ratio of prosecutions.

Most sex offenders in treatment programs are aged eighteen to thirty-five. A significant minority (mostly child molesters) are past fifty. How do the sex offenders enrolled in treatment programs differ from the remainder of sex offenders? At least five "sorting processes" distinguish the two groups. Some sex offenses are reported to the police; others are not. Most rapes and a wide range of lesser offenses go unreported. No man ends up in a treatment program as a result of an unreported offense. After an offense is reported, the perpetrator may or may not be apprehended and prosecuted. Those who escape arrest and prosecution no doubt differ in significant respects from those who reach the courts.

Of those prosecuted, a small number are found not guilty and a very large number (mostly minor offenders) receive suspended sentences or are placed on probation without assignment to a treatment program. Of the offenders remaining after those three sorting processes, some are sent to ordinary correctional institutions and others to treatment programs. Who will be sent to treatment programs depends in part on state law, in part on the judge, and in part on the availability of a treatment program.[33]

Finally, most treatment programs can (and do) reject or transfer to other institutions those offenders they deem unsuitable for treatment. The net effect of these five sorting processes is a population of program participants from which most of the very serious offenders and most of the very minor offenders have been screened.

Sex Offenders and Probation

Probation officers are generally underprepared to work with sex offenders because such efforts are complex and time intensive. Most officers lack specific training in the required interpersonal and professional skills, caseload size inhibits effective supervision, probation linkages with other social service agencies and providers are not optimal, female officers sometimes feel concerned about their own safety, and such offenders are "high-need" cases.

Enhanced probation services, through specialized caseload and electronic monitoring and intensive supervision, are increasingly used by probation officers to control sex offenders. As these strategies are more widely implemented across the nation, a smaller proportion of treatable sex offenders will be committed to prison facilities.

It is possible, of course, that tomorrow an alumnus of one of those treatment programs may commit a heinous lust-murder.[34] However, an alumnus of a local high school or a member of a church choir could do the same. Treatment programs are specifically designed to minimize the likelihood that an offender will commit any sex offense following release—either a crime of the grossly offensive type or a lesser offense like the ones the offender committed in the past.

Sex Offenders in Prisons

Attitudes toward sex offenders widely held by the public[35] as well as by legislators,[36] judges,[37] corrections officers,[38] and others in positions of power are largely influenced by traditional beliefs, and they are still changing today. The number

Minnesota's Sex Offender Program: A Model?

In Minnesota, more inmates are in prison for sex offenses than for any other category of crime. On January 1, 1996, 1,036 or 22 percent of the 4,720 inmates in state correctional facilities were serving time for sex offenses as their most serious offense.

The number of sex offenders sent to prison and the percentage of the total inmate population they represent have been increasing.

The January, 1996 data show a 250 percent increase in the number of sex offenders from 1981 to 1996 (see Figure 1-1).

Minnesota has developed a wide range of programming options for sex offenders. Most states do not incarcerate as high a percentage of inmates labeled as sex offenders. According to the Justice Department's Statistics, 9.4 percent of prisoners in the U.S. are incarcerated for sex offenses.

It is a commonly held belief that sex offenders return to prison for sex crimes after release more often than other offenders return to prison. Statistics do not indicate that this is the case. A follow-up study of 237 sex offenders released in 1991 shows that over 95 percent did not have convictions resulting in a return to prison for a new sex offense after three years.

These data confirm earlier reports. For example, 95 percent of 222 sex offenders released in 1988 did not have a conviction resulting in a state prison sentence for new sex offenses after a four-year follow-up.

A January, 1992 review of 1,243 sex offenders released from Minnesota correctional facilities since 1985 indicates that a total of 57 offenders or 4.6 percent returned to prison with a new sex offense. In 1994, the average sentence for sex offenders convicted of the most serious criminal sexual conduct was 161 months or over 13 and one-half years. Data from 1989 indicated that the average sentence in Minnesota was 84 months.

After reaching their mandatory release date, serious sex offenders are placed on supervised release, monitored intensively, and may be sent back to prison if they violate conditions of their release. About 15 percent of the sex offenders on supervised release are sent back to prison for not following their release conditions.

Since 1989, penalties for sex offenders have been increased substantially by Minnesota, doubling the presumptive sentence for first-time sex offenders convicted of serious criminal conduct and repeat sex offenders.

Modifications also include life sentences and mandatory minimum sentences for certain categories of repeat sex offenders.

A recent comparison shows time served in prison in Minnesota for rape is higher than all other 34 states in a national study.

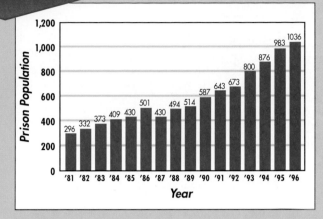

Sex offender prison population by year, January 1, 1981 to 1996.
SOURCE: Minnesota Department of Corrections.

Review teams in the department analyze public risk, monitoring cases to determine if they should be referred for possible commitment as a psychopathic personality. Upon their mandated release dates, public risk monitoring cases not referred for civil commitment or not civilly committed by the court are placed under the most strict surveillance available.

Other recent procedural improvements include:

- Notification of police chiefs and sheriffs of release of all offenders from state institutions.

- Establishment of a 24-hour-a-day, seven-day-a-week coverage system that helps ensure priority arrest warrants are issued immediately

New programs have been developed throughout the state to provide post-release programming for sex offenders released from correctional institutions. Participation in this programming is routinely required as a condition of release. Specialized approaches have been developed for sex offenders who have not completed treatment during their incarceration.

Specialized training for state and local corrections agents and probation officers who supervise sex offenders has been developed.

Probation officers are also required to report the address of sex offenders under their supervision to local law enforcement authorities.

State law requiring notification of victims of an inmate's prison release was expanded in 1991 to include notification of an inmate's transfer to minimum security. Notification occurs only at the victim's request.

The legislature has established the Community-Based Sex Offender Program Evaluation Project to gather the necessary information to develop effective and efficient mechanisms by which it can fund, monitor, and coordinate community-based sex offender programming.

As of this date, field research has produced information

Continued on page 358

(Continued from page 357)

Minnesota's Sex Offender Program: A Model?

on over 1,400 offenders placed on probation in the years 1987, 1989, and 1996. This information, when linked to the data regularly collected by the state Bureau of Criminal Apprehension (BCA), will allow the project to study the behaviors of sex offenders sentenced to probation in the com-

munity. Additional research has been initiated in conjunction with the State Department of Human Services, the BCA, and various counties throughout the state to add to the base of knowledge about sex offender behavior. ∎

SOURCE: Minnesota Department of Corrections in "Sex Offender Facts," *Backgrounder* (St. Paul; Minnesota Department of Corrections, 1996).

of sex offenders as prisoners in state corrections systems continues to climb, reaching a high of 81,400 at year-end 1993.[39] The number of offenders and arrest rates for sex-related crimes show declines from 1992–1994. The *UCR* for 1994 reflects data for arrests for forcible rape and sex offenses totaling 107,371, down 6.3 and 5.6 percent, respectively, from 1993. This excludes prostitution, which also declined slightly by 0.8 percent).[40] Whether this is a reflection of fear of AIDS, three-strikes laws, changes in demography, or a change in attitudes toward sexual activity remains to be seen. Despite the shift in rates, the climbing number of sex offenders committed to prison remains high. What should be done with them?

In correctional facilities providing more comprehensive treatment services to sex offender populations, treatment program elements ("modalities") are usually combined. Such modalities can include sex education, human sexuality, stress and anger management, social skills, substance abuse programs, how to identify and avoid high-risk situations, relapse prevention, and coping skills.

Long-term programs generally provide intensive and highly structured programs of at least two years, aftercare (up to a year), and follow-up services. Clients can be returned for refresher treatment ("tune-ups"), if necessary. Treatment with the so-called castration drug (depo-provera) provides the same effect as castration, without the need for surgery. Although its use is not common, it might be used as an adjunct to supervision.

Initial studies of the effectiveness of combined treatment are favorable. California reports rearrest follow-up rates (for sexual or other offenses) of 6 to 8 percent. Texas, using depo-provera as an adjunct to individual and group treatment, showed relapse rates for depo-provera–subjects to be one-third that for comparison with offenders not treated, and about 40 percent less than comparison cases after the drug was withdrawn. The Texas evaluation concludes that maintenance-level depo-provera treatment is beneficial for the compulsive sex offender.[41]

One outstanding example of a sensible and apparently successful program for the treatment of the sex offender is the 180 Degrees, Inc., program at a halfway house in Minneapolis. This program involves all prospective members in a *men's sexuality group.* There seems to be some hope in this program:

> After several years of operation, the program's long-term impact on its participants is not clear. Short-term statistics, however, are encouraging. Of the men who have participated in the sexuality group and who are no longer residents of the 180 Degrees, almost 75 percent successfully completed their

stay at the halfway house, 7 percent absconded from the program, and 18 percent were terminated administratively.[42]

The attitude toward the child molester, particularly those that involve ritual child abuse and mutilation in cults,[43] has activated many states to legislate extreme increases in the range of punishment for those types of offenses. Such attitudes are reinforced by continued recidivism reported almost daily in regard to these "headline" offenders. Although the history of the success with sexual offenders was initially poor, there is no hope for the future if additional new approaches to this age-old problem are not developed, tested, and tried.

$\mathcal{H}$IV and AIDS in Prisons

The AIDS pandemic growing in the United States has, of course, reached prisons, particularly through offenders with histories of injecting drugs, sharing needles, and engaging in unprotected sexual activities. Estimates of the extent of infection vary across states and institutions, but at least twenty-two thousand inmates had been diagnosed HIV positive, and almost five thousand with confirmed AIDS in 1994. The proportions of inmates carrying the virus that causes AIDS ranged from nearly zero to more than 27 percent in New York City prisons; the extent of infection in prisons is from six to seven times that of the general population.[44] Female inmates have higher rates of infection than do males.[45] The degree of prisoner-to-prisoner (intraprison) transmission to date appears to be less than previously suspected.[46]

AIDS infection will become increasingly problematic for correctional administrators for many reasons. First, the war on drugs has serious implications for concentration of HIV positive cases in prisons. As the National Commission on AIDS pointed out, "By choosing mass imprisonment as the federal and state governments' response to the use of drugs, we have created a de facto policy of incarcerating more and more individuals with **HIV infection**."[47]

Training staff on how to deal with HIV/AIDS is critical

—PHOTO BY SPENCER A. BURNETT, COURTESY OF NEW YORK CITY DEPARTMENT OF CORRECTIONS

The Commission estimated that the percentage of inmates in federal prisons incarcerated for drug offenses will rise from the current 47 percent to 70 percent by 1995.[48] Inmates sentenced to prison for drug law violations in 1980 received an average sentence of forty-seven months; by 1990, that figure had risen to eighty-one months.[49]

The current prison population increase will continue, disproportionately incarcerating such subpopulations at risk as young minorities who are intravenous drug injectors from urban areas. These groups have elevated infection rates as well as more frequent use of injected drugs, a high-risk behavior. As Vlahov stated:

> Available data on the geographical variation and temporal stability in serovalence in combination with data suggesting infrequent intraprison transmission appear reassuring, [but] HIV-1 infection remains a major prison health problem. Large numbers at risk for infection or already infected continue to enter correctional facilities.[50]

Thus, prison administrators can expect increases in the numbers of infected inmates, HIV-related illnesses and deaths in prisons, intraprison transmissions, and, inevitably, a growing stream of HIV-infected prisoners returned to the community through parole and other release mechanisms. Illegal drug use continues in prisons. About seven of every eight prisons in the nation tested an estimated total of 565,500 inmates for one or more illegal drugs between July 1, 1989, and June 30, 1990. In state facilities, 3.6 percent of the tests for cocaine, 1.3 percent for heroin, 2.0 percent for methamphetamines, and 6.3 percent for marijuana found evidence of drug use. In federal prisons, 0.4 percent of the tests for cocaine, 0.4 percent for heroin, 0.1 percent for methamphetamines, and 1.1 percent for marijuana were positive.[51]

HIV infection and resulting AIDS cases pose particular problems for corrections in terms of staff and inmates. Staff have been alarmed by the introduction of AIDS into prison, and initially little was done through education or training to reduce levels of irrational fear. Institutional policies will need to be developed and reconsidered in the areas of diagnosing, managing, and treating HIV infection.[52] Additional policy development and implementation will be necessary in the areas of staff training and education, inmate counseling, pre- and posttest counseling, voluntary (versus mandatory) testing, medical parole, and discharge and aftercare services (for parole and community supervision). Infection control policies will be necessary for dentists, nurses, physicians, security staff, and treatment.

AIDS AND SECURITY STAFF

Craig identified five communicable diseases frequently found in correctional facilities and presented procedures thought necessary to address HIV infection:

- Avoid blind pocket searches and reaching into blind crevices to lessen the possibility of needle-sticks and other puncture wounds, by using flashlights, mirrors, and other visual aids.

- Protective equipment should be provided and used, including latex gloves; masks, protective eye goggles, and gowns for invasive therapy by dentists or at autopsies; and one-way valve masks for emergency CPR equipment and procedures.

- Hand washing should be required after every contact with potentially infectious materials, and both sinks and disinfectants should be available.

- Infectious waste policies should be implemented that cover bodily wastes, particularly blood or body fluids, including used tampons.

- Exposure reporting procedures should be developed to document possible infection incidents and reduce chains of transmissions of blood- and airborne infectious agents (including Hepatitis B, HIV, tuberculosis, rubella, and Hepatitis A). Such procedures should include after-contact counseling, medical tests of possible contaminant sources, serial blood tests of exposed staff members, and appropriate medical intervention (such as the Hepatitis B immune globulin).

- Comprehensive infection control plans should be implemented, updated, monitored, and revised to maintain a healthy working environment, avoid litigation, and encourage officers to practice universal medical procedures.[53]

Adopting these policies will go a long way to ease staff anxiety and tension in prison settings.

AIDS AND INMATES

Perhaps the best single program for managing HIV infections revolves around educational programs to inform inmates of behaviors. Consensus on appropriate medical treatment within prison settings is that prisons should adopt existing community treatment as the standard of care.[54] At a minimum, special infirmaries should be established to prevent AIDS patients from becoming further victims of airborne infections.[55] Infirmaries[56] should also have drug treatment protocols that specify treatment with **antiviral drugs** (such as AZT) and drug therapy for such opportunistic infections as tuberculosis and pneumonia.

Correctional administrators should propose and encourage a medical-parole mechanism for AIDS patients no longer a threat to the public safety, for early

Needle Sharing and Condoms

Correctional administrators and investigators usually agree that major problems in prisons include the availability of illicit injectable drugs inside prison, and frequent voluntary and involuntary homosexual activity, including homosexual rape. Despite the clear evidence of the spread of AIDS through sharing dirty needles and anal intercourse, correctional personnel and managers are unreasonably resistant to providing prophylactics and bleach to inmates.

Men in prison who wish to engage in anal intercourse are usually sufficiently capable of bringing that act to a successful completion. If the act is forcible intercourse with a passive male coerced into receiving an unwanted intrusion and the HIV virus is spread, the matter of liability might mean considerable financial loss for the state, managing officer, and lowest-level correctional employee. Providing condoms to prisoners will soon be a constitutional right.

Dirty needles shared by prisoners can be easily and effectively sterilized by double rinsing of syringe and needle in common household bleach. Institutions with substantial availability of injectable illicit drugs should make distribution of household bleach a routine sanitary procedure. To do less is to invite liability and eventual punitive and exemplary damages that place them at risk, as well as to discourage prevention. Almost all states have some forms of these programs, but not all have written materials, reinforced by videotaped information on HIV and safer living, and verbal presentations made by an informed health professional, with a following question/answer period. Some institutions have English-only documents; others do not provide periodic updates or ongoing access to medical professionals steeped in HIV information. Some states have prerelease training sessions; others have developed extensive community-based support groups of HIV positive volunteers to ease the transition of AIDS cases back into the community. These components should be unified into an institutional policy and periodically updated. ∎

release back into the community by paroling authorities. Prerelease counseling[57] well in advance of the proposed release date would help inmates identify resources and service providers in the communities to which they will be released. Ideally, each institution should identify a community-based support group of HIV positive volunteers for inmate referral and ease of transition.

The cost of HIV and AIDS treatment in prison is unknown but in California approximates $86,000 per inmate per year. Existing social security and related medical insurance coverage would pay most of these costs if the offender were in a community setting. By managing medical care, corrections will develop an efficient health care system in prison, lessen stigma, reduce paranoia and staff-inmate tensions, and sharply curtail the potential for costly litigation.[58] Corrections faces a medical challenge unparalleled in American history. Innovation and leadership are required to overcome these problems. Figure 18-2 points out the number of deaths in prisons from homicide, suicide, and AIDS-related illnesses and the obvious rising number from the latter cause.

Geriatric Inmates: The Graying of American Prisons

The proportion of prisoners in the nation's institutions who are elderly is rapidly increasing, in part due to the tougher long-term sentences inherent in the current "get tough on crime" stance, but also because of the aging of the general population in America. In 1994, there were a total of 25,832 male inmates in state and federal institutions who were between fifty-five and seventy-five years old, and 620 over seventy-five years old. Female inmates numbered 1,141 between fifty-five and seventy-five years old, and only seventeen over seventy-five years old.[59] It has been estimated that by the twenty-first century, at least one in ten (about 125,000 inmates) will be age fifty or over.[60] The growth rate of older inmates (age fifty or above) in Florida already exceeds the growth rate of younger offenders.

FIGURE

18.2

Number of Inmate Deaths from Homicides, Suicides, and AIDS, 1988–1994

SOURCE: C. Camp and G. Camp, *The Corrections Yearbook 1995* (South Salem, NY: Criminal Justice Institute, 1995), p. 30.

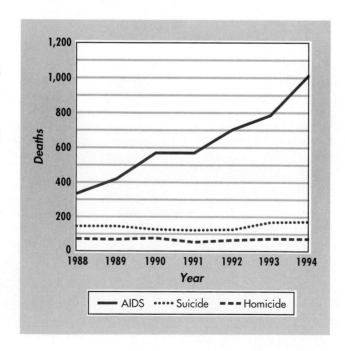

Elderly inmates are more likely to have committed crimes such as homicide and manslaughter, as well as sexual offenses. They are less likely to be imprisoned for robbery and burglary. Because of their significantly longer sentences, elderly inmates may be concentrated in prisons well beyond their proportions in the civilian population, which will pose problems for them as well as prison administrators. First, they will have health care problem concerns and need preventive health care programs that, if not provided, could be a source of considerable and, for correctional administrators, substantial litigation costs. At the least, they will suffer from depression and differing nutritional needs (less protein, fewer calories, and more soft food and fiber). Because taste sensations decline with aging, the elderly will request food richer in seasonings and will have a decrease in gastric acid and increase in gas production and constipation. Special diets will be needed.

In addition, growing old in prison will mean having to avoid exploitation and violence by younger inmates,[61] having to adjust new personal needs to prison life, and not having suitable programs (recreational, educational, or housing). Vulnerability to victimization, frailty, and isolation from outside relatives and friends will take their toll, as will fear of death, hopelessness, and being unable to cope when released.

Health care costs will increase significantly for hypertension, diabetes, stroke, cancer, and emphysema. Glasses, dentures, kidney dialysis, and heart surgery will be required. It has been estimated that by the year 2005, health care costs for elderly inmates will increase fourteenfold.[62] Many prisons will become geriatric centers,[63] and special staff as well as staff training will be necessary to treat this special-problem segment of the nation's offenders. Perhaps a nation that can explore space can find the necessary compassion to care for that small but increasing group as we enter the next century. Executive clemency, including pardons, may become a frequent act.

Geriatric prisoners, sentenced to life without hope of parole could live many years in the prisons of America…long after their dangerousness has passed. The courts of the land will be checking carefully to see that their rights are not violated, and it is certain that imprisonment costs will soar. Geriatric prisoners are "special people" and must be considered such when considering sentences that are too long (beyond what is cost effective).

Three Strikes and You're Out

Three strikes and you're out laws are sweeping the nation. It is clear that this is an idea that appeals to the public because it seems to be so tough. When the long-term costs in terms of operations and medical care are considered, it gives cause to thoughtful correctional professionals and legislators who seem to have fallen for an easy fix. California is now having their law reviewed by their Supreme Court—which seems to want it rescinded. A review of some of that state's apparent bill for three strikes includes:

- Costs for operation of the Department of Corrections will increase from $75 million in 1994/95 to $1.96 *billion* in 2001/02,

- $21 billion over the next decade for new construction,
- Rapid increase in geriatric inmates,
- Forced release of other inmates not on three strike conviction,
- Funding will most likely come from the state's education budget. ■

SOURCE: Peter Greenwod et al., *Three Strikes and You're Out: Estimated Costs and Benefits of California's New Mandatory Sentencing Law* (Santa Monica, CA: Rand Corporation, 1994).

Summary

The process of labeling is strong and pervasive in our society. Once labeled as mentally disordered, developmentally challenged, sex fiend, or just *old*,[64] a special category person's lot is rough indeed. Add to those heavy labels the added term *offender* and the problems multiply geometrically. Although mental illness is the nation's largest health problem, affecting one out of ten citizens, it is still frequently regarded with the snake pit philosophy of the Middle Ages, especially if some criminal act has been linked to the condition.

The developmentally challenged citizen is in a real dilemma if placed in a treatment program that requires measurable improvement as a condition of release. This concept led to laws in the 1930s that essentially gave developmentally challenged persons de facto life sentences if they were placed in an institution until they "improved."

The sex offender is involved in a situation in which society's sexual mores are in transition. Some behaviors that put many in prison just a few years ago are no longer considered criminal. That change has not removed the stigma of the label *sex offender*, however, and the tolerance of the outside world is low for those so labeled.

Inmates with AIDS, along with those who are getting a lot older in the prisons, cause serious problems with special handling procedures and huge medical bills.

These problems, along with the "right to treatment," seem at constant odds with one another. When treatment programs fail, blame is often placed on the attendant, the overworked and undertrained staff, the legislators, and the courts. In the final analysis, however, it is up to society to decide whether or not it wants to spend the time and money to provide care and treatment for its bottom-line "losers" and then to attempt to remove the labels and reintegrate those individuals into the mainstream. Without a firm commitment to change, the castoffs of society will continue to return to institutions and then be released to the public, either with no change or with a decided change for the worse.

We now move on to discuss some of the rights that prisoners, as human beings and American citizens, are entitled to receive both in confinement and as ex-offenders back in the community. We will also visit the ultimate right—the right to live—where we will examine the controversy that continues to surround the death penalty.

Review Questions

1. What spurred the growth of asylums in America?
2. How can one avoid criminal responsibility?
3. What are the most common sex offenses?
4. What would the American Psychiatric Association do with insanity acquittees?
5. What problems do developmentally challenged offenders pose for correctional administrators?
6. What types of former sex offenses have been decriminalized?
7. What recommendations have been offered for correctional processing of developmentally challenged offenders?
8. Can sex offenders be treated?
9. What can be done to reduce staff fear of AIDS?

10. Why are the "three-strikes" laws in trouble?

11. What should be done with geriatric prisoners?

Words to Remember

mentally disturbed

deinstitutionalize

incompetent to stand trial

criminally insane

not guilty by reason
of insanity

predict potential dangerousness

developmentally challenged

sex offenses

buggery

HIV infection

antiviral drugs

elderly inmates

geriatric prisoner

Endnotes

1. Kenneth Adams, "Who Are the Clients? Characteristics of Inmates Referred for Mental Health Treatment," *The Prison Journal* 72:1–2 (1992): 120–141.

2. G. Ives, *A History of Penal Methods* (London: S. Paul, 1914). Exploitation of the incarcerated developmentally challenged offenders by more aggressive and stronger inmates remains a problem in all facilities: mental institutions, juvenile centers, nursing homes, jails, and prisons. In 1980, Congress passed the Civil Rights of Institutionalized Persons Act, authorizing the attorney general to intervene in correctional settings if violations of inmates' civil rights are suspected. For an example of juvenile victimization, see C. Bartollas, S. Miller, and S. Dinitz, *Juvenile Victimization: The Institutional Paradox* (New York: Holsted Press, 1976), pp. 53–76. See also Freda Briggs, *From Victim to Offender: How Child Sexual Abuse Victims Become Offenders* (St. Leonards, AUS: Allen and Unwin, 1995).

3. J. Wilpers, "Animal, Vegetable or Human Being?" *Government Executive* (May 1973): 32.

4. Ibid., p. 33.

5. Adams, "Who Are the Clients?" p. 123.

6. Randy Revelle, former King County executive, while accepting the National Association of Counties award for the "6 East" project for mentally ill inmates at the King County Jail, 1982.

7. Henry Steadman et al., "Estimating Mental Health Needs and Service Utilization Among Prison Inmates," *Bulletin of the American Academy of Psychiatry and the Law* 19:3 (1991): 297–307. Canadian data from Laurence Motiuk and Frank Porporino, *The Prevalence, Nature and Severity of Mental Health Problems Among Federal Inmates in Canadian Penitentiaries* (Ontario: Correctional Service Canada, 1992).

8. This is a hotly debated point. First see S. Wessely and P. J. Taylor, "Madness and Crime: Criminology versus Psychiatry," *Criminal Justice and Mental Health* 1:3 (1991): 193–228. See also Mary Ann Finn, "Prison Misconduct Among Developmentally Challenged Inmates," *Criminal Behavior and Mental Health* 2:3 (1992): 287–299; Lynette Feder, "A Comparison of the Community Adjustment of Mentally Ill Offenders with Those from the General Prison Population," *Law and Human Behavior* 15:5 (1991): 477–493; and Bruce Link, Howard Andrews, and Francis Cullen, "The Violent and Illegal Behavior of Mental Patients Reconsidered," *American Sociological Review* 57:3 (1992): 275–292.

9. National Institute of Mental Health, *Directory of Institutions for the Mentally Disordered Offenders* (Washington, D.C.: U.S. Government Printing Office, 1972).

10. Valerie Hans, "An Analysis of Public Attitudes Toward the Insanity Defense," *Criminology* 24:2 (1986): 393–413. Among her more interesting findings were that the public wants insane lawbreakers punished, believes that insanity defense procedures fail to protect the general public, and wildly overestimates the use and effectiveness of the insanity defense. See also Bruce Arrigo, *The Contours of Psychiatric Justice* (New York: Garland, 1996).

11. Lisa Callahan et al., "The Volume and Characteristics of Insanity Defense Pleas: An Eight State Study," *Bulletin of the American Academy of Psychiatry and the Law* 19:4 (1991): 331–338.

12. Marnie Rice, Grant Harris, and Carol Lang, "Recidivism Among Male Insanity Acquitees," *Journal of Psychiatry and the Law* 18:3–4 (1990): 379–403.

13. Carmen Cirincione, Henry Steadman, and Margaret McGreevey, "Rates of Insanity Acquittals and the Factors Associated with the Insanity Pleas," *Bulletin of the American Academy of Psychiatry and the Law* 23:3 (1995): 399–409.

14. John Klofas and Ralph Weisheit, "Guilty but Mentally Ill: Reform of the Insanity Defense in Illinois," *Justice Quarterly* 4 (1987): 40–50.

15. Lisa Callahan, Margaret McGreevy, Carmen Cirincione et al., "Measuring the Effects of the Guilty but Mentally Ill (GBMI) Verdict: Georgia's 1982 GBMI Reform," *Law and Human Behavior* 16:4 (1992): 447–462.

16. American Psychiatric Association, *Standards for Psychiatric Facilities* (Washington, D.C.: American Psychiatric Association, 1981), pp. 17–18.

17. Lewis Carroll, *Alice's Adventures in Wonderland* and *Through the Looking Glass and What Alice Found There* (London: Oxford University Press, 1971), p. 123.

18. Bernard Rubin, "Prediction of Dangerousness in Mentally Ill Criminals," *Archives of General Psychiatry* 27 (September 1972): 397–407.

19. Miles Santamour and Bernadette West, *Sourcebook on the Mentally Disordered Prisoner* (Washington, D.C.: U.S. Department of Justice, 1985), p. 70.

20. Finn, "Prison Misconduct Among Developmentally Challenged Inmates," p. 296.

21. Severson identifies ten basic services necessary for inmate mental health. See Margaret Severson, "Refining the Boundaries of Mental Health Services: A Holistic Approach to Inmate Mental Health," *Federal Probation* 56:3 (1992): 57–63.

22. B. Farber, *Mental Retardation: Its Social Context and Social Consequences* (Boston: Houghton Mifflin, 1968).

23. B. Brown and T. Courtless, *The Developmentally Challenged Offender and Corrections* (Washington, D.C.: U.S. Government Printing Office, 1971). See also Miles Santamour, "Developmentally Challenged Offenders: Texas Program Targets Basic Needs," *Corrections Today* 52 (February 1990): 52, 92, 106.

24. *Ruiz v. Estelle*, 503 F. Supp. 1265 (S.D. Tex. 1980), aff'd in part. 679 F. 2d 1115 (5th Cir. 1982), cert. denied 103 S. Ct. 1438 (1983) at 1344.

25. Ibid., at 1344.

26. Richard C. Allen, "Reaction to S. Fox: The Criminal Reform Movement," in M. Kindred, ed., *The Developmentally Challenged Citizen and the Law* (Washington, D.C.: U.S. Government Printing Office, 1976), p. 645.

27. This area of legal procedure is rampant with charges of false accusation and victim's psychological trauma. See Andrew Soshnick, "The Rape Shield Law Paradox: Complaint Protection Amidst Oscillating Trends of State Judicial Interpretation," Journal of Criminal Law and Criminology 78:3 (1987): 644–698. See also Margaret Rieser, "Recantation in Child Sexual Abuse Cases," Child Welfare 70:6 (1991): 611–621, and Edwin Mikkelsen, Thomas Gutheil, and Margaret Emens, "False Sexual Abuse Allegations by Children and Adolescents," American Journal of Psychotherapy 46:4 (1992): 556–570.

28. The relationship between offender and victim is under intense study, particularly for stranger and serial rapists. See James LeBeau, "Patterns of Stranger and Serial Rape Offending: Factors Distinguishing Apprehended and At-Large Offenders," *Journal of Criminal Law and Criminology* 78:2 (1987): 309–326. See also Kate Painter, *Wife Rape, Marriage and the Law* (Manchester, UK: University of Manchester Press, 1991).

29. David O'Connor, "Hawaii Moves Closer to Legalizing Gay Marriages," *Bay Area Reporter* 22:29 (July 22, 1993): 12, and United Press International, "Florida Lesbians Sue for the Right to Marry," *Bay Area Reporter* 22:29 (July 22, 1993): 13.

30. See Patricia Cluss et al., "The Rape Victim: Psychological Correlates of Participation in the Legal Process," *Criminal Justice and Behavior* 10:3 (1983): 342–357.

31. David Finkelhor, "Removing the Child-Prosecuting the Offender in Cases of Sexual Abuse: Evidence from the National Reporting System for Child Abuse and Neglect," *Child Abuse and Neglect* 7:2 (1983): 195–205.

32. Jean Goodwin et al., *Sexual Abuse: Incest Victims and Their Families* (Boston: John Wright, 1982). See also Katherine Beckett, "Culture and the Politics of Signification: The Case of Child Abuse," *Social Problems* 43:1 (1996): 57–76.

33. Karl Hanson, Brian Cox, and Carolyn Woszczyna, "Assessing Treatment Outcomes for Sexual Offenders," *Annals of Sex Research* 4:3–4 (1991): 177–208; Fay Honey Knopp, Robert Freeman-Longo, and William Ferree Stevenson, *Nationwide Survey of Juvenile and Adult Sex Offender Treatment Programs and Models* (Orwell, CT: Safer Society Program, 1992).

34. Rhonda Reeves, "Approaching 2,000: Finding Solutions to the Most Pressing Issues Facing the Corrections Community," *Corrections Today* 54:8 (1992): 74–79.

35. Richard McCorkle, "Research Note: Punish or Rehabilitate? Public Attitudes Toward Six Common Crimes," *Crime and Delinquency* 39:2 (1993): 240–252.

36. Timothy Flanagan, Pauline Gasdow Brennan, and Debra Cohen, "Conservatism and Capital Punishment in the State Capitol: Lawmakers and the Death Penalty," *The Prison Journal* 72:1–2 (1992): 37–56, and Allen Beck et al., *Prisoners in 1994* (Washington, D.C.: Bureau of Justice Statistics, 1995), p. 11.

37. Anthony Walsh, "Placebo Justice: Victim Recommendations and Offender Sentences in Sexual Assault Cases," *Journal of Criminal Law and Criminology* 77 (1986): 1126–1141. Federal Bureau of Investigation, *Crime in the United States 1994: Uniform Crime Reports* (Washington, D.C.: U.S. Department of Justice, November 1995), p. 225.

38. John Weeks, Gary Pelletier, and Daniel Beaulette. "Correctional Officers: How Do They Perceive Sex Offenders?" *International Journal of Offender Therapy and Comparative Criminology* 35:1 (1995): 55–61.

39. Kathleen Maguire and Ann Pastore (eds.). *Sourcebook of Criminal Justice Statistics 1994* (Washington, D.C.: U. S. Department of Justice, 1995), p. 363.

40. Federal Bureau of Investigation. *Crime in the United States 1993: Uniform Crime Report* (Washington, D.C.: U. S. Department of Justice, 1994), pp. 11-13.

41. F. Brecher, *Treatment Programs for Sex Offenders.* (Washington, D.C.: U.S. Government Printing Office, 1978), pp. 1–12. The material for this section has been extracted from this document and reflects the current literature on the subject.

42. John Driggs and Thomas H. Zoet, "Breaking the Cycle—Sex Offenders on Parole," *Corrections Today* 49:3 (1987): 124.

43. Steven Glass, "An Overview of Satanism and Ritualized Child Abuse," *Journal of Police and Criminal Psychology* 7:2 (1991): 43–50, and Ben Crouch and Kelly Damphousse, "Newspapers and the Antisatanism Movement: A Content Analysis," *Sociological Spectrum* 12:1 (1992): 1–20.

44. Peter Brien and Allen Beck, *HIV in Prisons* (Washington, D.C.: U.S. Department of Justice, March 1996), p. 1.

45. National statistics released July 1993 indicate that, in 1992, more women developed AIDS from heterosexual intercourse than from intravenous drug use. Most of the infected females had had sex with men with histories of intravenous drug use., "California Bucks AIDS Trend," *San Francisco Chronicle*, July 26, 1993, p. A-14; and Scott Decker and Richard Rosenfeld, "Intravenous Drug Use and the AIDS Epidemic: Findings from a 20-City Sample of Arrestees," *Crime and Delinquency* 38:4 (1992): 492–509.

46. Harry E. Allen, "HIV Transmission Issues in Correctional Facilities," *National Social Sciences Journal* 2:1 (1992): 32–37.

47. National Commission on Acquired Immune Deficiency Syndrome, *Report: HIV Disease in Correctional Facilities* (Washington, D.C.: National Commission on Acquired Immune Deficiency Syndrome, 1992), p. 5.

48. Ibid., p. 8.

49. Reeves, "Approaching 2000," p. 78.

50. D. Vlahov, "HIV Infection in the Correctional Setting," *Criminal Justice Policy Review* 4:4 (1990): 309.

51. Caroline Wolf Harlow, *Drug Enforcement and Treatment in Prisons, 1990* (Washington, D.C.: U.S. Department of Justice, 1992), p. 1.

52. For a sobering view of consensual sex behaviors in a prison setting and implications for HIV transmission, see Victor Hassine, *Life Without Parole* (Los Angeles: Roxbury, 1996), pp. 71–89.

53. Rebecca Craig, "Six Steps to Stop the Spread of Communicable Diseases," *Corrections Today* 54:7 (1992): 104–109. See also Mary Coplin, "Managing the Challenge of HIV," *Corrections Today* 54:8 (1992): 104–107.

54. Reeves, "Approaching 2000," p. 76.

55. Mary Campbell, "Managing Exposure to Communicable Diseases," *Corrections Today* 54:3 (1992): 68–83; H. Parker Eales, "MDR Tuberculosis: Correction's Newest Communicable Danger," *Corrections Today* 54:3 (1992): 64–67; and H. Parker Eales, HIV and MDR-TB: A Tragic Combination," *The State of Corrections: Proceedings of the 1992 Annual Conferences* (Laurel, MD: American Correctional Association, 1993), pp. 48–50.

56. Joseph Paris, "Why an AIDS Unit?" *The State of Corrections: Proceedings of the 1991 Annual Conferences* (Laurel, MD: American Correctional Association, 1992), pp. 53–58.

57. Donald McVinney, "Counseling Incarcerated Individuals with HIV Disease and Chemical Dependency," *Journal of Chemical Dependency Treatment* 4:2 (1991): 105–118.

58. Patricia Satterfield, "A Strategy for Controlling Health Care Costs," *Corrections Today* 54:2 (1992): 190–194.

59. American Correctional Association, *1996 Directory: Juvenile & Adult Correctional Departments, Institutions, Agencies & Paroling Authorities* (Lanham, MD: American Correctional Association, June 1996), p. xxxii.

60. Sarah Bradley, "Graying of Inmate Population Spurs Corrections Challenges," *On the Line* 13 (March 1990): 5.

61. Richard Dugger, "The Graying of America's Prisons," *Corrections Today* 50 (June 1988): 26–34.

62. Bradley, "Graying of Inmate Population Spurs Corrections Challenges." See also Edith Flynn, "The Graying of America's Prison Population," *The Prison Journal* 72:1, 2 (1992): 77–98.

63. Gennaro Vito and Deborah Wilson, "Forgotten People: Elderly Inmates," *Federal Probation* 49 (March 1985): 18–24. See also Deborah Wilson and Gennaro Vito, "Long-Term Inmates: Special Need and Management Considerations," *Federal Probation* 52:3 (1988): 21–26.

64. Ann Goetting, "Racism, Sexism and Ageism in the Prison Community," *Federal Probation* 54:2 (1985): 10–22.

*R*ecommended Readings: Part IV

Allen-Hagen, Barbara. *Children in Custody 1989*. Washington, D.C.: U.S. Department of Justice, 1991.

American College of Physicians, National Commission on Correctional Health Care. "The Crisis in Correctional Health Care: The Impact of the National Drug Control Strategy on Correctional Health Services." *Annals of Internal Medicine* 117:1 (1992): 71–77.

American Friends Service Committee. *Struggle for Justice*. New York: Hill and Wang, 1971.

American Jail Association. *American Jails*. Quarterly publication of the American Jail Association.

Beck, Allen. *Profile of Jail Inmates, 1989*. Washington, D.C.: U.S. Department of Justice, 1991.

Branham, Lynne. *The Use of Incarceration in the United States: A Look at the Present and the Future*. Washington, D.C.: Criminal Justice Section, American Bar Association, 1992.

Cohen, Robyn. *Drunk Driving*. Washington, D.C.: U.S. Department of Justice, 1992.

Donziger, Steven. *The Real War on Crime*. New York: HarperCollins. 1996.

Greenfield, Lawrence, and Stephanie Minor-Harper. *Women in Prison*. Washington, D.C.: U.S. Department of Justice, 1991.

Harlow, Caroline Wolf. *Drug Enforcement and Treatment in Prisons, 1990*. Washington, D.C.: U.S.

Department of Justice, 1992.

Harry, Joseph. *Gay Children Grow Up*. New York: Praeger, 1982.

Hassine, Victor. *Life Without Parole*. Los Angeles: Roxbury, 1996.

Immarigeon, Russ, and Meda Chesney-Lind. *Women's Prisons: Overcrowded and Underused*. San Francisco: National Council on Crime and Delinquency, 1992.

Jankowski, Louis. *Jail Inmates, 1991*. Washington, D.C.: U.S. Department of Justice, 1992.

Krisberg, Barry, et al. "Reinventing Juvenile Justice: Research Directions." *Crime and Delinquency* 39:1 (1993):3–124.

Leinen, Stephen. *Gay Cops*. New Brunswick, NJ: Rutgers University Press, 1993.

McCoy, Clyde, and James Inciardi. *Sex, Drugs and the Continuing Spread of AIDS*. Los Angeles: Roxbury, 1995.

McMahon, Maeve. *The Persistent Prison: Rethinking Decarceration and Prison Reform*. Toronto: University of Toronto Press, 1992.

Mauer, Marc. "Americans Behind Bars." *Criminal Justice* 6:4 (1992): 12–18, 38–39. And "The International Use of Incarceration." *The Prison Journal* 75:1 (1995): 113–123.

National Council on Crime and Delinquency. *Juvenile Justice Policy Statement*. San Francisco: National Council on Crime and Delinquency 1991.

Palmer, Ted. *The Re-Emergence of Correctional Intervention*. Newbury Park, CA: Sage, 1992.

Quinlan, J. Michael, et al. "Focus on the Female Offender." *Federal Prisons Journal* 3:1 (1992): 3–68.

Simonsen, Clifford. *Juvenile Justice in America,* 3rd ed. New York: Macmillan, 1991.

Snell, Tracy. *Women in Jails 1989*. Washington, D.C.: U.S. Department of Justice, 1992.

Zimring, Franklin, and Gordon Hawkins. *Prison Population and Criminal Justice Policy in California*. Berkeley, CA: Institute of Governmental Studies Press, 1992.

Rights *of the* Sentenced Offender

CHAPTER NINETEEN

Offender Rights in Confinement

Overview

Ask the average person on the street what "rights" prisoners have coming to them when in confinement—or when released after their sentence has been served. After a few seconds of a blank stare, most would answer: "What do you mean *rights*? They don't have any." Part V will examine in some detail the sometimes mystical world of those rights that apply to inmates and ex-offenders. The incredible amount of litigation in institutions, the long battles for the lives of what appear to be killers who deserve to die, and the problems with the ex-prisoner trying to deal with society and carrying a heavy record for life cause us to wonder how this all came about. In this chapter we look at the convicted offender and, from both an historical and a current view, at some of the rights lost as well as the rights restored over time. In the next chapter, we enter the realm of the death penalty and the continuing controversy as to society's ability to take away the ultimate right—the convicted offender's life.

The Status of the Convicted Offender

When defendants have gone through the whole criminal justice process, including all appeals, and their sentences have been upheld, they officially acquire the status of *convicted offender*. They may already have spent a long time in prison as their appeals made their tedious way through the courts. But with the **final guilty verdict** in, the offenders' relationship to the correctional system undergoes a significant change. In this section, we examine offenders' new status and their rights during and after incarceration. Over the years, a body of folklore has grown up about the rights of prisoners and ex-prisoners. This chapter dispels some of those myths and clarifies recent developments.

> It has become common to think of courts imposing restrictions on unwilling prison administrators, but historically this would be inaccurate. The elaboration of rights for the punished has involved a sporadic negotiation among the courts, administrators, and legislatures.
>
> —David E. Duffee

Individual Rights Guaranteed by the "Bill of Rights"

A Right Against Unreasonable Searches of Person and Place of Residence

A Right Against Arrest Without Probable Cause

A Right Against Unreasonable Seizures of Personal Property

A Right Against Self-incrimination

A Right to Fair Questioning by the Police

A Right to Protection from Physical Harm Throughout the Justice Process

A Right to an Attorney

A Right to Trial by Jury

A Right to Know the Charges

A Right to Cross-examine Prosecution Witnesses

A Right to Speak and Present Witnesses

A Right Not to Be Tried Twice for the Same Crime

A Right Against Cruel or Unusual Punishment

A Right to Due Process

A Right to a Speedy Trial

A Right Against Excessive Bail

A Right Against Excessive Fines

A Right to Be Treated the Same as Others, Regardless of Race, Sex, Religious Preference, and Other Personal Attributes

A Right to Be Assumed Innocent Until Proven Guilty ■

SOURCE: Frank Schmalleger, *Criminal Justice Today*, 4th ed. (Upper Saddle River, NJ: Prentice Hall, 1996).

There was a time when a prison sentence often meant **civil death**, a cruel form of punishment expressly acknowledging a prisoner's permanent removal from free society. In a perverse sense, the civil death sentence benefited the prisoner's family: the "widows" of male prisoners were able to remarry and rebuild a shattered life. In the United States the inmate was considered a **slave of the state**[1] until 1974.[2] Today, except in rare cases, almost all convicted offenders eventually return to the community from which they came. Their families may try to stay together until they are released, when the ex-prisoners must begin to try again to cope with the free world.

⟨A⟩ Slave No More

In 1871, a Virginia Court decided the status of the inmate in *Ruffin v. Commonwealth*: "A convicted felon is one whom the law in its humanity punishes by confinement in the penitentiary instead of death.... For the time being, during his term of service in the penitentiary, he is a slave of penal servitude to the State ... for the time being, the slave of the State." In 1974, when the Court decided **Wolff v. McDonnell**, the legal status had shifted:

> Though his rights may be diminished by the needs and exigencies of the institutional environment, a prisoner is not wholly stripped of constitutional protections.... There is no iron curtain drawn between the Constitution

The once-common sight of prisoners breaking rocks will be seen again in Alabama

—COURTESY OF CORBIS–BETTMANN

and the prisons of this country… He may not be deprived of life, liberty or property without due process of law.

In a century, a slave had become an inconvenienced citizen. Imprisonment by its very nature deprives the offender of some constitutional rights. It is not clear, however, which rights must be completely sacrificed and which may be retained, perhaps in modified form. Prison officials have always been able to wield enormous power over the lives of incarcerated offenders.[3] In the days when the sole purpose of imprisonment was punishment, the rights of offenders seemed unimportant. Because offenders seldom returned to the community, neither they nor their families were likely to complain that the offenders' rights had been infringed.[4] As the philosophy of corrections moved toward reintegration, however, the complete deprivation of rights became intolerable.

With more than five million people[5] subject to the control of some kind of correctional authority in America each day, the status of those convicted offenders poses a significant problem. Correctional officials have been slow to draw up internal policies and procedures to guide their administrators in protecting the offenders' rights. Under the "hands-off" policy we mentioned in Chapter 8, the courts were reluctant to criticize decisions and procedures developed by correctional administrators. That policy was abandoned in the mid-1960s, opening the door to case after case regarding prisoners' rights, with no end in sight. Prison practices have ranged from the total loss of offenders' rights upon conviction to various degrees of loss, but the new movement is toward the standards recommended by the National Advisory Commission on Criminal Justice Standards and Goals a generation ago, which follow:

Each state should immediately enact legislation that defines and implements the substantive rights of offenders. Such legislation should be governed by the following principles:

Congress Staying Tough on Crime

Recent actions taken by the federal government reveal that legislators are staying the course when it comes to getting tough on crime. In addition to passing the critically important Prison Litigation Reform Act (PLRA), legislators are also focusing attention on monitoring sex offenders. According to Bill Collins, correctional attorney and editor of the *Correctional Law Reporter*, the PLRA will make it "more difficult for inmates to get issues to court and keep them there."

Collins added, "When you combine all this activity with the habeas reform act (signed by President Clinton as part of the compromise bill aimed at fighting terrorism and crime), it's been a big couple of weeks in Congress in terms of regulating inmate rights."

Passage of the PLRA is perhaps one of the most significant crime-related legislative actions taken since the 1994 Omnibus Crime Bill. The initiatives, which became federal law on April 26 when President Clinton signed the Balanced Budget Down Payment Act, II (H.R. 3019), could "make enormous strides in relieving the states of unnecessary federal judicial intervention, in the operation and management of prisons and jails," said Ariz. Gov. Fife Symington (R). The federal legislation is modeled on existing Ariz. law.

The PLRA is important largely due to its potential impact on jurisdictions currently operating under varying degrees of judicial authority, specifically consent decrees. "The new law could affect agencies that have been under a consent decree for over two years, allowing them to get out from under the decree," explained Collins.

The PLRA would also:

- Require the federal judiciary to pay for special masters;

- Curb so-called frivolous inmate lawsuits by requiring prisoners to pay court costs and filing fees;

- Crack down on "frequent filers" by not allowing a prisoner to file any more than 3 suits (while incarcerated) if his or her previous filings were dismissed on the grounds they were frivolous, malicious, or failed to state a claim upon which relief may be granted (unless the prisoner is under imminent danger of serious physical injury).

The new law is controversial and will no doubt provoke a slew of initial litigation around its Constitutional validity.

In other legislative action, on May 7, the House unanimously passed a measure modeled on NJ's "Megan's Law" (which requires that local officials be warned if and when sex offenders are released from prison and move into their community). Three days later, the Senate approved the measure on a voice vote.

The measure would require states to make public "relevant information" about child molesters and sexually violent offenders who are released from prison or placed on parole. It also would impose a life sentence without parole for any second, federal conviction for rape or serious sexual assault, and expanded federal jurisdiction over such crimes.

Prompted in part by a provision in the 1994 Crime Act, which provided for the registration (but made community notification optional) of sex offenders upon their release from prison, numerous states are responding to citizens' demands that they improve how sex offenders are tracked and monitored.

Laws requiring the registration of sex offenders are on the books in 47 states; fifteen states require community notification. Although many of the laws are held up in courts on the grounds that they violate the Constitution, the House's recent action indicates that legislators will continue to pass tough-on-crime legislation, regardless of the Constitutional challenges. ■

SOURCE: Editors, *Corrections Alert* 3:4 (May 20, 1996): p. 6.

1. Offenders should be entitled to the same rights as free citizens, except where the nature of confinement necessarily requires modification.

2. Where modification of the rights of offenders is required by the nature of custody, such modification should be as limited as possible.

3. The duty of showing that custody requires modification of such rights should be upon the correctional agency.

4. Such legislation should provide adequate means for enforcement of the rights so defined. It should authorize the remedies for violations of the rights of offenders, where they do not already exist.[6]

Community Ties: A Basic Need

The vestiges of civil death are probably most visible in correctional practices that pertain to the privilege of having visitors. There is continuous debate about whether having visitors is actually a **privilege** or is in fact a *right*. The practice of having visitors is not new; occasional visitors were allowed even as early as 1790 in the Walnut Street Jail. If a prisoner were diligent and good, he was allowed a visit from a close family member—but only once every three months, for fifteen minutes, through two grills, and under the scrutiny of a keeper.[7] This procedure may seem absurdly strict, but it closely resembles the current practice in some correctional institutions. The overriding security focus at most prisons dictates that visits be limited and subject to highly regimented conditions, likely to discourage close physical or emotional contact. The dehumanizing rules and procedures for visiting do not accord with modern goals of rehabilitation and correction. Although security is important in maximum security prisons, it could be tempered with humanity in such a personal thing as a visit from a friend or family member.

Limitations on visiting hours, restricted visitor lists,[8] overcrowded visiting rooms, and the constant presence of guards all contribute to the inmate's difficulty in maintaining ties with family and the outside world.[9] Most institutions are located far from large urban centers (where most inmates' families live), requiring long hours of travel and expense for visitors.[10] Not only **family ties** but friendships as well wither quickly under such conditions. This alienation creates serious problems for both the inmate and the institution. Typically, an inmate is allowed to receive a visitor once a week (in some places as seldom as once a month), usually a member of his or her immediate family. This is hardly representative of social life in contemporary America.

For the married inmate, family ties are inevitably weakened by long separation. With divorce frequent, the social consequences to the family, community, and institution are incalculable; imprisonment itself is grounds for divorce in some jurisdictions.[11] Institution officials often face severe problems caused by the deterioration of an inmate's family situation. When, for example, a wife does not write,

Family/Conjugal Visiting

During a conjugal, or what is most commonly called a "family visit," inmate, spouse, and children are allowed to spend time together on the prison campus, unsupervised and alone in private quarters, trailers, houses, and rooms. During this time, the couple may or may not engage in sexual intercourse.

European and Latin American countries have been the leaders in permitting conjugal visiting, but some states (e.g., California and Mississippi) have formal programs of conjugal visiting. Others (like Montana) permit the program without granting formal approval.

Advantages cited in some studies include lessening forced and voluntary homosexual acts within prison, maintaining a more normal prison environment, lowering tension levels, lessening attacks on correctional officers, reinforcing gender-appropriate roles, helping to preserve marriages, and (from the perspective of the prison administration) encouraging appropriate behavior by inmates hoping to earn a conjugal visitation pass.

Research on the relative effectiveness of conjugal visiting or unsupervised family visits in the United States has not been extensive, but conjugal visiting is believed to strengthen family ties, reduce homosexuality among inmates, lessen tensions between officers and inmates, make inmates easier to manage, and lessen isolation from the outside community. Opponents argue that it puts too much emphasis on the physical aspects of marriage, is unfair to the unmarried resident, raises welfare costs through increased family size, and decreases the intensity of punishment to offenders. ■

Juveniles learning to read, a right that could alleviate a major cause of crime

—COURTESY OF OHIO DEPARTMENT OF YOUTH SERVICES

or the inmate hears through the grapevine she has a lover, violence can and often does result—expressed in attacks against prison personnel,[12] another prisoner,[13] or even attempts to escape.

Deprived of even a semblance of normal relations with the outside, the inmate turns to the other inmates and the inmate subculture for solace. It seems ironic that inmates are cut off from both friends and relatives and drawn entirely into the company of criminals; yet some parole rules forbid the parolee to associate with known ex-offenders. Such paradoxical situations seem to run counter to the basic premises of American corrections. There is no better way to combat the inmate social system and prepare an inmate for freedom than by strengthening his or her ties with the outside world through visitations, family or conjugal visits,[14] home furloughs, telephone access, and mail.

Another form of visitation, employed in many foreign countries and at least six states, is the so-called **conjugal visit**. In Sweden, this is generally referred to as an unsupervised visit. The strong feelings generated over this issue pertain to the common belief that part of the inmate's punishment should be the loss of his or her sexual outlet. But in the Swedish system the sexual aspect of the visit is not questioned. As Torsten Eriksson, a former director of prisons in Sweden, once stated,

> The question whether an inmate shall be permitted to have sexual intercourse with his wife or a female inmate with her husband within the institution is the subject of considerable discussion in many countries. In the Latin American countries this is regarded as obvious and even necessary to the inmate's mental health; the Anglo-Saxons, on the other hand, usually regard it as an impossibility. In Sweden we generally allow unsupervised visits in the open institutions. An inmate may take a visitor to his private room, whether it is his father, mother, brother, sister, wife, fiancee, or someone else close to him. Since the inmate has a key to his room, nobody pays any attention if he locks himself in with his visitor. Moreover, unsupervised visits in special rooms may be permitted in closed institutions also. I do not know whether sexual intercourse

occurs during such visits, although I can always hazard a guess. In our opinion, sexuality is strictly a personal matter. We do not ask questions, we make no special provisions. We merely ask whether the individual inmate can be trusted to receive a visitor without supervision.[15]

It seems probable that our Anglo-Saxon heritage will prevent conjugal visitation[16] reforms in this country from reaching the openness of those in Sweden. The logical solution in the United States, one being used increasingly, is the **home furlough**. This permits the deserving prisoner to visit his or her family under unsupervised circumstances in a natural free world situation. The U.S. Army permits its major offenders incarcerated under maximum custody a seven-day leave each year to visit family. So far, when it has been used, the home furlough has not resulted in mass escapes or crime waves. This can be seen as but another step in the march toward community corrections. Ties with family and friends are critical to the rehabilitation of offenders, and correctional administrators must give them maximum opportunities to maintain those ties.

Use of the Mails

The mail system is closely tied to visitation as another way to maintain essential contact with the outside world. As in the case of visits, stated reasons for the limitation and censorship of mail are tied either to security or to the prison's orderly administration. Although the use of the mail system is a *right*, case law has established that correctional administrators can place reasonable restrictions on prisoners in the exercise of that right if there is a "clear and present danger" or **compelling state need**.[17] As with most situations behind the walls, in the past, mail rules were systematically stiffened to facilitate the institutions' smooth operation. If it became too great an administrative burden to read all the incoming and outgoing mail, the number of letters or the list of correspondents was reduced. Eventually, a small maximum of allowed letters and very restrictive lists of correspondents became the standard. As long as the prisoners could not turn to the courts, this practice did not create a stir. When the attorneys appointed to help prisoners began to see the unjustness of restrictions concerning mail and other so-called privileges, they began to question the rules and reestablish those privileges as *rights*.

How much mail should a prisoner receive? Administrators have usually restricted it to an amount that can readily be censored. During personnel shortages (in wars, for example), the amount of mail was often limited to one letter a month. Outgoing mail was similarly restricted. Communications with an attorney could be opened and read, but not censored unless the correspondence referred to plans for illegal activity or contained contraband. More recently, court decisions have found that most censorship of communications between inmates and their lawyers is unconstitutional;[18] this direction also appears in decisions regarding communications with the news media.[19]

Death row inmates frequently receive only photocopies of correspondence sent to them from persons other than attorneys. There is a clear and present danger of poisoning from chemicals sprayed on stationery at the inmate's request. Stamps can also be affixed to envelopes with a liquid poison. Finally, lethal poison can also be suspended in ink. Ironically, death row inmates cannot be allowed to kill themselves before their execution, although many do commit suicide.[20]

SOVEREIGN IMMUNITY

A judicial doctrine that precludes bringing suit against the government without its consent. Founded on the ancient principle that "the king can do no wrong," it bars holding the government or its political subdivisions liable for the torts of its officers or agents unless such immunity is expressly waived by statute or necessary inference from legislative enactment. The federal government has generally waived its nontort action immunity in the Tucker Act, 28 U.S.C.A. 1346(a)(2), 1491, and its tort immunity in the Federal Court Claims Act, 28 U.S.C.A. 1346(b), 2674. Most states have also waived immunity in various degrees at both the state and local government levels.

The immunity from certain suits in federal court was granted to states by the Eleventh Amendment to the United States Constitution.

Contraband by Mail

In the past, contraband was commonly described as any material that might be used for an escape or used to take advantage of other prisoners. Such items as matches, money, pornographic pictures, guns, knives, lubricants, drugs, and tools are generally considered contraband. Any item can be placed on the contraband list if it is seen as a threat to the prison's orderly operation.

The more recent definition of **contraband** is described as "any item found on the prisoner or in his or her cell that is not specifically authorized by the administration in written rules." This helps simplify the process and eliminate any controversy as to what is, or is not, contraband. (For example, if a prisoner is authorized two blankets, and three are found in a cell inspection, the third blanket is, by definition, contraband.)

When an inmate wishes to communicate with a second inmate, either a friend or jailhouse lawyer who is incarcerated at another institution, the courts have stuck to a hands-off policy, leaving that problem to the discretion of the administrators. The general policy has been to prohibit the passage of any correspondence between inmates. This policy continues to be under attack, however, and has been rejected by some states.[21] In most court cases, the test for permissibility of mail and literature has been the "clear and present danger" standard:

> We accept the premise that **certain literature** may pose such a clear and present danger to the security of a prison, or to the rehabilitation of prisoners, that it should be censored. To take an extreme example, if there were mailed to a prisoner a brochure demonstrating in detail how to saw prison bars with utensils used in the mess hall, how to make a bomb, or how to provoke a prison riot, it would properly be screened. A magazine detailing for incarcerated drug addicts how they might obtain a euphoric "high," comparable to that experienced from heroin, by sniffing aerosol or glue available for other purposes within the prison walls, would likewise be censored as restraining effective rehabilitation. Furthermore, it is undoubtedly true that in the volatile atmosphere of a prison, where a large number of men, many with criminal tendencies, live in close proximity to each other, violence can be fomented by the printed word much more easily than in the outside world. Some censorship or prior restraint on inflammatory literature sent into prisons is, therefore, necessary to prevent such literature from being used to cause disruption or violence within the prison. It may well be that in some prisons where the prisoners' flash-point is low, articles regarding bombing, prison riots, or the like, which would be harmless when sold on the corner newsstand, would be too dangerous for release to the prison population.[22]

The courts have also upheld restrictions on incoming newspapers and magazines that would permit receipt of such mail if "only the publisher" is the sender.[23]

Ohio took the lead in the reform of mail censorship, eliminating all of it in Ohio's prisons on August 3, 1973.[24] Under the Ohio system, both incoming and outgoing mail is merely inspected for contraband and delivered unread. Each inmate may write and receive an unlimited number of items of mail. The adoption of those standards has caused few if any problems. Most states, however, still inspect, electronically, incoming packages and open letters in order to look for contraband.

Religious Rights in Prison

The idea underlying the penitentiary was drawn from religious precepts. It thus seems ironic that there would be any conflict in providing freedom of religion in prisons, but this has indeed been the case. The early efforts to restore the criminal through penitence and prayer were conducted in small homogeneous communities. As immigration to America expanded, it became the most heterogeneous nation in the world. Because the United States was founded on a belief that freedom of worship could not be infringed by the government, the First Amendment addressed those issues: "Congress shall make no law respecting an establishment of religion, or prohibiting the free exercise thereof ...." It is the conflict between what constitutes an **established religion** and the individual's right to exercise it that has caused grief in the nation's prisons.

A clear example of this problem is the Black Muslim decision, which has dominated case law for over a decade. After a long string of cases,[25] the courts finally held that the Black Muslim faith did constitute an established religion and that the Black Muslims were therefore entitled to follow the practices the religion prescribed.[26] The resolution of the Black Muslim issue meant the standards applied there can be applied to any duly recognized religion.[27] This puts a strain on the prison administrator, who must allow equal protection for all inmates. The question of whether the state really grants each inmate "free exercise" simply by ensuring access to a minister of his or her particular faith is still unsettled. It is clear that totally free exercise of all religions would result in chaos in a closed environment such as a prison. In earlier cases, the test used to restrict a religious practice was the clear and present danger to the institution or its personnel, including inmates. In more recent years, the courts have relaxed the standards and now may require "reasonable and substantial justification."[28] Such tests have arisen over such related religious practices as inmates' wearing hats; eating special diets; having special feeding times; and wearing religious emblems, beards, and so on.

BLACK MUSLIM DECISION

In what has become titled "the Black Muslim decision," the court of appeals held that prison officials were not required to make available to prisoners Black Muslim publications that urged defiance of prison authorities and thus threatened prison security, unless properly interpreted by a trained Muslim minister. The resolution of the Black Muslim issue meant the standards applied there can be applied to any duly recognized religion.

Prison church service, the Walls, Huntsville, Texas

—*PHOTO BY ANDREW LICHTENSTEIN, COURTESY OF SYGMA*

Black Muslim leader, Malcolm X, in July 1963, speaks at a rally in New York Ciity

—*COURTESY OF AP/WIDE WORLD PHOTOS*

Generally, the courts have upheld restrictions of religious practice when there are reasonable and substantial justifications.[29] However, administrators have been alerted that religious freedoms are of special interest to the courts and will receive strong review, with the burden resting on the correctional administration to prove why the restrictions were imposed. Many inmates use religious programming for a variety of reasons, and access remains an important consideration.[30]

Acess to Court and Counsel

Access to the federal courts was not established as a constitutional right for inmates until 1940, in a case called *Ex Parte Hull*. In that decision, the U.S. Supreme Court established that "the state and its officers may not abridge or impair a petitioner's right to apply to a federal court for a writ of habeas corpus." Despite that clear ruling, the courts still maintained a strict hands-off policy in this regard until the 1964 case of *Cooper* v. *Pate*.[31]

Once the prisoners' right to use **jailhouse lawyers** was established in *Johnson* v. *Avery*,[32] inmates needed to be assured of an adequate supply of legal research materials. And in 1971, the case of *Younger* v. *Gilmore*[33] guaranteed the inmate writ writers such assistance. But the extent of provided materials has varied considerably, from complete law libraries[34] in the state prisons to the bare essentials elsewhere.[35] Meanwhile, other states allow law students to run legal clinics inside institutions, under the supervision of a law school faculty member qualified to practice in that jurisdiction. It seems the courts must continue to require that administrations offer adequate legal counsel to inmates, or they will have to live with the continued use of jailhouse lawyers and the problems that result.

The right to consult with counsel has been clearly established.[36] The problem, before *Gideon* and the cases it generated, was that most inmates could not afford a lawyer to defend them or prepare later appeals.[37] Early prison rules restricted the use of jailhouse lawyers, so few prisoners were able to file writs in the

RIGHT TO RELIGIOUS FREEDOM

Cooper v. Pate, a case dealing with freedom of religion, used Section 1983 of the Civil Rights Act. That strategy made the case a landmark decision in inmates' rights.

RIGHT TO LEGAL ASSISTANCE

Through a writ of certiorari, a court of appeals decision was reversed in favor of an inmate who had been disciplined for violating a prison regulation that prohibited inmates from assisting other prisoners in preparing writs. The court of appeals had reversed a district court decision that voided the regulation because it had the effect of barring illiterate prisoners from access to general habeas corpus. This decision established the "jailhouse lawyer" as a part of the modern correctional scene.

federal courts. After the courts established the right to counsel, those administrative agencies that could not or would not comply were covered by *Johnson v. Avery*. Though not all jurisdictions have been able to provide counsel for all inmates, the remedies incorporated in the court decisions have helped fill the void—while incidentally creating a flood of writs that have washed over the civil and appeals courts. See Table 19-1. Over the past two decades, the petitions filed in the U.S. district courts by federal prisoners increased 64 percent and by state prisoners increased 238 percent. The latter's civil rights suits increased by a whopping 389 percent!

The Right to Medical Treatment and Care

The issue of adequate medical care in our prisons has finally prompted a decision from the Supreme Court. Only when a constitutionally guaranteed right has been violated has the Court become involved in the provision of medical care. Because both medical programs and the backgrounds of prison medical personnel are extremely diversified, the quality of medical aid varies among institutions. Ironically, a nation that demands adequate medical care for all inmates is, at this writing, still struggling with providing adequate medical care for all of its citizens.

The U.S. Supreme Court has taken the position that inmates in state prisons should seek remedy in the state courts. In the 1976 case of *Estelle v. Gamble*,[38] that position was made even clearer. Although suits in the past have shown that prisoners' rights to proper diagnosis and medical treatment of illness have been violated on a grand scale, the courts have moved slowly in that area. In *Estelle v. Gamble*, however, the Court stated, "We therefore conclude that **deliberate indifference** to serious medical needs of prisoners constitutes the unnecessary and wanton infliction of pain proscribed by the Eighth Amendment. This is true whether the indifference is manifested by prison doctors in their response to the prisoner's needs or by prison guards in intentionally denying or delaying access to medical care or intentionally interfering with the treatment once prescribed."[39] This was a giant step forward in the provision of medical treatment, but it still falls short of the individual remedies provided by decisions in other areas. For example, the First Circuit U.S. Court of Appeals has ruled that inmates must receive "adequate

TABLE *19.1*

Petitions Filed in U.S. District Courts by Federal and State Prisoners, 1977–1994

Type of Petition	Federal			State		
	1977	*1987*	*1994*	*1977*	*1987*	*1994*
To vacate sentence	1,921	1,669	4,620	NA	7	0
Habeas corpus	1,745	1,812	1,441	6,866	9,542	11,918
Mandamus (Etc.)	542	313	491	228	276	397
Civil rights	483	725	1,140	7,752	22,972	37,925
Totals	4,691	4,519	7,700	14,846	32,797	50,240

SOURCE: Kathleen Maguire and Ann Pastore. *Bureau of Justice Statistics Sourcebook 1994* (Washington, D.C.: U.S. Department of Justice, 1995), p. 499.

medical care" but are not necessarily deserving "the most sophisticated care that money can buy."[40] Medical care in prison in relationship to the AIDS problem has been described as "a national disgrace."[41]

Gamble states a position of sympathy for complaints about the systemwide failure to provide adequate and humane medical care. The test of deliberate indifference, however, a requirement for evoking the Eighth Amendment, seems to be a major hurdle for most who choose to use *Gamble* as a basis for action. Mere negligence or malpractice leaves the prisoner with remedy only in a state civil case. Total deprivation of medical service seems to be the current standard for application of constitutional prohibitions.

Because of the relative ineffectiveness of using state and tort courts to remedy inadequate medical services and treatment in institutions, inmates have more recently begun to sue correctional administrators through **Section 1983 of the U.S. Code**. This section, passed in 1871 to protect the civil rights of recently freed slaves, allows petitioners to sue in a federal court without having first exhausted all existing state courts' remedies. The federal district and circuit courts are currently deciding a number of important cases, and some of those will eventually come before the U.S. Supreme Court.

TORT SUITS

A **tort** is a civil wrong. In corrections, the term *tort* typically means that the plaintiff alleges the defendant failed to perform a duty required by the defendant's position or owed to the plaintiff. The objective of the suit is usually compensation for damages. A tort case alleges the defendant was negligent, grossly negligent, or deliberately negligent. The same objectives are seen in medical malpractice suits brought by inmates against the facility and, in cases where the inmate has been attacked by others, for negligence in not protecting the inmate from attack.[42]

Not only are tort cases handled in state courts, but they are also time consuming. If the suit is lost by the state, damages and attorneys' fees may be awarded by the court. Fortunately, inmates are successful in lawsuits in less than 2 percent of the cases that go to trial.

CIVIL RIGHTS ACT "1983" SUITS

Title 42, Section 1983, of the U.S. Code, commonly known as the Civil Rights Act, reads as follows:

> Any person who, under color of any statute, ordinance, regulation, custom, or usage, in any state, or territory, subjects or causes to be subjected, any citizen of the United States or other person within the jurisdiction thereof to the deprivation of any rights, privileges, or immunities secured by the Constitution and laws, shall be liable to the party injured in an action at law, suit in equity, or other proper proceedings for redress.

One example of the use of Section 1983 to redress medical malpractice and mistreatment can be seen in *Tucker* v. *Hutto*,[43] a Virginia case in which Tucker's arms and legs became permanently paralyzed as a result of improper use of antipsychotic drugs while he was a patient at the Virginia State Penitentiary Hospital. The suit was initiated by the National Prison Project[44] and settled out of court for $518,000. Section 1983 suits can be an effective,[45] although unwelcome, avenue for defining and improving prisoner rights while under confinement.

Many times the federal courts have been forced to overlook the issue of constitutional rights in order to correct situations involving a flagrant disregard of the need for adequate medical service. That disregard has often produced prison riots in the past, and it will continue to be a factor in right-to-treatment cases over the next decade. Right to treatment is covered in detail in Chapter 22.

*I*nmates' Lawsuits

Prisoners frequently file lawsuits against confinement facilities and their administrators. Some suits address a single practice at one institution (such as child welfare services delivery) but others are class action suits addressing the totality of conditions of prison life, entered on behalf of all inmates similarly situated.

As of June 30, 1994, there were fourteen states whose entire correctional departments were under court ordered consent decrees for conditions of confinement or overcrowding, programming, medical and food services, or lack of mental health services.[47] In 1994, over fifty-seven thousand lawsuits were filed against some correctional unit. New York alone faced over ten thousand suits filed in 1994. The strengthening of offenders' rights was a major area of study for the National Advisory Commission. The issue is highly charged, and correctional authorities are understandably concerned that the press for rights may disrupt the programs at their institutions.[48] The standards suggested by the commission attempt to address the central problems:

> Each correctional agency immediately should adopt policies and procedures, and where applicable should seek legislation, to insure proper redress where an offender's rights are abridged.
>
> 1. Administrative remedies, not requiring the intervention of a court, should include at least the following:
>   a. Procedures allowing an offender to seek redress where he believes his rights have been or are about to be violated.
>   b. Policies of inspection and supervision to assure periodic evaluation of institutional conditions and staff practices that may affect offenders' rights.
>   c. Policies which:
>   (1) Assure wide distribution and understanding of the rights of offenders among both offenders and correctional staff.
>   (2) Provide that the intentional or persistent violation of an offender's rights is justification for removal from office or employment of any correctional worker.
>   (3) Authorize the payment of claims to offenders as compensation for injury caused by a violation of any right.
> 2. Judicial remedies for violation of rights should include at least the following:
>   a. Authority for an injunction either prohibiting a practice violative of an offender's rights or requiring affirmative action on the part of governmental officials to assure compliance with offenders' rights.
>   b. Authority for an award of damages against either the correctional agency or, in appropriate circumstances, the staff member

REMEDIES FOR VIOLATIONS OF RIGHTS

The first steps to remedy the almost standard practice of depriving convicted offenders of all rights have been taken, starting with the recognition that the Constitution does entitle those individuals to retain a substantial portion of their rights, even while incarcerated. The push for that recognition has come from the offenders themselves, often with the assistance of jailhouse lawyers, and has resulted in active and sympathetic judicial intervention. Writ of habeas corpus, designed as a tool for prisoners to test the legality of their confinement, has been the main weapon in the battle for prisoner rights.[46] The battle continues today, especially with regard to increased maintenance of community ties and the abolition of the death penalty.

Civil litigation abounds over correctional issues such as prison overcrowding, compensation for lost personal property, need for a special diet, and restoration of good-time credits, increasing every year at great expense and time consumed by institutional managers. Further, court litigation is not a speedy technique for resolving inmate needs. Finally, correctional administrators have become increasingly concerned with the impact of lawsuits on the institution, including the reluctance of correctional staff to take actions, decline in staff morale, officer stress, and general reluctance to comply with discretionary duties. In the search for alternatives to litigation, four basic approaches have been proposed: grievance boards, inmate grievance procedures, ombudsman, and mediators.

The **grievance board** is usually staffed by institutional employees, or an occasional concerned citizen, to accept and investigate inmate complaints and then propose solutions, as relevant, to correctional administrators.

The **inmate grievance** procedure is similar to the grievance board, except that inmates are selected to serve as part of the grievance committee, a procedure many correctional managers find unacceptable, as it might strengthen the influence of inmate grievance committee members over staff and other inmates.

The third alternative is the **ombudsman**, a public official who investigates complaints against correctional personnel, practices, policies, and customs and who is empowered to recommend corrective solutions and measures. Empowered to investigate, the ombudsman has access to files, inmates, records, and staff. The ombudsman (and office staff) tend to be impartial, have special expertise, and are independent of the correctional administrator. Reports are filed not only with the institutional manager, but also with the correctional department director and funding agent for the office of the ombudsman. There are at least seventeen correctional systems in the nation that operate with the ombudsman to protect inmates.

Mediators are relatively new on the correctional scene and represent a third party skilled in correctional work who agree to hear differences and to render a decision to remedy the condition that would be binding on both parties. Maryland, Rhode Island, Arkansas and, more recently, South Carolina have experimented with this approach.

An inmate might file a lawsuit in conjunction with any of these alternatives. The methods are seen as promising ways to avoid litigation over correctional issues. ∎

---

involved to compensate the offender for injury caused by a violation of his rights.

c. Authority for the court to exercise continuous supervision of a correctional facility or program including the power to appoint a special master responsible to the court to oversee implementation of offenders' rights.

d. Authority for the court to prohibit further commitments to an institution or program.

e. Authority for the court to shut down an institution or program and require either the transfer or release of confined or supervised offenders.

f. Criminal penalties for intentional violations of an offender's rights.[49]

The Americans with Disabilities Act

The Americans with Disabilities Act, commonly referred to as "**the ADA**," was passed in 1990 to protect the forty-three million Americans who are afflicted with some form of disability. The ADA prohibits discrimination, isolation, and political powerlessness in:

- Employment,
- Public services and transportation,
- Public accommodations, and
- Telecommunications services.

This sweeping act had grown out of the civil rights legislation of the 1960s and 1970s in regard to civil rights in general and vocational rehabilitation in particular. The ADA has noble goals and objectives, but may create some major problems to fully implement in corrections. As noted by Appel,

> Of the five titles contained in the ADA, Titles I and II have a direct effect on corrections. These two titles deal with employment practices and access to public-sector services.
>
> In corrections, three distinct groups are protected under the ADA: staff, inmates, and public, both visitors and volunteers. Each group must be considered in the design of inmate programs and the space in which programs take place.
>
> By definition, an individual with a disability has a physical or mental impairment that substantially limits one or more major life activities, has a record of such impairment, or is regarded as having such an impairment. Major life activities include functions such as caring for oneself, performing manual tasks, walking, seeing, hearing, speaking, working, learning, and breathing.
>
> The aging offender population ... the debilitating effects of alcohol and drug abuse, and injuries sustained through the violent behavior of inmates mean that corrections will be responsible for an increasing number of disabled offenders. At the same time, as the individuals with disabilities begin to feel empowered by the ADA to enter the corrections profession, corrections will find that an increasing number of staff and volunteers also will be disabled... .[50]

Among many others, corrections administrators are concerned with the question of how to meet the cost of providing the programs and design problems that stem from the ADA. Will these requirement be applied to the older facilities, many constructed of materials and with hallways and doorways that do not lend themselves to easy modification? Some solutions are simple and easy to obtain, such as moving programs to a floor-level room so that access is possible, adopting education that is computer based and can be done in living quarters or on the Internet, using special speech synthesizers for educational and program efforts and removing as many physical barriers as possible. Why should corrections use its resources to comply fully with ADA requirements, instead of minimum amount to comply? Appel feels it applies to three basic tenets of the correctional profession:

1. The ADA is the law, and as a law enforcement entity, corrections is bound to follow the spirit and letter of the law to the fullest extent possible.

2. The ADA is both just and fair, and it is the responsibility of government to set an example for others to follow. The integrity of the corrections agency and staff, as well as its programs are reinforced, which in turn results in inmates accepting the concepts.

3. The ADA will assist correctional institutions in helping inmates make positive changes in their behavior.

Despite the hardships that may accompany the ADA for correctional administrators, it is a right that has come to all Americans and is fair to be applied to correctional workers and inmates. The consequences, in terms of budgets and other major issues, will become apparent as it is implemented, and will take time to shake out. The ADA was only implemented in 1994, so it is barely off the ground. It will become necessary to monitor this act closely as it develops and has clearer guidelines for implementation and exceptions.

COURT MASTERS IN CORRECTIONS

Both a federal and a state court in which litigation over correctional issues has been filed may appoint a servant of the court, the **court master**, a functional adjunct whose task is to assist the court in whatever manner the court directs. Typically, the master oversees the day-to-day compliance of the institution to the decree of the court or the consent decree. A decree of the court implies that the defendant (correctional unit) lost the case and the court has issued orders that are to be implemented. A consent decree occurs where the complainants (inmates) or defendants agree to a set of actions that both would find acceptable.

Generally, masters monitor the lawsuit, report to the court, investigate complaints by inmates, have access to prisoners and their files, hold hearings, and write reports that inform the appointing judge on progress in the settlement of the orders. They also advise the court (through their special expertise in corrections, in particular) and help arrange compromises between the extremes of the demands of the inmates and the realities of prison administration.

When a master is appointed, correctional administrators tend to resist the intrusion of the master into the routine affairs of the institution. Some masters have their own reform agenda or fail to represent the correctional unit in securing compromise. Finally, the defendant (correctional system) must pay for the master and any staff, and there usually is little disincentive to the master's office running up long hours of work at high rates of compensation. Currently, masters are seen as providing correctional expertise to a court that has no competence in correctional administration. Future correctional administrators will need to develop positive working relationships with the court and negotiate with all parties to define clearly the powers, role, and scope of the master, to minimize any negative fallout from the appointment of an intervention agent.

REFORM BY LEGISLATION

Passage of meaningful reform legislation, especially in the corrections area, has been painfully slow. Even more difficult has been the provision of adequate funding to accomplish reform. The turbulence of the early 1960s prompted federal enactment of the Law Enforcement Assistance Act of 1965. That act, designed to test the value of granting federal funds to assist local law enforcement, was a symbol of things to come. After the release of the findings of President Lyndon Johnson's criminal justice commission, entitled *The Challenge of Crime in a Free Society* (1967), legislation was introduced to expand the Law Enforcement Assistance Act, with direct grants to state and local governments focusing on causation research, prevention, and control of crime. But the U.S. Senate moved slowly; the bill was deadlocked in committee when Congress was shocked from its apathy by the assassination of presidential aspirant Senator Robert Kennedy. This dramatic demonstration of the nation's need for more effective crime control prompted its quick passage.

The final version of the bill, known as the Omnibus Crime Control and Safe Streets Act of 1968, replaced direct grants to local governments with block grants to the states, but was otherwise passed substantially as submitted. This far-reaching act, implemented by the Law Enforcement Assistance Administration (**LEAA**), provided billions of dollars to states for action programs, research, education, evaluation, training, and administration of the criminal justice system. Amendments in 1970 created a category of funds especially earmarked for corrections. As part of LEAA, the Law Enforcement Education Program funneled more than $260 million to at least 300,000 criminal justice students from 1968 to 1981.

The policy change embodied in the act was a reaction to overemphasis on police needs in previous years, and it reflected a new awareness of the realities of

Sexual Harassment

Here are some frequently asked questions about sexual harassment:

Q: Is sexual harassment limited to conduct toward women?

A: Obviously not. This form of discrimination is gender based. Female supervisors who use their power to exact sexual favors from male subordinates similarly are harassing their subordinates on the basis of gender. Conduct that is motivated by a person's sex may give rise to sexual harassment. Moreover, the offensive conduct does not have to be explicitly sexual to be actionable.

Q: Does a complaint need to be lodged for an agency to investigate and take action?

A: No. The fact that a person fails to complain is not determinative. Agencies may take appropriate action when there is evidence of unwelcome conduct. In one instance, a male police sergeant was suspended for 5 days for making sexually suggestive remarks to a female subordinate even though the woman did not file a complaint. The chief took remedial action by suspending the sergeant. The chief's actions were upheld by the Board of Police Commissioners and a three-judge appellate court.

Q: Do inmates and others held in custody have the right to sue for sexual harassment?

A: Yes, sexual harassment of inmates by prison or jail employees is actionable. The inmate could sue for damages under Federal statute 42 U.S.C.§ 1983. A lawsuit brought under this law is based on a claim that a governmental entity deprived the individual of a constitutional right. Courts have held that prisoners are entitled to protection under the Eighth Amendment to be free from sexual harassment at the hands of prison staff. The plaintiff would need to allege facts demonstrating unlawful conduct in support of the claim.

Q: Should sexually explicit materials, such as posters and magazines, be banned from criminal justice facilities to avoid claims of hostile work environment?

A: That depends. A recent Federal court decision in California held as unconstitutional a fire department policy banning sexually oriented magazines in Los Angeles county firehouses as part of its sexual harassment policy. The court found that private possession, reading, and consensual sharing of such magazines is protected by the First Amendment to the Constitution. A critical element of the court's decision rested on the private nature of the possession and use of such materials. When sexually explicit materials are not private but are public, then their presence may rise to the level of actionable sexual harassment. Examples of public displays of such materials may include: obscene cartoons, sexually oriented pictures in the workplace, and sexually oriented drawings or graffiti on pillars and other public places in the workplace. ∎

SOURCE: Paula N. Rubin, "Civil Rights and Criminal Justice: Primer on Sexual Harassment." *NIJ Research in Action* (Washington D.C.: U.S. Department of Justice, 1995), p. 3.

local political structures. The criminal justice system, however loosely structured it may be, is still subject to the rules of any social system. When too much effort was expended on improving the police ability to catch criminals, judicial and correctional sectors were overwhelmed by the impact of their success. Most experts now recognize that corrections also must improve, or we will simply continue to recycle indefinitely the same or similar people through the system.

In the 1980s, a wave of political and fiscal conservatism swept the nation, contributing to the abandonment of early prison release mechanisms. An increasingly conservative makeup of the U.S. Supreme Court, encroachments on civil rights (search and seizure, evidence rules, right to privacy, etc.), and harsher prison sentences seemed to follow. The Congress (as well as state legislatures) also declared a war on drugs, and individual legislators adopted more punitive ideologies for the most base of reasons—to be elected to office or reelected as incumbents. Changes in sentencing practices, and a get-tough-on-crime movement, along with the war on drugs, have contributed to an unparalleled increase in the number of incarcerated Americans (estimated at over 1,050,000 as this book goes to press). We discuss these trends in detail in later chapters, but they reflect *negative* impacts on prison and correctional change brought about by past legislative actions: prison overcrowding, staggering prison construction and maintenance costs, unacceptable rates of incarceration, and a construction agenda that will lead to increasing commitments of the correctional dollar to support institutional sentencing and increased punishment.[51] Legislation, even that passed in a sincere but erroneous belief it will reduce crime, has serious public policy considerations seldom anticipated at the time of passage. It is a sad commentary on the political process to note that ideology can have such an overwhelming and negative impact on corrections in America.

REFORM BY EXECUTIVE ORDER

Not since 1929, when President Herbert Hoover established the National Commission on Law Observance and Enforcement (commonly known as the Wickersham Commission), had the executive office undertaken an in-depth examination of crime in America. The Great Depression, World War II, the war in Korea, and subsequent adjustments to peace all led a series of presidents to assign a low priority to criminal justice reforms.

The outbreak of violence on the streets of America in the early 1960s changed all that. From the embattled ghettos of Los Angeles and Detroit to the assassination of President Kennedy in Dallas, events highlighted the problems of crime and violence across the nation. On July 23, 1965, President Lyndon B. Johnson established the Commission on Law Enforcement and Administration of Justice with a mandate to examine every area of the American criminal justice system. The commission's report, *The Challenge of Crime in a Free Society*, and its more detailed papers have become the basic reference points for progress on all fronts of the criminal justice system.

The President's Commission confirmed in many respects the earlier Wickersham report. Many recommendations were found to be as pertinent in 1967 as they had been in 1929. At that time, the three thousand federal and state prisons, reformatories, workhouses, and county and city jails were cited for deficiencies in prisoner classification, employment, education, parole, and probation. They were characterized by outdated physical facilities, untrained and inadequate

Alabama to Make
Prisoners Break Rocks

ATHENS, Ala., July 28, 1995—The once-common sight of felons in chains breaking rocks under a searing sun is about to be a reality again here in Alabama, the state whose get-tough policy on convicts led to the resurrection of chain gangs in May.

The Commissioner of State Prisons, Ronald D. Jones, is preparing to have rocks trucked to at least three state penitentiaries so that chained inmates can break the stones into pea-sized pellets. The only goal of the program is to increase the level of punishment for prisoners, since state highway officials say they have no use for the crushed rock.

With final details being worked out, wardens have been told to be ready to start the rock program next week. Mr. Jones was not available to discuss the plans.

Ralph L. Hooks, the acting warden at Limestone Correctional Facility near Huntsville, where chain gangs have been revived, said that medium-security inmates assigned to the road crews there would also be required to break rocks.

He said that almost 400 inmates are already on chain gangs, working about 12 hours a day on the roads. The men, wearing leg irons, work in groups of five and are linked with eight-foot chains.

Chain gangs were discontinued nationally a half-century ago, but Mr. Jones revived the practice on May 3 as part of a policy that he and Gov. Fob James, Jr. adopted.

After Alabama reinstituted the gangs, Arizona and Florida said they were planning to do the same.

The Southern Poverty Law Center in Montgomery has filed suit in Federal District Court, saying that chain gangs constitute cruel and unusual punishment.

But Alabama is proceeding with its plans. On Thursday, sledge hammers were ordered for the rock-breaking project, in which 160 inmates in leg irons will work just outside the prison gates for 10 hours a day, resting every 20 minutes, Mr. Hooks said. They will have Saturdays and Sundays off.

Besides the prison in Limestone, the Staton Correctional Facility near Montgomery will also add a rock-breaking program, Mr. Hooks said. And today, the state said that it was planning a third rock-breaking project at Fountain Correctional Facility in Atmore in the southeastern part of the state.

Alabama has about 20,000 inmates, and most medium-security prisoners must spend one to three months on chain gangs. Officials said they are planning to extend that time to as much as six months. The amount of time a prisoner spends on a chain gang is decided by prison officials, not during the sentencing of a prisoner. During the months prisoners are assigned to the gangs, they are not allowed to smoke or watch television.

Mr. Jones also does not allow prisoners to drink coffee, except on Sundays. He also disconnected cable television in the prisons, and does not let prisoners have free postage stamps or their $1 monthly allowance.

He also banned vegetable gardening by inmates at Julia Tutwiler Prison for Women but lifted that ban after complaints from inmates, the public, and his wife.

Dalmus Davidson, a highway director in northeast Alabama, said that the Department of Corrections has asked him to provide rocks for the Limestone prison from quarries in the area.

Mr. Davidson said that the rock program would provide no financial benefit to the state, which already has contracts with quarries to crush rock in various sizes that can be used along highway shoulders and for some road construction. The broken rocks will remain at the prisons and be used to fill in dirt roads around the prison.

After the 1932 film classic "I Am a Fugitive from a Chain Gang" portrayed brutal conditions for prisoners, states were forced to remove leg irons from work crews.

Even so, popular culture has immortalized the image of Southern chain gangs and rock piles in movies like "Cool Hand Luke," released in 1967, and song lyrics like those of the Bobby Fuller Four's 1965 hit: "Breakin' rocks in the hot sun. I fought the law, the law won."

(Alabama cancelled its in-tandem chain gang program in February, 1996.)   ■

SOURCE: *The New York Times*, July 29, 1995, p.5.

staffs, and inmates beset by idleness. Identical problems, with few exceptions, were found in the massive study of corrections in America completed in 1967. The president's involvement, through his commission, pushed such issues as crime on the streets, corrections, and judicial processes to the top of the list for legislative proposals and action. Finally spurred to action, Congress provided federal funds to the states, through LEAA, to work on the problems.

Disturbed by the problems in their own states, a number of governors also began examining, evaluating, and improving the conditions of their criminal justice systems, especially the corrections sector (prisons). Using the citizens' task force concept as a model, they searched for ways to reform prison operations. Federal funding enabled them to implement many key suggestions from their state task forces. This was particularly important when a needed reform required more than state funds or a simple executive order. Notable among the citizens' task forces were those in Ohio and Wisconsin.

During the court terms when Warren Burger was chief justice, and in conjunction with the appointment of more conservative justices to the U.S. Supreme Court, the shift toward judicial recognition of prisoner rights slowed down.[52] Under the current Rehnquist court, it is expected that additional conservative decisions will be made. For example, in 1989, the U.S. Supreme Court acted as follows:

1. Upheld the tough and punitive federal sentencing guidelines,
2. Watered down the *Miranda* warnings to suspects,
3. Refused to establish a constitutional right to court-appointed counsel for death row inmates appealing their convictions and sentences, and
4. Held that sentencing a mentally retarded offender to death does not constitute cruel and unusual punishment.[53]

In 1993, the U.S. Supreme Court acted as follows:

1. Signaled possible intent to weaken the protection of rights of state prisoners, and
2. Rejected the grievous wrong standard in place of a flexible standard that would apply to requests to modify (escape from requirements) of consent decrees.[54]

The role of the federal courts in responding to inmate complaints is significant, and a new shift toward a liberal bent by the Supreme Court is likely to abate this conservative trend. The number of complaints filed in state and federal court over jail and prison conditions, violations of inmate civil rights, due process violations, mistreatment, and lack of treatment of inmates has increased every year for the last two decades.

Summary

Liability exposure of correctional administrators and managers has increased with several legal decisions. The sheriff, for example, has absolute liability for jail operations, whether or not he or she knew of the conditions.[55] The shield of the principle of sovereign immunity is gone; the state can do wrong. Third, many correctional systems have agreed to submit complaints to a mediator in an effort to avoid the time, cost, expenses, and damages of litigation. Whether that becomes a major trend will depend on the success of initial efforts in that direction. Finally, the gains made from the 1960s through the 1980s must be monitored to be certain that inmates' rights are not reversed by court decisions or by actions of correctional administrators to limit either access to the courts or the number of suits that may be filed. In the light of massive prison overcrowding, corrections must do everything possible to keep prisons from sliding back into the morass from which they have emerged over the last three decades.

As civil cases are increasingly filed in state and federal courts by inmates seeking to improve their lot in prisons and jails throughout the country, we sense an insurgent reactionary move in the political realm. Court appointees are more conservative, and the test used to determine if corrections can restrict conditions has partially slid from "clear and present danger" to "reasonable and substantial justification." Further, the proportion of offenders being committed to prisons is increasing, and legislatures have taken steps to see that the incarcerated remain in prison for longer periods. It is against this background that we point with enthusiasm to the comments of a former practitioner and expert witness, John P. Conrad:

> Prisoners' rights don't excite the public as a righteous cause. I want to propose that in the interest of the prisoners, the employees of the prison, and the general public, every prisoner has a right to conditions that won't make him a worse man. We know how hard it is to help prisoners to become better men, and many penal authorities have given up too easily on that task. But whatever prisons do, they must not make men needlessly worse. As to that requirement, there can be no competition of rights. Those who believe in justice as the essential virtue of social institutions in a democracy face only the difficulty of prodding prison bureaucracies into recognition of their plain duty. Every bureaucracy cares more about its survival than the performance of plain duties and of few can this be said more surely than those charged with the administration of prisons. Only the continuous vigilance of an informed public can assure that survival requires that performance of duty is manifest in the observance of rights.[56]

Clearly, the rights of prisoners have become a driving factor in planning by administrators, legislators, and jurists in regard to operations and conditions in America's jails and prisons. Next, we examine that most important of all rights— the right of convicted criminals sentenced to death—to live or die. The argument continues.

California's Inmate Bill of Rights

In 1975, California passed an Inmate Bill of Rights, defining by executive order and statute those personal rights accorded all prisoners. These included personal visits and the rights to marry and make out a will. The latter three were placed into state statutes. In 1994, the California legislature reduced prisoner rights to only those rights guaranteed in the California and U.S. Constitution. In 1996, personal visits were deleted from the statutes and became a privilege, to be granted as the California Department of Corrections might see fit. The administration's goal is also to curtail conjugal visits for sex offenders and violent criminals. ∎

SOURCE: Editorial, "Inmates Lose Right to Conjugal Visits Under New Legislation," *San Francisco Chronicle*, July 8, 1996,, p. A-17.

Review Questions

1. Why is it important for offenders to retain their ties with the community?
2. What is the difference between conjugal visits and unsupervised visits?
3. What is the name of the writ that tests the legality of confinement?
4. How have offender rights been developed by the courts?
5. What are four alternatives to litigation that inmates might use to secure their rights?
6. What have been the impacts of the more conservative courts on the definition of inmate rights?
7. What are the advantages and disadvantages of having the court master?
8. Give four indicators of rising conservatism in the U.S. Supreme Court.
9. What is the concept of *sovereign immunity* and how does it apply to corrections?

Words to Remember

final guilty verdict

civil death

slave of the state

Wolff v. *McDonnell*

privilege

family ties

conjugal visit

home furlough

compelling state need

contraband

certain literature

established religion

jailhouse lawyers

deliberate indifference

Section 1983 of the U.S. Code

tort

the ADA

court master

LEAA

grievance board

Endnotes

1. In *Ruffin* v. *Commonwealth*, 62 Va. (21 Grat.) 790, 796 (1871). See also *Wolff* v. *McDonnell*, 418 U.S. 539, 94 S. Ct. 2963 (1974). For a contrasting view, see Donald Wallace, "*Ruffin* v. *Virginia* and Slaves of the State: A Nonexistent Baseline of Prisoners' Rights Jurisprudence," *Journal of Criminal Justice* 20:4 (1992): 333–342.

2. *Cooper* v. *Pate*, a case dealing with freedom of religion, used Section 1983 of the Civil Rights Act. That strategy made the case a landmark decision in inmates' rights. (*Cooper* v. *Pate* 378, U.S. 546 [1964].) See Samuel Pillsbury, "Understanding Penal Reform," *The Journal of Criminal Law and Criminology* 80:3 (Fall 1989): 726-780.

3. And may again, according to Rudolph Alexander, "Slamming the Federal Courthouse Door on Inmates," *Journal of Criminal Justice* 21:2 (1993): 103–116.

4. See the history of litigation review in Anton Fowles, "Prisoners' Rights in English Law," in Bruno Holyst, ed., *Euro-Criminology*, Volume 3 (Warsaw: Polish Scientific Publishers, 1990), pp. 181–199. See also Tim Newburn, *Crime and Criminal Justice Policy* (Essex, U.K.: Longman, 1995).

5. See Allen Beck, Jodi Brown, and D. Gilliard, *Probation and Parole Population Reaches Almost 3.8 Million* (Washington, D.C.: U.S. Department of Justice, 1996), p. 7.

6. National Advisory Commission on Criminal Justice Standards and Goals, *Corrections* (Washington, D.C.: U.S. Department of Justice, 1973), p. 439.

7. Harry Elmer Barnes and Negley K. Teeters, *New Horizons in Criminology* 3rd ed. (Englewood Cliffs, NJ: Prentice Hall, 1959), p. 505.

8. Visiting lists may be restricted, and persons who have violated visiting regulations may be removed from the lists. See *Patterson* v. *Walters*, 363 F. Supp. 486 (W.D. Pa. 1973). In addition, any person who previously attempted to help an inmate escape may be required to visit via noncontact means. See *In re Bell*, 168 Cal. Rptr. 100 (App. 1980).

9. But see the evaluation of the New York Family Reunion Program in Bonnie Carlson and Neil Cervera, *Inmates and Their Wives: Incarceration and Family Life* (Westport, CT: Greenwood, 1992), and Ann Adalist-Estrin, "Strengthing Inmate-Family Relationships: Programs That Work," *Corrections Today* 57:7 (1995): 116–117.

10. Ohio Citizens' Task Force on Corrections, *Final Report* (Columbus: Ohio Department of Urban Affairs, 1972), p. C-66.

11. Velmer Burton, Francis Cullen, and Lawrence Travis, "The Collateral Consequences of a Felony Conviction: A National Study of State Statutes," *Federal Probation* 51:3 (1987): 52–60.

12. James Stephan, *Prison Rule Violators* (Washington, D.C.: U.S. Department of Justice, 1989); Jeffery Senese, Joe Wilson, Arthur Evans, et al., "Evaluating Jail Reform: Inmate Infractions and Disciplinary Response in a Traditional and a Podular/Direct Supervision Jail," *American Jails* 6:4 (1992): 14–23; Christopher Innes, *Violent State Prisoners and Their Victims* (Washington, D.C.: U.S. Department of Justice, 1990); and David Lowell and Ron Mishebone, "When Inmates Misbehave: The Costs of Discipline," *The Prison Journal* 76:2 (1996): 165–179.

13. R. W. Dumond, "The Sexual Assault of Many Inmates in Incarcerated Settings," *International Journal of the Sociology of Law* 20:2 (1992): 135–158; Victor Hassine, *Life Without Parole* (Los Angeles: Roxbury, 1996), pp. 71–76; and Stephen Donaldson, "The Rape Crisis Behind Bars," *The New York Times,* December 29, 1993, p. A-13.

14. George Kiser, "Female Inmates and Their Families," *Federal Probation* 55:3 (1991): 56–63, and Peter Breen, "Bridging the Barriers," *Corrections Today* 57:7 (1995): 98–99.

15. Torsten Eriksson, from an unpublished speech to a group in Sydney, Australia.

16. Columbus Hopper, "The Evolution of Conjugal Visiting in Mississippi," *The Prison Journal* 69 (Spring–Summer 1989): 103–109. States with conjugal visits are California, Connecticut, Minnesota, New York, Washington, and South Carolina. On occasion, Alabama has allowed conjugal visiting in selected institutions.

17. *Brown* v. *Wainwright,* 419 F. 2d 1308 (5th Cir. 1969); *Ortega* v. *Ragen,* 216 F. 2d 561 (7th Cir. 1954); and *Medlock* v. *Burke,* 285 F. Supp. 67 (E.D. Wis. 1968). These three decisions found insufficient jurisdiction for federal court interference on behalf of inmates against prison authorities. The *Brown* decision refused a prisoner's request that a three-judge court be convened to enjoin prison censors from removing postage stamps from his outgoing mail. In *Ortega* v. *Ragen,* civil rights action was denied to a prisoner alleging the warden's failure to deliver letters of appeal. The *Medlock* decision refused the prisoner's appeal for court intervention to prevent alleged deprivation of medical care. In 1980, the U.S. Bureau of Prisons reduced the number of letters per week that inmates could mail at the expense of the bureau but left intact its unrestricted mail-out policy for inmates paying their own postage.

18. *Palmigiano* v. *Travisono,* 317 F. Supp. 776 (D.R.I. 1970).

19. William Gilbertson, "Irked by Focus on Inmates, California Bans Interviews," *The New York Times,* December 29, 1995, p. A-8.

20. See the special death penalty theme issue of *Corrections Today* 55:4 (1993): 56–98; especially John Allard, "When There's No One to Say Goodbye," *Corrections Today* 55:4 (1993): 120–126.

21. Some courts have upheld the restriction of communications between inmates at different institutions for security reasons. *Schlobohm* v. *U.S. Attorney General,* 479 F. Supp. 401 (M.D. Pa. 1979).

22. *Sostre* v. *Otis,* 330 F. Supp. 941, 944–54 (S.D. N.Y. 1971). The district court upheld the prisoner's petition against prison officials for interfering with his receipt of literature.

23. *Guajardo* v. *Estelle,* 580 F. 2d 748 (5th Cir. 1978).

24. Executive Order Number 814 for incoming mail, 814A for outgoing mail. Office of the Governor, State of Ohio, August 3, 1973.

25. *Sewell* v. *Pegelow,* 304 F. 2d 670 (4th Cir. 1962); *Banks* v. *Havener,* 234 F. Supp. 27 (E.D. Va. 1964); and *Knuckles* v. *Prasse,* 435 F. 2d 1255 (3rd Cir. 1970). These three cases dealt with the right of Black Muslim inmates to freedom of religion. In *Knuckles* v. *Prasse,* the court of appeals held that prison officials were not required to make available to prisoners Black Muslim publications that urged defiance of prison authorities and thus threatened prison security, unless properly interpreted by a trained Muslim minister. In the *Sewell* decision, a clear instance of discrimination against a Black Muslim prisoner was brought before the court of appeals, which dismissed the case on the grounds that it properly came under the jurisdiction of the district court.

In *Banks* v. *Havener,* responding to a petition under the Civil Rights Act by Black Muslim prisoners, the district court held that the antipathy of inmates and staff occasioned by the Black Muslims' belief in black supremacy was alone not sufficient to justify suppression of the practice of the Black Muslim religion. See also *Hasan Jamal Abdul Majid* v. *Henderson,* 533 F. Supp. 1257 (N.D. N.Y., March 11, 1982).

26. Although correctional personnel originally feared them, the Black Muslims are paradoxically now viewed as a source of stability among inmates. See Keith Butler, "The Muslims Are No Longer an Unknown Quality," *Corrections Magazine* 4 (June 1978): 55–65.

27. Access to a minister is a constitutional right. See *Cruz* v. *Beto,* 405 U.S. 319 (1972).

28. See National Sheriffs' Association, *Inmates' Legal Rights* (Alexandria, VA: National Sheriffs' Association, 1987), pp. 64–66.

29. *Brown* v. *Johnson,* 743 F. 2d 408 (6th Cir. 1985).

30. Todd Clear, Bruce Stout, and Harry Daumer, "Does Involvement in Religion Help Prisoners Adjust to Prison?" *National Council on Crime and Delinquency Focus* (San Francisco: National Council on Crime and Delinquency Focus, 1992).

31. *Cooper* v. *Pate.* See also Rudolph Alexander, "Slamming the Federal Courthouse Door on Inmates," p. 112.

32. *Johnson* v. *Avery,* 393 U.S. 483, 484 (1969). Through a writ of certiorari, a court of appeals decision was reversed in favor of an inmate who had been disciplined for violating a prison regulation that prohibited inmates from assisting other prisoners in preparing writs. The court of appeals had reversed a district court decision that voided the regulation because it had the effect of barring illiterate prisoners from access to general habeas corpus.

33. *Younger* v. *Gilmore,* 92 S. Ct. 250 (1971).

34. Edward Parker and Dana Schwertfeger, "A College Library and Research Center in a Correctional Facility," *Journal of Offender Rehabilitation* 17:1–2 (1991): 167–179.

35. Gene Teitelbaum, *Inspecting a Prison Law Library* (New Albany, IN: W. Homer Press, 1989), and American Association of Law Libraries, *Correctional Facility Law Libraries: An A to Z Resource Guide* (Laurel, MD: American Correctional Association, 1991).

36. The U.S. Supreme Court has determined that death row inmates wishing to challenge their convictions and sentences have no constitutional right to a court-appointed counsel. See Michael Mello, "Is There a Federal Constitutional Right to Counsel in Capital Post-Conviction Proceedings?" *The Journal of Criminal Law and Criminology* 79:4 (1990): 1065–1104, for arguments in favor of such right. The other side is addressed by Donald Zeithaml, "Sixth and Fourteenth Amendments—Constitutional Right to State Capital Collateral Appeal: The Due Process of Executing a Convict Without Attorney Representation," *The Journal of Criminal Law and Criminology* 80:4 (1990). The case is *Murray* v. *Giarranto,* 109 S. Ct. 2675 (1989).

37. Jennifer Gararda Brown, "Posner, Prisoners, and Pragmatism," *Tulane Law Review* 66:5 (1992): 1117–1178.

38. *Estelle* v. *Gamble,* 97 S. Ct. 285 (1976). The standard for judging the adequacy of medical treatment is the level of care offered to free people in the same locality. The prison must furnish comparable services, and inmates may collect damages for inadequate medical treatment. See *Newman* v. *Alabama,* 559 F. 2d. 283 (1977). Medical treatment in jails is generally less adequate than that in prisons. See also American College of Physicians; National Commission on Correctional Care, "The Crisis in Correctional Health Care: The Impact of the National Drug Control Strategy on Correctional Health Services," *Annals of Internal Medicine* 117:1 (1992): 71–77. Also see Kenneth Kipnis et al., "Correctional Health Care—In Critical Condition," *Corrections Today* 54:7 (1992): 92–120. Also see B. Jayne Anno, *Prison Health Care: Guidelines for the Management of an Adequate Delivery System* (Washington, D.C.: U.S. National Institute of Corrections, 1991).

39. *Ibid.* In 1995, the U.S. district court in San Francisco ruled that the California Pelican Bay Prison inflicts unconstitutional cruel and unusual punishment on prisoners. See Bill Wallace, "Pelican Bay Prison Ruled Too Harsh," *San Francisco Chronicle,* January 12, 1995, p. A-7.

40. *United States* v. *DeColegro,* 821 F. 2d, 1st Circ., 1987.

41. Frederick Millen, "AIDS in Prison—A National Disgrace," *San Francisco Sentinel,* March 8, 1990, p. 7. See also Howard Messing, "AIDS in Jail," *Northern Illinois University Law Review* 11:2,3 (1991): 297–317. Especially useful is John R. Austin and Rebecca S. Trammell, "AIDS

and the Criminal Justice System," *Northern Illinois University Law Review* 11:2,3 (1991): 481–527. See also Susan Jacobs, "AIDS in Correctional Facilities: Current Staus of Legal Issues Critical to Policy Development," *Journal of Criminal Justice* 23:3 (1995): 209–221.

42. See *Farmer v. Brennan,* 114 S. Ct. 1970 (1994), and *Wilson v. Seiter,* 111 S. Ct. 2321 (1991), and Michael Vaughn and Rolando del Carmen, "Civil Liability Against Prison Officials for Inmate-on-Inmate Assault," *The Prison Journal* 75:1 (1995): 69–89.

43. In *Tucker v. Hutto,* entered as a civil case under 78–0161-R, Eastern District of Virginia, the trial judge approved the out-of-court settlement on January 5, 1979, just five days before the trial was to open. See also R. Allinson, "Inmate Receives $518,000 Damages Award," *Criminal Justice Newsletter* 10 (January 15, 1979): 7.

44. The National Prison Project, American Civil Liberties Union Foundation, 1346 Connecticut Avenue, N.W., Washington, D.C. 20036.

45. Office of Legal Policy, *Report to the Attorney General: Federal Habeas Corpus Review of State Judgements* (Washington, D.C.: U.S. Department of Justice, 1988).

46. Sue Davis and Donald Songer, "The Changing Role of the United States Court of Appeals: The Flow of Litigation Revisited," *Justice System Journal* 13:3 (1989): 323–340.

47. States under court order/consent decree were Alaska, Arizona, Connecticut, Georgia, Kansas, Kentucky, Mississippi, Missouri, Nevada, New Hampshire, Ohio, Pennsylvania, Rhode Island, and Virginia. American Correctional Association, *1996 Directory: Juvenile & Adult Correctional Departments, Institutions, Agencies & Paroling Authorities* (Landham, MD: American Correctional Association, 1996), p. xx.

48. Inmates suing over prison conditions can be expected to increase the volume of litigation, because prison overcrowding causes deterioration in the quality of life within the walls. The correlates are less privacy, recreation, work, and programs; more violence, assaults, physical and mental disorders, suicides, rules infractions, and disciplinary actions; and more violent deaths.

49. National Advisory Commission, *Corrections,* p. 70.

50. Alan Appel, "Requirements and Rewards of the Americans with Disabilities Act," in *Corrections Today* 57:2 (1995): 84-86.

51. J. Robert Lilly and Mathieu Deflem, "Profit and Penality: An Analysis of the Corrections-Commercial Complex," *Crime and Delinquency* 42:1 (1996): 3–20.

52. "Supreme Court Decisions May Signal Halt to Expansion of Prisoner's Rights," *Criminal Justice Newsletter* 5 (August 12, 1974): 1, and Rolando del Carmen, "The Supreme Court and Prison Excessive Use of Force Cases: Does One Test Fit All?" *Federal Probation* 56:2 (1992): 44–47.

53. See *The Journal of Criminal Law and Criminology* 80 (Winter 1990).

54. See *The Journal of Criminal Law and Criminology* 83:4 (1993).

55. *Tatum v. Houser,* 642 F. 2d 253 (8th Cir. 1981). For discussion of liability by various segments of the justice system, see the following: William Smith, Edward Rhine, and Ronald Jackson, "Parole Practices in the United States," *Corrections Today* 51 (October 1989): 22, 28; Michael Vaughn and Lisa Coombs, "Police Civil Liability Under Section 1983: When Do Police Officers Act Under Color of Law?" *Journal of Criminal Justice* 23:5 (1995): 395–415; Dale Sechrest and William Collins, *Jail Management and Liability Issues* (Miami, FL: Coral Gables Publishing, 1989); and John Watkins,"Probation and Parole Malpractice in a Noninstitutional Setting: A Contemporary Analysis," *Federal Probation* 53:3 (1989): 29–34.

56. John P. Conrad, "The Rights of Wrongdoers," *Criminal Justice Research Bulletin* 3:3 (1987): 6.

CHAPTER TWENTY

The Death Penalty: The Ultimate Right

Overview

Perhaps no subject in the field of corrections has had as much discussion at the individual, judge, church, or the correctional administrator levels than **capital punishment**. The arguments rage on, ranging from the aspects of morality, through to the fringes of justice, to the core of retribution and revenge. Is it right to kill someone in the name of the state for killing someone for the killer's own sake? We change the methods of execution to somehow make the act more acceptable to the general public. Popular films like *Dead Man Walking*[1] attempt to show both sides of this controversial ultimate punishment.

This chapter will explore the history, methods, offender crimes, and operation of the death penalty. Whether a person is for or against capital punishment often depends on who the offender is and who was(were) the victim(s). The student must keep an open mind about the death penalty and realize it has been around as long as societies have existed. Is it time to abolish the death penalty—or make it more efficient and sure? We will cover all the bases in this chapter, exploring a unique facet of American justice and a problem for corrections. Then, in the next chapter we will look at the ex-offender as he or she returns to society and attempts to overcome a criminal record.

> **I** am not convinced that capital punishment, in and of itself, is a deterrent to crime because most people do not think about the death penalty before they commit a violent or capital crime.
>
> —Willie L. Williams, Chief, LAPD

Origins of the Death Penalty

In earlier chapters, we made brief references to some of the issues regarding capital punishment, or the death penalty. The frequency with which the topic occurs demonstrates how intertwined it is with the other aspects of criminal justice. The term *capital punishment* general-ly refers to the **execution**, in the name of the state. The crimes for which this punishment has been imposed have varied over the centuries, but murder and rape have been the most common. The means by which the punishment has been carried out have varied even more.

In preindustrial society, the death penalty was relatively simple to carry out. Offenders were usually forced out into the wilderness (banished), where their demise was relatively certain. As human skills and culture advanced, their chances for survival in the wilderness increased, and the effectiveness of banishment diminished. Those persons often became outlaws and continued to prey on the social group. When society began to execute (rather than banish) individuals for serious transgressions (usually murder) based on *talion*, the impact of the death penalty returned to its original intent.

Society has always been able to devise countless imaginative and cruel methods for the destruction of a condemned offender. The condemned have been hanged, burned, flayed alive, boiled in oil, thrown to wild beasts, cruci-fied, drowned, crushed, sawed in half, impaled, stoned, shot, strangled, torn apart, beheaded, disemboweled, electrocuted, buried alive, smothered, gassed, and now, injected with lethal drugs. That list only partially exhausts the cre-ative methods that executioners have employed throughout history. In search of vengeance against the condemned, society has also resorted to all sorts of rit-ual punishment, with mutilation and degradation preceding the final coup de grace.

As noted earlier, executions were almost always administered as a public spectacle, in the hope they would serve as a warning and a deterrent to oth-ers. It could be argued that the human desire to obtain retribution for crimes was transferred from the individual to the state in a way that finally became repugnant to many enlightened societies. Still, long after the elimination of the more bloody forms of capital vengeance, controversy still centers on its possi-ble deterrent value. The arguments for and against the death penalty concern the issues of deterrence, excessive cruelty (Eighth Amendment arguments), equability (Sixth and Fourteenth Amendment considerations), and attitudes toward capital punishment.[2]

*T*he Death Penalty in America: A Long Trip, A Bumpy Road

The death penalty in its many forms was a matter for public observation until quite recently. It was thought that public executions would deter future crimes of the same type, and all crime in general. In the electronic media age, the idea of public executions has been advocated both for the same and the opposite reasons. It is unusual but not unexpected that both sides would use the same arguments.

On March 14, 1984, shortly before his death by lethal injection at Huntsville Prison, James David "Cowboy" Autry petitioned the Texas Board of Corrections to allow his execution to be televised. Twenty-six of forty-four tele-vision stations in Texas refused to show it, twelve said they would, and six were undecided. To see a death by execution in the family living room posed a number of philosophical and moral issues for the ambivalent American public in regard to the death penalty. The viewer would have seen the young, somewhat attractive Autry strapped down and injected with a lethal substance.

What they would not have seen was the forty-three-year-old mother of five, gunned down for a $2.70 six-pack of beer, or the forty-three-year-old former priest who picked up the phone to call for help and was also gunned down when Autry and his partner turned back. As it turned out, Autry died the way most offenders who have been executed in the United States have died—in the relative obscurity of a prison death house—at 12:40 A.M., the 7th of 351 persons to die since the moratorium on executions was lifted in 1976.[3] This issue rose again in 1991 in San Francisco—and almost exactly ten years later in North Carolina. As noted at the time in *The New York Times:*

> What is really being argued over in this case, as in the San Francisco case, is the power of television and the nature of the television audience. Print reporters are customarily among the observers at executions and have produced painful accounts of the condemned's last moments. No one nowadays argues that reporters be kicked out because of ulterior motives like selling newspapers or their possible influence on the debate over capital punishment.
>
> But those on the left as well as the right, who would bar television cameras lest the pictures add to the general coarsening of American life, know that for the mass audience a picture is worth innumerable words. They are not worried about people who read books. They are worried about the impressionables, the unlettered who compose so much of the television audience: the sort of folks who once might have picnicked at public hangings, and who nowadays may be tuning into Mr. Donohue . . .
>
> The argument for legal restraints on television ought not to be lightly dismissed, but to make it effective demands franker attention to the nature of genus

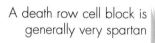

A death row cell block is generally very spartan

Americanus. Perhaps with television's help our society has become so anarchic that extensions of the First Amendment can only hasten America's unraveling. That uncomfortable possibility, well worth discussing, is usually skirted on camera, both by television personalities who want to stay popular and by political aspirants wooing the votes of people they do not esteem or deeply trust.[4]

The decades-long legal and moral issues have intensified, focusing on the questions of how, where, and why the death penalty should be used. After all, it was argued, why shouldn't executions in all their finality and horror be seen by the largest possible audiences? Isn't the purpose of capital punishment to *deter* other potential murderers? The rising popularity of "shock" television and radio may portend "executions for couch potatoes" in the twenty-first century—although we certainly hope that will not happen. Yet there is evidence that viewing an execution makes the audience less supportive of capital punishment.[5] See Figure 20-1 for the division of thought about the death penalty among the states.

As discussed in Part I, the death penalty was perhaps the earliest form of punishment and, until recent times, the most common. At one time in England there were over two hundred crimes for which the death penalty was imposed. The argument supporting the death penalty—its theoretical deterrent power—led to many public executions. This practice was finally stopped in England, legend has it, partly to curb the flourishing pickpocket business at the executions (picking pockets, ironically, was a capital offense).

The last public execution in the United States took place in Owensboro, Kentucky, on August 14, 1936.[6] It is estimated that over twenty thousand people crowded into the small Kentucky town to witness the spectacle. Various reform groups, disturbed that such a solemn event should take place in a holiday atmosphere, moved to have executions transferred behind the high stone walls of our

EXECUTIONS SINCE 1976 BY METHOD USED*

Method	States	Total
Lethal injection	32	194
Electrocution	11	123
Gas chamber	7	9
Hanging	4	3
Firing squad	2	2

*Some states authorize more than one method.

States with the Death Penalty (38)

Alabama	Louisiana	Oregon
Arizona	Maryland	Pennsylvania
Arkansas	Mississippi	South Carolina
California	Missouri	South Dakota
Colorado	Montana	Tennessee
Connecticut	Nebraska	Texas
Delaware	Nevada	Utah
Florida	New Hampshire	Virginia
Georgia	New Jersey	Washington
Idaho	New Mexico	Wyoming
Illinois	New York	
Indiana	North Carolina	Plus:
Kansas	Ohio	U.S. Government
Kentucky	Oklahoma	U.S. Military

States without the Death Penalty (12)

Alaska	Michigan	West Virginia
Hawaii	Minnesota	Wisconsin
Iowa	North Dakota	
Maine	Rhode Island	Plus:
Massachusetts	Vermont	District of Columbia

FIGURE

20.1

Status of the Death Penalty in the United States: 1996

SOURCE: Richard Deiter. *Twenty Years of Capital Punishment: A Reevaluation* (Washington, D.C.: Death Penalty Information Center, June 1996), pp. 7–9.

Six ways to carry out a
death sentence:

1. execution by hanging

—COURTESY OF CULVER PICTURES

2. execution by gas chamber

—COURTESY OF STATE OF CALIFORNIA
DEPARTMENT OF CORRECTIONS

1.

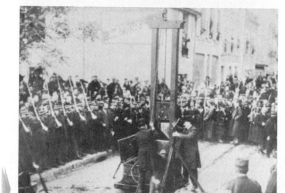

2.

3. execution by guillotine

—COURTESY OF CULVER PICTURES

4. execution by the electric
chair

—COURTESY OF GEORGIA DEPARTMENT
OF CORRECTIONS

3.

4.

5. execution by firing squad

—COURTESY OF CULVER PICTURES

5.

6. execution by lethal
injection

—PHOTO BY TED MATHIAS, COURTESY OF
AP/WIDE WORLD PHOTOS

6.

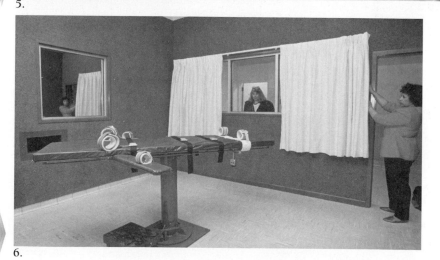

prisons. As the executions began to take place in private, methods were improved to make them more efficient. Without the emotional power of an execution before an audience, the grisly task became a sort of ritualistic slaughter. Over twenty-six hundred prisoners have died on the gallows, in the gas chamber, in the electric chair, by lethal injection, and by gunshot since Ramsey Bethea was hanged in Kentucky in 1936.

Better Ways to Die?

America's most innovative contribution to methods of execution was the invention of the electric chair. Although this invention was extolled as a more humanitarian way to kill the offender, many considered it merely a promotional scheme of the New York electrical company that developed it. The first electrocution was conducted at the Auburn Penitentiary in New York on August 6, 1890. The person who first died in this highly touted new device was William Kemmler, a murderer from Buffalo, New York. The first electrocution in the name of the state is vividly described in Drimmer:

> The warden rapped twice on the door. In the next room a lever clicked. A dynamo hummed to life somewhere. The witnesses heard an eerie whistling sound. Kemmler's shoulders shot up. Every muscle in his body went rigid. The leather thongs creaked as he strained against them, driven by a power far greater than his own. If he hadn't been strapped to the chair, the first surge of current might have hurled him clear across the chamber.

> The seconds ticked by. Kemmler's face had turned an intense red. Now an ashen pallor took place. He seemed to stare at the witnesses, but his eyes were glazed, the pupils dilated, unseeing. One of the fingers of his right hand had clenched so tight the nail had bitten into the flesh; blood was trickling down the arm of the chair.

> Spots appeared on his face, intensely red spots, like the mark of some terrible disease. Seventeen seconds had passed since the current had been turned on. Spitzka was leaning forward, close to Kemmler, but not touching him. "He's dead." MacDonald, by his side, nodded. The warden signaled Davis to shut off the electricity.

> Kemmler's body, released by the current, sagged like a rag doll. It was held upright in the chair only by the leather thongs. The warden loosened the strap on the convict's face, preparing to take off the headpiece. Then the thing happened that no man in that chamber would forget as long as he lived.

> As the warden bent over the slumped form in the chair, Kemmler's chest heaved. Durston stopped, paralyzed. Foam bubbled out of Kemmler's mouth. From his throat came a gurgling sound.

> "Quick, turn on the current!" Spitzka ordered.

> The warden pulled the headpiece strap taut. Almost immediately he signaled the electrician. In the bowels of the prison the dynamo began to hum

again. The rag doll in the chair sat up taut. Impelled by the fiery power of the current, it thrust itself forcefully against the straps restraining it. A wisp of smoke rose from the top of Kemmler's head and hovered in the air above him.[7]

Thus, finally, the end came to the first man to ride "Old Sparky." Opponents of the electric chair, including Thomas Edison, claimed that it must be excessively painful (a claim vehemently denied by prison administrators who used it).[8] The opposition advocated lethal gas as the most humane execution method. The first person to die in America in a prison gas chamber was a Chinese immigrant worker named Gee Jon. The crude system, gaining favor after a series of incredibly gruesome executions by electric chair, used cyanide gas. On February 8, 1924, Gee died in just six minutes. Again, Drimmer describes this first attempt at execution in a gas chamber:

> The signal came. The guard at the pump began to work it vigorously. In an instant, gas would begin to rise from the vent behind Gee's chair. Gee could hear the hiss of the gas behind him. His body was held fast by the straps, but he could turn his head and now he strove to do so.

> He never completed the movement. Witnesses observed his head suddenly sag backward, then forward. He appeared to lose consciousness. But for several minutes his head continued to bob, the movements growing weaker and weaker. His eyes remained open. At 9:46, six minutes after the guard had began pumping, the physician judged Gee was dead.[9]

Thus began yet another attempt to make state execution more humane, or at least not as awful to watch. Seven states eventually adopted the gas chamber as the execution of choice.

In an effort to make the execution of condemned criminals easier and cleaner still, lethal injection gained favor in the 1960s and 1970s. It seems that many states thought they could reinstate the death penalty more easily if it was seen to be less cruel and unusual. Again, Charles Brooks, a codefendant in a murder, was the first prisoner to die in this manner, executed December 6, 1982, in Oklahoma. Drimmer again provides a vivid description of the event:

> The chamber was small and brilliantly illuminated. With its two doctors, its medical technician and its neat gurney, it could almost have been mistaken for an emergency room in a hospital. Brooks looked frightened, but he needed no persuasion or pressure to get up on the gurney and stretch out. Six straps were attached to the mobile cot. The guards quickly secured them—two over his torso, one above the knees, another below and two over his ankles. A board projected from each side of the gurney and to these his arms were firmly fastened.

> From an opening in the red brick wall close by, two clear plastic tubes snaked. The technician took one, with a catheter needle attached, examined Brook's left arm, swabbed it with alcohol, and inserted the needle. A saltwater solution, the standard medium in giving anesthesia, began to flow into Brooks' arm.

The first drug was sodium thiopental, a quick-acting barbiturate. The second drug was Pavulon, a synthetic, often compared to curare, a plant extract South Americans use to dip their arrows into to paralyze their prey. Potassium chloride was the third member of the deadly trio. An electrolyte normally produced by the body, potassium regulates the action of the heart. Too much of it, however, will cause cardiac arrest.

It was 12:09 a.m. "We're ready," Warden Pursley said. The executioner had been waiting for those words. One after another he worked the three big syringes. Their contents poured into the IV tube and traveled toward the figure on the gurney.

The drugs began to take effect. Brooks "moved his head as if to say no," an eyewitness would say later. "Then he yawned and his eyes closed, and then he wheezed. His head fell over towards us, then he wheezed again." His arm bounced up and down. He opened and closed his hand several times.

One of the doctors placed a stethoscope over Brooks' heart. "A couple of minutes more," he said. At 12:16 a.m., the stethoscope was applied again. "I pronounce this man dead," the doctor said.[10]

It is interesting to note that more than twenty-seven states have passed legislation to use a lethal injection of chemicals as the latest, "most humane," form of execution as the primary or secondary option. Physicians' associations are expressing concern that their members, whose profession it is to save lives, may be asked by the state to take lives. It seems we are still seeking a way to make more humane the process, if not the practice, of execution.

The physical pain of the execution is probably the smallest concern of the offenders during their prolonged wait in the death house, a wait that often takes eight to ten years.[11] The mental anguish they must endure, which that long wait can only intensify, has been a primary focus of the recent widespread controversy surrounding the death penalty, as the more industrialized societies have moved to abolish it.[12] Methods used for executions, by state, are seen on p. 402. The number of executions peaked in the crime-laden 1930's as shown in Figure 20-2 when a total of 1,513 prisoners were executed,[13] an average of about 12 per month. Figure 20.2 demonstrates the sharp plunge in executions from 1930 to 1976. The increased number of appeals and rising

CHINA DRUG CRACKDOWN ORDERS MANY EXECUTIONS

BEIJING, June 26, 1996 (Reuters)—Hundreds of drug traffickers were believed to have been executed today as courts marked World Anti-Drugs Day by convicting 1,725 people nationwide and meting out some of their harshest sentences.

Among those convicted on the United Nations-declared day against drug abuse and trafficking, 769 were sentenced to death or life imprisonment, and many were taken immediately from the courtroom to the execution ground to be shot, the official New China News Agency said.

The news agency did not specify the number of executions, but China regularly executes most of those convicted of serious drug offenses. A total of 262 courts were called into session in the crackdown, it said.

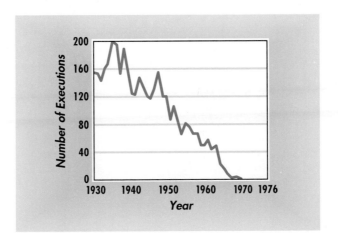

FIGURE

20.2

Persons Executed in the United States, 1930–1976

SOURCE: James Stephan and Tracy Snell, *Capital Punishment 1994* (Washington, D.C.: U.S. Department of Justice, February 1996), p. 2.

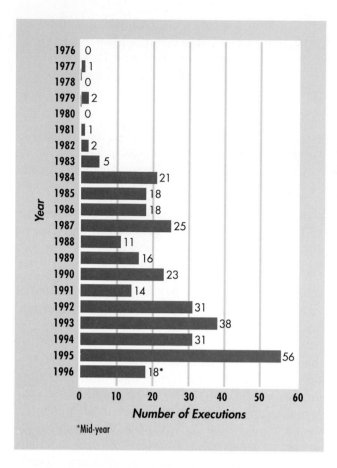

SOURCE: Editors, *Facts About the Death Penalty* (Washington, D.C.: Death Penalty Information Center, 1996).

FIGURE 20.3

Executions in the United States Since 1976

opposition to the death penalty peaked in the turbulent 1960s, and in 1972 the U.S. Supreme Court placed a moratorium on the death penalty while states considered legislation that could meet strict constitutional guidelines. That moratorium was dissolved in 1976, and executions began anew in 1977 with convicted murderer Gary Gilmore's cry of "Let's do it!" prior to execution before a firing squad in Utah. The number of executions since that one are shown in Figure 20-3.

The Execution Process Today

In Florida, when the governor signs a death warrant, the prison superintendent reads the warrant to the condemned inmate. The inmate then is taken from the death row cell to the death watch cell. Final preparation for the execution begins five days prior to the week of the scheduled execution. At this time, the condemned inmate and the administrative staff review the inmate's wishes for disposal of personal property, visits, last meal, and disposition of the body.

Executions are usually scheduled for 7 A.M. so as not to disrupt the institution's routine and to ensure the availability of the [Department of Corrections] secretary and the governor's staff before regular office hours.

The morning of the execution, the inmate is served a final meal and is showered. Because the method of execution in

Florida is electrocution, staff must shave the inmate's head and leg. The inmate is allowed a chaplain visit before being led down the hall to the execution chamber.

The assistant superintendent for operations and the chief correctional officer escort the inmate to the chamber. The superintendent leads the inmate into the chamber, where the maintenance superintendent and an electrician secure the straps around the head, chest, arm, and leg. The inmate is given an opportunity to make a final statement or read a prepared one before having the head gear put on.

The prison superintendent indicates to the executioner that the execution is to proceed. The executioner, an anonymous citizen hired by the Department of Corrections, is paid $150 per execution. He or she pulls a switch to activate

(Continued from page 406)

The Execution Process Today

the electrical equipment. The electrocution cycle lasts two minutes or less. A physician then verifies the inmate's death.

Twelve volunteer citizen witnesses and twelve media representatives are present in the viewing room at the execution. They are escorted into the room by two correctional officers, and a public information officer is available to assist them. The superintendent and assistant superintendent are also available to respond to reporters' inquiries.

Media representatives are selected from a pool of creden-tialed reporters and are required to provide information to all media representatives who are not able to attend.

In addition to the media attention, a contingent of supporters and opponents of the death penalty usually gathers across the street to demonstrate and hold vigils before and during the execution. Local law enforcement are on hand to maintain order. ∎

SOURCE: Kerry Flack, "In Florida: Day-to-Day Death Row Operations," *Corrections Today* 55:4 (1993): 78.

Arbitrary and Infrequent Punishment

To better understand the magnitude of the death penalty issue, we must examine the somewhat incomplete records[14] on the subject. The total number of U.S. executions between 1930 and 1994 (year-end) were 4,373. As we mentioned earlier, the death penalty has most often been prescribed for murder and rape.[15] One thus would reasonably expect a fairly high correlation between the number of such offenses and the number of executions. In the 1930s, the earliest period for which relatively reliable statistics are available, the average number of executions was about 165 per year. The number of murders and rapes reported per year during the 1930s averaged about 3,500 and 3,800, respectively, a ratio of about one execution to every forty-four **capital crimes** reported.[16]

Also significant is the number of executions in different states and regions. Most executions have taken place in the South. Eighty-three percent of the 257 executions between 1977 and 1994 were in the ten states of Texas (85), Arkansas (9), Louisiana (21), Mississippi (4), Alabama (10), Georgia (18), Florida (33), South Carolina (4), Virginia (24), and North Carolina (6). Industrial states that extend from Illinois to New York accounted for only 2 percent of the executions. The 13 remaining executions took place in states that were in the Southwest or Far West: California (2), Washington (2), Wyoming (1), Arizona (3), Oklahoma (3), and Utah (4). It is worth noting that half of those executed between 1977 and 1994 were minorities, 38 percent of whom were black.[17]

The number of executions per year dropped to only fourteen in 1991. The pace since then has picked up, most recently, at year-end 1996, with fifty-six. When we consider the thousands of murders and rapes reported during that period,[18] we must consider the comments of Justice William Brennan:

> When a country of over 200 million people inflicts an unusually severe punishment no more than fifty times a year, the inference is strong that the punishment is not being regularly and fairly applied. To dispel it would indeed require a clear showing of **nonarbitrary** infliction.[19]

A High-Volume Execution

ARKANSAS PREPARES FOR A TRIPLE-HEADER

Like most death-row cases, this one began a long time ago. On the night of Jan. 8, 1981, Don Lehman, wearing a T shirt and shorts, answered the front door of his custom-built home in Rogers, Arkansas. Four men wearing gloves and ski masks burst in. One of them grabbed his daughter, Vickie, by the hair, while the others grappled with Lehman. His wife, Virginia, tried to phone for help, but one of the men forced her into a corner. Don Lehman, 47, shot in the struggle, staggered into the bedroom, where his wife saw him fall onto the bed. One of the intruders, Virginia later testified, said, "Well, this one will finish him," and fired again. The men ransacked the house, found about $1,200 in an envelope and fled into the night.

After last-minute appeals, the state of Arkansas executed three men for the Lehman murder. Death by means of lethal injection was administered to Darryl Richley, 43, Hoyt Clines, 37, and James Holmes, 37. Little-noticed in this crime-disgusted environment, it was the first time since 1962 that a state executed three people at once. Arkansas, no slouch in the assembly-line department, executed two men just this past May, the first multiple execution since capital punishment was resumed in 1977. Multiple executions are seen as good for security; they even save a few dollars, what with the doctors and other staffers being around at one time. "I look forward to it," Richley told *Newsweek,* in a prison interview. "I'm getting out of here."

While some legal issues, like the question of a hypnotized witness, have trailed this case, prison officials concentrated on execution protocol. Based on their assigned prisoner numbers, Clines would be executed first, followed by Holmes and Richley. Richley and Clines quickly opted for injection over the electric chair, while Holmes, who had a phobia about needles, needed time to think about it. He finally decided the chair was even worse and selected injection. The executions took place in the death house at Cummins, Ark. Each prisoner is strapped to a gurney and a needle is placed in each arm—one for backup. Their bodies were released to the state medical examiner, who is required to perform an autopsy. After all, legally it is "a homicide," says deputy warden Tom Pitts.

Multiple executions were no big deal until the 1930s. (Actually, the largest on one day was in 1862 in Minnesota, when 38 Sioux Indians, convicted of rebellion, were hanged.) But the bulk method slowed in the 1930s, when states began substituting the gas chamber for electrocution or hanging. It seems that prison officials had to let the chamber air out for some time before sending another miscreant in. These days, death-penalty advocates would love to whittle down the nearly 3,000 people on death row

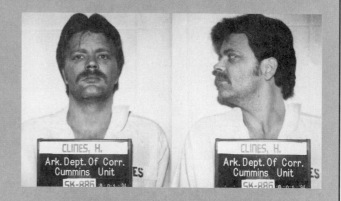

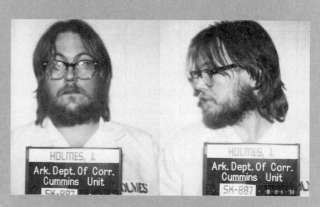

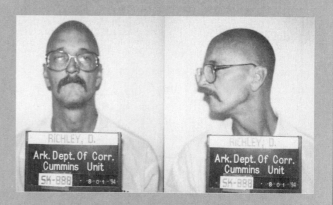

LETHAL WEAPON: It started with a doorbell rung one night 13 years ago and could end this week with needles in the arms of three death-row inmates

(Continued from page 408)

A High-Volume Execution

in large chunks, but that is not going to happen. In fact, the pace of executions this year is running behind last year's. Still, a coalition of anti-death-penalty groups said the triple execution "turns back the clock to a time when mass lynchings were the law of the land."

HYPNOTIC STATEMENT

The legal history of the Lehman case was tortuous—and again raised questions about whether the death penalty can be applied fairly. Defense lawyers discovered that prosecutors, without disclosing it at the trial, had hired an entertainer to hypnotize Vickie Lehman, who then gave statements more detailed than her original responses to police. After a series of appeals, the Eighth Circuit determined that any prosecutorial misconduct that occurred wasn't critical because Vickie's hypnotic statements weren't all that different—except in the case of a fourth defendant, Michael Orndorff. Those statements painted Orndorff as cavorting in the house while her father was dying, a picture that might have influenced the jury to impose the death sentence. The court ordered a new sentencing hearing but the state settled for life without parole for Orndorff, in part, it said, to spare the family.

To Clines, excluding Orndorff is proof that the death penalty is administered arbitrarily. "They're getting ready to execute an innocent man," he told Newsweek. "I've never denied being there. But I didn't kill anybody. I didn't even have a weapon." (Under the law, a participant at a felony where someone is killed can face the death penalty.) Clines expressed deep remorse before the clemency board last week. "I'm sorry this had to happen," he said. "I wish I could take it back; but I can't."

Lehman's family has never recovered. To Donette West, one of Lehman's daughters, the Orndorff case is proof that the state should execute the three other men before they "slip through the system." At the clemency hearing, a one-sentence statement by Lehman's mother, Thelma, 86, was read: "I hope they kill the durn devils." Vickie Lehman told the clemency board she is still single at 37 because she has never found a man to measure up to her father. His last words to her, she said, were whether she had heard the doorbell ring. ∎

SOURCE: *Newsweek*, August 8, 1996, p. 62.

Even if one agrees that the number of murders and rapes does not necessarily reflect the number for which the death penalty might have been imposed,[20] the difference is still staggering. As Justice Potter Stewart explained in *Furman*, the death penalty is "freakishly" or "spectacularly" rare in its occurrence. In a telling argument in *Furman* v. *Georgia*, Justice Brennan in 1970 summed up the arbitrary nature of the death penalty:

> When the punishment of death is inflicted in a trivial number of cases in which it is legally available, the conclusion is virtually inescapable that it is being inflicted arbitrarily. Indeed, it smacks of little more than a lottery system. The states claim, however, that this rarity is evidence not of arbitrariness, but of informed selectivity: Death is inflicted, they say, only in "extreme" cases.

> Informed selectivity, of course, is a value not to be denigrated. Yet presumably the states could make precisely the same claim if there were ten executions per year, or five, or even if there were but one. That there may be as many as fifty per year does not strengthen the claim. When the rate of infliction is at this low level, it is highly implausible that only the worst criminals or the criminals who commit the worst crimes are selected for this punishment. No one has yet suggested a rational basis that could differentiate in those terms the few who die from the many who go

to prison. Crimes and criminals simply do not admit of a distinction that can be drawn so finely as to explain, on that ground, the execution of such a tiny sample of those eligible. Certainly the laws that provide for this punishment do not attempt to draw that distinction; all cases to which the laws apply are necessarily "extreme." Nor is the distinction credible in fact. If, for example, petitioner Furman or his crime illustrates the "extreme," then nearly all murderers and their murders are also "extreme." Furthermore, our procedures in death cases, rather than punishment, actually sanction an arbitrary selection. For this Court held [that] juries may, as they do, make the decision whether to impose a death sentence wholly unguided by standards governing that decision, *McGautha v. California* 402 U.S. 183, 196-208 (1971). In other words, our procedures are not constructed to guard against the totally capricious selection of criminals for the punishment of death.[21]

This argument is further reinforced by the fact that the two crimes of murder and rape have accounted for nearly 99 percent of the executions in the United States since 1930, with 87 percent of the total for murder alone. In 1990s, almost every execution was for murder.

It appears that the original practice of *mandating* the death penalty for murder has become repugnant to American society as a whole. This is demonstrated by the reluctance of juries to convict in such cases, despite the earlier efforts of state legislators to pass laws that call for mandatory executions for certain types of murder.

The concept of **malice aforethought**,[22] usually an essential element of proof in the capital murder statutes, provided a rationale for juries to opt for a lesser penalty. The legislature finally recognized that juries were using this concept to avoid the death penalty and passed statutes that attempted to differentiate between the degrees of various capital crimes (for example, first- and second-degree murder and first- and second-degree rape), thus trying to restrict mandatory execution to the first offenses. In response, juries simply refused to convict in cases in which they felt—arbitrarily—that the death penalty was inappropriate. The further refinement of the distinction between capital and noncapital cases was abandoned by legislation in many jurisdictions, and juries were given legal discretion to continue the practice they had already established in fact. The sentence of death is now discretionary in every jurisdiction in which it is still used. Many states have done away with the death penalty entirely and others prescribe it only in very rare cases.

In those states with capital punishment, the prosecutor must decide to seek the death penalty, using the vast discretion inherent in that office. If the decision is not to pursue a death-eligible charge, the jury is usually prevented from imposing the sentence of death. There is consistent (but not unchallenged) evidence that race of the victim colors the prosecutor's decisions: victim-based discrimination has been found to be an important determinant in Texas,[23] the Chattahoochee Judicial District (Georgia),[24] and Kentucky,[25] but not in California.[26] Evaluations of prosecutorial discretion are ongoing.[27] We discuss the role of the prosecutor in more detail later.

As the power of imposing death moved from the impersonal and mandatory statutory approach to the hands of the jurors, the use of this final punishment declined to the point of insignificance. Of course, the decline was not so insignificant to the few who were still being executed by the state. Thus, in the 1960s, another series of cases appeared, attacking the death penalty on the grounds of **cruel and unusual** punishment.

The Eighth Amendment and the Death Penalty

American jurisprudence has borrowed much from the English law. The ban against cruel and unusual punishment embodied in the Eighth Amendment was lifted from the English Bill of Rights of 1689. As Justice Thurgood Marshall indicated in *Furman* v. *Georgia*,

> Perhaps the most important principle in analyzing "cruel and unusual" punishment questions is one that is reiterated again and again in the prior opinions of the Court: that is, the cruel and unusual language "must draw its meaning from the evolving standards of decency that mark the progress of a maturing society." Thus, a penalty which was permissible at one time in our nation's history is not necessarily permissible today.
>
> The fact, therefore, that the Court, or individual justices, may have in the past expressed an opinion that the death penalty is constitutional is not now binding on us.[28]

The reference to unusual punishment helps clarify the relationship between this particular amendment and the customs and practices of any given period. The death penalty was surely not an unusual punishment in the early nineteenth century.

Cruelty was examined by the Supreme Court in 1878 in *Wilkerson* v. *Utah*.[29] It was Utah's practice to punish premeditated murderers by shooting them at a public execution. In this case, the concept of the developing frontier and the execution practices being used in other areas around the world were examined.[30] The Court did not stick to the doctrine of traditional practice but examined contemporary thought on the matter of cruel punishment. It found that the case against Utah was not cruel in the context of the times, but it left open the door for future Court examinations of the cruelty issue:

> Difficulty would attend the effort to define with exactness the extent of the constitutional provision which provides that cruel and unusual punishments shall not be inflicted: but it is safe to affirm that punishments of torture . . . and all others in the same line of unnecessary cruelty, are forbidden by that amendment to the Constitution.[31]

Only with the introduction of the electric chair in New York was the issue of cruel and unusual punishment raised again. The 1890 case of *In re Kemmler* challenged the use of that new form of execution as cruel and unusual punishment, but the Court was unanimous in its decision that electrocution was not unconstitutional just because it was unusual. It also came very close to employing the due process clause of the Fourteenth Amendment in the case, giving early warning that it might do so at a later, more substantial hearing. In the 1892 case

FOURTEENTH AMENDMENT

All persons born or naturalized in the United States, and subject to the jurisdiction thereof, are citizens of the United States and of the state wherein they reside. No state shall make or enforce any law which shall abridge the privileges or immunities of citizens of the United States; nor shall any state deprive any person of life, liberty, or property, without due process of law; nor deny to any person within its jurisdiction the equal protection of the laws.

of *O'Neil* v. *Vermont*, the court again affirmed that the Eighth Amendment did not apply to the states, but this time there were three strong dissenting opinions. One of the dissenting justices wrote the following:

> That designation [cruel and unusual], it is true, is usually applied to punishments which inflict torture, such as the rack, the thumbscrew, the iron boot, the stretching of limbs and the like, which are attended with acute pain and suffering. . . . The inhibition is directed not only against punishments of the character mentioned, but against all punishments which by their excessive length or severity are greatly disproportionate to the offenses charged. The whole inhibition is against that which is excessive.[32]

This logic, though a minority attitude at the time, prevailed to dominate the 1910 landmark case of *Weems* v. *United States*[33] the first time the Court invalidated a penalty because they found it excessive. Clearly, excessive punishment had become as objectionable to the Court as what was inherently cruel.

Not until 1947 did the Court decide another significant case on the issue of whether the Eighth Amendment applied to the states. In the case of *Louisiana ex rel. Francis* v. *Resweber*,[34] the Court was virtually unanimous in its agreement that the infliction of unnecessary pain is forbidden by traditional Anglo-American legal practice. This unusual case involved a convicted murderer (Francis) who was sentenced to die in the electric chair. The electrical system malfunctioned at the execution, so Francis was not killed the first time the current passed through his body. Pleading that a second attempt at electrocution would be cruel and unusual punishment, Francis took his case to the Supreme Court. Although the case brought out many of the crucial Eighth Amendment issues, the Court stopped short of enforcing that amendment on the states, and Francis lost his appeal on a five-to-four split. He thus was finally executed, but his case paved the way for several that came in the 1960s.

The next significant case we note was the landmark 1972 case on capital punishment, **Furman v. Georgia**. The Court's decision was five to four in favor of a ban on using capital punishment as it was currently being practiced. Indeed, the justices were so widely divided on the issue that each wrote a separate opinion.[35] Only two of the justices (Brennan and Marshall) held that the death penalty was cruel and unusual punishment under all circumstances. The due process clause of the Fourteenth Amendment was evoked, leaving the states with the problem of passing legislation that met the Court's requirements, as described in the opinion of Chief Justice Warren Burger:

> The legislatures are free to eliminate capital punishment for specific crimes or to carve out limited exceptions to a general abolition of the penalty, without adherence to the conceptual strictures of the Eighth Amendment. The legislatures can and should make an assessment of the deterrent influence of capital punishment, both generally and as affecting the commission of specific types of crimes. If legislatures come to doubt the efficacy of capital punishment, they can abolish it either completely or on a selective basis. If new evidence persuades them that they acted unwisely, they can reverse their field and reinstate the penalty to the extent it is thought warranted. An Eighth Amendment ruling by judges cannot be made with such flexibility or discriminating precision.[36]

Although the minority opinion seemed to feel the Court had overstepped its jurisdiction, the tenor of the dissenting remarks made it clear they were willing to hear a new appeal when the findings in *Furman* were challenged. The high level of legislative activity in the states, seeking to reinstate the death penalty under the Court's new guidelines, suggested there would be a challenge in the near future.

Though *Furman* gave a new lease on life[37] to the over six hundred men who had been sitting on death row,[38] new death sentences continued to be handed down, awaiting final resolution of the issue.

THE 1976 DECISION

On July 2, 1976, five cases were decided as to whether certain state provisions were acceptable under the *Furman* decision. The statutes of three states (Texas, Florida, and Georgia) were affirmed, and the statutes of two others (North Carolina and Louisiana) were struck down. The case of *Gregg* v. *Georgia* is the model for those that were upheld. As noted in that decision,

> We think that the Georgia court wisely has chosen not to impose unneces-sary restrictions on the evidence that can be offered at such a hearing and to approve open and far-ranging argument. So long as the evidence intro-duced and the arguments made at the presentence hearing do not prejudice a defendant, it is preferable not to impose restrictions. We think it desirable for the jury to have as much information before it as possible when it makes the sentencing decision.

Finally, the Georgia statute has an additional provision designed to assure that the death penalty will not be imposed on a capriciously selected group of con-victed defendants. The new sentencing procedures require that the state supreme court review every death sentence to determine whether it was imposed under the influence of passion, prejudice, or any other arbitrary factor, whether the evidence supports the findings of a statutory aggravating circumstance, and "whether the sentence of death is excessive or disproportionate to the penalty imposed in sim-ilar cases, considering both the crime and the defendant." In performing its sen-tence review function, the Georgia court has held that "if the death penalty is only rarely imposed for an act or it is substantially out of line with sentences imposed for other acts it will be set aside as excessive." The court on another occasion stat-ed that "we view it to be our duty under the similarity standard to assure that no death sentence is affirmed unless in similar cases throughout the state the death penalty has been imposed generally . . .."[39]

The decision in *Gregg* set off a chain of legislative actions in state houses across the nation, aimed at providing death penalty statutes that would meet the Supreme Court's challenge. Again, they sought to activate the most cherished beliefs about the death penalty:

> No other punishment deters men so effectually from committing crimes as the punishment of death. This is one of those propositions which it is diffi-cult to prove, simply because they are in themselves more obvious than any proof can make them. It is possible to display ingenuity in arguing against it, but that is all. The whole experience of mankind is in the other direction.

The threat of instant death is the one to which resort has always been made when there was an absolute necessity for producing some result. . . . No one goes to certain inevitable death except by compulsion. Put the matter the other way. Was there ever yet a criminal who, when sentenced to death and brought out to die, would refuse the offer of a commutation of his sentence for the severest secondary punishment? Surely not. Why is this? It can only be because "All that a man has will he give for his life." In any secondary punishment, however terrible, there is hope; but death is death; its terrors cannot be described more forcibly.[40]

The abolitionists try to amass vast statistical bases to show the lack of correlation between statutes in various jurisdictions. Although such evidence is not without flaws, the abolitionists have a clear and convincing case that the death penalty is not useful as a deterrent to crime in America. What is the alternative to a death penalty in punishing offenders who have committed crimes such as murder and rape? Life imprisonment, without hope for parole, is considered the most logical substitute, though prison administrators claim that offenders who know they are in prison for life will feel they have nothing to lose if they commit further crimes behind the walls. In fact, there is an overwhelming body of evidence that the presence or absence of the death penalty has no effect on the homicide rate inside prisons. Murderers (who account for almost 99 percent of capital cases) are usually model prisoners. It has even been postulated that the death penalty itself creates an atmosphere which fosters violence in prison. The day of an execution is charged with extreme tension. The prisoners are often placed under more security than usual, and acts of violence in defiance of the authorities seem to be more prevalent.

Deterrence of the Death Penalty

While there are substantial claims that the death penalty may or may not act as a **deterrent** to others in an act of general deterrence, depending on the ideological position of the debater, one should realize that if the death penalty were a deterrent, no crime would occur. Retentionists point out that a lighthouse sits beside a dangerous rock-strewn coastline to warn ships away. The fact that a few ill-fated ships run afoul of the dangers the lighthouse proclaims is no reason to tear the lighthouse down—or to abolish capital punishment. For those ships the lighthouse warns away, there is no evidence of deterrence. Only the ones that ignore to their peril the lighthouse's warning will show up as "failures" of the deterrent effect.

PUBLIC OPINION AND THE DEATH PENALTY

There have been wide fluctuations in the American public's attitude toward the death penalty, as reflected in public opinion polls. Although most polls show strong support for the death penalty in the abstract (no alternative)—with a 77 percent showing in a 1993 poll—these opinions are somewhat softened when the public is given viable alternatives. As shown by Figure 20-4, support for the death penalty falls to only 41 percent when the alternative is no parole ever plus restitution. However, this fact seems to have as little impact on death penalty legislation as public opinion has on gun control.[41] Those who advocate the

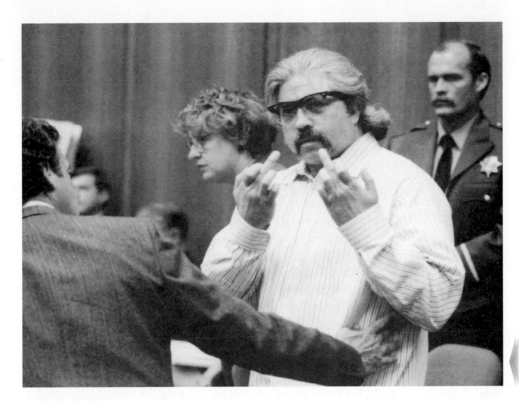

Polly Klas's murderer, Richard Allen Davis, gestured his contempt for the family of Polly Klas and TV cameras after his death penalty verdict was read

—PHOTO BY JOHN BURGESS/REUTERS, COURTESY OF ARCHIVE PHOTOS

death penalty claim there is no viable alternative that provides equal protection for society.[42] But the findings from the 1993 study, as shown in Figure 20-4 show that many would be supportive of the alternatives.

Many who oppose the life sentence as a replacement for the death penalty observe that the parole laws in many states make it possible for a "lifer" to get out in a relatively brief time.[43] Usually, those who receive life sentences become eligible for parole in thirteen years, but the national average served under a life sentence is currently less than seven years. The proposed answer to this argument is to remove the hope of parole from a prisoner given a life sentence (**life certain**), but that action would constitute an admission that certain prisoners could not be rehabilitated and would destroy the offenders' possible incentive to change their behavior patterns. The chance that an innocent person might be convicted also detracts from the acceptability of the irreversible death penalty.[44]

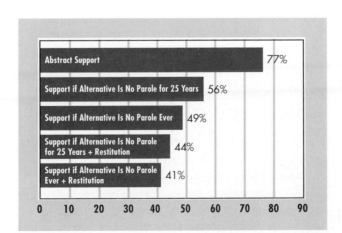

Abstract Support	77%
Support if Alternative Is No Parole for 25 Years	56%
Support if Alternative Is No Parole Ever	49%
Support if Alternative Is No Parole for 25 Years + Restitution	44%
Support if Alternative Is No Parole Ever + Restitution	41%

0 10 20 30 40 50 60 70 80 90

FIGURE

20.4

Support for the Death Penalty When Alternatives Are Presented

SOURCE: Richard D. Dieter, *Sentencing for Life: Americans Embrace Alternatives to the Death Penalty* (Washington, D.C.: Death Penalty Information Center, April 1993), p. 5.

The Controversy Continues

The U.S. Supreme Court has decided the death penalty is constitutional under certain circumstances and may be imposed if statutes meet the criteria that have emerged from case law. As such, it is not now considered as cruel and unusual punishment when used as a penal sanction, and its infrequency of application appears not to be an overwhelming obstacle for the Court.[45]

In the 1989 term of the U.S. Supreme Court, several capital punishment cases were decided, allowing for mentally retarded [developmentally disabled] offenders to be executed[46] and denying appointed counsel for death row inmates fighting their executions.[47] Those two decisions are seen as evidence of the general drift toward the conservative end of the legal continuum in which the corrections system now functions. The approval of Associate Supreme Court Justice Ruth Bader Ginsburg to replace Justice "Whizzer" White suggests the changing balance of the Court moving back toward a more liberal bent. With the reelection of President Clinton, he probably will have the chance to appoint more liberals to the Court in his term of office, and the Court will surely continue to move in that direction.

As yet unresolved is the controversial role of discretion in the decision to seek the death penalty. The prosecutor must enter a formal charge and may or may not seek the death penalty. One factor that affects the decision to seek the death penalty is the race of the victim. In South Carolina, for example, studies show that if the victim is white and the offender black, then the black offender is eight times as likely to face a death sentence as that same offender would face if the victim were black.[48] Keil and Vito found that, in Kentucky, blacks who killed whites, as compared to other homicide offenders, had more than an average chance of being charged with a death-eligible crime (by the prosecutor) and sentenced to die (by the jury). They also found thirteen cases in their study's time frame in which whites murdered blacks and prosecutors failed to seek the death penalty even once. Prosecutors have a **gatekeeper function** in the judicial system: if they choose not to seek the death penalty, it cannot be imposed by the jury. Keil and Vito suggest the following:

> It may be to the prosecutor's political and career advantage to treat murders in which the black kills a white more seriously than murders involving other racial combinations, even when such murders have the same legal attributes of seriousness. Juries may find it socially expedient to act in the same way in sentencing offenders to death.[49]

Radelet reaches a similar conclusion using status attributes (race, social class, economic status) in his study of executions since 1608.[50]

The Issue of Equability

The heart of the question of **equability** is whether the punishment is applied even-handedly across a jurisdiction. Are judges imposing similar sentences to offenders who have committed similar crimes?

Another related question involves the issue of whether or not the punishment fits the crime. This question arises in the case of a single court staffed by eleven judges, all of whom sentence offenders accused of driving under the influence of alcohol. One judge may routinely impose fines of $100 on all offenders to be sentenced; another sentencing judge may impose thirty days in jail plus thirty hours of community service. The other nine judges may place their offenders on probation, one condition of which may be compulsory attendance at meetings of Alcoholics Anonymous. Which, if any, of these punishments best fits the crime: a fine, jail time plus community service, or probation with mandatory attendance in an alcohol-avoidance program?

In terms of the death penalty, perhaps the question could best be phrased like this: "Are blacks who kill white victims more likely to receive a death sentence than white killers who murder black victims?" As we have noted, the answer is probably yes.

Behavioral science may not provide the most adequate basis for arguments against the equitable application of the death penalty for juveniles[51] or adults, but available evidence suggests that the death penalty is not evenly applied and may be wanton and freakish in its imposition. That conclusion, in more tentative form, can be found in the 1990 report by the General Accounting Office.[52] The minimum ages for application of capital punishment in 1994 are shown in Figure 20-5.

After a long and tortuous process, the Court has finally made clear what it feels are the boundaries for imposition of the death penalty. Despite its effort, many states still believe the death penalty is too harsh a punishment to impose. The arguments in the Supreme Court may be settled, at least for the time being, but the arguments continue in the wider area of society as a whole.

EQUITY

Freedom from bias or prejudice in the application of the law. Regarding the death penalty, the principle of equity would mean that capital punishment would be applied without favoritism to men and women and to blacks and whites alike.

Age Less than 18	Age 18	None Specified
Alabama (16)	California	Arizona
Arkansas (14)[a]	Colorado	Idaho
Delaware (16)	Connecticut[d]	Montana
Georgia (17)	Federal System	Louisiana
Indiana (16)	Illinois	Pennsylvania
Kentucky (16)	Kansas	South Carolina
Mississippi (16)[b]	Maryland	South Dakota[e]
Missouri (16)	Nebraska	Utah
Nevada (16)	New Jersey	
New Hampshire (17)	New Mexico	
North Carolina (17)[c]	Ohio	
Oklahoma (16)	Oregon	
Texas (17)	Tennessee	
Virginia (15)	Washington	
Wyoming (16)		
Florida (16)		

Note: Reporting by states reflects interpretations by state attorney general offices and may differ from previously reported ages.

[a] See Arkansas Code Ann.9-27-318(b)(1)(Repl. 1991).

[b] Minimum age defined by status is 13, but effective age is 16 based on an interpretation of U.S. Supreme Court decisions by the state attorney general's office.

[c] Age required is 17 unless the murderer is incarcerated for murder when a subsequent murder occurred; the age then may be 14.

[d] See Conn. Gen Stat. 53a-46a(g)(1).

[e] Juveniles may be transferred to adult court. Age may be a mitigating circumstance. No one under age 10 can commit a crime.

FIGURE

20.5

Minimum Age Authorized for Capital Punishment, 1994

SOURCE: James Stephan and Tracy Snell, *Capital Punishment* 1994 (Washington, D.C.: U.S. Department of Justice, February 1996), p. 2.

Death Row Populations Continue to Mount

With more than 2,890 prisoners on death rows across the nation and the number of executions growing, what will the reaction by the public be to an unprecedented number of executions that might be accomplished in the next few years? Administrators, politicians, legislators, and the public wrestle with what to do about the backlog of incarcerated evil. No one seems to be ready to deal with it, and so the appeals wend their ways through the courts at a staggering cost: about $4 million per case annually.[53] The major issue in regard to the death penalty in an era of shrinking resources is the relative cost of execution versus **life certain** without possibility of parole. What does this mean in terms of cost? Dieter makes a strong case for alternatives to the death penalty, at least as it is now administered and appealed, on an economic basis:

> Death penalty cases are much more expensive than other criminal cases and cost more than imprisonment for life with no possibility of parole. In California, capital trials are six times more costly than other murder trials. A study in Kansas indicated that a capital trial costs $116,700 more than an ordinary murder trial. Complex pretrial motions, lengthy jury selections, and expenses for expert witnesses are all likely to add to the cost in death penalty cases. The irreversibility of the death sentence requires courts to follow heightened due process in the preparation and course of the trial. The separate sentencing phase of the trial can take even longer than the guilt or innocence phase of the trial. And defendants are much more likely to insist on a trial when they are facing a possible death sentence. After conviction, there are constitutionally mandated appeals that involve both prosecution and defense costs.
>
> Most of these costs occur in every case for which capital punishment is sought, regardless of the outcome. Thus the true cost of the death penalty includes all the added expenses of the "unsuccessful" trials in which the death penalty is sought but not achieved. Moreover, if a defendant is convicted but not given the death sentence, the state will still incur the costs of life imprisonment, in addition to the increased trial expenses.
>
> For the states employing the death penalty, this luxury comes at a high price. In Texas, a death penalty case costs taxpayers an average of $2.3 million, about three times the cost of imprisoning someone in a single cell at the highest security level for 40 years. In Florida, each execution is costing the state $3.2 million. In financially strapped California, one report estimated the state could save $90 million each year by abolishing capital punishment. The New York Department of Correctional Services estimated that implementing the death penalty would cost the state $118 million [annually].[54]

Perhaps, in a time of economic turmoil, it is time to consider the cost of the death penalty in terms of both social and economic impact. Being sensible about the kinds of retribution we use is not necessarily being soft on crime.

Since the death sentence was imposed, the median time for the 4,173 prisoners who have been executed since 1930 has been about four years.[55] As Beamin Renshaw noted in 1982,

> Now again time is running out for a large proportion of individuals awaiting capital punishment. States have drafted and redrafted capital punishment measures, and the Supreme Court is overturning fewer and fewer on Eighth Amendment or other constitutional grounds. Further, many death row residents are exhausting their appeal processes under these statutes. Thus the situation is ripe for the nation to witness executions at a rate approaching the more than three per week that prevailed during the 1930s. We will then have a grim arena in which to conduct our national debate on the efficacy of the death penalty.[56]

That decision would not be good news for those who have traditionally taken over a decade to exhaust the appeals mechanisms. Executions will soon become more numerous, with less time between them. Whether this will dull the nation's senses to the death penalty or focus action against it has yet to be seen. As shown in Table 20-1, the latest data on time to execution for 1977–1994 show that most are still taking longer than before, bad news for hopes of expediting these cases. It will take more time to bring the long waits and delays down, if ever. It should be noted that elapsed time for blacks is still around 132 months, 10 months longer than for whites.

TABLE 20.1

Time from Death Sentence to Execution, by Race, 1977–94

Year of Execution	Number Executed			Average Elapsed Time from Sentence to Execution for		
	All Races*	White	Black	All Races*	White	Black
Total	257	156	99	97 mos	92 mos	106 mos
1977–83	11	9	2	51 mos	49 mos	58 mos
1984	21	13	8	74	76	71
1985	18	11	7	71	65	80
1986	18	11	7	87	78	102
1987	25	13	12	86	78	96
1988	11	6	5	80	72	89
1989	16	8	8	95	78	112
1990	23	16	7	95	97	91
1991	14	7	7	116	124	107
1992	31	19	11	114	104	135
1993	38	23	14	113	112	121
1994	31	20	11	122	117	132

NOTE: Average time was calculated from the most recent sentencing date. Some numbers have been revised from those previously reported.

*Includes Native Americans.

SOURCE: James Stephan and Tracy Snell. *Capital Punishment 1994* (Washington, D.C.: U.S. Department of Justice, 1996), p. 10.

Other Categories of Persons Under a Sentence of Death Are Growing

Prior to 1967, the last woman to have been executed legally in the United States was Elizabeth Ann Duncan, who died in the California gas chamber on August 8, 1962. Duncan was so infatuated with her son that she hired two killers to murder her daughter-in-law.

In 1984, Thelma Barfield was executed by lethal injection in North Carolina—hers the first execution of a woman in the state in twenty-two years and the first execution in the state since 1976. Despite the reluctance to execute women, the Supreme Court's desires for equity in imposing the death penalty seem to require that sex also be removed as a barrier. Of the 2,890 inmates on death row, at year-end 1994, only 1 out of 70, for a total of 41 on death row was a woman (see Table 20-2), even though about 1 out of 14 arrestees for murder was a woman in 1994. This unequal ratio of sentences to death for women who commit murder seems to be a harbinger for a more tough and **"equitable"** push for the death penalty for women in the future.[57]

Summary

At year-end 1994, 351 men and women had died by state execution since the day Gary Gilmore was shot through the heart in 1977. The U.S. Supreme Court streamlined and expedited its procedures for appellate review and seems to have tackled the issue of capital punishment head on. However, the death rows in thirty-seven states are packed, with a total of 2,729 persons sentenced to die by hanging, electrocution, lethal injection, gas, and the firing squad. Three states—

TABLE 20.2			
Women Under Sentence of Death, 12/31/94			
State	*Total*	*White*	*Black*
Total	41	27	14
California	6	4	2
Alabama	5	3	2
Illinois	5	2	3
Florida	4	3	1
Oklahoma	4	3	1
Pennsylvania	4	1	3
Texas	4	3	1
Missouri	2	2	0
North Carolina	2	2	0
Arizona	1	1	0
Idaho	1	1	0
Mississippi	1	1	0
Nevada	1	0	1
Tennessee	1	1	0

SOURCE: James Stephan and Tracy Snell. *Capital Punishment 1994* (Washington, D.C.: U.S. Department of Justice, 1996), p. 7.

New Hampshire, South Dakota, and Vermont—have the death penalty on the books, but have no inmates on death row. (New York approved a new capital punishment law in 1995.)

After it showed clearly what provisions it was willing to accept in regard to the death penalty in *Gregg*, the Supreme Court has been relatively supportive of the states' implementing them. It is clear, however, that the limited circumstances acceptable for the ultimate punishment must be administered on a scrupulously equitable basis or the Supreme Court may hold that even such limited application of the sanction of death is unconstitutional. The matter of equity is the one that must be watched over the next few years, as the number of convictions continues to grow. The increasing violent crime on the streets seems to be being countered by harder sentencing in the courts to be include death.

All but 16 of the 351 inmates executed since the lifting of the ban on capital punishment in 1976 have been executed in states in the Deep South. The southern **tradition of retribution** seems to be ready now to spread to the rest of America. That attitude has already spread to states like Washington and California. As we continue the decade of the 1990s and head toward the twenty-first century, the Supreme Court of all the United States is keeping a sharp eye on the pattern of executions that seems restricted to one geographical region. The Supreme Court will need to rethink the matter of equity and, perhaps, take action to correct it.

Next we look at what some consider "Life on the street" in regard to the rights of ex-inmates who try to make it back in the free world—not an easy task in a "get-tough" society, even though it is essential that the cycle of punishment must end.

We can hope that, someday, we will choose to work toward improved and innovative correctional programs that leave the death penalty ritual for future anthropologists and historians to ponder. The legacy may well stand as an example of the callous disregard for the value of human life in the twentieth century. This seems especially sad when we have such major social problems as the homeless, AIDS, education and health care, and continue to spend hundreds of millions of dollars to execute a tiny fraction of those who commit capital crimes. One way to modify such a legacy lies in efforts to improve the entire criminal justice system to make sure all offenders are treated equitably.

In the next chapter, we will examine the rights and challenges that face those individuals who have served their time and now find themselves back on the hard streets of America with a record and many restrictions. The rights of the ex-offender are very poorly understood by most Americans, and we shall try to clear up much of that confusion and misunderstanding. With millions of ex-offenders and ex-inmates back in society, it is important for the student of corrections to know what their rights and restrictions are.

*R*eview Questions

1. Explain the guidelines that came out of *Furman* v. *Georgia*.
2. Prepare an argument for the retention of the death penalty, and then prepare an argument against it.
3. How does the race of the victim affect being charged with a capital crime?
4. Why should the number of executions increase sharply in the future?
5. What does the economic situation do to impact the death penalty?
6. Who were the first to die in America by electrocution, by the gas chamber, by the use of lethal injection? What are your reactions to each form?

Words to Remember

capital punishment

execution

capital crimes

nonarbitrary

malice aforethought

cruel and unusual

Furman v. *Georgia*

deterrent

life certain

gatekeeper function

equability

equitable

tradition of retribution

Endnotes

1. Tim Robbins, director, *Dead Man Walking* (Hollywood, CA: Gramercy Polygram Film Productions, 1995). This film was nominated for a number of Academy Awards. Susan Sarandon was awarded the Oscar for best actress in 1995 for her portrayal of a nun who tried to help save a condemned man's soul by encouraging him to admit to having committed the crimes for which he was incarcerated.

2. The most readable discussion of these issues can be found in P. Lewis et al., "A Post-*Furman* Profile of Florida's Condemned—A Question of Discrimination in Terms of the Race of the Victim and a Comment on *Spinkellink v. Wainwright*," *Stetson Law Review* 9 (Fall 1979): 1–45. The general public strongly supports the death penalty. Dwayne Smith and James Wright, "Capital Punishment and Public Opinion in the Post-*Furman* Era: Trends and Analyses," *Sociological Spectrum* 12:2 (1992): 127–144. Even many violent offenders support the death penalty (for others): Dennis Stevens, "Research Note: The Death Sanction and Inmate Attitudes," *Crime and Delinquency* 38:2 (1992): 272–279. But see Robert Bohm, "Retribution and Capital Punishment: Toward a Better Understanding of Death Penalty Opinion," *Journal of Criminal Justice* 20:3 (1992): 227–236, and Richard Dieter, *Sentencing for Life: Americans Embrace Alternatives to the Death Penalty* (Washington, D.C.: Death Penalty Information Center, 1993).

3. Death Penalty Information Center, *Facts About the Death Penalty* (Washington, D.C.: Death Penalty Information Center, August 2, 1993), p. 1.

4. Walter Goodman, "Resolved: The Death Penalty Is a Good Thing." *The New York Times*, June 13, 1994, p. B4.

5. Gary Howells, Kelly Flanagan, and Miriam Hogan, "Does Viewing a Televised Execution Affect Attitudes Toward Capital Punishment?" *Criminal Justice and Behavior* 24:1 (1995): 411–414.

6. Harry Elmer Barnes and Negley K. Teeter, *New Horizons in Criminology* (Englewood Cliffs, : Prentice Hall, 1959), p. 308.

7. Frederick Drimmer, *Until You Are Dead: The Book of Executions in America* (Secaucus, NJ: Carol Publishing, 1990), pp. 18–19.

8. Correctional personnel required to participate in an execution are an ignored component of capital punishment. See Dean Gursky, "The Aftermath of an Execution: An Interview with Jennie Lancaster," *Corrections Today* 50 (December 1988): 76–84; Reid Payne, Roger Pray, and Louis Damis, "Utah Stress Education Program Helps Staff Deal with Executions," *Corrections Today* 52 (July 1990): 160–169; and Daniel Vasquez, "Trauma Treatment," *Corrections Today* 55:4 (1993): 70–72.

9. Drimmer, *Until You Are Dead*, pp. 82–83.

10. Ibid., pp. 107–109.

11. Barnes and Teeters, *New Horizons in Criminology*, p. 309. In 1988, the average wait from conviction to execution was six years and eight months but, by 1991, it had increased to eighty-five months, just over seven years. See Lawrence Greenfield, *Capital Punishment* 1991 (Washington, D.C.: U.S. Department of Justice, 1992), p. 13.

12. For a good reference to this controversy, see Ernest van den Haag and John Conrad, *The Death Penalty: A Debate* (New York: Plenum, 1983). See also Roger Hood, *The Death Penalty: Worldwide Perspective* (Oxford: Clarendon Press, 1989); H. Wayne House and John Howard Yoder, *The Death Penalty Debate: Two Opposing Views of Capital Punishment* (Dallas:

Word, 1991); Lawrence Wood, *Alone Among Its Peers: The United States' Refusal to Join the International Movement to Abolish Capital Punishment* (Buffalo: State University of New York at Buffalo, 1991); and Enid Harlow, David Atlas and Jane Rocamora, *Indictment of Capital Punishment in the United States* (New York: Amnesty International, 1995).

13. Greenfield, *Capital Punishment 1991*, p. 12.

14. Raymond Paternoster, *Capital Punishment in America* (New York: Lexington, 1991); Stewart Tolnay, E. M. Beck, and James Massey, "Black Competition and White Vengeance: Legal Executions of Blacks as Social Control in the Cotton South," *Social Science Quarterly* 73:3 (1992): 627–644; and Adelberto Aguirre and David Baker, *Race, Racism and the Death Penalty* (Berrien Spring, MI: Van de Vere Publishing, 1991).

15. Congress authorized the imposition of the death penalty for presidential assassination and certain drug-related murder. See Peggy Tobolowsky, "Death and Drugs: Congress Authorizes the Death Penalty for Certain Drug-Related Murders," *Journal of Contemporary Law* 18:1 (1992): 47–73, and Charles Williams, "The Federal Death Penalty for Drug-Related Killings," *Criminal Law Bulletin* 27:5 (1991): 387–415.

16. J. Edgar Hoover, *Uniform Crime Reports* (Washington, D.C.: U.S. Government Printing Office, 1931–1939). A rough average of such crimes known to the police is presented.

17. Editors, Death Penalty Information Center, *Facts About the Death Penalty*, p. 3.

18. James Stephan and Tracy Snell, *Capital Punishment 1994* (Washington, D.C.: U.S. Department of Justice, February 1996), p. 10.

19. Justice William J. Brennan, *Furman v. Georgia*, 408 U.S. 238 (1976).

20. The U.S. Supreme Court has rendered three decisions that further restricted the application of the death penalty. In 1977, the case of *Coker v. Georgia* (433 U.S. 584) decided that the death penalty was "grossly disproportionate punishment" for the crime of rape of an adult woman, even though the offender had been previously convicted of rape and was, at the time of the crime, an escapee from prison. The second case (*Roberts v. Louisiana*, 431 U.S. 633) was decided in 1977 and prohibited the mandatory death penalty following conviction for the killing of a firefighter or police officer in performance of his or her duties. The last cases (*Lockett v. Ohio*, 434 U.S. 889, and *Bell v. Ohio*, 434 U.S. 887) were 1978 decisions, striking down Ohio's death penalty statute for "impermissible restricting the mitigating factors that may be considered on behalf of an offender at sentencing."

21. Brennan, *Furman v. Georgia*.

22. *Malice aforethought* means malice in fact or implied malice in the intent of one who has had time to premeditate an act that is unlawful or harmful. This issue is wrapped around the plea of not guilty by reason of insanity. See William A. Schabas, "International Norms on Execution of the Insane and the Mentally Retarded," *Criminal Law Forum* 4:1 (1993): 95–117.

23. Paige Ralph, Jonathan Sorensen, and James Marquart, "A Comparison of Death-Sentenced and Incarcerated Murderers in Pre-*Furman* Texas," *Justice Quarterly* 9:2 (1992): 185–209.

24. Death Penalty Information Center, *Chattahoochee Judicial District: Buckle on the Death Belt: The Death Penalty in Microcosm* (Washington, D.C.: Death Penalty Information Center, 1992); see also Death Penalty Information Center, *Killing Justice: Government Misconduct and the Death Penalty* (Washington, D.C.: Death Penalty Information Center, 1992).

25. Gennaro Vito and Thomas Keil, "Capital Sentencing in Kentucky: An Analysis of Factors Influencing Decision Making in the Post-*Gregg* Period," *The Journal of Criminal Law and Criminology* 79:2 (1988): 483–508. See also Thomas Keil and Gennaro Vito, "The Effects of the *Furman* and *Gregg* Decisions on Black-White Execution Ratios in the South," *Journal of Criminal Justice* 20:3 (1992): 217–226.

26. Stephen Klein and John Rolph, "Relationship of Offender and Victim Race to the Death Penalty in California," *Jurimetrics Journal* 32:3 (1991): 33–48.

27. Franklin Zimring, Austin Sarat, Robert Emerson, et al. "Symposium: Research on the Death Penalty," *Law and Society Review* 27:1 (1993): 9–175, and Mark Small, "A Review of Death Penalty Caselaw: Future Directions for Program Evaluation," *Criminal Justice Policy Review* 5:2 (1991): 114–120.

28. Justice Thurgood Marshall, *Furman v. Georgia*. Actually, the U.S. Supreme Court shifted from the earlier standard (concerned only with historical techniques for imposing punishment) to the "emerging standards" doctrine in 1910 (*Weems v. United States*, 217 U.S. 349).

29. *Wilkerson v. Utah*, 99 U.S. 130 (1878). The State Supreme Court of Utah upheld a

lower-court decision sentencing a prisoner convicted of murder in the first degree to be shot publicly.

30. Roelien Therou, Julia Sloth-Nielsen, and Hugh Corder, eds. *Death Penalty by Decree: South Africa and the Death Penalty* (Plumstead, SA: Society for the Abolition of the Death Penalty in South Africa, 1991), and Wenyuan Qi, "The Reality and Prospects of the Penal Policy of China: An Outline," *Arborg 1995* (Copenhagen: Copenhagen Institute, 1995), pp. 143–149.

31. Justice Nathan Clifford, *Wilkerson v. Utah*, 99 U.S. 130 (1878).

32. Justice Stephen Field, *O'Neil v. Vermont*, 1944 U.S. 323 (1892).

33. *Weems v. United States*, 217 U.S. 349 (1910). This decision represented a broad interpretation of the Eighth Amendment, asserting that "cruel and unusual punishment" could apply to prison sentences of a length disproportionate to the offense.

34. *Louisiana ex rel. Francis v. Resweber*, 329 U.S. 459 (1947). The State Supreme Court of Louisiana denied a writ of habeas corpus against a second attempt to execute a prisoner convicted of murder, the first attempt at electrocution having failed because of mechanical difficulty.

35. For briefer analysis of the varied opinions, see F. C. Rieber, "Supreme Court Bars Death Penalty as It Is Now Imposed by the States," *American Journal of Corrections* 35 (1973): 10–14. See also Louis D. Bilionis, "Moral Appropriateness, Capital Punishment, and the Lockett Doctrine," *Criminal Law and Criminology* 82:2 (1991): 283–333.

36. Chief Justice Warren Burger, *Furman v. Georgia*.

37. Genarro Vito and Deborah Wilson, "Back from the Dead: Tracking the Progress of Kentucky's *Furman*-Commuted Death Row Populations," *Justice Quarterly* 5:1 (1988) 101–111.

38. They included such notable figures as Sirhan Sirhan, the convicted killer of Senator Robert Kennedy, and Charles Manson, leader of the group of mass killers in California known as the "Family."

39. *Gregg v. Georgia*, 428 U.S. 153 (1976).

40. Sir James Stephen (as quoted in *Furman v. Georgia* by Justice Marshall).

41. Hans Zeisel and Alex Gallup, "Death Penalty Sentiment in the United States," *Journal of Quantitative Criminology* 5 (1989): 285–296. See also M. Dwayne Smith and James Wright, "Capital Punishment and Public Opinion in the Post-*Furham* Era: Trends and Analyses," *Sociological Spectrum* 12:2 (1992): 127–144; Thomas J. Keil, and Gennaro F. Vito, "Fear of Crime and the Attitudes Toward Capital Punishment: A Structured Equations Model," *Justice Quarterly* 8:4 (1991): 447–464; and David Kopel, *Guns: Who Should Have Them?* (Amherst, NY: Prometheus, 1995).

42. In a telephone survey of respondents in Ohio, Skovron et al. found disapproval of the death penalty's being used on juveniles: Sandra Evans Skovron, Joseph Scott, and Francis Cullen, "The Death Penalty for Juveniles: An Assessment of Public Support," *Crime and Delinquency* 35 (1989): 546–561. William Carlsen reports that Californians solidly support the death penalty for adults (82 percent favor, versus 14 percent opposed), but life in prison without the possibility of parole as an alternative to capital punishment is favored by 67 percent of the respondents. William Carlsen, "Support for the Death Penalty—Sometimes," *San Francisco Chronicle*, March 28, 1990, p. A-9. The war against drugs has been spread to the death penalty. See Charles J. Williams, "The Death Penalty for Drug-Related Killings," *Criminal Law Bulletin* 27:5 (1991): 387–415. See also Shirley Dicks, *Young Blood: Juvenile Justice and the Death Penalty* (Amherst, NY: Prometheus, 1995).

43. Dieter, *Sentencing for Life: Americans Embrace Alternatives to the Death Penalty*.

44. H. Bedeau and M. Radelet, "Miscarriages of Justice in Potentially Capital Cases," *Stanford Law Review* 40 (1987): 21–179. See also Elizabeth Rapaport, "The Death Penalty and Gender Discrimination" *Law & Society Review* 25:2 (1991): 367–383, and Michael Radelet, Hugo Bedeau, and Constance Putnam, *In Spite of Innocence: The Ordeal of 400 Americans Wrongly Convicted of Crimes Punishable by Death* (Boston: Northeastern University Press, 1992).

45. Small, "A Review of Death Penalty Caselaw."

46. *Perry v. Lynbaugh*, 109 S. Ct. 2934 (1989).

47. *Murray v. Geirranto*, 109 S. Ct. 2765 (1989).

48. Raymond Paternoster and Ann Marie Kazyaka, "The Administration of the Death Penalty in South Carolina: Experience over the First Few Years," *South Carolina Law Review* 39:2 (1988): 245–411.

49. Thomas Keil and Gennaro Vito, "Race and the Death Penalty in Kentucky Murder Trials: An Analysis of Post-*Gregg* Outcomes," *Justice Quarterly* 7:1 (March 1990): 189–207.

50. Michael Radelet, "Executions of Whites for Crimes Against Blacks: Exceptions to the Rule?" *Sociological Quarterly* 30:4 (1989): 529–544. A more recent study was conducted by Thomas J. Keil and Gennaro F. Vito, "The Effects of the *Furham* and *Gregg* Decisions on Black-White Execution Rates in the South," *Journal of Criminal Justice* 20:3 (1992): 217–226. See also Keil and Vito, "Capital Sentencing in Kentucky."

51. Gregory Leong and Spencer Eth, "Behavioral Science and the Juvenile Death Penalty," *Bulletin of the American Academy of Psychiatry and the Law* 17:3 (1989): 301–309. But see also Victor Streib and Lynn Sametz, "Capital Punishment of Female Juveniles," paper presented at the 1988 annual meeting of the American Society of Criminology, November 1988. See also Amnesty International, USA, *United States of America: The Death Penalty and Juvenile Offenders* (New York: Amnesty International, 1991).

52. General Accounting Office, *Death Penalty Sentencing: Research Indicates Pattern of Racial Disparities* (Washington, D.C.: U.S. General Accounting Office, 1990).

53. Martha Carter, *Cost of the Death Penalty: An Introduction to the Issue* (Lincoln: Legislative Research Division, Nebraska Legislature, 1995).

54. Richard C. Dieter, *Millions Misspent: What Politicians Don't Say About the High Costs of the Death Penalty* (Washington, D.C.: Death Penalty Information Center, October 1992). But see Elizabeth Rapaport, "The Death Penalty and Gender Discrimination," *Law and Society Review* 25:2 (1991): 367–383.

55. Streib and Sametz, "Capital Punishment of Female Juveniles," p. 1.

56. Beamin H. Renshaw III, "Death Row Prisoners: 1981", *Bureau of Justice Statistics Bulletin* (Washington, D.C.: U.S. Department of Justice, July 1982), p. 1.

57. James Stephan and Tracy Snell, *Capital Punishment 1994* (Washington, D.C.: U.S. Department of Justice, February 1996), p. 10.

CHAPTER TWENTY-ONE

The Rights of Ex-Offenders

Overview

In the past two chapters, we have discussed the rights of offenders who are incarcerated and face execution. These rights are important and they are carefully monitored. What about those persons who have finally done their time and now find themselves back in their former neighborhood, but with a record and a stigma? There are literally millions of citizens on the streets of America who have been placed under correctional supervision of some kind at some point in their lives. (There are over five million who are under active correctional supervision, from incarceration to parole and probation.) This chapter deals with the sometimes gray area of the ex-offender and what they face in trying to reintegrate into society. This task is one that has many bumps in the road back to being a productive and useful citizen, but many more make that trip and succeed than we often give credit to. This chapter considers the restrictions on ex-offenders and the current status of efforts to give them additional rights. We start with some of the myths and legends about these efforts.

The Legend of the Ex-Con

The highly stylized version of the **ex-con** presented in the movies and on television usually depicts a tough streetwise, scar-faced thug who is able to survive on wits and muscle, with a good-looking and willing woman not too far in the background. The ex-con is often depicted as a person to be feared and never trusted. With a granite jaw and shifty eyes, he talks out of the corner of his mouth and prefers a life of crime. The real-life ex-offender, of course, is something quite different from our legendary ex-con of

Young, unskilled, poorly educated, the typical offender has few marketable capabilities to offer potential employers. Unable to find or keep a job upon his release from prison, the offender often returns to crime—the only "business" he knows. Breaking the cycle of recidivism is a difficult task, involving many complex contributing factors. One of these is employment potential. Effective programs for building relevant job skills do ease the offender's reentry into society.

—Gerald M. Caplan, former Director, National Institute of Justice

movie and mystery novel fame. Newly released ex-offenders found in most cities are young, with little experience outside prison walls; they are male or female, poor, with only the funds they managed to acquire while in prison; uneducated, with less than a high school diploma; former illicit drug users;[1] and frightened, having spent several years away from a rapidly changing world. After release from prison, these individuals must start a new life and make it in the free world while being watched by the correctional authorities, local police, employers, friends, and family. They often return to the same social and environmental conditions that gave rise to their trouble in the first place. The wonder is not that so many ex-offenders recidivate but that more do not do so.[2] If we add to this already heavy burden the legal and administrative restrictions placed on ex-offenders, it becomes evident that the happy-go-lucky ex-con is indeed a legend invented for the reading and viewing public.[3]

Collateral Consequences of a Conviction

Conviction for an offense carries with it the punishment imposed by statute. In addition, the convicted offender must carry several other disabilities and disqualifications that result from the conviction per se. Many state and federal statutes restrict some of the rights and privileges ordinarily available to law-abiding citizens in the nation. They include the rights to vote, to hold offices of private and public trust, to assist in parenting, to be on jury duty, to own firearms, to remain married, and to have privacy. Those and other rights may be lost upon conviction. They are collectively called **collateral consequences** of criminal conviction.

Just how many citizens face collateral consequences is unknown, but a conservative estimate is that there are at least fifty million persons living in our societies who have been arrested for some offense in the nation, and at least fourteen million of them have been convicted of a felony.

Even after offenders have served their sentences, these secondary handicaps continue to plague them in the form of **social stigma**, loss of civil rights, and administrative and legislative restrictions. Each of these areas interacts with the others, and their overall effect is to prevent the successful reintegration of ex-offenders into the free community. The problems first surface when ex-offenders attempt to find employment,[4] as this account by one such job seeker illustrates:

> Now if you're out there on the bricks and looking for work, Joe, don't bother applying for any of those jobs I told you about and you'll save yourself a bundle of heartaches. Whenever you apply for any job, my advice is not to mention your record. That's right, lie to 'em. If they have a place on the employment application where it asks you if you've ever been convicted of a crime, put down N-O, no! If you don't, you're screening yourself out of 75 percent of all jobs, and damned near 100 percent of the better jobs. You have to look ahead too, Joe. Big Willie, the "trustyland" barber, has a brother working for one of the big steel companies. A friend got him the job, white collar too. That was seven, eight years ago. He's still on the same job, but guys who have only been with the company two or three years are moving right up the line to higher job classifications and better pay. Why? His boss told him why. He's got a record, and the company knows it's on his original

employment application. His boss told him he was terribly sorry, that wasn't his fault, but the higher-ups passed him up because fifteen years ago he served two years in prison. See, Joe, crime don't pay, because they ain't never going to let you up once they got you down. That's just the way it is.

Go ahead and tell 'em if you want to, Joe. You're taking a chance no matter what you do. If you tell 'em you don't get the job most of the time. If you don't tell 'em, and they find out, they fire you. You know Louie, the cellhouse clerk? He got a job and didn't tell 'em about his record. Louie's parole officer came around checking on him and blowed the job for Louie. How do you like them apples? And Gabby, the four block runner, went out and got a job that'll knock you out. He was hired as a credit investigator! Yeah, handling confidential financial reports all day long. While he was still on parole too. His parole officer was an OK guy and said more power to 'em. Well, it took about two months because the employment application investigation isn't handled by regional offices but is done by the main office in New York. One day his boss calls him in, red faced and all, and says to him, why didn't you tell us? Louie says, if I'd told you, would you have hired me? His boss says, of course not! Louie was canned.[5]

The greatest dilemma faced by the ex-offender in search of a job is obvious.

STIGMA

The stigma of a prison record is to ex-offenders a millstone to be worn around their necks until death. Though we pride ourselves that we have advanced beyond the eye-for-an-eye mentality of the past, we do not show it in the treatment of our offenders who have allegedly paid their debt to society. Aaron Nussbaum pointed out some of the problems of stigma for the discharged prisoner:

> It is a grim fact that total punishment for crime never ends with the courts or jails. None can deny that a criminal record is a life-long handicap, and its subject a "marked man" in our society. No matter how genuine the reformation, nor how sincere and complete the inner resolution to revert to lawful behavior, the criminal offender is and remains a prisoner of his past record long after the crime is expiated by the punishment fixed under the criminal codes.

> This traditional prejudice and distrust stalks him at every turn no matter what crime he may have committed or the nature of the punishment meted out to him. It strikes at the first offender as ruthlessly, and with as deadly effect, as upon the inveterate repeater or the professional criminal. It pursues those alike who have served time in imprisonment, of long or short duration, and those who have been merely cloaked with a criminal record in the form of a suspended sentence, a discharge on probation, or even a fine.[6]

One needs **self-esteem** to survive in the competitive atmosphere of the free world. Thus the diminished self-esteem of the offender makes it difficult to bridge the gap between institutional life and the community.[7] It is the search for self-esteem and status that leads many ex-offenders back to the circle of acquaintances that first led them afoul of the law. The personal disintegration encouraged by the fortress prisons of America makes the discharged offender both a social and an economic cripple. We can only hope that the new techniques in corrections, designed to strengthen self-esteem and produce reasonable readjustment in the community, will help offset that effect, as will increased use of community corrections and intermediate punishments.

THE TRANSITION PERIOD

Many ex-inmates, particularly those having served longer sentences, face a difficult transitional period when released back into the communities of America, under parole supervision or not. Not only do they have breaks in their employment histories that are difficult to explain to potential employers, but many are taken aback by the cost of food and services on the outside, especially as inflation has more than doubled the cost of housing, food, and other basic commodities since their incarceration. Because of those problems, many ex-offenders need intensive assistance from reintegration services, such as community residential centers and halfway houses.[8] In the Federal Bureau of Prisons, a large portion of prerelease inmates in fact spend their last six months in halfway houses, where they receive training in how to fill out employment applications, how to get and hold a job, how to deal with family problems and crises, where to secure services available in their communities, how to manage money, and so on. Such services will be even more important as states decrease or eliminate parole services, while even more inmates are incarcerated and sentences are extended. The concept of charging ex-offenders fees for parole services may even further aggravate the situation.[9] It seems obvious that few will be eager or able to pay for their own parole.

LOSS OF CIVIL RIGHTS

Though most people recognize that released prisoners do not automatically regain all their civil rights, there is widespread confusion as to which rights are permanently lost and which suspended, and what machinery is available to regain them. Sol Rubin, a lawyer and writer on penology, discussed the offender's loss of the rights to vote and engage in certain kinds of employment:

> [W]hen a convicted defendant is not sentenced to commitment, but is placed on probation, and receives a suspended sentence, he should lose no civil rights. This is a recommendation of the Standard Probation and Parole Act published as long ago as 1955.

> It is a contradiction of the purposes of probation and parole that this view does not prevail. A California case cites the following instruction to a new parolee: "Your civil rights have been suspended. Therefore, you may not enter into any contract, marry, engage in business, or execute a contract without the restoration of such civil rights by the Adult Authority." A look at the rights restored by the Adult Authority at the time of release on parole is just as sad, hardly more than that on release he may be at large. He may rent a habitation, he is told, buy food, clothing, and transportation, and tools for a job; and he is advised that he has the benefit of rights under Workman's Compensation, Unemployment Insurance, etc.

> When the sentence is commitment, the principle of *Coffin v. Reichard* ought to apply, that a prisoner retains (or should retain) all rights of an ordinary citizen except those expressly or by necessary implication are taken away by law.[10]

To determine the current status of collateral consequences, Burton, Cullen, and Travis surveyed the fifty states' and the District of Columbia's statutes, case law, and attorneys general in a systematic review of the specific privileges, immunities, and rights that felons might lose after conviction. The basic results are found in Tables 21-1 and 21-2. The researchers found that states are generally becoming less restrictive in depriving felons of their civil rights.

TABLE 21.1

Restrictions of Felony Offenders' Civil Rights

Restrictive vs. Less Restrictive, by Right and Jurisdiction

Jurisdiction	Voting Permanently Lost vs. Restorable	Parental Rights Yes vs. No	Divorce Permanently Yes vs. No	Public Employment Permanently Lost vs. Restorable	Juror Permanently Lost vs. Restorable	Holding Office Permanently Lost vs. Restorable	Firearm "Violent" Felony vs. "Any" Felony	Criminal Registration Yes vs. No	Civil Death Yes vs. No
Alabama	X	X	X	X	X	X		X	
Alaska			X		X		X		
Arizona		X					X	X	
Arkansas	X		X		X	X	X		
California		X			X	X[1]	X	X	
Colorado		X							
Connecticut			X				X		
Delaware				X	X	X	X		
D.C.			X		X	X[1]	X		
Florida	X				X	X	X	X	
Georgia			X		X	X	X		
Hawaii					X		X		
Idaho			X		X				X
Illinois			X				X		
Indiana		X	X		X		X		
Iowa	X			X	X	X	X		
Kansas		X					X		
Kentucky	X				X	X	X		
Louisiana			X						
Maine						X[1]	X		
Maryland			X		X				
Massachusetts		X				X[1]	X		
Michigan		X					X		
Minnesota			X						
Mississippi	X	X	X	X		X	X	X	X
Missouri					X				
Montana					X		X		
Nebraska					X		X		
Nevada	X	X			X	X	X	X	
New Hampshire			X				X		
New Jersey			X		X	X			
New Mexico	X				X	X	X		
New York			X		X	X	X		X
North Carolina									

TABLE 21.1

Restrictions of Felony Offenders' Civil Rights *(Con't)*

Restrictive vs. Less Restrictive, by Right and Jurisdiction

Jurisdiction	Voting Permanently Lost vs. Restorable	Parental Rights Yes vs. No	Divorce Permanently Yes vs. No	Public Employment Permanently Lost vs. Restorable	Juror Permanently Lost vs. Restorable	Holding Office Permanently Lost vs. Restorable	Firearm "Violent" Felony vs. "Any" Felony	Criminal Registration Yes vs. No	Civil Death Yes vs. No
North Dakota			X						
Ohio			X		X	X			
Oklahoma			X		X		X		
Oregon		X					X		
Pennsylvania			X		X		X		
Rhode Island	X	X	X	X	X	X			X
South Carolina				X	X	X			
South Dakota		X	X						
Tennessee	X	X	X		X	X		X	
Texas			X		X	X	X		
Utah			X		X			X	
Vermont			X						
Virginia	X		X		X	X			
Washington									
West Virginia			X					X	
Wisconsin		X				X	X		
Wyoming		X			X				

X = right is restricted or jeopardized

1 – right is restricted for specific offenses

SOURCE: Velmer Burton, Francis Cullen, and Lawrence Travis, "The Collateral Consequences of a Felony Conviction," *Federal Probation* 51:3(1987): 55.

Some eleven states permanently disenfranchise the felon unless he or she is pardoned[11] or restored to citizenship through the vacating of the original sentence, expungement of record, or other judicial procedure unique to the jurisdiction. In the survey, over three-fourths of the jurisdictions restored the right to vote after specific periods of time had elapsed. Other major findings were as follows:

1. In sixteen states (nearly one-third of the jurisdictions surveyed), courts may terminate parenting rights on the conviction or incarceration of a parent.

2. More than half (twenty-eight states) permit divorce for conviction of or imprisonment for a felony.

3. Thirty percent of the jurisdictions permanently bar convicted felons from public employment in their home states, unless pardoned or restored to full citizenship.

4. If one is a felon in nineteen states, one may not hold public office.

TABLE *21.2*

Restricted Rights of Jurisdiction

Number of Rights That Are Restricted	Jurisdictions
9	None
8	Mississippi
7	Alabama and Rhode Island
6	Nevada and Tennessee
5	Arkansas, California, Florida, Iowa, and New York
4	Delaware, District of Columbia, Georgia, Indiana, Kentucky, New Mexico, Texas, and Virginia
3	Alaska, Arizona, Idaho, Massachusetts, New Jersey, Ohio, Oklahoma, Pennsylvania, South Carolina, Utah, and Wisconsin
2	Connecticut, Hawaii, Illinois, Kansas, Maine, Maryland, Michigan, Montana, Nebraska, New Hampshire, Oregon, South Dakota, and Wyoming
1	Colorado, Louisiana, Minnesota, Missouri, North Dakota, Vermont, and West Virginia
0	North Carolina and Washington

Rights considered were in the areas of voting, parenting, divorce, public employment, jury duty, holding public office, owning firearms, criminal registration, and civil death.

SOURCE: Velmer Burton, Francis Cullen, and Lawrence Travis, "The Collateral Consequences of Felony Conviction," *Federal Probation* 51:3 (1987): 52–60.

5. Almost every state forbids a felon from possession of a firearm.

6. Only eight states require the felon to register as a former offender, and only four states continue the practice of civil death.[12]

Recognition of the inequities of such denials is expressed in the provisions of Section 306.1(1) of the American Law Institute's Model Penal Code:

No person shall suffer any legal disqualification or disability because of his conviction of a crime or his sentence on such conviction, unless the disqualification or disability involves the deprivation of a right or privilege which is:
   a. necessarily incident to execution of the sentence of the court; or
   b. provided by the Constitution or the Code; or
   c. provided by a statute other than the Code, when the conviction is of a crime defined by such statute; or
   d. provided by the judgment, order, or regulation of a court, agency, or official exercising a jurisdiction conferred by law, or by the statute defining such jurisdiction, when the commission of the crime or the conviction or the sentence is reasonably related to the competency of the individual to exercise the right or privilege of which he is deprived.[13]

RIGHT TO WORK VERSUS NEED TO WORK

Ex-offenders are often faced with the cruel paradox that they must have employment to remain free, even though the system denies them employment because they have a record.[14] Many studies have shown that employment is one of the most important factors in the successful reintegration of ex-offenders into the community.[15] In the past, ex-offenders could move on to a new territory and establish a new identity, thus escaping the stigmatization that goes with a prison record. On the advancing frontiers of early America, the new settlers asked few questions and judged individuals on their present actions rather than past records. But today computers record every aspect of our lives,[16] and privacy has become less a right than a very rare privilege. To many people, the informational expansion is a boon; to ex-offenders it often represents a catastrophe. Even citizens who find themselves involved in an arrest that does not result in conviction may suffer the worst consequences of a record, including the failure to obtain a job, or its loss.

There appear to be two levels where action is necessary to alleviate this crushing burden for the ex-offender. At the community level, barriers to employment that work against the poor and uneducated must be overcome; that is, more realistic educational requirements for jobs must be negotiated. (Degrees and diplomas are often used as screening devices for jobs that do not require them.) A structural framework must be constructed in which the community has jobs to fill, training to give, and a willingness to offer both to offenders and ex-offenders. These conditions can be met only by basic changes in society, not by programs for the individual. The use of ex-offenders as parole officer agents by some states is an example of such a favorable development.

At the individual level, the offender must overcome his or her personal handicaps. Many recent programs are aimed at the employability of the offender and ex-offender, often the young, the unemployed, and the unskilled (frequently also members of minority groups), who comprise the bulk of official arrest statistics.

In community-based programs to help in the employment of offenders and ex-offenders, it must be assumed that the person has the capability for regular employment but is unfamiliar with and inexperienced in certain of the required behavioral skills.[17] In other words, behavioral training, rather than therapy, is needed. It must also be assumed that if offenders learn to handle themselves in the community while under correctional control, they will be able to do so when those controls have been lifted. In planning employment assistance for offenders and ex-offenders who may need it, program planners are faced with questions like the following:

- Should supportive services be provided in-house or be contracted?
- How good a job should be sought ("dead end," having job mobility, on a career ladder, etc.)?
- Who should be trained, and what kind of training should be offered?
- What kind of and how much training should be provided in the institutions? When?

To answer those questions, a comprehensive service program should include the following:

- Assessment of the client's skills and abilities;
- Training in job-hunting and job-readiness skills and in acquiring acceptable work attitudes;
- Job training and basic education, if necessary;
- Job development and job placement;

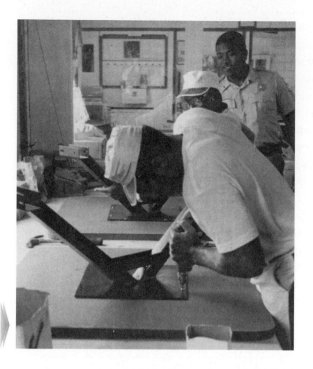

A job—the ultimate rehabilitation

—COURTESY OF THE GEORGIA DEPARTMENT OF CORRECTIONS

- Follow-up with employee and employer after placement; and
- Other supportive services, as required (medical or legal aid).

RESTRICTED TRADES: BARRIERS TO EMPLOYMENT

Although there are still some barriers to employment in general for ex-offenders, today's standards are more likely to apply to the individual and his or her offense. Ex-offenders as an identified class (or minority) are appealing more and more to the courts. The 1990s continued to work toward improvements in that area, especially in the removal of **employment restrictions** for ex-offenders based simply on their being ex-offenders.[18] It is not only the general unemployment picture that most severely affects the ex-offender. When work is scarce for all, the ex-offender finds it more and more difficult to find any kind of employment. This tends to highlight the overall problem, in all aspects of society, that results from a criminal record. The slow-growing economy of the 1990s, combined with increased levels of crime and incarceration, has slowed down progress.

The National Alliance for Business and the Probation Division of the Administrative Office of the U.S. Courts operate a partnership venture designed to test a delivery system for ex-offender training services and employment. The model is designed to use existing resources, which are coordinated to attain the model's objectives. The alliance provides technical assistance to localities attempting to implement the model, and it is proving to be a promising operation.[19]

The Problem with a Record

As we have seen, the person with a record of conviction is at a major disadvantage when trying to integrate with the community. The deprivation of rights and bars to employment are related to that record, and so it is vital to know what having a record means in the age of information. It seems that a record, even a record of mere contact with the criminal justice system, is extremely difficult to shed once it has been acquired. This record becomes the basis for special attention by the police and difficulty with credit agencies. Once the record has been placed in the computers, it can be retrieved whenever requested by an authorized agency and, inevitably, by some unauthorized agencies.

One way to overcome the problem of a record is to construct a system that will annul the conviction after certain specifications are met. The National Council on Crime and Delinquency[20] makes the following provision in its Model Act for Annulment of Conviction of Crime:

> The court in which a conviction of crime has been had may, at the time of discharge of a convicted person from its control, or upon his discharge from imprisonment or parole, or at any time thereafter, enter an order annulling, canceling, and rescinding the record of conviction and disposition, when in the opinion of the court the order would assist in rehabilitation and be consistent with the public welfare. Upon the entry of such order the person against whom the conviction had been entered shall be restored to all civil rights lost or suspended by virtue of the arrest, conviction, or sentence, unless otherwise provided in the order, and shall be treated in all respects as not having been convicted, except that upon conviction of any subsequent crime the prior conviction may be considered by the court in determining the sentence to be imposed.
>
> In any application for employment, license, or other civil right or privilege, or any appearance as a witness, a person may be questioned about previous criminal record only in language such as the following: Have you ever been arrested for or convicted of a crime which has not been annulled by a court? Upon entry of the order of annulment of conviction, the court shall issue to the person in whose favor the order has been entered a certificate stating that his behavior after conviction has warranted the issuance of the order, and that its effect is to annul, cancel, and rescind the record of conviction and disposition. Nothing in this act shall affect any right of the offender to appeal from his conviction or to rely on it in bar of any subsequent proceedings for the same offense.[21]

This kind of proposal has aroused interest but little action for adult felons in state legislatures. Because annulment is, in fact, the only reasonable way to protect the ex-offender from questions about prior convictions, some courts are getting around the legislative inaction by failing to enter the record of conviction and keeping an informal "**vest-pocket**" record.[22]

The problem of a criminal record in this country is especially critical whenever an arrest does not result in a conviction. In most foreign countries, an arrest with no conviction cannot be used against the person in later actions. In the United States, in most jurisdictions, employment applications can include questions about an arrest, regardless of whether or not there was a conviction. Even a pardon, exonerating the suspect from guilt, does not remove the incident from the record. Not surprisingly, the current attack on this perpetual record is based on the cruel and unusual punishment clause of the Eighth Amendment.[23] Another legal approach is reflected in recent suits claiming that prisoners and ex-offenders are being discriminated against as a class, instead of being treated on the basis of individual merit.

It is a truism that we find hard to accept that the protections of the Bill of Rights against police and other official abuse are for all of us, the criminals and the non-criminals. But when we consider the tens of millions who have a record of arrest, perhaps as many as 50 million, it is clear that the civil rights of those who are in conflict with the law are, indeed, in the most pragmatic way, the interest of all. We are in an era of struggle for civil rights, for blacks, for women, for the mentally ill, for the young, even the delinquent young. Perhaps we are in a period of civil rights for homosexuals and others whose sexual practices are unreasonably subject to legal condemnation.

It is timely, indeed, that we awake to the excesses in punishing those in conflict with the law. It is a field of great discrimination, and must be remedied, just as much as other discriminations must be remedied. Not all people with a criminal record are vicious or degraded to begin with, or if their crime was vicious, are they doomed to remain as they were; unless, of course, we strive by discrimination and rejection to make them so.[24]

REGISTRATION OF CRIMINALS

Registration of criminals has been a practice ever since society started imprisoning individuals. In ancient times, registration was used to identify prisoners in penal servitude: prisoners were branded or marked to decrease their already minimal chances of escape. Because penal slaves had no hope of ever being free, the markings were a sign of their permanent status. The "yellow card" was later used in European countries to identify former prisoners who were lucky enough to have lived through their sentences.[25] The registration of felons has also been a widespread practice in America, especially at the local level. A problem with local registration is that it tends to single out offenders for special attention from authorities to which they would not otherwise be subject. Most of these requirements are obsolete today. As information on offenders and arrested persons is placed into computer data banks, a public official can easily query the computer to check the status of almost anyone.

A public notification of a sex offender's residence

—*PHOTO BY JIM LOTT, COURTESY OF SEATTLE TIMES*

The most common form of local registration concerns sex-related offenses. The **sex offender file** is used to check out former offenders in the event of similar crimes. That kind of file is no doubt an asset to law enforcement, but it becomes a real problem for the ex-offender who is seriously trying to conform. Such inquiries are legitimate for law enforcement personnel; however, the discretion with which they are conducted can make a great difference to the ex-offender.

This problem was recently highlighted in the state of Washington, where legislation allows for community notification when a predatory sex criminal is about to be released and considered to be still dangerous under the state's Community Protection Act, passed and implemented in 1990. The release of Joseph Gallardo, a convicted sex offender, with police notification to the community under the act and the citizen anger it engendered, apparently resulted in the arson of the ex-offender's home and his being badgered out of the state and, subsequently, out of a second state. No matter how one might feel about the crimes committed by such offenders, it seems clear that the practices used to notify (and often enflame) communities will almost certainly end up being challenged in the Supreme Court before this kind of behavior is ultimately approved or banned. This is noted in a thoughtful and strong front-page article, presented here in its entirety with permission of the *Seattle Times*:

> A Lynnwood arson yesterday not only destroyed the home of a man labeled a sex offender but focused attention on the strengths and weaknesses of a unique state law.
>
> The law allowed police to broadcast the man's whereabouts and purported danger, leading to a large community meeting protesting Joseph Gallardo's release from prison. A few hours later, Gallardo's house was torched.
>
> In 1990 the [Washington] state Legislature passed the Community Protection Act in response to a spate of horrible sex crimes.
>
> The year before, Earl Shriner had raped, stabbed and sexually mutilated a Tacoma boy, 7, and left him for dead. The same year, Wesley Allen Dodd killed three boys in the Vancouver area for sexual gratification.
>
> The public wanted vengeance, and the Legislature gave it to them.
>
> The Community Protection Act requires sex offenders to register with sheriffs' offices when they are released from custody or treatment programs. The police have the option of notifying citizens about the offender's release and where he or she lives.
>
> Since 1990, 7,033 sex offenders have registered statewide. Most—1,657— are in King County, followed by Pierce County with 1,047, Snohomish County with 673 and Spokane County with 609.
>
> The police have not notified citizens about most of these offenders because there are too many and the majority are not considered violent.
>
> But when police have decided an offender warrants notification, the public response has often been more aggressive and violent than anticipated.
>
> John Curtis Peterson received death threats and was evicted from a Bothell mobile-home park after police alerted citizens to his release in 1990. The

thirty-one-year-old child rapist moved to Kitsap County but was forced to leave after citizens posted fliers with his photograph. He lost three jobs before he eventually moved from the state.

Tacoma residents also hounded two convicted sex offenders that year, picketing the home of 18-year-old Bobby Bonnell and hurling a rock through a window of Bill Aschenbrenner's home.

In Kent's Timberlane community, citizens shadowed a convicted rapist in 1991 by recording his movements on a computer and posting updates of his activities at a local market. Eggs were thrown at his grandparents' home, where he lived, and the family received death threats. In retrospect, some Timberlane residents now think they went overboard.

Joyce Owens, who was actively involved in the predator watch and who had threatened to use a gun on Travis Lee Sickle if he ever got near her grandchildren, recalled things got ugly. "I don't think it was handled properly," she said. "It seemed like a bunch of vigilantes. I'm not saying people shouldn't have been upset, but it should have been handled more appropriately. We should have discussed it thoroughly and decided on proper steps instead of going off half-cocked."

Police do not know how many offenders have faced such harassment, but they do acknowledge that treatment varies from county to county because the law allows agencies to set guidelines for notifying the public. In Kitsap County, for example, the police regularly provide local newspapers with a list of registered offenders. In contrast, the King County sheriff's department has only notified the public of about five offenders.

"The rule of thumb here—the person must have an extensive history, especially with strangers; no treatment; and a history of assaulting or raping other inmates," said King County Sheriff Casey Johnson.

The wide discrepancy between agencies has critics. "It's implemented very differently throughout the state so one's privacy depends on the county in which one lives," said John La Fond, a professor at the University of Puget Sound School of Law. La Fond also said the law generates hysteria, "which can in turn lead to an increased sense of insecurity and fear, and also cause citizens to take rash and illegal steps."

That sentiment is echoed by Jerry Sheehan, legislative director of the American Civil Liberties Union. "I don't see one whit of evidence of any additional community security created by this notification process," he said. "It only causes anxiety and fear, without any additional benefits to the community." Sheehan also argued that the law creates a false sense of security by focusing on strangers—when, in fact, most sex offenders are family members or acquaintances.

In Snohomish County, for example, only 4 percent of the 1,058 felonious sexual assaults were carried out by strangers. Most, 43 percent, were by teachers, coaches, and other acquaintances. Natural parents were the offenders 22 percent of the time, followed by other relatives, 15 percent, and stepparents, 9 percent, said Bill France, a child advocate in the Snohomish County Prosecutor's Office.

Yet the law is not likely to change. Although the Community Protection Act is pending review by the Washington State Supreme Court, the notification aspect of it has not been challenged. What is challenged is the portion of the act that allows the state to lock up violent offenders deemed likely to reoffend—even if they have served their prison sentence and haven't committed another crime.

Meanwhile, Governor Mike Lowry [yesterday] said he plans to work with the state Legislature to enact tougher penalties for sex offenders. "Frankly, sexual predators are [the most] dangerous people I can think of," Lowry told a standing-room-only crowd at the Everett Community College. "Yet no one knows how to treat them," he added.

Snohomish County Sheriff Jim Scharf took one of the audience microphones to address Lowry, who was holding a routine town meeting. In his opinion, Scarf said, convicted child molesters should be sentenced to life in prison without parole. "Lock 'em up and they'll never get out," Scharf said, winning cheers and applause from the crowd of more than 300. "It is a travesty in our society to let these people be free."

Several other speakers also implored Lowry to help keep neighborhoods safe for children. "We're not a group of vigilantes. We're a group of terrified parents," said Brian Levesque, of Lynnwood, who helped [Sunday's] rally against Gallardo. Outside the meeting, Levesque criticized Lowry for "talking a lot and saying very little."

The law is aimed at dangerous sexual offenders and, to lock them up indefinitely, they must be "predators" who prey on strangers. For that reason, police could not commit Gallardo. His rape victim was 10-year-old daughter of a friend, not a stranger, said Jim Townsend, Snohomish County's chief criminal deputy prosecutor. "The predator statute is very limited," he said. "I think the statute raised expectations that we'd be able to deal with these situations—but the system did as well as it could with this case."[26]

The practice of registering felons seems to be matter of interest again, mainly because of the mobility of our present American society, and is now in force in at least eight jurisdictions. The furor around the Washington state law will surely raise the issue to a level of prominence again. Registration may be much more subtle than the practice of branding with a scarlet letter,[27] but it also has the potential to become a permanent stigma. There is considerable room to improve on these tactics in an age of modern informational techniques.

EXPUNGEMENT AS A RESPONSE

It is clear that the debilitating effect of a criminal conviction is often heightened, rather than reduced, when the ex-offender returns to the free society. Some states have recognized that fact and attempted to develop **expungement** statutes, which erase the history of criminal conviction and completely restore the ex-offender's rights, thus removing the stigma of a criminal record. This idea was first developed in 1956, at the National Conference on Parole:

The expunging of a criminal record should be authorized on a discretionary basis. The court of disposition should be empowered to expunge the record

ANNULMENT
An annulment is a judicial proceeding that nullifies, abolishes, cancels, and abrogates a judgment or former judicial proceeding. An annulment results in a legal statement that the arrest and conviction never existed, and deprives the former judgment of all force currently or in the future.

of conviction and disposition through an order by which the individual shall be deemed not to have been convicted. Such action may be taken at the point of discharge from suspended sentence, probation, or the institution upon expiration of a term of commitment. When such action is taken the civil and political rights of the offender are restored.[28]

The American Law Institute also saw the need for some way to vacate a conviction record in selected cases. A section of the Institute's Model Penal Code was compiled in 1961, recommending the court use its authority to erase a record when an offender "has been discharged from probation or parole before the expiration of the maximum thereof" or "when the defendant has fully satisfied the sentence and has since led a law-abiding life for at least five years."[29]

These early recommendations of expungement did not specify procedures for the expungement order and did not go into great detail in identifying the real issues. The Model Act for Annulment proposed by the National Council on Crime and Delinquency, containing the comprehensive provisions for expungement quoted earlier, would give the ex-offender better protection than the Model Penal Code. But it remains too limited in its application and fails to recommend adequate procedures. Its effect on someone who is convicted is clear, as it takes effect only after conviction. But it does not help the individual who is arrested and not convicted. Any viable annulment statute must also permit erasure of an arrest record.

Over two decades ago, the American Bar Association Project on Standards for Criminal Justice made the following points regarding the need to remove the record stigma. Those statements are still valid, but general adoption of these points has been agonizingly slow:

> Every jurisdiction should have a method by which the collateral effects of a criminal record can be avoided or mitigated following the successful completion of a term on probation and during its service.

> The Advisory Committee is not as concerned with the form which such statutes take as it is with the principle that flexibility should be built into the system and that effective ways should be devised to mitigate the scarlet letter effect of a conviction once the offender has satisfactorily adjusted.[30]

Clearly, there is growing support for the principle that ex-offenders (especially those who have demonstrated they are in fact reformed) should be given a means of eliminating the brand of the felon. Though expungement is not the only answer to the problem of the burden and consequences of a criminal record, a sensible approach to the method is sorely needed.[31]

Restoring Offenders' Rights

Some states restore civil rights when parole is granted; others do so when the offender is released from parole. In still others, it is necessary for a governor to restore all rights, usually through a pardon. Pardons can be full or conditional; the former generally applies to both the punishment and the guilt of the offender, and blots out the existence of guilt in the eyes of the law. It also removes an offender's disabilities and restores civil rights. The conditional pardon usually falls short of the remedies available in the full pardon, is an expression of guilt, and does not obliterate the conviction but may restore civil rights.

The U.S. Supreme Court decisions on pardons and their effects are directly contradictory, and thus state laws usually govern pardons. While pardons are not frequent in the nation at this time, it is reasonable to expect they may become more frequent as prison overcrowding becomes more critical.

California's procedures for **pardon** illustrate the latter. What is required for a pardon in California?

California's procedures illustrate some of the steps required for a pardon. Generally, the offender must have led a crime-free existence for ten years following release from parole. The offender must initiate a petition for pardon in a superior court (also called a court of common pleas in other jurisdictions). A formal hearing is held, and the presiding judge solicits opinions from the local district attorney and chief law enforcement officer in the jurisdiction. A computer search is made for any arrests and convictions. The local probation department prepares a prepardon hearing report. If the preponderance of evidence is favorable and no arrest or conviction record is found, the petition is approved by the superior court and is forwarded to the governor's office. The governor may then order the equivalent of a parole board (Board of Prison Terms) to prepare an investigation that would contain a recommendation for pardon. If the report is favorable, the governor may pardon the petitioner, thereby restoring to him or her all of the rights and immunities of an ordinary citizen. It is evident that most ex-offenders, though no doubt preferring a pardon, may favor even more having the crime and conviction put as far behind them as possible. They may also not have the perseverance to endure such an involved and expensive procedure. Finally, statistics show that almost all ex-offenders are rearrested within the ten-year time period, even if there is no further action by criminal justice system officials. No wonder so few ex-offenders seek and receive pardons!

Clemency and the President

The U.S. Constitution (Article II, Section 2) authorizes the President to grant executive clemency for federal offenses. Petitions are received and reviewed by a pardons attorney who makes recommendations. Clemency may be a reprieve, revision of a fine or penalty, commutation of a sentence, or a full pardon. A pardon, which is generally considered only after the completion of a sentence, restores all basic civil rights and may aid in the restoration of professional credentials and licenses which were lost due to the conviction. A commutation is a significant reduction in the sentence. Outcomes for clemency applications are listed below for the years shown:

EXECUTIVE CLEMENCY GRANTED/DENIED

Year	Pardons	Commutation	Denied
1980	155	11	500
1985	32	3	279
1990	0	0	289
1994	0	0	785

SOURCE: K. Maguire and A. Pastore, *Sourcebook of Criminal Justice Statistics 1994* (Washington, D.C.: U.S. Department of Justice, 1995), p. 507.

President Richard M. Nixon was pardoned by his successor, President Gerald Ford

—PHOTO BY FABIAN BACHRACH, COURTESY OF FPG INTERNATIONAL

$\mathcal{S}$ummary

Laws that deprive ex-offenders of civil rights are vestiges from distant times and contradict both the principles of reintegration and the purposes of correction. It seems sensible and fair that all laws depriving ex-offenders of civil rights should be abolished until and unless it is proved the public's safety and protection require them. Doing so would advance the goals of corrections and reintegration and is more defensible than is the continuing disenfranchisement of currently law-abiding persons.

Many organizations contend that when convicted felons have paid their debt to society, they should have a chance to start over with a clean record. This belief has been translated into statutes that provide for the annulment and expungement of criminal records in a number of states, but many of them lack adequate mechanisms to implement the provisions. These efforts seem to get derailed today by extremely violent crimes, especially those involving predatory sex offenders, that have frightened the public and inflamed them to press for tougher measures to control those who return to society with this stigma. This group of ex-offenders is small, but has great impact on the public and the criminal justice system. The vast majority of ex-offenders (living today in almost every community in America) need to have a way to deal with the problems of never-ending stigma. Only when the general public has fully accepted the idea of a fresh start for the ex-offender will our legislators pass the revisions necessary to make the statutes fully effective.

Review Questions

1. What are the collateral consequences of a conviction? Discuss.

2. How could expungement improve the reintegration process for ex-offenders?

3. Why does registration of criminals have such a drastic effect on the ex-offender? What are the alternatives?

4. What will be the outcome of registration of predatory sex offenders? How do you feel about this practice?

Words to Remember

ex-con

collateral consequences

social stigma

self-esteem

employment restrictions

"vest-pocket" record

"yellow card"

sex offender file

expungement

pardon

Endnotes

1. Lawrence Greenfield estimated that two-thirds of offenders in state prisons for drug offenses were convicted for possession (up 107 percent over 1980). The other third were convicted of sales and manufacture, up 180 percent (1988 over 1980). See Lawrence Greenfield, *Prisoners in 1989* (Washington, D.C.: Bureau of Justice Statistics, 1990), p. 9.

2. Over four-fifths of state prison inmates were recidivists in 1986. See Christopher Innes, *Profile of State Prison Inmates, 1986* (Washington, D.C.: Bureau of Justice Statistics, 1988), p. 1.

3. Dennis Massey, *Doing Time in American Prisons: A Study of Modern Novels* (Westport, CT: Greenwood Press, 1989). See also Ken Smith, *Inside Time* (London: Herrap, 1989). Ken Smith's poetry (artist-in-residence at Wormwood Scruggs Prison in the United Kingdom) depicts the prison as a place of danger, tedium, and darkness.

4. R. H. Walkman, *Employment Services for Ex-Offenders Field Test: Summary Report* (Washington, D.C.: U.S. Department of Justice, 1985). Walkman's primary finding of interest was that employment decreased recidivism among ex-offenders. See also Michael Eisenberg, *Special Release and Supervision Programs: Two Year Outcome Study: Project Rio* (Austin: Texas Board of Pardons and Paroles, 1989). Project RIO resulted in a 5 percent reduction in recidivism and costs savings (program costs subtracted from avoided operating costs) of $14.5 million over two years. Chris Hale, Dima Sabbagh, David Cantor, et al., "Unemployment and Crime," *Journal of Research in Crime and Delinquency* 28:4 (1991): 397-429 (a special section devoted to unemployment and crime); E. Britt Patterson, "Poverty, Income Inequality, and Community Crime Rates," *Criminology* 29:4 (1991): 755-776 (shows strong association between poverty and certain kinds of crime); and Anthony J. Bossoni, *Post-Release Assistance Programs for Prisoners: A National Directory* (Jefferson, NC: McFarland, 1992), (a state-by-state listing of approximately twelve hundred agencies and assistance programs in the United States).

5. Georgetown University Law Center, *The Closed Door: The Effect of a Criminal Record on Employment with State and Local Public Agencies* (Springfield, VA: National Technical Information Service, 1972), p. v. See also Thomas J. Young, "Regional Differences in the Collateral Consequences of a Felony Conviction," *International Journal of Comparative and Applied Criminal Justice* 15:1 (1991): 121-124 (shows significant differences in regard to restricted rights for a felony conviction).

6. Harry Elmer Barnes and Negley K. Teeters, *New Horizons in Criminology* 3rd ed. (Englewood Cliffs, NJ: Prentice Hall, 1959), p. 544.

7. Michael Braswell, "Correctional Treatment and the Human Spirit: A Focus on Relationship," *Federal Probation* 53:2 (1989): 49-60. See also Michael T. French and Gary A.

Zarkin, "Effects of Drug Abuse Treatment on Legal and Illegal Earnings," *Contemporary Policy Issues* 10:2 (1992): 98-110 (compares the impact of length of time in drug treatment and post-treatment legal and illegal earnings).

8. Ann Yurkanin, "Meeting Offenders Halfway: An Interview with J. Brian Riley," *Corrections Today* 51:1 (April 1989): 16-20.

9. For a parallel discussion of fees in probation, see Christopher Baird, Douglas Holien, and Audrey Bakke, *Fees for Probation Services* (Madison, WI: National Council on Crime and Delinquency, 1986). See also Gordon Bazemore, "New Concepts and Alternate Practice in Community Supervision of Juvenile Offenders: Rediscovering Work Experience and Competency Development," *Journal of Crime and Justice* 14:1 (1991): 27-52. Also Walter T. Hessler, "The Released Prisoner and His Difficulties to Be Accepted Again as a 'Normal' Citizen," *Eurocriminology* 4 (Warsaw, Poland) (1992): 61-68 (illustrates that steps to reintegration of former prisoners is not unique to the United States).

10. Sol Rubin, "The Man with a Record: A Civil Rights Problem," *Federal Probation* 34:3(1971): 4.

11. Kathleen Dean Moore, *Pardons: Justice, Mercy, and the Public Interest* (New York: Oxford University Press, 1989).

12. Velmer Burton, Francis Cullen, and Lawrence Travis, "The Collateral Consequences of a Felony Conviction: A National Study of State Statutes," *Federal Probation* 51:3 (1987): 52-60.

13. American Law Institute, *Model Penal Code: Proposed Official Draft* (Philadelphia: American Law Institute, 1962), p. 43.

14. There is a potential liability in disclosing a parolee's background to a prospective employer if it results in the client not getting the job. See Rolando del Carmen and Eve Trook-White, *Liability Issues in Community Service Sanctions* (Washington, D.C.: U.S. Department of Justice, l986), pp. 19-21. See also David E. Barlow, Melissa Hickman Barlow, and Theodore G. Chicicos, "Long Economic Cycles and the Criminal Justice System," *Crime, Law, and Social Change* 19:2 (1993): 143-169 (examines the relationship between long cycles of capitalist activity and formation of public policy on criminal justice).

15. For a discouraging note on the impact of fiscal constraints on ex-offender programs, see Danesh Yousef, "Baton Rouge Ex-Offenders' Clearinghouse: A Casualty of Misguided Savings," *International Journal of Offender Therapy and Comparative Criminology* 33:3 (1989): 207-214. See also Ted Chiricos, "Unemployment and Punishment: An Empirical Assessment," *Criminology* 29:4 (1991): 701-724 (an attempt to explain the relationship between unemployment and imprisonment).

16. U.S. Bureau of Justice Statistics, *Public Access to Criminal History Record Information* (Washington, D.C.: U.S. Bureau of Justice Statistics, 1989).

17. Jeffrey Mark Jackson, *Effects of a Skills Training Intervention with Juvenile Delinquents* (Ann Arbor, MI: University Microfilm International, 1988).

18. See Reynoso's dissenting opinion in *Heatherington v. California*, 147 Cal. 300 (1978). Here, Judge Reynoso argued that ex-offenders should not be denied the right to work simply because of the prior felony conviction. (Judge Reynoso was recalled from the California Supreme Court in 1987 in part because of a conservative backlash against the chief justice of the time.) See also J. Robert Lilly and Paul Knepper, "The Corrections-Commercial Complex," *Crime & Delinquency* 39:2 (1993): 150-166, and their examination of a concept of subgovernment influence on correction policy.

19. National Alliance of Business, *Employment and Training of Ex-Offenders: A Community Approach* (Washington, D.C.: National Alliance of Business, 1983). See also William G. Saylor and Gerald G. Gaes, *PREP Study Links UNICOR Work Experience with Successful Post-Release Outcome* (Washington, D.C.: U.S. Bureau of Prisons, 1991). [initial findings from the PREP (Post-Release Employment Project), which show excellent results].

20. The National Council on Crime and Delinquency was founded in 1907 (685 Market Street, Suite 620, San Francisco, California 94105).

21. National Council on Crime and Delinquency, *Annulment of a Conviction of Crime, a Model Act* (Paramus, NJ, 1962). See also Bureau of Justice Statistics, *Criminal Justice Information Policy: Juvenile Records and Recordkeeping Systems* (Washington, D.C.: U.S. Bureau of Justice Statistics, 1988).

22. A vest-pocket record is an informal record that the court keeps unofficially and holds over the defendant for a set period of time.

23. "Excessive bail shall not be required, nor excessive fines imposed, nor cruel and unusual punishment inflicted."

24. Rubin, "The Man with a Record," pp. 6-7.

25. Most European countries have required residents to carry identification cards for population control purposes. A "yellow card" (identification card of yellow color) was, in many countries, a sign of an ex-offender.

26. Linda Keene, "Legal Dilemma: Rapist's Rights vs. Public's Right to Know," *Seattle Times*, July 13, 1993, p. 1. Reprinted with permission of the *Seattle Times*.

27. The scarlet letter was a scarlet "A" that the Puritans required known female adulterers to wear around the neck as a punitive mark. The practice is fully described in Nathaniel Hawthorne's novel *The Scarlet Letter*.

28. Georgetown University Law Center, *The Closed Door*, p. 58.

29. American Law Institute, *Model Penal Code: Proposed Official Draft*, p. 136.

30. Georgetown University Law Center, *The Closed Door*, p. 61.

31. For a discussion of executive clemency, including pardon, commutation of sentence, reprieve, remission of fines and forfeitures, restoration of rights, and amnesty, see Center for Policy Research and Analysis, *Guide to Executive Clemency Among American States* (Washington, D.C.: National Governors' Association, 1988).

Recommended Readings: Part V

Amnesty International, USA. *United States of America: The Death Penalty and Juvenile Offenders.* New York: Amnesty International, USA, 1991.

Bailey, William C. "Murder, Capital Punishment, and Television: Execution Publicity and Homicide Rates." *American Sociological Review* 55:5 (1990): 628-633.

Bilionis, Louis D. "Moral Appropriateness, Capital Punishment, and the Lockett Doctrine." *Criminal Law and Criminology* 82:2 (1991): 283-333.

Bowker, Arthur L., and Robert E. Schweid. "Habilitation of the Retarded Offender in Cayahoga County." *Federal Probation* 56:4 (1992): 48-52.

Burton, Velmer, Francis Cullen, and Lawrence Travis. "The Collateral Consequences of a Felony Conviction: A National Study of State Statutes." *Federal Probation* 51 (1987): 52-60.

Center for Policy Research and Analysis. *Guide to Executive Clemency Among American States.* Washington, D.C.: National Governors' Association, 1988.

Conley, Ronald W., Ruth Luckasson, and George N. Bouthilet, eds. *The Criminal Justice System and Mental Retardation: Defendants and Victims.* Baltimore: Brookes, 1992.

Drimmer, Frederick. *Until You Are Dead: The Book of Executions in America.* Secausas, NJ: Carol, 1990.

Eisenberg, Michael. *Special Release and Supervision Programs: Two Year Outcome Study: Project RIO.* Austin: Texas Board of Pardons and Paroles, 1989.

Freeman-Longo, Robert E. and Fay Honey Knopp. "State-of-the-Art Sex Offender Treatment: Outcomes and Issues." *Annals of Sex Research* 5:3 (1992): 141-160.

Haines, Herb. "Flawed Executions, the Anti-Death Penalty Movement, and the Politics of Capital Punishment." *Social Problems* 39:2 (1990): 125-138.

House, H. Wayne, and John Howard Yoder. *The Death Penalty Debate: Two Opposing Views of Capital Punishment.* Dallas: Word, 1991.

Innes, Christopher. *Profile of State Prison Inmates, 1986.* Washington, D.C.: Bureau of Justice Statistics, 1988.

Keil, Thomas J., and Gennnaro F. Vito. "Fear of Crime and the Attitudes Toward Capital Punishment: A Structured Equations Model." *Justice Quarterly* 8:4 (1991): 447-464.

Keil, Thomas J., and Gennnaro F. Vito. "The Effects of the *Furham* and *Gregg* Decisions on Black-White Execution Rates in the South." *Journal of Criminal Justice* 20:3 (1992): 217-226.

Mair, Katharine J. "The Nature of the Act: A Neglected Dimension in the Classification of Sex Offenders." *British Journal of Criminology* 33:2 (1993): 267-275.

National Advisory Commission on Criminal Justice Standards and Goals. *Corrections.* Washington, D.C.: U.S. Department of Justice, 1973.

National Institute of Corrections. *The Handicapped Offender.* Washington, D.C.: U.S. Department of Justice, 1982.

President's Commission on Law Enforcement and Administration of Justice. *Task Force Report: Challenge of Crime in a Free Society.* Washington, D.C.: U.S. Government Printing Office, 1967.

Rapaport, Elizabeth. "The Death Penalty and Gender Discrimination." *Law & Society Review* 25:2 (1991): 367-383.

Schabas, William A. "International Norms on Execution of the Insane and the Mentally Retarded." *Criminal Law Forum* 4:1 (1993): 95-117.

Smith, M. Dwayne, and James Wright. "Capital Punishment and Public Opinion in the Post-*Furham* Era: Trends and Analyses." *Sociological Spectrum* 12:2 (1992): 127-144.

U.S. Office of the Pardon Attorney. *Civil Disabilities of Criminal Felons: A State-by-State Survey (October 1992).* Washington, D.C.: U.S. Office of the Pardon Attorney, 1992.

Williams, Charles J. "The Federal Death Penalty for Drug-Related Killings." *Criminal Law Bulletin* 27:5 (1991): 387-415.

Corrections
as a Profession

CHAPTER TWENTY-TWO

Custody Functions *and* Tasks

Overview

The primary mission for any confinement facility, prison or jail, is to "protect the public." That prime directive sometimes has been, and is, carried to the extreme. Whether from fear, ignorance, apathy, or poor training, custody staff are defensive of their role and defensive of their tactics. Emotions in a high-security cell block can run high, with tensions spawning inappropriate behaviors on both sides of the bars. The custody staff are the front lines of corrections and deserve a lot of respect for what they do. If the entire staff of the institutions cannot work together, they will fail separately—with the prisoners as the winners in the long run.

The question that drives many of the attitudes of the custody staff is, "Why don't they let us just *control* these criminals?" The answer to that question is not easy to find and often wrong from both perspectives. When prisons and jails sometimes have only two or three persons on shift, or in a cell block for hundreds of prisoners, it is hard to remember things like courtesy and kindness to hardened criminals. That might not be politically correct, but it is reality on the midnight shift.

Custody came with the first tribe member who was asked to guard a thief until punishment was meted out. The long history of custody far outstrips the short time that "treatment" has been on the scene. The latter has only been on the correctional scene since the early 1930s in any organized fashion. The long-standing battles about custody and treatment started at the beginning and have continued, somewhat subdued, since that time. While outwardly the arguments seem to be over one or the other philosophy of corrections, they are more often seen in conflict over budgets, manpower, and turf. This part looks at the various organizational components of corrections to see what they do and how they might do it better. Custody comprises by far the largest part of that organization system, and we start with it.

> Our endeavors to control violence, in whatever setting, should be shared similarly by what we know about treating violent behavior. . . . Criminal behavior is learned behavior and ignoring its origin is wrong.
>
> —Joseph D. Lehman

Institutions: Bureaucratic Control

The prevailing management climate for corrections institutions is **bureaucratic control**, especially in state institutions. In most major correctional facilities, the inmate population is usually controlled by a combination of coercive rules that prohibit certain kinds of behavior and punishments that are meted out when the rules are broken. Bureaucratic organization is insulated by rules, and violations are punished in the name of equity.

In institutions that hold thousands of prisoners, each with personal problems, the bureaucratic style seems to be the only functional way to cope with control: the process takes precedence over the individual, and prisoners become faceless commodities to be housed, worked, fed, secured, and released. This nineteenth-century model stresses warehousing and processing offenders. Any rehabilitation is incidental, a welcome but low-priority by-product, because the bureaucratic style clearly conflicts with any emphasis on rehabilitation. The separate functions of the rigid and formalized organizations create an impoverished climate for behavioral change.[1]

Custody: A Twenty-Four-Hour Impact

Impacts on the behavior and attitudes of imprisoned persons are usually those that come from staff who have direct and continuous contact with them. Administrative and treatment staff have very limited interaction with inmates on a day-by-day basis. But custody staff are with them twenty-four hours a day. If the whole institutional staff is not working as a team, then months of discipline can fall by the wayside in one session. Conversely, months of professional counseling can be destroyed by a single custody officer's actions. The term **custody** refers to the level of immediate control exercised over offenders within correctional institutions. The levels can range from maximum, or close, to medium and minimum.

Maximum, or close, custody usually means the inmate cannot be trusted to move from one area to another, in the general prison or in the cell blocks, without being escorted by a correctional officer. It also implies that inmates will not be allowed "contact visits" or be allowed to associate with other prisoners freely or without supervision. They are also limited in their contacts with other persons in general. The ratio of correctional officers to inmates in most maximum or close areas is usually quite high, as many as one for every four inmates. (Death Row inmates are usually considered as close custody and therefore are very expensive to house, especially with their time from conviction to execution running over tens years on the average. See Chapter 19.)

Medium and minimum custody levels generally accommodate less risky or dangerous offenders or those closer to the end of their sentences. Generally speaking, the difference between medium and minimum is the presence of a high fence and armed guard towers surrounding the former, with reasonably free movement within the facility for both. The inmates classified as medium in an enclosed institution are allowed in what is referred to as "General Population." Staff-to-inmate ratios generally decrease, with one to eight or twelve not too uncommon. Inmates classified as minimum in a fenced or walled prison are often used on institutional jobs with very little supervision or observation (e.g., groundskeeping, sweeping, and cleanup). Minimum custody inmates are often placed in honor camps or farms with low levels of supervision, for some period of time prior to release. This is a system that can reimpose a higher level of security at any time. This is both a carrot and a stick, a reward for good behavior and a loss of privileges for misbehavior. Most custody staff see this as a control mechanism and a pathway to "graduated release." Generally speaking, administrators will err on the "side of the angels" and assign a higher level of custody when there is any doubt, especially until the inmate has gotten established in the institution.

Custody and control have traditionally been the warden's dominant concerns. Until very recently, the warden's principal adviser was almost always the chief of the guard force, depicted in the prison films of the 1930s to 1950s as "the Captain." The hard-nosed prison guard was the main instrument of control, the stereotyped **screw** (often farmers working in the off-season at a rural institution, with little compassion and a heavy hand), earlier guards did not give priority to rehabilitation. Even though much better trained and educated **correctional officers** have now replaced the old-time guards in almost all prisons, many institutions still follow the same oppressive custodial procedures, especially in times of unrest. Until the cause-and-effect relationship between autocratic organizational styles and institutional disturbance is openly acknowledged, the advocates of rigid custodial control will retain their influential role.

Since the average length of tenure for chief administrators of our jail and prison systems is less than three years and custody staff remain much longer—usually a career of twenty to thirty years, it seems that some better way to manage custody and control still needs to be found.[2]

*C*orrectional Officers and Jailers: On the Front Lines

Although custody staff have been called "guards," "jailers," "prison guards," "turnkeys," "screws," "hacks," "detention officers," "correctional officers," or "security staff," for purposes of this text we choose to use the term correctional officer. Whatever the title used, it refers to those women and men charged with control, movement management, and observation of the inmates in the jails and prisons of America. There were over 237,006 line-level custody staff working in our state, federal, and local adult prisons in America, of which only 15.6 percent were supervisory.[3] Also, there are 117,900 line officers in jails and local detention facilities in midyear 1993, which represented 71.3 percent of the total staffing.[4] The proportion of female officers in the prison systems was about 18 percent[5] and almost 25 percent in local jails and detention facilities.[6] About 30 percent of correctional officers were classified as nonwhite in prisons[7] and about the same ratio of nonwhites for local jails and detention facilities.[8] (See Figure 22-1.)

Relatively little research has been conducted about American correctional officers who are not supervisory staff. That is further compounded by the relatively high average turnover rates among correctional officers, now averaging almost 12 percent (see Figure 22-2), down but still high. The average turnover in various state systems ranges runs from about 5 percent to over 50 percent.[9] Much remains to be learned about why some people are attracted to institutional custody work, how long they remain employed, their salaries, and why they choose to leave. Those questions are important because correctional officers, who spend

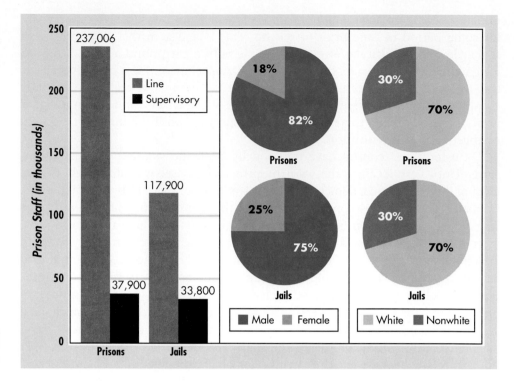

Staffing of Prisons
and Jails, 1994

SOURCE: ACA. *1996 Directory: Juvenile and Adult
Correctional Departments, Institutions, Agencies &
Paroling Authorities* (ACA, Lanham, Maryland,
1996), p. xxiv.

more time with inmates than anyone, form the backbone of institutional efforts to
secure, control, and rehabilitate those offenders sent to the correctional institutions of America. Also needed are more extensive studies of prison wardens and
superintendents.[10]

Administration's Problem: Punish, Control, or Rehabilitate?

The lack of coordination and articulated inter- and intrasystems outlined in the
previous chapters suggests some of the reasons correctional administrators are
often harried and hampered in their efforts to secure, control, and correct inmates.
Although the public is willing to espouse reformatory goals for corrections, it is

F I G U R E

22.2

Agency Average Turnover
Rate for Correctional
Officers, 1990–1994

SOURCE: C. Camp and G. Camp, *The Corrections
Yearbook 1995: Adult Corrections* (South Salem,
NY: Criminal Justice Institute, 1995), p. 77.

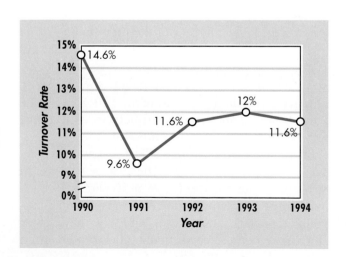

not willing to provide the support and funding that would make such reform a legislative priority. That inconsistency places dedicated correctional administrators in an awkward position: they can implement only the most meager of programs, and even then they must maintain an overall emphasis on control and punishment. Regardless of the approach to the problem, some aspect of operations will suffer.[11] If required to increase the number of security guards, the administrator must obtain the necessary funds by decreasing the support for some treatment program. And if the administrator tries to amplify the treatment programs, it must usually be done at the expense of the custody staff.

Unionization and the Correctional Officer

Unionization, found in almost every sector of business and industry, has in recent decades spread to the ranks of state and federal employees. The union movement has extended to the "sworn" officers charged with the police, fire, and correctional protection of the public. Police officers and firefighters have established collective bargaining agencies in most urban departments, with improved working conditions and better pay as a result. Prohibited in many states by law from going on strike to back up their demands, however, law enforcement and fire protection officers have used a unique strategy involving massive outbreaks of **blue flu** to emphasize their plight. In the correctional field, the union movement has taken root more slowly.

Because many jurisdictions forbid government employees from striking, other tactics are employed to create power negotiation in collective bargaining. Correctional officers have also resorted to "blue flu," the practice of uniformed personnel's taking sick leave en masse to back up their demands for improved working conditions, salary increments, and other items on their agenda. This method permits negotiating leverage without forcing the employees to strike, an illegal act.

As agents of public protection became more successful in their demands, their counterparts in the correctional institutions took notice. The great move in the late 1960s toward more professionalism and the sharp increases in prisoner populations, community corrections, and other programs pointed up some of the needs of the long-neglected correctional officer. Initial efforts to organize met with disapproval from administrators, often because of limited budgets and already overtaxed security forces in the crowded prisons. Most administrators wanted the few available funds to be used for new personnel, not pay raises for the officers they already had. In some cases the correctional officers did go on strike, and their duties were assumed by administrative and office personnel.[12]

Because correctional institutions tend to be widely scattered, especially local jails and juvenile facilities, the growth of the union movement has been slow and fragmented. In addition, as we have suggested, the goals of the collective bargaining agencies sometimes do not correspond to the administration's rehabilitation goals. Organization and collective action have brought many benefits to correctional officers so far, but they will get little sympathy from the administrators and the public until they show concern for the overall mission of the institution as well as their personal needs.

Earl Warren (1891–1974) was the Chief Justice of the United States Supreme Court for sixteen years (1953–1969) and became famous as a liberal leader in cases involving civil rights. One of his first major decisions was the landmark case in civil rights, *Brown v. Board of Education* in Topeka, Kansas, which put an end to segregated schools. Chief Justice Warren's Court presided over many landmark decisions in the field of criminal justice, such as *Gideon v. Wainwright, Miranda v. Arizona,* and *Mapp v. Ohio.*

Inmate Organization: The Social System

Prisons are total institutions[13] in which the resident's every activity, moment, movement, and option are carefully regulated by the correctional staff. Inmates are given little individual responsibility and autonomy, important characteristics of everyday life in a modern achievement-oriented society. The tight regime compounds their personal inadequacies rather than correcting them. Cut off from ordinary social intercourse and their families and friends, then isolated in bastionlike prisons, inmates are quickly taught by the other residents how to exist in that environment. As we described earlier, the process of learning how to exist in prison—learning appropriate attitudes and behaviors, the norms of prison life—is called prisonization. This process leads to the adoption of the folkways, mores, customs, and general culture of the prison's inmates.[14]

Prisonization can be imported into prisons by former inmates. It also occurs spontaneously even in newly opened institutions: the process is handed down from prisoner to prisoner, remaining a strong force that is later transmitted between prisons, working against the rehabilitation goals of even the most enlightened administrator. It impedes rather than facilitates treatment efforts, preventing inmates from acquiring the skills, talents, attitudes, and behavior necessary for successful adjustment in free society.

Indeed, the opposite tends to occur: Inmates are infantilized[15] rather than matured. That situation led the President's Commission on Law Enforcement and Administration of Justice to note that "the conditions in which [inmates] live are the poorest possible preparation for their reentry into society, and often merely reinforce in them a pattern of manipulation and destructiveness."[16] The other development results from the abolition of parole in many jurisdictions as a mechanism for the early release of rehabilitated prisoners and those who have benefited from their terms of imprisonment. In this case, motivating inmates to participate in institutional programs has suffered, rehabilitation programs have been less effective, and considerable tension has been created between inmates and correctional staff.[17]

As part of the process of prisonization, inmates learn codes and roles, and they are subjected to a reward and punishment system that encourages them to act appropriately. Prison codes emphasize a number of specific behaviors: loyalty to other inmates ("never rat on a con"); maintenance of calm ("keep cool"; "don't start feuds"); avoidance of trickery or fraud ("always share with your cellmates"; "sell hoarded goods at the going rate"); manliness ("don't complain"); and quick-wittedness in prison dealings ("don't be a sucker"; "guards are screws, never to be confided in or trusted").

Inmates who conform to these expectations become real men who can be trusted and are looked up to by other inmates. They share in the privileges available in prisons, and they can count on support if another inmate attacks them physically. Those who violate the normative structure become outcasts and are referred to by various descriptive and unpleasant names (e.g., "rat," "snitch," "fag," "merchant," "fink," "punk").

Two recent developments in America's jails and prisons have exacerbated those problems. The first is the rise of gangs in prisons. Most of these gangs are based on street gang origins and are racial and ethnic in nature, grouping together for power and protection. There are four major gangs in California's prisons, for

Profiles of Texas: Seven Major Gangs

Texas prisons contend with seven major gangs. Each insists on a lifetime commitment; once committed to one of these organizations, death is the only way out. Each prison gang is highly structured and operates under a specific "constitution" or set of rules. What follows is a brief description of these gangs and their histories.

TEXAS SYNDICATE

The Texas Syndicate began in the California Department of Corrections in the mid-1970s. It is mostly comprised of Hispanic inmates who migrated to California from Texas, although a few white inmates have been accepted. Through violent acts, the gang made a reputation for itself as a group to be feared and respected among general population inmates.

On release from the California Department of Corrections, gang members returned to Texas and continued their illegal activities. Many were subsequently incarcerated in Texas. Since arriving in our agency, the gang has been suspected of involvement in more than forty-eight inmate homicides and numerous other nonfatal assaults on staff and inmates.

The Texas Syndicate is structured along paramilitary lines and has a set of strictly enforced rules: violations may result in death. The group's members are known to have been incarcerated in California, New Mexico, Arizona, Florida, Illinois, and the Federal Bureau of Prisons.

MEXIKANEMI

Mexikanemi, or MM, is the largest and fastest-growing prison gang in the Texas Department of Criminal Justice (TDCJ). Mexikanemi is an Aztec term for "free or liberated Mexican." The group originated in Texas prisons in the early 1980s. It initially started as a group of inmates interested in their cultural background, but it rapidly transformed into a prison gang involved in extortion, narcotic trafficking, and assaults on inmates and staff.

The gang is structured along hierarchical lines, with a president (its founder), a vice president, and three generals, each of whom is responsible for a specific region in the state. Generals can appoint members under them to run activities in specific facilities.

The gang's constitution states that "in being a criminal organization, we will function in any aspects or criminal interest for the benefit or advancement of the gang. We will traffic in drugs, contracts of assassinations, prostitution, robbery of high magnitude and anything we can imagine."

ARYAN BROTHERHOOD OF TEXAS

This group, comprised of white racist inmates, originated in the TDCJ in the early 1980s and should not be mistaken with other groups with similar names found across the country.

The Aryan Brotherhood of Texas has been involved in assaults and murders of inmates in our agency and also conspired to have a state judge assassinated. Operating under a structure resembling a steering committee or a commission, this group has extended its illegal activities to the outside.

TEXAS MAFIA

The Texas Mafia is mostly comprised of white inmates, but a few Hispanics have been accepted. The gang has an extensive background in narcotics; many of its members are involved in producing crystal methedrine and have ties with motorcycle gangs. The group is very violent and has been involved in inmate homicides and staff assaults. It has a close working relationship with the Texas Syndicate.

NUESTRO CARNALES

This group has fewer than one hundred members. However, they have established a reputation for violence by being involved in several inmate assaults, including one homicide. Formed along a hierarchy structure with one recognized leader, this group is attempting to gain a foothold in the community as well as maintaining its status inside the prison walls. This gang appears to have strong ties with the Texas Syndicate.

HERMANOS DE PISTOLEROS LATINOS

Composed of 174 members within TDCJ, this group has posed security problems for the agency by being involved in numerous illegal activities, including inmate assaults and inmate homicides. An additional 104 members have been released to the community and will have an impact for outside law enforcement agencies. This group appears to have ties with the Texas Syndicate and has been known to discuss joint illegal activities with that group.

RAZA UNIDA

This group is the most recent to be identified as a disruptive group with TDCJ. With a membership of only sixty-four inmates, this group has yet to achieve the status and respect afforded the other prison gangs by the inmate population. However, they are rapidly gaining notoriety due to their recent assaults on inmates at various facilities within the agency. Classification of inmates from one specific region has assisted the group in forming and evolving into a prison gang. ∎

SOURCE: Salvador Buentello. "Texas Turnaround: New Strategies Combat State's Prison Gangs."*Corrections Today* 54:5, May 1992, p. 59.

example, two Chicano gangs (ghetto Chicanos or "Nostra Familia" and the Mexican Mafia or "EME"); the Black Brotherhood (often based on gang affiliation such as "Crips" or "Bloods"); and the Aryan Brotherhood (includes most bikers, white supremacists, and others like the Skinheads). Gangs with many variations on these themes are found in jails and prisons nationwide (see the accompanying box for an example from Texas). Conflicts between the gangs have led to stabbings, murder outside prison, rape, blackmail, and exploitation of nonaligned prisoners. All prison gangs are organized strictly to take part in only antisocial and criminal behavior. Many administrators have ordered **lockdowns** that confine prisoners to their cells in order to avoid bloodshed and violence, leading to criticism from legislators and other staff.[18] Jail and prison overcrowding has made matters worse, and many an administrator has resigned because of a sense of hopelessness.

We stress again that the importance of prisonization lies in its negative impact on attempts to provide rehabilitative programs which encourage inmates to engage in legitimate noncriminal activities.

Custody as a Way of Life

The "assistant superintendent for custody" or "security programs," also known as the "deputy warden for custody," or the "captain of custody" in jails, is one of the most important figures in any correctional facility. His or her main responsibility is to develop ways of accounting for the whereabouts of all prisoners at all times. Techniques have become more humane and permissive in recent years, but in most institutions the count is still the principal method of determining the prisoners' whereabouts, and counts are sometimes conducted as often as every two hours. Preoccupation with counting and recounting prisoners makes it difficult to conduct meaningful programs or permit individualized operations. To some extent, however, outside work details and opportunities for educational and vocational training and furloughs have been included in more streamlined counting methods. Today, counts are often called in to a central office in the prison's control room and tabulated against the daily tally of inmates, in some cases using barcoded wristbands, access cards with magnetic data stripes, and computers.[19]

Security involves much more than just inmate control in a major correctional institution

—COURTESY OF GEORGIA DEPARTMENT OF CORRECTIONS

Although the count is more sensibly administered, it still remains the most important task for which the custody staff is responsible.

Another function of the custody staff is to establish and maintain security procedures. Security procedures, at a minimum, include the inspection of persons and vehicles passing in and out of the institution, usually at a sally port at entry and exit points. The sally port is an area enclosed by a double gate. A vehicle or individual enters through the first gate, which is then closed. Before the second gate is opened, the search for forbidden articles (contraband) is made. After the search is completed, the second gate is opened and the individual or vehicle passes through that gate. At no time may both gates be open, and many gate systems are mechanically adjusted so it is impossible to open them both at the same time. Sometimes a visitor feels it is as hard to get into the institution as it is to get out. The fear that inmates and visitors will try to smuggle in contraband or other items to assist escape pervades the maximum security prison. Searches of vehicles and the requiring of visitors to pass through electronic metal detectors have become standard practices and procedures at major institutions.

Unfortunately, under the assumption that all inmates are alike, similar security practices have also been adopted by medium and minimum security prisons. It took over a century before America was prepared to build a prison without massive walls; it may take even longer to convince old-guard custody personnel that less stringent security measures may serve as well to ensure control.[20]

DISCIPLINE AND INMATE TRAFFIC CONTROL

Rules and regulations for inmates are usually aimed at strict traffic control. Prisoners' movements are carefully planned and controlled in every detail. In the past, all prisoners were awakened, moved to work, and fed at the same time, always under the eye of custody personnel. That degree of planning has slackened in many institutions: the trend is toward more reasonable controls over inmate traffic within the walls.

The suggestion that, when inmates are treated as if they are dangerous they will become dangerous, is generally considered valid. One way to avoid that problem is for staff and inmates to maintain meaningful communications. If the custody staff loses contact with inmates, the latter only responds to the inmate subculture. All too often, such limited interaction results in violence among the inmates. The most effective controls over inmate traffic and movement may well be those that guide our behavior in the free community.

The most recently available report on prison rule violators analyzed the characteristics of state prison inmates charged with infractions of institutional rules. Despite an increase of 64 percent in state prison populations from the previous study conducted ten years earlier, some 54 percent of prisoners had infractions charged to them in both studies. A summary of the data is reported in Tables 22-1 and 22-2. Other important aspects of this study are as follows:

- Younger inmates and those with more extensive criminal careers or drug histories were the most likely to have violated **prison rules**.

- Inmates housed in larger prisons or maximum security prisons have higher percentages of rule violations than do prisoners in other types of facilities.

- More than 90 percent of the inmates charged with violating prison rules were found guilty in prison administrative proceedings.

- The 90 percent and above rate of guilty decisions occurred for different racial/ethnic, age, and sex categories and did not vary by size or security level of the prison.

- Inmates serving their first sentence to prison had a lower average annual rate of infraction (1.0) than did recidivists (1.6), regardless of how long they had served on their current sentence. A higher percentage of male inmates (53 percent) than female inmates (47 percent) were charged with rule breaking. On an average annual basis, however, women had a higher prison infraction rate than men (2.0 average violations per year versus 1.4 for men).

- Inmates who used drugs prior to admission were more likely to violate prison rules than were nonusers of drugs, 57 percent compared to 37 percent.

TABLE 22.1

State Prison Inmates Charged with Violating Prison Rules During Their Current Sentence, by Drug-Use History, 1994

Characteristic	Percentage of Inmates Charged with Violating Prison Rules During Current Sentence	Percentage of Charged Inmates Found Guilty
All inmates	52.7	94.0
Ever used drugs		
No	37.3	92.5
Yes	63.7	94.2
Ever used drugs regularly		
No	43.0	92.4
Yes	57.5	94.7
Used drugs in month before admission offense		
No	43.4	92.6
Yes, less than once a week	58.2	92.7
Yes, at least once a week	55.2	95.3
Yes, daily or almost daily	61.3	94.9
Under drug influence at time of admission offense		
No	40.1	93.2
Yes	59.9	95.3

SOURCE: James Stephan, *Prison Rule Violators* (Washington, D.C.: U.S. Government Printing Office, December 1989), p. 4.

TABLE 22.2

Average Number of Prison Rule Violations per Inmate per Year, by Admission Offense, 1989

Admission Offense	Average Annual Number of Infractions per Inmate
All inmates	1.5
Violent offenses	1.4
Murder	0.9
Manslaughter	0.8
Rape/sexual assault	1.1
Robbery	1.9
Assault	1.5
Kidnapping	1.1
Property offenses	1.8
Burglary	2.0
Arson	1.2
Motor vehicle theft	2.3
Fraud	1.0
Larceny	1.5
Stolen property	2.0
Drug offenses	0.9
Possession	0.9
Trafficking	0.9
Public-order offenses	1.1
Weapons	1.1
Other public-order	1.1

SOURCE: James Stephan, *Prison Rule Violators* (Washington, D.C.: U.S. Government Printing Office, December 1989), p. 4.

- Whites and blacks committed infractions at the same rate—approximately 1.5 violations per inmate per year. White and black rule violators reported nearly identical distributions of punishments received for rule violations. The most common penalties were solitary confinement or segregation and loss of good-time credit.[21]

More recent studies of rule violation behaviors found that the pattern and types of misconduct were the same for males and females in a state prison, although levels of infractions were lower for women. Younger prisoners began their "misconduct careers" sooner.[22]

A second study focused on major and minor ("serious" and "regular") infractions in a medium security prison and found the ratio to be about one to three, respectively. Minor infractions include such activities as theft of food, horseplay, lying, and use of abusive language to a correctional officer. More serious offenses include homicide, assault, possession of a weapon, and threatening to set a fire. The average processing cost of an infraction is estimated to be about $970 for each infraction charged resulting in a finding of guilty.[23]

The figures tend to show that the problems with inmate infractions do not seem to have increased any faster than the growing population and that disciplinary actions may deter many other rule infractions.

Traffic control is but one aspect of the rules designed to regulate inmate behavior. The same factors that apply to discipline in any situation apply to discipline in jails and prisons:

> Despite the most sincere, intelligent, and painstaking efforts by capable officers to maintain good discipline, disciplinary problems will arise in any jail (corrections institution). If there are group problems such as racial conflicts, strikes, disturbances or riots, they must be dealt with firmly and without hesitation.
>
> The capable and experienced jail [corrections] officer can stop most outbreaks before they get started by constantly analyzing and correcting conditions that cause bitterness and unrest, and by spotting and segregating inmate ringleaders and agitators who are fomenting trouble.
>
> The word discipline is not intended here to suggest negative or punitive action. Rather, it means close supervision of inmates with an understanding of their problems and frustrations, backed up by thorough knowledge of inmates' personalities, potentialities, and characters.[24]

Some of the archaic rules employed at many correctional institutions and jails may have been necessitated by the earlier widespread use of poorly educated and untrained rural personnel as "prison guards." Many of those individuals were already instilled with the idea of the "convict bogey" before undertaking correctional work, a situation that precluded meaningful interaction with inmates, even those with rehabilitation potential. The gap between the cultural backgrounds of basically urban prisoners and rural guards was often filled by unnecessarily severe discipline. Correctional administrators must acknowledge the problems with such cultural differences in order to best utilize the personnel they are able to attract.

While most jurisdictions are now able to offer more reasonable salaries, corrections is still perceived by many as a low-prestige and transitory occupation. "I'll just work here until things get better and I can get a real job" is often the attitude. Unfortunately, administrators have had a difficult time convincing their untrained or unmotivated officers that more progressive correctional methods could be much more effective. The administrators, therefore, are left with a staff clearly in a warehousing role.

It should be noted, however, that most correctional officers are dedicated and humane persons, and maximizing their potential is an important challenge to concerned administrators. The situation with regard to educating those officers is improving. Most states now offer extensive preservice training to ensure a minimal level of competence in the officers before they are placed on the job. This basic course ranges from 40 to 640 hours of preservice training. In-service training is generally 40 hours annually, but many states provide 80 hours.[25] As this trend continues, salaries, the quality of personnel, and working conditions will improve. The tendency to use outdated and counterproductive forms of discipline should decrease accordingly, and the correctional officer, long recognized as the single most important agent for change in institutions, will be able to realize his or her[26] potential contribution to the rehabilitation approach. This can best be done by meeting correctional training standards, as shown by Table 22-3.

CONTRABAND AND SHAKEDOWNS

In early years of corrections in America's jails and prisons, contraband was officially defined as any item that could be used to break an institution's rule or to assist in escape. In practice, the term usually ended up referring to anything the

TABLE *22.3*

Training Requirements for New Correctional Officers* 1994

	Pre-Service	In-Service		Pre-Service	In-Service
Alabama	400	40	Nebraska	160	40
Alaska	240	40	Nevada	160	24
Arizona	288	24	New Hampshire	240	40
Arkansas	240	40	New Jersey	400	NA
California	240	40	New Mexico	280	40
Colorado	144	40	New York	283	40
Connecticut	471	181	North Carolina	160	18
Delaware	240	40	North Dakota	120	40
Dist. of Col.	240	80	Ohio	280	40
Florida	411	40	Oklahoma	240	40
Georgia	160	40	Oregon	200	40
Hawaii	340	40	Pennsylvania	160	40
Idaho	320	40	Rhode Island	320	40
Illinois	240	40	South Carolina	270	40
Indiana	120	40	South Dakota	140	40
Iowa	144	40	Tennessee	120	40
Kansas	200	80	Texas	120	40
Kentucky	120	40	Utah	440	40
Louisiana	120	40	Vermont	40	40
Maine	70	4	Virginia	160	24
Maryland	228	18	Washington	160	30
Massachusetts	160	40	West Virginia	120	40
Michigan	640	40	Wisconsin	280	80
Minnesota	280	40	Wyoming	120	80
Mississippi	160	40	Federal	160	40
Missouri	160	43			
Montana	120	40	**Average**	**224**	**43**

*New correctional officers must complete an average of 224 hours of training. Annually thereafter, an average of 43 hours of training is required.

SOURCE: C. Camp and G. Camp, *The Correcting Yearbook 1995: Adult Corrections* (South Salem, NY: Criminal Justice Institute, 1995), p. 85.

custody staff designated as undesirable for possession by the inmates. Such banning power is unrestricted. It can start with a particular object, such as a knife, and extend to anything that might conceivably be made into a knife—a policy that has placed some relatively innocuous items on contraband lists. The following definition illustrates the extensive power held by correctional officers.

Any item that is not issued or not authorized in the jail is contraband. Control of contraband is necessary for several reasons:

1. To control the introduction of articles that can be used for trading and gambling
2. To control the collecting of junk and the accumulation of items that make housekeeping difficult
3. To identify medications and drugs and items that can be used as weapons and escape implements

Controlling contraband requires a clear understanding of what contraband is, of regulations that are designed to limit its entry into the jail, and of effective search procedures. The definition of contraband just given is simple and clear. However, this definition can become useless if the jail attempts to supplement it with a long list of approved items. If the jail permits prisoners to have packages, the problem of contraband control will be made difficult, since the list of authorized items may grow long.[27]

What appears to be a relatively simple definition is often then complicated by long lists of approved and forbidden items. Overdefinition can result only in a bureaucratic nightmare for correctional officers who must continuously search for contraband. A broad and clear definition, followed by the use of common sense by trained correctional officers, will usually result in better control and less conflict over what is or is not contraband. An excessively long contraband list is often seen as a challenge to the inmate and an indication of suppression by prison administrators.

Such items as guns, however, are clearly dangerous contraband, and prison administrators must continually check packages, visitors, and correctional officers to detect such material. This is usually accomplished using modern metal-detecting and X-ray equipment.

The generally accepted way of defining contraband in the 1990s is to use the affirmative approach. For example, "contraband is any item, or quantity of an item, that is not specifically authorized by the institution rules." This clearly defines what is not contraband and leaves the decision as to what is contraband to the inmate. Contraband is more often found to be the acquisition of excess items that are authorized, rather than those items that are dangerous per se (e.g., extra blankets, extra books, hoarded food). Contraband in this sense is seen as power to the inmate, plus a way to beat the system and show fellow inmates that the forbidden can be done. That power is used to trade favors or show favoritism to more powerful inmates. Contraband is often used as currency (cigarettes and matches, for example), just as we use barter on the outside.

Because the loss of contraband is the loss of power, searches and shakedowns are another source of potential conflict with inmates in security institutions. The most common type of search to prevent contraband entry into and movement within institutions is the **frisk search.** This type of search is used whenever prisoners enter or leave the institution and when institutional personnel suspect a prisoner may be hiding contraband on his or her person. Figure 22-3 shows the proper procedures for a frisk.

When it is suspected that a prisoner has had access to drugs, weapons, or other items that can be secreted on the body or in a body cavity, and a frisk reveals nothing, a strip search may be conducted. The strip search is ordinarily made in a location where the prisoner will not be observed by other inmates and subjected to ridicule. The basic strip search requires only the visual observation of the entire body and orifices. If a more extensive body cavity search is merited, it must be conducted with the knowledge and permission of the chief administrator of the facility (superintendent, sheriff, etc.). A body cavity search must be conducted by qualified medical personnel. Failure to follow those procedures can result in serious lawsuits against the institution.

Plastic capsules or vials inserted in the inmate's rectum are one way to hide ("**keester**" or "keestering") drugs and other small items of contraband, and so when there is probable cause, body cavities may need to be examined. The strip search frequently follows visits, either for every inmate or on a random sample

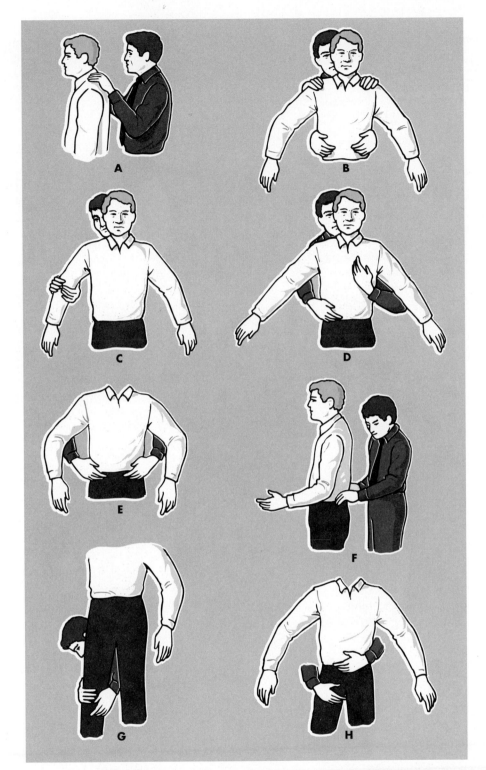

FIGURE

22.3

The Frisk Search

SOURCE: Nick Pappas, *The Jail: Its Operation and Management* (Lompac, CA: Federal Prison Industries, 1971), p. 23.

basis. In the past, frequent strips were used to debase and abuse prisoners, a practice that greatly increased prison tension and resulted in many legal actions against offending staff. Frisks are a necessary part of institutional security, but if strip searches are made an everyday routine, the procedure soon degrades not only the searched but the searcher as well.

As rules prohibiting contraband grow more detailed, inmates seek ways to secrete those items in the living area and throughout the institution. There is

California Electrified Fences: A New Concept in Prison Security

The move to replace continuously staffed guard towers with lethal electrified perimeter fences could very well become a national trend because of state governments' urgent need to reduce operating costs.

In November 1993, the California Department of Corrections (DOC) activated an electrified fence model at Calipatria State Prison in Imperial County. Since then, another 23 have been installed, one is under construction, and more new prisons with electrified fences are being planned. Electrified fences have been installed at adult facilities for men and women throughout California's agricultural areas, foothills, deserts, coastal and urban areas, and a few at higher elevations.

At most of the facilities included in the California Statewide Electrified Fence Project, traditional perimeter guard towers are spaced at distances that allow correctional officers to use deadly force to prevent escapes. At newer facilities, as many as 109 towers (or 48.3 staff positions over three watches) can be deactivated. Using lethal fences greatly reduces the need for tower staff.

BASIC DESIGN

The electrified fence is installed between two parallel, chain-link perimeter security fences. It consists of 15 to 18 stainless-steel stranded wires, horizontally oriented and installed on insulators attached to metal fence posts. The wires are spaced at various intervals; they are close together (eight inches) at the lower portion of the fence and gradually increase in spacing toward the upper portion (13 inches). The top wire is one foot higher than the two perimeter security fences. A concrete-grade beam elevates the bottom wire to approximately 13 inches above the finish grade and prohibits anyone from crawling under the fence.

Circular, stainless-steel detection rings, attached to the lower electrified fence wires, trigger an alarm if the wires are spread vertically and come in contact with an adjacent ring/wire.

The electrified wires are charged with more than 5,000 volts and very low amperage many times the dosage normally considered lethal. Specifically designed control cabinets step up the voltage from 480 volts. Sensor cabinets monitor current flow and loss of voltage, and detect when someone or something touches the fence. The electrified fence carries only an appreciable current flow (i.e., amperage) when an object contacts the wires; therefore, operation of the fence requires minimal electrical power consumption.

The electrified fence typically is divided into four to six separate zones for location monitoring and emergency response. Because the cost of the fence increases as the length of the perimeter and the number of zones increase, a facility with a perimeter of 7,000 feet typically would be divided into four electrified fence zones.

Graphic alarm annunciation panels are located in the continuously staffed sally port guard tower and the central control room. Panels display alarm status by zones and indicate high temperatures, open doors on control cabinets, and other operational conditions. Information is transmitted to outside patrol vehicles and watch commanders.

A computer system logs alarm and fence status information to generate various status and historical reports. The reports serve as valuable aids in forecasting maintenance, troubleshooting and tracking operating status. Reports can be printed out chronologically, by zone or by type of alarm.

California DOC's safety features for the electrified fence include:

- at least 10 feet of space between the electrified fence and the exterior perimeter security fence;
- security glazing panels to eliminate accidental contact at sally ports where the electrified fence terminates;
- interlock panels that de-energize power, ground the high voltage fence wires, and verify that the fence has been deactivated before maintenance or emergency response crews go between perimeter fences;
- high voltage test meters used for maintenance or emergency response personnel to provide an additional independent check that the fence has been deactivated prior to staff entry between perimeter fences;
- graphic warning signs on the inner and outer perimeter security fences in English and Spanish; and
- annual safety and operations training for security and maintenance personnel.

CONCLUSION

California's program has greatly reduced the need for tower staff, saving the state an average of $1.5 million a year per "electrified" prison. "The electrified fence clearly is meeting our goal of providing cost-effective perimeter security," Carruth says. "A final resolution to the environmental problem will make the program a complete success." ■

SOURCE: Brian Hoffmann, Gary Straughn, Jack Richardson, and Allen Randall, "California Electrified Fences: A New Concept in Prison Security," *Corrections Today* 58:4 (1996): pp. 66–68.

virtually no limitation to the ingenuity employed in hiding contraband in prisons. Ironically, the older—and presumably more "secure"—institutions and plants lend themselves best to secret hiding places. The process could almost be seen as a game, with correctional officers periodically searching the same old spots. The need for shakedowns (searching of an entire cell or cellblock) is lessened when contraband rules are made realistic and humane; prohibiting such items as family pictures and toothpicks creates a needless irritant. The shakedown also has greater effect if used only to locate items that represent a clear and present danger to the institution, not just for the sake of what inmates call "Mickey Mouse" harassment.

Prevention of Escape

Maximum security jails and adult prisons were built as though they had to contain the most dangerous creature imaginable. "A jail or prison is designed to be as strong as the strongest inmate" is an old correctional chestnut. The high walls, corner towers, and armed guards are external signs of preoccupation with escape. The nature of most jail and prison populations, although changing to harder types, does not seem to justify that model. Escape is a serious concern for administrators, however, and although there were in excess of eighty-five hundred escapes in 1994, about 72 percent of the escapees were recaptured quickly.[28] Escapes in 1994, while it may seem to be a rather large number to most people, they were mostly walkaways from minimum security or community programs and represented only .02 percent of the average daily population. When we consider the increasingly dangerous nature of the incarcerated inmate, this is actually a very good record (but bad news when they do escape!). It is a mistake to think that U.S. jails and prisons are seething with oppressed and vicious criminals just waiting their chance to get out and ravage the innocent.

The conception of inmates as highly dangerous, when coupled with the extreme overcrowding of institutions, increases the concern of many correctional officers about the possibility of escape.[29] The issue is complex but revolves around two problems. The first is the philosophy of mass treatment, firmly established since the time when lockstep and silence were required for all prisoner movements. The second reason is political. Seasoned superintendents know that frequent escapes will be extremely damaging to their records, and so they take extreme measures to prevent them—directed toward all prisoners rather than toward the few who might actually try to escape. In a few prisons, however, administrators have begun to realize that a tax evader and an ax murderer do not have the same potential for escape attempts.

THE MILITARY MODEL

The need for an organized and effective custody and control force in jails and prisons has instilled a paramilitary flavor in most security staffs. The adoption of militaristic organizational structures and procedures early in corrections history made it easier to train a force with limited background to do a specific job. The **paramilitary approach** is seen in the uniforms, titles, and procedures of custody personnel. Training is directed to the mission of security, and there is little emphasis on interaction with inmates. The model of the aloof but efficient guard has emerged, and the hiring of custody personnel is rarely based on the applicant's ability to work with people. To a great extent, correctional hiring practices inhibit those people who can best fulfill the newer mission of rehabilitation. The seniority system and the growing power of correctional officer unions often discourage the infusion of custody personnel with behavioral science backgrounds.

Willy Sutton (1901–1980) was a bank robber and escape artist in the 1930s and 1940s and was caught by accident in 1952 when the battery failed on his escape vehicle. When asked why he robbed banks, he is alleged to have answered, "Because that's where the money is."

Frequent and good training is the most effective way to upgrade the quality of custody personnel

—*COURTESY OF THE PENNSYLVANIA DEPARTMENT OF CORRECTIONS*

In order to provide the best entry-level personnel, and to maintain a level of quality and growth in their staff, many jurisdictions have established rigid training standards along the lines recommended by the American Correctional Association. Such requirements will ensure all staff are eventually exposed to methods that are not simply "more of the same."

To reflect the population in institutions, personnel should actively recruit from minority groups, women, young persons, and prospective indigenous workers and see that employment announcements reach those groups and the general public.

It is useful to conduct a task analysis of each correctional position (to be updated periodically) to determine the tasks, skills, and qualities needed. Hands-on testing based solely on relevant features, to assure that proper qualifications are considered for each position, helps the administrator know what is needed and can be provided by training. Those procedures will lead to an open system of selection in which any testing device is related to a specific job and is a practical test of a person's ability to perform, at an acceptable standard, the tasks identified for that job.

These are a few of the steps that might help span the presently large communication gap between keepers and kept. Correctional officers and custody staff spend more time with the inmate population than does anyone else in the institution. They should relate well to others because they can be the most positive agents of change in that corrections subsystem.[30] They can also destroy any efforts toward change attempted by a treatment staff that tries to bypass them. A move away from the military/police image to the correctional image is critical to effective change in the institutional setting.

UPGRADING CORRECTIONAL PERSONNEL

The most important rehabilitative tool is the impact of one person on another. Thus a primary goal for the correctional system is the recruitment, training, and retention of employees who are able—physically, emotionally, educationally, and motivationally—to work as a team.

In the correctional system it is hard to hire or keep qualified personnel, including the nation's prisons and jails. There is no real reason for the correctional officer and jailer to complain about salaries in the field. The national average entry-level starting pay shown in Figure 22-4 of about $19,900 (around $21,500 after probation) is not bad when we consider that the current minimum qualifications for applicants is usually only a high school diploma or equivalent (GED) and no criminal record.

As we are entering the twenty-first century, national unemployment rates have reached new lows, and some jail and prison jobs go begging. This will make young people interested in possibly seeking jail and prison custody jobs. As corrections competes with a growing economy, it will become more difficult to hire young people. Because of the persistent problem of unfilled slots on most shifts, supervisors ask officers on duty to work another shift (work "doubles"). That situation leads to overtired staff and high overtime budgets, but legislators are seldom willing to increase expenditures for staff. They fear that correctional officers are just padding the roles, or perhaps are trying to avoid the costs of providing fringe benefits to more employees. The concept of audits for "minimum critical staffing" has been tried many times, but budget needs still seem to override attempts at rationalizing staffing patterns.[31]

Perhaps more important than salary is the custody employees' sense of public rejection, reinforced in some institutions by the belief (whether true or false) that the administrators and professional staff do not consult them, treat them fairly, or care what they think.[32] New channels of communication must be opened between administrators and employees, as well as between employees and inmates. Administrators should meet with staff to discuss employee problems; custodial and treatment staff should also coordinate.[33] These meetings should be regularly scheduled and formally integrated into institutional procedures.

Historically, correctional institutions probably have done a more effective job in custody and security than in any other aspect of the institutional program. In the 1990s, the custodial staff are finally looking at more efficient and effective ways to provide better security through one of the new technologies or management theories. And, we hope, they are leaving the officers alone to develop more interactive security strategies and tactics with the inmates and to foster better relationships with treatment staff. The pitfalls in exercising that responsibility include opportunities for the excessive use of force by some personnel, the debilitating effects of excessive routinization on inmates, and the frustration of treatment programs in which security needs are seen as paramount. Those negative possibilities become probabilities because the custodial portion of the institutional program is carried out by the persons least trained in treatment techniques.

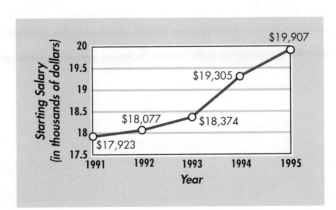

FIGURE

22.4

Average Starting Salaries for Correctional Officers, 1991–1995

SOURCE: C. Camp and G. Camp, *The Corrections Yearbook 1995: Adult Corrections* (South Salem, NY: Criminal Justice Institute, 1995), p. 81.

Unit Team and Other Methods to Avoid Compartmentalization

In regard to ongoing conflicts between custody and security, a few final comments seem appropriate to show the student it is not hopeless. Many institutions already adhere to these concepts, and only the overcrowding and violence are keeping progress in the slow lane.

First, policies should be developed jointly to define the relationships between critical custody and security functions in regard to get all staff involved in jointly meeting rehabilitative program goals and custody needs for their institutions. The obvious dichotomy between custody and treatment must be erased and greater recognition given to the fact that each is supportive of the other. This kind of activity has been instituted in many institutions as "unit team" management, in which all members of the team of a given cellblock, tank, pod, or wing work as a team to provide custody, security, and rehabilitative services in a single coordinated package. Clarification must be made of the essential roles of all aspects of the institutional program so that none can be unduly hampered by the needs of one over the others.

Second, policies and guidelines for institutional rules and regulations should be developed and all present rules and regulations revised to ensure that the demands of security do not negate the objectives of treatment. In policy formation and in specific rules, the principle of clear and present danger should apply; if the regulation is required for the safety of the institutional community, it should be kept. If not, it should be abolished. Those policies should provide for periodic review of institutional compliance. At each institution, a permanent

Custody personnel must be prepared for response to all emergencies, such as escape attempts, hostage situaions, and even riots

—PHOTO BY SPENCER A. BURNETT, *COURTESY OF THE NEW YORK CITY DEPARTMENT OF CORRECTIONS*

Who Should Take Command in a Prison Riot?

The level of command during a prison riot depends on several factors:

- Knowledge of the facility.
- Effects on the chain of command.
- Breadth of experience, responsibility, and communication.
- Links between responsibility and authority.
- The administrative framework.

Some of these factors favor assigning command to the warden, but others indicate the central office administrator or the commissioner may be more appropriate in particular situations.

THE WARDEN

Because details vary from one facility to the next, one unit to the next, and one shift to the next, some agencies feel that overall authority should remain in the hands of the warden, who has greater overall knowledge of the facility. This knowledge may enable him or her to more quickly assess the situation and recognize the consequences of different courses of action.

To many corrections administrators, another compelling argument for keeping riot resolution in the hands of the warden concerns maintaining the chain of command in the aftermath. Taking away the warden's authority during a disturbance, it is argued, may undermine his or her subsequent authority; midlevel managers, correctional officers, and inmates alike will view the central office, not the warden, as the real authority. Allowing the warden to remain in command for the riot's duration reaffirms the commitment of the central office to his or her leadership.

However, if the warden is new, someone else who has spent more time at the facility (a central office administrator, for example) may be more familiar with it. Each situation must be weighed individually. In some cases, a team approach may be warranted to capitalize on the knowledge and skill of each individual.

CENTRAL OFFICE ADMINISTRATOR

Because of their experience across a range of situations, central office administrators may have a more developed understanding of resolution strategies. They are more likely, as well, to have greater insight into the effects of disturbances on the department or corrections as a whole than those whose primary identification may be with a particular facility. Additionally, their experiences in dealing with agencies and resources outside the department can be brought to bear, if necessary.

THE COMMISSIONER

In other cases, it is argued that because the commissioner bears ultimate responsibility for the resolution, decisionmaking authority should reside in his or her hands. Moreover, in agencies in which the decisionmaking power tends to be concentrated in the central office, existing practice may dictate that the commissioner take direct charge of the resolution. The commissioner can follow the procedures he or she and others in the central office have established. By contrast, in decentralized departments in which wardens have greater latitude, it may be more advantageous for the warden to remain in command. ∎

SOURCE: Bert Useem, C. Camp, G. Camp, and Revie Dugan, *Resolution of Prison Riots* (Washington, D.C.: U.S. Department of Justice, October 1995).

---

standing committee, representing all major services, should be made responsible for implementing guidelines and policies.

Third, in cases where force has been used on an inmate, in addition to an investigation by the institution and/or an outside agency, a report should routinely be submitted to the corrections authority by the prison physician and by the inmate himself or herself.

Finally, the correctional authority should respond to requests from families that they be permitted to visit and see an inmate if they believe excessive force has been used against him or her. If they desire an outside physician to examine the prisoner, their request should be granted without delay, in accordance with rules to be promulgated by the correctional authority. Copies of all "Use of Force" reports should be filed with the correctional authority and be made available for inspection by the inmate's family, attorney, and, with the inmate's written permission, other appropriate people.

Summary

Even though the official policy of the institution may be humane, the people who are in direct contact with the inmates may have an entirely different view of their role, sometimes leading to degrading and even brutal treatment of inmates. Recruitment and hiring standards, practices, and procedures have not established sufficiently high educational or personality standards for the position of corrections officer. Salaries authorized by most legislatures for custodial personnel, while improving, are not yet high enough to attract and retain treatment-minded persons with high levels of education. It speaks well for today's correctional personnel that relatively few have been identified as brutal persons and excessive force litigation is rare. The nature of the situation, however, lends itself to individual expressions of punitiveness.[34]

One of the most vexing problems of prison management concerns the sometimes adversarial relationship between custody and treatment staffs. Both under the law and in fact, the primary emphasis in corrections is on custody and security. This attitude is, unfortunately, reinforced by the increasingly higher levels of violence in the inmates imprisoned and jailed, as well as fear of unpredictable behavior by many offenders convicted for drug-related offenses. These issues are adding fuel to a "get-tough" attitude by the custodial staff. Thus the deputy warden, associate superintendent for custody, or jail captain becomes the institution's chief operating officer.

Disciplinary infractions and other security considerations can prevent, hamper, or terminate inmate involvement in academic, vocational, educational, and other recommended activities (recreation, Alcoholics Anonymous, visiting, drug therapy, and so on). Furthermore, many important services are usually not available at night; thus inmates who work during the day are excluded. Adequate staffing could permit the expansion of treatment services to the evening hours and weekends.

Treatment-oriented and custody oriented personnel at all levels express concern about the conflict between security and program needs. Although institutional rules and regulations are vital to the correctional process, unnecessary rules that regiment even minor aspects of daily life can impede the development of individual responsibility. For example, even properly conducted lockdowns, shakedowns, and strip searches are inherently humiliating and engender inmate bitterness and resentment toward custody personnel. In a cell shakedown, the inmates' possessions are sometimes knocked to the floor and trampled. It is true that occasional thorough searches of persons and premises are necessary to protect the institutional community. Nevertheless, the basic principles of human dignity need to be observed in their interaction and conduct.

It is recognized by all involved in corrections that custody and security are necessary but are not the only correctional goals. The next chapter deals with treatment as another essential component of corrections.

Review Questions

1. What is the primary focus of the bureaucratic style of prison management?
2. Where have prison guards been obtained in the past? How does this situation create problems?
3. Why has the military model been so popular in the prisons?
4. Why do disciplinary and security considerations so greatly affect treatment programs? How can that issue be resolved?

5. What are the effects of imprisonment on inmates? Staff?

6. In what ways have the roles and positions of correctional officers improved over the last two decades?

7. What are the problems with prison gangs? What is their makeup?

8. Give a description of unit team management. How does it work?

Words to Remember

bureaucratic control

custody

"screw"

correctional officers

unionization

blue flu

lockdowns

prison rules

frisk search

"keester"

paramilitary approach

Endnotes

1. Clifford English, "The Impact of the Indeterminate Sentence on an Institutional Social System," *Journal of Offender Counseling, Services and Rehabilitation* 8 (Fall–Winter 1983): 69–82.

2. Camille G. Camp and George M. Camp, *The Correctional Yearbook 1995: Adult Corrections* (South Salem, NY: Criminal Justice Institute, 1995) p. 68.

3. American Correctional Association, *1996 Directory: Juvenile & Adult Correctional Departments, Institutions, Agencies & Paroling Authorities* (Lanhan, MD: American Correctional Association, 1996), pp. xiv–xv.

4. Craig Perkins et al. *Jails and Jail Inmates 1993–94.* (Washington, D.C.: U.S. Department of Justice, April 1995), p. 8.

5. American Correctional Association, *1996 Directory.*

6. Perkins et al. *Jails and Jail Inmates.*

7. American Correctional Association, *1996 Directory.*

8. Perkins et al. *Jails and Jail Inmates.*

9. Ibid., p. 76. See also Thomas A. Wright, "Correctional Employee Turnover: A Longitudinal Study," *Journal of Criminal Justice* 21:2 (1993): 131–142.

10. Frances Cullen, E. Latessa, V. Burton, and L. Lombardo, "The Correctional Orientation of Prison Wardens," *Criminology* 31:3 (1994): 69–92. On correctional officers, see Kuotsai Liou, "Role Stress and Job Stress Among Detention Case Workers," *Criminal Justice and Behavior* 22:4 (1995): 425–436, and Maria Peters, Bram Brunk, and Wilmar Schaufeli, "Social Interaction and Feelings of Inferiority Among Correctional Officers," *Journal of Applied Social Psychology* 25:12 (1995): 1073–1089.

11. John Hepburn and C. Albonetti, "Role Conflict in Correctional Institutions: An Empirical Examination of the Treatment-Custody Dilemma Among Correctional Staff," *Criminology* 17 (February 1980): 445–460. See also Nancy Jurik and M. Mushenko, "The Internal Crisis of Corrections: Professionalism and the Work Environment," *Justice Quarterly* 3 (1986): 457–480; Craig Robertson and Melvin Ray, "Public Attitudes Toward Prison Capacity Extension in Mississippi," *American Journal of Criminal Justice* 19:1 (1994): 99–115; and Steven A. Anderson, "A Model for Ranking the Punitiveness of the States," *Journal of Quantitative Criminology* 8:2 (1992): 217–232.

12. Correctional officers have gone on strike in Washington State and in institutions in the Ohio state system. Whenever that happens, administrative personnel or state police are required temporarily to fill the correctional officers' posts. Although police strikes have been found to have a limited impact on the rates of reported crime, little is known about institutional disturbances and rule violations in prison whenever correctional officers strike.

13. See David Shichor and Harry Allen, "Correctional Efforts in the Educated Society: The Case of Study Release," *Lambda Alpha Epsilon* 39 (June 1976): 18–24. See also Sally Chandler Halford, "Thoughts on Jail Management," *American Jails* V:5 (1992): 21–25.

14. Donald Clemmer, *The Prison Community* (New York: Rinehart, 1940), Anthony Scacco, *Rape in Prison* (Springfield, IL: Charles C. Thomas, 1975), and Victor Hassine, *Life Without Parole* (Los Angeles:Roxbury, 1996).

15. Shichor and Allen, "Correctional Efforts in the Educated Society," p. 21.

16. President's Commission on Law Enforcement and Administration of Justice, *The Challenge of Crime in a Free Society* (Washington, D.C.: U.S. Government Printing Office, 1967), p. 159.

17. Steve Daniels, "Prison Gangs: Confronting the Threat," *Corrections Today* 49 (1987): 66, 126, 162; Salvador Buentello, "Texas Turnaround: New Strategies Combat State's Prison Gangs," *Corrections Today* 54:5 (1992): 58–61; and Russell Craig and David Rausch, *An Historical, Philosophical, and Pragmatic Approach to Penology* (Lewiston, NY: Edward Millin Press, 1994).

18. English, "The Impact of the Indeterminate Sentence on an Institutional Social System," pp. 70–71. See also Peter Nacci and Thomas Kane, "Sex and Sexual Aggression in Federal Prisons: Inmate Involvement and Employee Impact," *Federal Probation* 48 (1985): 46–52.

19. David Hagar, "Computers Aid Rehabilitation in New Zealand," *Corrections Today* 49 (1987): 118, and Peter Nacci, Kevin Jackson, and Karry Cothorn, eds., "The Future of Automation and Technology," *Corrections Today* 57:4 (1995): 66–120 (theme issue).

20. Ernst van den Haag, "Prisons Cost Too Much Because They Are Too Secure," *Corrections Magazine* 6 (April 1980): 39–43. See also Don Gibbons, *The Limits of Punishment as Social Policy* (San Francisco: National Council on Crime and Delinquency, 1988). See also Herman Franke, "The Rise and Decline of Solitary Confinement: Social-Historical Explanations of the Long-Term Penal Changes," *British Journal of Criminology* 32:2 (1992): 125–143, and Ronaldo V. del Carmen, "The Supreme Court and Prison Excessive Use of Force Cases: Does One Test Fit All?" *Federal Probation* 56:2 (1992): 44–47.

21. James Stephan, *Prison Rule Violators* (Washington, D.C.: U.S. Government Printing Office, December 1989).

22. Amy Craddock, "A Comparative Study of Male and Female Prison Misconduct Careers," *The Prison Journal.* 76:10, 1996): 60–80.

23. David Lovell and Ron Jemelka, "When Inmates Misbehave: The Costs of Discipline," *The Prison Journal* 76:2 (1996): 165–179.

24. National Sheriff's Association, *Jail Officer's Training Manual* (Alexandria, VA: National Sheriff's Association, 1984), p. 95. See also Ted Heim, "The University Role in Training Jail Personnel: The Washburn Experience," *American Jails* VII:1 (1993): 18–20, and Pamela Steinke, "Using Situational Factors to Predict Types of Prison Violence," *Journal of Offender Rehabilitation* 17:1 (1991): 119–132.

25. Camp and Camp, *The Correctional Yearbook 1995*, p. 85.

26. Lois Sawyer, "On the Question of Having Women Guards in Male Prisons," *Corrective and Social Psychiatry and Journal of Behavior Technology Methods and Therapy* 33 (1987): 154–159. See also Joann B. Morton et al., "Women in Corrections," *Corrections Today* 54:6 (1992): 76–180; Pamela K. Wuthrow, "Pros and Cons: Women's Views on Working in Corrections," *Corrections Today* 54:6 (1992): 84–92; Marjorie H. Young, "Keys to Success: What Works for Women in Juvenile Corrections," *Corrections Today* 54:6 (1992): 106–111; and Patricia Van Voorhis, Francis T. Collen, Bruce G. Link, et al., "The Impact of Race and Gender on Correctional Officers' Orientation to the Integrated Environment," *Journal of Research in Crime and Delinquency* 28:4 (1991): 472–500.

27. Nick Pappas, *The Jail: Its Operation and Management* (Lompoc, CA: Federal Prison Industries, 1971), p. 23.

28. Camp and Camp, *The Correctional Yearbook 1995*, pp. 23–24.

29. For a discussion of prison security, see *Corrections Today* 57 (July 1995). See also M. Wayne Huggins, Edward F. Reynolds, James E. Dare, et al., "Accreditation," *Corrections Today*

54:3 (1992): 40–62, and David M. Bogard, "Smart Security: Making the Right Technological Choices," *Corrections Today* 55:2 (1993): 74–80.

30. Carol Fewell, "Successful Strategies: Integrating Health Care and Security Functions," *Corrections Today* 50 (1988): 20–22. See also Kathy Briscoe and Joyce Kuhrt, "How Accreditation Has Improved Correctional Health Care," *American Jails* VI:4 (1992): 48–60.

31. John Shuiteman, "Playing the Numbers Game: Analysis Can Help Determine Manpower Requirements," *Corrections Today* 49 (1987): 40–42. See also Mary K. Stohr and Linda L. Zupan, "Street-Level Bureaucrats and Service Provision in Jail: The Failure of Officers to Identify the Needs of Inmates," *American Journal of Criminal Justice* 16:2 (1992): 75–94.

32. Frances Cheek and Marie Di Stefano Miller, "Reducing Staff and Inmate Stress," *Corrections Today* 44 (1982): 72–76, 78. See also John T. Super, T. H. Blau, B. Charles, et al., "Using Psychological Tests to Discriminate Between 'Best' and 'Least Best' Correctional Officers," *Journal of Criminal Justice* 21:2 (1993): 143–150.

33. Michael Sherrill and Peter Katel, "New Mexico: An Anatomy of a Riot," *Corrections Magazine* 6 (April 1980): 6–24. See also Steven Dillingham and Montgomery Reid, "Can Riots Be Prevented?" *Corrections Today* 44 (1982): 54–56. See also American Correctional Association, "After Atlanta and Oakdale: ACA Pays Tribute to Federal Officials, Staff," *Corrections Today* 50 (1988): 26, 64. See also Stephen C. Light, "Assaults on Prison Officers: Interactional Theme," *Justice Quarterly* 8:2 (1991): 217–242.

34. Susan Zitzer, "Veteran Correctional Professional Exhibits Dedication to Job," *Corrections Today* 57:9 (1995):82.

CHAPTER TWENTY-THREE

Management *and* Treatment Functions *and* Tasks

Overview

In the last chapter, we focused attention on such custody issues as contraband, security, personnel, and discipline. These issues are, understandably, the dominant concerns of correctional administrators and their management staff and consume great amounts of administrative time as well as large fiscal allocations by state or local correctional institutions. That leads us to explore the development of management styles in corrections and the application of these styles to the major strategic processes of corrections—custody and treatment. Custody was seen as having a long history of a bureaucratic style of management, while treatment might be seen as trying to apply a more personal style within a professional setting, contrasting to the oppressive environment of a correctional facility.

Corrections might be likened to a major business with external and internal challenges. But it must also have a system of administration and control that protects society and attempts to treat inmates in a humane fashion and return its clients to a community setting ready to be reintegrated. As theories of formal organization and in concepts related to administrative leadership and behavior evolved, corrections has changed, producing new styles of management and spawning new environments for administrators. Correctional management has evolved along pathways that run generally parallel to administrative science in most public and private fields of endeavor.

Concepts for operation of organizations and the roles of their managers have changed radically in the past century, starting with Frederick Taylor's scientific management movement. This model portrayed the administrator as a highly skilled technician whose role was to ensure the smooth operation of such organizational processes.[1] The industrial age required that work be simplified and made efficient by constant supervision and time management. From that vantage point, the ideal executive was seen as a rational

> **A**fter a decade of empirical and ideological attacks on treatment philosophy and in light of a "get tough" movement that has sponsored harsh renovations of criminal codes, a number of commentators have been moved to ask, "Is rehabilitation dead?"
>
> —Cullen, Cullen, and Wozniac

individual manipulating the levers of a human/machine interface. The task was to keep correcting deficiencies by rearranging the span of control, the line of command, or the interrelationships of the structural components. Taylor's emphasis was on the anatomy of the system as symbolized by the organizational chart. He ignored the basic human tendency to resist conforming as if the worker were just another mechanical part, a fact that contributed greatly to the early demise of the scientific management movement.

The so-called human relations movement which followed in the 1930s proclaimed somewhat pompously (it now seems) that the needs and goals of the human participants within formal organizations exert a powerful influence and management would do well to recognize and accommodate them. It was argued that the workers' need to find rewarding social satisfactions in their relationships with one another operates as a strong determinant of morale and, therefore, of production. Earlier research findings soon reinforced that position.

One contribution of the human relations school of thought was an elaboration of the idea of **informal organization** that takes into account how the actual dynamics of status and influence differ from the static lines and boxes on

A Catalog of Prison History

1773 Connecticut converts copper mine to underground prison, called Newgate, in Simsbury.

1787 The Pennsylvania Prison Society is founded.

1790 Philadelphia's Walnut Street Jail, one of the country's first penal institutions, opens.

1793 Mary Weed takes post as principal keeper of Walnut Street Jail, serving until 1796.

1819 Auburn prison in New York opens, using silent, or congregate, system.

1825 Auburn-style prison (Sing Sing) opens at Ossining, New York.

1829 Eastern Penitentiary opens, designed by John Haviland, at Cherry Hill.

1870 American Prison Association publishes its guidelines as the *Declaration of Principles*.

1873 First separate women's prison opens: Indiana Women's Prison, Indianapolis.

1874 Fort Leavenworth prison opens for military offenders.

1876 Nation's first reformatory opens under the direction of Zebulon Brockway at Elmira, New York.

1891 Congress approves Three Prisons Act to build three federal penitentiaries (USP Leavenworth, USP Atlanta, and McNeil Island, a former territorial jail, now a Washington State prison).

1901 The first separate reformatory is built exclusively for women at Bedford Hills (Westfield), New York.

1906 Federal prison at Leavenworth opens.

1914 Thomas Mott Osborne is appointed warden of Sing Sing Prison in Ossining, New York.

1927 First woman serves as a federal warden: Mary Belle Harris, at Federal Institution for Women, Alderson, West Virginia.

1929 Hawes-Cooper Act passes, placing restrictions on the sale of prison-made goods.

1930 Federal Bureau of Prisons is established.

1930 First training school for federal prison guards opens in New York City.

1933 Alcatraz becomes a federal penitentiary.

1935 Ashurst-Sumners Act passes, prohibiting interstate shipment of prison-made products.

1965 Prisoner Rehabilitation Act signed by President Johnson.

1971 Riot at Attica, New York.

1971 First African American to serve as a federal warden: Lee Jett, Federal Corrections Institution, Englewood, Colorado.

1974 Robert Martinson publishes his controversial article on rehabilitation ("What Works: . . .").

1977 *Dothard* v. *Rawlinson* strikes down minimum height and weight requirements for officers.

1980 New Mexico Prison riot at Santa Fe.

1980 The Civil Rights of Institutionalized Persons Act is passed.

1987 Cuban detainees riot in federal facilities in Georgia and Louisiana.

1993 First female director, Federal Bureau of Prisons: Kathleen Hawk. ∎

SOURCE: Marilyn McShane and Frank Williams III, *Encyclopedia of American Prisons* (New York: Garland, 1996), p. xxv.

an organizational chart. Secretaries, it was pointed out, may exercise great influence, though they have little formal status, because they can control the access of people and information to their superiors. In the correctional institution, the warden, superintendent, or chief jailer would often relate better to shift lieutenants or line staff than to so-called "treatment," or other noncustodial staff, even though the latter may be placed higher in rank and pay in the *formal* organizational structure.

In recent years, more sophisticated theories and research methodologies have been brought to bear on the informal side of organization life. Just as prisons came to be conceived of as social systems, generic theories of organization began to define all of the systems within which workers join together to accomplish work goals as "complex" and "open."[2]

Concern for the psychological and social ingredients of organization life emphasized the responsibility of management to create conditions under which participants could use their capacities fully and creatively. Attention was given to the dilemma of satisfying concurrently the legitimate requirements of the individual and the organization. In contrast with the former preoccupation with hierarchy and the downward flow of authority, modern theorists argue that organizations should be seen as composites of problem-solving groups in which the leaders are primarily concerned with generating wide participation among the members and in which the decision-making power is shared with the members.[3]

Some recent formulations concerning management techniques seem especially applicable to developments in the field of corrections and therefore help provide a context for much research. Schein pointed out that the work styles of managers reflect the assumptions they make about people. He set forth four views[4] about the nature of humankind that seem to have been operative in correctional management:

1. The first view sees people as rational and economic in nature, primarily motivated by materialistic rewards, requiring from management a firm structure of incentives and controls in order to carry out predetermined tasks.

2. The second view sees the worker as social, primarily motivated by a need for meaningful relationships with others, requiring from management a concern for personal feelings and a structuring of work to bring about satisfying human interactions and group experiences.

3. The third view sees humankind as potentially self-actualizing. After satisfying lower-level needs, such as survival, self-esteem, and autonomy, people respond to internal forces in seeking a sense of achievement and meaning in their work. The function of management, under this view, is to facilitate the efforts of correctional staff members to use their energies in creative and productive ways.

4. The fourth view sees the worker as complex and, though capable of self-actualization, highly varied in responding to different situations. This view challenges management to develop diagnostic skills and wide flexibility in meeting the needs, and thereby maximizing the contribution, of different organization members under constantly changing circumstances.

Certain aspects of these views can be found in both historic and contemporary correctional administration. The staffs of large routinized institutions have generally been treated by management as rational-economic. Smaller institutions (especially those for juvenile offenders) and community-based correctional programs have moved toward the view that employees are motivated by social as well as economic satisfactions. Some of the most interesting experimental programs (for example, institutional efforts to develop **therapeutic communities** and demonstrations of intensive treatment on probation or parole)[5] have given the staff many opportunities for self-actualization. And some managers do view their staff as complex and seek to use varied skills and methods in working with them, along the lines suggested by Schein.

We must remember, of course, that correctional administrators have managerial relationships not only with staff but also with offenders. Indeed, it is the balancing and harmonizing of the two sets of relationships that create some of the most difficult problems, perhaps because administrators (consciously or unconsciously) adopt one view of people when dealing with staff and another when dealing with offenders. Consider, for example, the dynamics that might occur in an institution in which the management treated staff as motivated by social and economic needs while viewing inmates as capable of responding only to coercion.[6]

The historic and contemporary picture of correctional management's view of offenders seems even more varied than its view of staff. Many offenders have been, and still are, viewed as responding only to force or threat of force. Both the time-honored penal work programs,[7] which offer opportunities for small earnings on a sliding scale, and the practice of reducing the time of incarceration (giving good time) for conforming behavior stem from a rational-economic view of inmates.

One of the most significant developments in correctional rehabilitation—the use of **small-group process** to bring about changes of attitude and behavior—seems to rest on the concept that offenders are social humans. Other innovations, such as work or educational furloughs, have overtones of both the self-actualization and the complex views of offenders. Our position is that correctional management will be most effective if it is generally consistent in its view of all participants, whether staff or offenders, and if it seeks to develop approaches to them based on the assumption that participants, although complex, can be capable of self-actualization.

Another formulation from management theory that seems useful in assessing trends in correctional administration is the typology of organization and management styles suggested by Likert.[8] Distinguishing basically between authoritative and **participative organizations**, Likert posited four approaches to management, each with specified consequences for the motivation of participants, their job satisfaction, communication, decision making, production, and other variables. The four types, which Likert viewed as stages of development from ineffective and pathological to effective and healthy management, are as follows:

1. exploitive-authoritative
2. benevolent-authoritative
3. participative-consultative
4. participative-group

It appears that aspects of all four approaches are found in contemporary correctional organizations. The general trend, however, has been away from type 1, which is illustrated by the traditional prison with its dependence on coercive uses of authority, and into types 3 and 4, through a mixture of benevolently applied authority and limited democratization of the management process. The use of inmate advisory councils, the delegation of case management authority to probation and parole officers, and the involvement of junior staff in long-range planning are examples of the **participative-consultative** practices adopted in many correctional agencies, particularly those based in or closely tied to the community. The general pattern in corrections, however, seems closer to Likert's benevolent-authoritative type than to any of the other three.

Some progressive correctional programs operate along lines similar to Likert's fourth type, participative-group. Examples of such an approach can be found in the New Jersey Highfields Experiment, the Pinehills Project in Utah, and the California Community Treatment Project. Though differing from one another in many ways, these and similar experimental ventures distribute influence and decisional power widely among the staff and the offenders involved and use the group process extensively in guiding program operation.

Correctional administrators should seek to develop participation at all levels within their organizations. It should be recognized, however, that much empirical research is needed (both in correctional administration and in generic management processes) to refine understanding of how participative techniques may be employed successfully and how they may be adapted to the realities of particular programs.[9] As we already noted, precipitous efforts to democratize correctional organizations not only tend to be dangerous but are usually also destined to fail. The introduction of participative methods into programs that are oriented toward the goals of revenge and restraint requires great sensitivity to the forces at work in the organization and in its environment.

Above all, corrections and correctional institutions are a product of the people's will and legislative action to resolve a perceived problem in society. The early prisons and penitentiaries had no problem with the "lock 'em up" wishes of society. In the twentieth century, however, we have been struggling to determine just

Sanford Bates

— *COURTESY OF FEDERAL BUREAU OF PRISONS*

what we really want to do with, to, or for our offenders. As noted in Chapter 4, this "model muddle" continues to be a problem for the correctional administrator. As a manager, the correctional leader must contend with a staff that is bifurcated into those who are mainly concerned with security and custody and those who are concerned with programs and treatment. As we are entering the twenty-first century, we need to understand the problems faced by administrators who are required to accomplish both while dealing with overcrowding, budget cuts, a changing clientele, and the myriad other issues facing them in the last decade of the century. As we discussed in Chapter 21, custody's primary role is to protect society. Treatment efforts attempt to return inmates to society prepared to serve it in a humane fashion. As changes in theories of formal organization and in concepts related to administrative leadership and behavior evolved, corrections changed, producing new styles of management and proliferating new environments for administrators. Correctional management has evolved along pathways that run generally parallel to administrative science in all fields of endeavor.

Living within the prisons but seldom part of the management and administrative components are the inmates, who are involuntarily sentenced to prison facilities and, for the most part, eager to be released. In the better prison systems, inmates receive humane treatment and handling designed to prepare them for their eventual return to society. For most inmates, however, the demands of custody and the philosophical orientations of administrators and staff will mean denial of treatment opportunities. This chapter deals with current status of treatment: programs and policies designed to lessen criminal inclinations and tendencies while strengthening motivations to adopt law-abiding behavior.

The Treatment Model: Alive or Dead?

Treatment services, which generally include vocational training, education, counseling, teaching, casework, religious activities, and clinical activity, are believed to play a significant role in offender rehabilitation. In the past, especially in the larger institutions, the allocation of resources and personnel for treatment bore little, if any, relation to that assumed significance. As a national average, the resources allocated for **treatment services** amounted to only about 10 percent of the expenditures of the institutional staffs. The disproportionate distribution of resources as early as the 1960s was well addressed by that era's *Manual of Correctional Standards*:

> Over the past thirty years, there has been increasing recognition that a major function of a correctional agency is to influence change in the attitude and behavior of the offender. The disciplines of psychiatry, psychology, and social casework have provided corrections with tools which are useful in stimulating change.[10]

Part of the disproportionate allocation of resources is a basic difference in nature between treatment and custody operations. Staff on the custody side must work 24 hours a day, 7 days a week, 365 days a year. Treatment staff, on the other hand, usually work only 8 hours a day, 5 days a week, and have holidays, vacations, and weekends off. When a custody officer is sick or takes vacation, he or she *must* be replaced (the common term is **back-filled**) by another corrections officer, often on overtime, because "minimal critical staffing" must be

A one-to-one HIV/AIDS education program for inmates

—PHOTO BY JOHN CHIASSON, COURTESY OF GAMMA LIAISON

maintained in order to protect the public. That protection is still the primary mission of corrections. When treatment staff are sick or take vacation, their position usually goes unfilled until they return to work. Because each 24-hour post requires 5.4 to 5.6 full-time staff, the ratio will always seem heavily weighted toward custody staff.

As Figure 23-1 shows, the ratio of inmates to line correctional officers, possibly due to economic conditions and slashed budgets across the nation, has begun to increase toward the lows of the late 1980s. This may result in continued battles between custody and treatment over limited personnel funds. The dramatic difference between the number of custody and line staff in corrections can be seen in Figure 23-2, based on figures as of January 1, 1995.[11] The detailed breakout of treatment staff reported by 50 agencies is shown in Table 23-1.

In the entire corrections system, a very small percentage of institutional personnel are employed in social work or psychological services, and the number of psychiatrists in corrections is infinitesimal. Diagnostic work-ups and testing processes tend to consume the workday of those involved in these services. Also, treatment personnel must often spend long hours sitting on disciplinary hearing courts, classification and reclassification committees, and honor placement committees. Thus a minute staff has almost no time to spend on ongoing treatment with inmates. In addition, correctional administrators and the treatment staff frequently have to contend with the deeply ingrained antagonism of the staff members who are oriented toward custody, security, and maintenance of calm.[12]

Only in recent times has the associate superintendent for treatment (or deputy warden for treatment) been selected from candidates with training in the social sciences, rather than through the promotion of a faithful custody supervisor. This is important, as the typical rank-and-file custody person was usually not someone who had earned the job through training and education, but through experience and staying out of trouble. Thus a person with a high school education (or less) was often placed over psychiatrists, psychologists, medical doctors and nurses, social workers, and educators who possessed far more academic credentials. Understandably, these roles created many problems as treatment became more important.

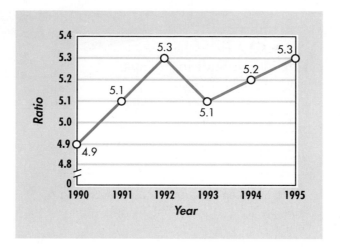

FIGURE

23.1

Ratio of Inmates to Line Correctional Officers, 1990–1995

SOURCE: C. Camp and G. Camp, *The Corrections Yearbook 1995: Adult Corrections* (South Salem, NY: Criminal Justice Institute, 1995), p. 83.

Influence of the Prison Environment

The traditional prison (the archetype of all correctional organizations) was an **autocracy**. Its single purpose was to maintain custody over the inmates. To accomplish this, it developed a rigid and highly stratified hierarchy along the lines of a military organization. Authority and status were related to rank, from the warden to the guard. Each separate institution became its own small kingdom and the warden became the king.

Staff tended to be highly protective of that structure, holding to the closely defined prerequisites and prerogatives attached by custom to its various positions and levels. The reorganization of many correctional institutions within the last few decades added another kind of hierarchy, the noncustodial personnel, to the framework of the organization. A deputy warden in charge of treatment, heading a battery of professional and specialized services, was given formal authority and position equal to those of the deputy warden in charge of custody.

Business managers, heads of prison industries, and directors of honor camp programs were added, according to local needs. The special authority connected with worker function and specialization was fitted into the structure alongside the traditional authority of rank and seniority held by custodial personnel. These trends led to major redistributions of power and authority in the formal organization and resulted in a variety of stresses and adjustments in the informal organization of most institutions.[13]

BACKFILLING

To cover a personnel shortage on the next shift, a correctional officer is asked to stay on duty when his or her shift would end. The correctional officer would then work through the next shift (a "double"), in effect working sixteen hours straight (or twenty hours if the agency works on a "four days, ten hours plan"). Union rules ordinarily would require overtime pay, frequently for time and one-half for the first four hours and double-time for the remainder. While this can become extremely costly in a short period of time, it is necessary when the post to be filled is part of "minimum critical staffing," which indicates that the post *must* be filled to maintain a proper level of security. This is the budget planner's worst nightmare.

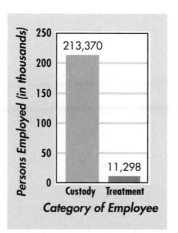

FIGURE

23.2

Relative Numbers of Custody and Treatment Staff in Prisons, January 1, 1996*

*Includes psychiatrists, psychologists, social workers, caseworkers, recreation therapists, and counselors.

SOURCE: C. Camp and G. Camp, *The Corrections Yearbook 1995: Adult Corrections* (South Salem, NY: Criminal Justice Institute, 1995), pp. 71, 84–85.

TABLE *23.1*

Treatment Staff in Prisons

	Psy-chiatrists	Psy-chologists	Social Workers	Case-workers	Recreation Therapists	Coun-selors
Alabama	0	21	4	0	0	0
Alaska	1	14	0	0	0	2
Arizona	7.5	25	1	44	1	28
Arkansas	2	14	7	18	0	7
California	96	171	0	0	8	1,161
Colorado	1	16	30			
Connecticut	5	11	36		30	327
Delaware	1	.8				
Dist. of Col.	5	22	5	119	7	3
Florida	33	61	21	212		75
Georgia	20	30	0	0	166	674
Hawaii	2	1	8	0	0	0
Idaho	0	11	23	0	3	8
Illinois	0	15	4	57	137	284
Indiana	4	23	2	0	0	68
Iowa	4	12	0	11	10	93
Kansas						
Kentucky	7	11		2	1	
Louisiana	8	3	52		1	12
Maine		8	1	25		6
Maryland	6	40	30	0	0	0
Massachusetts						347
Michigan		83	6		1	71
Minnesota	0	7	36	72	5	0
Mississippi	1	4	0	16	1	0
Missouri	0	40	0	20	0	8
Montana	1	10	9	5	7	6
Nebraska	0	6	0	143	24	74
Nevada	8	27	3	55	2	
New Hampshire	1	7	6	26	1	
New Jersey	2	58	94	0	6	40
New Mexico	2	31	3	75	4	
New York	1	45			164	911
North Carolina	3	72	18		18	
North Dakota	2	1	2	21	1	10
Ohio	0	33	0	245	83	0
Oklahoma	4.6	17	1	0	1	0
Oregon					18	209
Pennsylvania	1	88			105	244
Rhode Island	0	4	1	0	0	24
South Carolina	3	11	72	120	30	12
South Dakota						
Tennessee	3	4	4	83	2	53
Texas	45	170	18	106	28	6
Utah	3	11	43	10	2	
Vermont	0	4	0	25	0	
Virginia	5	30	19		28	238
Washington	2	21	12	0	71	220
West Virginia	2	6	0	0	6	35
Wisconsin	1	60				
Wyoming	1	1	0	1	0	23
Federal	28	295	8	971	8	
Total	**322**	**1,656**	**579**	**2,482**	**980**	**5,279**

SOURCE: C. Camp and G. Camp. *The Corrections Yearbook, 1995* (South Salem, NY: Criminal Justice Institute, 1995), pp. 84–85.

In addition, these developments have tended to confuse and affect the expanded number of environments in which to make decisions and to restrict choices that would be made by other administrators in the prison. The environment of correctional organizations has changed drastically as they have evolved from their traditional form. In the authoritarian prison, all significant decisions were made at or very near the top of the hierarchy. Moreover, those decisions were made according to simple and well-understood criteria. Such values as good control and safe custody have a concrete quality when compared with such vague prescriptions as "helping each individual to the extent that he is able to help himself" or individualizing treatment according to the needs and problems of each inmate.[14] One effect of adding more complex and nebulous criteria to the administrator's decision-making matrix has been to force the actual making of decisions downward toward the level of functional operations. The more difficulty that administrators have encountered in harmonizing treatment and custodial values in statements of policy and procedure, the more they have left the responsibility for making significant decisions to their subordinates.

Even while the prison was being established as the dominant organizational form for adjudicated offenders, other approaches developed. Institutions for juveniles, although influenced by their adult counterparts, tended to be smaller, less monolithic, and more committed to the goal of individual treatment. Probation and parole organizations, operating in the free community, produced fewer encapsulated, formal, and **hierarchical management** structures. Nevertheless, certain characteristics of penitentiaries and reformatories have conditioned the process of management and the style of managers in all correctional settings.

PERCEPTIONS AND CORRECTIONAL MANAGEMENT

Three pervasive themes have run through correctional management. First, the goals of restraint and reformation have helped reinforce correctional administrators' perceptions of offenders as morally, psychologically, physically, and educationally inferior human beings who must be upgraded and, in the meantime, controlled. As a result of that perception, correctional administrators focus the resources at their command primarily on the individual offender.

Because the offender is the principal target of organizational activity, little effort is made to mobilize and co-opt community resources, a function that is the very essence of the reintegration model of correctional intervention. That management posture has many consequences, such as the division of offenders into caseloads for purposes of treatment and supervision; recruitment of varied specialists (therapists) whose efforts are seldom coordinated; and, as we mentioned earlier, the scarcity of well-conceived efforts to work cooperatively with such community institutions as the schools, employment services, and neighborhood centers. As Richard Cloward pointed out,

> In order to ease the process of reintegration in the community, we shall have to give much greater attention than we do now to our aftercare [parole] programs. Since the real struggle between conformity and deviance takes place back in the community, the aftercare program is strategic. Yet aftercare tends to be the weakest program in most correctional systems. Somehow correctional administrators are reluctant to allocate funds for aftercare if that means reducing the scope of prestigious clinical activities within the institution itself. Professional personnel, in turn, often tend to shun aftercare work.

George J. Beto (1916–1991) was known as "Walking George" to the inmates of the Texas Department of Corrections, which he headed from the 1960s to the 1970s. He was the creator of the "control model" of correctional administration and respected for making the Texas system one of the best in the nation under his leadership. He was also jokingly called "the most sued man in Texas." Beto was instrumental in introducing the high school equivalency (GED) into the Texas system as part of his plan to control and rehabilitate. The Windham school district became the first nongeographic school district to be located in a prison system, offering GEDs, adult basic education, vocational training, and college credits. He was the first to integrate the Texas prison population and to hire the first black correctional officers into that system.

Somehow the thought of spending one's time working with families, teachers, and employers in the interests of mobilizing social opportunities for [an offender] seems distasteful; such activities do not carry the same prestige as therapeutic activities. But whatever the reasons, aftercare programs seem to get short shrift in the allocation of personnel and money.[15]

A second persistent attribute of correctional management has been a **gradualism approach** to program development and change. This approach has been characterized by a somewhat frivolous subscription to "new" ideas and generally nonrigorous, nonscientific rules of thumb for determining what to delete from the old system and what to add to it. The predominant conservatism of system managers has militated against deviations from familiar ways, encouraged the avoidance of risk, and has led to tokenism in the launching of new measures.

Correctional administrators are not so much responsible for that condition as they are victims of two realities: society's uncertainty about the causes and solutions of the crime problem, and the present inability of social science and research to provide a solid frame of reference for considering alternative courses of action and estimating their consequences.[16] Nevertheless, in any effort to understand how correctional executives might be effective innovators, it is necessary to confront the difficulties and frustration that currently surround the process of change.

It is important to note that there are numerous small-scale examples of change in correctional organization and programming that run counter to the general pattern we have described.[17] Some experimental programs have been firmly supported by theoretical premises and have been evaluated objectively. Some correctional administrators and consultants have made an effort to make change additive rather than fragmentary. Some executives in the system have attempted to move toward change along relatively rational lines while still coping skillfully with a plethora of "irrational" forces in their environments. It is that growing edge of innovation, of improved dissemination of knowledge, and of close connection between discovery and implementation of technique that offer hope for gains in the near future.

The third and final theme, which has its roots in the prison culture of the past and still runs through correctional management today, is the syndrome of

Inmate Program Involvement

One of the fears of correctional experts when states began to shift to determinate sentences was that, since the best motivator for inmate program participation appeared to be the need to convince releasing authorities of prisoners' reform through completion of prison treatment programs, determinate sentences would render treatment programs underenrolled if not superfluous. After all, if inmates were "playing the reform game" to convince a parole board of their readiness for release, and the parole board's discretion to release was abolished, inmates might very well stop participating in any treatment programs.

This fear has been proven unfounded. The rates of program participation in Illinois, Minnesota, and Connecticut,

for example, remained about the same or increased somewhat. How much of the noted participation was voluntary, however, remains in question. Prison administrators need concrete criteria for making decisions about transfers to less secure institutions, institutional job and housing assignments, furlough eligibility, and awarding of meritorious good-time credits based on program participation. The incentives for inmate involvement may have changed, but participation rates and levels appear to be unaffected by the determinate sentence. ∎

isolationism and withdrawal. That condition has helped conceal from the public the realities of life in institutions and probation and parole agencies, and has thus acted to perpetuate stereotypes and myths. Prisons, after all, were designed and located to keep criminals out of the sight and mind of the larger populace. Prison administrators found it expedient to honor that mandate. When community-based correctional programs gingerly sought to gain a foothold, their managers seemed intuitively to avoid exposure to public scrutiny and judgment. Whereas the police tend to publicize aggressively their views of crime and punishment, the leaders of corrections tend to avoid public debate, particularly debate centering on controversial issues.[18]

That tendency has had serious consequences. The correctional field has had little success in developing public understanding and support for needed changes. Simplistic or erroneous conceptions of the nature of crime and its treatment have flourished, partly because there have not been effective spokespeople for more sophisticated interpretations, especially at times of "opportunity" when conflict or crisis have awakened the interest of an otherwise apathetic public.[19]

PRESSURES TOWARD INTEGRATION OF SERVICES

One of the most important developments in American corrections over the past three decades has been a movement toward the **centralization** and integration of services in some of the more progressive systems. The concept of a coordinated correctional system possessing a variety of rehabilitative services and custodial facilities was in direct contradiction to the historic pattern in which the head of each penal institution reigned almost as a monarch, typically under the large umbrella of a multipurpose administrative board. As one researcher pointed out almost fifty years ago:

> The trend is marked and distinct. Increasing centralization of authority and responsibility is evident in correctional organizations. The movement is in the direction away from decentralization. . . . The single state department with a

Executive team meeting in Warden's office at a prison

—*PHOTO BY MIKE DAVIES, COURTESY OF THE ORANGE COUNTY CORRECTIONS DIVISION, ORLANDO, FL*

"Unit team" meeting at a prison

—*PHOTO BY MIKE DAVIS, COURTESY OF THE ORANGE COUNTY CORRECTIONS DIVSION, ORLANDO, FL*

professional administrator is doubtless the most satisfactory administrative form developed to date. More extensive authority and direction over corollary functions— probation, parole, local jails—reflect the growing unity of correctional administration.[20]

Generally, most of the significant innovations in correctional practice have occurred within professional centralized administrative systems whose parts were related through a coherent framework of policy and whose programs were implemented through planning, research, and varied staff services. Many states (Minnesota, Iowa, and Colorado for example), are implementing Community Corrections Acts to construct, coordinate, fund, and unify local and state correctional systems.[21] The field of corrections needs more unification.[22]

Yet, although movement toward centralization of correctional services within jurisdictions has been a major trend, the correctional services of the nation as a whole remain balkanized. Different levels of government operate the same services. There are schisms between services for juveniles and services for adults, between institutional facilities and community-based programs. The jails are more attached to the world of law enforcement than to the corrections establishment. The correctional field is still undecided on whether a board or a single administrator can provide more effective management for correctional systems and programs. It is also divided on whether the administration of field parole services should be controlled by the boards that make release decisions or by the departmental structures which administer institutional services.[23]

CLASSIFICATION: FOR SECURITY OR TREATMENT?

Classification is a relatively recent innovation in corrections and may be found more often in parole supervision. The classification process can frequently intensify the conflict between treatment and custody staffs if it is not carefully handled. In most correctional classification processes (either at the individual institution or at a central classification facility), there is more concern with the danger that the new inmates might present to the institution than there is with the possibility they might respond to treatment. As a result, new inmates are often assigned to higher custody grades than their backgrounds warrant, until

James V. Bennett (1894–1978) was another leading penal reformer who lead the Federal Bureau of Prisons for almost three decades, from 1937–1964. He personally led a sweeping reorganization of the federal system and implemented several innovations in prison administration and programming that brought an international reputation to this outspoken advocate of "individualized treatment" for the rehabilitation of offenders. His report in 1928 called for the establishment of a "coordinated system of federal correctional institutions,"—a centralized bureau that would manage and operate federal prisons. His reputation as an advocate of rehabilitation was matched by his ability as a shrewd administrator. His rehabilitation approach became known as the "medical model" for corrections.

they can prove themselves. This security-oriented concept of classification often excludes inmates from participation in the programs that could lead to their rehabilitation. Their early treatment, in fact, may be restricted to health care, an essential program as most offenders are in poor physical condition when they enter the institution.

Summary

Although many claim the treatment model is dead, that does not mean rehabilitation cannot work if done effectively and in a team spirit. Despite the cries that "nothing works in corrections" in the early 1990s, there has been considerable empirical data suggesting that some programs do work if they are done well and are carefully monitored and documented. The findings of Paul Gendreau, who reviewed over eighty studies of North American rehabilitation programs, are reviewed by Frelberg:

> The most successful programs in reducing recidivism rates, he said, are those that employ behavioral modification techniques that reward pro-social behavior and "target those antisocial attitudes and values that fuel criminal behavior."
>
> In an interview, Gendreau said these techniques vary. In some corrections settings, prisoners are given more privileges or money for pro-social behavior. In many cases, he said, there are efforts to influence an offender's thinking by using role playing to change his or her values.
>
> Effective rehabilitation programs also tend to allow clients to have some say in establishing the rules, according to Gendreau. They teach offenders skills they can use to keep from committing crimes again. Family therapy can also be helpful, he said.
>
> According to Gendreau, several types of treatment have been "shown to be failures," including psychodynamic and nondirective individual therapies, pharmacologic approaches and legal sanctions and punishment.
>
> He said there are no data indicating that financial restitution, shock incarceration—the disciplinary "boot camps" that are now being established in an increasing number of states—or electronic monitoring to keep tabs on an offender's whereabouts "produce any reduction in recidivism whatsoever."
>
> In contrast, positive reinforcements outweigh punishing sanctions in successful rehabilitation programs by a 3 to 1 ratio, Gendreau said.
>
> Gendreau said his evaluation of rehabilitation studies shows that community-based programs such as halfway houses are somewhat more effective than prison and other institutional-based treatment. Also, programs carried out after 1980 have been more effective than pre-1980 efforts.
>
> "What I think we are seeing is that we know more about rehabilitation, we are getting better at it," he said.
>
> Gendreau said rehabilitation programs show very little effect on low-risk clients—offenders who would be unlikely to violate the law again with or without treatment.

PRISON MANAGEMENT AS A PROFESSION

With prison management now recruiting more women and minorities, the profile is now more diverse. Over the years, prison management has become more professional. Managers and staff belong to professional associations (e.g., the American Correctional Association) and college programs now deal with subjects and degrees directly applicable to corrections. National standards and accreditation programs at jails and prison contribute to a growing professionalism for prison managers. This has had a "trickle-down" effect on the staff and the whole system.

UNIT TEAM MANAGEMENT

This innovative management concept requires that staff assigned to a wing, ward, module, pod, or other residential unit of a prison accept collective responsibility for managing the unit. Correctional officers, for example, may provide counseling when treatment officers are absent from the unit, or treatment personnel may undertake custodial staff functions as necessary. The joint responsibility for managing the unit blurs traditional roles of custody and treatment, provides staff with experience and insight into additional roles and job enrichment, and lessens social distance between staff and inmates.

"But the data is very strong," he said. "There's study after study that indicates that if you . . . target medium- to high-risk clients for intervention, then you'll see some very dramatic reductions in recidivism by using primary behavioral strategies."[24]

It sometimes seems that with the correctional administrator driving a two-horse team—a Shetland pony (treatment) on the left and a Clydesdale (custody) on the right—it will never be possible to turn the wagon in the direction of treatment and rehabilitation. The drug epidemic, overcrowding, and more dangerous inmates put a heavier pack on the back of the treatment side of the hitch. Treatment may be in a coma and will awake in the next century with replicable programs that will work. If we fail to keep an eye on the programs that seem to be rehabilitating prison inmates, we will repeat the failures of the past and continue to build jails and prisons ad infinitum.

Review Questions

1. Why are there more correctional officers than treatment staff?
2. Is classification more properly a security or a treatment function? Why?
3. Why is treatment more likely to be available for juveniles than for adult offenders?
4. Explain why corrections in general has so few spokespersons.
5. What motivates inmates to participate in prison treatment programs?

Words to Remember

informal organization

therapeutic communities

small-group process

participative organizations

participative-consultative

treatment services

back-filled

autocracy

hierarchical management

gradualism approach

isolationism and withdrawal

centralization

Endnotes

1. Frederick W. Taylor, *The Principles of Scientific Management* (New York: Harper, 1911).
2. Daniel Katz and Robert Kahn, *The Social Psychology of Organizations* (New York: John Wiley, 1966).
3. Rensis Lickert, *New Patterns of Management* (New York: McGraw-Hill, 1961).
4. Edgar Schein, *Organizational Psychology* (Englewood Cliffs, NJ: Prentice Hall, 1965).
5. Kim English, Susan Chadwick, and Suzanne Puller, *Colorado's Intensive Supervison Probation* (Denver: Colorado Division of Criminal Justice, 1994). See also Raymond Sakumoto, *Report of a Statistical Study and Evaluation of the Juvenile Intensive Supervision Program* (Honolulu: University of Hawaii at Manoa, 1995).
6. Schein, *Organizational Psychology*.
7. Lynn McAuley, "Correctional Industries Help Solve Hawaii's Labor Shortage," *Corrections Today* 56:6 (1994): 81–86; Bob Sanders, "Joint Venture Program Benefits Inmates, Employers," *Corrections Today,* 56:6 (1994): 88–90; and John Conroy, "New York

Program Succeeding in Today's Competitive Climate," *Corrections Today* 56:6 (1994): 94–96.

8. Lickert, *New Patterns of Management*.

9. Office of Development, Testing, and Dissemination, *Putting Research to Work: Tools for the Criminal Justice Professional* (Washington, D.C.: U.S. Department of Justice, 1984), and James Macguire, D. Bloomfield, C. Robinson, and B. Rooson, "Short-Term Effects of Probation Programs: An Evaluation Study," *International Journal of Offender Therapy and Comparative Criminology* 39:1 (1995): 23–42.

10. American Correctional Association, *Manual of Correctional Standards,* 3rd ed. (Washington, D.C., 1966), p. 17.

11. Camille G. Camp and George M. Camp, *The Corrections Yearbook 1995*: *Adult Corrections* (South Salem, NY: Criminal Justice Institute, 1995), pp. 71, 84–85.

12. See Rob Wilson, "Who Will Care for the 'Mad' and the 'Bad'?" *Corrections Magazine* 6 (February 1980): 5–17. See also Michael T. Charles, "The American Jail," *American Jails* VI:1 (1992): 24–31, and Henry J. Steadman, Edward J. Holobean, Jr., and Joel Dvoskin, "Estimating Mental Health Needs and Service Utilization Among Prisoner Inmates," *Bulletin of the American Academy of Psychiatry and the Law* 19:3 (1991): 297–307. But see the outstanding commentary, Russell Eisenman, "A Psychologist Looks Back on His History of Work with Young Offenders," *Corrections Today* 55:5 (1993): 16, 18, 224, and Kurt Olsson, "Prison Chaplin Goes Beyond the Expected," *Corrections Today* 57:3 (1995): 84.

13. For an understanding of the bases of power in prison, see John Hepburn, "The Exercise of Power in Coercive Organizations: A Study of Prison Guards," *Criminology* 23 (1985): 145–164. See also Sally Chandler Halford, "Thoughts on Jail Management," *American Jails* V:6 (1992): 11–13. See also Ronald Waldron and A. Turner, "Reinventing Corrections Through Project Management," *Journal of Contemporary Criminal Justice* 11:3 (1995): 177–186.

14. Elmer K. Nelson, "The Gulf Between Theory and Practice in Corrections," *Federal Probation* 18 (1954): 48, and Malcom Miller and Julian Buchanon, "Probation: A Crisis of Activity and Purpose," *Probation Journal* 42:4 (1995): 195–198.

15. Richard Cloward, "Social Problems, Social Definitions, and Social Opportunities," paper prepared for the National Council on Crime and Delinquency, New York, 1963, pp. 9–10 (mimeographed). This earlier position is being reexamined in light of recent legal developments, influx of funds, and spread of services available for offenders; also see Valerie Hildebeithel, "Addressing the Needs of the Mentally Ill Inmate in Lehigh County Prison," *American Jails* VI:5 (1992): 60–62. And see Matthew Hiller and D. Simpson, "Compulsory Community-Based Substance Abuse Treatment and the Mentally Ill Criminal Offender," *Prison Journal* 76:1 (1996): 22–59.

16. But see the excellent evaluation of Joan Petersilia, *The Influence of Criminal Justice Research* (Santa Monica, CA: Rand Corporation, 1987). And Jeffrey Fagan and M. Forst, "Risks, Fixers and Zeal: Implementing Experimental Treatment for Violent Juvenile Offenders," *Prison Journal* 76:1 (1996): 22–59.

17. See David Busby, "A Combination That Worked for Us," *Federal Probation* 48 (March 1984): 53–57; Freddie Smith, "Alabama Prison Option: Supervised Intensive Restitution Program," *Federal Probation* 48 (March 1984): 32–35; and Fagan and Forst, "Risks, Fixers and Zeal."

18. Francis Cullen and Karen Gilbert, *Reaffirming Rehabilitation* (Cincinnati: Anderson, 1982). Also see Tom McEwen, *NIJ Survey of Probation and Parole Agency Directors* (Washington, D.C.: U.S. Department of Justice, 1995).

19. An essay on the impacts of "low profilism" in corrections can be found in John Irwin and James Austin, *It's About Time* (San Francisco: National Council on Crime and Delinquency, 1987). See also Carl C. Bell, "Inmate Health Care Threatens U.S. Communities," *American Jails* VI:3 (1992): 97–98, and Steve Donziger, *The Real War on Crime* (New York: HarperCollins, 1996), pp. 194–219.

20. Richard McGee, "State Organization for Correctional Administration," in Paul Tappan, ed., *Contemporary Corrections* (New York: McGraw-Hill, 1951), p. 89. The National Academy of Corrections in the National Institute of Corrections conducts many advanced correctional management seminars to teach leadership in corrections. The current mailing address for the National Academy of Corrections is 1790 30th Street, Suite 140, Boulder, Colorado 80301.

21. Kay Harris, "Key Differences Between Community Corrections Acts in the United States," *Prison Journal* 76:2 (1996): 192–238.

22. For an excellent blueprint for unification, see E. Kim Nelson, R. Cushman, and N. Harlow, *Unification of Community Corrections* (Washington, D.C.: U.S. Department of Justice, 1980).

23. John Hepburn and L. Goodstein, "Organizational Imperatives and Sentencing Reforms," *Crime and Delinquency* 32 (1986): 339–365.

24. Peter Frelberg, "Rehabilitation Effective If Done Well, Studies Say," *APA Monitor* (September 1990): 17–19. See also David Pisapio, "Offender Responsivity to Intensive Supervision," *Forum* 7:3 (1995): 42–44; Sharon Williams, "A National Strategy for Managing Sex Offenders," *Forum* 8:2 (1996): 33–35; and Robert Grieser, "Public and Private Sector Partnerships in Prison Industries and Offender Employment," *Forum* 8:2 (1996): 43–45.

CHAPTER TWENTY-FOUR

Specialized Functions *and* Tasks

Overview

The treatment model for corrections is seen in the three basic services first offered to prisoners: religious, medical and educational. The development of those services is traced in this chapter, along with an analysis of some more recent treatment innovations. Much of the public still views any "special programs" for inmates as a form of coddling, and many politicians have responded to this view by rejecting new and promising rehabilitation techniques created by behavioral scientists. Instead, they choose to favor "wars"—(against crime, criminals, drugs, ad infinitum)—as the easiest way to garner votes from the uninformed, often uncaring public. In fact, the protection of society, not the pampering of offenders, is also the basic reason for treatment and specialized programs in corrections. If at least some of the sources of an individual's criminality can be dealt with before he or she is referred back to the community, or released from aftercare back to the community, corrections should achieve that. Inmates are most strongly influenced by those persons who spend the most time with them. At present, it is the correctional officers and custody staff who are most likely to exert that influence, rather than rehabilitative and treatment programs designed by specialists.

We discussed the many sharp splits between treatment and custody in the previous chapters, a gap that is slowly being bridged in many jurisdictions, both state and local prisons. In those programs, often using unit team concept, the treatment staff is directly involved with the custody staff, both to accomplish control and to be instrumental in rehabilitation. This process actually begins with initial correctional classification.[1] The treatment model in corrections is under attack again,[2] however, as the violence on the nation's streets pushes legislators for more punitive answers. The model of unit team management, pioneered by the federal system, combines the skills of all the staff and works to

> **W**e have witnessed a major revolution in criminal justice practices since Martinson's famous proclamation of "nothing works" in the mid-1970s. That statement praised the death of rehabilitation and rejoiced at the dawning of the new epoch of punishment . . . it is time to stop hiding behind the smoke screen of "doing justice," reducing costs, and reducing recidivism.
>
> —Professor Paul Gendreau

provide a climate that helps in rehabilitation. In this chapter, we shall look at the kinds of programs for specialized services that have been traditional and the people who provide them, as well as some new approaches that show positive results.

The Three Traditional Basic Services

The basic services provided by the treatment side of corrections can be bundled together as health and **medical services**, religious services, and educational and training programs for inmates. What follows is an outline of these services and programs.

HEALTH AND MEDICAL SERVICES

Even in the earliest days of American prisons, certain times were set aside for **sick call**. Of course, the treatment provided was less than one would expect to receive at a clinic in the community. In many cases, prisoners use sick call merely to obtain a brief respite from prison labor or from the dull routine. Time wasted on **goldbrickers** is time the medical staff cannot give those who really need care. Because the correctional funnel selects out all but the most serious and manipulative offenders, the cream of society does not often end up in prisons. Those who are imprisoned usually have numerous medical and dental needs.

Medical services are often a source of inmates' complaints and frequently become a real headache for administrators. In many areas throughout the country, qualified medical personnel are generally in short supply, and that shortage is felt even more acutely in correctional institutions. To supply the total medical care for which

Dialysis nurse providing kidney dialysis care

—COURTESY OF FEDERAL BUREAU OF PRISONS, SPRINGFIELD

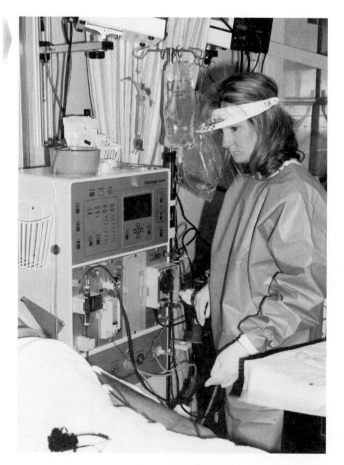

Managing Infectious Diseases

Like other institutional settings, correctional facilities are potential breeding grounds for infectious diseases. Outbreaks of disease in correctional facilities create risks for both the inmate population and the general public.

TUBERCULOSIS

One of the most threatening infectious diseases facing correctional systems today is tuberculosis (TB). For 1994, the Texas Department of Criminal Justice (TDCJ) estimated 62 cases of TB per 100,000 in Texas prisons, versus 14 per 100,000 in the free community.

In recent years, TB has become even more of a menace through the evolution of multi-drug resistant tuberculosis (MDR-TB), which occurs when strains of the TB bacteria resist one or more therapeutic drugs. Even after full treatments, which can last up to two years, MDR-TB has only a 50 percent cure rate. Coupled with HIV/AIDS, the survival rate is dismal.

The number of TB strains—such as MDR-TB—is on the upswing. In 1994, the Texas Department of Health reported 136 cases of MDR-TB in Texas' general population, while nine cases were diagnosed in Texas correctional facilities.

From 1990 to 1992, the New York Department of Corrections experienced an outbreak of MDR-TB involving at least 19 correctional facilities and two hospitals that treated the inmates. More than 40 inmates were diagnosed with MDR-TB; some cases resisted as many as six treatment drugs. By 1993, 36 inmates were dead, with 85 percent of the deaths occurring a month after diagnosis. Several correctional employees were infected, and one died. No successful drug therapy was ever found. The agency was widely criticized for its delayed response to diagnosis and isolation of the first infected individual. As a result, New York State instituted mandatory annual TB testing for all inmates and staff, routine testing for drug susceptibility to all positive TB cultures and other preventive and management practices, such as education and training.

In Texas, TB testing for inmates has been mandatory since 1993. New inmates are tested as they arrive and once a year thereafter. Also, TDCJ must provide TB screening to any employee who requests it.

Only one known TB outbreak has occurred in the Texas prison system, and that was among participants in the mentally retarded offenders program in Beaumont in 1994. Fifteen people contracted pulmonary TB; all recovered.

HIV/AIDS

As with other correctional systems across the country, Texas faces increasing incidence of HIV/AIDS in its inmate population. Though less than 2 percent of the prison population is HIV-positive, AIDS was the leading cause of death among Texas inmates in 1994, claiming 138 lives. The second most common inmate killer, heart disease, caused 64 deaths.

Prisoners are not required to be tested for HIV unless a medical professional suspects HIV infection; however, the number of inmates tested has risen from 31 in 1985 to more than 14,700 in 1995. Slightly more than half of HIV-positive inmates were intravenous drug users.

Texas law does not mandate segregation of HIV-positive inmates, but TDCJ may use "protective custody" if contact with other inmates presents a threat to the HIV-positive inmate, or "special housing" if the warden feels the inmate's violent and/or risky behavior endangers other inmates.

The *Ruiz* v. *Estelle* settlement over conditions in state prisons imposed several occupational and public health requirements on prison facilities, such as standards for ventilation, humidity and temperature. Some institutions have added isolation cells with negative air pressure to alleviate the risk of airborne disease transmission. Over the course of the *Ruiz* litigation, the cost of modifying heating, humidity and ventilation systems was about $21.5 million. ∎

SOURCE: Editors, *Managing Infectious Diseases (Bulletin)*, Texas Department of Criminal Justice, 1995.

---

an institution is responsible, it is often necessary to combine the services of full-time medical employees, contractual consultants, and available community resources.[3] Even with all these efforts, inmates and the public often tend to look down on any medically trained person who is willing to become involved with a correctional institution. Any doctor who accepts the prison physician's relatively low income and standard of living, it is thought, must have been a failure in the community.

Proper medical care is important to the overall rehabilitation effort. In many cases, the condition of the offender's health is one of the main reasons that authorities decided to opt for the prisoner's placement in a correctional institution instead of a road camp unit. Poor diet, drug abuse, a history of inadequate medical attention, and other debilitating conditions are not uncommon among inmates. Once they have been restored to reasonable health, it is often easier to work on the causes behind their problems.[4]

Major medical problems now faced by jail and prison inmates include **hepatitis A and B**, HIV infection, mental illness, geriatric inmates, prenatal care, rubella (measles), and drug-resistant tuberculosis. Drug-dependent inmates,[5] frequent transfers of inmates among facilities, and overcrowded living conditions are conducive to rapid transmission of these diseases that could result in epidemics, especially multidrug-resistant tuberculosis. Tuberculosis is easily airborne transmitted, and even dormant carriers can transmit the bacillus. Tuberculosis transmission from inmates to staff has already been documented. And staff could spread the infection to family and friends (tertiary infection), bringing this serious disease into the outside community. Inmates (and staff) should have tuberculin skin tests on a routine basis[6] because the incidence of the disease has increased dramatically.[7] The potential cost of such disease and health problem is clearly shown in the data on prison health bills in the state of Texas, as detailed in Figure 24-1.

In the most progressive prisons, cosmetic corrective medicine plastic surgery is available on request of the treatment staff, to reshape the offender's self-image and thus increase his or her self-confidence. As a matter of fact, in a survey the authors conducted of over one hundred types of treatment, it was noted that **plastic surgery** appeared to be one of the most effective rehabilitation treatments.

Another major service for the offender is found in the dental clinic because most prisoners have very bad teeth. Even in an institution fortunate enough to have good dental care facilities, dental service can take many months as prisoners' teeth have suffered from long neglect and need extensive work. The effects of dental treatment are similar to those of plastic surgery: improved appearance enhances the offender's feelings of confidence and well-being, and he or she may be relieved of chronic pain and irritation as well.

RELIGIOUS ASSISTANCE AND SERVICES

From 1790 until today, one service that has traditionally been available to the incarcerated felon is religious assistance and guidance. Solitary meditation in the Walnut Street Jail was intended to make offenders realize the error of their sinful ways and make them penitent. Penitence was often encouraged by visits from the

FIGURE
24.1

Prison Health Bills in Texas, Fiscal 1996

SOURCES: John Sharp, Texas comptroller of public accounts, and Texas Department of Criminal Justice.

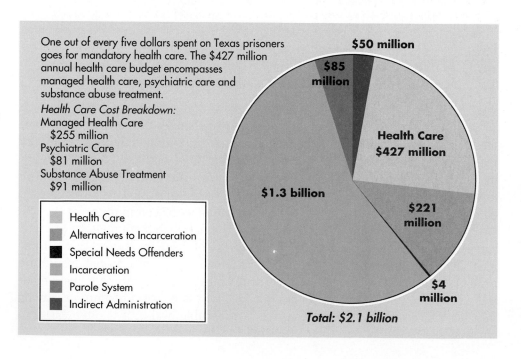

One out of every five dollars spent on Texas prisoners goes for mandatory health care. The $427 million annual health care budget encompasses managed health care, psychiatric care and substance abuse treatment.

Health Care Cost Breakdown:
Managed Health Care
   $255 million
Psychiatric Care
   $81 million
Substance Abuse Treatment
   $91 million

Legend:
- Health Care
- Alternatives to Incarceration
- Special Needs Offenders
- Incarceration
- Parole System
- Indirect Administration

$50 million
$85 million
Health Care $427 million
$221 million
$4 million
$1.3 billion
Total: $2.1 billion

Chuck Colson, former Nixon aide, now active in prison ministries, talks with inmates at Powhattan Correction Center

—PHOTO BY DAVID BURNET, COURTESY OF CONTACT PRESS IMAGES

local ministers and priests. Later, the large institutions of the early 1800s created the need for a full-time chaplain on the premises.

The **correctional chaplaincy** has been and is currently the least sought-after position among ministers, who evidently prefer to serve more conventional congregations. Part of the problem, too, is the remote location of most prisons and a widespread public belief (shared by many administrators) that religion in prisons should be confined to the chaplain's traditional duties.[8] A movement has sprung up to establish a core of clinically oriented clerics, but the correctional field is less attractive to them than are other kinds of institutions. There is a definite need to upgrade the role of the correctional chaplain in order to attract the best into the institutions. The role of the chief chaplain can be enhanced if it becomes accredited by the Association for Clinical Pastoral Education. With that background, the chaplain can develop programs,[9] recruit and train chaplaincy candidates, and even use seminary students to augment his or her resources.

The new and growing special-interest groups inside prisons, those whose religious orientation is toward a particular ethnic group, culture, or subculture, do not agree with the traditional religious outlets. As we noted in Chapter 19, their right to pursue their faiths while confined has been firmly established. The traditional correctional institution has provided Protestant, Roman Catholic, and (sometimes) Jewish chaplains as representatives of the three major religious groups in the United States because it was not feasible to have a cleric for each and every religion observed by different inmates. The chaplains attempt to offer ecumenical services and have tried to provide worship for all prisoners. However, the

CHAPLAINS

What does a modern chaplain do in a prison environment? The image of a chaplain delivering a sermon from a pulpit does not describe the many and difficult duties of a prison chaplain. Most chaplains feel they have been called to this service, but they do the bulk of their ministry behind the scenes, offering spiritual hope to the depressed, lost, and often forgotten inmates. They come from many faiths but often find themselves providing religious and counseling services to inmates with religious backgrounds far different from their own. These servants of faith represent humanity and hope behind the bars of prison.

Jobs in Corrections

Correctional job titles and descriptions vary according to the structure and needs of each institution and agency. However, certain categories remain fairly constant and can give you an idea of the types of jobs available and the many directions your career can take. Check with your agency for more specific job descriptions and requirements.

Budget administrator: Performs or supervises work in one or more phases of budgeting.

Chaplain: Offers religious guidance and spiritual counseling to inmates. Requires ordination by a recognized ecclesiastical body; chaplains may be called upon to minister to inmates not of their faith.

Computer specialist: Manages or performs design, use, and maintenance of computer systems. Requires knowledge and familiarity with computers, computer-based systems, and programming.

Correctional institution administrator: Manages or helps manage correctional institutions, systems, or programs. Requires knowledge of penological theories, principles, and techniques as well as the problems, methods, and techniques of institutional management.

Correctional officer: Supervises the treatment and custody of offenders in correctional institutions.

Employee development specialist: Plans, supervises, or leads programs designed to train and develop employees and consults with or guides management concerning employee training and development issues. Requires an understanding of employee development objectives and techniques of education and training.

Facility manager: Manages and maintains buildings, grounds, and other facilities. Requires managerial skills and a broad technical knowledge of operating capabilities and maintenance requirements of various kinds of physical plants and equipment.

Financial manager: Maintains financial staff services such as auditing and credit analysis; coordinates financial policies and procedures.

Food service manager: Manages and supervises the operation of the institution's or department's food services, including the storeroom, kitchen, dining rooms, bakery, and procurement. Often requires certification as a registered dietitian and familiarity with federal, state, and local health codes and sanitary standards.

Health system administrator: Responsible for the administrative management of a health care delivery system and use of all available resources to provide the best possible patient care.

Industrial specialist: Assists or manages a prison industry. Requires practical knowledge of how an industry operates and the materials and facilities necessary.

Juvenile care worker: Supervises the treatment and custody of juvenile offenders in correctional or rehabilitation facilities.

Medical officer: Performs professional and scientific work in one or more fields of medicine. Requires the degree of doctor of medicine and, in most states, a current license to practice medicine.

Ombudsman: Acts as an unbiased liaison between inmates and facility administrators; investigates inmate complaints, reports findings, and helps achieve equitable settlements of disputes between inmates and correctional administration.

Psychologist: Works with inmates and corrections professionals offering counsel regarding the capacities, traits, interests, and activities of human behavior. Requires professional training in psychological principles, theories, methods, or data to practical situations and problems.

Personnel manager: Either directs or advises a personnel management program or provides staff leadership and technical guidance.

Probation/parole officer: Advises and counsels individuals who are on probation or parole; enforces and monitors compliance to rules imposed on the offender by either the court or parole board. Requires a bachelor's degree in social science, human behavior, or criminal justice.

Recreation specialist: Plans, organizes, and administers programs that promote inmates' physical, creative, artistic, and social development. Requires a general knowledge of the principles and techniques of recreation.

Safety manager: Offers technical advice on or manages occupational safety programs, regulations, and standards. Requires knowledge of the techniques of safety and pertinent aspects of engineering, psychology, and other factors affecting safety.

Teacher: Leads classes on various pertinent subjects for both juvenile and adult offenders. Requires a bachelor's degree plus certification by state education authority in specific subject area.

Training instructor: Administers or supervises training program development and instruction. Requires a combination of knowing how to lead a training program and a practical knowledge of the subject matter being taught.

Job categories and descriptions are based on information from Occupations Within the Federal Bureau of Prisons. ∎

SOURCE: Jody K. Spertzel, "A Correction Career Guide," *Corrections Today* 55:1 (1993): 37.

more vocal members of the smaller sects have protested that arrangement. The number of members of the Islamic faith who are incarcerated has grown considerably. As the need for religious service to these Muslims increases, local Imams are beginning to be more active in that ministry.

It is possible, if the chaplain's salary and image can be sufficiently upgraded, that ministers trained in the behavioral sciences will become part of the contemporary prison scene, a far cry from the Walnut Street missionaries whose sole function was to provide Bible reading and prayer. The new chaplains might well play an integrated part in the treatment team in future rehabilitation programs.

EDUCATIONAL AND TRAINING PROGRAMS
FOR INMATES

In most state correctional systems, education of incarcerated inmates is a legislative mandate. The largest group of treatment personnel are the teachers, who usually far outnumber those in counseling services. Although most institutions have some kind of educational program, there are marked differences in kind and extent. Early efforts were aimed simply at teaching prisoners to read. With 12 million people in the United States considered to be **functionally illiterate** (cannot read, write, or compute above the third grade level), it is not too surprising that those at the bottom of the barrel have literacy problems in even greater measure.

Today, most inmates are able to achieve at least a high school education (or **GED**) through institutional programs, and the more progressive institutions are offering courses at the two-year and four-year college level.[10] It is acknowledged that lack of education is a serious handicap when those people return to the free world: former offenders who cannot get jobs because of insufficient education are likely to return to crime. For that reason, education has long been regarded as a primary rehabilitative tool in the correctional field. The gap between the need for educational services and the provision of adequate educational and vocational training is wide, however.[11]

One of the first barriers to effective educational programs is, once again, the problem of administrative considerations: operational requirements, security needs, shortage of teachers, shortage of educational materials, tight budgets, and

Howard Gill (1890–1989) directed the construction of the Massachusetts Correctional Institution at Norfolk and became its first superintendent in 1927. This radically different facility, for those times, was praised by Edwin Sutherland, the dean of American criminology, as the "most noteworthy achievement in the field of penology in the United States in the last generation." Gill founded the Institute for Correctional Administration at American University, one of the first centers to provide professional training for prison managers.

Literacy and Its Impact on Re-offending

The federal prison system, known as the Federal Bureau of Prisons (FBOP), established a mandatory literacy program in 1982 requiring sixth grade reading as the minimum literacy standard. This was changed to eighth grade reading in 1986 and General Education Development certificate (GED) in 1991. The adult basic education program has been very successful: when completion rates are compared from 1981 to 1990, an encouraging 724 percent increase has occurred in the number of inmates achieving basic literacy.

Three recent studies of the effects of education on reoffending are also encouraging. Fairchild reported on all three.

On the first, there was only a 15 percent reoffending rate for New Mexico inmates who had completed at least one year of college, compared to 68 percent for the general population. Fairchild found zero recidivism for college graduates versus a reoffending rate of 55 percent for the general prison population studies at a California prison. Finally, Fairchild reported that none of the first two hundred Indiana reformatory inmates earning a college degree offered by a university extension program returned to the reformatory. ■

a lack of inmate motivation.[12] Inmates and staff are often handicapped by unsuitable or out-of-date textbooks, often below the level of the street sophistication of the average adult prisoner. Inmates who are prevented from attending classes for disciplinary reasons[13] may miss enough to be required to forgo the rest of the term. Denying education as part of disciplinary action devalues its effectiveness as a treatment component and doubles the punishment factor.

The classes held in most institutions are conventional and relatively old fashioned, in contrast with those that use the new learning technology and innovations available to students at all levels on the outside. Most prisoners have had little formal education and probably resisted whatever teaching they were exposed to. Material that bored them as children or truant teenagers is not likely to hold them enthralled as adults. What mature felons neither want nor need are "Dick and Jane" readers or other textbooks designed for children. Inmates may be actually or functionally illiterate, but they are adults in the main, and are in possession of a lot of street smarts. To be given such materials is embarrassing and difficult for them. But because of the low priority and minimal funds assigned to education in most institutions, it is those useless texts that prisoners are often provided, usually by public schools that no longer use them. Small wonder that most prison programs are neither accredited nor enthusiastically supported by inmates. Inmates prefer listening and reading modes for learning.[14] The learning disabled (from 7 to 25 percent of institutional populations) may respond best to tape recorders, television, and computers.[15]

The surprising fact is that some educational services not only survive but even contribute to the inmates' rehabilitation.[16] In Ohio, the Department of Rehabilitation and Correction was finally able to establish a complete school district composed entirely of the educational programs within the state prison system. In the states of New York and Washington, education programs are contracted with local community colleges and they provide excellent programs, from adult basic education[17] to degree programs in the institutions. **Project Newgate**, a program bringing the first years of college into the prisons, along with instructors and a complete curriculum, was the model for such programs in the 1970s.

Prison Release Programs

Work, occupational training, and education are three major objectives for which inmates are allowed to leave the prison. In most states, the legal mechanism for allowing an inmate to leave prison is the furlough program: the legislature extends the limits of confinement to include placement in the community while the prisoner pursues some common and identifiable correctional goal.

Furlough candidates are usually screened carefully and supervised by an agency. Although the extent of recidivism among furlough users is unknown, it is generally believed to be low. One reason for the low recidivism probably is that furloughees in most jurisdictions remain inmates and can be returned to prison easily if they show overt signs of being unable to conform their behavior to community expectations.

Oklahoma has used home furlough (house arrest of inmates) as a mechanism to reduce prison overcrowding, and the recidivism rate is markedly low. More states are exploring the opportunities of increasing furlough programs to extend the limits of confinement for low-risk inmates and plan to couple house arrest with electronic monitoring, unscheduled drug and alcohol testing, and supervision fees. This approach may become a major prison-release mechanism in the next decade. ■

Two other education-related programs that have been attempted, with varying results, are work/training release or furlough and educational release. In educational release, inmates are allowed to leave the institution to attend college, high school, or vocational-technical schools during the day, though they must return to the institution or an approved site when not at school or at night. The use of educational release became quite widespread in the United States, but the programs were usually curtailed due to highly visible failures or budget cuts. In the work/training-release program, an inmate may be allowed to leave the limits of confinement to secure education and a job; this enables offenders to develop a work history, learn a trade, support dependents, or even make restitution to the victim of their crimes. Of the 184,300 furloughs in 1994, only 394 inmates failed to return or committed another crime, a .2 percent failure rate.[18]

Education, medical care, and religious practice have served as the basic treatment programs in America's prisons since the days of the Walnut Street Jail. In recent years, this limited three-sided approach to treatment has expanded to include a wide variety of programs aimed at the rehabilitation of incarcerated offenders.

THE VOCATIONAL-REHABILITATION MODEL

Vocational and technical training in prisons has been available to prisoners ever since the industrial prison was established in the early 1800s. That early training, however, was aimed not at prisoner rehabilitation but at institutional profit. Later, at the Elmira Reformatory, the concept of training for the purpose of teaching a trade to ex-offenders was introduced, and it has slowly taken root over the years.

A major setback to adequate **vocational training** came with the passage of restrictive federal laws on the interstate transport of prison industry goods. Those laws, passed in the mid-1930s, sounded the death knell for many work programs in state prisons. Only in the past twenty years have institutions begun to reemphasize vocational training programs.

The waste of prisoners' time in idleness is staggering. Neil Singer conducted an analysis of potential inmate economic benefits in 1973 and found that 208,000 felons in prison could earn an average of $8,038 each year, or $1.67 billion in total.[19] Now, a generation later, and with today's prison population of

IDENTIFYING SUICIDE RISKS

Suicide is one of the leading unnatural causes of death in corrections. The following are the most common signs or risk indicators for potential suicide in prisons and jails:

1. Any pronounced mood or behavioral change;
2. Receipt of bad news, such as divorce or death of a loved one;
3. A history of mental illness or chemical dependency;
4. A terminal illness, such as cancer or AIDS;
5. Rape or threats of sexual assault;
6. Being incarcerated for the first time and facing a very long sentence;
7. A family history of suicide;
8. Too much or too little sleep;
9. Increase or loss of appetite or weight;
10. Talk about death or preoccupation with death or suicide.

approximately 883,000, that amount could be estimated at closer to $7.2 billion (in 1973 dollars)! Such economic realities should cause legislators, managers, and citizens to wince when they appraise current forms of treatment. In addition, the evidence is strong that participation in prison training programs significantly lowers inmate misconduct behavior.[20]

The goals of vocational training, when aligned too closely with institution-oriented goals, can have some problems. As noted by Guynes and Grieser,

> Vocational training consumes both raw materials and staff instructional time. When these costs are imposed on industries, the institutional cost reduction goals are endangered.
>
> The development of good work habits in a real-world environment requires production with a minimum of "featherbedding." In a correctional environment, this is contrary to the need to maximize the number of inmates on the work force (i.e., reduce idleness).
>
> In order to maximize inmates' capacity to learn to manage their pay, adequate salaries must be provided. While this goal is compatible with the institutional goal of cost reduction (to the degree that the offender is then responsible for room and board and commissary needs), the associated managerial expense may well increase product costs rather than reduce them. Certainly, the increased salary required to provide gate money runs counter to reducing the state's incarceration expenses.[21]

A common problem with prison industries is their multiple goals, for they sometimes shift and are always ambiguous. The prison administrator may believe the goal of prison industries to be generation of profits, shop managers are convinced it is to train inmates, and inmates believe it is "make work" and that they will receive some wage unrelated to productivity.[22] Leadership in resolving those conflicting goals was exerted by Congress in 1979, when it passed the Prison-Industries Enhancement Act, selectively repealing portions of the federal laws limiting prison industries. Since then, over twenty states (such as Arizona, Minnesota, Washington, and Kansas) have authorized some form of private sector involvement with state penal industries, such as in the areas of data processing, hotel chain reservations, and manufacturing. Many of these private industry efforts must deal with insurance, initial plant investment costs, and quality control problems. It remains to be seen how effective private industry will be in collaborating with prisons,[23] but such efforts are welcome signs in times of prison overcrowding.

These procedures, taken together, offer a realistic solution to one of the most serious problems impeding the successful return of offenders to an employment-oriented society. To assist in this effort, many professionals work in the field of corrections to provide treatment. The most prominent are discussed in the following sections.

Exciting programs working with companies in South Carolina, California, and Connecticut have formed successful projects with state and local correctional agencies. Some positive features of these collaborations include:

1. A cost-competitive, motivated work force, which can continue to work after release from prison;
2. The proximity of a prison-based feeder plant to the company's regular facility;
3. Financial incentives, including low-cost industrial space and equipment purchase subsidy, that are offered by correctional officials;

Mary Belle Harris (1874–1957) had a lengthy career in corrections and pioneered development of evaluation and classification of inmates. She was the first superintendent for the women's federal prison at Alderson, West Virginia that opened in 1925. Her management style underscored:

1. Too many staff members utilize lack of information as an excuse for doing nothing.
2. For the average run of problems, the less attention paid to peculiarities, the better.
3. Employment of parolees serves as a model to others being asked to do so.
4. No work should be used as punishment as it degrades the positive concept of labor.
5. Judges should visit facilities to which they send individuals.
6. Inmates should be given tasks they can attain to know success and achievement.

4. Safe work environment due to the presence of security personnel and a metal detector that keeps weapons out of the shop area, and;

5. The partial return to society of inmate earnings to pay state and federal taxes, offset incarceration costs, contribute to the support of the inmate's families, and compensate victims.[24]

Professionals in the Field of Corrections

PSYCHOLOGISTS

Psychology is concerned with measuring and evaluating an individual's intellectual capability and his or her ability to cope and adjust in society. The use of mass testing, popularized in World War I, clearly had possibilities for prisons. With the advent of the first classification program in New Jersey in 1918, the psychologist became a dominant force in the classification process. Today, IQ tests and other measurements developed by psychologists have become standard in classification and treatment decisions. Psychologists have continued to outnumber other professionals who seek to determine the cause of and cure for criminal behavior. With their relatively straightforward measurements and questionnaires, psychologists are generally more acceptable to the correctional staff than psychiatrists are.[25]

PSYCHIATRISTS

Although psychiatrists became involved in prison activity early in the development of treatment programs, the correctional team has not readily accepted their presence. It is often difficult for the mission-oriented custody staff to accept the abstract, seemingly indecisive approach that is the hallmark of psychiatric treatment. The correctional officer would prefer to have all offenders with psychiatric problems relegated to mental institutions.[26] That distrust of prison psychiatrists also stems from an awareness that competent psychiatrists in private practice can make several times the salaries offered by prisons.

Another stumbling block to really effective psychiatric service in prison is the institutional environment itself: many psychiatrists would argue that little can be done in the way of treatment inside the monolithic institutions. Their efforts in prisons, as a result, stress diagnosis rather than treatment. This combination of environment and role may mean that some state systems have very few full-time psychiatric staff members and others have none. To gain maximum help from the psychiatrist, the whole function of most prisons would have to be changed. The new pattern envisioned by the psychiatrist would be along the lines of the hospital model, in which treatment diagnoses can be seen through to completion. An alternative might be a small urban-based short-term treatment facility for handling moderately disturbed offenders.

SOCIOLOGISTS

Sociologists have been latecomers into correctional treatment programs. They are especially helpful in identifying and developing the roles and structures of the prison subcultures and groups which interact with the administrative personnel. Many of the current research projects in prisons and other areas of correctional treatment are being directed by sociologists. This group of professionals has also

DIAGNOSTIC AND RECEPTION CENTERS

Diagnostic and reception centers are generally to be found as separate facilities or units within a correctional facility or system. Newly admitted inmates are sent there to go through intensive evaluation and classification, orientation, and reassignment to the proper facility and level of custody. Modern reception centers differ from earlier models, reflecting new realities as to the types of inmates and viable options in the present day. Most centers are now called "reception and evaluation" (R and E) centers. These new procedures are more receptive to overall system requirements and options.

been helpful in determining the social factors that cause offenders to commit or repeat crimes. The findings and recommendations from many sociological studies are helping to push corrections back into the community.

Sociologists have also worked their way into administrative positions in corrections, where they can exert more influence on the complex organization and its programs. Many higher education programs in corrections are housed in university sociology departments; here criminology is handled as an integral part of the discipline of sociology.

SOCIAL WORKERS

Social work became particularly important in the spectrum of corrections when it began to emphasize rehabilitation. The **caseworker** is essential in the presentence investigation phase, and many probation officers and parole officers received their training in social work. It seems reasonable that the social worker became more involved in institutional programs as those programs developed an emphasis on treatment. Social workers had already taken their places in school programs, hospitals, and mental health institutions, among others. The basic concepts of social casework can be successfully applied in the authoritarian atmosphere of the prison.[27] The social worker has the training to help the offender adapt to the prison situation inside the walls.

Barnes and Teeters, in their classic text on criminology, list four prerequisites for effective casework in prison:

Essential Eligibility Requirements: ADA

If an inmate is "qualified" for participation in a program or activity, excluding the inmate or limiting his or her participation would violate one or more of the general prohibitions of discrimination in 28 C.F.R. §35.130....

(b)(1) A public entity, in providing any aid, benefit, or service, may not, directly or through contractual, licensing, or other arrangements, on the basis of disability:

(i) Deny a qualified individual with a disability the opportunity to participate in or benefit from the aid, benefit, or service;

(ii) Afford a qualified individual with a disability an opportunity to participate in or benefit from the aid, benefit, or service that is not equal to that afforded others;

(iii) Provide a qualified individual with a disability with an aid, benefit, or service that is not as effective in affording equal opportunity to obtain the same result, to gain the same benefit, or to reach the same level of achievement as that provided to others;

(iv) Provide different or separate aids, benefits, or services to individuals with disabilities or to any class of individuals with disabilities than is provided to others unless such action is necessary to provide qualified individuals with disabilities with aids, benefits, or services that are as effective as those provided to others;

(b)(2) A public entity may not deny a qualified individual with a disability the opportunity to participate in services, programs, or activities that are not separate or different, despite the existence of permissibly separate or different programs or activities.

(b)(7) A public entity shall make reasonable modifications in policies, practices, or procedures when the modifications are necessary to avoid discrimination on the basis of disability, unless the public entity can demonstrate that making the modifications would fundamentally alter the nature of the service, program, or activity.

(b)(8) A public entity shall not impose or apply eligibility criteria that screen out or tend to screen out an individual with a disability or any class of individuals with disabilities from fully and equally enjoying any service, program, or activity, unless such criteria can be shown to be necessary for the provision of the service, program, or activity being offered.

(d) A public entity shall administer services, programs, and activities in the most integrated setting appropriate to the needs of qualified individuals with disabilities. ∎

SOURCE: Paula Rubin and Susan McCampbell, *The Americans With Disabilities Act and Criminal Justice* (Washington D.C.: U.S. Dept. of Justice), p. 3.

First, it must be accepted by the administration that there are constructive elements in a prison experience; second, that these elements can be translated into a sound correctional program; third, that the staff dedicate itself to the task of helping the inmate find maturity as a mark of social responsibility; fourth, that the administration provide the structure or climate in which the case worker can operate effectively.[28]

SOCIAL CASEWORK IN PRISON

Social workers in prison settings serve many functions and roles. Inmates encounter social workers at intake and classification, in assignment to treatment programs, in correctional counseling and crisis intervention, in reality therapy and responsibility training, and in behavior modification and group counseling sessions. Social workers also work closely with families of inmates, coordinate volunteers in corrections, and translate inmate concerns to other correctional staff and administrators. Clearly, the role of the social caseworker is especially suited to working out inmate problems.

The Reintegration Model

The movement toward treatment and corrections in the community has highlighted the need to make programs inside the walls relate to circumstances in the outside world. Crime cannot be controlled by the reformation of prisoners alone. There must be continued reformation and reintegration efforts in the community.

Toward that end, many of the barriers shutting off the prison from the community have come down in the last decade. The treatment concept has been

Marion Federal Prison, Illinois, 1988. Inmates eating together

—PHOTO BY SUSAN MEISELAS, COURTESY OF MAGNUM PHOTOS, INC.

Questions Most Frequently Asked About ADA

1. Does the ADA apply to corrections facilities?

Yes. Title II of the ADA applies to all public entities including state and local governments and the agencies that operate under their auspices. This includes jails, detention centers, and prisons. This section of the law covers all programs, services, and activities provided by the state or local government through its agencies.

2. Do short-term holding facilities (i.e., less than 1 year) have fewer obligations under the ADA than long-term facilities?

The ADA applies regardless of how long an inmate with a disability remains in custody. However, the length of an inmate's incarceration would certainly be a consideration in evaluating whether or not a modification to a facility's policies, practices, or procedures would fundamentally alter the nature of the service, program, or activity. Remember also that while public entities are not generally required to provide personal devices (for example, wheelchairs or hearing aids) or personal services (for example, attendants), this is not true for correctional facilities and other custodial entities.

3. During an intake evaluation, can an inmate be asked if he or she is HIV positive or has AIDS?

Public entities may not make unnecessary inquiries into the existence of a disability. If it is necessary to know whether an inmate who uses a wheelchair can perform manual work to determine eligibility for inmate work programs, then it might be permissible to ask. However, if asking about this disability is done as a general matter and not in connection with providing services, it could be challenged under the ADA as irrelevant. As a good practice, the agency should also be sure that medical information about inmates, such as their HIV or AIDS status, remains separate and confidential.

4. Is the correctional facility required to provide a sign language interpreter for a hearing-impaired inmate who wishes to attend Alcoholic Anonymous (AA) or Narcotics Anonymous meetings? What if the inmate's attendance at these meetings is court-ordered?

Generally, the corrections facility will be required to provide effective communication through auxiliary aids and services that enable the inmate to participate in such meetings in a meaningful way. This is true regardless of whether attendance is mandatory (court-ordered) or voluntary. An inmate cannot be required to pay the costs of auxiliary aids required by the ADA.

Remember, auxiliary aids that are *effective* are required. When interacting with deaf or hard-of-hearing inmates, writing notes for short exchanges may be effective, but for interactions such as an AA meeting, disciplinary hearings in which the inmate may lose privileges, participation in the facility's GED programs, or visits with an attorney, interpreters will most likely be more appropriate. Primary consideration must be given to the request of the person with the disability.

5. Does the ADA require that a law library contain duplicate volumes in Braille to accommodate inmates with vision impairments?

Correctional facilities are only required to provide auxiliary aids and services where necessary to enable an inmate with a disability to participate in programs, services, and activities. Doing so will not be required if it fundamentally alters the nature of the program, service, or activity, or if it causes undue financial and administrative burdens on the agency. An undue burden is significant difficulty or expense based on all of the resources available for use in the program. While duplicating an entire library might constitute an undue burden, printing relevant cases or portions of books might be in order. Similarly, it might be possible to provide persons to read to visually impaired inmates, or recorded books. Auxiliary aids need only provide equal opportunity to participate in a program, service, or activity. They do not have to be the most expensive accommodation.

6. Would a program that gives credit toward early release based on hard manual labor violate the ADA because it screens out inmates whose disability prevents them from participating in this program?

Probably. This is also a matter for consideration for the "boot camp" programs that are gaining popularity in many states and localities. Remember, this may be a denial of equal opportunity for inmates with disabilities to benefit from participation in this type of program, service, or activity.

One solution is to find another way for inmates who cannot participate in "hard labor" to get "good time" credit by performing other tasks. For example, inmates with mobility impairments might be able to

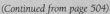

(Continued from page 504)

Questions Most Frequently Asked About ADA

work as readers for inmates with vision impairments; inmates with vision impairments might be able to earn credit by working in the laundry.

7. Can all inmates with disabilities be put in the same cell block? In other words, can I dedicate a corrections facility to persons with disabilities?

Generally, no. Remember, one of the goals of the ADA is to integrate persons with disabilities into the mainstream of society. This includes a community within a society, even a prison community. Inmates with disabilities should be classified and housed the same as inmates without disabilities with the same classification status *unless* housing the inmate in that location would pose a direct threat to the safety of staff or other inmates. Of course, the ADA does not require the integration of vulnerable prisoners who prefer to be segregated.

Inmate classification systems may consider an inmate's disability as an override to change housing location if a threat exists, but disability should not be a primary factor in determining the inmate's classification.

8. May inmates with mobility impairments be put together on the first floor for easy evacuation in case of fire?

Safety issues will permit some flexibility in segregating inmates with disabilities. Although it is possible to keep inmates with mobility impairments in ground floor accommodations for safer evacuation purposes, it is a good idea to integrate these inmates among other inmates on the ground level.

9. Does the ADA give inmates working in correctional facilities rights as employees under Title I?

Probably not. Two Federal courts recently held that inmates working for prison industries were not entitled to minimum wage under the Fair Labor Standards Act. The courts reasoned that there is no employee-employer relationship between an inmate and the correctional facility for which he or she performs hard labor. It would seem that, by analogy, the same could apply to the ADA. However, no court has yet addressed this issue specifically.

10. How does the ADA affect the providing of special education services to inmates over the age of 22?

The ADA does not preempt other federal or state laws to the extent that those laws meet the ADA requirements or expand upon them. While the ADA was probably never meant to encompass special education, it does require reasonable modifications to be made regardless of the individual's age.

Remember, any classes offered, whether special education or otherwise, need to be accessible to inmates with disabilities who wish to participate. Access includes physical accessibility; the ability to participate in the program, service, or activity; and effective communication.

SOURCE: Paula Rubin and Susan McCampbell, "The Americans with Disabilities Act and Criminal Justice: Providing Inmate Services," *Research in Action* (Washington, D.C.: U.S. Department of Justice, 1994), pp. 4–5.

expanded to encompass the efforts of community-oriented professionals, and community volunteers have begun to give offenders the support and guidance needed to ensure successful reintegration.[29] The main objective of the reintegration model is to return the offender to the community as a responsible and productive citizen, rather than a feared and shunned "ex-con" with little hope for success. Institutions dedicated to that objective have learned to overcome deficits in funding and personnel by using the ingenuity of prison staff and the resources available in the community. Teachers and graduate students are encouraged to offer courses on topics that will help reintegrate the inmate, including such subjects as social problems, mental health, and the use of community resources.[30]

Other assistance and support by outsiders help reduce the feeling of isolation and stigma that inevitably overtakes the incarcerated offender. No discussion of treatment would be complete without at least a mention of some of the various treatment modalities used in both prison and community corrections.

Some treatment programs can be found in every institution, although the treatment personnel might be given titles that would not reflect the particular training or discipline of a **counselor**. Those treatment modalities cannot be covered in depth in an introductory course but include transactional analysis, psychodrama, behavior modification, individual and group psychotherapy, therapeutic communities, emotional maturity instruction, and guides to "better living."[31]

In many institutions, the barriers are coming down for traffic in both directions ("the door swings both ways"). Outside activity by inmates and prison personnel ranges from touring lecture programs to work and educational furloughs. The latter programs serve as a method of graduated release back to the community. The rationale for graduated release has its roots in the problems faced by the newly released inmate. Release is a very stressful time for inmates, especially when they emerge directly from an institution. Inmates know they have failed in the past and fear they will fail again. Without a chance to ease back into society in stages, as happens in graduated release, the inmate feels very vulnerable if he or she has been inside the walls for a long period of time. The released prisoner needs new social skills and a chance to catch up with a rapidly moving society.

The **reintegration model** allows the inmate to take on increasing responsibilities until he or she is ready for complete acceptance by the community. It is the wave of the future, and treatment programs built around such a comprehensive and integrated plan will have much higher potential for success than the old custody/control methods. The true reintegration model recognizes the need to give the ex-offender a reasonable means of support. Hence good vocational training is important.

Summary

Corrections has undergone great change in the years since the emphasis shifted from custody to rehabilitation. Public safety demands that the convicted offender emerge from our correctional system a better person, certainly no worse, than when he or she entered it. That high expectation has stimulated the search for more effective ways to handle offenders. One reason for the pressure to create community-based corrections has been the recognition that prisonization can actually aggravate an offender's criminality.

It is clear the future of corrections lies in community-based programs. A major obstacle, however, is the prominence of the institutional model, with its physical plants and other programs already in operation, whereas no organized community program has yet gained widespread acceptance. So far, most community programs have emerged as demonstration projects or individual experiments, rather than as the products of systematic interaction among police, courts, and conventional correctional services.[32]

Incarceration clearly is a series of destructive situations for the offender: the custody model intensifies the likelihood of physical danger, deprivation of human values, and loss of self-esteem. It is a basic humanitarian concept that only offenders who pose a threat to society should be subjected to the trauma of incarceration. This last issue demands, of course, a valid system of diagnosis, classification, and evaluation.

One weakness apparent in analyzing the administrative or management functions in correctional agencies is that the superintendents, supervisors, and counselors are promoted from within the ranks because of their abilities as professionals or practitioners, with little regard for their training or qualifications as administrators. Or, if they have received training, it is too specialized in nature, too related to a specific field. Although those who find themselves in such positions do the best they can to perform adequately as administrators, they are nevertheless handicapped by their training or background.

Within the serious problems of the correctional institution, the correctional treatment process has many elements—from the more formalized approach of the social scientists, the medical professionals, and the educators to the efforts of community volunteers and release programs, and intelligent and humane corrections officers. The key to treatment is an organized program designed to prepare the inmate for successful reintegration within the free society. It is obvious how important the cooperation and understanding of the security and custody staff can be in the success of any of the efforts described as "treatment." As the single most influential agent of change, the correctional officer is the keystone to the success or failure of any kind of treatment program. A cooperative effort by custody and treatment staffs is the essence of an effective institutional program. But treatment cannot end at the prison gate. To ensure maximum success, the treatment must be continued and reinforced in the community. Community programs are discussed in Chapter 27. The next part discusses the various systems that provide corrections and treatment in America, from jails and detention systems to the new wave of privatization.

Review Questions

1. What are five common health problems found in prisons?
2. How are religious services delivered inside prisons?
3. Does education lower recidivism when inmates are paroled?
4. What kinds of inmates are given furloughs?
5. What jobs are available in prisons for staff? Inmates?

Words to Remember

medical services   correctional chaplaincy   vocational training
sick call   functionally illiterate   caseworker
goldbrickers   GED   counselor
hepatitis A and B   Project Newgate   reintegration model
plastic surgery

Endnotes

1. Ray Nelson, "Isolation of Staff from Inmates," *Corrections Today* 46:4 (1984): 106–108,110. See also Carol Fewell, "Successful Strategies: Integrating Health Care and Security Functions, *Corrections Today* 50:6 (1988): 20–22, and B. Jane Anno, "The Cost of Correctional Health Care: Results of a National Survey," *Journal of Prison and Jail Health* 9:2 (1990): 105–133.

2. Donald Evans, "Parole Board Under Attack in Ontario," *Corrections Today* 57:4 (1995): 151–152.

3. Several states contract with health maintenance services for comprehensive health care skills. Not only do such private organizations recruit and pay physicians, nurses, dentists and

psychiatrists, but most also assist in defending against lawsuits and carry malpractice insurance. One example is the Prison Health Services, Inc., of Wilmington, Delaware. See also recent issues of *Corrections Today* for listings of advertised services.

4. The relationship between ingestion of drugs and crime appears quite strong. See, in particular, the National Institute of Justice reports *Prisoners and Drugs: 1983)* and *Prisoners and Alcohol: 1983* (Washington, D.C.: U.S. Department of Justice, 1985). See also Bernard Gropper, *Probing the Links Between Drugs and Crime* (Washington, D.C.: U.S. Department of Justice, 1985), and Toni Atmore and Edward Bauchiero, "Substance Abuse: Identification and Treatment," *Corrections Today* 49 (1987): 22, 24, 26, 110. See also Donald McVinney, "Counseling Incarcerated Individuals with HIV Disease and Chemical Dependency," *Journal of Chemical Dependency Treatment* 4:2 (1991): 105–118.

5. Drug abuse is widespread among prison inmates but treatment programs are in short supply. See Donald Dowd, S. Dalzell, and Margaret Spencer, "The Sentencing Controversy: Punishment and Policy in the War Against Drugs," *Villanova Law Review* 40:2 (1995): 301–427.

6. California Department of Health Services, *Tuberculosis Transmission to Employees at a State Prison* (Berkeley: California Department of Health Services, 1991).

7. U.S. Department of Health and Human Services, *Control of Tuberculosis in Correctional Facilities: A Guide for Health Care Workers* (Washington, D.C.: U.S. Department of Health and Human Services, 1992). See also H. Parker Eams, "MDR Tuberculosis: New Tuberculosis Strain Demands Immediate Attention," *Corrections Today* 54:3 (1992): 64–66; Mary Campbell, "Proper Precautions: Shutting the Door on Infectious Diseases," *Corrections Today* 54:3 (1992): 68–74; and Patricia Satterfield, "Creative Strategies for Controlling Health Care Costs," *Corrections Today* 54:2 (1992): 190–194.

8. Jody Spertzel, "Rev. Henry Bouma: Chaplain's Ministry Links Facility with Community," *Corrections Today* 55:3 (1993): 91.

9. Arthur Pace, "Religious Volunteers Form Partnership with the Military's Chaplaincy Program," *Corrections Today* 55:5 (1993): 114–116.

10. Oklahoma prisoners have low tested educational levels, and many are reading-disadvantaged adult offenders (up to 40 percent of a prison's population). Computer-assisted instruction has been installed at six correctional facilities. See Frank McKane, "The Effect of Computer Assisted Instruction on Reading for Disadvantaged Offenders," Oklahoma Correctional Research Symposium (Oklahoma City: Oklahoma Criminal Justice Research Consortium, 1993), p. 12.

11. Richard Lawrence, "Classrooms vs. Prison Cells: Funding Policies for Education and Corrections," *Journal of Crime and Justice* 18:2 (1995): 113–126.

12. See the special feature issue on education found in *Corrections Today* 49 (June 1987), and Hans Toch, "Reintegrating Inmates Through Education," *Federal Probation* 51 (September 1987): 61–66. See also Steven Schlossman and Joseph Spillane, *Bright Hopes, Dim Realities: Vocational Innovation in American Correctional Education* (Santa Monica, CA: Rand Corporation, 1992), and Robert J. Di Vito, "Survey of Mandatory Education Practices in State Penal Institutions," *Journal of Correctional Education* 42:3 (1991): 126–132.

13. William Reed, "Motivation of Inmates for College Enrollment and the Effect of Higher Education and Vocational Training upon Inmate Discipline," *Education* (Santa Monica, CA: Rand Corporation, 1992). See also Ted Palmer, "Treatment and the Role of Classification: A Review of the Basics," *Crime and Delinquency* 30 (1984): 245–268.

14. T. L. Felton, "The Learning Modes of the Incarcerated Population," *Journal of Correctional Education* 45:3 (1994): 118–121.

15. Eva Fisher-Bloom, "The Import of Learning Disabilities in Correctional Treatment," *Forum* 7:3 (1995): 20–26.

16. Carolyn Buser, Peter Leone, and Mary Bannon, "Segregation: Does Education Stop Here?" *Corrections Today* 49 (1987): 16–18.

17. See Rick Linden and Linda Perry, "The Effectiveness of Prison Educational Programs," *Journal of Offender Counseling, Services and Rehabilitation* 6 (1982): 43–57.

18. C. Camp and G. Camp, *Correctional Yearbook 1995: Adult Corrections* (South Salem, NY: Criminal Justice Institute, 1995), p. 65.

19. Neil Singer, *The Value of Inmate Manpower* (Washington, D.C.: American Bar Association Commission on Correctional Facilities and Manpower, 1973). See U.S. Government

Accounting Office, *Federal Prisons: Inmate and Staff Views on Education and Work Training Programs* (Washington, D.C.: U.S. Government Accounting Office, 1993), pp. 3–4. Inmates are particularly keen to work in the Bureau of Prison Industries (UNICOR). See also the special correctional education theme issue, *Corrections Today* 55:1 (1993): 36–81.

20. Kathleen Maguire, "Prison Industry Programs and Inmate Institutional Behavior," *Forum* 8:1 (1996): 39–42.

21. Randall Guynes and Robert C. Grieser, "Contemporary Prison Industry Goals," *A Study of Prison Industry: History, Components, and Goals* (Washington, D.C.: U.S. Department of Justice, January 1986), p. 25.

22. Joint Subcommittee on the Economic Productivity of the Prison Population and on Work Release Programs, *Report to the Governor and General Assembly of Virginia* (Richmond: Senate Document 22, 1982). But see the U.S. Government Accounting Office, *Federal Prisons*, p. 4.

23. Gail Funke et al., "The Future of Correctional Industries," *Prison Journal* 42 (1981): 37–51. See also Joan Mullen, Kent Chabotar, and Deborah Carrow, *The Privatization of Corrections* (Washington, D.C.: U.S. Department of Justice, 1985), and Charles Logan, "The Propriety of Proprietary Prisons," *Federal Probation* 51 (September 1987): 35–40.

24. George Sexton, *Work in American Prisons: Joint Ventures with the Private Sector* (Washington, D.C.: U.S. Department of Justice, November 1995), p. 2.

25. Ibid.

26. See Stephen Hardy, "Dealing with the Mentally Disturbed and Emotionally Disturbed," *Corrections Today* 46 (June 1984): 16–18, 126, and Sol Chanales, "Medical and Psychiatric Responses to Prisoners," *Journal of Counseling, Services and Rehabilitation* 8 (1983): v–viii. See also George A. Harris, ed., *Tough Customers: Counseling Unwilling Clients* (Laurel, MD: American Correctional Association, 1991).

27. Daniel Juda, "On the Special Problems of Creating Group Cohesion Within a Prison Setting," *Journal of Offender Counseling, Services and Rehabilitation* 8 (1983): 47–60.

28. Harry Elmer Barnes and Negley K. Teeters, *New Horizons in Criminology*, 3rd ed. (Englewood Cliffs, NJ: Prentice Hall, 1959), pp. 472–473. See also Edward W. Gondolf, "A Victim-Based Assessment of Court-Mandated Counseling for Batterers," *Criminal Justice Review* 16:2 (1991): 214–226.

29. Edward Latessa, Larry Travis, and Harry E. Allen, "Volunteers and Paraprofessionals in Parole: Current Practices," *Journal of Offender Counseling, Services and Rehabilitation* 8 (1983): 91–107.

30. David Onek, *Pairing College Students with Delinquents: The Minnesota Intensive Case Monitoring Program* (San Francisco: National Council on Crime and Delinquency, 1994).

31. Gregory Falkins, M. Pendergast, and D. Anglin. "Drug Treatment in the Criminal Justice System" *Federal Probation* 58:3 (1994): 37–44, and Patrick Kinkade and D. Jenkins, "Problems in Establishing Alternative Programs in Existing Correctional Institutions," *Federal Probation* 58:3 (1994): 37–44.

32. Kay Harris, "Key Differences Among Community Corrections Acts in the United States," *Prison Journal* 76:2 (1996): 129–238.

*R*ecommended Readings: Part VI

American Correctional Association. *The Effective Correctional Officer*. Laurel, MD: American Correctional Association, 1992.

Anno, B. Jaye. "The Cost of Correctional Health Care: Results of a National Survey." *Journal of Prison & Jail Health* 9:2 (1990): 105–133.

Chaiken, Jan, et al. *The Impact of Fiscal Limitation on California's Criminal Justice System*. Santa Monica, CA: Rand Corporation, 1981.

Cohen, Jacqueline. "Incapacitating Criminals: Recent Research Findings." *Research in Brief*, pp. 1–5. Washington, D.C.: U.S. Department of Justice, 1983.

Cullen, Francis T., Edward J. Latessa, and Velmer S. Burton, Jr. "The Correctional Orientation of Prison Wardens: Is the Rehabilitative Ideal Supported?" *Criminology* 31:1 (1993): 69–92.

Currie, Elliott. *What Kind of Future? Violence and Public Safety in the Year 2000.* San Francisco: National Council on Crime and Delinquency, 1987.

Del Carmen, Ronaldo V. "The Supreme Court and Prison Excessive Use of Force Cases: Does One Test Fit All?" *Federal Probation* 56:2 (1992): 44–47.

DeLuca, H. R., Thomas J. Miller, and Carl F. Wiedemann, "Punishment vs. Rehabilitation: A Proposal for Revising Sentencing Practices," *Federal Probation* 55:3 (1991): 24–27.

Di Vito, Robert J. "Survey of Mandatory Education Practices in State Penal Institutions," *Journal of Correctional Education* 42:3 (1991): 126–132.

Esparaza, David, C. Curry, and B. Orozco. *The Three Strikes and You're Out Law: A Preliminary Assessment.* Sacramento, CA: Legislative Office, 1995.

Franke, Herman. "The Rise and Decline of Solitary Confinement: Social-Historical Explanations of the Long-Term Penal Changes." *British Journal of Criminology* 32:2 (1992): 125–143.

Gondolf, Edward W. "A Victim-Based Assessment of Court-Mandated Counseling for Batterers." *Criminal Justice Review* 16:2 (1991): 214–226.

Greenwood, Peter, and Frank Zimring. *One More Chance: The Pursuit of Promising Intervention Strategies for Chronic Juvenile Offenders.* Santa Monica, CA: Rand Corporation, 1985.

Harris, George A., ed. *Tough Customers: Counseling Unwilling Clients.* Laurel, MD: American Correctional Association, 1991.

Harris, Kay. "Key Differences Among Community Corrections Acts in the United States." *Prison Journal* 76:2 (1996): 129–238.

Harris, Patricia M., Liz Mealy, Herman Matthews, et al. "A Wilderness Challenge Program as Correctional Treatment." *Journal of Offender Rehabilitation* 19:3,4 (1993): 149–164.

Huggins, M. Wayne, Edward F. Reynolds, James E. Dare, et al. "Accreditation." *Corrections Today* 54:3 (1992): 40–62.

Light, Stephen C. "Assaults on Prison Officers: Interactional Theme." *Justice Quarterly* 8:2 (1991): 217–242.

McCulloh, Robert. *A Comparative Analysis of Juvenile Justice Standards and the JJDP Act.* Washington, D.C.: U.S. Department of Justice, 1981.

McVinney, Donald. "Counseling Incarcerated Individuals with HIV Disease and Chemical Dependency." *Journal of Chemical Dependency Treatment* 4:2 (1991): 105–118.

Morton, Joann B., et al. "Women in Corrections." *Corrections Today* 54:6 (1992): 76–180.

Petersilia, Joan. *Expanding Options for Criminal Sentencing.* Santa Monica, CA: Rand Corporation, 1987.

Schlossman, Steven, and Joseph Spillane. *Bright Hopes, Dim Realities: Vocational Innovation in American Correctional Education.* Santa Monica, CA: Rand Corporation, 1992.

Selkey, William L., and Steven A. Anderson. "A Model for Ranking the Punitiveness of the States." *Journal of Quantitative Criminology* 8:2 (1992): 217–232.

Simonsen, Clifford. *Juvenile Justice in America,* 3rd ed. New York: Macmillan, 1991.

Steadman, Henry J., Edward J. Holobean, Jr., and Joel Dvoskin. "Estimating Mental Health Needs and Service Utilization Among Prisoner Inmates." *Bulletin of the American Academy of Psychiatry and the Law* 19:3 (1991): 297–307.

Steinke, Pamela. "Using Situational Factors to Predict Types of Prison Violence." *Journal of Offender Rehabilitation* 17:1 (1991): 119–132.

Stohr, Mary K., and Linda L. Zupan. "Street-Level Bureaucrats and Service Provision in Jail: The Failure of Officers to Identify the Needs of Inmates." *American Journal of Criminal Justice* 16:2 (1992): 75–94.

Super, John T., T. H. Blau, B. Charles, et al. "Using Psychological Tests to Discriminate Between 'Best' and 'Least Best' Correctional Officers." *Journal of Criminal Justice* 21:2 (1992): 143–150.

Sweeney, Laura T., and Craig Haney. "The Influences of Race on Sentencing: A Meta-Analytic Review of Experimental Studies." *Behavioral Sciences & the Law* 10:2 (1992): 179–195.

Turner, Susan, and Joan Petersilia. "Work Release in Washington: Effects on Recidivism and Courtroom Costs." *Prison Journal* 76:2 (1996): 138–164.

Van Voorhis, Patricia, Francis T. Cullen, Bruce G. Link, et al. "The Impact of Race and Gender on Correctional Officers' Orientation to the Integrated Environment." *Journal of Research in Crime and Delinquency* 28:4 (1991): 472–500.

Wright, Thomas A. "Correctional Employee Turnover: A Longitudinal Study." *Journal of Criminal Justice* 21:2 (1993): 131–142.

PART SEVEN

Correctional Systems

CHAPTER TWENTY-FIVE

State *and* Local Systems

*O*verview

In past chapters, we have examined the philosophies, clients, and the functions and tasks of the operators of America's prisons. We have seen the male/female and racial allocations to the facilities that make up systems that cost the taxpayers over $21 billion to operate each year. (See Figure 25-1 for breakdown of these system costs.) This chapter will take you into the basic functions and characteristics of the state prisons, using as our vehicle male adult offenders, who constitute 93 percent of the population. Women inmates are discussed in Chapter 16. While they are not an insignificant part of daily state and local adult prison activity, the male inmate and institution will be used here as a demonstration of how most of the systems are operated.

*S*tate Correctional Institutions: The Core of the System

This chapter explores the state and certain large-city, locally operated systems for housing the well over 1,035,000 adult sentenced male and female offenders in the 1,449 adult state and local prisons in America as of 1994[1] (see Table 25-1). Juvenile institutions, detention centers, jails, workhouses, and other facilities for misdemeanants and minor offenders are not included. The major correctional institutions contained in the state systems are maximum, medium, and minimum security prisons, most of which are modeled after the nineteenth-century concepts in the Auburn penitentiary.

These institutions form the core of most state correctional programs charged with the simultaneous, and often conflicting, functions of punishment and reform. Most are short on money and personnel, but they are still expected to prevent their graduates

The endurance of these monolithic structures is surpassed only by the tenacity of the assumptions and attitudes on which they were founded: the cause of crime is located in the individual offender; he should be punished for his acts; behavior is modifiable; and isolated institutions are appropriate settings in which to modify an individual's behavior. America has created a theory, reformation by confinement, and the system has been unwilling to abandon it although it has proved unworkable.

—William G. Nagel,
The New Red Barn

from returning to crime. Security and custody are the primary emphases in these prisons, and their environments are isolated both physically and philosophically from the mainstream of life. James V. Bennett, a former director of the Federal Bureau of Prisons, described the ironic situation forty years ago:

> Even our modern prison system is proceeding on a rather uncertain course because its administration is necessarily a series of compromises. On the one hand, prisons are expected to punish; on the other, they are supposed to reform. They are expected to discipline rigorously at the same time that they teach self-reliance. They are built to be operated like vast impersonal machines, yet they are expected to fit men to live normal community lives. They operate in accordance with a fixed autocratic routine, yet they are expected to develop individual initiative. All too frequently restrictive laws force prisoners into idleness despite the fact that one of their primary objectives is to teach men how to earn an honest living. They refuse a prisoner a voice in self-government, but they expect him to become a thinking citizen in a democratic society. To some, prisons are nothing but "country clubs" catering to the whims and fancies of the inmates. To others the prison atmosphere seems charged only with bitterness, rancor, and an all-pervading sense of defeat. And so the whole paradoxical scheme continues, because our ideas and views regarding the function of correctional institutions in our society are confused, fuzzy, and nebulous.[2]

Correctional institutions are both a blessing and a curse. Reflecting a positive and humane movement away from the cruel punishments of the eighteenth century, they provided an **alternative to death** and flogging. But in terms of reforming inmates so they can lead a noncriminal life in the free world, prisons have obviously failed. Still, the public's perceived need for security and the prison's effectiveness in isolating offenders from society have unfortunately made this system the primary answer to criminal behavior. The 958,704 male and female inmates confined in state correctional institutions for adults at the start of 1995 were distributed in maximum, medium, and minimum security institutions.[3] We project that by the year 2000 prison population (state, federal, and local city systems) will have grown to approximately 1.8 million Americans. (See Figure 25-1.)

Maximum security facilities house approximately 11 percent of state inmates. **Close/high-security facilities** house another 10.4 percent on the average. In comparison, **medium custody prisons** house some 41.4 percent of state inmates. More than 89 percent of medium security institutions were constructed after 1925.[4] As shown in Figure 25-2, the vast majority of correctional institutions fall into the categories of medium, minimum, multi-level, and community-based. Only 5.7 percent are maximum, and only 4.8 percent are high/close.

Minimum security prisons typically have neither the barbed wire nor the double fence, and armed posts are very rare. (As the types of prisoners have become more violent and dangerous, many minimum security institutions have had to put fences and razor wire around them to make the public feel safer.[5] This "cosmetic" security makes little operational sense because the inmates are typically outside the institution on work details all day.) Much of the available housing is open-dormitory style. About 26 percent of the prison population resides in minimum custody cells or blocks, to include honor farms and camps. More than 60 percent of minimum security institutions were constructed after 1950. The remaining 11 percent of prison inmates are in community facilities or unclassified.

State Institutions by Security Level, 1995

	Multi.	Max.	Close/Hi	Med.	Min.	C'm'n'ty	Recept.	Total
AL	3	0	0	7	9	10	2	31
AK	11	0	1	1	0	1	0	14
AZ	3	3	7	13	16	1	2	45
AR	2	1	1	6	4	0	1	15
CA	29	0	0	0	0	56	0	85
CO	1	1	1	5	9	0	1	18
CT	0	5	1	5	8	6	1	26
DE	3	0	1	0	2	0	0	6
DC	3	1	0	4	1	11	0	20
FL	39	1	0	48	0	38	4	130
GA	0	4	11	50	0	5	6	76
HI	7	0	0	0	2	0	0	9
ID	0	1	0	2	3	3	0	9
IL	2	4	0	11	7	11	0	35
IN	1	1	3	7	6	3	1	22
IA	3	1	0	3	5	20	0	32
KS	6	1	0	0	2	0	0	9
KY	0	1	0	8	6	0	0	15
LA	10	0	0	0	2	5	1	18
ME	2	2	0	0	2	3	0	9
MD	1	3	0	6	10	5	1	26
MA	5	1	0	8	4	5	0	23
MI	12	4	3	11	7	17	2	56
MN	1	1	2	3	1	0	0	8
MS	2	0	0	1	0	17	1	21
MO	3	2	3	3	6	2	1	20
MT	2	0	0	0	1	0	0	3
NE	4	0	0	0	2	2	1	9
NV	0	1	0	5	10	2	0	18
NH	3	0	0	0	0	0	0	3
NJ	0	2	0	9	1	0	0	12
NM	1	1	1	4	7	0	1	15
NY	9	10	0	31	16	0	2	68
NC	5	3	5	34	56	0	0	103
ND	1	0	0	0	1	0	0	2
OH	12	1	6	4	5	0	0	28
OK	6	1	0	1	8	8	1	25
OR	0	1	0	4	6	0	1	12
PA	0	0	6	10	4	15	1	36
RI	0	1	1	2	2	1	1	8
SC	0	0	0	9	13	7	3	32
SD	1	1	0	1	3	0	0	6
TN	1	2	3	3	4	3	4	20
TX	3	14	6	33	7	4	2	69
UT	4	0	0	0	0	0	0	4
VT	0	0	0	6	2	0	0	8
VA	42	0	0	0	0	0	0	42
WA	5	0	1	3	4	17	0	30

Continued on page 518

TABLE *25.1*

State Institutions by Security Level, 1995 *(Con't)*

	Multi.	Max.	Close/Hi	Med.	Min.	C'm'n'ty	Recept.	Total
VV	2	1	0	1	2	3	0	9
WI	1	3	0	4	18	0	1	270
WY	2	0	0	0	2	0	0	4
	253	80	63	366	286	281	42	1,371

SOURCE: C. Camp and G. Camp, *The Corrections Yearbook 1995: Adult Corrections.* (South Salem, NY: Criminal Justice Institute, 1995), pp. 34—35.

The general trend today is toward medium rather than maximum security.[6] Most medium security prisons were built in the twentieth century, in accordance with the new concepts of behavioral science. In fact, most of the medium security correctional institutions were built in the last twenty-five years. Although many of the ideals of early prison reformers could be realized in some medium security institutions, the primary emphasis still remains on security. The medium security correctional institution may well become the last resort in most state systems, as it offers much the same security as the maximum security prison does, but without the latter's oppressive and dehumanizing atmosphere and cost. The minimum security prison is intended to provide a model of reality for inmates who are near the ends of their sentences. Unfortunately, because minimum security inmates are assigned to service more secure institutions or to help satisfy interagency state agreements, those facilities all too frequently tend to sacrifice individual programs for the needs of the major institutions, farms, forest fire fighting, or work projects. The percent of inmates held in various classification levels is shown in Figure 25-3. Again, the vast majority are being held in medium and minimum custody status.

FIGURE

25.1

Annual Cost of Prisons in the United States, 1996

(Includes salaries and benefits, administrative and operations costs, maintenance and repair expenditures, and "other.")

SOURCE: American Correctional Association, *1996 Directory* (Lanham, MD: American Correctional Association, 1996) pp. xiv-xvii.

Total: $21,144,803,152

- State Systems: $17.7 billion
- Federal Bureau of Prisons: $2.3 billion
- NY City Dept. of Corrections: $716 million
- District of Columbia: $214 million
- Cook County: $120 million
- Philadelphia: $104 million

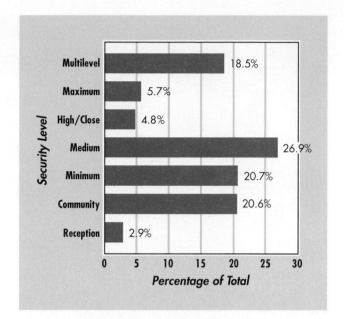

FIGURE

25.2

Security Levels of All
Institutions on
January 1, 1995

SOURCE: C. Camp and G. Camp, *The Corrections
Yearbook 1995: Adult Corrections* (South Salem,
NY: Criminal Justice Institute, 1995), p.35.

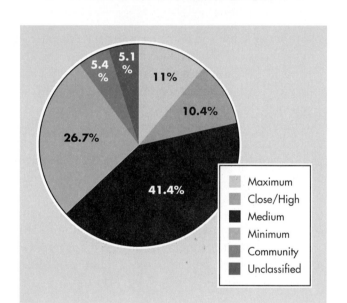

FIGURE

25.3

Percentage of Inmates
in Custody Levels
on January 1, 1995

SOURCE: C. Camp and G. Camp, *The Corrections
Yearbook 1995: Adult Corrections* (South Salem,
NY: Criminal Justice Institute, 1995), p. 23.

Organization of State Systems

Of all the thousands of various types of correctional facilities in America, public and private, adult and juvenile, community and city, public and private, only 16 percent of them are under the control of state agencies. It is not surprising that the correctional "system" in most states is not really systematized at all. Organizational rigidity has handicapped meaningful revision and modernization of corrections. Rehabilitation and reintegration require that organizational structures be concerned with more than just institutional programs. In at least six states, that organizational need has been met by exercising control over all correctional activities at the state level.

Corrections at the state level generally is organized into a separate department of corrections (with a cabinet-level secretary or director appointed by the

An example of a modern maximum security prison

governor) or a division within a larger state department. Most correctional administrators consider the separate department to be more effective, and having the director at the cabinet level adds great flexibility and prestige to the correctional operation. Without an intermediate level of organization, the director of a separate department has the ability to move more freely at the policy-making level. An autonomous department is able to control the allocation of personnel and fiscal resources, using economy-of-scale purchasing and operating with minimum competition from other divisions within the same department. Centralized control also has the advantage of providing effective administrative functions that are unique to correctional problems.

Corrections is a human resource organization. As such, it is not amenable to analysis by the use of charts or the development of expenditure measures and empirical criteria. Human resources management presents special problems. One of the better descriptions of human resource management was written twenty years ago:

Managing a human resource organization is probably even more difficult than managing other public agencies because many traditional management

Filling Our Prisons

If we imprison youthful violent offenders for life, rather than into their thirties, we will do so in the twilight of their criminal careers, while other young offenders take their place. If we are primarily interested in preventing crime, rather than in punishing offenders, we need to address crime prevention by youngsters who are growing into the high-crime cohort. "Three Strikes for Life" laws will eventually fill our prisons with

geriatric offenders, whose care will be increasingly expensive when their propensities to commit crime are at the lowest.   ■

SOURCE: Jerome H. Skolnick, "What Not to Do About Crime—The American Society of Criminology 1994 Presidential Address," *Criminology* 33:1 (1995):9.

tools are not directly applicable. Data describing effects of the correctional process relate to behavior or attitudes and are subject to subjective, frequently conflicting interpretations. The feedback loops necessary for judging the consequences of policies are difficult to create and suffer from incomplete and inaccurate information. There has not been in corrections an organized and consistent relation between evaluative research and management action.

The management of corrections as a human resource organization must be viewed broadly in terms of how offenders, employees, and various organization processes (communications, decision making, and others) are combined into what is called "the corrections process."[7]

The corrections process must include a system of multilevel programs and facilities to provide the spectrum of services required to make a statewide program work. Most state correctional systems are concerned only with the principal institutions and parole services, leaving the majority of correctional problems in the state to units of local government.

Development of State Systems

Each type of state correctional system has developed as a matter of historical accident as much as in response to a state's particular needs. As might be expected, the large industrial prisons are more in evidence in the major industrial states, generally in the area between Illinois and New York. Most of these institutions were built early in the prison movement and were designed to take advantage of the cheap labor force inmates represented. They were the hardest hit by the restrictions the government later placed on prison industries in the 1930s.

At present, the industry allowed in the giant institutions does not provide full employment for large inmate populations.[8] In an effort to spread the few jobs among the many inmates, supervisors try to slow down production and make the work last as long as possible. These procedures are not likely to provide the inmate with a model for job success on the outside. The general picture of activity in the one-time industrial prisons is one of idleness and boredom. Despite even the most dedicated attempts by the staff[9] inside and outside the institutions, there are just not enough meaningful jobs or other programs to help the thousands crowded into the likes of Raifords (Florida), Attica (New York), and Soledad (California) of the country.

The **agricultural prison** was begun in the southern states. Those farms became very profitable ventures for the states and thus have been slow to change. Prisoners who served on public works and state farms replaced the pre–Civil War slave labor in many states, not only in the South. Here again, authorities may have rationalized that the training received from farm work helped prepare offenders for return to a basically agrarian southern economy, but the intent was to use free labor to produce farm products. Cheap prison labor was often leased out to farm owners at a great profit to both the farmer and the state that collected the fee. The use of prison farms has become less profitable, however, with the advent of highly mechanized farming methods in most agricultural states.

Other regions of the country have designated certain institutions as farm oriented. The food produced in those institutions has been used to feed the rest of the institutions in the state. Many states have now begun to abandon that practice,

PROFILE OF FELONS CONVICTED IN STATE COURTS, 1992

White defendants were 52 percent of those convicted of a felony in state courts, black felons were 47 percent, and persons of other races (American Indians, Alaskan Natives, Asians, and Pacific Islanders), 1 percent.

Among persons convicted of a felony, white felons were less likely than blacks to be sent to prison: 42 percent of convicted white defendants received a prison sentence, 56 percent of black defendants, and 52 percent of defendants of other races.

Among persons sentenced to prison, blacks received a state prison sentence seven months longer than that of whites: eighty-one months for blacks and seventy-four months for whites.

Sir Thomas Beever (1726–1814) designed and operated the Gaol at Wymondham, in Norfolk, England. Though little known by most correctional students, his work at the gaol was noted by the Philadelphia Society for Alleviating the Miseries of Public Prisons from a pamphlet in 1790. This resulted in the Pennsylvania Act of April 5, 1790, which created the first penitentiary in the United States at the Walnut Street Jail.

A prison farm in the South, not too long ago

PHOTO BY DANNY LYON, COURTESY OF MAGNUM PHOTOS

as it has been realized that farming experience is of little value to the primarily urban inmate found in most contemporary prisons. Another problem with prison farms has been the pressure from farm organizations, whose members argue that competition from the state is unfair, much as union workers protested about prison manufacturing industries in the early part of this century.

Many states have chosen to set up **work camps** and other forms of prisoner activity appropriate to their particular needs. Lumber camps have been used, as have road prisons or camps to construct and maintain roads. Recent versions of the work camp have been geared to provide a combination of hard work in the outdoors and programmed treatment aimed at preparing the offender for release. It is considered more beneficial for offenders to do time in the relatively healthful atmosphere of a small work camp than to languish in the idleness and boredom of the prison.

INMATES IN STATE PRISONS

In 1983, the U.S. Department of Justice conducted a national survey of inmates in state correctional facilities in the United States and found an estimated 381,955 offenders under the jurisdiction of state governments.[10] Since that study was conducted, the population of state prisons has skyrocketed to over 958,000, an increase of over 250 percent!

An overwhelming majority of the inmates (ninety-three of every one hundred) were males. The number of white male inmates to black males has been decreasing at the state level, and now constitutes 35 percent of the total versus 48 percent for African Americans. All other minority males (Hispanics and others) is now only 16 percent of the state prison populations. The average age was about thirty years, and about 6 percent of the total population was at least age fifty, reflecting the graying of America's general population as well as its inmates. It is interesting to note that a survey of thirty-six adult agencies showed an average of 4.1 percent of their adult male populations were non-U.S. citizens.

As a group, state prison inmates were less educated than their counterparts in the civilian population. At least 60 percent of the inmates had not received a high school diploma or GED, in contrast with 36 percent of the general population eighteen years of age or older.

In terms of their criminal offenses, almost 27.1 percent were classified as violent in 1994. The average sentence length imposed was nine years,[11] although 9 percent of the prisoners were incarcerated under life sentences. One in three had incurred at least one other sentence, in addition to the instant offense, and one in four had served time as a juvenile offender.

As seen in Figure 25-4, all but one of prison inmate categories shown have declined or stayed flat, with the exception of inmates involved with drugs. This is consistent and continues to grow in that single category as we approach the year 2000.

In 1994, 931,711 adult male inmates were housed in state facilities whose maximum capacities totaled 772,551 (see Table 25-2). California is the largest state correctional system (see Table 25.3), but Louisiana has more inmates per 100,000 residents than any other state.[12]

To keep abreast of the crush of new commitments, states have launched a brick-and-mortar construction binge: the number of prisons beds constructed each year is astounding. Prison beds are expensive to build. In general, the lower the security level, the cheaper the bed, with minimum security costs averaging $32,346 versus $79,958 for maximum security. Prison bed construction costs for 1994 alone will be recorded at about $5.0 billion. The cost of incarceration for adults averages $53.24 per inmate, or in excess of $49 million a day to house, feed, control, and care for the nation's adult state male inmates. Despite the construction, remodeling, redesigning, and renovations, American prisons remain overcrowded. The U.S. Supreme Court may have to examine again the realities of imprisonment in the late 1990s and the Eighth Amendment. Table 25-2 shows the number and percentage of state prisoners as a percent of reported capacity from 1989 to 1994. The national picture of prisoners under the jurisdiction of federal and state correctional agencies on three different dates and the percentage of increase in each state and region, as well as the federal system, is reflected in population as a percentage of reported capacity, as shown in Table 25-3.

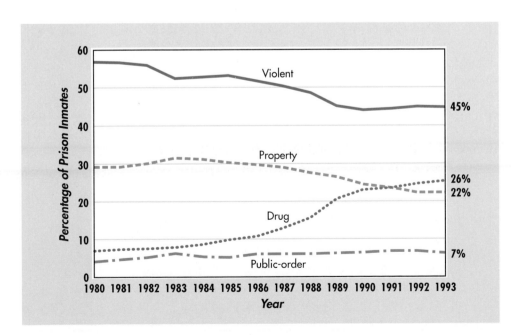

FIGURE
25.4

Percentage of Prison Inmates Classified as Violent, Charged with Property and Drug Abuse, and Incarcerated for Disruption of Public Order, 1980–1993

SOURCE: Allen Beck and Darrell Gilliard, *Prisoners in 1994* (Washington, D.C.: U.S. Department of Justice, 1995), p. 10.

Vocational training also helps build a new facility

TABLE *25.2*

State Prison Population as a Percentage of Reported Capacity, 1989–1994

	State Prisons
Highest capacity 1994	772,751
Lowest capacity 1994	704,004
Net change in capacity, 1993—94	
Highest	63,641
Lowest	54,559
Population housed as a percentage of capacity	
Highest	
1989	107%
1990	115
1991	116
1992	118
1993	118
1994	117
Lowest	
1989	127%
1990	127
1991	131
1992	131
1993	129
1994	129

SOURCE: Allen Beck and Darrell Gilliard, *Prisoners in 1994* (Washington, D.C.: U.S. Department of Justice, 1995), p. 7.

TABLE *25.3*

Prisoners Under the Jurisdiction of State or Federal Correctional Authorities, June 30, 1995, December 31, 1994, and June 30, 1994, by Region and State

Region and Jurisdiction	Total 6/30/95	Total 12/31/94	6/30/94	Percentage of Capacity 6/30/95
U.S. total	1,104,074	1,055,073	1,014,670	403
Federal	99,466	95,034	93,708	31
State	1,004,608	980,039	920,962	372
Northeast	158,184	153,072	150,702	295
Connecticut	15,005	14,380	14,427	325
Maine	1,459	1,474	1,468	112
Massachusetts	11,469	11,293	11,166	180
New Hampshire	2,065	2,021	1,895	180
New Jersey	25,626	24,632	24,471	323
New York	68,526	66,750	65,962	377
Pennsylvania	29,844	28,302	27,082	247
Rhode Island	3,132	2,919	3,049	190
Vermont	1,058	1,301	1,182	135
Midwest	190,170	184,508	178,339	307
Illinois	37,790	36,531	35,614	320
Indiana	15,699	15,014	14,828	270
Iowa	5,892	5,137	5,090	201
Kansas	8,927	6,371	6,090	269
Michigan	41,377	40,631	40,220	434
Minnesota	4,764	4,575	4,573	103
Missouri	18,940	17,898	16,957	356
Nebraska	2,801	2,711	2,449	168
North Dakota	610	536	522	90
Ohio	43,168	43,074	41,168	387
South Dakota	1,780	1,708	1,636	245
Wisconsin	10,832	10,022	9,206	198
South	446,498	422,455	395,491	474
Alabama	20,082	19,573	19,096	459
Arkansas	8,825	8,643	8,916	349
Delaware	4,651	4,488	4,324	406
District of Col.	10,484	10,949	11,033	1,722
Florida	61,882	57,168	56,052	437
Georgia	34,111	33,425	30,292	468
Kentucky	11,949	11,066	10,724	310
Louisiana	24,840	24,063	23,333	573
Maryland	21,441	20,998	20,887	398
Mississippi	12,446	10,930	10,631	447
North Carolina	26,818	23,648	22,650	357
Oklahoma	17,605	16,831	16,306	536
South Carolina	19,481	18,999	19,646	510
Tennessee	14,933	14,401	14,397	284
Texas	127,092	118,195	100,136	659
Virginia	27,310	26,968	24,822	412

Continued on page 526

TABLE 25.3

Prisoners Under the Jurisdiction of State or Federal Correctional Authorities, June 30, 1995, December 31, 1994, and June 30, 1994, by Region and State *(Con't)*

Region and Jurisdiction	Total 8/30/95	Total 12/31/94	Total 8/30/94	Incarceration Rate on 6/30/95
South				
West Virginia	2,438	2,332	2,244	134
West	**209,756**	**200,004**	**198,430**	**348**
Alaska	3,031	3,292	3,120	293
Arizona	20,907	19,748	18,830	473
California	131,342	125,605	124,813	402
Colorado	10,757	10,717	9,954	287
Hawaii	3,583	3,333	3,246	218
Idaho	3,240	2,811	2,861	278
Montana	1,801	1,764	1,654	207
Nevada	7,487	8,993	6,745	488
New Mexico	4,121	3,712	3,704	234
Oregon	7,505	6,936	6,723	199
Utah	3,272	3,045	2,948	166
Washington	11,402	10,833	10,650	210
Wyoming	1,308	1,217	1,174	271

SOURCE: Darrell Gilliard and Allen Beck, *State and Federal Prisons Report Record Growth During Last 12 Months* (Washington, D.C.: U.S. Department of Justice, 1995), p. 5.

There were many repeat offenders: two-thirds had a prior sentence to probation or incarceration, and more than half had been sentenced at least twice. These data suggest the difficulties faced in the state systems and indicate the inefficiency and general failure of current uncoordinated correctional systems. As we approach the year 2000, with over one million persons in state prisons, it is clear that the problems for harried correctional administrators are only beginning. Fortunately, some of these problems are being addressed in actions in the Supreme Court.

LOCAL ADULT CITY-OPERATED PRISONS

In calculating the numbers of inmates in adult prisons, one must not forget the **Big Four**, a group of institutions that house populations larger than those in most states. These four are as follows:

1. **Cook County Department of Corrections**
2. **New York City Department of Corrections;**
3. **Washington, D.C., Department of Corrections**
4. **Philadelphia prison system**

These four systems are have a total of thirty-nine adult prisons and a large number of other institutions and programs. One seldom thinks of cities as needing their own correctional systems, but these four very large cities have chosen to do so. Their operations are similar to the state prisons, but they allow inmates to be housed nearer to home. It may be that some of the other megacities may get into the corrections game as well, but most have shown little interest. Many local jail systems are already so overcrowded that most do not have time to plan that far ahead. The trends of the big four should be followed carefully. The percentages of the types of offenses and the sentence length for them in 38 states is shown in Table 25-4. The big four follow a similar pattern.

TABLE *25.4*

Maximum Sentence Length (in months) for New Court Commitments to U.S. Prisons in Thirty-eight States, by Offense, Sex, and Race, 1992

Most Serious Offense	*All*	*Median*	*Mean*	White Male *Median*	White Male *Mean*	Black Male *Median*	Black Male *Mean*
All offenses	100%	48	67	36	64	48	73
Violent offenses	28.4	72	104	61	99	75	113
Homicide	4.2	240	188	180	162	288	221
Murder and nonnegligent manslaughter	2.8	433	240	1,188	225	420	266
Murder	2.3	Life	279	Life	275	1,176	295
Nonnegligent manslaughter	0.5	132	152	120	118	156	174
Negligent manslaughter	1.3	96	122	72	103	120	150
Unspecified homicide	0.1	240	192	300	183	240	201
Kidnapping	0.6	96	123	84	114	120	141
Rape	2.1	120	144	108	143	120	153
Other sexual assault	3.5	72	99	72	101	72	99
Robbery	10.0	72	99	60	93	72	105
Assault	7.4	48	74	42	66	60	81
Other violent	0.7	48	60	36	55	60	68
Property offenses	30.8	36	53	36	54	36	54
Burglary	12.9	48	65	48	65	48	67
Larceny-theft	8.1	24	40	27	42	24	41
Motor vehicle theft	2.3	36	41	36	40	36	44
Arson	0.6	60	81	60	79	60	92
Fraud	3.7	36	47	36	50	36	46
Stolen property	2.3	36	45	36	46	36	45
Other property	0.9	36	42	36	42	36	42
Drug offenses	30.8	40	58	36	51	48	63
Possession	5.5	36	53	36	46	48	57
Trafficking	20.0	48	61	36	53	48	68
Other drug	5.3	24	48	24	47	36	51
Public order offenses	9.0	24	38	24	35	30	42
Weapons	2.5	36	45	30	39	36	47
Driving while intoxicated	2.6	24	28	24	29	24	26
Other public order	3.8	24	40	24	40	24	41
Other offenses	1.1	24	45	24	40	30	53

SOURCE: Kathleen Maguire and Ann Pastore (eds.). *Source Book of Criminal Justice Statistics, 1994* (Washington, D.C.: U.S. Department of Justice, 1995), p. 555.

ARE PRISONS "CRUEL AND UNUSUAL PUNISHMENT"?

Whether they are state or local, male or female, the problems of institutionalization are ever present in our prisons. Understaffing, underbudgeting, and the lack of citizen interest often become excuses for allowing conditions to deteriorate to the lowest levels. Beginning in the 1970s, both state and federal courts were asked to examine the operations and policies of correctional facilities and personnel to ensure compliance with the Eighth Amendment's prohibition against cruel and unusual punishment. By February 1983, the courts had declared unconstitutional the entire prison systems of Alabama, Florida, Mississippi, Oklahoma, Rhode Island, Tennessee, Texas, and all the male penal institutions of Michigan. In addition, at least one (or more) facilities in another twenty-one states were operating under either a court order or a consent decree as a result of inmate crowding and/or the conditions of confinement. Yet another seven states were involved in ongoing litigation relating to overcrowding and/or the conditions of release from prison. Finally, in eight states, the courts had appointed receivers or masters to operate the state prison system or facility, had ordered the emergency release of inmates because of crowding, or had designated specific prisons to be closed.[13] The courts took those actions only as a last resort and when it was clear the affected states had relinquished their responsibility to protect the constitutional rights of the inmates under their custody and care. Correctional construction began in earnest as a response to prison overcrowding. Between 1987 and 1992 alone, 298 new prisons were added to correctional systems.[14] The average age of convicted felons in 1992, as shown in Table 25-5, was 30 years of age.

TABLE 25.5

Average Age of Convicted Felons in State Courts, 1992

Most Serious Conviction Offense	Average Age (in years)	
	Mean	*Median*
All offenses	30 yr	28 yr
Violent offenses	29 yr	27 yr
Murder	28	25
Rape	33	31
Robbery	26	25
Aggravated assault	30	28
Other violent	33	31
Property offenses	29 yr	27 yr
Burglary	27	25
Larceny	29	27
Fraud	31	30
Drug offenses	30 yr	29 yr
Possession	31	30
Trafficking	30	28
Weapons offenses	29 yr	27 yr
Other offenses	31 yr	30 yr

SOURCE: Patrick Langan and Robyn Cohen. *State Court Sentencing of Convicted Felons, 1992* (Washington, D.C.: U.S. Department of Justice, 1996), p. 17.

The states, understandably, have reacted with great indignation over the Supreme Court's intruding into the domain of the executive branch at the state level.[15] Where does the Court get the right to intervene in such matters? The Civil Rights Law of 1871 provides for the principal method of allowing such inmate complaints into the federal courts.[16] That statute provides that citizens denied constitutional rights by the state may sue in the federal court. Originally designed to protect the newly freed slaves in the post–Civil War era, the statute was generally forgotten until a landmark case in 1961 revived interest in it. It was not until 1964, however, that the Court finally ruled in favor of a prisoner's seeking relief in federal court by way of the 1871 act.

The procedure has been tentative and careful, each step breaking new ground for prisoners' rights:

> These decisions provided almost all of the legal groundwork necessary for "conditions suits." They all came while Earl Warren was chief justice. But under Warren Burger, the Supreme Court has shown even more interest in prison cases. In some areas, it has extended prisoners' rights; in others it has held the line. But it has held fast to one principle: no one must interfere with the right of inmates to take their complaints to federal courts.

> With these sketchy guidelines, federal district judges have been feeling their way. In the first cases dealing with specific prison practices, the judges would balance the constitutional rights of the prisoners against the prison officials' legitimate interests in security, rehabilitation, and order. If the officials' defense was not sufficient, then the practice would be ordered changed. If such a ruling was upheld on appeal by one of the eleven U.S. Circuit Courts of Appeal, then it became a binding precedent within that circuit and was available to guide judges in other circuits. Only if the U.S. Supreme Court issues a ruling on a case is the precedent binding across the nation— although approval can be implied when the Court declines to hear an appeal. The Supreme Court has declined appeals on all the broad condition suits that have been brought before it. District court judges have generally built upon each other's decisions in these areas.

> This judicial activism has not taken place in a vacuum, of course. In most areas of constitutional law inmates have ridden on the coattails of more popular causes such as school desegregation and voting rights for minorities. The extension of the class-action suit has made broad-based challenges to prison conditions possible. Increased activism among lawyers and the growth of legal aid programs was an important factor.[17]

The states are not giving up easily, however, and have appealed these decisions. Each case is different, of course, but they have all been slowed in their immediate impact by the issuance of a decision of the Fifth Circuit Court of Appeals, written in regard to the Alabama order.

> This seemingly inexorable march toward greater judicial activism was slowed when the Fifth Circuit Court of Appeals issued its ruling on the state's appeal of the Alabama order. In an opinion by a three-judge panel, written by Judge J. P. Coleman, a former governor of Mississippi, the appeals court affirmed the basic finding of unconstitutionality, but it reduced the scope of Johnson's original order. The court ordered a new hearing on the judge's requirement of sixty square feet of space per inmate in new construction. It dissolved the Human Rights

PRIVACY

The issue of privacy in prison is almost an oxymoron, but it raises many legal, social, and administrative concerns. Privacy was recognized as a right as early as 1890, and its importance to human dignity is self-evident. Privacy was one of the major human rights that came under full attack in the "total institution." Overcrowding of prisons exacerbates the loss of privacy, and prison administrators must work hard to avoid costly and time-consuming litigation efforts in regard to privacy.

State Prisons Find a New Source of Financing: Their Inmates

Darryl E. Gilyard lost his legs after the garbage truck on which he was riding was hit by another truck in 1984. He lost his freedom after a court convicted him in 1989 of shooting and killing a friend in a drug-related murder.

And he lost almost $100,000 on June 6 when a Circuit Court judge in Cole County, Mo., about 100 miles down the Missouri River from here, ruled that Mr. Gilyard had to reimburse the state for the cost of his imprisonment.

While Mr. Gilyard's money is the result of a $4.3 million insurance settlement for his injury, his case is just an extreme example of a trend in which states are trying to make prisoners pay for everything from filing lawsuits to room and board.

With the number of inmates in state prisons having tripled since 1980, to one million, and political pressure bringing tighter budgets, state officials say they are justified in going after even token payments from inmates, most of whom have few resources. In 1995, states passed more than two dozen laws intended to regain some costs of incarceration.

Arizona requires an inmate to pay a utility fee if he has a television or other "major electrical appliance." Connecticut has a law similar to Missouri's, forcing inmates to pay the expense of their confinements. New Hampshire compels prisoners to repay the cost of state-provided lawyers. And Texas demands part of an inmate's wages earned from any work program outside the prison.

"Inmates should be made to pay for their crimes—literally," said Donna Lyons, who follows the topic for the National Conference of State Legislatures in Denver. "It's symbolic, it's an issue of accountability as well as a fiscal issue."

In addition to the one million inmates in state prisons, Federal prisons hold 100,000 prisoners and local jails about 500,000.

"We try to get as much of our buck back as we can," said Michael Arra, a spokesman for the Department of Corrections in Arizona, where prisoners are limited to three electrical appliances and must pay a $2 monthly utility fee. "It's what the taxpayers expect and demand."

So far, few of the laws have been tested in court, but critics contend that, even if the legislation should pass constitutional muster, the concept remains bad public policy and is unnecessarily punitive to those who have already lost their freedom.

"It's unfair," said Jenni Gainsborough, a spokeswoman for the American Civil Liberties Union Prison Project in Washington. "When you deprive someone of their liberty and lock them up, the state takes on the responsibility of providing for their care. It's just political pandering, showing how tough you are on crime by being tough on prisoners."

Ms. Gainsborough said the overwhelming majority of prisoners were so poor that programs intended to obtain money from inmates would most likely cost more to administer than they would bring in. A more efficient path, she said, would be to find alternatives to imprisonment that involve productive employment. She acknowledged that politics made such a program unlikely.

Mr. Gilyard is an exception. A former Golden Gloves boxer, Mr. Gilyard receives a monthly insurance payment of $5,256 for his injury.

After Judge Thomas Brown of Circuit Court ruled that he must pay the cost of his confinement—$12,000 yearly—he was ordered to pay the state $97,724.61 to cover expenses to date. Judge Brown also authorized the state to begin withholding the monthly cost of confinement, about $1,000, from his insurance check.

Mr. Gilyard's lawyer said the ruling would be appealed.

If it is not overturned, Mr. Gilyard, 43, who is serving a life sentence without parole at the Jefferson City Correctional Center, would have to pay an additional $360,000 if he lived another 30 years.

Lee Nation, Mr. Gilyard's lawyer, said the court decision was unfair because his client had been awarded the money to redress a wrong and the state had taken away some of that compensation.

"Obviously, he would rather have legs and no money than money and no legs," Mr. Nation said. "You're singling out someone because he's a cripple." ∎

SOURCE: Editors, *The New York Times*, July 7, 1996, p. 1.

Committee and dismissed the hired consultant, although it said the judge could appoint a single monitor for each prison "to observe, and to report his observations to the court, with no authority to intervene in daily prison operations." The court also overturned Judge Johnson's order forbidding the state to require women visitors to prisons to stand over a mirror and drop their underwear as part of a routine search for contraband.

The most significant part of Judge Johnson's order, that dealing with idleness, was also cut back. Rehabilitation programs, the court said, could not be required.

Because the order that each inmate be assigned to a job "should not impose any real burden" on prison officials, it let that part stand. But it ruled that it could not be used as a precedent in future cases. "If the state furnishes its prisoners with reasonably adequate food, clothing, shelter, sanitation, medical care, and personal safety, so as to avoid the imposition of cruel and unusual punishment, that ends its obligations under Amendment Eight," the decision stated.[18]

Realistically, we must acknowledge that the prison has little control over who will be committed. Nor does it exercise much control over sentence length,[19] parole eligibility, minimal sentence proportion to be served,[20] or legislative allocations. The current prison situation is a result in part of the high-risk age category (sixteen to twenty-nine) that the baby boom has brought about, the more conservative response to crime, the public's fear of crime and criminals, increased sentence lengths, and the higher failure rates of parolees who must then be returned to prison. Yet the cruel and unusual punishment conditions continue.

One other response by corrections was to add more correctional personnel. Slightly more than 117,000 persons were employed in state correctional facilities in 1985, an increase of 21 percent over the number in 1979. As a result, the staff-to-inmate ratio rose from 4.1 to 1 to 5.4 to 1 overall. On January 1, 1995, there were more than 213,000 custodial staff employees; the agency average of inmates to line-level staff was back down to 5.1 to 1, a 6 percent decrease since 1985.[21]

Correctional opportunities will continue to increase, and students will be sought who have the skills and willingness to work in the prisons of tomorrow. There is clearly a need for active citizen support for corrections, especially at the state level, and for active monitoring of our prison conditions.

Classification and Assignment in State Prisons

Most state codes provide for the separation or classification of prisoners, their division into different grades with promotion or degradation according to merit or demerit, their employment and instruction in industrial pursuits, and their education. Most also stipulate that reformation of prisoners is a primary goal, though there are some exceptions. California, for example, now advocates punishment.

In most systems, the **initial classification** determines the institution to which an inmate will be assigned. The receiving institution then determines whether the individual shall remain in maximum security or be transferred to a medium or minimum security penitentiary. (Each state has at least one maximum security institution.) Most states base their transfer decisions on a perception of the individual's ability to handle the lowest level of security. Also important is an evaluation of the individual's ability to adjust to a program geared primarily to work, to academic or vocational training, or to the needs of older offenders.[22] A classification committee usually participates in making these decisions.

The classification process continues at the institutional level. Although each receiving institution emphasizes different programs, each has some version of education, counseling, and the other ingredients of a total program. Theoretically, individuals are assigned according to their needs but, realistically, assignments are too often made to conform to **institutional needs**. For example, an inmate may genuinely want to learn welding. If the welding class is filled, as it often may be, but there is a vacancy in the furniture shop, the inmate may be assigned to the furniture

MIXED GENDER STAFFING AND OBSERVATION
Many prison facilities continue to allow observation of inmate's genitalia and bodily functions by correctional officers and other prison staff of the opposite gender. This is usually explained away as necessary for security purposes, and that this is a professional duty akin to female nurses and male patients. A few states have prohibited the practice as a final invasion of privacy of the prisoner.

Jeremy Bentham (1748–1832) was the creator of the "panopticon" plan for prisons, consisting of a huge structure covered by a glass roof. A central cupola with cell blocks radiating out like spokes of a wheel allowed the guards to see into the cells. The U.S. government built several of these monsters. The first was at Richmond, Virginia, in 1800, and the last was Statesville Prison in Illinois in 1919. Bentham believed that more light would help control inmates, long before the electric light bulb was invented.

Razor wire has replaced barbed wire in prison fences

shop; no effort would be made to offer additional welding instruction. Also, inmates will often be assigned to a maintenance operation, such as food service or janitorial work, that is unlikely to conform to their own vocational ambitions. An essential element of effective classification is a periodic review of the inmate's progress through the recommended program.[23] All institutions allow for this reevaluation, usually called reclassification. The purpose is to adjust the program in accordance with the inmate's progress and needs. Realistically, though, decisions are all too frequently made on the basis of the available vacancies and institutional needs.

Institution personnel may genuinely wish to provide the recommended program for an inmate; however, the need to keep the institution going inevitably shapes decisions. Personnel may rationalize maintenance assignments on the basis that many inmates need the experience of accepting supervision, developing regular work habits, learning to relate to coworkers, and the like. All of that may be true, but the treatment staff members are no less frustrated than the inmates are when prescribed programs are ignored. The classification and assignment process just described is only a composite of what the more effective programs provide. The average sentence compared to the time to be served for a felony varies widely. As shown in Figure 25-5, even violent offenders were likely to serve only about 46 percent of their sentence in 1992.

TRAINING IN STATE SYSTEMS

One other way to improve the ability of state systems to react to a rapidly changing environment is to improve the requirements for entry-level staff, and then to improve the training of staff who are already in the system. The federal system has always had the advantage of high entry standards (now a bachelor's degree is required) and excellent training programs for staff. Most state systems require only the following:

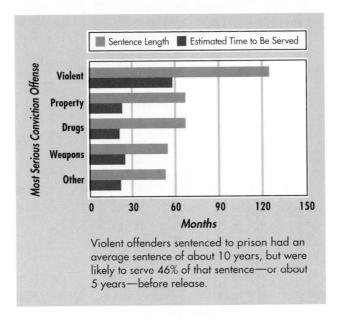

FIGURE

25.5

Average Sentence to State Prison and Estimated Time to Be Served for a Felony, 1992

SOURCE: Patrick Langan and Robyn Cohen, *State Court Sentencing of Convicted Felons, 1992* (Washington, D.C.: U.S. Department of Justice, 1996), p.2.

Violent offenders sentenced to prison had an average sentence of about 10 years, but were likely to serve 46% of that sentence—or about 5 years—before release.

1. high school diploma or GED
2. no record of prior felony convictions
3. minimum age of twenty-one (some states accept eighteen)
4. valid driver's license (of that state)

These seem to be quite minimal requirements for a job that commands so much influence over the lives and rights of inmates. Some of the more progressive states are beginning to raise these standards. California and Florida, for example, require extensive background investigations. California estimates it will need about three thousand new corrections officers a year for the next few years to keep up with massive construction programs. Florida has a training program that amounts to over five hundred hours, which must be completed before the employees can pass their probation periods.

The general rule is for employees to have at least eighty hours of training within their probationary period, usually six months. Some jurisdictions get around that requirement by making most of the training on-the-job activity. Most states try to provide at least some training. Before the efforts of the 1970s and subsequent lawsuits, most training amounted to the employee being handed a set of keys and told to go to work. Some states now work closely with their community colleges to provide preservice and postservice training, especially in the social sciences. Others have state training academies that provide basic and ongoing training.

The need to have better trained staff has caused the growth of many private and nonprofit agencies to start training academies for preemployment programs for corrections officers. Some of these programs have concentrated on finding interested minorities and women, and have done quite well. Others have tried the same approach but, lacking rigid standards, careful screening, and close association with the correctional agencies, they have failed.

Many administrators of correctional programs at the state level would like to raise entry-level standards to require a two-year degree and promotional qualifications in line with that base point (e.g., a bachelor's degree for captains, master's degree for superintendents). They have a long battle ahead. Those already in the system are

INMATES PAY INTO FUND FOR CRIME VICTIMS

More than $518,000 was collected from wages of working inmates during the beinnium to fund services for crime victims.

The Minnesota Deparment of Corrections deducts between 5 and 10 percent from the pay inmates earn working in correctional industry jobs. All inmates whose biweekly gross wages are over $50 are subject to the deduction.

Funds are used for a variety of programs that assist crime victims and witnesses throughout the state.

The surcharge began in 1985 in accordance with state law authorizing the withholding policy. A recent law requiring that other mandated deductions be made first, such as court-ordered victim restitution and child support payments, may impact the amount collected through this surcharge in future years.

usually afraid of the proposed requirements and oppose the raising of such standards. Their attitudes are enhanced by union activity that is primarily based on seniority, not training. It seems that some progress could be made if the incumbents were given a liberal opportunity to be "grandfathered" into the new programs. Training in the future high-tech prisons is essential; it is an area to watch carefully in the future.

Summary

The state and local adult correctional systems in America are as diverse as the states and cities themselves. We have given an overview of some of the problems facing correctional administrators when they try to model a unified and coordinated system of corrections within the framework of fragmented and antiquated institutions and procedures. The prison remains the core of most state correctional systems, despite its patent failure as a means of rehabilitation and reintegration of offenders (the current goals of corrections). Classification of inmates and subsequent assignment and reassignment are still based more on the institution's needs and security than on individual needs. A few states have seen the advantage of a correctional system that is controlled by the state, but most are still moving toward an autonomous department of corrections for increasingly larger percentages of offenders who now fall under state control.

Movements to absorb all correctional programs under the state's supervision and control encounter almost insurmountable political and practical obstacles at every step. New concepts are also hampered by the massive overcrowding in state institutions, causing funding to go for bricks and mortar rather than for managerial or administrative improvements.

Capacities of institutions also reflect the continuing problems created by overcrowding and growth. Populations that range from 81 percent to 193 percent of capacity ratings have become commonplace, averaging 131 percent of capacity.[24] Obviously all of the major systems are extremely and critically overcrowded.

Longer sentences and stiffer enforcement measures have filled existing beds faster than they can be built. Alternatives to confinement have been used for all but the very few, and those few are not those we want out on the streets. Although the new institutions are being constructed, in the majority of cases, to constitutional standards in regard to square footage and other considerations, there seems to be little doubt that the single cells will soon become double-bunked. The taxpayers are beginning to rethink the allocation of funds to build more and more prisons, often at a total cost of up to $200,000 per bed.

State correctional systems have inherited the legacy of a sometimes well-intentioned but often inhumane past. The purposes for which many of the crumbling old institutions were built and the procedures for operating these facilities are no longer in tune with society or behavioral science. The cry to tear down the monuments is a valid one, but practicalities dictate that the flood of inmates must be kept somewhere, and public safety takes precedence over innovative solutions. Although many new programs outside the prisons are being attempted, they must be proved effective before they will be widely accepted. Moreover, the types of inmates now being placed in prisons do not lend themselves to lower security levels.

Much progress is being made, sometimes at the prodding of citizens' groups like the 1970s Ohio Citizens' Task Force on Corrections,[24] whose investigations uncovered the conditions in a typical state system of that era. But the death in 1981 of the Law Enforcement Assistance Administration, shrinking state budgets, and get-tough attitudes from a public tired of being victimized make change much more difficult. In the next chapter we examine a truly centralized and integrated correctional system, the Federal Bureau of Prisons.

Review Questions

1. Characterize the current state inmate population in the nation.
2. How much time do state inmates generally spend in prison?
3. What makes a prison cruel and unusual punishment?
4. Why are alternatives to incarceration beginning to be so necessary for correctional administrators?
5. What impact does overcrowding have on the reform of institutional programs in state systems?
6. How are inmates classified?
7. Has the institutional inmate/staff ratio gone up or down? Why?
8. What are three likely trends in state correctional facilities over the next ten years?

Words to Remember

alternative to death

maximum security facilities

close/high security facilities

New York City
   Department
   of Corrections

institutional needs

work camps

agricultural prison

Cook County
   Department
   of Corrections

Big Four

Philadelphia prison system

medium custody prisons

initial classification

Washington, D.C.,
   Department of Corrections

Endnotes

1. Allen Beck and Darrell Gilliard, *Prisoners in 1994* (Washington, D.C.: U.S. Department of Justice, 1995), p. 3.

2. Quoted in Harry Elmer Barnes and Negley K. Teeters, *New Horizons in Criminology,* 3rd ed. (Englewood Cliffs, NJ: Prentice Hall, 1959), pp. 461–462.

3. Allen Beck and Darrell Gilliard, *Prisoners in 1992* (Washington, D.C.: U.S. Department of Justice, 1993), p. 1.

4. Camille G. Camp and George M. Camp, *The Correctional Yearbook 1995: Adult Corrections* (South Salem, NY: Criminal Justice Institute, 1995), p. 22.

5. For an analysis of the impact of locating a low-security federal institution, see George Rogers and Marshall Haimes, "Local Impact of a Low-Security Federal Correctional Institution," *Federal Probation* 51 (September 1987): 28–34.

6. In 1994, about one-third (34.2 percent) of the new prison beds added through construction or renovation were in medium security facilities. Camp and Camp, *The Correctional Yearbook 1995*, p. 40.

7. National Advisory Commission on Criminal Justice Standards and Goals, *Corrections* (Washington, D.C.: U.S. Government Printing Office, 1973), p. 440.

8. But see the October 1986 issue of *Corrections Today* 48, particularly pp. 12–66. See also Gerald Farkas and Margaret Hambrick, "New Partnership: Industries and Education/Training Benefit Institutions and Inmates," *Corrections Today* 49 (1987): 52–54.

9. See the special theme issue of *Corrections Today* 55:3 (1993): 80–110.

10. Bureau of Justice Statistics, *Prisoners in 1983* (Washington D.C.: U.S. Department of Justice, May 1984).

11. Allen Beck et al., *Survey of State Prison Inmates 1991* (Washington, D.C.: U.S. Department of Justice, 1993), p. 7.

12. D. Gilliard and A. Beck, State and Federal Prisons Report Record Growth During Last 12 Months (Washington, D.C.: U.S. Department of Justice, 1995), p.5.

13. Bureau of Justice Statistics, *Report to the Nation on Crime and Justice* (Washington, D.C.: U.S. Department of Justice, 1983), p. 80.

14. Camp and Camp, *The Correctional Yearbook 1993*, p. 47.

15. Ibid., p. 43.

16. This is Chapter 42 of the U.S. Code, Section 1983: Every person who under color of any statute, ordinance, regulation, custom, or usage of any State or Territory, subjects or causes to be subjected, any citizen of the United States or other person within the jurisdiction thereof to the deprivation of any rights, privileges, or immunities secured by the Constitution and laws, shall be liable to the party injured in an action at law, suit in equity, or other proper proceeding for redress.

17. S. Gettinger, "Cruel and Unusual Prisons," *Corrections Magazine* 3 (December 1977): 3–6.

18. Ibid., p. 10.

19. In 1994, the average sentence served was twenty-seven months. Camp and Camp, 1995 p. 16.

20. To understand some of the ways prison staff can shorten the length of incarceration time, even in states with determinate sentencing, see John Hepburn and Lynne Goodstein, "Organizational Imperatives and Sentencing Reform Implementation: The Impact of Prison Practices and Priorities on the Attainment of the Objective of Determinate Sentencing," *Crime and Delinquency* 32 (1986): 339–365.

21. Camille Camp, and George M. Camp, *The Corrections Yearbook 1987* (South Salem, NY: Criminal Justice Institute, 1987), pp. 44–45. See also Camp and Camp, 1995 note 1, p. 80.

22. Gennaro Vito and Deborah Wilson, "Forgotten People: Elderly Inmates," *Federal Probation* 49 (1985): 18–24.

23. Gilliard, *Prisoners in 1992*, pp. 4–5.

24. Harry Allen, *Final Report by the Ohio Citizens' Task Force on Corrections* (Columbus: State of Ohio, 1971).

The Federal System

Overview

With the proclamation shown in the box below, the federal government went into the business of corrections in a big way. The history of incarcerating offenders for violations of federal law is long and interesting. With the power of the federal government (and the federal purse) behind it, the Federal Bureau of Prisons became an innovator and leader in correctional management and operations. The Federal Bureau of Prisons is an entirely separate system from the state and local correctional agencies. It is designed and intended to deal only with those who have violated federal laws. Since the federal system, like the juvenile system discussed in Chapter 17, slowly developed as an independent entity, a review of its background and history is necessary and useful in understanding where this system came from and where it might be going.[1]

The Use of State Facilities

Prior to 1930, federal prisoners were sent to state and local institutions to serve their sentences. One of the first acts of Congress was to pass a bill (*An Act to Establish the Judicial Courts of the United States*) that encouraged the states to pass laws providing for the incarceration of federal law violators in state institutions. Most of the states did pass such laws, and all federal offenders sentenced to one year or more served their sentences in state facilities. Offenders who were sentenced to terms of less than one year or those being held in detention awaiting trial were usually confined in local jails, a practice that continues today on a limited scale, primarily due to lack of space in federal facilities.

In 1870, Congress established the **Justice Department**. A general agent in the Department of Justice was placed in charge of all federal prisoners in state and local institutions. Later, the

That there is hereby established in the Department of Justice a Bureau of Prisons . . . responsible for the safekeeping, care, protection, instruction and discipline of all persons charged with or convicted of offenses against the United States.

—Acts approved by President Herbert Hoover, May 14 and May 27, 1930

general agent became the superintendent of prisons, responsible to an assistant attorney general for the care and custody of all federal prisoners.

The state prisons became seriously overcrowded in the period that followed the Civil War. With increased numbers of both state and federal prisoners, many states became reluctant to take federal prisoners when they could not even care properly for their own. Consequently, in some states only federal prisoners from that specific state were accepted. In states where neither suitable nor adequate facilities were available, transporting federal inmates to appropriate facilities involved lengthy travel and high costs. In 1885, there were 1,027 federal prisoners in state prisons and approximately 10,000 in county jails. By 1895, those numbers had risen to 2,516 federal prisoners in state prisons and approximately 15,000 in county jails.

On March 3, 1891, the U.S. Congress passed a bill (*An Act for the Erection of United States Prisons and for the Imprisonment of United States Prisoners, and for Other Purposes*) authorizing the construction of three penitentiaries, although funding was not approved until later. The establishment of federal prison facilities was considered necessary because of the states' growing reluctance to house federal prisoners, the exclusion of federal prisoners from contract labor, and the increasing number of federal and state offenders.

Early Federal Prison Facilities

Until 1895, all military prisoners were confined at Fort Leavenworth, Kansas. The War Department then decided to house its prisoners in several military installations. Consequently, the Department of Justice acquired the surplus military prison at Fort Leavenworth in eastern Kansas. For the first time, federal prisoners, those transferred from state institutions as well as new commitments, were confined in a federal facility. In short order the Department of Justice realized the prison, adapted from former quartermaster warehouses, was inadequate. Therefore, on July 10, 1896, Congress appropriated funds for the construction of the previously authorized penitentiary, capable of holding twelve hundred inmates, to be built three miles from the prison at Fort Leavenworth. The site for the new penitentiary was the Fort Leavenworth military reservation. Because the penitentiary was built by convict labor, construction took many years and was not completed until 1928.

A second penitentiary at McNeil Island, Washington, was constructed between 1892 and 1895. The federal government designated it as a **U.S. penitentiary** in 1907. A third penitentiary at Atlanta, Georgia, was built in 1899.[2] The Auburn style of architecture, characterized by multitiered cell blocks and a fortresslike appearance, was adopted in all three of these penitentiaries.

Between 1900 and 1935, American prisons, including federal institutions, were primarily custodial, punitive, and industrial. Overcrowding at the federal prisons during this period left few resources for anything but custodial care. Nevertheless, there were significant developments during the early 1900s that have affected the operation of federal institutions to the present day, including passage of

1. the *White Slave Act* in 1910 (interstate commerce of prostitution)
2. the *Harrison Narcotic Act* in 1914 (taxing and records must be kept on controlled substances)
3. the *Volstead Act* in 1918 (prohibition of the sale and consumption of alcohol)
4. the *Dyer Act* of 1919 (interstate transportation of stolen vehicles)

The federal medical center, Carswell Air Force Base, Fort Worth, Texas, acquired from the U.S. Air Force in 1994

—COURTESY OF THE FEDERAL BUREAU OF PRISONS, CARSWELL

All of these acts brought a larger number of people under federal criminal jurisdiction. The number of offenders incarcerated under those statutes swelled the federal prison population beyond the available physical capacity. Largely because of the population increase in federal prisons, Congress authorized in 1925 a reformatory for "male persons between the ages of seventeen and thirty," which was constructed in Chillicothe, Ohio.[3]

By the 1920s the number of federal female prisoners being housed in state facilities warranted the building of special federal facilities for women. In 1927 a new five hundred-bed female institution opened at **Alderson**, West Virginia.

In 1929, when overcrowding reached a critical stage in the New York City area, the state and local authorities ordered all federal prisoners removed from the Tombs and the Raymond Street Jail. Responding to this crisis, a federal detention center was built in a newly constructed three-story garage and called the Federal Detention Headquarters.

The Bureau of Prisons Is Born

In 1929, Congress created the House Special Committee on Federal Penal and Reformatory Institutions. After extensive deliberations, it offered the following recommendations:

1. Establishment of a centralized administration of federal prisons at the bureau level;

2. Increased expenditure for federal probation officers, to be appointed by federal judges and exempt from civil service regulations;

3. Establishment of a full-time parole board;

4. Provision of facilities by the District of Columbia for its prisoners;

Linda Allen, in 1978, became the first woman correctional officer at the U.S. penitentiary at McNeil Island, Washington (now a Washington state correctional facility), breaking the barrier to female officers at a high-security institution. Now that this is commonplace at state and federal prisons, there are issues to consider in the recruitment, placement, and retention of these highly qualified females.

5. Transfer of all military prisoners held in civil prisons to Fort Leavenworth military barracks;

6. Removal of the minimum age of prisoners at the U.S. Industrial Reformatory at Chillicothe, Ohio;

7. Expeditious establishment of the two narcotic treatment farms previously authorized;

8. Passage of H.R. 11285 authorizing road camps for federal offenders;

9. Provision of additional employment opportunities for federal offenders;

10. Employment of an adequate number of nonfederal jail inspectors and linking payments for those facilities to conditions and programs found in them, and;

11. Construction of institutions to include two additional penitentiaries, a hospital for the care of the criminally insane, and a system of federal jails and workhouses in the more congested parts of the country.

Legislation was drafted, passed, and signed into law by President Herbert Hoover on May 14, 1930, creating the Federal Bureau of Prisons within the Department of Justice. Sanford Bates was appointed by President Hoover to be the first director of the Bureau of Prisons. The selection of Bates signified that the attitude toward penal administration in the federal government had shifted away from one that depended on political patronage.

EARLY GROWTH OF THE FEDERAL BUREAU OF PRISONS

It was soon obvious that three penitentiaries, two reformatories (one for young men and one for women), a jail, and eight camps did not meet the growing needs of the federal prison system. Federal prisoners with sentences of a year and less

Razor wire has taken the place of massive walls in modern prisons

—*COURTESY OF THE FEDERAL BUREAU OF PRISONS..*

could not be legally confined in the penitentiaries, and many were unsuitable for open camps. It was decided to build new structures or remodel existing structures to serve as regional jails.

In the early 1930s the old New Orleans Mint was modified for use as a federal jail. A new regional jail was opened at La Tuna, Texas, primarily to house the influx of immigration violators. A similar institution was opened near Detroit at Milan, Michigan. Another penitentiary was added at Lewisburg, Pennsylvania, and a men's reformatory was constructed west of the Mississippi River at El Reno, Oklahoma. A hospital for mentally ill prisoners (and for those with chronic medical ailments), was opened at Springfield, Missouri. The crime wave of the 1930s, combined with the expanding role of the federal government in crime control, brought the old military prison on Alcatraz Island in California under the control of the Department of Justice and historical fame.

RECENT DEVELOPMENTS

Public attitudes toward criminals and the appropriate societal response to them were influenced by many factors during the 1980s. Chief among those were increasing crime rates and the growing problems in administering prisons. Inmate disruptions at Attica and other institutions provided opportunities for the public to reexamine the prison's goals.[4] After a 1987 uprising by 1,000 Cuban inmates held at the **Oakdale** facility in Louisiana and 1,400 held at the Federal Penitentiary in Atlanta, there was a public outcry. The Cubans, part of the **Mariel** of 100,000 refugees admitted into the country in 1980, had taken hostages and overrun both facilities after hearing on their radios that 2,500 "undesirable" [Marielito] Cubans were about to be deported to Cuba. A siege of both facilities went on for eleven days, ending with the release of the eighty-nine hostages unharmed. The decision by the Department of Justice that no one would be held responsible for the millions of dollars in damage to the institutions was widely criticized. Former Attorney General Meese responded as follows:

Hugo (Lafayette) Black (1886–1991) was an associate justice of the U.S. Supreme Court from 1937–1971. Justice Black followed a course marked by the absolute defense of civil right as literally defined in the Bill of Rights and the Constitution. He was, as a senator, a strong supporter of President Franklin Roosevelt's plan to expand the U.S. Supreme Court by six justices and was appointed by the president in 1937. He was an obdurate supporter of the First Amendment and often was in conflict over issues involving freedom of speech, press, and religion with fellow justices who leaned toward more governmental authority.

The state of California has added a central, electrified fence to razor wire to provide lethal security

—*COURTESY OF STATE OF CALIFORNIA DEPARTMENT OF CORRECTIONS*

[T]he [incarcerated Mariel] Cubans did not come out ahead of the government in the agreement ending the 11-day crisis. . . . When details of the agreement that freed the 89 hostages are fully understood, it will become clear it was fair and proper.

You will learn as we proceed in this matter . . . in no institution will people be able to gain by an uprising.[5]

The neoclassical call for law and order prompted a public debate about crime and criminals similar to what had occurred in the 1930s. In response to this public concern, the Bureau of Prisons devised a comprehensive master plan. Four objectives for the Bureau of Prisons were established in the bureau's master plan:

1. Increasing program alternatives for offenders who do not require traditional institutional confinement, thereby minimizing the negative effects of imprisonment, lessening alienation from society, and reducing economic costs to the taxpayer;

2. Enhancing the quality of the correctional staff by providing increased training opportunities, better working conditions, and heightened professional challenges to inspire continuous personnel growth and satisfaction;

Women as High-Security Officers

Historically, women have been underrepresented in corrections. Those women who did work in corrections traditionally were placed in clerical or other support service positions, and some served as correctional officers. Few women have served in supervisory or upper management positions.

While gender bias in correctional facility employment certainly still exists, the situation has changed. The "new" correctional philosophy is that women should be hired, trained, and promoted to all positions—and at all security levels, including maximum security.

For years, the Federal Bureau of Prisons has had a gender-neutral hiring policy for all positions except correctional officers at high-security male institutions (penitentiaries). As a result, the Bureau has witnessed steady growth in the numbers of women in its workforce. In January 1992, the gender-neutral policy was extended to all positions, with full implementation expected by 1994.

The trend toward gender-neutral hiring in maximum-security institutions is also evident in the State corrections. Forty-five States use women to staff at least one male maximum-security prison or unit. Twenty-four of these allow women to be eligible for all correctional posts; policy is gender-neutral with respect to hiring women in these settings. In 15 States, women are not permitted to work certain maximum-security posts; these usually involve supervising showers or performing strip searches. Seven States have highly restrictive policies with respect to using women to staff male maximum-security prisons. Of these, six States exclude women correctional officers from positions within housing units, and one State excludes women completely from maximum-security prisons.

Based on 20 years of experience as a correctional administrator and a lengthy review of the current literature, I have encountered several myths about women in the workplace.

- Women do not want to be promoted. They would rather follow than lead.

- Advancement for women is precluded by domestic issues, such as a lack of mobility and a preoccupation with child care.

- Women simply cannot do the work that men can do in correctional settings because they do not have the skills needed to advance in the organization.

These myths have caused me to reflect on personal experiences in which gender bias has occurred. For example, while warden at the United States Penitentiary, Lompoc, California, I was asked to comment on the possibility of women working in "contact" positions at the maximum-security level. At first, I felt women could not handle the pressures associated with a maximum-security institution. However, after reviewing the available literature on the topic, I changed my mind. ∎

SOURCE: Richard H. Rison, "Women as High-Security Officers: Gender Neutral Employment in High-Security Prisons." *Federal Prisons* 3:3 (1994): 19–20.

3. Improving present physical plants and incorporating new facilities into the system to increase the effectiveness of correctional programs, and;

4. Expanding community involvement in correctional programs and goals because, in the final analysis, only through successful reintegration into the community can the ex-offender avoid reverting to crime.

A significant development during the 1970s and 1980s was the assignment of responsibility for the planning and management of inmate programs to treatment teams under the concept of **unit management**. Though the staff makeup of the teams varied among institutions, they usually consisted of a caseworker, a correctional counselor, and an educational representative. Also introduced was the functional unit approach, or unit management, in place of traditional casework programming. The unit management system provides for semiautonomous unit teams.

The bureau's rehabilitation programs and their increasing sophistication were challenged in the mid-1970s by academicians, researchers, and practitioners who pointed out the bankruptcy of results obtained from traditional rehabilitation programming.[6] Accordingly, in 1975 the medical model of corrections in the Federal Bureau of Prisons was deemphasized, and in its place was substituted a philosophy of rehabilitation, retribution, deterrence, and incapacitation.

The 1970s found the Bureau of Prisons with more new facilities than it had at any time since the 1930s. A steady increase in inmate population during the first five years of the decade dictated the acquisition of additional and modernized

Many types of handcuffs, chains, and leg irons are used in a prison

—*COURTESY OF FEDERAL BUREAU OF PRISONS*

facilities, to reduce overcrowding, to create more humane and safe living conditions, and close the three old penitentiaries at McNeil Island, Washington; Atlanta, Georgia; and Leavenworth, Kansas.[7]

The Federal Bureau of Prisons experienced as much change in the 1970s as it did in any other time in its history; yet many of the activities of the bureau for the most part remain unchanged. This apparent contradiction can be explained as the result of contradictory input from the Congress, public, professional corrections personnel, and others who, on the one hand, wish prisons to be secure and protective of the public and, on the other, wish in some way to reform or change the individual.

Organization and Administration

The Federal Bureau of Prisons provides administration at the central office in Washington, D.C., and via five **regional offices**. The central office comprises the director's office and four divisions: Correctional Programs; Administration; Medical and Services; and Industries, Education, and Vocational Training. Each division is headed by an assistant director. There is also an Office of General Counsel and an Office of Inspections, both of which report to the director.

The five regions are headed by regional directors and are located in Atlanta, Dallas, Philadelphia, Burlingame (San Francisco), and Kansas City, Missouri.

INMATE POPULATIONS EXPLODE

The inmate population of the Federal Bureau of Prisons was 95,034 at year-end 1994, and reached over 100,000 by year-end 1995[8] (see Figure 26-1). Federal court sentencing of offenders to longer terms of confinement for serious crimes and the effort to combat organized crime and drug trafficking greatly contributed to sharp inmate population increases in 1993. The percentage of inmates serving sentences for drug law violations increased to a whopping 67 percent of the population for minimum security, 69.7 percent for low security, 56.1 percent for medium security and 33.9 percent for high security federal facilities. That constitutes an overall average of 57 percent of the total population at the end of 1994.[9] The decline in the rates of some crimes has been minimized or eliminated from federal data, primarily due to policy at the Department of Justice in the 1970s in the

FIGURE

26.1

Inmate Population
Growth

SOURCE: Annual report of the Federal Bureau of Prisons, 1995.

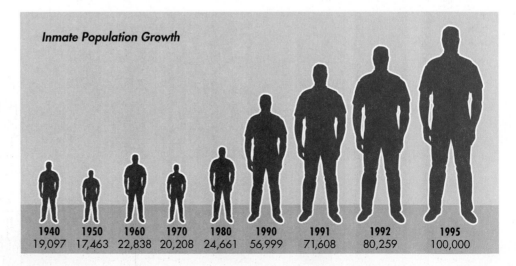

Inmate Population Growth

1940	1950	1960	1970	1980	1990	1991	1992	1995
19,097	17,463	22,838	20,208	24,661	56,999	71,608	80,259	100,000

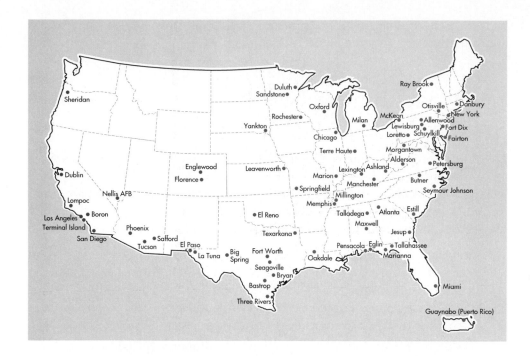

FIGURE

26.2

Federal Facilities, Year-end, 1994

Bureau of Prisons to no longer house juvenile offenders, who made up a large portion of those convicted of auto theft.[10] Figure 26-2 shows the locations of federal correctional facilities throughout the United States, at year-end 1994.

Community Programs

Prison space is a scarce and costly resource, to be used in situations where the interests of society must be protected. Because of the continuing record-high prison population growth in the federal system as well, the use of alternatives to incarceration for nonviolent offenders is essential. A large number of prisoners are confined in Bureau of Prisons' contract facilities. Approximately 80 percent of eligible offenders released to the community are regularly released through community treatment centers. These centers are used for offenders who are near release as a transition back to home, job, and community. Time is used to find a job, locate a place to live, and reestablish family ties.

The Community Correctional Center project was implemented in Washington, D.C., in 1983. The project uses imprisonment alternatives such as community service, work, and victim restitution when recommended by the U.S. district court. The center is available to federal courts in the District of Columbia, Maryland, and Virginia for sentenced offenders who are not a risk to the community and who may be in custody up to one year. A second community correctional center was opened in Detroit, Michigan, in September 1985.

All persons adjudicated under the Juvenile Justice and Delinquency Prevention Act are placed under contract in local and state facilities as well as in such facilities as boys' ranches, group homes, or foster homes. Most adult inmates sentenced to serve less than six months are confined in local jails.

A small number of federal inmates are housed in state prisons. Those inmates are housed in state facilities primarily for protection, as most have cooperated with the federal government in providing testimony. More state beds are being sought as federal inmate populations grow, but very few spaces are available.

A Model Inmate Classification System

The Bureau of Prisons' inmate classification system has been in effect since April 1979. Variables such as severity of offense, history of escapes or violence, expected length of incarceration, and type of prior commitments are used to determine an inmate's security level. The federal system groups the seventy-nine institutions into five security levels: **minimum**, **low**, **medium**, **high**, and **administrative** as follows:

1. *Minimum:* Minimum security institutions, also known as Federal Prison Camps have dormitory housing, a relatively low staff-to-inmate ratio, and no fences. These institutions are work and program oriented, and many are located adjacent to larger institutions or at military bases, where inmates help serve the labor needs of the institution or base.

2. *Low:* Low-security federal correctional institutions (FCIs) have double-fenced perimeters, mostly dormitory housing, and strong work and program components. The staff-to-inmate ratio in these institutions is higher than in minimum-security facilities.

3. *Medium:* Medium-security FCIs have strengthened perimeters (often double fences with electronic detection systems), cell-type housing, a wide variety of work and treatment programs, and an even higher staff-to-inmate ratio than low-security institutions, providing even greater internal controls.

4. *High:* High-security institutions, also known as U.S. penitentiaries (USPs) have secure perimeters (either walled or double-fenced), multiple- and single-occupant cell housing, and close staff supervision and movement controls.

5. *Administrative:* Administrative facilities are institutions with special missions, such as the detention of noncitizen or pretrial offenders, the treatment of inmates with serious or chronic medical problems, or the containment of extremely dangerous, violent, or escape-prone inmates. Administrative facilities are capable of holding inmates of all security categories.[11]

Data on inmates of the Federal Bureau of Prisons by inmate security level are shown in Table 26-1.

The Federal Bureau of Prisons is now responsible for carrying out the judgments of federal courts whenever a period of confinement is ordered. In their major institutions, ranging from minimum to maximum security, over 12,000 employees were at work in 1986, and this number grew to 26,489 at year-end 1994, with 74 percent male and 26.6 percent female. In its growth projections, the bureau planned to have 88 facilities on line by 1995, in hopes of providing for the huge increases in populations.[12] Over 100,000 inmates are currently confined in federal institutions. All sentenced offenders who are medically able are required to complete regular daily work assignments. In addition, all offenders have opportunities to participate in educational, vocational training, work, religious, and counseling programs.

The classification system, designed to place offenders in the least restrictive institution possible, that is, nearest to their homes, has proven effective.

TABLE *26.1*

Federal Bureau of Prisons
Statistics by Inmate Security Level

	Min.	Low	Med.	High
Sentence Length (years)				
Average sentence length	5	6.5	10	15
Sentence Imposed (as % of Population)				
Under 1 year	5.1%	1.4%	0.4%	0.5%
1—3 years	27.5	12.9	6.1	1.3
3—5 years	21.4	15.1	9.3	3.6
5—10 years	29.3	28.6	23.3	13.5
10—15 years	13.6	26.2	24.5	18.1
15—20 years	1.8	9.4	16.6	15.8
Over 20 years	1.2	5.9	18.8	31.8
Life sentence	0.1	0.5	1.0	15.4
Offense (as % of Population)				
Drug/Liquor	67.0%	69.7%	56.1%	33.9%
Robbery	1.5	6.6	15.8	33.9
Property offenses	6.8	4.7	4.6	4.4
Extortion, bribery, and fraud	12.9	3.3	2.1	1.0
Violent offenses	0.3	1.8	3.8	10.3
Arms, explosives, arson	7.6	7.0	11.8	12.0
All others	4.2	6.4	8.7	15.5

SOURCE: FBOP. *State of the Bureau* (Washington, D.C.: U.S. Department of Justice, 1995), p. 67.

Minimum security inmates account for 40 percent of the federal inmate population, low-security 29 percent, medium-security 24.6 percent, and high-security 12.4 percent.[13] That means more inmates can be moved into such open institutions as prison camps. The effect is that higher security level institutions become more humane through reduced crowding.

UNICOR: Federal Prison Industries, Inc.

Federal Prison Industries, Inc., with the corporate trade name UNICOR, is a wholly owned government corporation that sells its products and services to other federal agencies. UNICOR's mission is to support the Federal Bureau of Prisons through the gainful employment of inmates in diversified work programs.

Eligible inmates confined in the federal prison system are employed by UNICOR. The industrial operations located in most federal institutions constructively employ inmates and assist in preparing them for employment opportunities upon release.

Occupational training is also offered through UNICOR and includes on-the-job training, vocational education, and apprenticeship programs. There are hundreds of formal training programs in various trades offered by federal institutions. Apprenticeship programs, registered with the U.S. Department of Labor's Bureau of Apprenticeship and Training, exist at about two-thirds of the federal institutions.

An active program of plant modernization and expansion of industries was begun in 1983 and continues apace in hopes of providing meaningful activity for the expected increases in population. As it continues, it will ensure modern production capacity far into the future.

Education and Training: Inmates and Staff

The Federal Bureau of Prisons provides academic and occupational training programs to prepare inmates for employment upon release. Enrollment is voluntary, but program options are extensive, ranging from Adult Basic Education (ABE) through college courses. Occupational training programs include accredited vocational training, apprenticeship programs, and preindustrial training.

A mandatory literacy program has been implemented for inmates since 1983, requiring all federal inmates to function at a sixth grade educational level. Those who could not are required to enroll in the ABE program for a minimum of ninety days. In 1986, the standard was raised to an eighth grade literacy level, the nationally accepted functional literacy level. In 1991, the *Crime Control Act of 1990* (Public Law 101-647) directed the Federal Bureau of Prisons to have a mandatory functional literacy program for all mentally capable inmates in place. The bureau voluntarily raised the standard to twelfth grade and required participation for a minimum of 120 days. All promotions in Federal Prison Industries and in institution work assignments were made contingent upon the inmate's achieving literacy.

The Adult Basic Education program has been quite successful. Certificates for completion of the General Education Development (GED) program have been awarded to thousands of inmates. English as a Second Language (ESL) is also provided for all who need it. Projects are funded by UNICOR to provide job training in such fields as computer sciences, business, diesel mechanics, water treatment, petroleum technology, graphic arts, and food service.

Staff training provides every bureau employee with the knowledge, skills, and abilities required to assure high standards of employee performance and conduct. The staff training network is composed of the Staff Training Operations Office, Washington, D.C.; a Staff Training Academy at the Federal Law Enforcement Training Center in Glynco, Georgia; a Management and Specialty Training Center in Denver, Colorado; and a Food Service and Commissary Training Center at the Federal Correctional Institution in Fort Worth, Texas. All new employees are required to undergo four weeks of formal training during their first forty-five days with the Bureau of Prisons.

Federal Female Offenders

The Bureau of Prisons continues to focus on improving programs and services for female offenders. It operates seven co-correctional facilities, and all-female institutions located in FPC Alderson, in West Virginia, FPC Bryan and FMC Carswell in Texas, FCI Butner in North Carolina, FCI Danbury in Connecticut, and FCI Dublin in California.

Apprenticeship training programs have been accredited by the Women's Bureau of the U.S. Department of Labor, Bureau of Apprenticeship and Training.

Holistic Health Comes to Prison

Maria stopped in her tracks, noticing the onset of the first stages of the panic attack that usually preceded her seizures. Her heart was beating rapidly, and she felt afraid. She began to regulate her breathing and tried to connect with the feeling of being centered and grounded.

She turned to her friend Rosa and asked for help. Rosa saw at once what Maria needed and began to speak calmly, instructing her to focus on her breathing and concentrate on staying fully present in her body. As contractions passed through Maria's body, Rosa stayed with her. The seizure passed quickly, and Maria gradually regained consciousness without any of the fear and distress that usually accompanied her seizures. She felt grateful for Rosa's help and for the breathing and centering techniques they had both learned in the prison's holistic health program.

This is but one of the success stories of the Prison Integrated Health Program (PIHP), serving the entire prison population—both inmates and staff—at the Federal Correctional Institution (FCI), Dublin, California. This innovative volunteer program began in 1990 as a stress management workshop for 20 long-term inmates. The program was taught by Kathy Park, an artist and somatic education teacher, under my supervision as Clinical Director of Health Services. From a two-session stress management workshop taught by one volunteer, the holistic health program at Dublin has expanded dramatically in the years since.

The volunteer organization Prison Integrated Health Program was created by its co-directors in spring 1991 to bring together teachers (along with community resources) to develop comprehensive holistic health programming for FCI, Dublin, and to serve as a model for a new approach to health promotion and disease prevention in correctional facilities.

Central to the program is the belief that health is a function of physical, mental, emotional, and spiritual well-being: only by addressing all aspects of people's lives through a holistic approach can we change behavior, prevent disease, reduce symptoms, and promote health. PIHP has developed the first holistic health program in a Federal women's prison. It has already inspired the creation of similar programming in several other jails and prisons nationwide.

PIHP is co-directed by volunteers Kathy Park and Wendy Palmer, who is a teacher of meditation, conflict resolution, and intuition. Its core teaching staff currently consists of five facilitators, an auxiliary staff of 25, and many guest speakers—all volunteers. PIHP is a sponsored project of the San Francisco Women's Centers, a nonprofit organization. It is independently funded by individual donations and foundation grants and has received many in-kind donations of books, tapes, and art supplies. PIHP has also assembled a national advisory board of professionals concerned with holistic health issues, including renowned authors George Leonard (*Mystery*) and Clarissa Pinkola Estes (*Women Who Run With the Wolves*).   ■

SOURCE: Tracy Thompson, "Holistic Health Comes to Prison." *Federal Prisons* 3:3 (1994). 55—56.

These programs assist in preparing women for nontraditional careers as auto mechanics, electricians, plumbers, painters, and bricklayers. Apprenticeship programs are offered for women in a large number of different trades. Federal facilities housed about seventy-three hundred female offenders in 1994, 7.7 percent of the total population of federal inmates.[14]

Community Corrections in the Federal System

The Federal Bureau of Prisons' Community Corrections and Detention Division is responsible for the development and implementation of policies and procedures related to the administration of approximately six hundred community corrections centers and detention contract facilities nationwide. This is organized around the central office in Washington, D.C., the six regional offices that oversee thirteen management center administrators and the activities of thirty-three community corrections offices (CCOs) throughout the United States.

Women in federal institutions may participate in holistic programs that include meditation

—PHOTO BY JIM KETSDEVER/VALLEY TIMES, COURTESY OF CONTRA COSTA NEWSPAPERS/CCN

Each CCO has a community corrections manager, who is responsible for the development, administration, and routine oversight of residential and nonresidential services provided through contractual agreements with federal, state, county, and city governmental agencies and through contracts with private agencies. Services provided by these agencies include prerelease programs, short- and long-term detention, juvenile and adult boarding, and home confinement programs such as those using electronic monitoring.

Expansion of new programs and facilities include Intensive Confinement Centers (ICCs), urban work camps, transitional drug abuse treatment programs, and comprehensive sanctions centers. Since more than 27 percent of its inmate population consists of foreign nationals, the bureau is constantly active in finding and obtaining additional contract bed space for this group.

Changing Population of Federal Institutions

A former governor of Georgia, Lester Maddox, is credited with saying (when asked how to improve that state's correctional system), "What we need here is a better class of prisoner." The Federal Bureau of Prisons was looked upon for years as dealing with just the "cream of criminals." Whether true or apocryphal, the times are changing, and the federal system has some real problem inmates to deal with today. They are now experiencing some of the serious overcrowding and violence problems that have long been the fate of the state facilities. In 1984, Congress created the U.S. Sentencing Commission as an independent body, located in the judicial branch of the government. The Commission began its work in 1985 and submitted new guidelines that have dramatically altered sentencing practices in the federal criminal justice system. A summary of their impact follows:

1. "Straight" probationary sentences (i.e., sentences that require no form of confinement) will be reduced significantly.

TABLE 26.2

Federal Bureau of Prisons
Year-End 1994

General Data

Institution Rated Capacity

Total	68,221
Percentage of capacity occupied	126%

Inmates Under Bureau Jurisdiction

Total	95,034
In Bureau institutions	85,573
Other*	9,461
Sentenced	89.2%
Unsentenced	10.8

Average Cost of Confinement per Inmate (FY 1994)

Daily	58.50
Annual	$21,352

Staff-to-Inmate Ratio 1:2.6

White	61.8%
Other	2.8

Inmate Characteristics

Average Age 37

Gender

Male	92.5%
Female	7.5

Race

White	61.8
Black	35.4
Other	2.8

Ethnicity

Hispanic	26.7%
Non-Hispanic	**73.3**

Citizenship

United States	74.8%
Mexico	8.9
Colombia	4.4
Cuba	2.9
Dominican Republic	1.6
Nigeria	1.0
Other	5.1

Type of Commitments

U.S. Code	96.3%
Probation violation	1.7
Parole violation	1.0
State territorial	0.6
D.C. Superior Court	0.4

Median Months Expected to be Served

All offenses	63
Drug offenses	71
Robbery	91
Property offenses	48
Extortion, fraud, and bribery	22
Violent offenses	142
Firearms, explosives, and arson	51
White-collar offenses	17
Immigration	20
Sex offenses	74
National security	51
Continuing criminal enterprise	152

Inmate Status

Inmates by Security Level

Minimum	40.0%
Low	29.0
Medium	24.6
High	12.4

*Includes inmates in Community Corrections Centers, State boarders, juveniles, and other contract categories.
SOURCE: FBOP, *State of the Bureau* (Washington, D.C.: U.S. Department of Justice, 1995), p. 67.

2. For especially serious crimes, such as drug offenses and crimes against persons, probationary services will decline dramatically.

3. For other crimes, like property offenses, the proportion of sentences involving some form of probation will not change appreciably, although probation with a condition of confinement may be substituted for straight probation.

4. Average time served for violent offenses will increase substantially. For most property crimes, average time served will remain largely unchanged. Exceptions are burglary and income tax fraud, where average time served will go up.

5. Federal prison populations will grow markedly by the end of this century, more as a result of the Anti-Drug Abuse Act of 1986 and the career offender provision of the Comprehensive Crime Control Act of 1984 than as a result of the guidelines.[15]

Drugs and Federal Prison Populations

There has been an explosion of arrests and convictions and increasingly longer sentences for possessing and selling drugs. A Justice Department study, completed last summer, but not released until February, found that of the 90,000 federal prison inmates, one fifth are low-level drug offenders with no current or prior violence or previous prison time. They are jamming the prisons. The federal prison population, through mandated and determinate sentences, has tripled in the past decade. It will rise by 50% by the century's turn, with drug offenders accounting for 60% of the federal prison population. Yet as Jeffrey Fagan concluded, following his own field research and a review of the literature on the effect of criminal sanctions on drug selling:

As long as demand for drugs remains high, and the likelihood of marginal gains from drug selling are sufficient to neutralize motivations to avoid crime or participate in illicit work, offenders in socially and economically marginal neighborhoods may continue to perceive economic benefits from participation in the drug economy." ■

SOURCE: Jerome H. Skolnick, What Not to Do About Crime—The American Society of Criminology 1994 Presidential Address," *Criminology* 33:1 (1995): 9.

The changes have had a major impact on the correctional administrators in the Bureau of Prisons in the form of a massive increase in the numbers and types of inmates confined in federal institutions, institutions that are already overcrowded. The statistical data for the Federal Bureau of Prisons, at year-end 1994, is summarized on the previous page, in Table 26-2.

Summary

One objective of the Federal Bureau of Prisons is to be a model for state and local corrections. The bureau has attacked some of the major issues head on and has made notable progress. But there are no simple solutions to the long-festering problems of corrections, whether state or federal. Much hard work lies ahead—for the bureau and for all other correctional agencies in the United States.

One of the bright spots on the horizon is the increasing use by the courts and corrections of community-based treatment as a humane, less costly alternative to incarceration for selected offenders. A substantial percentage of offenders, however, are not suitable for treatment in the relative freedom of community-based programs. Into that category fall many multiple offenders who have long histories of serious, often violent, crimes.

To achieve maximum correctional benefits for all offenders, the Bureau of Prisons has sought to develop a balanced approach, recognizing that no single all-purpose treatment method can be expected to produce effective results. One of the main challenges of the future undoubtedly will be to sustain the present level of public and legislative interest, which demands a concerted effort by the correctional community and by concerned citizens.

Review Questions

1. Explain the various kinds of institutions in the federal prison system.
2. What forces led to the shift in philosophy of the Federal Bureau of Prisons in the 1970s?
3. Outline the FBOP institutional security classification system.

4. Why does the bureau have such an advantage over state systems in evaluating programs?

5. Why has the prison population of the Federal Bureau of Prisons increased over the last few years?

Words to Remember

Justice Department	Mariel group	medium security level
U.S. penitentiary	regional offices	high security level
Alderson	minimum security level	administrative security level
Oakdale	low security level	unit management

Endnotes

1. With kind permission from the bureau, this chapter has drawn heavily from the U.S. Department of Justice, *The Development of the Federal Prison System* (Washington, D.C.: U.S. Government Printing Office, 1979), and the Federal Bureau of Prisons Annual Report, and various items from other Federal Bureau of Prisons publications. The authors appreciate their cooperation and assistance.

2. The facility is now part of the prison system of the state of Washington.

3. This facility is currently an Ohio correctional institution.

4. Between November 21 and 23, 1987, eighty-nine federal prison staff were seized as hostages at the Atlanta Penitentiary and at the Alien Detention Center at Oakdale, Louisiana. The uprisings have been described as the most disruptive episodes in the history of the Bureau of Prisons. Hostages were eventually released after the attorney general agreed to review each case of the Marielitos, Cubans who arrived in the nation during the Mariel boat lift. See "After Atlanta and Oakdale," *Corrections Today* 50 (1988): 26, 64–65.

5. Associated Press, "Meese Defends Prison Deal," *Seattle Times,* December 5, 1987, p. A2.

6. See Harry Allen and Nick Gatz, "Abandoning the Medical Model in Corrections: Some Implications and Alternatives," *Prison Journal* 54 (Autumn 1974): 4–14, and Simon Dinitz, "Nothing Fails Like a Little Success," in Edward Sagarin, ed., *Criminology: New Concerns* (Beverly Hills, CA: Sage, 1979), pp. 105–118.

7. Only McNeil Island has been closed, and has since been sold to the state of Washington to help solve some of its prison overcrowding. The institutions at Atlanta and Leavenworth still serve the overcrowded system.

8. In addition, the Office of General Counsel in the Federal Bureau of Prisons administers and oversees the inmate grievance program, initiated in 1974. Approximately fourteen thousand grievances were filed in fiscal year 1982; inmates were granted relief in 20 percent of those filings. U.S. General Accounting Office, *Prison Expansion: Staffing New Facilities Will Be a Challenge for BOP* (Washington, D.C.: U.S. General Accounting Office, May 12, 1992), p. 1.

9. Sue Kline, "A Profile of Female Offenders in the Federal Bureau of Prisons," *Federal Prison Journal* 3:1 (1992): 33–36.

10. Ibid., p. 34.

11. Federal Bureau of Prisons, *State of the Bureau: Emergency Preparedness and Response* (Washington, D.C.: U.S. Department of Justice, 1994), p. 45.

12. Ibid.

13. Ibid.

14. Ibid.

15. National Institute of Justice, "The Impact of the Federal Sentencing Guidelines," *NIJ Reports: Research in Action* (Washington D.C.: U.S. Department of Justice, September 1987), p. 2.

CHAPTER TWENTY-SEVEN

Community-Based Systems

Overview

Our examination of the correctional system has led us through systems at local, state, and federal systems levels. Programs representing the systems in the public sector that are direct tax-supported entities. These have had easily defined territorial boundaries (such as a city, county, or state). We venture now into the realm of community-based systems, correctional activities typically without walls, subsidized in part by private funds, and that generally have a contract with one or more subsystems of corrections. We begin this discussion of community corrections with a brief review of incarceration and the inmate's exit from prison.

The manifold implications of the concept of community corrections pivot around a profound idea: official reactions to the convicted offender should be related to the community forces which contribute to criminality, which are involved in the definition of crime as a social problem, and which largely determine whether or not "rehabilitation" programs will produce his integration within the control system regulating the behavior of noncriminals.

—Elmer H. Johnson, criminologist

Prisons: At a Turning Point

For over two centuries, jails, prisons, reformatories, juvenile detention, training schools, and other secure facilities have embodied the primary societal response to criminal behavior in America. The public is becoming increasingly aware, especially in these times of limited budgets, that the institutions are inefficient, ineffective, and expensive.[1] Unrelieved confinement may be necessary for a reasonable percentage of the inmate population. But to house all of the rest in bleak and cheerless places is a waste not only of human potential but also of costly security measures. More recently, as we noted in Part III, the correctional system has expanded to include five components: (1) jails and detention facilities, (2) probation, (3) intermediate sanctions, (4) imprisonment, and (5) parole

The five have grown separately, often in competition for the same limited fiscal, physical, and personnel resources. In recent years, authorities have recognized that an effective utilization of scarce resources demands their coordination and consolidation.

Crime and the American Way

We are a nation both afraid of and obsessed with crime. Each day, newspapers tell another story of innocence shattered: the Oklahoma City bombing, the drowning of two young boys in a South Carolina lake by their mother, the brutal stabbings of Nicole Brown Simpson and Ronald Goldman. In the evenings, our televisions are saturated with real-crime dramas such as *America's Most Wanted* and *Unsolved Mysteries*. Since the 1960s, hundreds of different crime bills have been passed by Congress and state legislatures. We have fought a war on drugs. Annual expenditures on police have increased from $5 billion to $27 billion over the past two decades. We have built more prisons to lock up more people than almost every country in the world. We are the only country in the West to employ capital punishment and to use the death penalty against teenagers. Yet Americans in record numbers still report that they feel unsafe in their streets and in their homes.

We have leveled our supposedly strongest weapons at crime, to the tune of about 100 billion tax dollars per year, but we have not accomplished much. Crime rates have not gotten worse—as many would have you believe—but neither have they gotten much better. ■

SOURCE: Steven R. Donziger, ed., *The Real War on Crime* (New York: HarperCollins, 1996), p. 1.

Still badly fragmented and divided in many ways, the correctional services in the United States are slowly, and often reluctantly, beginning to move toward the creation of an organized system. Foremost in that movement is the shift away from the total institution toward alternatives to incarceration.

The current trends in prison construction, against continuous overpopulation, reflect a more punitive, conservative, and hard-line approach to crime and criminals. The crime rates in the United States began to decrease in 1975 and have actually continued to do so. The National Crime Victimization Study indicates that crime fell almost 30 percent overall between 1975 and 1994. This is due, in part, because the baby boomers have moved through the high-risk ages of sixteen to twenty-nine. Also, the selective incapacitation of the highest-risk offenders for longer periods of incarceration may achieve the suppressive effects[2] sought by its advocates.[3]

Selective incapacitation is characterized as a sound concept in theory, but a nightmare in practice (see Chapter 6). Struckoff quotes Walker's five questions about selective incapacitation:

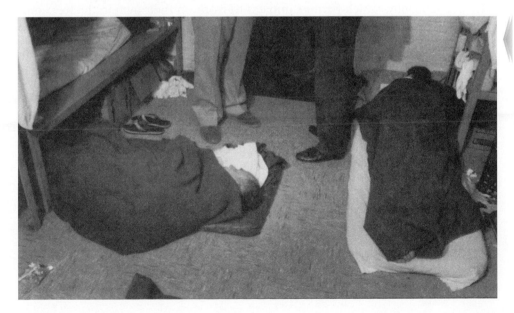

Overcrowding in jails leads to sleeping anywhere space allows

—PHOTO BY MARK LUDAK, COURTESY OF IMPACT VISUALS

1. Can we correctly estimate the amount of crime reduction?

2. Can we accurately identify chronic offenders and predict their future behavior?

3. Can we afford the monetary costs of implementing selective incapacitation should it involve massive new detention center construction?

4. Can we implement a policy of consistent selective incapacitation without violating constitutional rights?

5. What will the side effects be?[4]

Clearly the jury is still out on this controversial attempt to link incarceration to crime reduction. As Struckoff says, "A vigorously joined debate continues on this topic, because it will affect police, prosecutors, judges, legislators, the public, and the correctional community."[5]

The correctional pendulum swings slowly, and probably will continue to swing for many decades. But if the movement is toward the "hard line of increased incarceration" today, it also can swing in the opposite direction in the future. In today's correctional environment, the main aim remains to achieve the greatest possible use of supportive treatment in the community. The custodial institutions have failed because most of them have virtually no access to community treatment programs, professional services, or public support. . . and neither time nor resources to do *inside* the overcrowded prisons.

Perhaps it would be better to raze all the prisons and start over again, but that cannot be done until workable alternatives have been firmly established. The number of alternatives is growing, however, and attempts to evaluate the effectiveness of such programs are under way.

REENTRY INTO THE COMMUNITY FROM THE INSTITUTION

One of the earliest programs for releasing prisoners before their full sentences expired was the result of the first work-release legislation. The use of offenders for community work programs had its origins in ancient Rome, where prisoners aided in the construction of massive public works. Those workers, however, had no hope for release; their work was just another form of slave labor. The work-release philosophy, which permits inmates to work on their own in the free community, dates back to a 1913 Wisconsin statute that allowed misdemeanants to continue to work at their jobs while serving short sentences in jail. North Carolina applied the principles of the Wisconsin statute to felony offenders in 1957, under limited conditions; Michigan and Maryland soon followed suit with similar acts.

In 1965, Congress passed the Federal Prisoner Rehabilitation Act, which provided for work release, furloughs, and community treatment centers for federal prisoners. This act, an excerpt of which is found in the accompanying correctional brief served as a model for many states.

Institutional work release is not intended to be a substitute for parole, but it can be a valuable tool for the correctional administrator and the parole officer who must eventually supervise an individual who has participated in work release. The work-release program is not really an alternative to incarceration. Rather, it is a chance for offenders to test their work skills and personal control over their behavior in the community. And it allows them to spend the major part of the day away

Federal Prisoner Rehabilitation Act

The Attorney General may extend the limits of the place of confinement of a prisoner as to whom there is reasonable cause to believe he will honor this trust, by authorizing him, under prescribed conditions, to:

1. visit a specifically designated place or places for a period not to exceed thirty days and return to the same or another institution or facility. An extension of limits may be granted only to permit a visit to a dying relative, attendance at the funeral of a relative, the obtaining of medical services not otherwise available, the contacting of prospective employers, or for any other compelling reason consistent with the public interest; or

2. work at paid employment or participate in a training program in the community on a voluntary basis while continuing as a prisoner of the institution or facility to which he is committed. . . .

The willful failure of a prisoner to remain within the extended limits of his confinement, or to return within the time prescribed, to an institution or facility designated by the Attorney General, shall be deemed an escapee from the custody of the Attorney General. ∎

SOURCE: American Academy of Political and Social Science, *The Future of Corrections: The Annals* (Washington, D.C.: American Academy of Political and Social Science, 1969), p. 65.

---

from the institution. Because offenders must still return to the institution, the type work-release program may be considered only a partial alternative.

Work release has other benefits besides allowing inmates to be outside the walls for a period of time each day. The income derived from the work can be used in a number of ways. If the inmates have families, the earnings can be used to keep them off welfare rolls or to augment the assistance they might be receiving. Inmates can also reimburse victims for their loss if the judge has required it;[6] or they may be able to build a nest egg for the time when they will be released. One of the main fringe benefits is that their community becomes aware of their ability to maintain a job without creating problems for themselves or others. Also, their association with stable coworkers in the free world may provide them support and

A metropolitan correction center

—*COURTESY OF THE FEDERAL BUREAU OF PRISONS*

guidance[7] that they could not find inside the walls. In the American tradition, the ability to "do a good day's work" both heightens the offenders' self-esteem and commands respect from others. Most Scandinavian prisons have factories attached to them, allowing inmates to work at real-world jobs for pay equal to that earned by the outside worker.

Another form of **partial incarceration** is the furlough. Both work release and furlough extend the limits of confinement to include unsupervised absences from the institution. Furloughs and home visits have been allowed for many years on an informal basis. The death of a family member or some other crisis situation was the most common reason for the home furlough. As states have passed legislation making furloughs a legal correctional tool, furloughs have been used for a number of purposes, including a home visit during holidays or just before release, so that the return to the free world becomes a graduated process. Education has been another reason for extensive use of the furlough; it often allows the inmate to be in residence at the school during the week and he or she returns to the correctional institution on the weekend. One benefit of home furloughs, obviously, is decreased sexual tension in institutions. More uses for the furlough will be explored as correctional administrators gain experience with it. A major roadblock to progress in such programs has been a few highly publicized and sensationalized failures. Those failures,[8] combined with the general increase in violent and dangerous inmates coming out of the prisons, make it difficult to promote any kind of furlough program.

HALFWAY HOUSES AS ALTERNATIVES TO INCARCERATION

The search for alternatives to incarceration led to the development of the **halfway house** (now known as a community residential center), a place where offenders can benefit from work or education in the free world while residing in the community.[9]

Counseling for inmates in a drug rehabilitation center

—PHOTO BY JOHN GRIFFIN, COURTESY OF THE IMAGE WORKS

The interest in the halfway house as an alternative to imprisonment has grown in recent years. Although the original halfway houses served as residences for homeless, unemployed men or women released from prison, they have since been used for a variety of purposes. Small residences offering shelter have been managed by prison aid societies for over a century. In recent years, more attention has been given to halfway houses as the possible nuclei of community-based networks of residential treatment centers, drug-free and alcohol-free living space, or as prerelease guidance centers.

In 1961 the U.S. Bureau of Prisons established prerelease guidance centers in major metropolitan areas. The offender is sent to these centers from a correctional institution several months before he or she is eligible for parole. Staff personnel are selected on the basis of their treatment orientation and aptitude for counseling. The offender is allowed to work and attend school in the community without supervision, and he or she participates in a number of programs in the halfway house itself. This approach has been copied by many states and appears to be a viable program when properly staffed and supervised. As other possible uses for the halfway house are explored and outcomes are verified,[10] the units will offer not only short-term residency before the prisoner's placement on parole but also noninstitutional residence facilities[11] for a number of different classes of offenders.[12] At that point, halfway houses will constitute the first true alternative to institutional incarceration in the community.

THE PRIVATE SECTOR IN COMMUNITY CORRECTIONS

The roles of the private for-profit and private nonprofit sectors in institutional jails and prisons will be discussed in more detail in Chapter 28. The idea of involving these sectors comes as a shock to many people, but the concept of having government services provided by contracting in the private sector was actually the primary method of obtaining these services for the first hundred or so years in the United States. Transportation, fire protection, police, and even armies were often provided on contract. The second century for the United States saw a change toward providing services through bureaucratic, governmental agencies. In recent years, however, the cost of government-provided services has risen so high that many services are now moving back to the private sector.

There have been a number of precedents for privsion of private sector services to the correctional field. Health care, food service, education, mental health, transportation, and training have been provided by contractors to many systems. From the time of John Augustus, most juvenile and adult halfway houses and other services have been provided by private or charitable organizations. As the need for more community corrections has grown, many entrepreneurs have become involved in the boom industry of corrections. Many of these entrepreneurs are now expanding across state borders and operating facilities and operations like a franchise.

The main advantage that is held by these providers is the ability to expand and contract their operations as needs change. When a government invests in the building of a major correctional facility in the community, it is obliged to staff it and operate it even if it is not cost-effective to do so. The entrepreneurs of community corrections can modify an existing facility, provide staff on a contract basis, use community resources for professional services and, then close it down or use it for some other purpose when no longer needed. The federal community corrections programs house over three thousand inmates in 330 contracted community correctional centers. Most states contract for their community corrections, so the business is burgeoning.

WILLIE HORTON

a convicted murderer, made a great impact on all community corrections programs when in June 1986, under Massachusetts state law, he was granted a 48-hour furlough and never came back. In April 1987, Horton broke into a house and brutally murdered the owner over a seven-hour period. When the owner's fiancee returned, Horton gagged her, savagely raped her twice, and stole the owner's car. He was sentenced to two consecutive life terms in Maryland. The release program after 76 prisoners on furlough walked away, was finally canceled. This program became a major political issue in Governor Dukakis' failed run at the presidency. Ads featuring the crimes of Willie were run by the Bush campaign managers.

One of the major issues for the contractor concerns liability for potential public safety issues. Most government agencies are **self-insured**. This insurance protects them with the resources of the entire government entity. The private sector operator, however, must have some type of liability insurance to cover the same problems. With the incredible growth of litigation in the United States, government agencies have become targets for attorneys looking for new markets. This has caused insurance rates to skyrocket and has affected operations by the private sector.[13] The small operator has been put in a squeeze, and the large ones are hurting as well. We shall see in Chapter 28 how this aspect of private corrections influences some of the efforts by private operations to move into jails and prisons.

Diversion: Keeping the Offender Out of the System

Some jurisdictions have established policies to minimize assignment of certain nondangerous or problematic offenders to the justice system. This is particularly true of mentally disordered[14] and drug-[15] and alcohol-[16] disabled offenders. Diversion from the criminal justice system has taken place in one form or another since social controls were first established. In most cases, informal diversions merely means official exercise of discretion at some point in the criminal process.

More formal diversions include suspension of the criminal process in favor of some noncriminal disposition. Less than 25 percent of the reported offenses in America result in an arrest, and only about one-third of those arrests result in a criminal conviction, an indication that preconviction diversion is not uncommon.

Diversion may occur at a number of points in the criminal justice system. The primary points are prior to police contact, prior to official police processing, and prior to official court processing. Three basic models emerge to determine which agency might be responsible for diversion: **community-based diversion** programs, **police-based diversion** programs, and **court-based diversion** programs. Although each of these models usually involves more than one agency or group, programs will generally be grouped according to who initiates the action and is primarily responsible for its implementation.

Most diversion programs now in effect constitute informal responses to the ambiguities of existing legislation. The value of such programs is difficult, if not impossible, to estimate. Their goals and procedures must be clearly articulated and integrated into the rest of the criminal justice system.

COMMUNITY-BASED DIVERSION PROGRAMS

Diversion projects are most effective when integrated into a community-based correctional system with many levels of supervision and custody. The currently informal options on an accountable basis must be formalized without making the process too rigid. If community-based programs are too restricted, they will become mere "institutions without walls." Diversion is seen as the first threshold of the community corrections system, designed to remove as many offenders as possible from the process before their conviction and criminalization.

Programs aim toward providing a total or partial alternative to incarceration and are improvements. But they do not eliminate the stigma of a conviction record. Diversion programs tied to treatment and services in the community, however, both avoid the problems of incarceration and remove the criminal label. These programs are seen not as a substitute for probation services but as a method of filling the gap between offenders eligible for probation and cases in which the charges can be dropped. Diversion should be accompanied by a formalized agreement with offenders as to what they are to do in return for the elimination of their arrest records. A set of alternative treatment services and residential reinforcements may be needed to help diverted individuals handle their problems. The diverted individuals should have the programs and services available to all other categories of offenders and ex-inmates being treated in the local network.

POLICE-BASED DIVERSION PROGRAMS

Police agencies have practiced diversion, informally, by using their power of discretion at the time of an offender's arrest. Several programs have been established to encourage more diversions on a formal basis. Police have been reluctant in the past to formalize their practice of discretion because of public opinion criticizing such actions as being too soft. Most formalized programs are aimed at the youthful offenders in an effort to keep them from beginning a career of crime.

Another example of diversionary tactics at the police level is to use family crisis intervention. This approach, which has been used in several large cities, is especially important as domestic violence laws across the country are being toughened. Laws often now result in the arrest of both parties. There are indications that the police, by identifying conflict situations at an early stage of development, can prevent the escalation of violence. A general model involves the use of specially trained family crisis intervention officers to respond to family disturbances; the officers attempt to resolve the conflict on the scene. If they cannot, the antagonists are arrested[17] and, in some jurisdictions, referred to a community agency instead of jail.

COURT-BASED DIVERSION PROGRAMS

The courts are involved with diversion in several ways. One method is to use civil commitment for individuals who presumably can be treated more efficiently in a hospital situation. However, the constitutionality of civil commitment procedures has been questioned, and their continued use is doubtful. A more common and reasonable use of diversion by the courts is found in pretrial intervention programs, which have been funded extensively by the U.S. Department of Labor. The general pattern of such actions, at the end of the prescribed period of the continuance, is to allow (1) dismissal of pending charges based on satisfactory project participation and demonstrated self-improvement; (2) extension of the continuance to allow the program staff more time to work with the person (usually for an additional thirty to ninety days); or (3) return of the defendant to normal court processing, without prejudice, because of unsatisfactory performance in the program.

Diversion is especially appropriate for the public drunk and the first-time drug abuser. The current alternative to incarceration for the public drunk is to send him or her to a detoxification center. Voluntary attendance at detoxification centers demonstrates the willingness of many problem drinkers to accept treatment, if only for free room and board.

The severity of criminal sanctions and public reaction to most drug offenses makes the diversion of drug abuse cases a sensitive area. With the country awash with illegal drugs, and drug use by the general population quite high, the wave of enforcement activity has made it difficult to divert all but the least violent of users,

WORK-RELEASE PROGRAMS

Over sixty-two thousand offenders were in work-release programs at the end of 1993. Work release is any program in which inmates of jails or prisons are allowed to work in the community with minimal restriction, are compensated at the prevailing minimum wage, and must serve their nonworking hours in a secure facility. This program was first used in 1906. Local sheriffs in Vermont issued "day passes" to inmates, allowing them to work all day without correctional supervision in the local community. The first state-sanctioned work-release program was in Wisconsin in 1913.

leaving the hard cases to sweat it out in institutions that seldom provide meaningful programs. Most diversion programs for drug users are concentrated on juveniles and are aimed at the first-time arrestees.

The spectrum of diversionary programs is geared toward the same goal: provision of a reasonable alternative to incarceration in large punitive prisons.[18] Again, as in the development of many other aspects of correctional services, such programs often begin as independent actions by concerned professionals and community groups. As a result of earlier efforts, community corrections acts (CCAs) have been authorized as a "statutory medium" for including citizens and bringing funding to local governments and county agencies to plan, develop, and deliver correctional services and sanctions at the local level.[19] At least twenty-two states have passed such enabling legislation, encouraging intermediate sanctions, advocacy for juveniles, involving local community organizations, victim/offender reconciliation, victim restitution, employment services, and county residential facilities, among many others. Some private state contracts with prison agencies for county programs offer to leave control at the community level. Subsidiaries can be provided, or a superagency can be structured to meet the needs of *all* offenders throughout the state. The best implemented CCAs are in Colorado and Florida. Both of these states offer model programs that could be copied by other jurisdictions.

Probation and Parole: A Changing Role in the Community

Probation and parole have been the traditional modes of retaining or releasing offenders into the community. Probation gives nondangerous convicted offenders a chance to remain in their community and work toward an eventual release from supervision. Parole has been developed for institutionalized offenders who are ready to return to the community under supervision before their sentences have expired. Both programs were discussed in detail in Part III. Essential to successful community-based corrections is the coordination of activities and services available for all offenders, whether on diversion, probation, or parole. These programs presently function as separate, often uncoordinated, entities, each under the control of different local units of government. As comprehensive community-based correctional systems are developed, the traditional role of probation and parole officers will give way to that of "**change agents**." Such agents will have an array of correctional treatment and service alternatives at their disposal, with the ability to move offenders as needed from one type of program to another (as opposed to the narrow options of returning offenders to court or prison, or ignoring their problems entirely).

The overcrowding of our jails and prisons has caused the courts to take a chance by placing more and more violent offenders on probation. Those cases are now under supervision by probation agencies in record numbers. The problem is seen as out of control by many probationers and resulting in another Catch-22 situation akin to guerrilla warfare. An overextended probation system may cause more danger to the public than the more publicized prison system. As noted by Cochran:

> Because not all probationers will obey the law, reality requires probation agencies to have an arsenal of risk-control tools at their disposal. These tools

may include urine analysis, electronic monitoring, curfews, house arrest, and intensive supervision programs, to name but a few. However, the most important and effective resource continues to be the skilled individual probation officer, who appropriately enforces the conditions of probation and holds offenders accountable for their behavior.[20]

ADJUNCTS TO INSTITUTIONALIZATION:

AN INTERMEDIATE STEP

The sharp distinction between treatment methods in the institution and community-based treatment has become blurred as more and more offenders are released under supervision. The most effective response to their differential needs is to develop a spectrum of custody and supervision modalities. The problems of bridging the gap between the institution and the community have been recognized since the earliest prisons began to release offenders on "tickets-of-leave" in the mid-nineteenth century. The efforts of Ireland's Sir Walter Crofton gave prisoners a chance to work in the community for a period of time before their release. The concept of work release has since become an important adjunct to institutional programs. Under such programs, offenders are allowed to work at jobs in the community and still receive the benefit of certain programs available at an institution. Work release may often be the first step toward some form of residential and custodial facility in the community for offenders who are able to function at their job but are still in need of supervised treatment. Such community-based facilities are usually referred to as halfway houses (discussed earlier) because residents are considered to be halfway out of the institution.

Community residential centers (halfway houses) are often operated by private organizations under state supervision. As funds have been made available from various sources, halfway houses have acquired different organizational and ideological orientations. Some states have begun to take a much closer look at their funding of halfway house programs and require a better accounting of results. Halfway houses are often located in depressed neighborhoods in older buildings that were originally designed for some other purpose.[21]

The increasing use of diversionary and probationary alternatives to imprisonment resulted in the development of halfway-in houses for offenders who need supportive residential treatment but who are not dangerous enough to be sent to prison. An integrated system of the future might place halfway-out and halfway-in offenders in the same residence, with the emphasis on the kinds of treatment provided rather than the type of offender. The two categories may well be joined by a third as the new reintegration centers become part of the correctional system. In the future, residential care and custody will most likely emphasize referral to available community services and programs, rather than just personal contact with the offender.

The **community correctional center** (CCC) is the most appealing step in recent years toward a community-based institution. Developed in a number of models, such centers are usually fairly open and located in the community, utilizing community resources for their services. CCCs serve a variety of purposes, including detention, treatment, holding, and prerelease, and are based in a variety of facilities ranging from existing jails to hotels and motels. With growing support, the CCCs will offer a specific and integrated set of services.

Turning Point Program

The Turning Point Program is part of the Talbert House, Inc., a nonprofit multiservice agency that consists of thirteen programs in four areas: victim assistance, chemical dependency, mental health, and criminal corrections. The Turning Point Program consists of a 40-bed, 28-day chemical dependency treatment program for men and women serving sentences for multiple DUI offenses.

After 30-day jail incarceration, select offenders are relocated to the program site, a community residential confining program that permits visits but not leaves. The program is a comprehensive treatment regimen focused on drug and alcohol addiction and includes individualized alcohol treatment, family counseling, and educational services. AA (Alcoholics Anonymous) and NA [Narcotics Anonymous] are required. Turning Point participants were less likely after treatment to be arrested than comparison groups; the comprehensive treatment reduced DUI behavior. ∎

SOURCE: Robert Langworthy and Edward Latessa, "Treatment of Chronic Drunk Drivers: The Turning Point Project," *Journal of Criminal Justice* 21:3 (1993): 265-276.

IS CHEAPER BETTER?

As we mentioned earlier, proponents of community-based corrections have often touted exaggerated claims for their results. Upon examination, however, it appears that community programs are no more and no less effective than institutional corrections. But from a financial standpoint, community-based corrections are proving to be more practical.[22] In the community-based exemplary project conducted in Des Moines, Iowa, it was found that residential corrections programs were approximately four times cheaper than the ongoing state institutional programs.[23] In community-based programs that do not require a residential facility, the cost differential is even more pronounced.

Economics is not the only measure of a correctional program, however. The principal objective of such programs is to protect the public. Only when it is definitely established that shifts from institutional to community corrections can be accomplished with no increased danger to the public should they be made. It is clear that treatment in the community is more humane, and it protects the offender from institutionalization. It has been shown that subjecting offenders to custodial coercion in the fortress prisons places them in physical danger, destroys their community ties, and reduces their self-esteem. A system is hard to fault that avoids those problems, costs less, is more (or equally) effective, and still protects the community. It is basically for these reasons that the movement toward community corrections has gained such great support in the past decade. Improvements and increased success for the programs that are now in an experimental stage will make the community-based programs the keystone of corrections in the decades to come.

THE INTEGRATED CONTRACT MODEL:
A POSSIBLE COMPROMISE

We need not review the general procedures of processing offenders from arrest through parole; nor need we elaborate on the existence of varied alternatives to formal processing. They are sketched in Figure 27-1 and are assumed to exist to divert offenders for reintegration purposes. Our focus is on the offender after pleading or being adjudicated guilty of a felony.[24]

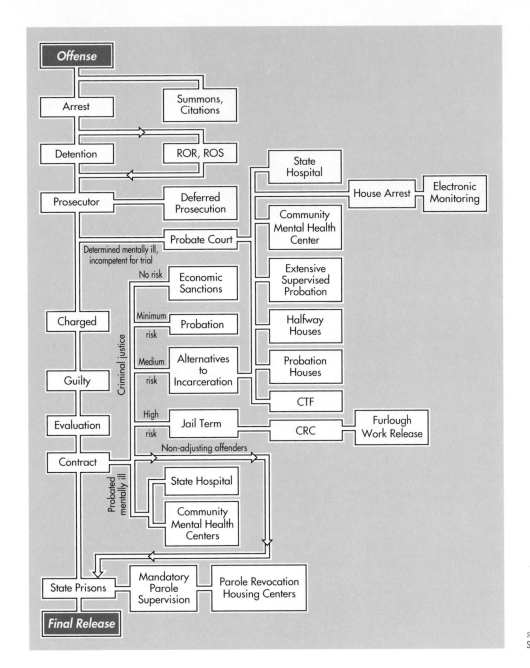

SOURCE: The authors are indebted to Dr. Richard Seiter for the original model of this concept.

FIGURE

27.1

A Reintegration Model

With the **integrated contract model**, once guilt has been determined, and before disposition of the instant case, the judge would formally preside over and participate in the offender's choice of either punishment or reintegration. In this initial decision, the defense attorney would continue to provide legal advice and protect the offender's rights. The prosecuting attorney should remain an active player and also participate in the final contract.

Upon conviction of those offenders not opting for punishment, the state's department of corrections would institute a comprehensive reintegration plan predicated on maximum delivery of services, victim restitution, the least restrictive environment, and a detailed program for dealing with the offender. Various options would include behavior modification, intrusive therapy, halfway houses, house arrest, probation hostels for chemically dependent offenders, restitution, community treatment centers, electronic monitoring,

A counselor works with female offenders

—PHOTO BY FRANK SITEMAN, COURTESY OF UNIPHOTO PICTURE AGENCY

community reintegration centers, and education/vocation furlough programs. The individualized plan would be presented to the court in the form of a proposed contract. Both the defense and prosecuting attorneys could consent to or dissent from the plan; the court would retain authority for development of the final contract.

Once the contracts were approved and signed by all parties, the court would formally dispose of the offender by his or her commitment as a probationer to the state's department of corrections. Their responsibility would include implementation of the contract, provision of services, and supervision, the levels of which could be varied in accordance with the offender's progress toward defined goals within the contractual time period. Serious deviation from the contract, absconding, and technical violations would be governed by at least the *Morrissey* conditions outlined in the landmark case (see Chapter 13). The court would retain the right to revoke formally the reintegration contract and to impose prison as the alternative.

There would be five categories of offenders for whom this would not be necessary, and mandatory prison terms would be required for those offenders who

1. perpetrate murder in the first degree;
2. commit any crime in which a firearm is used;
3. are third-time felony conviction offenders;
4. are rapists, or;
5. are convicted as large-scale drug dealers.

The philosophy of prison would be incapacitation; sentence lengths would be determinate, with minor reductions for good-time behavior. Recidivists would receive multiples of the determinate sentence. Inasmuch as parole would not exist as a mandatory requirement and sentences would be determinate, a paroling agency would not be necessary. However, ex-prisoners desiring assistance would be eligible for all of the services, available to probationers on a voluntary basis.

At present, that system is much more concept than reality. Yet the various elements that are its foundation exist in most jurisdictions today. The major difference between the social justice model and the standard criminal justice model is the establishment of graduated and integrated levels of correctional treatment, related less to the offense than to the offender's individual problems and needs.

THE LEASE SYSTEM IN THE SOUTH

The system of leasing prisoners out to farms for labor, with the state relinquishing almost all supervision to the lessee, was prevalent in the post–Civil War period in the United States. While the lease system was not totally confined to the South, it is associated with that region because of its widespread use there. The leasing out of convicts was a solution to the abolishment of slavery in the war-torn South, and it provided revenue to the operators of prisons. The profit motive led to harsh and cruel conditions and became known as the "new slavery." In 1908 the federal government became interested in the appalling conditions under the lease programs, but they persisted until the mid-1930s, when they finally ceased.

Most social agencies now are taking this approach on a piecemeal basis, but the added element of coordination and control would ensure that all programs could contribute to the offender's rehabilitation. The social justice model seems to represent a logical conclusion for the present evolutionary trend in corrections. Like it or not, the correctional system today is under heavy fire; the emphasis is on accountability. Explanations must be given for the billions spent on corrections, rehabilitation, and processing of offenders. Excuses and glib platitudes are no longer the currency of the times. Results are.

Summary

In the eyes of some, the answer to all correctional problems appears to lie in the closing down of America's prisons. But the total problem is not that simple to state or to solve. When we speak of alternatives to incarceration, we speak of a carefully selected group of accused or convicted offenders. The primary mission of the correctional system remains the protection of the public. All programs must be designed or proposed with that mission in mind, or they will be doomed to early failure and public rejection. All the systems described in this chapter have been designed to meet the needs of certain categories of offenders. We do not propose that *all* offenders be given the chance for diversion or community treatment or any of the other described programs. What seems to be needed, however, is a system that offers as many alternatives to incarceration as possible for the individuals who appear to have some promise of benefiting from them and who will present little, if any, danger to the community. The residual population may be required to remain in maximum security institutions until new treatments are found for them. Institutions for those residual inmates can be made more humane, more treatment oriented, and more closely tied to the community. The community should be encouraged to also come into the institution, providing models of behavior and friendship ties for the offenders who must remain incarcerated. The prison, in a modified form, still has a valuable place in the correctional system for the estimated 15 to 20 percent of convicted offenders who require more restrictive levels of control. For most convicted and diverted offenders, however, the use of either partial or total alternatives is a more reasonable response than incarceration.

Review Questions

1. What are the traditional components of a correctional system? What are some recent additions?
2. Why is graduated release so beneficial to both the community and the offender?
3. Should all offenders be given the chance for diversion from the criminal justice system? Why or why not?
4. What is the primary mission of any correctional system?
5. Describe the contract model of corrections.
6. What are likely to be the major trends in corrections in the next decade? In prisons?
7. How can community corrections be coordinated to provide services?

*W*ords to Remember

partial incarceration   community-based diversion   halfway house

police-based diversion   integrated contract model   self-insured

court-based diversion   community correctional center   change agents

*E*ndnotes

1. James Galvin, "What Does Incarceration Really Cost?" *Criminal Justice Newsletter* 14 (August 29, 1983): 5. Estimates of the annual cost of incarcerating an inmate in Minnesota range from $20,500 to $48,650, depending on the institution. The average cost is $34,000. See American Correctional Association, *1996 Directory* (Lanham, MD: American Correctional Association, 1996), pp. 240-242.

2. Daniel Glaser, "Supervising Offenders Outside of Prison," in James Q. Wilson, ed., *Crime and Public Policy* (San Francisco: Institute for Contemporary Studies, 1983), pp. 207-227.

3. Alfred Blumstein, "Prisons, Population, Capacity and Alternatives," in Wilson, *Crime and Public Policy*, pp. 229-250. See also Lawrence Greenfield, *Prisoners in 1989* (Washington, D.C.: U.S. Department of Justice, 1990), pp. 7-9.

4. David R. Struckoff, "Selective Incapacitation," *Corrections Today* 49 (February 1987): 30.

5. Ibid., p. 32.

6. James Bridges et al., "The Case for Creative Restitution in Corrections," *Federal Probation* 43 (September 1979): 28-35. See also Burt Galaway, "Probation as a Reparative Sentence," *Federal Probation* 46 (September 1983): 9-18, and Jean Warner and Vincent Burke, eds., *National Directory of Juvenile Restitution Programs: 1987* (Washington, D.C.: U.S. Department of Justice, 1987).

7. The longer a work-release participant remains employed in the same work-release job after earning parole status, the greater is the potential for parole success. Kyu Man Lee, *The Wichita Work Release Center: An Evaluative Study* (Ann Arbor, MI: University Microfilms International, 1983). See also Mike Goss, "Serving Time Behind the Front Door," *Corrections Today* 52 (July 1990): 80-84.

8. David Anderson, *Crime and the Politics of Hysteria: How the Willie Horton Story Changed American Justice* (New York: Random House, 1995).

9. Roy Fisher and Charles Wilson, *Authority or Freedom? Probation Hostels for Adults* (Hants, U.K.: Gover, 1982). See also James Bonta and Laurence Motiuk, "The Diversion of Incarcerated Offenders to Correctional Halfway Houses," *Journal of Research in Crime and Delinquency* 24 (1987): 302-323, and Edward Latessa and Lawrence Travis, "Residential Community Correctional Programs," in J. Byrne and A. Lurigio, eds., *Smart Sentencing? An Examination of the Emergence of Intermediate Sanctions* (Beverly Hills, CA: Sage, 1991).

10. Marc Levinson, "In South Carolina, Community Corrections Means the Alston Wilkes Society," *Corrections Magazine* 9 (1983): 41-46. In Florida, presentence investigation reports are prepared by the Salvation Army. See also Bobbie Huskie and Arthur Lurigo, "An Examination of Privately Operated Intermediate Punishments in the United States," *Corrections Compendium* 17:12 (1992): 1, 3-8.

11. Daniel Glaser, "Supervising Offenders Outside of Prison," p. 212.

12. James Beck, "An Evaluation of Federal Community Treatment Centers," *Federal Probation* 43 (September 1979): 36-41, and Paul Gendreau, Mary Shilton, and Patrick Clark, "Intermediate Sanctions: Making the Right Move," *Corrections Today* 57:1 (1995): 28-65.

13. For example, the Pioneer Human Services agency in Seattle experienced a tripling of their liability rates in a one-year period.

14. Maryland Governor's Office, *Administration Report to the State/Local Criminal Justice/Mental Health Task Force* (Baltimore: MD: Maryland Office of Justice Administration, 1995), and James Byrne and Faye Taxman, "Crime Control Policy and Community Corrections Practice," *Evaluation and Program Planning* 17:2 (1994): 227-233.

15. A. Barthwell, P. Bokos, and J. Bailey, "Interventions/Wilmer: A Continuum of Care for Substance Abusers in the Criminal Justice Systems," *Journal of Psychoactive Drugs* 27:1 (1995): 39-47.

16. California Department of Corrections, *Overview of Substance Abuse Programs* (Sacramento: California Department of Corrections, 1995).

17. Richard Tolman and Arlene Weisz, "Coordinated Community Incarceration for Domestic Violence: The Effects of Arrests and Prosecutions on Recidivism of Women Abuser Perpetrators," *Crime and Delinquency* 41:4 (1995): 481-495, and Christopher Carlson and Frank Nidey, "Mandatory Penalties, Victim Compensation, and the Judicial Processing of Domestic Abuse Assault Cases," *Crime and Delinquency* 41:1 (1995): 132-149.

18. James Galvin, "Midwest Group Provides Community Options," *Criminal Justice Newsletter* 14 (August 15, 1983): 1-2. See also his "Missouri Community Corrections Bill," *Criminal Justice Newsletter* 14 (August 15, 1983): 3, and Kay Harris, "Key Differences Among Community Corrections Acts in the United States: An Overview," *The Prison Journal* 76:2 (1996): 192-238.

19. Kay Harris, "Key Differences Among Community Corrections Acts in the United States: An Overview."

20. Donald Cochran, "Corrections' Catch 22," *Corrections Today* (October 1989): 18.

21. Harry E. Allen et al., *Halfway House: Program Model* (Washington, D.C.: U.S. Department of Justice, 1979). See also Bobbie Huskey, "Community Residential Centers," *Corrections Today* 54:8 (1992): 70-73, and Rhonda Reeves, "Future Forecast: Examining Community Corrections' Role in the Justice System," *Corrections Today* 54:8 (1992): 74-79.

22. Department of Court Services, *A Handbook of Community Corrections in Des Moines* (Washington, D.C.: U.S. Department of Justice, 1973), p. 145. For cost statements for probation, intensive supervised probation, and imprisonment, see Billie Erwin and Lawrence Bennett, *New Dimensions in Probation: Georgia's Experience with Intensive Probation Supervision* (Washington, D.C.: U.S. Department of Justice, 1986). The per day costs are $.76, $4.37, and $30.43, respectively. See also Betsy Fulton and Susan Stone, "Intensive Supervision: Evaluating Programs Across the Nation," *Corrections Today* 54:8 (1992): 80-87.

23. Estimating the costs of any correctional program is fraught with problems. It is very difficult to estimate human costs, recidivism costs, land costs, and lower taxes because the land does not yield tax revenue. Welfare payments to offenders' families, loss of property to victims, suffering and loss of income of victims, the cost of a life or a truncated life expectancy because of victim injury, and so on, are difficult to estimate. One should consider such cost statements only as estimates.

24. Much of this section was drawn from Nick Gatz and Harry Allen, "Abandoning the Medical Model in Corrections: Some Implications and Alternatives," *Prison Journal* 54 (Autumn 1974): 4-24. See also Edward Latessa and Harry Allen, *Corrections in the Community* (Cincinnati: Anderson, 1997), pp. 419-425.

CHAPTER TWENTY-EIGHT

Private Sector Systems

Overview

The words above were written a decade ago and foretold the continuing overcrowding problem that the student has seen as a constant issue throughout this text. The state, city, and federal correctional administrators wrestled with this issue when the populations of their combined institutions was about *one-third* of what is being reported herein. This chapter deals with what has become another major factor in trying to keep up with the tidal wave of populations under the supervision of criminal justice agencies—privatization of correctional services and facilities.

As will be seen, privatization is neither a new idea nor one that occurred only in the last decade. The major challenge for privatization, however, is to provide for the incarceration of the populations of convicted felons in long-term, secure facilities by a private company for profit. The state of Tennessee was the first to consider the privatization of its entire adult prison system. One of the first and largest of the providers of privately operated adult correctional facilities made an offer to take over the complete management and operation of the beleaguered Tennessee system. For a number of reasons, that bid was not accepted, and Tennessee poured millions into upgrading what they had. This chapter will discuss the pros and cons—and the vast growth—of privatization and its role in the twenty-first century. We have seen this issue grow from a paragraph to an entire chapter in the past few editions of this text. It seems fitting that this chapter is the last before our final review, as it seems to be related to almost every other topic in the text.

Prison supply, especially at current prices, is unable to meet demand. The resultant overcrowding, combined with taxpayer reluctance to bear the costs of new construction and added operational expenses, creates a dilemma for penology. Commercial prisons, privately owned and operated under government contract, may offer at least a partial solution.

—Charles Logan and Sharla P. Rausch

The Private Sector in Community Corrections

The idea of involving the private sector[1] in providing management and operation of correctional facilities may come as some kind of shock to many people. But the concept of having government services provided by contracting with the private sector was actually the primary method of obtaining those services for the first hundred or so years in the United States. Transportation, fire protection, police, and even armies were often provided on contract. It was only in the nation's second century that services were provided through bureaucratic agencies. In recent years, however, the cost of government-provided services has risen so high that many services are now moving "back to the future" for correctional services being provided through the private sector.

There have been a number of precedents in the correctional field: health care, food service, education, mental health, transportation, and training have been provided by contractors to many systems. From the time of John Augustus, most juvenile and adult halfway houses and other services have been provided by private for-profit, private nonprofit, or charitable organizations. As the need for more community corrections has grown, primarily due to overcrowded jails and prisons, many entrepreneurs in the private for-profit and nonprofit sectors have become involved in the "boom" industry of community-oriented corrections. Many of those entrepreneurs are now expanding across state borders and operating prisons like a franchise.

These agencies provide services both in institutions and follow-up services in local community facilities or outpatient programs, especially for drugs and alcohol addiction, basic adult education and literacy, and development of life skills. An example of this kind of program is the **Correctional Recovery Academy** (CRA) offered by CiviGenics of Milford, Massachusetts.[2] These and many other types of specialized private services are offered by private providers at literally thousands of locations across the nation. Such networks tend to ease the correctional problems by furnishing (1) alternatives to incarceration in the community, (2) meaningful programs inside the prisons to help prepare inmates for a better life when they are released, and (3) a bridge from incarceration to the free society that will assist in that difficult transition.

PRIVATIZATION OF HEALTH CARE

Privatization of prison health services is especially appealing to those systems that have difficulty in recruiting and retraining qualified health care staff. The management and operation of the health care operations then becomes the responsibility of the contractor. The state is still ultimately responsible for ensuring that the health care services provided to inmates is adequate, however.

Some Historical Considerations

EARLY HISTORY

From an historical perspective, private involvement in corrections during the 1870–1930 era was neither notable nor distinguished. Even before this era, some states would lease out their entire prison populations to private bidders who would contract to provide food, custody, and clothing to inmates for a flat fee per inmate annually in return for the labor of the inmates. Contractors would use the inmates to farm or harvest crops, much like the "slaves of the master." The state would make a profit and could avoid the cost of building additional and adequate facilities, hiring correctional staff, feeding and clothing inmates, and otherwise assuming such care, custody, and provisioning as would have been required. In brief, prisons became "profit centers" for those states willing to lease out their

Correctional Recovery Academy

Correctional recovery is the criminogenic equivalent of addiction recovery. It is the theoretical foundation of the Correctional Recovery Academy.

The Correctional Recovery Academy (CRA) is a comprehensive instructional program to train inmates in a battery of cognitive and psycho-social skills that are essential for a life free of criminal and drug habits. To date, the CRA curriculum has been utilized by three state Departments of Corrections (Georgia, Massachusetts, and Rhode Island), with delivery to sixteen prison sites throughout the nation.

The Academy marries two proven social learning methodologies. One is Recovery Training, a form of group counseling for relapse prevention developed at the Harvard School of Public Health. Its clinical developer has crafted for CiviGenics, a new curriculum called Correctional Recovery Training (CRT), expressly for inmate-addicts. CRTs synthesize a variety of relapse prevention exercises and instructions with elements of progressive residential treatment (modularized Therapeutic Community elements with "real-world" applicability).

CiviGenics staff have enjoyed long-term working relationships with internationally respected practitioners of both prison treatment and relapse prevention. CRA sites have been the proving grounds for state-of-the-art treatment models.

The CRA typically operates 5 days per week—Monday through Friday between the hours of 8:00 a.m.–9:00 p.m., in separate housing units within the institution. Inmates participate in a structured weekly schedule consisting of recovery classes, ongoing violence-reduction sessions, weekly peer support groups, planned recreational activities, Twelve-Step Fellowship meetings, Academy meetings, individual study and seminars. Individual counseling focuses on the inmate's specific needs and formulates an individual treatment plan and a discharge plan.

The Correctional Recovery Academy partners with public agency personnel to support their priorities and protocols. At the same time the CRA effectively involves an interdisciplinary staff with the shared concern of security and recovery. ■

SOURCE: CiviGenics, *Statement of Corporate Capabilities*, (Milford, MA, CiviGenics, 1996), p.24.

---

convict populations. Costs incurred by contractors were significantly below those of having to hire free world labor or, in the pre–Civil War era, buying more slaves who would have had to be fed, clothed, housed and disciplined more attentively than mere criminals.

During the 1879–1930 era, when industrialization was under full steam in this nation, leased inmates were put to work building roads, railroads, trestles, wagons, shoes and boots, and other consumables easily sold on the open markets. To protect profit margins, lessors would transport inmates in rolling cages, where they lived without sanitary and bathing facilities and were worked from dawn to dusk under the watchful eye of heavily armed guards not motivated to use the least amount of force to achieve production quotas. Inmates attempting to escape were killed or beaten, placed in leg irons, forced to wear ball-and-chain restraints, dressed in distinctive garb, and had attenuated life expectancies. Food was abysmal and in short supply, and health care nonexistent. Seeking redress in court was impossible, and avenues of appeal and protest were closed.

The suffering of inmates under these conditions is well recognized. What is not as obvious is the large percentage of inmates leased out who died under contract arrangements, a figure frequently exceeding 50 percent in a given year. Loss of workers through death, however, had little consequence. Prison administrators were not concerned or condemned, and the media rarely covered those events. If a shortage of laborers occurred, prison administrators would lease out newly arrived prisoners who were quickly placed into harness and assigned to labor gangs. Not all states, of course, were this brutal in their approach to prisoners, and perhaps this description best fits only some states in the Deep South after the Civil War, when their prisons were filled with former slaves confined for law-violating

---

EARLY PRISON LABOR EFFORTS

At the Walnut Street Jail and Newgate, the prisons were established on the premise that work was reformative and potentially profitable. Piecework and other forms of manufacture were attempted to help finance the operations of these facilities. Those early efforts at prison labor failed, however, both in terms of economics and reformation. Their demise gave way to the Auburn system of silence and labor. These eventually developed into the industrial prisons of America as well as the agricultural prisons of the South.

behavior. This was one of the most odious chapters in the early history of American corrections, and the residue of feelings and sentiments about leasing inmates through private sector involvement continues to color, even if unfairly, the arguments about privatization of corrections.

MORE RECENT DEVELOPMENTS

As noted, **privatization** is by no means a new concept in the field of corrections. Many services provided to state, federal, and local correctional facilities have come from the private sector almost from the beginning of such services. The criminal justice system often appeared to be stumbling around like a clumsy giant. It can impose lengthy prison terms, and even execute a few criminals. It can slap offenders on the wrist with fines and suspended sentences. However, it seems able to do little in between, although changing, but government moves very slowly. In this century, probation and parole were used as the most frequent options to incarceration. Their ability to supervise and control offenders became the standard for the community. But we have seen that both of these options have been under fire as of late for charges of ineffectiveness.

The development of intermediate sanctions has provided three major options for direct private sector involvement in corrections: (1) treatment programs, (2) supervised release and low-security custody, and (3) **technologies for surveillance** of offenders not incarcerated. It is the operation of these three options that provides the greatest area of potential growth opportunity for privatecontractors, not the operation of high-security correctional facilities.

PRIVATE SECTOR TREATMENT PROGRAMS

Supervised treatment programs imposed as a condition of probation, include drug and alcohol abuse treatment and job training programs. Virtually nonexistent thirty years ago, such programs are now commonplace components of the criminal justice system. Almost all are private and many are run for profit, deriving both their clients and their incomes from contracts with local governments. Some are designed as long-term residential facilities and others as outpatient clinics. Program philosophies vary widely: some are organized with strict, military-like discipline; others are based on religious beliefs; some are devoted to group therapy; others stress rugged individualism and self-reliance. The growing desire to respond to the widespread demand to treat drug abuse has rekindled interest in these types of programs, and we can expect their numbers to increase.

Private sector programs handle a large number of criminal offenders. For every offender housed in a privately managed jail or prison, there are hundreds in privately run noncustodial programs operating under contract with state and local governments. Despite their numbers and importance, these private programs are largely ignored in discussions of privatization of corrections. This may be because such programs are regarded as merely service providers rather than penal programs. Or it may be because their roles as agents of state control are obscured because client participation is primarily voluntary.

If we broaden our frame of reference to consider them as forms of punishment or substitutes for incarceration, we must realize that these new treatment programs are also integral components of the correctional system that extend the reach of the criminal sanction and expand the array of penalties the state can impose. As such, they are part of a much expanded menu of punishments that can be used in concert with each other. In the aggregate, they also constitute an impressive extension

THE EMPLOYER MODEL OF PRISON INDUSTRY

Of the six models of prison industries, the "employer model" seems to be the most appealing. This model is dominated by small to medium-size businesses that employ prisoners directly at a facility on the prison grounds. These businesses sell their products on the open market (e.g., cloth products, computer processing, ceramics), and prisoner employees can be fired if they do not produce. Despite protests from organized labor groups, these ventures are growing and help the inmates learn the value of real work.

Prisoners at Kyle New Vision
Chemical Dependency
Treatment Center

—*COURTESY OF WACKENHUT
CORRECTIONS CORPORATION*

of state control that is also exempted from due process standards required of public agencies.

LOW-SECURITY CUSTODY PROGRAMS

Another important development in corrections in recent years has been the growth of low-security custodial facilities. Many of the most innovative types of low-security custody have been designed and implemented by advocates of privatization, and many of the most successful of such institutions are operated by private contractors. Today, this form of custody constitutes one of the fastest-growing areas of corrections and the most important segment in the business of private, for-profit contractors.

The juvenile justice system, in particular, has come to rely on private contractors to provide such low-security custodial facilities. This, in turn, has increased government's flexibility in dealing with juveniles and expanded its capacity to commit them into custody. California, Florida, Massachusetts, Michigan, Pennsylvania, Rhode Island, and Washington, among others, all rely heavily on private contractors to care for their wards. In a number of states, placement in out-of-home settings constitutes a major component of the state's juvenile corrections policy; in some, private placements outnumber placements in public facilities. It must be stressed that these private custodial placements are not simply more efficient versions of state-run programs. Although these programs have redirected some juveniles who would otherwise have been placed in secure public institutions, they also target groups that once would not have been placed in custody at all. In short, such programs add a new intermediate level of sanctioning to the state's repertoire.

Private contractors have played a similar role in developing low-security facilities for adult offenders, and there is a growing differentiation between what the private and public sector facilities have to offer. The private sector is developing more facilities at the low end of the spectrum, such as community work-release centers, prerelease centers, short-term detention facilities, restitution centers, return-to-custody facilities, residential treatment facilities, and the like.

The pressure to expand community corrections also has had a clear impact on the expanding penal options through the involvement of the private sector. Connecticut law, for example, provides for a network of public and private agencies to offer community services, including custody at the local level, for offenders who could otherwise be imprisoned. Colorado has come to depend on an extensive network of private vendors to provide minimum security facilities. Private sector involvement in community corrections is increasing, and there are indications that it will continue to grow, especially as prison populations exceed capacity highs and pressures mount to increase alternatives that are more flexible and less costly. Time will tell if this "net-widening" effect of such expanded services will actually reach enough of the problem clients in the community who would not normally have been served.

SURVEILLANCE AND CONTROL TECHNOLOGIES

New technologies are yet another area that has emerged as a response to the growing concern with crime. Only a few years ago, chemical testing was performed by state laboratories in a costly and time-consuming manner. Now private drug testing companies can offer fast, cheap, and reliable tests to detect a large variety of illegal substances. But expanded use of cheap and reliable drug tests has increased the likelihood of detection of illegal substances which, in turn, has raised the number of probation and parole violators, helping to transform probation and parole officers from social workers to law enforcement officers. The upsurge in the numbers returned to custody has, in turn, generated demands for specialized low security custodial facilities and new forms of confinement. In short, new technology has placed burdens on the correctional system and affected traditional roles.

Private contractors have also introduced a variety of electronic devices that monitor the movement of people. These devices can be used for surveillance and offer the possibility of confinement without custody, as was seen in Chapter 11. Developed by specialized security firms and still in its infancy, **electronic monitoring** has a vast potential as an effective and inexpensive intermediate form of punishment. For instance, it can supplement if not replace work-release facilities and be used to confine drunk drivers to their homes and places of work.

The Era of Expansion of Privatization

The long history of private sector involvement in community programs has resulted in far less controversy than the furor that has erupted from the private companies that have grown quickly to provide the kinds of management and operations shown in Table 28-1. These operations, while constituting less than 2 percent of the total beds for adult incarcerated persons in the United States, represent an incredibly rapidly growing industry. Figure 28-1 illustrates the juvenile correction population by type of supervision in 1993. It can be seen that two-thirds of these juveniles are placed on probation supervision. Some of the reasons for this growth are as described by Equitable Securities Research as follows:

1. The number of adults under correctional supervision has grown from 1.9 million in 1980 to 5.1 million in 1994.

2. Approximately 11 million adults and 2 million juveniles are arrested annually in the United States.

LEGAL LIABILITY FOR PRIVATE CORRECTIONAL CONTRACTORS

Legally, the government is ultimately responsible for what happens in a prison or a community corrections facility. The state can contract away the duties, but it cannot contract away responsibility. The government serves as a safety net for private contractors, many of whom could not handle the weight of civil rights and tort suits generated in a correctional environment. Effective monitoring by state and local officials is the answer for both parties.

Private Adult Correctional Facility Census Summary for December 31, 1995

Management Firm	Rated Capacity of All Facilities Under Contract*	# Facilities Under Contract	Rated Capacity of Facilities Now In Operation	Prisoner Populations on 6/30/95	% Occupancy for Facilities In Operation	New Facilities to Open within 12–18 Months	Expansion Anticipated within 12–18 Months
Alternative Programs, Inc.	240	1	240	240	100.00	0	0
The Bobby Ross Group	1,832	3	1,832	1,218	66.48	0	0
Capital Correctional Resources	1,056	2	1,056	912	86.36	0	0
Cornell Corrections, Inc.	1,328	3	860	789	91.74	0	468
Corrections Corporation of America	30,610	42	20,457	16,888	82.55	9	10,153
Correctional Systems	30	1	30	28	93.33	0	0
Dove Development Corporation	1,002	2	762	406	53.28	0	240
Esmor Correctional Services, Inc.	1,970	6	870	810	93.10	3	1,100
Fenton Security, Inc.	228	2	228	155	67.98	0	0
Group 4 Prison & Court Services, Ltd.	1,395	4	795	790	99.37	1	600
The GRW Corporation	100	1	100	50	50.00	0	0
Management & Training Corporation	2,978	4	2,978	2,609	87.61	0	0
Mid-Tex Detention, Inc.	1,207	3	1,207	1,142	94.61	0	0
RECOR	144	1	144	102	70.83	0	0
Securicor	800	1	0	N/A	N/A	1	800
U.S. Corrections Corporation	3,018	6	2,918	2,760	94.59	0	100
Wackenhut Corrections Corporation	15,657	22	9,039	8,458	93.57	7	6,618
TOTALS	63,595	104	43,516	37,357	85.85	21	20,079
% Changes Since 12/31/94	29.38	15.38	41.19	30.26	–		

3. The number of people between the ages of fourteen and twenty-four is expected to dramatically increase during the next fifteen years. People in this age group are the most likely to violate the law.

4. One out of one hundred violent crimes committed in the United States in 1992 resulted in a criminal serving a prison sentence.

5. From June 1994 to June 1995, the United States added 89,707 new state and federal prison beds, approximately 1,725 new prison beds per week.

6. By 1996, it was estimated that the United States would have added 104,449 new state and federal beds, approximately 2,000 new prison beds per week.

7. As of December 31, 1994, the U.S. state-level prison population was at 119 percent of rated capacity.

Proponents of private corrections would argue that:

1. Private corrections companies have demonstrated the capacity to perform the same services as government agencies and at a 10–15 percent savings to the taxpayer.

2. The most experienced and best capitalized private providers will garner a comparatively larger percentage of future business.[3]

It is especially interesting to note that these sentiments originated from an *investment* company. In earlier editions of this text, we jokingly indicated that corrections seemed to be a "growth industry" which, if one could buy stock, would be rated high as an investment. Now that off-hand prediction has come true, as the private sector correctional companies are rated as highly favorable investments. Critics of private sector involvement are quick to identify value conflicts in the issues around privatization of corrections. Terms like **punishment for profit, the correctional/industrial complex,** and "shrewdness pays" have been used to describe private sector participation in corrections. For example, as recently as January 1996, Lilly and Deflem argued that:

> The major problem that may evolve from the large-scale involvement of private trade and commerce in criminal justice is that the latter's administration will no longer be under state-controlled supervision. This danger can be termed the **monetary colonization of criminal justice**, which points to the fact that when success-oriented mechanisms of the economic system enter into the corrections domain, concerns for profit, efficiency competition, and

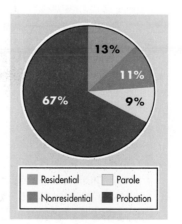

SOURCE: U.S. Bureau of Justice Statistics, *Juvenile Correctional Populations* (U.S. Government Printing Office, Washington, D.C., 1995), p. 2.

FIGURE

28.1

U.S. Juvenile Corrections Population, 1993

13%
11%
67%
9%

Residential   Parole
Nonresidential   Probation

money may radically alter the latter's normative goals. In a democracy, justice issues, in large measure, are suppose to rely on the legitimate consensus of the people whose actions are regulated (or at least to be subject to their critique through participation in democratic public bodies); thus it is no small concern when economic interests drive justice decisions . . . most of the recent studies on penality have paid scant attention to its broader social contexts. Whatever the reasons, whether the rise of a conservative ideology, the appeals and rewards of government research contracts, or private consulting or moral philosophy, little attention has been given to the influential connections that conventional penality has with trade and commerce. It is in part for this reason that we argue that an important portion of the political and economic context of penality has been neglected.

To ignore business in any form of analysis which seeks to explain general patterns in criminal justice, especially patterns of punishment capable of generating profit, is a serious error. To ignore, for example, the potential impact of $22 billion in annual sales, or the potential explanatory value of more than 300 U.S. corrections or corrections-connected companies (some with direct connections to the military-industrial complex), is to be analytically myopic and politically naive.[4]

Strong words from the field of justice, but words that require one to rethink at least some of the reasons to rush to privatization. But, first, what happened in the past? How did American corrections get into this current situation?

Lilly and Delflem, in their "correctional complex" arguments, include correctional officers as well as private corrections providers, unions of state and entrepreneurs, and legislators and businessmen (both of whom might profit). This discussion of the "correctional complex" is not just another antiprivatization tirade. It seems roughly equivalent to Sutherland's attempt to expand on the range and scope of the definition of criminal behavior to include white-collar and corporate crime, namely, savings and loan looting and racketeering, hazardous materials dumping, homicide during arson for profit, pollution of baby foods, wire fraud, and cyberfraud, among others.

Correctional Privatization: Issues and Evidence

It is now widely understood that, first, privatization arrangements cast *government* and not a private firm as the entity that establishes public priorities and that, second, they involve the efforts to achieve public goals by reliance on *private* rather than public means. Despite considerable evidence regarding various types of privatization which demonstrates that they can yield meaningful cost benefits, however, new privatization proposals routinely encounter significant opposition. Importantly, one really cannot appreciate the significance of the privatization trends today without having a basic understanding of what is so different today, from as little as fifteen years ago. In 1980, there was not a single privatized jail or prison here or abroad.

To be sure, the private sector was a major player in managing correctional facilities for juveniles. Minimum security facilities for adults in the community, such as halfway houses, community correctional facilities, and work-

Private Corrections: Corporate Demon?

Critics who oppose privatization for reasons other than their narrow and obvious vested interest would be prudent to consider one historical and one modern fact. The historical fact is that the traditional monopoly government has enjoyed in the correctional arena cannot reasonably be said to have served the interests of confined persons or the general public interest either efficiently or effectively. Indeed, even were one to focus exclusively on the history of American corrections since the holding of the Supreme Court in *Monroe v. Pape* marked the beginning of modern Section 1983 jurisprudence, one would find tens of thousands of cases brought by prisoner plaintiffs. To be sure, the frequency with which prisoner plaintiffs prevail in their continuing flood of cases is low in relative as well as absolute terms. Nevertheless, the number and the scope of successes prisoner plaintiffs have achieved clearly reveal that state-created deprivations of constitutional rights in the nation's correctional system are far from uncommon. It is thus difficult to advance a claim that the traditional governmental monopoly has worked so well and so smoothly that all right-minded persons should join together to attack the present challenge to the status quo.

The modern fact is no less important. The modern fact is that correctional privatization has not produced either the wave of litigation critics imagined it would produce or the deficient delivery of correctional services many critics anticipated. To the contrary, prisoner litigation initiated against private corrections firms has been minimal, and the available research routinely reports that privatization has resulted in a combination of financial and service benefits.

So where is the corporate demon against whom privatization critics have directed their oppositional rhetoric? Has the demon earned its reputation by failing to fulfill promises of lower correctional costs? No. Has the demon earned its reputation by failing to fulfill promises of improved correctional services? No. Has the demon earned its reputation by

acts or omissions to act that have in turn prompted a flood of successful—or for that matter even unsuccessful—civil suits? No. And does this analysis reveal that the demon can with immunity brush aside any concerns prisoner rights advocates might have purely or partly because the demon is a private rather than a public creature? No.

In short, then, correctional privatization does not stand as a cure for the ills which so trouble the nation's correctional system. The corporate demon of the nightmares of privatization critics, however, has no real-world counterpart. This, of course, does not mean that the day will not come when the greed or the ineptitude of a private corrections firm will not emerge to challenge the greed or the ineptitude one finds described in many volumes of cases involving government-managed correctional facilities. Indeed, greed and ineptitude not being uncommon in our society, it is altogether probable that the day will come when a private corrections firm will consciously or stupidly ignore the constitutional rights of prisoners in its effort to do well and at the expense of doing good. As this analysis demonstrates, however, if that unhappy day does come, the state of law is such that those who suffer deprivations at the hands of their private keepers will be able to respond more efficiently than they could had the same deprivations been caused by public keepers. For those who share this author's view that the exercise of governmental power, whether that power is exercised by public or by private persons, should always be subject to as complete a panoply of legal remedies as is reasonable, the expansion of prisoner rights which flows with privatization should not be trivialized or ignored as the privatization debate continues.∎

SOURCE: Charles W. Thomas, "Prisoners' Rights and Correctional Privatization: A Legal and Ethical Analysis," *Business & Professional Ethics Journal* (Vol. 10, Spring 1991), pp. 34–35.

release centers were also serviced by the private sector. As mentioned earlier, there is a long tradition of services provided by the private sector in secure adult facilities (e.g., food services, medical services, and work programs). Any notion that the full-scale privatization of secure adult correctional facilities might be a viable option, however, still seemed alien to most and absurd to more than a few, only a decade ago.

The precise moment when this concept of privatization of secure adult facilities was born is subject of much debate. The foundation was probably laid on or near the date in 1983 when **Corrections Corporation of America** (CCA) was formed in Nashville, Tennessee. The first local contract for a secure county facility was awarded to CCA in 1984. The first state-level contract was awarded to U.S. Corrections Corporation (USCC) in 1985 by Kentucky. The first federal-

A Corrections Corporation of America facility

—PHOTO *COURTESY OF CORRECTIONS CORPORATION OF AMERICA*

level contract of any size went to CCA from the Immigration and Naturalization Service in 1984. Soon there was a rush of private companies to get into this new field, and the number of beds and companies grew apace (see Table 28-1 on page 576). By awarding contracts for four 500-bed facilities, including design, construction, and management (two were awarded to CCA and two to the new Wackenhut Corrections Corporation, WCC), the Texas Department of Corrections moved the private corrections industry into a much larger arena for privatization of correctional facilities. The first overseas venture involved a joint venture with the CCA and the Corrections Corporation of Australia. The industry had moved from a novel idea to a viable alternative to the monopoly previously enjoyed only by government agencies. Frequently, resistance by correctional agencies was strong.

Associations and unions representing the status quo moved aggressively to protect the considerable benefits they had garnered for their memberships. These obstacles aside, the status quo was under attack from the sheer numbers, virtually forcing policy makers to reassess budgets and seek cost-beneficial alternatives to the same old thing. Success by privatization in the newest service delivery areas and favorable assessments by those brave enough to try these new concepts provided many with cause to reject recommendations by nay-sayers and antiprivatization lobbies.

The result was rapid growth in this new niche of the private services sector. In just the five-year span between 1990 and 1995, the contract capacity for private secure adult correctional facilities grew from 15,300 to 63,595, an increase of over 415 percent! (See Figure 28-2.) The number of private facilities distributed over 18 states reached 92. (See Figure 28-3.)

Whether a person opposes or embraces the idea of privatization of secure adult facilities at the local, state, or federal level, there are many core issues to be addressed that have shaped the debate about correctional privatization. The parameters of the debate have been set by a small number of questions which, unless answered in the affirmative, would preclude privatization altogether, would recommend against it, or would limit its scope. These policies include the following:

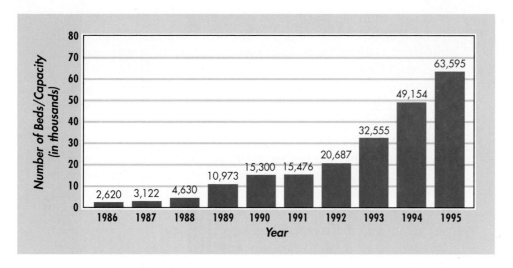

FIGURE

28.2

Ten-year Growth in Rated
Capacity of Private Secure
Adult Correctional
Facilities, 1986–1995*

*Based on private estimates of rated capacities of
all secure private facilities. Estimates include all
facilities in operation and under construction.

SOURCE: Charles W. Thomas. *Correctional
Privatization: The Issues and Evidence.* (Center for
Studies in Criminology and Law, University of
Florida, Gainsville, FL. 1996) p. 29.

1. *As a matter of law, is it possible for government to contract with a private
   entity for operation of a jail or prison?* At least when the debate began
   in the early 1980s in the United States, privatization opponents
   often argued that any full-scale management contracts would be
   declared to be unlawful on constitutional grounds. Privatization
   proponents argued that there were no constitutional problems
   which were not subject to resolution.

2. *Will any jurisdiction be prepared to take the potentially* **consequential
   risks** *that would necessarily be associated with awarding facility management contracts without which there could be no concrete tests of the potential
   benefits of correctional privatization?* Privatization opponents reasoned
   that few or no jurisdictions would explore private alternatives or that, if
   isolated experiments were pursued, the evidence would come from

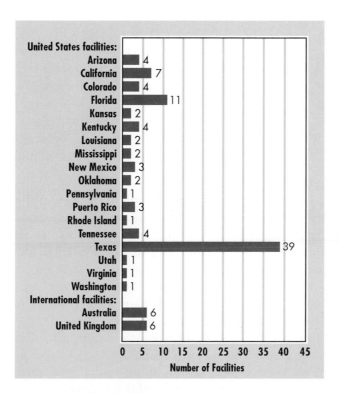

FIGURE

28.3

Number of Private
Facilities by Geographical
Location*

*The geographical location of facilities does not
necessarily indicate contracting decisions made by
agencies in these jurisdictions. Some states are
contracting for the housing of their prisoners in
other jurisdictions. Some states are providing sites
only for federal facilities. Estimates include both
facilities in operation and those under construction.

SOURCE: Charles W. Thomas. *Correctional
Privatization: The Issues and Evidence.* (Center for
Studies in Criminology and Law, University of
Florida, Gainsville, FL. 1996) p. 31.

such atypical facilities as to have no persuasive value. Privatization proponents could do little more than cross their fingers and hope that the pressures confronting at least some jurisdictions would encourage meaningful tests of their theory.

3. *Is there tangible evidence that contracting with a private entity for the management and operation of a jail or a prison can yield cost savings?* Privatization opponents continue to argue that private firms cannot possibly provide the full array of essential services at a cost below government agency costs and remain profitable. From the very beginning of the debate, privatization proponents contended that the private sector could provide all essential services at a cost significantly below government agency costs and still achieve acceptable levels of profitability.

4. *Is there evidence that contracting with a private entity for the management and operation of a jail or a prison can yield correctional services that are at least equal to those government agencies provide?* Privatization opponents continue to argue that the private sector lacks both the expertise and the motivation necessary to provide high-caliber correctional services. Privatization proponents claim that private firms can deliver a full range of correctional services at a quality level that is at least equal to what government agencies can offer.

5. *If there is evidence that contracting with a private entity for the management and operation of a jail or a prison can yield cost savings, does equally tangible evidence reveal that the savings can be achieved without a corresponding decrease in the quality of correctional services?* Privatization opponents claim that any cost savings resulting from contract awards to private firms will necessarily be by reductions in the quality of employees, the quality of correctional services, or both. Privatization proponents are persuaded that the private sector can provide services the quality of which is at least equivalent to those of the public agencies and still provide meaningful cost savings.

6. *If there is evidence that contracting with a private entity for the management and operation of a jail or a prison can yield cost savings without a corresponding decrease in the quality of correctional services, does the evidence suggest that such benefits are limited to specialized types of correctional settings?* Privatization opponents are of the opinion that any involvement of the private sector will of practical, if not legal, necessity be limited to special categories of facilities and/or of the prisoner population (e.g., small facilities, minimum security prisoners, female prisoners, parole violators). Privatization proponents increasingly often advance the contrary conclusion that the potential benefits of contracting out are not limited by any factors whatever.[5]

Fewer than fifteen years ago, these questions neither did nor could have answers that were based on any kind of hard evidence, for the simple reason that there were no privatized jails or prisons. There was, however, supportive evidence from a broad spectrum of privately supplied noncorrectional service delivery areas for which privatization was growing in appeal and for fiscal necessities. Private facility management for the housing of juvenile offenders provided valuable experience for the next steps toward adult jails and prisons. Experience gained from the provision of individual services required in jails and prisons (food and medical services, for example), and from full-scale management of nonsecure adult facilities provided broad inside knowledge for expansion to full-scale operations. The key

The Modern Correctional Facility: A Visit

In the course of initiating coverage on the private correctional industry we have visited four prisons, among them Corrections Corp. of America's Middle Tennessee facility, and Wackenhut's Moore Haven Correctional Facility in Central Florida near Lake Okeechobee. Neither facility was what we expected, and probably not what most investors would imagine them to be. Herein is a brief description:

Much of what we saw at the Moore Haven facility resembled CCA's Middle Tennessee facility. Moore Haven is surrounded by chain link fences topped with razor wire. The building is constructed of cinder blocks painted in neutral colors and electronically secured doors viewable through Plexiglas. The first thing one notices inside are the floors, which are impeccably clean. No dirt is visible on any surface. The next thing one notices is inmates sharing the halls and clustered in adjacent rooms engaging in various classes. We were compelled to wonder what kind of control exists.

"Does anyone have a gun?" we ask Warden Chester Lamden.

"There are no guns inside the facility," he says. We then enter the prisoner's living/working areas through secured doors. Now, nothing separates our business-suited group from inmates clad in prison garb.

Being inside a prison feels like being on a navy ship. Everything is regimented. Among corrections officials is a clearly defined hierarchy starting with the warden and assistant warden, working its way down through functional specialists like chief of security and head of inmate programs to section supervisors, shift supervisors, and finally line officers. Even among the inmates there is a hierarchy within activities like drug treatment programs, where inmates frequently serve in administrative capabilities. In the interaction we witnessed between inmates and guards, inmates' behavior was decidedly deferential. They were polite, even solicitous. Everyone, guard and inmate alike, was addressed as "mister."

Inside the living areas, the immediate impression is of openness. Both the Florida facility and the Middle Tennessee facility were built based on a modern understanding of corrections management. Dorms are rectangular. Minimum/medium security beds are arranged dorm-style with up to 80 inmates living in a communal area. Inmates requiring higher levels of security may be housed in cells arrayed around the perimeter of a central living area, each with a locked door. Such inmates live two to a cell, a more secure but more expensive arrangement. Both dorm area and individual cells provide easy site lines to every spot within the area from a central point. Gone were the stereotypical long corridors of facing cells.

After our tour of Moore Haven, we entered the warden's office to speak further with Mr. Lamden, his regional supervisor Ross Maggio, and Brenda Williams, who directs inmate programs within the facility. We tried to stick to objective topics but it was difficult to avoid the philosophical: Does the system coddle prisoners? For instance, should the facility be air conditioned? Virtually all facilities run by public companies are, we were informed. It is the opinion of the group, an opinion shared by counterparts at Corrections Corp., that providing a reasonable level of comfort reduces tension and results in lower operating costs. This philosophy lies at the heart of the private prison movement.

Ms. Williams quickly reviewed the various programs under her supervision: drug treatment, computer training, high school equivalency diplomas, living skills, horticulture—and she objected vigorously when we unwittingly change the subject before she described them all. She was obviously proud of the work she does, believing it to be a service both for inmates and society as a whole.

All three representatives from Moore Haven, as well as their counterparts at the Corrections Corp. facility, believe that reinstitution of practices like chain gangs and rock splitting by states like Alabama are counterproductive. They pointed out that most inmates are released eventually, and believe that increasing an inmate's level of hostility while adding nothing to their employable skills is destructive for everyone.

As analysts, it is not our business to weigh in on issues of public policy. As people, we cannot help but agree. ∎

SOURCE: Barry Bryant and Jennifer Childe, *Private Corrections Industry*. (Rodman and Renshaw, Chicago, IL, 1996), p. 9.

question that remained, however, was whether any of that limited experience with privatization could be generalized effectively, if and when the opportunity for full-scale operation of adult jails and prisons became a reality. Opponents and proponents of this giant step could claim whatever they wanted to and had no fear of anyone proving them wrong. Opponents and proponents of privatization today are still free to claim whatever they want to, but they must be prepared to face a rapidly growing body of research evidence if they overstate their case.

Privately managed adult facilities now house a diverse prisoner population in both small and large facilities. The largest facility now in operation is a 1,704-bed state prison in Texas that is operated by the Management and Training Corporation. That distinction will soon fall to the Corrections Corporation of America, when it opens a 2,000-bed Texas facility. But that will be leap-frogged by a New Mexico facility of 2,200 beds to be managed by the Wackenhut Corrections Corporation. As we saw in Table 28-1, the number of jurisdictions electing to hold their prisoners in privately managed facilities has grown nationally and internationally at a substantial rate. Critics predicted that no maximum security facility could be privatized, but Corrections Corporation of America opened a privately managed maximum security facility in Leavenworth, Kansas, in 1992. Numerous other privately managed facilities house significant numbers of maximum security classified prisoners. The evidence regarding such control problems as inmate-on-inmate assault, inmate-on-staff assaults, minor disturbances, riots, and escapes simply does not support claims that private correctional employees would be incapable of maintaining effective control at these facilities.[6]

Privately Managed Juvenile Facilities

In 1993, the last available data at publication, there were approximately 2 million juvenile arrests. In that same year, the juvenile corrections population (defined as juveniles adjudicated and in a secure facility, in a community environment, on probation or on parole) had more than 400,000 juveniles in the system.

At the end of 1993, there were approximately 54,000 juveniles incarcerated, 48,000 in nonresidential programs, 290,000 on probation, and 40,000 on parole, for a total of 432,000. There are estimates of 700,000 admissions to residential facilities every year (this includes detention centers, reception centers, training schools, and ranches) in the United States. The average length of stay ranges from fifteen days at a detention center to thirty-two weeks at a training school. Approximately 80 percent of all juveniles confined in residential facilities are male and between the ages of fourteen and seventeen. This seems a viable population in which the private correctional industry might have a serious interest.

As we have noted, many juvenile programs in the community have been traditionally contracted to private for-profit as well as private non-nonprofit agencies. As with adult facilities, there is a growing trend toward juvenile beds in secure facilities as well. There are approximately forty-three hundred juvenile beds which are managed by the five publicly traded private management companies. (See Table 28-2.)

Three of the companies that manage adult correctional facilities (Corrections Corporation of America, Wackenhut Corrections Corporation, and Esmor Correctional) have contracted for youthful offender programs. These programs deal primarily with the older juveniles and less with treatment, a focus in the typical residential programs that both Children Comprehensive Services and Youth Services operate. The youthful offender programs that are managed by adult corrections companies have lower per diem charges on the average (approximately $65–$80 per day), when compared to residential programs run by primarily juvenile service providers ($85–$180 per day). To date, private corrections companies concentrating on the adult market have chosen not to compete with the companies that concentrate entirely on juvenile programs.

The juvenile corrections area has traditionally been extremely short of beds, and this trend is clearly one that will continue. A second factor is the rising number

TABLE *28.2*			
Publicly Traded Private Management Companies			
Company	*Number of Juvenile Facilities Under Contract*	*States Where Juvenile Facilities Are Located*	*Total Juvenile Beds Under Management*
Youth Services	18	LA, TN, MD, SD, MO UT, AZ, NM, & TX	1,988
Corrections Corp.	7	TN, KS, IN, & FL	1,005
Children's Comp. (CCS)	5	AL, CA, FL, & TN	469
Esmor Correctional	3	FL	774
Wackenhut Corrections	1	TX	96*
Total	34		4,332

*Wackenhut Corrections also has a design and construction contract for a 112-bed juvenile facility in New Brunswick, Canada.

SOURCE: Charles Thomas, *Correctional Privatization: The Issues and the Evidence.* (Privatization of Correctional Services Conference, Toronto, Canada, 1996), pp. 22-34.

of youthful crimes of violence that might be better dealt with in more secure facilities. This is a market that is almost sure to attract the private sector as an area that has great potential and the flexibility afforded to jurisdictions with growing needs for juvenile beds and programs.

TRAINING NEEDED FOR STAFF IN BOTH ADULT AND JUVENILE PROGRAMS

The need to have better trained staff has impacted the growth of many private and nonprofit agencies and has prompted some entrepreneurs to start training academies for preemployment programs for adult and juvenile corrections officers.

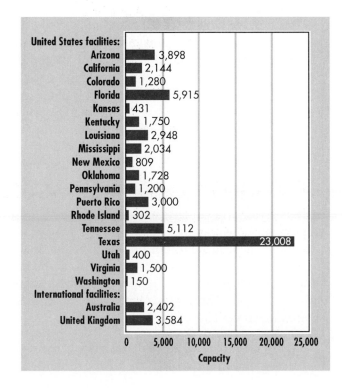

FIGURE *28.4*

Rated Capacities of Private Facilities by Geographical Location*

*Estimates include both facilities in operation and those under construction.

SOURCE: Charles Thomas, *Private Adult Correctional Facility Census* (Center for Studies in Criminology & Law, University of Florida, Gainesville, FL, March 15, 1996), p. 30.

Some Hidden Costs of Corrections

- **Capital costs:** land purchases, construction, major equipment, depreciation or amortization.
- **Finance costs:** service and interest on bonds.
- **Opportunity costs:** taxes or rent forgone from alternative uses of land or buildings.
- **Employment (fringe) benefits:** insurance, longevity bonuses, retirement contributions, unfunded pension payouts.
- **Unemployment and workers' compensation costs.**
- **External administrative overhead:** prorated share of the expenses of centralized executive offices (governor, mayor, etc.) or administrative offices (e.g., personnel services, central purchasing, data processing, general services administration).
- **External oversight costs:** inspections, program monitoring, administrative or judicial reviews and appeals of decisions, auditing, and other comptroller services.
- **Legal service costs,** including public funds for inmate plaintiffs and defendants as well as for defense of government.
- **General liability costs:** successful legal claims, punitive

damages, fines, court costs, premiums for general liability insurance or costs of administering a self-insurance plan.
- **Property insurance costs:** premiums or self-insurance costs for fire, theft, and casualty protection (or risk cost of uninsured losses).
- **Staff training costs** (when provided or subsidized by another agency).
- **Transportation costs:** transportation services, vehicles, vehicle maintenance, fuel, parts, related costs (when provided by other departments).
- **Food costs** (when other government agencies provide surplus food or subsidies).
- **Interagency personnel costs** (when personnel are borrowed from other agencies for routine purposes or emergencies).
- **Treatment or program costs** (when other agencies provide hospitalization, medical and mental health care, education, job training, recreation, counseling, or other treatment programs and services.   ∎

Some of these programs have concentrated on searching out interested minorities and females, and have done quite well. Others have tried the same approach but, lacking rigid standards, careful screening or close association with the correctional agencies, they have failed.

Most of the largest of the private adult corrections companies have excellent training facilities and programs that compare with the best offered by state-operated training facilities. Others have yet to develop the kinds of training facilities and programs that meet the industry standards or avoid the criticism of opponents for failing to develop quality staff equal to public agencies. This area is one of the weak spots for the private service and facility providers, and must be carefully addressed to avoid criticism and litigation.

Summary

There is a vast array of facts and arguments one must take into account to avoid adopting an unrealistic perspective on the privatization movement and its future directions. The data are just beginning to be amassed and become large enough to see some clear patterns and directions. This is the first time we have been able to gather enough information to put together a comprehensive chapter on this important topic. The future of privatization seems to be very promising and Thomas illustrates this by the following:

Growth in contracting for the management of secure correctional facilities grew far more rapidly in the past decade than virtually everyone

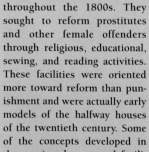

EARLY PRIVATELY OPERATED FACILITIES FOR WOMEN

Private "houses of refuge" for women were created throughout the 1800s. They sought to reform prostitutes and other female offenders through religious, educational, sewing, and reading activities. These facilities were oriented more toward reform than punishment and were actually early models of the halfway houses of the twentieth century. Some of the concepts developed in these privately operated facilities were later adopted for use in state reformatories. This early use of the private sector for special category prisoners was a forerunner of many of today's private sector community correctional operations.

thought it would. Still, it is also true that only slightly more than 2 percent of all prisoners in the United States are presently being housed in private facilities.

Although private facilities are now in operation or under construction in seventeen states, and although private facilities presently house prisoners for the benefit of at least twenty-two states, it is important to note that a majority of American jurisdictions have not awarded any local or state-level contracts. Those that have refrained from contracting include numerous states which have both large prisoner population and significant problems caused by their prisoner populations being above 100 percent of the highest design capacity of their systems (e.g., Georgia, Illinois, Michigan, Ohio, and New York).

Most privatization initiatives have involved contract awards that were intended to expand the capacity of correctional systems. Although the potential cost savings and performance improvements which could flow from decisions to privatize existing facilities are considerable, obvious political considerations reduce the appeal of this kind of contracting. This is an obstacle for privatization proponents. The obstacle could become troublesome where general population growth tends to moderate.

The appeal of many types of privatization are considerable beyond the boundaries of the United States. However, it remains true that facility management contracts have been awarded in only two other nations, Australia and the United Kingdom.

Opposition both to the enactment of legislation authorizing privatization and to exercising existing statutory authority remains strong in many jurisdictions. It is highly improbable that any amount of positive research evidence will persuade some local- and state-level corrections agencies to adopt a less adversarial position. It is even less likely that public employee unions will assume a nonadversarial posture.

Despite these and other risks and obstacles, it is still true that that the progress of privatization in corrections has been remarkable. Key demonstrations by the private sector have resulted in the following realities:

1. The hypothesis that the management of jails and prisons is a core function of government that cannot be delegated to the private sector has been invalidated.
2. The hypothesis that the private sector would never receive consequential contract awards from governmental agencies has been invalidated.
3. The hypothesis that private management firms would be incapable of achieving and maintaining profitability and still provide cost-effective services has been invalidated.
4. The hypothesis that private management firms would never have the expertise to manage either large facilities or facilities housing prisoners with high security classifications has been invalidated.[7]

What has been proven is that private management firms can provide professional-caliber services in all types of correctional settings and facilities and do so at a highly competitive cost.

This all suggests that we have seen little more than the leading edge of the fundamental transformation of the way public policy makers conceptualize the relationship between government agencies and the delivery of correctional services. Increasingly, we will see policy makers encouraging or requiring agencies to allocate more of their efforts to correctional planning and to reduce their involvement as direct service providers. No responsible policy maker can any longer view the management of correctional facilities as a monopoly to which public agencies and their employees are automatically entitled. The evidence that the public interest is better served by competition between alternative providers is far too strong for such an archaic strategy to prevail.

There are many viewpoints in the controversy over the public or private provision of correctional management over full-scale jails and prisons. The arguments have been shown here, in this new chapter, to stimulate the student's interest in this battle as we enter the twenty-first century. What has been done in the past has not been necessarily bad or good but, rather, what was possible and seemed practical for the times. Consider the old saying, "The surest sign of insanity is doing the same thing over and over . . . and expecting different results." Perhaps the next decade, in a new century, will see the reinvention of corrections into a model of public and private cooperation to achieve new goals and objectives for the beleaguered system that the student has studied for these twenty-eight chapters. In the next and final chapter, we summarize the major issues of corrections today and cautiously predict what will come next.

Review Questions

1. What are the primary reasons for the private sector to become involved in prisons and jails?
2. How many beds are being supplied by the private sector in adult prisons?
3. What are the major arguments against privatization of adult jails and prisons?
4. What are the major arguments in favor of privatization of correctional services?
5. What is meant by the term commercial/correctional complex?

Words to Remember

Correctional Recovery Academy

punishment for profit

the correctional/industrial complex

technologies for surveillance

consequential risks

the monetary colonization of criminal justice

Corrections Corporation of America

privatization

electronic monitoring

Endnotes

1. This section is extracted from Malcolm M. Feeley, "The Privatization of Prisons in Historical Perspective," *Criminal Justice Research Bulletin* 6:2 (1991): 6–8.

2. CiviGenics is a criminal justice service company founded by a consortium of nationally recognized security, criminal justice, treatment, and education experts. It offers products and

services that are high-quality, cost-effective solutions to escalating public safety concerns of communities across the nation.

3. Editors, Equitable Research Corporation, *Report of Private Corrections,* (New York City, NY: Equitable Research Corporation, 1996), p. 1

4 J. Robert Lilly and Mathieu Deflem. "Profit and Penality: An Analysis of the Corrections-Commercial Complex," *Crime and Delinquency* 42:1 (1996): 3–20.

5 Charles W. Thomas, *Correctional Privatization: The Issues and the Evidence,* paper presented at Privatization of Correctional Services Conference, Toronto, Canada, July 10–11, 1996.

6. Ibid.

7. It should be noted that large portions of this chapter are extracted, paraphrased, and generously provided by Charles W. Thomas, Director, Center for Studies in Criminology and the Law, University of Florida, and author of the fine documents of the Private Corrections Project. The authors are extremely grateful for his kind support and sharing of his writings and data for this important new chapter.

*R*ecommended Readings for Part VII

Blumstein, A., J. Cohen, and D. Nagle. *Deterrence and Incapacitation: Estimating the Effects of Criminal Sanctions on Crime Rates.* Washington, D.C.: National Academy of Sciences, 1978.

Chapman, Jane Robert. *Women Employed in Corrections.* Washington, D.C.: U.S. Government Printing Office, 1983.

Cohen, Jacqueline. *Incapacitating Criminals: Recent Research Findings.* Washington, D.C.: U.S. Department of Justice, 1983.

Cory, Bruce, and Stephen Gettinger. *Time to Build? The Realities of Prison Construction.* New York: Edna McConnell Clark Foundation, 1984.

Erwin, Billie, and Lawrence Bennett. "New Dimensions in Probation: Georgia's Experience with Intensive Probation Supervision." *Research in Brief.* Washington, D.C.: National Institute of Justice, 1987.

Feeley, Malcolm M. "The Privatization of Prisons in Historical Perspective." *Criminal Justice Research Bulletin* 6:2 (1991): 6–8.

Gibbons, Don. *The Limits of Punishment as Social Policy.* San Francisco, CA: National Council on Crime and Delinquency, 1988.

Glick, Ruth, and Virginia Neto. *National Study of Women's Correctional Programs.* Washington, D.C.: U.S. Department of Justice, 1977.

Greenwood, Peter, and Frank Zimring. *One More Chance: The Pursuit of Promising Intervention Strategies for Chronic Juvenile Offenders.* Santa Monica, CA: Rand Corporation, 1985.

Hershberger, Gregory. "The Development of the Federal Prison System." *Federal Probation* 43 (December 1979): pp. 13–23.

Kinkade, Patrick T., and Matthew C. Leone. "Issues and Answers: Responses to Controversies Surrounding Privatization." *The Prison Journal* 72:1, 2 (1992): pp. 28-54.

Kinkade, Patrick T., and Matthew C. Leone. "Prison Privatization and Conjugal Visitation: A Nexus of Opportunity?" in L. Mays and T. Gray, etc. *Privatization and the Provision of Correctional Services.* Cincinnati: Anderson, 1994.

Lilly, J. Robert, and Mathieu Deflem. "Profit and Penality: An Analysis of the Corrections-Commercial Complex." *Crime and Delinquency* 42:1 (1996): pp. 3-20.

Logan, Charles H., and Sharla P. Rausch. "Punish and Profit: the Emergence of Private Enterprise Prisons." *Justice Quarterly* 2:3 (1985): pp. 308-318.

McCarthy, Belinda, ed. *Intermediate Punishments.* Monsey, NY: Criminal Justice Press, 1987.

Morris, Norval, and Gordon Hawkins. *The Honest Politician's Guide to Crime Control.* Chicago: University of Chicago Press, 1970.

Noonan, Susan, and Edward Latessa. "Intensive Probation: An Examination of Recidivism and Social Adjustment." *American Journal of Criminal Justice* XI (1987): 45–61.

Petersilia, Joan. *Expanding Options for Criminal Sentencing*. Santa Monica, CA: Rand Corporation, 1987.

Seiter, Richard P., Harry E. Allen, Evalyn Parks, and Eric Carlson. *Halfway Houses*. Washington, D.C.: U.S. Government Printing Office, 1977.

Sexton, George E. *Work in American Prisons: Joint Ventures with the Private Sector.* Washington, D.C.: U.S. Department of Justice, 1995.

Thomas, Charles W. "Prisoner Rights and Correctional Privatization: A Legal and Ethical Analysis." *Business and Professional Ethics Journal* 10:2 (1991), pp. 3-45.

Thomas, Charles W. *Correctional Privatization: The Issues and Evidence* (monograph). Toronto: The Fraser Institute, July 1996.

U.S. Department of Justice. *Prevention of Violence in Correctional Institutions*. Washington, D.C.: U.S. Government Printing Office, 1972.

U.S. Department of Justice. *The St. Louis Detoxification and Diagnostic Evaluation Center.* Washington, D.C.: U.S. Government Printing Office, 1992.

PART EIGHT

The Future *of* Corrections

29. Corrections Enters
the 21st Century

CHAPTER TWENTY-NINE

Corrections Enters *the* Twenty-first Century

Correctional History: As the Twenty-first Century Approaches

More than twenty years of our searching for relevant, current, and interesting materials to share with teachers and students about corrections has been both intellectually rewarding as well as professionally disappointing. Sometimes it is hard to look so closely at a field we both care for so deeply and observe the often glacial progress of corrections. This chapter is our chance to pass along some of our personal and professional concerns for the future, as well as our thoughts on the directions the field may take as it enters the new millenium. While the viewpoints expressed here may seem ascerbic at times, we do believe that corrections is at a crossroads and that this generation of leaders and students can make a real impact if they decide to commit to excellence.

The last two decades began with mixed signals. The executioner was back from forced retirement, the treatment model was prematurely declared dead, and flat and harsher sentencing had found its way back into more and more state legislation. Parole came under heavy attack and was abandoned in many states, and the public seemed to acquire an even "get-tougher attitude." In the United States, the number of adult prison residents more than quintupled from 196,000 in 1970 to over 1,054,000 in 1995, and there appears to be no end in sight for that kind of continuing growth. Such growth is taxing systems that do not work all that well at best—but are staggered by overcrowding, violence, and insufficient budgets. Our projections of the numbers of prisoners likely to be found in the reformatories, correctional institutions, and prisons of the nation by 2010 can be found in Figure 29-1. Based on the rate of growth from 1993 to 1994, America could have almost 4 million adults incarcerated by the year 2010!

Humanity owes a debt of gratitude to that philosopher who, from the obscurity of his isolated study, had the courage to scatter among the multitude the first seeds, so long unfruitful, of useful truths.

—Cesare Beccaria, 1764

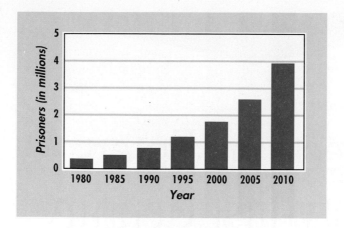

FIGURE
29.1

Prisoners in America
(in millions), 1980–2010
(est.)

SOURCE: Adapted from Allen Beck and Darrell Gilliard, *Prisoners In 1994* (Washington, D.C.: U.S. Department of Justice, 1995), p. 5.

The public still seems neither concerned about nor aware of the growing cancer of overcrowding and violence in the nation's jails and prisons. The thirty-six hours of rage and horror that riveted them to their television screens on the first weekend of February 1980 gave them a short-lived "wake-up call." Live and on television, the New Mexico State Prison took its place in the sordid history of prison riots, along with the many other incidents that brought to the public's attention the conditions of fortress jails and prisons of America over the next two decades.

It is ironic that much of the progress in corrections is overshadowed by such incidents as the New Mexico or earlier Attica prison riot. In stark contrast to these grisly events, the U.S. Penitentiary at Leavenworth announced that one of its inmates, a thirty-eight-year-old bank robber, became the first prisoner ever to be inducted into the elite Phi Beta Kappa scholarship society. The inmate earned a bachelor of science degree in psychology after five years of study in courses offered by the University of Kansas at Leavenworth, finishing with a grade-point average of 3.97 out of a possible 4.0. The more likely candidate for headlines in the 1980s was the serial killer Ted Bundy as he waited for execution and appealed over and over to the Supreme Court for clemency.

As corrections enters into the twenty-first century, the pattern seems to be one step ahead and two steps back. The changes underway are dynamic, but they offer a confused and often contradictory picture. We have examined many of the more promising innovations in the previous twenty-eight chapters. But the future of corrections belongs to those who have mastered the knowledge and skills needed to implement and apply real change in a system that often resists change at almost every level. Unless the most intelligent and informed leaders of corrections decide to take action, the next edition of this text no doubt will open with a story about yet another prison riot caused by the apathy and ignorance of the public, politicians, and correctional bureaucrats. Such malaise does not infect all, or even most, correctional leaders. But enough of them tolerate or ignore these conditions (just trying to make it to their retirement) so that correctional history seems to repeat itself relentlessly.

The last few decades have been a time of continuing if not escalating social change, a change reflected in the operation of correctional programs. The ongoing industrialization of America eventually exacerbated urbanization, corporate downsizing and layoffs, and the resulting problems connected with densely populated poverty-ridden slums and under- or unemployed workers. Rising crime in hard-pressed urban centers contributed to a mass exodus into the suburbs (sometimes called "white flight") by those who could afford to move. The inner cities became wastelands of neglect and street crime. The much touted American dream became a nightmare of idleness, drugs, and despair. Left were the poor, the old, the uneducated, minority groups, crime, drugs, and little social or economic capital. Inner cities became places to fear and avoid.[1] Then so-called street crime became a political issue.

Over three decades ago, presidential hopeful Barry Goldwater alerted the nation to law and order as a campaign issue in the 1964 general elections. Lyndon Johnson was elected, but he too got the message. Something had to be done about crime in the streets. Hence he appointed a commission to look into the problems of "crime in a free society." The task force reports of that commission, especially the report on corrections, detailed what was already common knowledge to practitioners in the field. Failure and confusion were reported at all levels of the system. With high recidivism rates from institutions, adult prisons and juvenile institutions were depicted as schools of crime. There seemed to be no clear alternatives to more and more incarceration. All this at a time when fewer than 200,000 adults were incarcerated in the United States.

All of these points were merely variations on the themes contained in the Wickersham Commission report of 1931 and several other "blue-ribbon" commissions and reports in between. As in the past, most correctional administrators expected the 1967 commission reports to end up on dusty shelves, stimulating little or no action. Fortunately, the federal government had provided the means for doing something about this commission's recommendations.

The Law Enforcement Assistance Act of 1965 (Public Law 89-197) was enacted to provide funds for the development of programs that would reduce crime in the streets (see Chapter 4). The initial success of that legislation led to the development of the *Omnibus Crime Control and Safe Streets Act of 1968* (Public Law 90-351). This legislation, implemented with generous funding by the Congress, pumped billions of dollars into the nation's fight against crime. Important to the field of corrections was the specific requirement that at least 20 percent of the money given to the Law Enforcement Assistance Administration (LEAA) be spent on action programs in corrections. This federal funding was matched by significant permanent funds from the states as well, ensuring continuation of at least some of the most promising pilot programs and projects. The successor to the LEAA, the Office of Justice Programs, continues those efforts.

Correctional institutions continue to be a kind of out-of-focus microcosm of the free society from which the inmate comes. It is not surprising that many issues which swept the cities of the 1960s spread to the prisons of America. The 1960s saw great advances in civil rights, but radical groups to the left and right perceived the changes as occurring either too slowly or too quickly. The results exacerbated polarization between the races and caused especially serious problems in the institutional setting. Divisions along racial, political, and ideological lines are strongly accentuated by the total institution. Many of the riots and disturbances in the prisons have been aimed at achieving narrow political ends rather than really trying to improve conditions in that particular system.

The pressure-cooker environment of an overcrowded, underfunded, and understaffed total institution means that the slightest friction can explode the surface calm almost immediately into uncontrollable violence. Thus the highly volatile issues of the last four decades continue to produce serious crises in the jails and prisons of the United States. As correctional administrators are told to turn more and more alternatives to incarceration, the prisons are filled with the residual hard-core and radicalized problem offenders as their cadre, further increasing the risk of prison violence.[2] The serious overcrowding of the prisons exacerbates the problems of the administrators and leaves a living time bomb on their hands. We have seen the relationship between violent, dangerous, and difficult inmates change dramatically over the last twenty years. In some maximum security institutions, the ratio is almost 80 to 90 percent hard-core, violent criminals to property offenders. We predict that more supermaximum prisons will be built in the next decade to control and manage such volatile and dangerous inmates.

NEWER CHALLENGES

The conservative, get-tough philosophy in criminal justice administration that resurfaced in the early 1980s viewed all offenders as predatory criminals, inherently evil and irredeemable. They were thought to voluntarily commit crime and were not deterred by a justice system that only occasionally arrested a few offenders and them gave them slaps on the wrists by placing them on probation. A sense of moral outrage was coupled with a political crusade against drugs, creating a concept of a "War on Drugs." One must ask, "If we are at war with drugs, who is the enemy?" But catchy sound bytes are always good for the latest crusade against crime. We have had lots of them: "Safe Streets Acts," "Zero Tolerance," "Lock 'Em Up and Throw Away the Key," "Take Back the Streets," "Light the Night," "Three Strikes and You're Out," and "Just Say No." The hard-line approach has led the nation to incredibly overcrowded prisons and unanticipated expenditures never before seen on such a scale, as well as widespread corruption and goal displacement among some law enforcement agencies. Yet seldom have the leaders been brave enough to address the basic underlying causes that create wave after wave of offenders entering the high crime rate ages of fifteen to twenty-four.[3]

"Killer Kids," street gangs, drive-by shootings, prison gangs, and deteriorating urban environments are only symptoms of the problem. What is the underlying disease? Current national criminal justice policy could be likened to treating terminal cancer by rattling bones, engaging in exorcism, and labeling the dying as "wicked." Much is said but little is done about understanding the "basic pathology" (urban blight, racism, ghetto mentality, poverty, and generations of welfare and unemployment), followed by developing and delivering curatives (economic enterprise zones, business expansion, hiring local residents, Big Brother/Sister programs), or lowering susceptibility to this "social cancer" (giving up smoking, life-style alterations, or diet modifications). Possible justice policies equivalents might be encouraging parents not to use drugs, drink, or smoke in their children's presence; parenting classes; child and spousal abuse care centers; and school aide volunteering. In brief, correctional policy has been preempted by a political agenda that fails to prevent crime and reintegrate offenders. Until a new consensus on political objectives develops, and the great experiment on the War on Drugs can be viewed as ineffectual, corrections may have to become a proactive leader in addressing new solutions to both old and current problems. We begin this ending with an examination of crime trends and law enforcement responses.

CRIME TRENDS

Our investigation of crime trends in the nation revealed that crime rates and number of crimes are actually coming *down* from the historical and demography-driven highs of the 1970s. National victimization studies suggest that the decline began at least two decades ago; the Uniform Crime Reports show decreases starting about over half a decade before. Thus the crime decreases began before the "hardest line" approach and could not have resulted from the "law and order" legislation of the recent past, as seen in the chain gang and "three-strikes" legislation. Change in crime rates tend to take place long after the implementation of new policy, not the quick fix that is desired by the public and the politicians.

Yet new crimes are emerging, particularly the so-called high-technology crimes, and include the savings and loan lootings, mail and wire fraud, computer hacking, and computer sabotage. Terrorism—particularly by domestic extremist groups—is on the increase. Law enforcement has responded—somewhat slowly at first but more rapidly now as policing roles have expanded and new technology has been adopted—with such high-technology investigative techniques as DNA testing, sex offender databanks, and computer-enhanced photography. One result will be an increase in the number of persons being convicted in the future due to enhanced investigative skills—and the subsequent further increase in prison populations as the correctional filter widens at the bottom.

Other important events and trends that are likely to increase the ranks of Americans under correctional supervision include the coming demographic bulge of the post–baby boom children who will enter the high crime and high-commitment years of seventeen to twenty-nine (the "echo boom"). One can easily predict an increase of juvenile offending, particularly within areas of local drug trade involvement and crimes of violence, as well as the spread of juvenile gangs. It is not unreasonable to also expect a sharp increase in computer-related crime by this first generation raised on computer games and with a PC in almost every home and school at their disposal. An alarmed public, especially when incited by irresponsible media and politicians, is likely to respond with even more punitiveness. This could lead to more efforts to lower the age at which juveniles are processed as adults, waivers to criminal courts, and bind-overs by juvenile courts for trial as an adult. The return of chain gangs and prison stripes are other indicators of punitiveness.

COMMUNITY SUPERVISION WILL CHANGE

Public fear, perceptions of increased violence and "wilding" by youths, and media focus will impact on community supervision, accelerating changes already in progress or under consideration. The shift from casework and helping to surveillance, already underway, will increase. Supervision focus will intensify in the areas of risk assessment and risk control; there will be more demand for "offender accountability" and victim compensation. Thus we can reasonably predict increased use of assessment and prediction devices and instruments and enhanced use of strategies that will diversify supervision methods and caseload size, such as electronic monitoring, house arrest, intensive supervision, community work orders, and restitution. These are seen in Figure 29-2.

Supervision strategies will increasingly be linked to computerized surveillance. It is even probable that wristlet and anklet devices will contain computer chips that permit identification and location of clients by using existing cellular telephone systems. One certain development: a much extended period of boot camp aftercare, probably linked with telemetry, and permitting return to institutional training for those among the "community barracks" who show evidence of possible recidivism or technical violations for breaking supervision conditions and rules.

WILDING

A behavior brought to light when a woman in Central Park in New York City was attacked, raped, and almost killed, by a roving gang of teenagers looking for no more than someone to assault for the thrill of it.

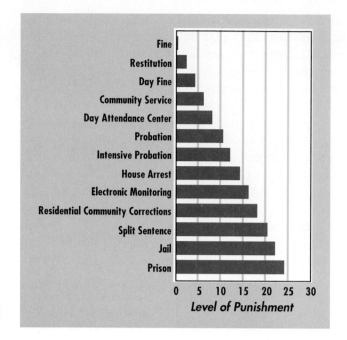

FIGURE

29.2

A Range of Sentencing
Options, Ranked by Level
of Punishment

SOURCE: Edward Latessa and Harry Allen,
Corrections in the Community (Cincinnati:
Anderson,1997), p. 614.

PRISON POPULATION TO INCREASE

The current tendency to "demonize" drug users and offenders and respond with righteous indignation at the more heinous crimes evidenced by widely publicized (but fortunately rare) rapes, child molestation, mutilations, murders, drunk drivers, and assaults will probably continue. Fighting crime has taken on almost religious overtones, likened somewhat to apocalyptic and eschatological events.[4] One can reasonably predict increased rates of jail and prison incarceration, including a rapidly rising percentage of incarcerated females in prison. In turn, it is obvious that more prisons will need to be constructed. It is hoped that these will be medium security rather than supermax institutions. More public funds will be needed to expand bed space. We already need to bring seventeen hundred new beds on line each week, each bed costing over $54,000, a figure that will no doubt increase over time. Even with private prison sector involvement,[5] more prison cells are likely to be built. More cells will mean more correctional officers. Corrections is a growth industry.

The length of time offenders would serve in prison is likely to increase as states turn to habitual offender and three-strike acts. Congress has already allocated prison construction funds for states willing to require offenders to serve 85 percent of their original sentence. Finally, parole as an early-release mechanism is under attack and has been abolished in eleven jurisdictions, including the federal system. These trends have unfavorable implications for correctional administrators and can be seen in increased warehousing of inmates, gangs formation and expansion, an increasingly old and geriatric population, and more prisoners with HIV infection and terminal-phase AIDS. We turn first to HIV infection.[6]

THE GRAYING OF AMERICA'S PRISONS REVISITED

The number and proportion of inmates in American prisons over the age of fifty is steadily increasing, reflecting the graying of America in general. Longer and mandatory minimum sentences imposed by the courts, when coupled with the increasing incarceration rate per one thousand arrests, will mean that an older

HIV Infection

Approximately 2 percent of the nation's prison inmates are infected with HIV, the virus that causes AIDS. The ratio is higher for women in prison, due to the emerging link between injecting illegal drugs and past records of prostitution. The infection rate is at least 27 percent in local areas with high rates of narcotics and drug abuse, such as in the Northeast. All state, federal, and the District of Columbia prisons have at least some inmates with HIV. AIDS accounted for 34 percent of the inmate deaths in 1994[6] and, it is predicted, will account for one in three by the year 2000; currently, one in every four inmates has used a needle to inject illegal drugs.

Managing the challenge of HIV in prisons will require medically adequate treatment, staff and inmate education, training in infection control and case management programs, antituberculosis regimens, counseling, prison drug research centers, medical parole, and community residential centers (CRCs). California's prison intramural HIV program costs $86,000 per inmate a year, a much greater cost than treatment in private sector CRCs. Much remains to be done in the next decade. ∎

prison population will pose administrative challenges to corrections. This situation will only be exacerbated by the latest "Three Strikes and You're Out," "Life Without Hope of Parole," and "Life for a Life"[7] laws that are being passed at state and federal levels. As these inmates are incarcerated for life, the future portends the possibility of tens of thousands of inmates growing old in prison across the country. This will make prisons the largest "old age homes" in the nation. Time will tell if this policy will be effective in reducing crime in any cost-effective manner.

Increasingly fearful and frail, geriatric inmates will eventually require special housing with appropriate modification to accommodate wheelchairs and walkers. Special diets lower in salt and fat will be needed for inmates, along with eyeglasses and aids for the visually impaired, prescription drugs, and specialized recreation units. Limited care and convalescent unit programs will need to be made increasingly available. Staff will need special training about the potential liabilities associated with violations of the Americans with Disabilities Act (ADA) and that will no doubt require policy changes in the institutions. Retrofitting of cell blocks, passage ways, dormitories and dining areas will be needed. In corrections, new employment opportunities and challenging work will face the new correctional staff.[8]

BOOT CAMPS AS EARLY RELEASE MECHANISMS?

Boot camp (shock incarceration) programs began in 1983 and now total seventy-five camp programs across thirty-six jurisdictions, including the federal government, and growing. Almost twelve thousand inmates graduated and were released back into the community, generally under intensive supervision and as step-down, regular supervision. Some states, such as Georgia, have elaborate boot camp programs that permit the supervising agency to return nonconforming clients to an institution for retraining ("tune-up") before return to the community. Given the political popularity and widespread belief in the ability of the military model to bring discipline to an offender's life, boot camp programs may well become a major alternative to parole as well as a mechanism for more effective delivery of drug abuse treatment. No doubt community supervision will be expanded to include longer-term "community barracks" and treatment.

MORE CAUTIOUS PREDICTIONS

As American corrections heads with fits and starts into the twenty-first century, prison populations are at an all-time high and growing. In addition, a greater percentage of the population is incarcerated in the United States than in any other major Western democracy. Per bed construction costs are soaring to as high as $100,000 per cell. The per capita costs to the taxpayers for the nation's total criminal justice system averaged slightly over $216 in 1987, but should approximate $400 by the year 2000.

Though such statistics tend to be quite unnerving, extrapolations based on current trends for the year 2000 are even more ominous. In the last edition of this text, we predicted the national prison population would reach 1.2 million by the start of the twenty-first century. We were wrong. America reached that level in early 1996. California prisons, with a mere 6 percent growth rate, were predicted to exceed a population of 100,000 by the year 1996. As this edition goes to press, the level had already exceeded 136,000. Even with modest inflation rates, construction costs per bed could soar to as much as $150,000, not including debt service charges. The average annual cost per inmate could reach $50,000. Although these are straight-line projections, they seem to be happening and, even if they are off by a factor of one-half, they are useful indicators of some of the fiscal and space problems that corrections may experience at the turn of the century. We offer projections of the size of the major correctional components for 2000 in Figure 29-3. The lighter columns are current sizes, the next largest are the optimist's view, and the sky-scrapers are projections based on current trends.

POLICY OPTIONS AND IMPLICATIONS

Jails, departments of corrections, and juvenile systems have no choice but to accept those inmates the courts commit. The problems of scarcity of beds, prison overcrowding, lawsuits, and Eighth Amendment prohibitions (to say nothing of the problems of meeting minimum standards in the current accreditation movement) must dictate proactive administrative policies to protect institutions and inmates. Prisons can be constructed and renovated, but voters can defeat bond issues, resist taxes, and oppose prison construction in their local areas. It is becoming clear that the nation's resources are finite and that corrections will have

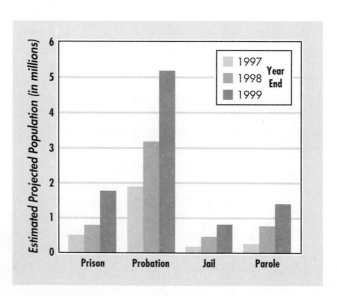

FIGURE

29.3

Projected Correctional Populations to the Year 2000

SOURCE: Harry Allen and Edward Latessa, "The State of Corrections in the New Millenium," paper presented at the annual meeting of the Southern Criminal Justice Association, Gatlinburg, Tennessee, September 30, 1995.

to do more with less. This is true in every segment of the government and industry and means that we must roll up our sleeves and do it better.

Corrections agencies will need to adopt a variety of defensive policies: probation subsidies to strengthen local corrections, paying counties to retain short-sentence offenders in lieu of committing them to state correctional facilities, split sentencing, use of paraprofessionals and volunteers, shock probation and shock parole, community-based residential facilities, and probation services for courts on an "as requested" basis. Use of high-technology solutions to many problems needs a concerted effort to coordinate with the manufacturers in developing as yet unheard of devices to help. These measures can only slow the crisis: they cannot eliminate the problem. The courts have used a somewhat remarkable process for diverting and deferring the costs from local government levels—and bucking the problem up to the state level. That simple process is commitment to state institutions.

As present trends continue, policies designed to purchase local correctional services from the private sector seem to be a viable option (see Chapter 28). Innovations include probation and diversion agencies and programs, halfway houses, community corrections centers, women's detention centers, jails, workhouses, and other community-based correctional programs. Adopting these programs can be accomplished piecemeal through subsidies, purchase of service plans, and cost-sharing programs. They can be done on a regional basis initially through planning commissions and consolidation. They are being done in the several states that have Community Corrections Acts.

Perhaps no more important policy implication for the future of corrections can be found in the growing problems of violence and America's youth. These problems are pointed out in the preface of a famous 1993 report "Violence and Youth." We must get to the root causes of violence in order to save a generation of children.

Violence and Youth

Although violence involving youth is hardly a new phenomenon in the United States, both the quantity and quality of this violence have undergone a dramatic change within the past 10 to 15 years. Mere statistics cannot tell the story, but the following observations will suggest how much the parameters of the problem have altered:

■ Homicide is the most common cause of death for young African-American females as well as for young African-American males. The probability of a young Africa-American female dying by homicide is four times that of a non-African-American female. A young African-American male is 11 times more likely to die by homicide than a non–African-American male.

■ Children can buy handguns on street corners in many communities. In part because of this ready availability of firearms, guns are involved in more than 75 percent of adolescent killings. "Get rid of the guns," said a teenage girl from a violent neighborhood in Washington, D.C., when asked what adults could do to stop the violence in her community.

■ The intensity of violence involving children and youth has escalated dramatically. In testimony presented to APA, Mireille Kanda, MD, who was then Director of Child Protection Services at Children's National Medical Center in Washington, D.C., noted that the rate of penetrating trauma caused by violence seen in her emergency department increased 1,740 percent between 1986 and 1989.

■ Children are becoming involved in violence at ever-younger ages. In a study of first and second graders in Washington, D.C., 45 percent said they had witnessed muggings, 31 percent said they had witnessed shootings, and 39 percent said they had seen dead bodies. A 17-year-old African-American girl from Boston told a state task force that she had attended the funerals of sixteen friends aged 14 to 21 who had died by violence. ■

SOURCE: American Psychological Association Commission on Youth and Violence, *Youth and Violence* (New York: American Psychological Association, 1993), pp. 12–13.

Summary and Final Comments

It is extremely difficult to decide when to stop writing about the fascinating, complex, and dynamic field we call corrections. But, reluctantly, we now close with a last few observations. This text was designed to give you a broad view of the history, processes, systems, clientele, and problems shaping the functions and facilities that constitute corrections in America. In the beginning, we asked the questions, "What is corrections?" It should be apparent now that corrections remains a goal in search of a discipline, a discipline that works. The history of corrections is long, but in America we are actually dealing with only a score of years longer than two centuries of experience. Clearly, we are all still learning what it takes to make corrections work.

In the short term, as we enter the next century, we predict that Americans will come to realize the practical limits of law enforcement as a solution to crime, much like community-oriented policing reflects growing realization that the "thin blue line" needs the political and philosophical clout of citizens, community leaders, other agencies, and much support to get the job done. If there is a thin blue line, our first line of defense against crime, that line is the *citizen* with law enforcement as the agent of that effort. And so it is with corrections. We can no longer continue to allow corrections to be the "invisible empire" where what is done is done out of sight and mind of the citizens whom corrections serve. To stand alone is not possible; we must become "partnerships with people" to serve and protect all the community when the offender returns, in 95 percent of the cases.[9]

A second new focus will have to be on crime prevention, drug prevention, and treatment. These efforts pose untapped potential in lowering crime as well as reducing the demand for drugs. The war on drugs cannot be won, but we can win battles one person at a time, if we care enough to do it. The drug court is promising a mechanism for ending the battles.

Third, we predict that mandatory minimum sentencing will come under increasing criticism and will, by the year 2010, be recognized as another correctional promise unfulfilled. If imprisonment increases the probability of reoffending, sentences to long mandatory periods of incarceration may well increase recidivism in the long run. We have no doubts that most prisoners have earned their incarceration. But are long mandatory sentences worth the price some of these offenders will extract from society on release if we don't correct them?

Finally, we predict a broad resurgence for maintenance of constitutional protection such as the exclusionary rule and prohibition against cruel and unusual punishment. The excessive use of asset forfeiture in connection with drug law violations has already sparked renewed interest in regard to individual rights.

How do we stop this effort without missing an issue or detail for the student and instructor? That, of course, is an impossible task. We have tried our best to make this a book for the twenty-first century, and hope that a homey parable, "A Story of Two Brothers," by our valued colleague Steven Donziger helps sum up this exciting era:

> The best lesson we can learn about the American criminal justice system comes from a story of two brothers who wanted to earn some extra money. In the heat of the summer they decided to open a stand to sell tomatoes. The brothers drove all night to a farm and purchased a truckload of tomatoes for 50 cents per pound. Early the next morning they opened their stand. They sold their product for 50 cents a pound. Demand proved enormous, and by

the end of the day they had sold all their supply. At first the brothers were impressed with the fullness of the cash drawer. But when they compared the earnings to the money they had spent to buy the tomatoes, they discovered that they had earned nothing at all. Including the cost of the overnight haul, they had actually lost money.

The young men were undaunted and they decided to try again. To ensure a profit next time, they decided to do things differently. Next time they decided to buy more tomatoes.

For the past twenty years, criminal justice practices and policies have been much like the business practices of the brothers: so profoundly ill-conceived that they are destined to fail. As the failures have accumulated, the justice system has responded by adding more of the same policies.[10]

The issues and challenges posed to students and professionals in corrections who are the future and present professionals are controversial and complex. But if we don't shrink away from valid controversy, these issues and challenges can be solved by dedicated, trained, and educated persons who are willing to propose constructive criticism and logical solutions. The student and new staff must learn to ask "Why?" and refuse to accept the answer, "It's always been done that way." As Walter C. Reckless was known to have said over many decades of working with corrections, "The fields are ripe unto harvest and we need hands to bring it in." It is with this spirit that we urge serious students to consider pitching in and providing the hands to help bring in the harvest of improved corrections in America. Both of us have enjoyed bringing this text to thousands of students in the past two decades, and we look forward to doing our small parts in the next century.

Endnotes

1. Jerome Skolnick, "What Not to Do About Crime," *Criminology* 33:1 (1995): 465–491, and Harry Allen, "The American Dream and Crime in the Twenty-first Century," *Justice Quarterly* 12:3 (1995): 427–445.

2. Victor Hassine, *Life Without Parole* (Los Angeles: Roxbury, 1996), pp. 27–34, 71–76, and 107–111.

3. Steven Donziger, *The Real War on Crime* (New York: HarperCollins, 1996), pp. 63–99.

4. Jeffrey Kaplan, "America's Last Prophetic Witness: The Literature of the Rescue Movement," *Terrorism and Political Violence* 5:3 (1993): 58–77; M. Borg, *Meeting Jesus Again for the First Time* (San Francisco: HarperCollins, 1994); and J. Crossan, *Who Killed Jesus? Exposing the Roots of Anti-Semitism in the Gospel Story of the Death of Jesus* (San Francisco: HarperColllins, 1995).

5. J. Robert Lilly and Mathieu Deflem, "Profit and Penalty: An Analysis of the Corrections-Commercial Complex," *Crime and Delinquency* 42:1 (1996): 3–20.

6. Camille Camp and George Camp, *The Corrections Yearbook 1995: Adult Corrections* (South Salem, NY: Criminal Justice Institute, 1995), p. 30.

7. Peter Moon, "Jail-for-Life Policy Negates Values of Prison Reforms," *The Globe and the Mail*, June 26, 1995, p. A-8.

8. Edward Walsh, "Geriatric Care Becoming a Big Concern for Prisons," *San Francisco Chronicle*, July 15, 1996, p. A-7.

9. Fox Butterfield, "Idle Hands Within the Devil's Own Playground," *The New York Times*, July 16, 1995, p. E-3.

10. Steven Donziger, *The Real War on Crime,* p. 195.

Glossary

The authors are grateful to the Law Enforcement Assistance Administration for the publication of the *Dictionary of Criminal Justice Data Terminology*, from which many of the following terms and definitions have been extracted. It is in the spirit of that effort to standardize criminal justice terminology that we have decided to include this section. We hope that students, especially those new to the field, will take the time to read and absorb the meanings of these tools of the trade. To obtain more detailed information about the terms in this glossary, the student should write to U.S. Department of Justice, National Criminal Reference Service, Washington, D.C. 20531.

Abscond (corrections). To depart from a geographical area or jurisdiction prescribed by the conditions of one's probation or parole, without authorization.

Abscond (court). To intentionally absent or conceal oneself unlawfully in order to avoid a legal process.

Acquittal. A judgment of a court, based either on the verdict of a jury or a judicial officer, that the defendant is not guilty of the offense(s) for which he or she has been tried.

Adjudicated. Having been the subject of completed criminal or juvenile proceedings, and convicted, or adjudicated a delinquent, status offender, or dependent.

Adjudication (criminal). The judicial decision terminating a criminal proceeding by a judgment of conviction, acquittal, or by a dismissal of the case.

Adjudication (juvenile). The juvenile court decision, terminating an adjudicatory hearing, that the juvenile is a delinquent, status offender, dependent, or that the allegations in the petition are not sustained.

Adjudicatory hearing. In juvenile proceedings, the fact-finding process wherein the juvenile court determines whether or not there is sufficient evidence to sustain the allegations in a petition.

Adult. A person who is within the original jurisdiction of a criminal, rather than juvenile, court because his or her age at the time of an alleged criminal act was above a statutory specified limit.

Alias. Any name used for an official purpose that is different from a person's legal name.

Alternative Facility. An alternative place of limited confinement that may be an option for certain kinds of offenders. Such facilities may include treatment settings for drug-dependent offenders, minimum security facilities in the community that provide treatment and services as needed, work/study-release centers, and halfway houses or shelter-type facilities. All of these are less secure than the traditional jail, but offer a more stimulating environment for the individual.

Appeal. A request by either the defense or the prosecution that a case be removed from a lower court to a higher court in order for a completed trial to be reviewed by the higher court.

Appearance. The act of coming into a court and submitting to the authority of that court.

Appearance, first (initial appearance). The first appearance of a juvenile or adult in the court that has jurisdiction over his or her case.

Appellant. A person who initiates an appeal.

Arraignment. The appearance of a person before a court during which the court informs the individual of the accusation(s) against him or her and during which he or she enters a plea.

Arrest. Taking a person into custody by authority of law for the purpose of charging him or her with a criminal offense or initiating juvenile proceedings, terminating with the recording of a specific offense.

Arson. The intentional destruction or attempted destruction, by fire or explosive, of the property of another or of one's own property with the intent to defraud.

Assault. Unlawful, intentional inflicting, or attempted or threatened inflicting, of injury upon another.

Assault, aggravated. Unlawful, intentional causing of serious bodily injury with or without a deadly weapon or unlawful intentional attempting or threatening of serious bodily injury or death with a deadly weapon.

Assault, simple. Unlawful, intentional threatening, attempted inflicting, or inflicting of less than serious bodily injury, in the absence of a deadly weapon.

Assault with a deadly weapon. Unlawful, intentional inflicting, or attempted or threatened inflicting, of injury or death with the use of a deadly weapon.

Assault on a law enforcement officer. A simple or aggravated assault, in which the victim is a law enforcement officer engaged in the performance of his or her duties.

Assigned counsel. An attorney, not regularly employed by a government agency, assigned by the court to represent a particular person(s) in a particular criminal proceeding.

Attorney/lawyer/counsel. A person trained in the law, admitted to practice before the bar of a given jurisdiction, and authorized to advise, represent, and act for other persons in legal proceedings.

Backlog. The number of pending cases that exceeds the court's capacity, in that they cannot be acted upon because the court is occupied in acting upon other cases.

Bombing incident. The detonation or attempted detonation of an explosive or incendiary device with the willful disregard of risk to the person or property of another, or for a criminal purpose.

Bondsman-secured bail. Security service purchased by the defendant from a bail bondsman. The fee for this service ranges upward from 10 percent and is not refundable. *The bail bondsman system, which permits a private entrepreneur to share with the court the decision on pretrial release, has been criticized for many years and is becoming obsolete in more progressive jurisdictions.*

Booking. A police administrative action officially recording an arrest and identifying the person, the place, the time, the arresting authority, and the reason for the arrest.

Burglary. Unlawful entry of a structure, with or without force, with intent to commit a felony or larceny.

Camp/ranch/farm. Any of several types of similar low security confinement facilities, usually in a rural location, which contain adults or juveniles committed after adjudication.

Case. At the level of police or prosecutorial investigation, a set of circumstances under investigation involving one or more persons; at subsequent steps in criminal proceedings, a charging document alleging the commission of one or more crimes; a single defendant; in juvenile or correctional proceedings, a person who is the object of agency action.

Case (court). A single charging document under the jurisdiction of a court; a single defendant.

Caseload (corrections). The total number of clients registered with a correctional agency or agent during a specified time period, often divided into active and inactive or supervised and unsupervised, thus distinguishing between clients with whom the agency or agent maintains contact and those with whom it does not.

Caseload (court). The total number of cases filed in a given court or before a given judicial officer during a given period of time.

Caseload, pending. The number of cases at any given time that have been filed in a given court, or are before a given judicial officer, but have not reached disposition.

Cash bail. A cash payment for situations in which the charge is not serious and the scheduled bail is low. The defendant obtains release by paying in cash the full amount, which is recoverable after the required court appearances are made.

CCH. An abbreviation for computerized criminal history.

Charge. A formal allegation that a specific person(s) has/have committed a specific offense(s).

Charging document. A formal written accusation, filed in a court, alleging that a specified person(s) has/have committed a specific offense(s).

Check fraud. The issuance or passing of a check, draft, or money order that is legal as a formal document, signed by the legal account holder but with the foreknowledge that the bank or depository will refuse to honor it because of insufficient funds or a closed account.

Chief of police. A local law enforcement officer who is the appointed or elected head of a police department.

Child abuse. Willful action or actions by a person causing physical harm to a child.

Child neglect. Willful failure by the person(s) responsible for a child's well-being to provide for adequate safety, food, clothing, shelter, education, and supervision.

Citation (to appear). A written order issued by a law enforcement officer directing an alleged offender to appear in a specific court at a specified time in order to answer a criminal charge.

Citizen dispute settlement. The settlement of interpersonal disputes by a third party or the courts. Charges arising from interpersonal disputes are mediated by a third party in an attempt to avoid prosecution. If an agreement between the parties cannot be reached and the complainant wishes to proceed with criminal processing, the case may be referred to court for settlement.

Commitment. The action of a judicial officer ordering that an adjudicated and sentenced adult, or adjudicated delinquent or status offender who has been the subject of a juvenile court disposition hearing, be admitted into a correctional facility.

Community facility (nonconfinement facility, adult or juvenile). A correctional facility from which residents are regularly permitted to depart, unaccompanied by an official, to use daily community resources such as schools or treatment programs, or to seek or hold employment.

Community service. A period of service to the community as a substitute for, or in partial satisfaction of, a fine. This disposition is generally a condition of a suspended or partially suspended sentence or of probation. The offender volunteers his or her services to a community agency for a certain number of hours per week over a specified period of time. The total number of hours, often assessed at the legal minimum wage, is determined by the amount of the fine that would have been imposed or that portion of the fine that is suspended.

Complaint. A formal written accusation made by any person, often a prosecutor, and filed in a court, alleging that a specified person(s) has/have committed a specific offense(s).

Complaint denied. The decision by a prosecutor to decline a request that he or she seek an indictment or file an information or complaint against a specified person(s) for a specific offense(s).

Complaint granted. The decision by a prosecutor to grant a request that he or she seek an indictment or file an information or complaint against a specified person(s) for a specific offense(s).

Complaint requested (police). A request by a law enforcement agency that the prosecutor seek an indictment or file a complaint or information against a specified person(s) for a specific offense(s).

Conditional diversion. At the pretrial stage, suspension of prosecution while specific conditions are met. If conditions are not satisfied during a specified time period, the case is referred for continued prosecution.

Conditional release. The release of a defendant who agrees to meet specified conditions in addition to appearing in court. Such conditions may include remaining in a defined geographical area, maintaining steady employment, avoiding contact with the victim or with associates in the alleged crime, avoiding certain activities or places, participating in treatment, or accepting services. Conditional release is often used in conjunction with third-party or supervised release.

Confinement facility. A correctional facility from which the inmates are not regularly permitted to depart each day unaccompanied.

Convict. An adult who has been found guilty of a felony and who is confined in a federal or state confinement facility.

Conviction. A judgment of a court, based either on the verdict of a jury or a judicial officer or on the guilty pleas of the defendant, that the defendant is guilty of the offense(s) for which he or she has been tried.

Correctional agency. A federal, state, or local criminal justice agency, under a single administrative authority, of which the principal functions are the investigation, intake screening, supervision, custody, confinement, or treatment of alleged or adjudicated adult offenders, delinquents, or status offenders.

Correctional day program. A publicly financed and operated nonresidential educational or treatment program for persons required, by a judicial officer, to participate.

Correctional facility. A building or part thereof, set of buildings, or area enclosing a set of buildings or structures operated and administrated by a government agency for the custody and/or treatment of adjudicated and committed persons, or persons subject to criminal or juvenile justice proceedings.

Correctional institution. A generic name proposed in this terminology for those long-term adult confinement facilities often called prisons, "federal or state correctional facilities," or "penitentiaries," and juvenile confinement facilities called "training schools," "reformatories," "boys, ranches," and the like.

Correctional institution, adult. A confinement facility having custodial authority over adults sentenced to confinement for more than a year.

Correctional institution, juvenile. A confinement facility having custodial authority over delinquents and status offenders committed to confinement after a juvenile disposition hearing.

Corrections. A generic term that includes all government agencies, facilities, programs, procedures, personnel, and techniques concerned with the investigation, intake, custody, confinement, supervision, or treatment of alleged or adjudicated adult offenders, delinquents, or status offenders.

Count. Each separate offense, attributed to one or more persons, as listed in a complaint, information, or indictment.

Count, institutional. A specific time in the day at which all inmates are counted physically, or are accounted for by documentation.

Counterfeiting The manufacture or attempted manufacture of a copy or imitation of a negotiable instrument with value set by law or convention, or the possession of such a copy without authorization, with the intent to defraud by claiming the copy's genuineness.

Court. An agency of the judicial branch of government, authorized or established by statute or constitution, and consisting of one or more judicial officers, which has the authority to decide on controversies in law and disputed matters of fact brought before it.

Court of appellate jurisdiction. A court that does not try criminal cases but that hears appeals.

Court of general jurisdiction. Of criminal courts, a court that has jurisdiction to try all criminal offenses, including all felonies, and that may or may not hear appeals.

Court of limited jurisdiction. Of criminal courts, a court of which the trial jurisdiction either includes no felonies or is limited to less than all felonies and which may or may not hear appeals.

Credit card fraud. The use or attempted use of a credit card in order to obtain goods or services with the intent to avoid payment.

Crime (criminal offense). An act committed or omitted in violation of a law forbidding or commanding it for which an adult can be punished, upon conviction, by incarceration and other penalties, or for which a corporation can be penalized, or for which a juvenile can be brought under the jurisdiction of a juvenile court and adjudicated a delinquent or transferred to adult court.

Crime Index offenses (index crimes). A Uniform Crime Reports (UCR) classification that includes all Part I offenses with the exception of involuntary (negligent) manslaughter.

Crimes against business (business crimes, commercial crimes). A summary term used by the National Crime Panel reports, including burglary and robbery (against businesses).

Crimes against households (household crimes). A summary term used by the National Crime Panel reports, including burglary (against households), household larceny, and motor vehicle theft.

Crimes against persons. A summary term used by UCR and the National Crime Panel NCP reports, but with different meanings:

> UCR
> Murder
> Nonnegligent (voluntary) manslaughter
> National Crime Panel
> Forcible rape
> Robbery (against persons)
> Aggravated assault
>
> NCP
> Negligent (involuntary) manslaughter

Forcible rape
Aggravatated assault
National Crime Panel
Simple Assault
Personal Larceny

Crimes against property (property crime). A summary term used by UCR, both as a subclass of the Part I offenses and as a subclass of Crime Index offenses, but with different meanings:

As a subset of UCR Part I offenses
Robbery
Burglary
Larceny—theft
Motor vehicle theft

As a subset of UCR Crime Index offenses
Burglary
Larceny—theft
Motor vehicle theft

Crimes of violence (violent crime). A summary term used by UCR and the National Crime Panel, but with different meanings:

As a subset of UCR Index Crimes
Murder
Nonnegligent (voluntary) manslaughter
Forcible rape
Robbery
Aggravated assault

As a subset of National Crime Panel crimes against persons
Forcible rape
Robbery (against persons)
Aggravated assault
Simple assault

Criminal history record information. Information collected by criminal justice agencies on individuals, consisting of identifiable descriptions and notations of arrests, detentions, indictments, informations, or other formal criminal charges, and any disposition(s) arising therefrom, including sentencing, correctional supervision, and release.

Criminal justice agency. Any court with criminal jurisdiction and any other government agency or subunit that defends indigents, or of which the principal functions or activities consist of the prevention, detection, and investigation of crime; the apprehension, detention, and prosecution of alleged offenders; the confinement or official correctional supervision of accused or convicted persons; or the administrative or technical support of the above functions.

Criminal proceedings. Proceedings in a court of law undertaken to determine the guilt or innocence of an adult accused of a crime.

Culpability. The state of mind of one who has committed an act that makes him or her liable to prosecution for that act.

Defendant. A person against whom a criminal proceeding is pending.

Defense attorney. An attorney, hired by the defendant or appointed by the court, who represents the defendant in a legal proceeding.

Delinquency. Juvenile actions or conduct in violation of criminal law and, in some contexts, status offenses.

Delinquent. A juvenile who has been adjudicated by a judicial officer of a juvenile court as having committed a delinquent act, which is an act for which an adult could be prosecuted in a criminal court.

Delinquent act. An act committed by a juvenile for which an adult could be prosecuted in a criminal court but for which a juvenile can be adjudicated in a juvenile court or prosecuted in a criminal court if the juvenile court transfers jurisdiction.

De novo. Anew, afresh, as if there had been no earlier decision.

Dependency. The legal status of a juvenile over whom a juvenile court has assumed jurisdiction because the court has found his or her care by parent, guardian, or custodian to fall short of a legal standard of proper care.

Dependent. A juvenile over whom a juvenile court has assumed jurisdiction because the court has found his or her care by parent, guardian, or custodian to fall short of a legal standard of proper care.

Detention. The legally authorized holding in confinement of a person subject to criminal or juvenile court proceedings until the point of commitment to a correctional facility or release.

Detention center. A government facility that provides temporary care in a physically restricting environment for juveniles in custody pending court disposition.

Detention facility. A generic name proposed in this terminology as a cover term for those facilities that hold adults or juveniles in confinement pending adjudication, adults sentenced for a year or less of confinement, and in some instances postadjudicated juveniles, including facilities called "jails," "county farms," "honor farms," "work camps," "road camps," "detention centers," "shelters," "juvenile halls," and the like.

Detention facility, adult. A confinement facility of which the custodial authority is forty-eight hours or more and in which adults can be confined before adjudication or for sentences of a year or less.

Detention facility, juvenile. A confinement facility having custodial authority over juveniles confined pending, and, after adjudication.

Detention hearing. In juvenile proceedings, a hearing by a judicial officer of a juvenile court to determine whether a juvenile is to be detained, to continue to be detained, or to be released, while juvenile proceedings are pending in his or her case.

Diagnosis or classification center. A functional unit within a correctional institution, or a separate facility, that evaluates persons held in custody in order to determine to which correctional facility or program they should be committed.

Dismissal. A decision by a judicial officer to terminate a case without a determination of guilt or innocence.

Disposition. The action by a criminal or juvenile justice agency that signifies that a portion of the justice process is complete and jurisdiction is relinquished or transferred to another agency or that signifies that a decision has been reached on one aspect of a case and a different aspect comes under consideration, requiring a different kind of decision.

Disposition, court. The final judicial decision, which terminates a criminal proceeding by a judgment of acquittal or dismissal, or which states the specific sentence in the case of a conviction.

Disposition hearing. A hearing in juvenile court, conducted after an adjudicatory hearing and subsequent receipt of the report of any predisposition investigation, to determine the most appropriate disposition of a juvenile who has been adjudicated a delinquent, a status offender, or a dependent.

Disposition, juvenile court. The decision of a juvenile court, concluding a disposition hearing, that a juvenile be committed to a correctional facility, placed in a care or treatment program, required to meet certain standards of conduct, or released.

Diversion. The official halting or suspension, at any legally prescribed processing point after a recorded justice system entry, of formal criminal or juvenile justice proceedings against an alleged offender, and referral of that person to a treatment or care program administered by a nonjustice agency or a private agency, or no referral.

Driving under the influence—alcohol (drunk driving). The operation of any vehicle after having consumed a quantity of alcohol sufficient to potentially interfere with the ability to maintain safe operation. This is usually determined by a blood alcohol reading high enough to ascertain the status of being legally drunk in that jurisdiction.

Driving under the influence—drugs. The operation of any vehicle while attention or ability is impaired through the intake of a narcotic or an incapacitating quantity of another drug.

Drug law violation. The unlawful sale, transport, manufacture, cultivation, possession, or use of a controlled or prohibited drug.

Early release. Release from confinement before the sentence has been completed. Early release to supervision means less jail time and, with more rapid turnover, lower jail populations and capacity requirements. Early release may come about through parole, time off for good behavior or work performed, or modification of the sentence by the court. The last procedure is usually associated with sentences to jail with a period of probation to follow. Although there are some objections to its use, "probation with jail" is a common disposition in some jurisdictions. More often than not, these sentences are in lieu of a state prison term.

Embezzlement. The misappropriation, misapplication, or illegal disposal of legally entrusted property with intent to defraud the legal owner or intended beneficiary.

Escape. The unlawful departure of a lawfully confined person from a confinement facility or from custody while being transported.

Expunge. The sealing or purging of arrest, criminal, or juvenile record information.

Extortion. Unlawful obtaining or attempting to obtain the property of another by the threat of eventual injury or harm to that person, the person's property, or another person.

Felony. A criminal offense punishable by death or by incarceration in a state or federal confinement facility for a period of which the lower limit is prescribed by statute in a given jurisdiction, typically one year or more.

Field citation. Citation and release in the field by police as an alternative to booking and pretrial detention. This practice reduces law enforcement costs as well as jail costs.

Filing. The commencement of criminal proceedings by entering a charging document into a court's official record.

Finding. The official determination of a judicial officer or administrative body regarding a disputed matter of fact or law.

Fine. The penalty imposed on a convicted person by a court requiring that he or she pay a specified sum of money. The fine is a cash payment of a dollar amount assessed by the judge in an individual case or determined by a published schedule of penalties. Fines may be paid in installments in many jurisdictions.

Forgery. The creation or alteration of a written or printed document that, if validly executed, would constitute a record of a legally binding transaction, with the intent to defraud by affirming it to be the act of an unknowing second person. Defining features: Making or altering a written or printed document or record. Act being falsely attributed to an unknowing second person. Intent being to deprive illegally a person of property or legal rights.

Fraud. An element of certain offenses consisting of deceit or intentional misrepresentation with the aim of illegally depriving a person of property or legal rights.

Fugitive. A person who has concealed himself or herself or fled a given jurisdiction in order to avoid prosecution or confinement.

Group home. A nonconfining residential facility for adjudicated adults or juveniles or those subject to criminal or juvenile proceedings, intended to reproduce as closely as possible the circumstances of family life and at the minimum, providing access to community activities and resources.

Recommended conditions of use.

Classify government facilities fitting this definition as *community facilities.*
Annotation.

Group home is variously defined in different jurisdictions. Most of the facilities known by this name are privately operated, though they may be financed mainly from government funds. Classification problems unique to private facilities have not been dealt with in this terminology, although most recommended standard descriptors for publicly operated facilities are also applicable to the private sector. See *correctional facility* for recommended standard descriptors. The LEAA (Law Enforcement Assistance Administration) series "Children in Custody" defines *group home* as one which allows juveniles extensive contact with the community, such as through jobs and schools, so long as none or fewer than half are placed there on probation or "aftercare/parole." It is distinguished from *halfway house* in this series by the percentage of residents on probation or parole.

Halfway house. A nonconfining residential facility for adjudicated adults or juveniles or those subject to criminal or juvenile proceedings, intended as an alternative to confinement for persons not suited for probation or needing a period of readjustment to the community after confinement.

Recommended conditions of use.

Classify government facilities fitting this definition as *community facilities*.

Annotation.

Halfway house is variously defined in different jurisdictions. Most of the facilities known by this name are privately operated, though they may be financed mainly from government funds. Classification problems unique to private facilities have not been dealt with in this terminology, although most recommended standard descriptors for publicly operated facilities are also applicable to the private sector. See *correctional facility* for recommended standard descriptors. The series "Children in Custody" defines *halfway house* as one which has 50 percent or more juveniles on probation or aftercare/parole, allowing them extensive contact with the community, such as through "jobs and schools." It is distinguished from *group home* in this series by the percentage of residents on probation or parole.

Hearing. A proceeding in which arguments, evidence, or witnesses are heard by a judicial officer or administrative body.

Hearing, probable cause. A proceeding before a judicial officer in which arguments, evidence, or witnesses are presented and in which it is determined whether there is sufficient cause to hold the accused for trial or whether the case should be dismissed.

Homicide. Any killing of one person by another.

Homicide, criminal. The causing of the death of another person without justification or excuse. *Equivalent terms* (defined for the Uniform Crime Reports): criminal homicide, murder (often used as a cover term for murder and nonnegligent manslaughter), nonnegligent manslaughter, voluntary manslaughter, negligent manslaughter, and vehicular manslaughter.

Homicide, excusable. The intentional but justifiable causing of the death of another or the unintentional causing of the death of another by accident or misadventure, without gross negligence. Not a crime.

Homicide, justifiable. The intentional causing of the death of another in the legal performance of an official duty or in the circumstances defined by law as constituting legal justification. Not a crime.

Homicide, willful. The intentional causing of the death of another person, with or without legal justification.

Indictment. A formal written accusation made by a grand jury and filed in a court, alleging that a specified person(s) has/have committed a specific offense(s).

Information. A written formal accusation, filed in a court by a prosecutor, that alleges a specific person has committed a specific offense.

Infraction. An offense punishable by fine or other penalty, but not by incarceration.

Inmate. A person in custody in a jail or correctional institution.

Institutional capacity. The officially stated number of inmates or residents that a correctional facility is designed to house, exclusive of extraordinary arrangements to accommodate overcrowded conditions.

Intake. The process during which a juvenile referral is received and a decision is made by an intake unit to file a petition in juvenile court, to release the juvenile, to place the juvenile under supervision, or to refer the juvenile elsewhere.

Intake unit. A government agency or agency subunit that receives juvenile referrals from police, other government agencies, private agencies, or persons and screens them, resulting in closing of the case, referral to care or supervision, or filing of a petition in juvenile court.

Jail. A confinement facility, usually administered by a local law enforcement agency, intended for adults but sometimes also containing juveniles, that holds persons detained pending adjudication and/or persons committed after adjudication for sentences of a year or less.

Jail (sentence). The penalty of commitment to the jurisdiction of a confinement facility system for adults, of which the custodial authority is generally limited to persons sentenced to a year or less of confinement.

Judge. A judicial officer who has been elected or appointed to preside over a court of law, whose position has been created by statute or by constitution and whose decisions in criminal and juvenile cases may only be reviewed by a judge or a higher court and may not be reviewed *de novo*.

Judgment. The statement of the decision of a court that the defendant is convicted or acquitted of the offense(s) charged.

Judicial officer. Any person exercising judicial powers in a court of law.

Jurisdiction. The territory, subject matter, or person over which lawful authority may be exercised.

Jurisdiction, original. The lawful authority of a court or an administrative agency to hear or act upon a case from its beginning and to pass judgment on it.

Jury, grand. A body of persons who have been selected and sworn to investigate criminal activity and the conduct of public officials and to hear the evidence against an accused person(s) to determine whether there is sufficient evidence to bring that person(s) to trial.

Jury, trial (jury, petit; jury). A statutorily defined number of persons selected according to law and sworn to determine certain matters of fact in a criminal action and to render a verdict of guilty or not guilty.

Juvenile. A person subject to juvenile court proceedings because a statutorily defined event was alleged to have occurred while his or her age was below the statutorily specified limit of original jurisdiction of a juvenile court.

> *Annotation.*
> Jurisdiction is determined by age at the time of the event, not at the time of judicial proceedings, and continues until the case is terminated. Thus a person may be described in a given data system as a juvenile because he or she is still subject to juvenile court proceedings, even though his or her actual age may be several years over the limit. Conversely, criminal process data systems may include juveniles if the juvenile court has waived jurisdiction. Although the age limit varies in different states, it is most often the eighteenth birthday. The variation is small enough to permit nationally aggregated data to be meaningful, although individual states

should note their age limit in communications with other states. The UCR defines a juvenile as anyone under eighteen years of age. See *youthful offender.*

Juvenile court. A cover term for courts that have original jurisdiction over persons statutorily defined as juveniles and alleged to be delinquents, status offenders, or dependents.

Juvenile justice agency. A government agency, or subunit thereof, of which the functions are the investigation, supervision, adjudication, care or confinement of juveniles whose conduct or condition has brought or could bring them within the jurisdiction of a juvenile court.

Juvenile record. An official record containing, at a minimum, summary information pertaining to an identified juvenile concerning juvenile court proceedings, and, if applicable, detention and correctional processes.

Kidnapping. Unlawful transportation of a person without his or her consent or without the consent of his or her guardian, if a minor.

Larceny (larceny-theft). Unlawful taking or attempted taking of property, other than a motor vehicle, from the possession of another.

Law enforcement agency. A federal, state, or local criminal justice agency of which the principal functions are the prevention, detection, and investigation of crime and the apprehension of alleged offenders.

Law enforcement agency, federal. A law enforcement agency that is an organizational unit, or subunit, of the federal government.

Law enforcement agency, local. A law enforcement agency that is an organizational unit, or subunit, of local (county, city, borough) government.

Law enforcement agency, state. A law enforcement agency that is an organizational unit, or subunit, of state government.

Law enforcement officer (peace officer, police officer). An employee of a law enforcement agency who is an officer sworn to carry out law enforcement duties or is a sworn employee of a federal prosecutorial agency who primarily performs investigative duties.

Law enforcement officer, federal. An employee of a federal law enforcement agency who is an officer sworn to carry out law enforcement duties or is a sworn employee of a federal prosecutorial agency who primarily performs investigative duties.

Law enforcement officer, local. An employee of a local law enforcement agency who is an officer sworn to carry out law enforcement duties or is a sworn employee of a local prosecutorial agency who primarily performs investigative duties.

Law enforcement officer, state. An employee of a state law enforcement agency who is an officer sworn to carry out law enforcement duties or is a sworn employee of a state prosecutorial agency who primarily performs investigative duties.

Level of government. The federal, state, regional, or local county or city location of administrative and major funding responsibility of a given agency.

Manslaughter, involuntary (negligent manslaughter). Causing the death of another by recklessness or gross negligence.

Manslaughter, vehicular. Causing the death of another by the grossly negligent operation of a motor vehicle.

Manslaughter, voluntary (nonnegligent manslaughter). Intentionally causing the death of another with reasonable provocation.

Misdemeanor. An offense usually punishable by incarceration in a local confinement facility for a period of which the upper limit is prescribed by statute in a given jurisdiction, typically limited to a year or less.

Model Penal Code. A generalized modern codification of that which is considered basic to criminal law, published by the American Law Institute in 1962.

Monitored release. Recognizance release with the addition of minimal supervision of service; that is, the defendant may be required to keep a pretrial services agency informed of his or her whereabouts, and the agency reminds the defendant of court dates and verifies the defendant's appearance.

Motion. An oral or written request made by a party to an action, before, during, or after a trial, that a court issue a rule or order.

Motor vehicle theft. Unlawful taking, or attempted taking, of a motor vehicle owned by another with the intent to deprive the owner of it permanently or temporarily.

Murder. Intentionally causing the death of another without reasonable provocation or legal justification, or causing the death of another while committing or attempting to commit another crime.

Nolo contendere. A defendant's formal answer in court to the charges in a complaint, information, or indictment in which the defendant states that he or she does not contest the charges and which, though not an admission of guilt, subjects the defendant to the same legal consequences as does a plea of guilty.

Offender (criminal). An adult who has been convicted of a criminal offense.

Offender, alleged. A person who has been charged with a specific criminal offense(s) by a law enforcement agency or court but has not been convicted.

Offense. An act committed or omitted in violation of a law forbidding or commanding it.

Offenses, Part I. A class of offenses selected for use in UCR, consisting of those crimes that are most likely to be reported, that occur with sufficient frequency to provide an adequate basis for comparison, and that are serious crimes by nature and/or volume.

> *Annotation.*
> The Part I offenses are:
> 1. Criminal homicide.
>   a. Murder and nonnegligent (voluntary) manslaughter
>   b. Manslaughter by negligence (involuntary manslaughter)
> 2. Forcible rape
>   a. Rape by force
>   b. Attempted forcible rape
> 3. Robbery
>   a. Firearm
>   b. Knife or cutting instrument

        c. Other dangerous weapon

        d. Strongarm

  4. Aggravated Assault

        a. Firearm

        b. Knife or cutting instrument

        c. Other dangerous weapon

        d. Hands, fist, feet, etc.—aggravated injury

  5. Burglary

        a. Forcible entry

        b. Unlawful entry—no force

        c. Attempted forcible entry

  6. Larceny-theft (larceny)

  7. Motor vehicle theft

        a. Autos

        b. Trucks and buses

        c. Other vehicles

  8. Arson

Offenses, Part II. A class of offenses selected for use in UCR, consisting of specific offenses and types of offenses that do not meet the criteria of frequency and/or seriousness necessary for Part I offenses.

  Annotation.

The Part II offenses are:

    Other assaults (simple,* nonaggravated)

    Arson*

    Forgery* and counterfeiting*

    Fraud*

    Embezzlement*

    Stolen property: buying, receiving, possessing

    Vandalism

    Weapons; carrying, possessing, etc.

    Prostitution and commercialized vice

    Sex offenses (except forcible rape, prostitution, and commercialized vice)

    Narcotic drug law violations

    Gambling

    Offenses against the family and children

    Driving under the influence*

    Liquor law violations

    Drunkenness

    Disorderly conduct

    Vagrancy

    All other offenses (except traffic law violations)

    Suspicion*

    Curfew and loitering law violations (juvenile violations)

    Runaway* (juveniles)

Terms marked with an asterisk (*) are defined in this glossary, though not necessarily in accord with UCR usage. The UCR does not collect reports of Part II offenses. Arrest data concerning such offenses, however, are collected and published.

Pardon. An act of executive clemency that absolves the party in part or in full from the legal consequences of the crime and conviction.

Annotation.

Pardons can be full or conditional. The former generally applies to both the punishment and the guilt of the offender and blots out the existence of guilt in the eyes of the law. It also removes his or her disabilities and restores civil rights. The conditional pardon generally falls short of the remedies of the full pardon, is an expression of guilt, and does not obliterate the conviction. (U.S. Supreme Court decisions on pardons and their effects are directly contradictory, and thus state laws usually govern pardons.)

Parole. The status of an offender conditionally released from a confinement facility, prior to the expiration of his or her sentence, and placed under the supervision of a parole agency.

Parole agency. A correctional agency, which may or may not include a parole authority and of which the principal function is the supervision of adults or juveniles placed on parole.

Parole authority. A person or a correctional agency that has the authority to release on parole those adults or juveniles committed to confinement facilities, to revoke parole, and to discharge from parole.

Parolee. A person who has been conditionally released from a correctional institution before the expiration of his or her sentence and who has been placed under the supervision of a parole agency.

Parole violation. A parolee's act or a failure to act that does not conform to the conditions of his or her parole.

Partial confinement. An alternative to the traditional jail sentence, consisting of "weekend" sentences, that permit offenders to spend the work week in the community, with their families, and at their jobs; furloughs, which enable offenders to leave the jail for a period of a few hours to a few days for specified purposes—to seek employment, take care of personal matters or family obligations, or engage in community service; or work/study release, under which offenders work or attend school during the day and return to the detention facility at night and on weekends.

Penalty. The punishment annexed by law or judicial decision to the commission of a particular offense, which may be death, imprisonment, fine, or loss of civil privileges.

Percentage bail. A publicly managed bail service arrangement that requires the defendant to deposit a percentage (typically 10 percent) of the amount of bail with the court clerk. The deposit is returned to the defendant after scheduled court appearances are made, although a charge (usually 1 percent) may be deducted to help defray program costs.

Person. A human being, or a group of human beings considered a legal unit, which has the lawful capacity to defend rights, incur obligations, prosecute claims, or be prosecuted or adjudicated.

Personally secured bail. Security that is put up by the defendant or the defendant's family. This arrangement is generally out of reach of the less affluent defendant.

Petition (juvenile). A document filed in juvenile court alleging that a juvenile is a delinquent, a status offender, or a dependent and asking that the court assume jurisdiction over the juvenile or that the juvenile be transferred to a criminal court for prosecution as an adult.

Petition not sustained. The finding by a juvenile court in an adjudicatory hearing that there is not sufficient evidence to sustain an allegation that a juvenile is a delinquent, status offender, or dependent.

Plea. A defendant's formal answer in court to the charges brought against him or her in a complaint, information, or indictment.

Plea bargaining. The exchange of prosecutorial and/or judicial concessions, commonly a lesser charge, the dismissal of other pending charges, a recommendation by the prosecutor for a reduced sentence or a combination thereof, in return for a plea of guilty.

Plea, final. The last plea to a given charge, entered in a court record by or for a defendant.

Plea, guilty. A defendant's formal answer in court to the charges in a complaint, information, or indictment, in which the defendant states that the charges are true and that he or she has committed the offense as charged.

Plea, initial. The first plea to a given charge, entered in a court record by or for a defendant.

Plea, not guilty. A defendant's formal answer in court to the charges in a complaint, information, or indictment, in which the defendant states that he or she is not guilty.

Police department. A local law enforcement agency directed by a chief of police or a commissioner.

Police officer. A local law enforcement officer employed by a police department.

Population movement. Entries and exits of adjudicated persons, or persons subject to judicial proceedings, into or from correctional facilities or programs.

Predisposition report. The document resulting from an investigation by a probation agency or other designated authority, which has been requested by a juvenile court, into the past behavioral, family background, and personality of a juvenile who has been adjudicated a delinquent, a status offender, or a dependent, in order to assist the court in determining the most appropriate disposition.

Presentence report. The document resulting from an investigation undertaken by a probation agency or other designated authority, at the request of a criminal court, into the past behavior, family circumstances, and personality of an adult who has been convicted of a crime, in order to assist the court in determining the most appropriate sentence.

Prior record. Criminal history record information concerning any law enforcement, court, or correctional proceedings that have occurred before the current investigation of, or proceedings against, a person; or statistical descriptions of the criminal histories of a set of persons.

Prison. A confinement facility having custodial authority over adults sentenced to confinement for more than a year.

Prisoner. A person in custody in a confinement facility or in the personal custody of a criminal justice official while being transported to or between confinement facilities.

Prison (sentence). The penalty of commitment to the jurisdiction of a confinement facility system for adults, whose custodial authority extends to persons sentenced to more than a year of confinement.

Privately secured bail. An arrangement similar to the bail bondsman system except that bail is provided without cost to the defendant. A private organization provides bail for indigent arrestees who meet its eligibility requirements.

Probable cause. A set of facts and circumstances that would induce a reasonably intelligent and prudent person to believe that an accused person had committed a specific crime.

Probation. The conditional freedom granted by a judicial officer to an alleged offender, or adjudicated adult or juvenile, as long as the person meets certain conditions of behavior. One requirement is to report to a designated person or agency over some specified period of time. Probation may contain special conditions, as discussed in the definition of suspended sentence. Probation often includes a suspended sentence but may be used in association with the suspension of a final judgment or a deferral of sentencing.

Probation agency (probation department). A correctional agency of which the principal functions are juvenile intake, the supervision of adults and juveniles placed on probation status, and the investigation of adults or juveniles for the purpose of preparing presentence or predisposition reports to assist the court in determining the proper sentence or juvenile court disposition.

Probationer. A person required by a court or probation agency to meet certain conditions of behavior and who may or may not be placed under the supervision of a probation agency.

Probation officer. An employee of a probation agency whose primary duties include one or more of the probation agency functions.

Probation (sentence). A court requirement that a person fulfill certain conditions of behavior and accept the supervision of a probation agency, usually in lieu of a sentence to confinement but sometimes including a jail sentence.

Probation violation. An act or a failure to act by a probationer who does not conform to the conditions of his or her probation.

Prosecutor. An attorney employed by a government agency or subunit whose official duty is to initiate and maintain criminal proceedings on behalf of the government against persons accused of committing criminal offenses.

Prosecutorial agency. A federal, state, or local criminal justice agency whose principal function is the prosecution of alleged offenders.

Pro se (in propria persona). Acting as one's own defense attorney in criminal proceedings; representing oneself.

Public defender. An attorney employed by a government agency or subdivision, whose official duty is to represent defendants unable to hire private counsel.

Public defender's office. A federal, state, or local criminal justice agency or subunit of which the principal function is to represent defendants unable to hire private counsel.

Purge (record). The complete removal of arrest, criminal, or juvenile record information from a given records system.

Rape. Unlawful sexual intercourse with a person, by force or threat of force, without legal or factual consent.

Rape, forcible. Sexual intercourse or attempted sexual intercourse with a person against her/his will, by force or threat of force.

Rape, statutory. Sexual intercourse with a person who has consented in fact but is deemed, because of age, to be legally incapable of consent.

Rape without force or consent. Sexual intercourse with a person legally of the age of consent but who is unconscious or whose ability to judge or control his/her conduct is inherently impaired by mental defect or intoxicating substances.

Recidivism. The repetition of criminal behavior; habitual criminality.

Annotation:

In statistical practice, a recidivism rate may be any of a number of possible counts of instances of arrest, conviction, correctional commitment, and correctional status changes, related to the number of repetitions of these events within a given period of time. Efforts to arrive at a single standard statistical description of recidivism have been hampered by the fact that the term's correct referent is the actual repeated criminal or delinquent behavior of a given person or group; yet the only available statistical indicators of that behavior are records of such system events as rearrests, reconvictions, and probation or parole violations or revocations. It is recognized that these data reflect agency decisions about events and may or may not closely correspond with actual criminal behavior. Different conclusions about degrees of correspondence between system decisions and actual behavior consequently produce different definitions of recidivism, that is, different judgments of which system event repetition rates best measure actual recidivism rates. This is an empirical question, and not one of definition to be resolved solely by analysis of language usage and system logic. Resolution has also been delayed by the limited capacities of most criminal justice statistical systems, which do not routinely make available the standardized offender-based transaction data (OBTD) that may be needed for the best measurement of recidivism. Pending the adoption of a standard statistical description of recidivism and the ability to implement it, it is recommended that recidivism analyses include the widest possible range of system events that can correspond with actual recidivism and that sufficient detail of offenses charged be included to enable discrimination among degrees of gravity of offenses. The units of count should be clearly identified and the length of community exposure time of the subject population stated.

Recidivism is measured by: (1) criminal acts that resulted in a conviction by a court, when committed by individuals who are under correctional supervision or who have been released from correctional supervision within the previous three years, and by (2) technical violations of probation or parole in which a sentencing or paroling authority took action that resulted in an adverse change in the offender's "legal status."

Neither of these formulations is endorsed as adequate for all purposes. Both limit the measure and concept of recidivism to populations that are or have been under correctional supervision. Yet the ultimate significance of data concerning the repetition of criminal behavior often depends on the comparison of the behavior of unconfined or unsupervised offenders with the behavior of those with correctional experience.

Referral to intake. In juvenile proceedings, a request by the police, parents, or other agency or person that a juvenile intake unit take appropriate action concerning a juvenile alleged to have committed a delinquent act or status offense or to be dependent.

Release from detention. The authorized exit from detention of a person subject to criminal or juvenile justice proceedings.

Release from prison. A cover term for all lawful exits from federal or state confinement facilities primarily intended for adults serving sentences of more than a year, including all conditional and unconditional releases, deaths, and transfers to other jurisdictions, excluding escapes.

> Transfer of jurisdiction
> Release on parole
> Conditional release
> Release while still under jurisdiction of correctional
>   agency, before expiration of sentence
> *Discretionary*
> Release date determined by parole authority
> *Mandatory*
> Release date determined by statute
> Discharge from prison
> Release ending all agency jurisdiction
> Unconditional release
> *Discretionary*
> Pardon, commutation of sentence
> *Mandatory*
> Expiration of sentence
> Temporary release
> Authorized, unaccompanied temporary departure
>   for educational, employment, or other authorized purposes
> Transfer of jurisdiction
> Transfer to jurisdiction of another correctional agency or a court
> Death
> Death from homicide, suicide, or natural causes
> Execution
> Execution of sentence of death

In some systems release on "parole" represents only discretionary conditional release. It is recommended that mandatory conditional releases be included, as both types describe conditional releases with subsequent parole status.

Release on bail. The release by a judicial officer of an accused person who has been taken into custody, upon the accused's promise to pay a certain sum of money or property if he or she fails to appear in court as required, a promise that may or may not be secured by the deposit of an actual sum of money or property.

Release on own recognizance. The release, by a judicial officer, of an accused person who has been taken into custody, upon the accused's promise to appear in court as required for criminal proceedings.

Release, pretrial. A procedure whereby an accused person who has been taken into custody is allowed to be free before and during his or her trial.

Release to third party. The release, by a judicial officer, of an accused person who has been taken into custody, to a third party who promises to return the accused to court for criminal proceedings.

Residential treatment center. A government facility that serves juveniles whose behavior does not necessitate the strict confinement of a training school, often allowing them greater contact with the community.

Restitution. Usually a cash payment by the offender to the victim of an amount considered to offset the loss incurred by the victim or the community. The amount of the payment may be scaled down to the offender's earning capacity, and/or payments may be made in installments. Sometimes services directly or indirectly benefiting the victim may be substituted for cash payment.

Retained counsel. An attorney, not employed or compensated by a government agency or subunit or assigned by the court, who is privately hired to represent a person(s) in a criminal proceeding.

Revocation. An administrative act performed by a parole authority removing a person from parole, or a judicial order by a court removing a person from parole or probation, in response to a violation by the parolee or probationer.

Revocation hearing. An administrative and/or judicial hearing on the question of whether or not a person's probation or parole status should be revoked.

Rights of defendant. Those powers and privileges that are constitutionally guaranteed to every defendant.

Robbery. The unlawful taking or attempted taking of property that is in the immediate possession of another, by force or the threat of force.

Robbery, armed. The unlawful taking or attempted taking of property that is in the immediate possession of another, by the use or threatened use of a deadly or dangerous weapon.

Robbery, strongarm. The unlawful taking or attempted taking of property that is in the immediate possession of another by the use or threatened use of force, without the use of a weapon.

Runaway. A juvenile who has been adjudicated by a judicial officer of a juvenile court as having committed the status offense of leaving the custody and home of his or her parents, guardians, or custodians without permission and failing to return within a reasonable length of time.

Seal (record). The removal, for the benefit of the subject, of arrest, criminal, or juvenile record information from routinely available status to a status requiring special procedures for access.

Security. The degree of restriction of inmate movement within a correctional facility, usually divided into maximum, medium, and minimum levels.

Security and privacy standards. A set of principles and procedures developed to ensure the security and confidentiality of criminal or juvenile record information in order to protect the privacy of the persons identified in such records.

Sentence. The penalty imposed by a court on a convicted person, or the court decision to suspend imposition or execution of the penalty.

Sentence, indeterminate. A statutory provision for a type of sentence to imprisonment in which, after the court has determined that the convicted person shall be imprisoned, the exact length of imprisonment and parole supervision is afterward fixed within statutory limits by a parole authority.

Sentence, mandatory. A statutory requirement that a certain penalty shall be imposed and executed upon certain convicted offenders.

Sentence, suspended. The court decision postponing the pronouncement of sentence upon a convicted person or postponing the execution of a sentence that has been pronounced by the court.

Sentence, suspended execution. The court decision setting a penalty but postponing its execution.

Sentence, suspended imposition. The court decision postponing the setting of a penalty.

Shelter. A confinement or community facility for the care of juveniles, usually those held pending adjudication.

Sheriff. The elected or appointed chief officer of a county law enforcement agency, usually responsible for law enforcement in unincorporated areas and for operation of the county jail.

Sheriff, deputy. A law enforcement officer employed by a county sheriff's department.

Sheriff's department. A law enforcement agency organized at the county level, directed by a sheriff, that exercises its law enforcement functions at the county level, usually within unincorporated areas, and operates the county jail in most jurisdictions.

Speedy trial. The right of the defendant to have a prompt trial.

State highway patrol. A state law enforcement agency whose principal functions are the prevention, detection, and investigation of motor vehicle offenses and the apprehension of traffic offenders.

State highway patrol officer. An employee of a state highway patrol who is an officer sworn to carry out law enforcement duties, primarily traffic code enforcement.

State police. A state law enforcement agency whose principal functions may include maintaining statewide police communications, aiding local police in criminal investigations, training police, guarding state property, and patroling highways.

State police officer. An employee of a state police agency who is an officer sworn to carry out law enforcement duties, sometimes including traffic enforcement duties.

Stationhouse citation. An alternative to pretrial detention, whereby the arrestee is escorted to the precinct police station or headquarters rather than the pretrial detention facility. Release, which may occur before or after booking, is contingent upon the defendant's written promise to appear in court as specified on the release form.

Status offender. A juvenile who has been adjudicated by a judicial officer of a juvenile court as having committed a status offense, which is an act or conduct that is an offense only when committed or engaged in by a juvenile.

Status offense. An act or conduct that is declared by statute to be an offense, but only when committed or engaged in by a juvenile, and that can be adjudicated only by a juvenile court.

Subjudicial officer. A judicial officer who is invested with certain judicial powers and functions but whose decisions in criminal and juvenile cases are subject to *de novo* review by a judge.

Subpoena. A written order issued by a judicial officer requiring a specified person to appear in a designated court at a specified time in order to serve as a witness in a case under the jurisdiction of that court or to bring material to that court.

Summons. A written order issued by a judicial officer requiring a person accused of a criminal offense to appear in a designated court at a specified time to answer the charge(s). The summons is a request or instruction to appear in court to face an accusation. As an alternative to the arrest warrant, it is used in cases on which complaints are registered with the magistrate or prosecutor's office.

Supervised release. A type of release requiring more frequent contact than monitored release does. Typically, various conditions are imposed and supervision is aimed at enforcing these conditions and providing services as needed. Some form of monetary bail also may be attached as a condition of supervised release, especially in higher-risk cases.

Suspect. A person, adult or juvenile, considered by a criminal justice agency to be one who may have committed a specific criminal offense but who has not been arrested or charged.

Suspended sentence. Essentially a threat to take more drastic action if the offender again commits a crime during some specified time period. When no special conditions are attached, it is assumed that the ends of justice have been satisfied by conviction and no further action is required, as long as the offender refrains from involvement in new offenses. Suspended sentences may be conditioned on various limitations as to mobility, associates, or activities or on requirements to make reparations or participate in some rehabilitation program.

Suspicion. Belief that a person has committed a criminal offense, based on facts and circumstances that are not sufficient to constitute probable cause.

Theft. Larceny, or in some legal classifications, the group of offenses including larceny, and robbery, burglary, extortion, fraudulent offenses, hijacking, and other offenses sharing the element of larceny.

Third-party release. A release extending to another person the responsibility for ensuring the defendant's appearance in court. This may be a person known to the defendant or a designated volunteer. Third-party release may be a condition of unsecured bail, with the third party as a cosigner.

Time served. The total time spent in confinement by a convicted adult before and after sentencing, or only the time spent in confinement after a sentence of commitment to a confinement facility.

Training school. A correctional institution for juveniles adjudicated to be delinquents or status offenders and committed to confinement by a judicial officer.

Transfer hearing. A preadjudicatory hearing in juvenile court in order to determine whether juvenile court jurisdiction should be retained or waived for a juvenile alleged to have committed a delinquent act(s) and whether he or she should be transferred to criminal court for prosecution as an adult ("bound over").

Transfer to adult court. The decision by a juvenile court, resulting from a transfer hearing, that jurisdiction over an alleged delinquent will be waived and that he or she should be prosecuted as an adult in a criminal court.

Trial. The examination of issues of fact and law in a case or controversy, beginning when the jury has been selected in a jury trial, the first witness is sworn, or the first evidence is introduced in a court trial and concluding when a verdict is reached or the case is dismissed.

Trial, court (trial, judge). A trial in which there is no jury and a judicial officer determines the issues of fact and law in a case.

Trial, jury. A trial in which a jury determines the issues of fact in a case.

UCR. An abbreviation for the Federal Bureau of Investigation's Uniform Crime Reports Program, published each year and based on voluntary reports from law enforcement agencies nationwide.

Unconditional discharge. As a posttrial disposition, essentially the same as unconditional diversion. No savings are obtained in criminal justice processing costs, but jail populations may be reduced; conditions of release are imposed for an offense in which the defendant's involvement has been established.

Unconditional diversion. The cessation of criminal processing at any point short of adjudication with no continuing threat of prosecution. This type of diversion may be a voluntary referral to a social service agency or program dealing with a problem underlying the offense.

Unsecured bail. A form of release differing from release on recognizance only in that the defendant is subject to paying the amount of bail if he or she defaults. Unsecured bail permits release without a deposit or purchase of a bondsman's services.

Venue. The geographical area from which the jury is drawn and in which trial is held in a criminal action.

Verdict. In criminal proceedings, the decision made by a jury or judicial officer in a court trial, that a defendant is either guilty or not guilty of the offense(s) for which he or she has been tried.

Verdict, guilty. In criminal proceedings, the decision made by a jury in a jury trial, or by a judicial officer in a court trial, that the defendant is guilty of the offense(s) for which he or she has been tried.

Verdict, not guilty. In criminal proceedings, the decision made by a jury in a jury trial, or by a judicial officer in a court trial, that the defendant is not guilty of the offense(s) for which he or she has been tried.

Victim. A person who has suffered death, physical or mental suffering, or loss of property as the result of an actual or attempted criminal offense committed by another person.

Warrant, arrest. A document issued by a judicial officer that directs a law enforcement officer to arrest a person who has been accused of an offense.

Warrant, bench. A document issued by a judicial officer directing that a person who has failed to obey an order or notice to appear be brought before the court.

Warrant, search. A document issued by a judicial officer that directs a law enforcement officer to conduct a search for specified property or persons at a specific location, to seize the property or persons, if found, and to account for the results of the search to the issuing judicial officer.

Witness. A person who directly perceives an event or thing or who has expert knowledge relevant to a case.

Youthful offender. A person, adjudicated in criminal court, who may be above the statutory age limit for juveniles but is below a specified upper age limit, for whom special correctional commitments and special record sealing procedures are made available by statute.

Index of Authors

C

D

Subject Index

First-generation jails, 165
First juvenile court, 327
First women's prison, 294
500 Delinquent Women (Glueck/Glueck), 308
Flogging, 9-11, 22, 37, 516
Flopped, use of term, 242
Florida Community Control Program (FCCP), 206-7
Folkways, 3-4
Food service, 506
Food service manager, 496
Forcible rape, 80, 82, 84, 192, 354
   See also Sex offenders
Ford v. Wainwright, 345
Formal criminal charge, filing of, 136-38
Fornication, 354
Fortune Society, 146
Fourteenth Amendment, 135, 136, 142, 144, 411
Fourth Amendment, 143, 333
Free will, 9
Friedensgeld, 7, 9
Frisk search, 462-63
Front-end solutions, and overcrowding, 196, 231, 246
Functionally literate, 497
Furloughs, 207, 456, 499, 558
   home, 379
   for male offenders, 279-80
Furman v. Georgia, 409, 411-13

Gangs, 325-26, 454-56, 596
Gaolbirds, 20-21
Gaols, 20-21
Gas chamber, 404
General Education Development (GED), 467, 497, 548
Geriatric inmates and offenders, 362-63
"Get right with God" concept, 7
Get-tough legislation, 65, 218
Gideon v. Wainwright, 135, 382
Girl Scouts Beyond Bars, 309
Glossary, 605-29
Goldbrickers, 492
Good-time credits, 126, 243
Good-time laws, 241
Good-time policies, 125, 127
Gothic-style monoliths, 227
Gradualism approach, 484
Grand jury, appearance before, 138
Great Law, The, 24-26
Gregg v. Georgia, 413
Grievance board, 386
Guilty but mentally ill (GBMI), 348

Habeas corpus, 478
Habitual-offender statutes, 108-9
Halfway houses, 109, 209, 429, 558-59, 563
Hammurabic Code, 5
Harrison Narcotic Act (1914), 538
Hawes-Cooper Act, 44-45
Health and medical services, 492-94
   cost of, 287
Health system administrator, 496
Hedonistic calculus, 18-19
Hepatitis A and B, 494
Hermanos de Pistoleros Latinos, 455
Heroin abuse, 284-85
Hierarchical management, 483
High-security institutions, 225-29, 516, 546
High-technology crimes, 597
HIV infection:
   and correctional staff, 360
   cost of treatment in prison, 362
   management of, in correctional facilities, 493
   in prisons, 359-62, 598-99
"Holdback" jail inmates, 265
Hole, the, *See* Solitary confinement
Home furloughs, 379
Hospice of San Michele, 19, 23-24
House arrest/home detention, 68, 200, 206-7
Hulks, 22-24
Human Cage, The, 226
Human law, 11

Illinois Penitentiary, 227
Imprisonment, 61, 69, 217-37
   classification, 222-25, 486-47
   cost of, 69
   crime statistics and, 92
   future of, 232-33
   maximum security prisons, 225-29
   medium and minimum security prisons, 229-31
   prison overcrowding:
      alternatives to, 231-32
      effects of, 222
   prison populations, 217-22
   rise in, 224
   for white-collar criminals, 88
   See also Correctional institutions;
      Jails; Prisons
Incapacitation, 58-61
   selective, 59
Incarceration:
   shock, 247-48
   See also Female offenders; Jails; Male offenders
Incarceration rates, 117
Incidence of crime, 77-97
Incompetency to stand trial, 109, 347
Indeterminate punishments, 66
Indeterminate sentencing, 38-39, 63, 116
Index crimes, 78, 82
Indiana Reform Institute for Women, 294
Indictment, 138
Industrial prisons, 43-45
Industrial specialist, 496
Infectious diseases, managing, 493
Informal organization, 475-76
Information, grand jury, 138
Initial appearance, 136
Initial classification, 531
Inmate deaths:
   federal jails, 272
   from AIDS, 270

Treatment model, 63, 479-80
Trial, 138
    by ordeal, 8
Tuberculosis, management of, in prisons,
    493, 494
Tucker Act, 379
Tucker v. Hutto, 384
Turning Point Program, 564

U

UNICOR (Federal Prison Industries, Inc.),
    547-48
Uniform Crime Reports (UCRs), 79, 80, 102-3,
    317, 597
Uniform Juvenile Court Act (1968), 333
Unionization, 453
Unit team, 468-69
    management, 487
United States Code, Chapter 42, Section 1983,
    140, 144
U.S. Bureau of Prisons, *See* Bureau of Prisons
U.S. Code, Section, 384, 1983
U.S. Congress, 539
    and crime, 376
    establishment of Justice Department,
        537-38
U.S. Constitution, 25, 143
U.S. Corrections Corporation (USCC), 579
U.S. Federal Courts Study Committee, 148
U.S. Parole Commission, 243
U.S. Supreme Court, 47-48, 140, 144, 383,
    384, 390
    and death penalty, 406, 411, 416
    and inmates' right to treatment, 346
    justices' caseload vs. constitutional
        rights, 151
    landmark cases of 1960s/1970s, 150
    makeup of, 151-52
    pardons, 441-42
    role of, 142
Utilitarianism, 18
Utilitarian view, of retribution, 56

V

Vendetta, 4
Vera Institute of Justice, 173
Vest-pocket record, 435
Victimless crimes, 293-94
Violence:
    domestic, 85
    and juvenile delinquency, 318-22
    juvenile victims of, 322-25
    and youth, 601
Vocational-rehabilitation model, 499-501
Volsted Act (1918), 538
Voluntary turnover, 456

W

Wackenhut Corrections Corporation (WCC),
    580, 584
Walled prisons, 226
Walnut Street Jail, 25-27, 30, 494, 497, 572
    riots at, 46
War on Crime, 218
War on Drugs, 53, 67, 217, 596
    effects of, 69
    and female offenders, 299-301
Ward, 317
Wardens, 110, 469
Warren Court, 143
Washington, D.C., Department of Corrections,
    526-27
Washington State Penitentiary (Walla Walla), 49
Weekend confinement, 165, 174
Weekenders, 174
Weems v. United States, 412
Wergeld, 7, 9
Western Penitentiary, 30-31, 36
Wethersford Prison (Connecticut), 35
Whipping, 10-11, 57, 354
White-collar crime, 86-88
White Slave Act (1910), 538
Wickersham Commission, 66, 390, 595
Wilkerson v. Utah, 411
Wolff v. McDonnell, 374-75
Women:
    correctional officers, 546
    and crime fighting, 312
    as high-security officers, 542
    influence of women's liberation
        movement, 299
    in jail, 301-2
    in prison, 302
    See also Female offenders
Women presidents, American Correctional
    Association, 299
Work camps, 522
Workhouses, 13, 20, 43
Work release programs, 556-58, 561
Writ of certiorari, 384
Wyatt v. Stickney, 149
Wyndomham Penitentiary, 20

Y

Yellow card, 436-39
Younger v. Gilmore, 382
Youth gangs, 325-26, 454-56, 596